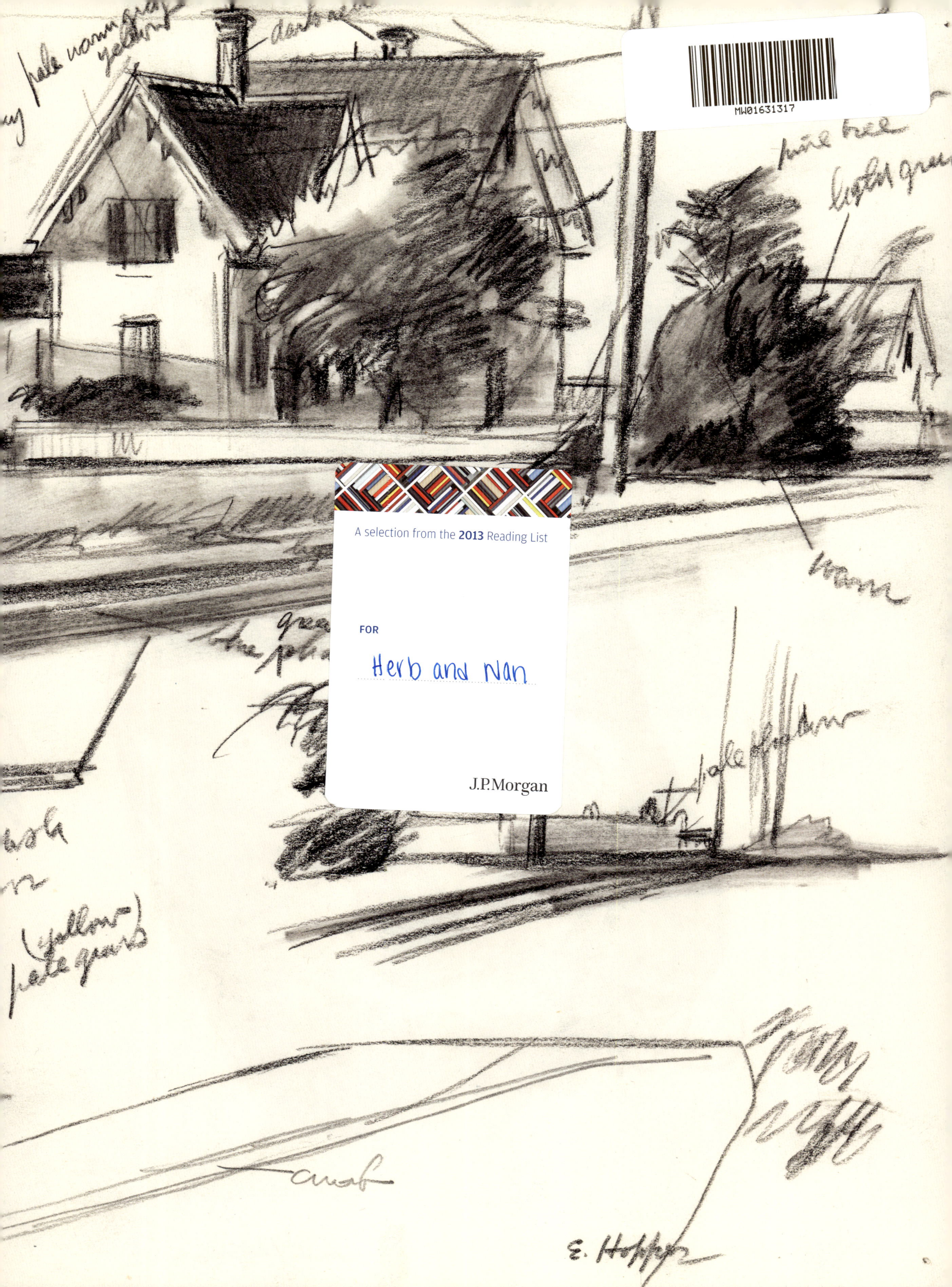

pine tree
E. Hopper

CARTER E. FOSTER

with contributions by

DANIEL S. PALMER
NICHOLAS ROBBINS
KIMIA SHAHI
MARK W. TURNER

Hopper

Drawing

Whitney Museum of American Art, New York
Distributed by Yale University Press, New Haven and London

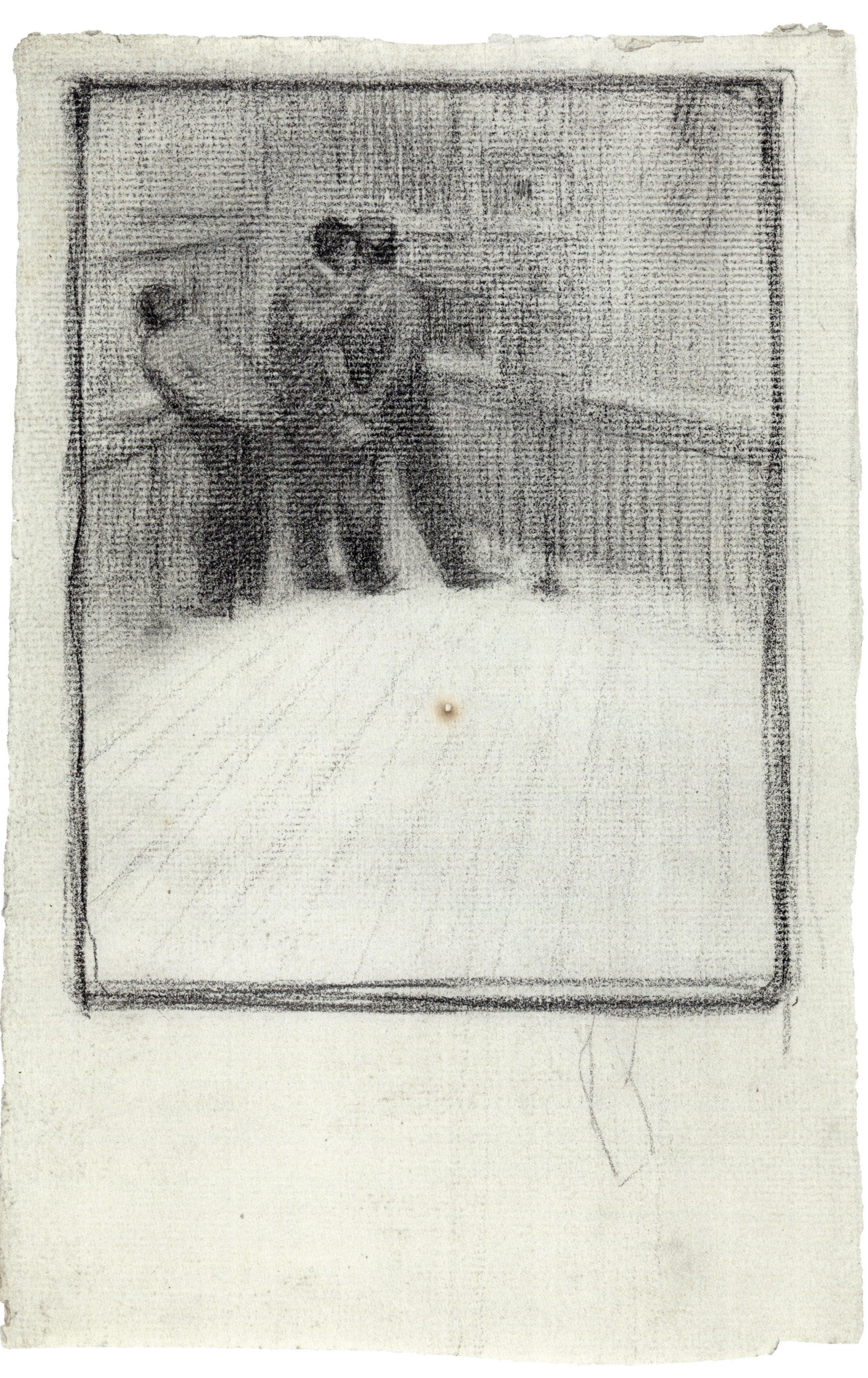

Contents

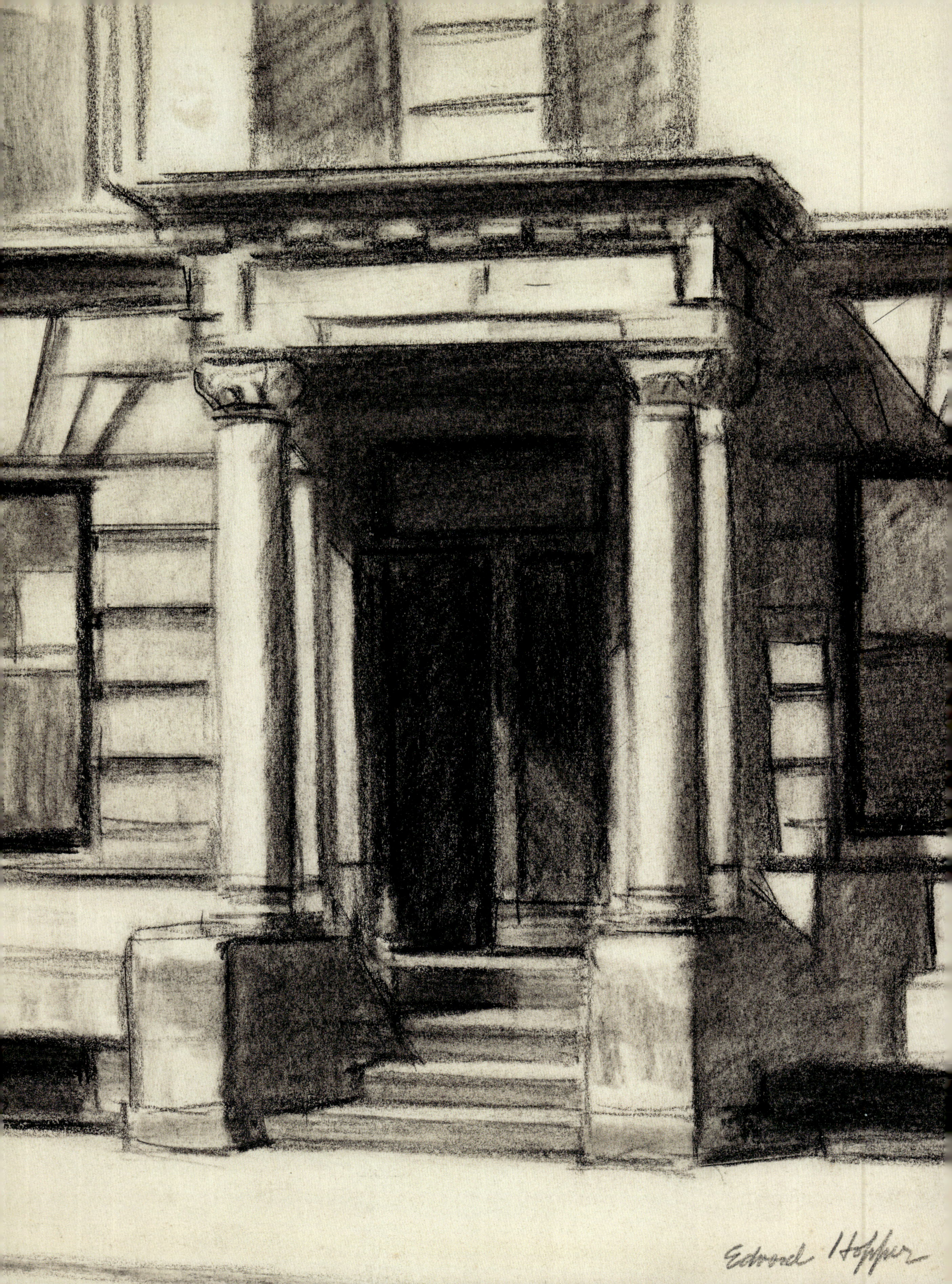
Edward Hopper

FOREWORD

Today, Edward Hopper is one of America's most iconic artists. His work is in great demand for exhibition around the world. In the last decade, his art has been the subject of two international retrospectives and other major exhibitions in Europe and Asia. Indeed, he is one of the few early twentieth-century American artists—along with Georgia O'Keeffe and Alexander Calder—with a present-day global reputation. While the current popularity of his work may seem unsurprising to contemporary viewers, this has not always been the case. Hopper began as a "local" artist, though his ambitions, if rarely articulated, were always greater. I daresay his art continues to have a fundamental local specificity from which it derives much of its power.

Hopper's art was the product of his innate interest in and attention to visual fact. As Carter E. Foster, curator of this exhibition, points out, Hopper's nuanced observation, evident in the ten-year-old artist's earliest drawings of the Hudson River waterfront in Nyack, New York, found a natural fit in his later training with inspiring urban realist American painters such as Robert Henri. Henri, who espoused the preeminent connection between art and daily life—especially the street life of New York—had a profound influence on the young Hopper. As Henri said in 1901, "What you must express in your drawing is not 'what model you had,' but 'what were your sensations.'"[1] Hopper would echo this approach in perhaps his most celebrated statement (of which there are not many), written three decades later on the occasion of his first retrospective at the Museum of Modern Art: "My aim in painting has always been the most exact transcription possible of my most intimate impressions of nature."[2] For Hopper, like Henri, true art began not with the copying and imitation of other art (the prevalent academic training of the day) but in connecting one's immediate environment with personal imagination. As Foster notes in this volume, "Hopper's drawings, especially his studies for major oils, are the material record linking the observed world and his subjective transformation of it." Hopper's nature and nurture were tied to the specifics of place and time, and drawing was his vehicle for transcribing and transfiguring those specifics.

While Hopper made three trips to Europe—in 1906–07, 1909, and 1910, residing mostly in Paris—which profoundly influenced his art and his use of drawing to inform his painting, and a number of visits to Mexico in the 1940s and 1950s (travels that had little influence on his art), he was essentially a creature of habit. Hopper immersed himself in the subjects of New York City and Cape Cod, Massachusetts, where together he spent almost the entirety of his seventy-year career. Over time, he concentrated his powers of observation and his efforts to achieve an art that transcended the particulars of place. (It is noteworthy that in 1913, for the *International Exhibition of Modern Art*—known as the Armory Show—which introduced America to avant-garde art, Hopper submitted one painting, *Sailing* from 1911. That he chose a painting which had as its source his childhood depictions of boating scenes, rather than one of his Parisian paintings, is telling.)

Hopper's extensive exhibition history largely reflects the local nature of his art and life. After leaving his childhood home and studying at the New York School of Illustrating and the New York School of Art, he exhibited his work at the MacDowell Club in New York, along with other Henri peers and students. By 1918 he had found his artistic home at the Whitney Studio Club, the Museum's precursor. There he became associated with a group of downtown New York bohemian artists (many of whom were also connected to Henri), participated in life drawing classes, socialized, and made use of the Club's library.

Hopper had his first one-man exhibition at the Studio Club in 1920 and was included in eight subsequent exhibitions before it closed in 1928 to make way for the Whitney Museum of American Art, which would open in 1931. During the 1920s, Hopper's work was presented in Philadelphia, Boston, and Chicago, giving him national presence. In 1932 his painting *Room in New York* (1932) was exhibited in the first Whitney Biennial, and his work continued to be shown in Whitney Biennials and Annuals throughout his life. In the early years, when the Biennials presented painting alternately with works on paper and sculpture—from 1932 to 1956—Hopper regularly exhibited his watercolors. Hopper's three lifetime retrospectives were all held in New York—the first at the Museum of Modern Art (1933), the others at the Whitney Museum (1950 and 1964).

The single major exhibition of Hopper's work abroad during his lifetime was as one of four artists featured in the American Pavilion at the Venice Biennale in 1952. The *New York Times* review of the Pavilion identifies Hopper's particular geographically based sensibility: "Foreigners recognized, and rightly, something authentically American in the pathos of his landscapes, a germ of loneliness which they detect in our literature."[3] This American sensibility should be understood not as merely the product of locale but as something derived through the agency of observation, the accumulation of fact, and the distillation of detail that Hopper absorbed, transmuted, and transmitted in his drawing: the very essence that we have come to recognize as what Foster terms the "Hopperesque."

When Hopper died in 1967, there were some 2,500 drawings in the artist's estate—the overwhelming majority of his extant drawings. After his wife, Josephine, died a year later, these along with his complete artistic holdings were bequeathed to the Whitney Museum at Edward's direction. *Hopper Drawing*, appropriately titled to encompass both the process and the object, is the first exhibition to concentrate on the artist's drawings and creative process.

Over the years, the Whitney has organized numerous exhibitions devoted to specific aspects of Hopper's art: his figures; relationship to film, photography, and literature; work in Paris; prints; and illustrations, among others. Yet an exploration of his drawings, which constitute a vast portion of the Hopper bequest and are fundamental to understanding his art, has not until now been broached. Hopper exhibited his drawings infrequently during his lifetime, perhaps because he considered so few "finished." While he may have discarded large numbers of working drawings, he also saved many. Now, through the intensive study that Foster has conducted, it is clear that these drawings are the underpinnings of his relatively small output of paintings. Together they form, as Foster calls it, a kind of "connective tissue" which runs through his practice throughout the many decades of his career.

Providing an overview of Hopper's approach to drawing, this exhibition examines his method as he assiduously and intuitively used suites of drawings to "find" and "construct" a work. Analogously, Foster focuses on key masterworks, including *Soir Bleu* (1914), *Early Sunday Morning* (1930), *New York Movie* (1939), *Office at Night* (1940), and *Nighthawks* (1942), to analyze and formulate how the person, the place, the mind, and the hand are linked. He demonstrates that Hopper was not a reporter but rather a synthesizer who used drawing as a record to be tempered by his memory and imagination. As Foster perceptively writes, "Memory and the act of remembering are often his implicit subjects." This is further suggested in the way that Hopper revisited some subjects throughout his career—the theater, the bedroom, the road, et cetera. In addition, Foster presents new research using historic photographs of New York to elucidate what Hopper saw, drew, and painted. What we in turn see is a New York that is today largely gone, never completely existed, and now exists only thanks to Hopper and his consummate imagination. Hopper's work has such broad international appeal because, although it began with the local, it isn't about specific places but is concerned instead with an idea of America, the modern condition, and the look and experience of silence. It is about space and time, things in transition, and ultimately the impossibility of capturing pure idea in pigments on canvas.

I would like to thank several generations of Hopper scholars, many of whom were resident at the Whitney Museum—beginning with Lloyd Goodrich, who devoted so much of his art historical career to Hopper, as well as Gail Levin and Deborah Lyons. It is on their foundation that all Hopper scholarship is built. Carter E. Foster stands next in this line of Whitney Hopper scholars, having participated in the organization of the first survey of the artist's work to be presented in Italy. With the inception of *Hopper Drawing*, Foster proves himself to be a scholar who apprehends not only the range of Hopper's work but its very depth in all senses of the word. My congratulations and thanks to Carter for this major endeavor.

It is a timely and much needed advance in Hopper scholarship. His curatorial assistant, Nicholas Robbins, provided critical support at every turn of this undertaking. For this and his accomplished text "The Road," I extend my great appreciation. The Whitney is delighted to share this exhibition with the Dallas Museum of Art and the Walker Art Center, Minneapolis, and I am grateful to Maxwell L. Anderson, Eugene McDermott Director at the Dallas Museum of Art, and Olga M. Viso, director at the Walker Art Center, for their enthusiasm and for their commitment to this project.

An exhibition of this scope would not be possible without the tremendous generosity of its lenders and of the many foundations and individuals who offered their support. I am enormously grateful to the National Endowment for the Arts, The Dietrich Foundation, The Selz Foundation, Barney A. Ebsworth, Steve Martin and Anne Stringfield, The Robert Lehman Foundation, Jane Carroll, The Aaron I. Fleischman Foundation, Arlene and Robert Kogod, Sarah and Seth Glickenhaus, and an anonymous donor. I would also like to thank the Tianaderrah Foundation, for their crucial support of the conservation of many of the drawings in this exhibition, as well as the Wyeth Foundation for American Art and Furthermore: a program of the J. M. Kaplan Fund for their kind support of this important publication.

ADAM D. WEINBERG
Alice Pratt Brown Director

1 Robert Henri, "An address to the students of the School of Design for Women, Philadelphia," 1901, in *The Art Spirit* (Philadelphia and New York: J. B. Lippincott, 1951), 55–56.
2 Edward Hopper, "Notes on Painting," in Alfred H. Barr, Jr., et al., *Edward Hopper: Retrospective Exhibition, November 1–December 7, 1933*, exh. cat. (New York: Museum of Modern Art, 1933), 17.
3 Stuart Preston, "Art Survey by Nations," *New York Times*, July 20, 1952, sec. 10, 2, quoted in Gail Levin, *Edward Hopper: An Intimate Biography* (New York: Rizzoli, 2007), 451.

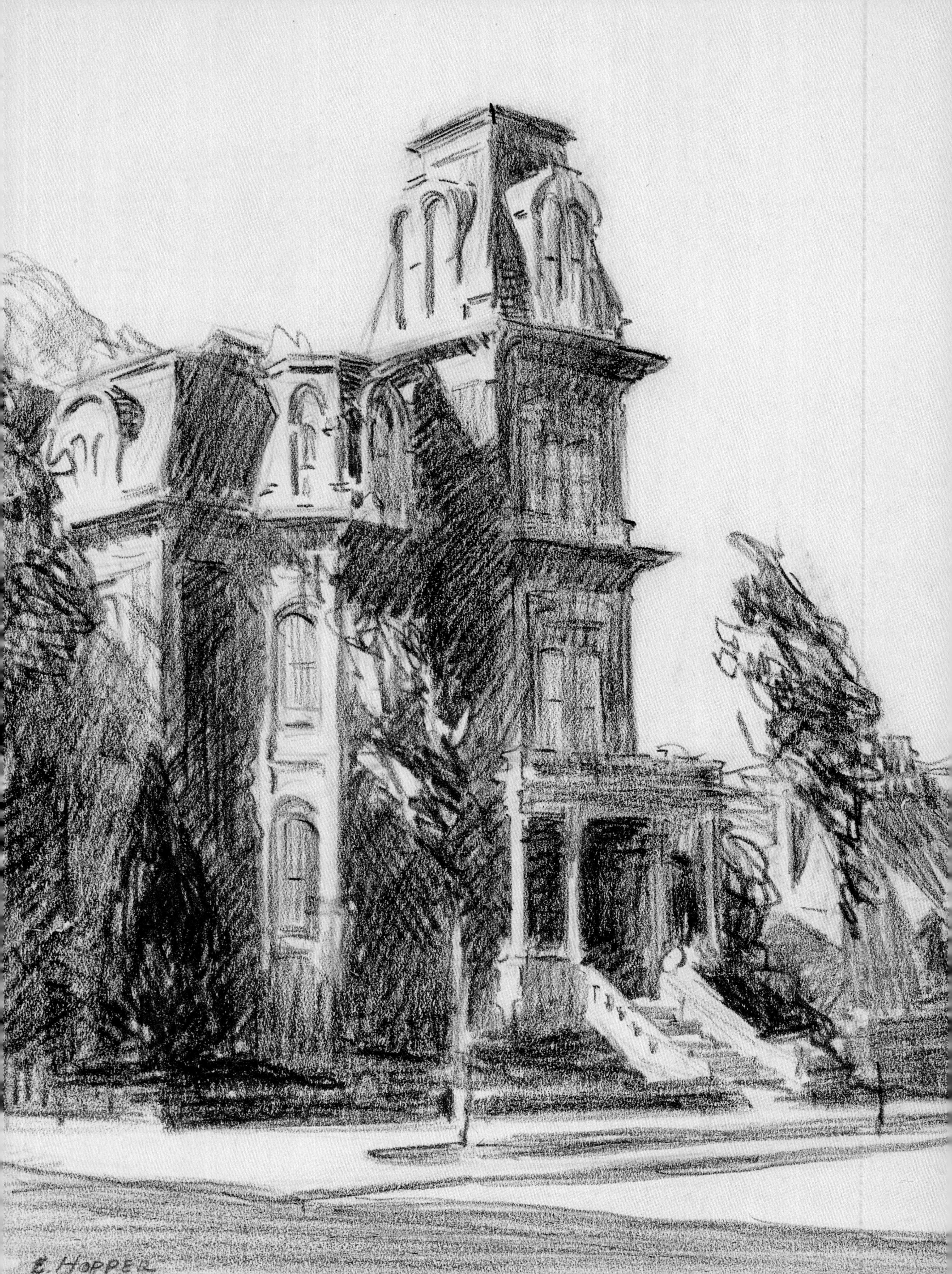
E. HOPPER

ACKNOWLEDGMENTS

It has been a privilege to delve into the practice of an artist as great as Edward Hopper, and a rare opportunity to initiate research on an extensive but relatively unknown body of work: the Whitney Museum of American Art's unparalleled collection of the artist's drawings, bequeathed to the Museum by his widow, Josephine. I express my deep gratitude to Adam D. Weinberg, Alice Pratt Brown Director, whose unshakable belief in the importance of art and artists in the world guides us all at the Whitney; and to chief curator and deputy director for programs Donna De Salvo, who has taught me to think big about art and history and to be fearless in analyzing and presenting it. I was lucky to work with a devoted and extraordinarily capable team of researchers, assistants, and interns whose contributions to this catalogue and exhibition run deep. Most important, I must thank curatorial assistant Nicholas Robbins, who labored tirelessly and enthusiastically on every aspect of this project with me and who contributed an original and beautifully conceived essay; his sharp intellect and attention to detail are reflected throughout this publication and made it an incredibly gratifying collaboration. Our two thorough research assistants, Daniel S. Palmer and Kimia Shahi, helped track down innumerable scholarly minutiae and comparative material, adding to the breadth of the main essays as well as the research notes and bibliography; both also made significant individual contributions to the catalogue; our intern Sarah Humphreville diligently and ably helped with much in the final stages. Rory O'Dea updated hundreds of Hopper cataloguing records and helped, especially, in dating or redating many drawings during his tenure at the Whitney as project researcher, drawings, Collection and Documentation Initiative. Others who worked on the project at various stages include former curatorial assistants Margot Norton and Kristin Sarli; and former curatorial interns Andrew St. Louis, Elizabeth Bidart, Jennifer Harris, Kathleen McEvily, and Jake DeMartini. I must single out Sean Leatherbury, who helped us find—in a true eureka moment—additional photographs of the building on Seventh Avenue that inspired *Early Sunday Morning*.

Anyone working on Hopper is indebted to the fundamental research of Gail Levin; her biography of the artist and catalogue raisonné were constantly open during every phase of our work, and her many other writings gave invaluable direction. Friend and colleague Carol Troyen, curator at the Museum of Fine Arts, Boston, has been a wonderful source of insight and information about Hopper for several years, and her own scholarship on the artist is much appreciated. Judith Barter, curator at the Art Institute of Chicago, has also written wonderfully on Hopper; her belief in our project and her support in lending *Nighthawks*—surely one of the most wanted paintings in the world—is deeply appreciated. Fellow Whitney curator Chrissie Iles offered lively insights, support, and encouragement as she watched my research evolve. I would like to give special thanks to Brian O'Doherty, whose poetic, beautiful, and revelatory writing on Hopper greatly inspired my own wish to understand something of this great painter's artistic process; O'Doherty's peerless 1964 essay on the artist (revised and republished in 1973), based on their friendship and personal connection, will always be the starting point for anyone who wishes to delve into the essence of Hopper's creative genius.

At the Whitney, I have been preceded in my research and appreciation of Hopper by former curator, director, and friend to the artist, Lloyd Goodrich; his former colleague Anita Duquette, manager of rights and reproductions, who oversees many aspects of the Hopper legacy, and to whom I am so grateful for her input and guidance at every level; Gail Levin, former curator, Hopper Collection; and Deborah Lyons, former adjunct associate curator, Hopper Collection. Our library staff, led by Carol Rusk, Irma and Benjamin Weiss Librarian, also helped tirelessly in support of our project, in particular assistant archivist Kristen Leipert and assistant librarian Ivy Blackman. Others who helped with our research and with this catalogue in invaluable ways include: Geoff Alexander at the Academic Film Archive of North America; Wendy Hurlock Baker and Joy Weiner at the Archives of American Art, Smithsonian Institution; Jennifer Belt and Michael Slade at Art Resource; Dilys Blum and Laura L. Camerlengo at the Philadelphia Museum of Art; Cora Cahan and Allison Mui at the New Victory Theater (formerly known as the Republic and Minsky's); Mark Callahan at the Silver School of Social Work, New York University; Robert Delap and Marilyn Kushner at the New-York Historical Society; Rachel Engler; Jeffrey Fraenkel, Amy Whiteside, and Karin Johnson at Fraenkel Gallery; Patricia Sherwin Garland and Elizabeth Hodermarsky at the Yale University Art Gallery; Mellissa Huber; Danielle King and Deborah Wye at The Museum of Modern Art; Matthew Knutzen and Thomas Lisanti at the New York Public Library; Philip Koch; Anna Kuehl at the Corcoran Gallery of Art; Kathy McLeister at the Theatre Historical Society of America; Russell Merritt at the University of California, Berkeley; Hope Morrill at the Cape Cod National Seashore; Francis Morrone; Ricki Moskowitz at The Willem de Kooning Foundation; Linda Briscoe Myers at the Harry Ransom Center, the University of Texas at Austin; Alexander Nemerov; Didier Ottinger at the Musée national d'art moderne, Centre Georges Pompidou; Mary Siccio at the Nickerson Archives, Cape Cod Community College; James M. Sousa at the Addison Gallery of American Art, Phillips Academy; and David Wright at the Wellfleet Historical Society.

This catalogue came together through the combined, outstanding efforts of Beth A. Huseman, director of publications at the Whitney; our editor, David Updike; Brian Reese, former publications assistant; Anita Duquette and Kiowa Hammons, rights and reproductions assistant; production coordinators Nerissa Dominguez Vales and Sue Medlicott of The Production Department; and our brilliant designer, Mark Nelson, and the team at McCall Associates, including David Zaza and Marijane K. Moosoolian. I would also like to thank Mark Turner for contributing his insightful and incisive essay to the catalogue, and for his support and enthusiasm for the project.

Exhibitions are always collaborations, and the various Whitney departments that helped shape and implement this project worked enthusiastically to bring it to successful fruition. Christy Putnam, associate director for exhibitions and collections management, heads our able team of registrars and art handlers, including Chris Ketchie and Graham Miles. I especially acknowledge our paper preparator Kelley Loftus, particularly for her wise and thoughtful solutions for the display of fragile drawings; and freelance preparator Eliza Proctor, art handler Gregory Reynolds, and head preparator Joshua Rosenblatt, all of whom helped us generously and extensively with research and access to our collection. I am also grateful to conservators Stephanie Lussier and Clara Rojas Sebasta, who reviewed all of the Whitney's Hopper drawings and conserved many of the works in this exhibition. The Museum's conservation staff, led by Carol Mancusi-Ungaro, with Matthew Skopek and Eleonora Nagy, provided much advice and expertise.

Maura Heffner, exhibitions manager, coordinated the exhibition and its tour, along with registrars Seth Fogelman and Melissa Cohen, and I am grateful for their guidance at every step of the exhibition's planning, as well as for the crucial assistance of Barbi Spieler, head registrar, permanent collection. I would also like to thank Beverly Parsons, project registrar, for her invaluable and extensive contributions to the project. I further thank our talented exhibition designer, Mark Steigelman, and his colleague Anna Martin for their incredible resourcefulness, attention to detail, and good taste.

Our outstanding development team raised substantial financial support for this exhibition, led by Alexandra Wheeler, deputy director for development. I would like to thank Stephanie Adams, director of individual and planned giving; Hillary Strong, director of foundations and government relations; Jessica Vodofsky Sigalow, former manager of foundations and government relations; Morgan Arenson, manager of foundations and government relations; Betty Stolpen, senior major gifts coordinator; Courtney Bassett, major gifts officer; and Kasey Sherrick, manager of corporate sponsorships.

At the Whitney, I also gratefully acknowledge the efforts of the following individuals and their colleagues: Kathryn Potts, associate director, Helena Rubinstein Chair of Education; Anne Byrd; Gene McHugh, Kress Interpretation Fellow; Margie Weinstein, manager of education initiatives; Emily Arensman, coordinator of public programs; Joel Snyder, manager of member benefits and relations; Jeffrey Levine, chief marketing and communications officer; Stephen Soba, communications officer; Amanda Angel, communications manager; Sarah Hromack, head of digital media; Elyse Mallouk, digital content manager; Hilary Greenbaum, head of graphic design; Meg Forsyth, graphic designer; Jen Leventhal, administrative coordinator; Justin Romeo, executive coordinator to the director; Farris Wahbeh, manager, cataloguing and documentation; Nick Holmes, general counsel; Gina Rogak, director of special events; Wendy Barbee-Lowell, manager of visitor services; and John Balestrieri, director of security. In addition to those already mentioned, I express thanks to my fellow curators for their wonderful collegiality and deep talent: Barbara Haskell, Dana Miller, David Kiehl, Elisabeth Sussman, Jay Sanders, and Scott Rothkopf; and to other colleagues in the curatorial department: Emily Russell, our tactful and devoted department manager; and Brooke Cheyney, former curatorial assistant.

The Whitney is fortunate to have such esteemed partners for the exhibition's tour: at the Dallas Museum of Art, I am grateful to director Maxwell L. Anderson, to Jeffrey Grove, senior curator of modern and contemporary art, and to Sue Canterbury, curator of American art, who oversaw the exhibition there; at the Walker Art Center, I thank director Olga M. Viso, chief curator Darsie Alexander, curator Siri Engberg, and Betsy Carpenter, curator of collections and the curator in charge of the show's presentation in Minneapolis.

Last, and most important, I would like to thank all of the lenders, private and institutional, whose willingness to participate in our project and to part with their artworks made this exhibition possible, as well as the foundations and individuals whose extraordinarily generous support of the exhibition and catalogue was crucial to our undertaking. I am very grateful to Daniel Dietrich, Aaron I. Fleischman, and Mr. and Mrs. Larry Magid for the loans of their beautiful Hopper works, as well as to the two lenders who wish to remain anonymous. James Reinish of James Reinish and Associates was incredibly generous with his time and knowledge of all things Hopper and helped in too many ways to mention here—I am most appreciative of his efforts, good humor, and enthusiasm. Jane Wyeth also helped a great deal with loans and other support, as did Marc Porter.

I also thank my museum colleagues at other institutions for their support of this project and assistance with loans: Brian T. Allen and James M. Sousa, Addison Gallery of American Art, Phillips Academy; James Cuno, Douglas Druick, and Judith Barter, The Art Institute of Chicago; Nannette V. Maciejunes, Columbus Museum of Art; Sally Kurtz, The Dayton Art Institute; Peter Findlay and Rebecca Hoffman, Peter Findlay Gallery; Ellen Lee, Indianapolis Museum of Art; Gary Tinterow, formerly of The Metropolitan Museum of Art; Glenn Lowry, Ann Temkin, Cora Rosevear, Connie Butler, Esther Adler, and Kathy Curry, The Museum of Modern Art; Lisa Petrulis and Jennifer Lanman at the Swope Art Museum; Elizabeth Glassman and Cathy Ricciardelli, Terra Foundation for American Art; Olga Viso and Pamela Caserta, Walker Art Center; Patricia McDonnell, Wichita Art Museum; Christina Olsen, Williams College Museum of Art; and Jock Reynolds, Helen Cooper, and Patricia Garland Stewart, Yale University Art Gallery.

CARTER E. FOSTER
Steven and Ann Ames Curator of Drawing

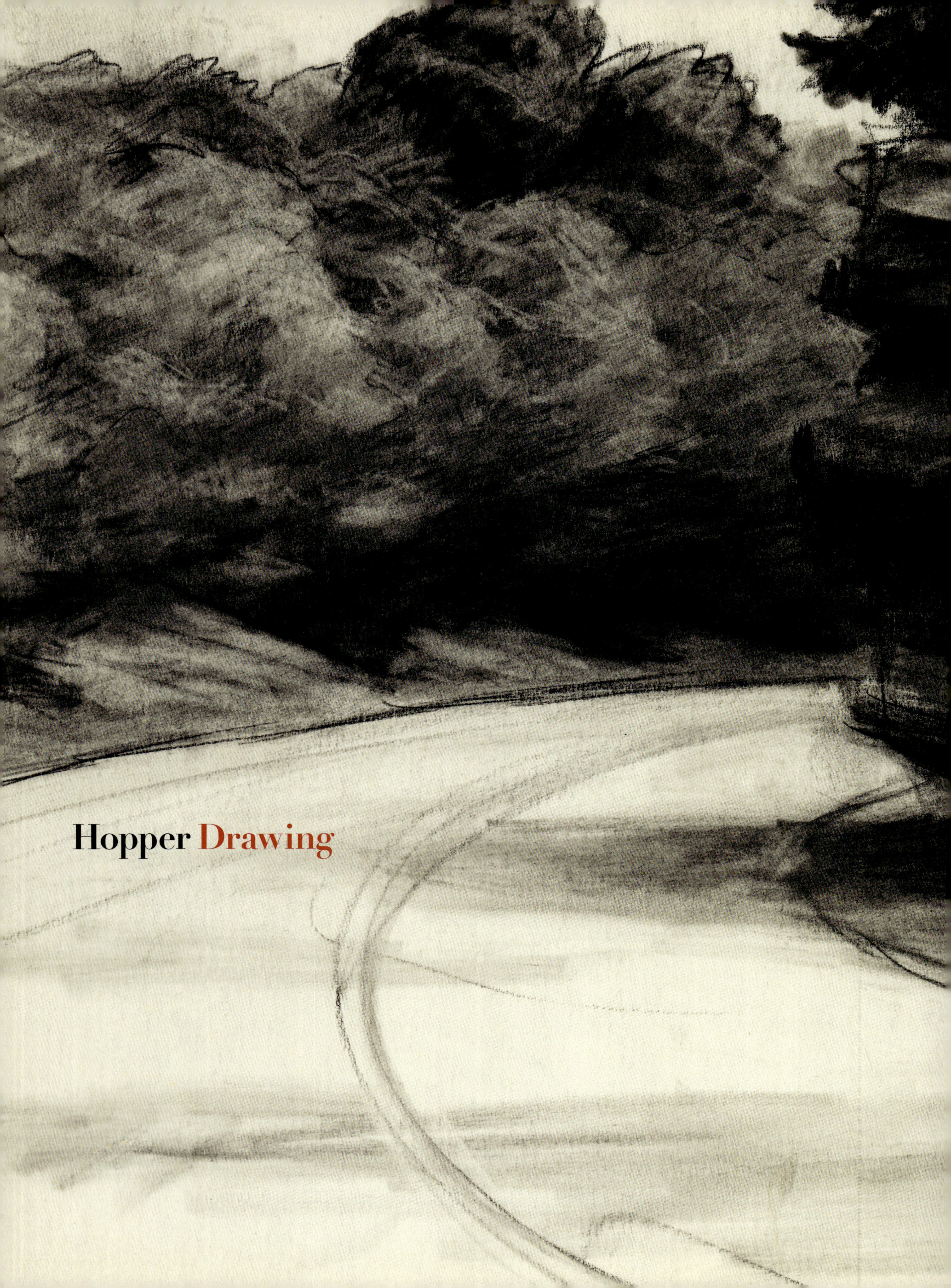

Hopper Drawing

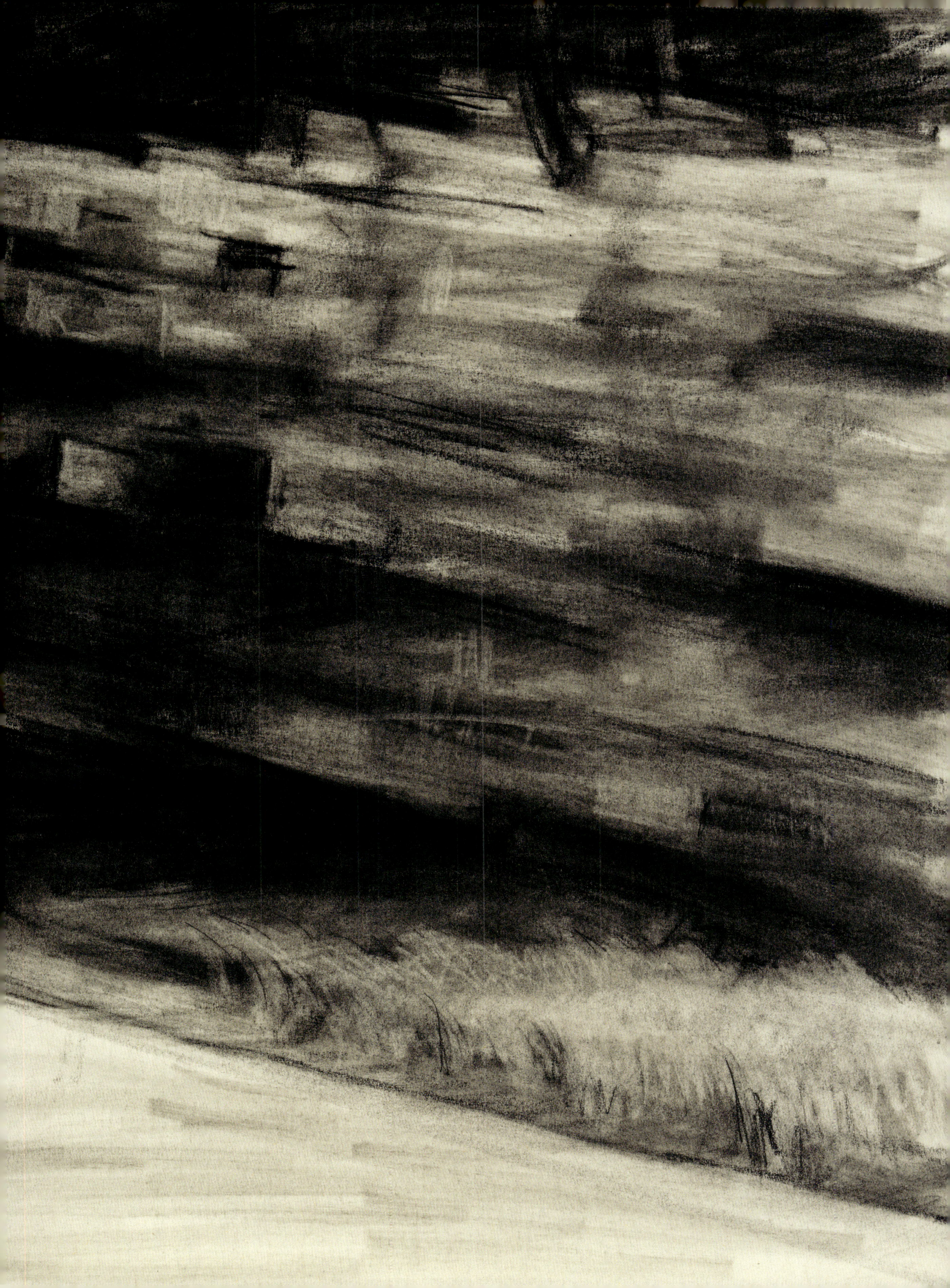

Hopper's Drawings

CARTER E. FOSTER

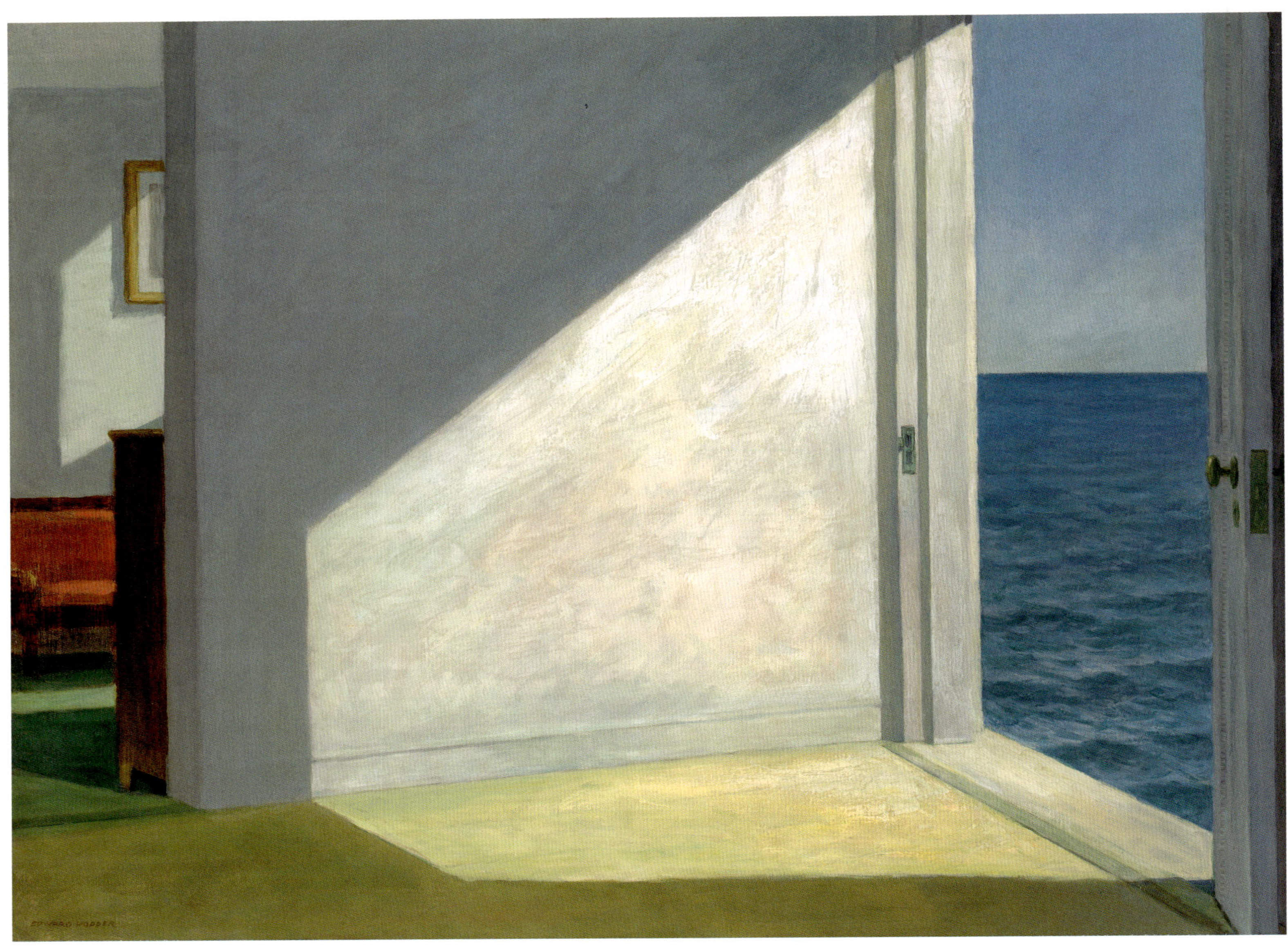

Drawing, Painting, Memory, and Imagination

Edward Hopper's *Rooms by the Sea* (fig. 1) suggests an allegory of vision and looking. As with many of the artist's paintings of rooms (especially his late ones), the chamber and the light slanting into it from an opening evoke the mind and the eye: light taken in and refracted, information relayed to and processed by the brain.[1] Comparisons to common printed diagrams demonstrating vision are apt (fig. 2). Hopper deepens the symbolism by rhyming the primary polygon of light in the fore room with a similarly angled trapezoid in the rear chamber. This patch of light indexes an unseen window—the other open "eye"—and falls across a picture in a frame. The picture on the wall is Hopper's self-conscious acknowledgment of the role of painters as creators of "windows on the world," one of the most enduring metaphors for representation in Western art. Hopper's rooms open onto a view of the expansive ocean, visible through the doorway in a simple seascape of light and dark blue creating a flat horizon. Here again Hopper alludes to the painter's practice: The horizon line is fundamental for creating pictorial space on a flat surface—for rendering in painting (and drawing) the space we inhabit in the world and the way we perceive and understand ourselves in it. Hopper once stated emphatically that he wished to paint himself,[2] and in *Rooms by the Sea*, with its multiple references to viewing, views, pictures, and seeing, he seems to do just that by visually and symbolically cataloguing his métier. Hopper painted this work in the house he designed himself on Cape Cod in Massachusetts, and it invokes that specific place without depicting it precisely.[3] The seaside house had a spacious open studio room with an oversize window where he painted, and a smaller, domestically scaled bedroom area in back. In this painting, Hopper also created one of his most directly surreal images by eliminating any suggestion of land and combining sea with house, with no visible terrestrial connection.[4]

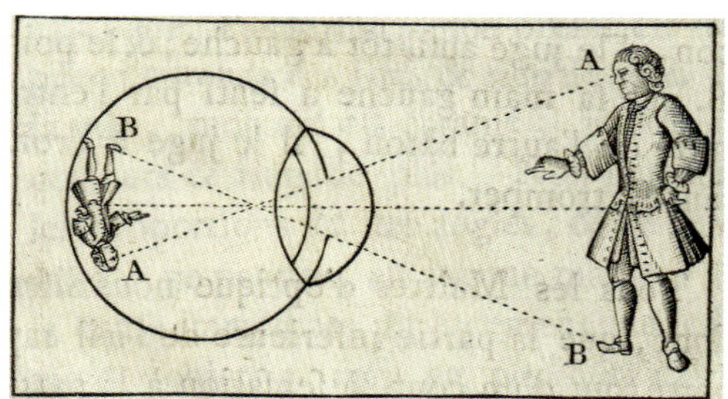

This strange and beguiling disjunction is a reflection of the way he processed the world by painting it—synthesizing his observations and transforming them. His goal in painting was to represent the connection between the interiority of his subjective mind and what he observed in the exterior world, and this lies at the core of his art. In *Rooms by the Sea* the interior looks out—through doorway and window—onto the expansive world in a visual metaphor for the kind of art Hopper made and admired. By eliminating the land, Hopper allows the painting to be read as an allegory, but he was also simply combining familiar elements he lived with on Cape Cod—a large room filled with light, a view of the ocean, common household furniture.[5]

What we know of Hopper's conception of painting comes from his own statements, and he was, famously, a man of few words. There are a handful of published writings, several important letters, and conversations recorded by others, most notably Lloyd Goodrich and Brian O'Doherty.[6] The way he composed and made his paintings is intimately tied to his drawing practice, and this intersection is the chief subject of the present exhibition and catalogue. Hopper's drawings, especially his studies for major oils, are the material record linking the observed world and his subjective transformation of it. He discussed this link in a consistent way throughout his long career. The most concise and direct quote about his practice is a sentence from "Notes on Painting," the short essay he wrote for his 1933 exhibition at the Museum of Modern Art: "My aim in painting has always been the most exact transcription possible of my most intimate impressions of nature."[7] A few years later he similarly explained: "My aim in painting is always, using nature as the medium, to try to project upon canvas my most intimate reaction to the subject as it appears when I like it most; when the facts are given unity by my interest and prejudices."[8] He offered a richer elucidation when he shared with O'Doherty a quote by Goethe that he carried in his wallet: "The beginning and end of all literary activity ['For literary substitute artistic. It works for that too'] is the reproduction of the world that surrounds me by means of the world that is in me, all things being grasped, related, re-created, molded, and reconstructed in a personal form and an original manner."[9] Each of these statements gives, in essence, equal importance to the world and to the artist; their combination creates the art. Hopper wanted to paint himself by painting the world;

1. *Rooms by the Sea*, 1951
Oil on canvas, 29 ¼ × 40 in. (74.3 × 101.6 cm)
Yale University Art Gallery, New Haven; bequest of Stephen Carlton Clark, B.A. 1903 1961.18.29

2. Diagram of image inverted in the retina, from Voltaire (François-Marie Arouet) (1694–1778), *Elémens de la philosophie de Neuton* (Amsterdam: Etienne Ledet & Compagnie, 1738), p. 71

paint was the (imperfect) medium through which he "molded and reconstructed in a personal form" his observations of the world that surrounded him. Painting's materiality, while imperfect, held great importance to Hopper as the medium through which he created this personal form.[10]

In art historical terms, the direct rendering in a chosen medium of an observed subject is usually referred to as painting or drawing "from life" or "from nature." Hopper had his own phrase for this: "from the fact." In multiple interviews, he used these words to convey, in simple, nonmetaphorical language, how he employed empirical observation as the starting point for all of his work.[11] He found subjects out in the world and could find inspiration no other way.[12] Hopper was extremely self-critical and keenly aware of the limitations of painting in trying to achieve his stated goals—limitations he described quite poetically as a form of "decay": a struggle between what was in his head and the limits of oil and canvas.[13] "You start with the canvas and you have an idea up here," he said to O'Doherty in 1962, tapping his head. "It isn't very clear, but it has definition. As soon as you start putting it on canvas, every concrete element is driving it away from the idea. You can't project your mind onto the canvas, because there are concrete things that interfere, technical things. It's *decaying* from your original idea."[14] Painting was a struggle for Hopper, and the relatively few mature oils he produced over a long life reflect this.[15] His difficulty stemmed in part from his perception that the materiality of painting was at odds with the ethereality of thought and imagination: "Just to paint a representation or a design is not hard. But to express thought in painting is.... The thought is fluid, but when you put something on canvas that is concrete and it tends to direct the thought. The more you put on canvas the more you lose control of the thought. I've never been able to paint what I set out to paint."[16] One can imagine that for Hopper, his most successful paintings were ones where he felt he lost the least control over what he saw in his head.

Although Hopper painted in oil "from the fact" (that is, out in nature, *en plein air*) fairly regularly in the earlier part of his career,[17] by the mid-1930s he had shifted his practice, synthesizing observations made out in the world in his studios in Truro, Massachusetts, and on Washington Square in New York. He sometimes referred to this process as "improvising."[18] His watercolors were always executed from life and form a distinct oeuvre; beautiful and accomplished, they lack the tension and narrative ambiguity of his great paintings.[19] At the core of his drawing practice are the groups of studies for single paintings that record the conceptual development of his canvases, sometimes in great nuance and detail. The specifics of this process will be examined in other essays, especially as related to *Early Sunday Morning* (see fig. 164), *Nighthawks* (see fig. 166), and *New York Movie* (see fig. 214); for those works we have enough evidence of what Hopper saw, what he drew, and what he painted to understand in detail the syntheses he made.

More generally, Hopper's process relates to memory and the way it functions. He used memory almost like a technical tool because it was a natural filter for eliding and combining observations made in the world into a cohesive work of art back in the studio. These elisions could be described as the most potent sites of his "intimate reactions to the subject,"[20] though it is not always possible to know what those sites are in a specific work; they may in fact be the entire painting. In some cases, by comparing the drawings to the painting we can see the evolution clearly and know what he changed as he bent the subject into a personal vision. Some suites of preparatory studies illustrate almost literally and step-by-step the transformation that occurred in the artist's mind as he changed "the fact" into art. O'Doherty has written eloquently and convincingly of Hopper's use of memory, suggesting that the wide appeal of his work relates to the universality of "the intimate memory-traces all of us possess, persisting from experiences."[21] He suggests, in other words, that we as viewers sense instinctively Hopper's use of memory in creating his work, since memory is a process and phenomenon with which all human beings are familiar. Because Hopper used memory as a filtering tool, he leads the spectator to the uncanny sensation of knowing something without recognizing it specifically. His tendency to simplify and distill his images (both as he developed them in drawing and as he painted them on canvas) shifted his works from the specific toward the general. But his imagery's grounding in empiricism always underpins this simplification, even when it veers toward the abstract and surreal.[22] Hopper indicated to O'Doherty that he was aware of memory operating when he painted, explaining that his favored quote from Goethe "applies to painting from the memory."[23] O'Doherty suggested the term "memory-image" to describe the precursor to the painted image that Hopper described to him as occurring in his head, noting also that "the dynamics of remembering and of forgetting are, of course, part of the process that refines [Hopper's] imagery."[24] Memory by definition infuses observed reality with one's own subjectivity; if Hopper's great paintings successfully depict and are in a sense *of* memory itself, they necessarily contain both. Hopper made a sharp distinction between "imagination" and "invention," associating the latter with abstract art.[25] He could not abide this mode because for him it dealt "narrowly with harmonies or dissonances of color and design" rather than "the vast field of experience and sensation.... One must say guardedly, human experience, for fear of having it confounded with superficial anecdote."[26] Taken together, Hopper's drawings and paintings form a record of human experience distilled into a form that was for him necessarily a "recognizable image from life."[27] Perhaps the fact that he returned to the same subjects again and again reflects his own attempt to narrow this "vast realm" into something he could manage.

Hopper's Drawings, His Artistic Estate, and the Whitney Museum

"I don't care so much for my drawings," Hopper wrote to Alfred H. Barr, Jr., in 1933 when the latter was organizing the artist's first retrospective at the Museum of Modern Art.[28] That show would include oils, watercolors, and etchings only. Hopper showed drawings publicly only a few times during his career. He sent a group of nude life studies from the early 1920s to the Frank K. M. Rehn Galleries at 683 Fifth Avenue in New York for a show in 1929, which his wife, Jo, dutifully recorded in the Record Books.[29] There were seventeen drawings in the 1950 Whitney Museum of American Art show organized by Lloyd Goodrich, all lent by the artist.[30] When the Addison Gallery of American Art in Andover, Massachusetts, devoted a fascinating exhibition in 1940 to analyzing Hopper's process through his painting *Manhattan Bridge Loop* (see fig. 153), the artist allowed his studies, at the gallery's request, to be included and ended up donating them to the institution.[31] Hopper very occasionally gave drawings away and sold a few through his gallery over the course of his lifetime.[32] Hopper regularly gave Jo drawings as gifts, which he inscribed and dedicated to her. In 1950 Hopper allowed editors from the periodical *American Artist* to go through his "portfolios" for a short article, from which they chose to publish seven sheets, apparently the first time any of his drawings were reproduced.[33] Goodrich included twenty-one drawings in the 1964 Whitney retrospective; as in 1950, none were reproduced in the catalogue.[34] In most of these circumstances, Hopper seems to have been accommodating the requests of others who showed an interest in his drawings. He considered them mostly studio material and generally spoke of them negatively.[35] In 1964, he declined a publisher's offer to create a book about his drawings.[36] When O'Doherty asked to see a sketch for *Sun in an Empty Room* (see fig. 385) while visiting the Hoppers in Truro in the early 1960s, the artist showed it to him reluctantly and called it "a piece of tripe."[37] But Hopper's behavior is as important to consider as his stated opinions: he kept a huge percentage of the thousands of drawings he made over the course of a long career. Clearly they were important to him—perhaps not as art objects, but certainly as records of his process and thought. When Jo died in 1968 and the Hopper bequest came to the Whitney

Museum, drawings were by far the most voluminous part of this extraordinary donation, numbering more than 2,500. Along with the drawings acquired by two others close to Jo Hopper, the Whitney collection seems to represent nearly the totality of Hopper's surviving drawn oeuvre.[38]

The Whitney began the task of accessioning, photographing, and cataloguing Hopper's artistic estate in 1969, a process overseen by researcher Elizabeth Tweedy Streibert. With an admirable accuracy and precision she recorded the basic information for hundreds of drawings and linked groups of studies to related paintings. When a group of museum representatives viewed works from the Hopper bequest in a Manhattan storage facility in 1969, they reported that "portfolios of drawings, watercolors, etc. were just noted and not counted or investigated."[39] A few weeks later the museum completed a summary inventory that seems to reflect (to some degree at least) the general categories and groups of drawings as the artist had kept them. By far the largest group was "preliminaries for oils." Watercolors were stored separately, as were nude life studies and drawings dedicated to Jo. Other groups of drawings were counted but not assigned to any category. About half of the drawings were made before 1906, during the artist's childhood and years as a student. As the drawings were accessioned, Streibert indicated in her catalogue sheets that groups of them were kept together by the artist—not surprisingly, they are generally suites of studies for specific paintings, although none of the material seems to have been rigorously organized beyond that.

An Overview of Hopper's Drawing Practice

Childhood and Juvenilia, 1892–99

Hopper signed and dated drawings as early as 1892, when he was ten years old. Hundreds of sheets survive from his boyhood in Nyack, New York. Boats and ships of all varieties were his favorite subject; he had plenty of opportunity to study them firsthand from his hometown on the Hudson River (fig. 3). He favored graphite pencil in much of this work from the early and mid-1890s, as he progressed rapidly from diagrammatic renderings of steamships (fig. 4) and horse-drawn fire wagons (fig. 5) to more sophisticated attempts at three-dimensional modeling and foreshortening (fig. 6). At eleven or twelve, in 1894, the aspiring draftsman rendered a cylinder in charcoal with a full range of tonal modeling, the light falling on both exterior and interior surfaces and creating multiple shadows, plays of light that Hopper handled quite well given his age (fig. 7). No doubt copied from an artist's manual, it shows ambition, discipline, and direction. Other early sheets feature small vignettes that nod in the direction of commercial illustration, the arena toward which his parents encouraged him and from which he would make a living in the first half of adulthood (fig. 8). In an 1898 study of a large ship (fig. 9), Hopper demonstrates his facility with pen and ink, a medium he used with frequency between about 1897 and 1908 (and which he eventually abandoned in favor of chalk and charcoal). By late adolescence, Hopper already showed promising technical skill.

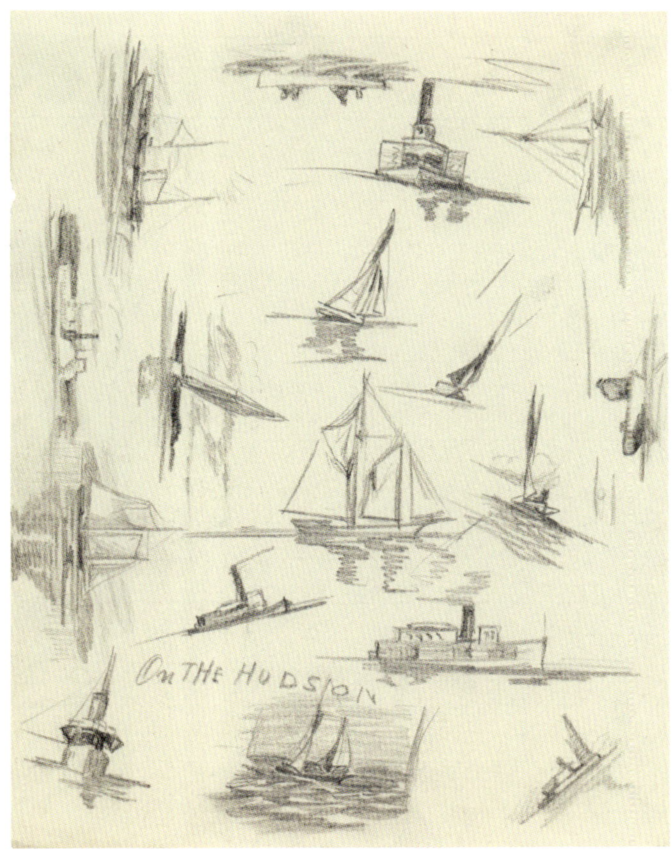

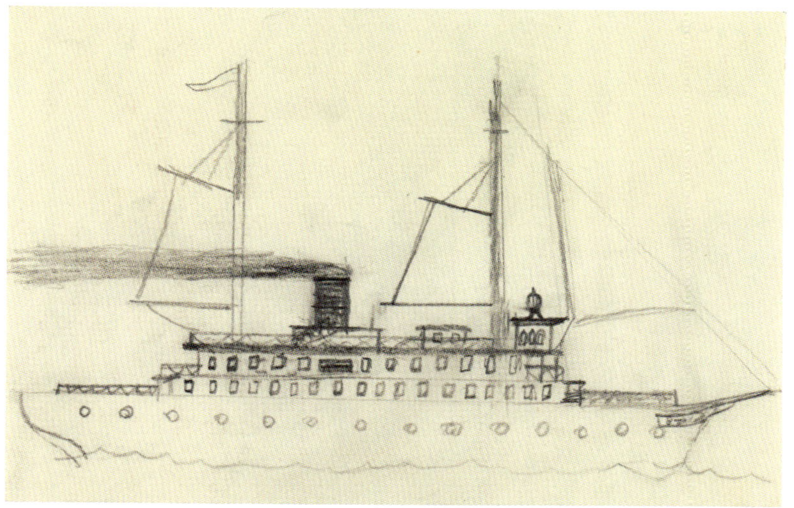

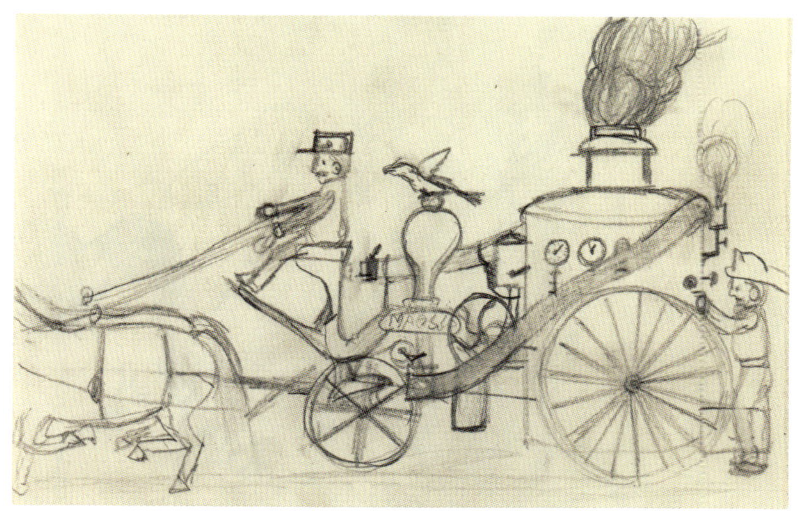

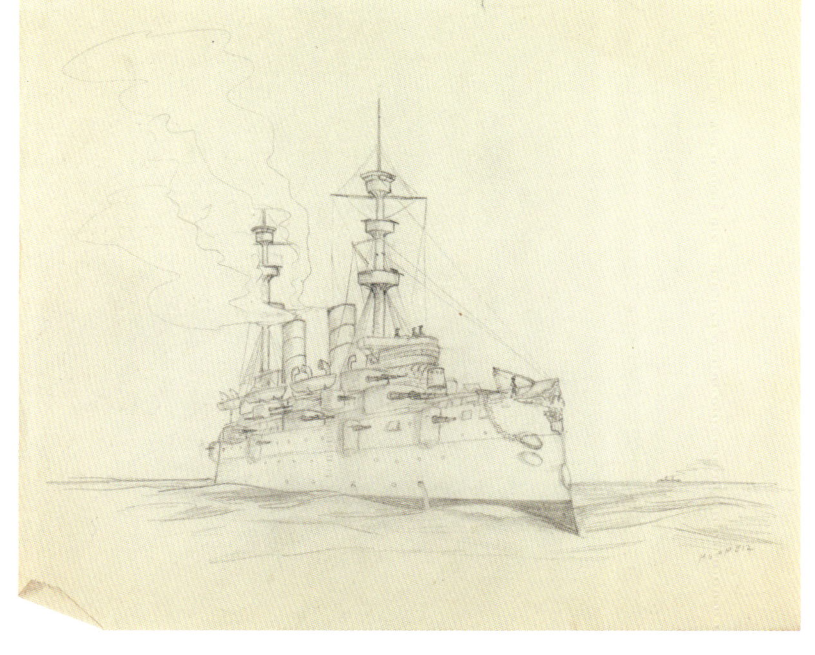

3. *On the Hudson*, 1895–99
Graphite pencil on paper, $9\frac{15}{16} \times 7\frac{7}{8}$ in. (25.2 × 20 cm)
Josephine N. Hopper Bequest 70.1553.88

4. *Large Steamer with Sails*, 1892–95
Graphite pencil on paper, $4\frac{1}{4} \times 6\frac{11}{16}$ in. (10.8 × 17 cm)
Josephine N. Hopper Bequest 70.1554.10

5. *Fire Engine and Two Fire Fighters* (recto), 1896
Graphite pencil on paper, $4\frac{1}{4} \times 6\frac{11}{16}$ in. (10.8 × 17 cm)
Josephine N. Hopper Bequest 70.1553.133a–b

6. *Battleship at Sea*, 1892–95
Graphite pencil on paper, $7\frac{15}{16} \times 9\frac{15}{16}$ in. (20.2 × 25.2 cm)
Josephine N. Hopper Bequest 70.1557.1

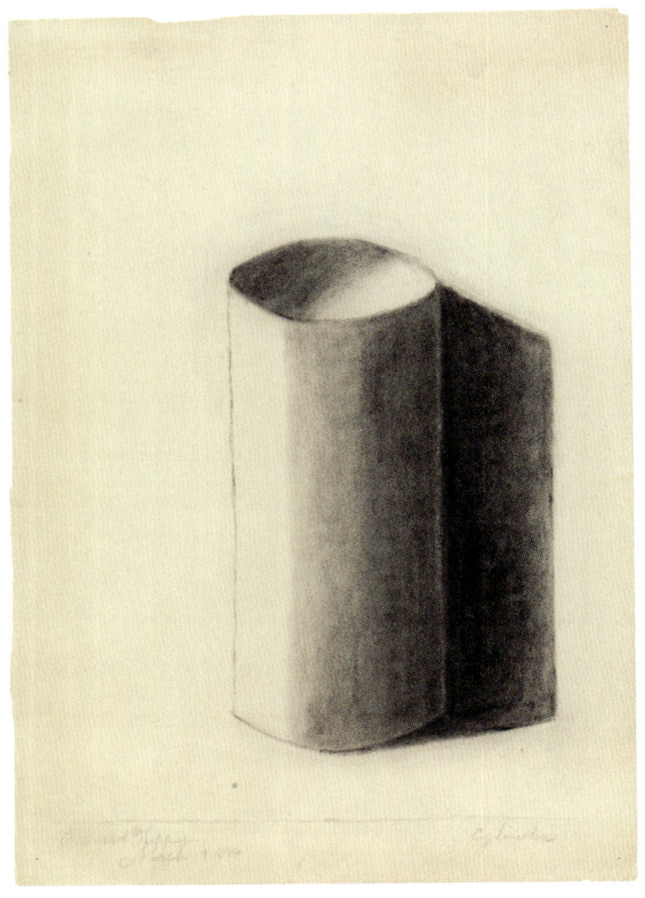

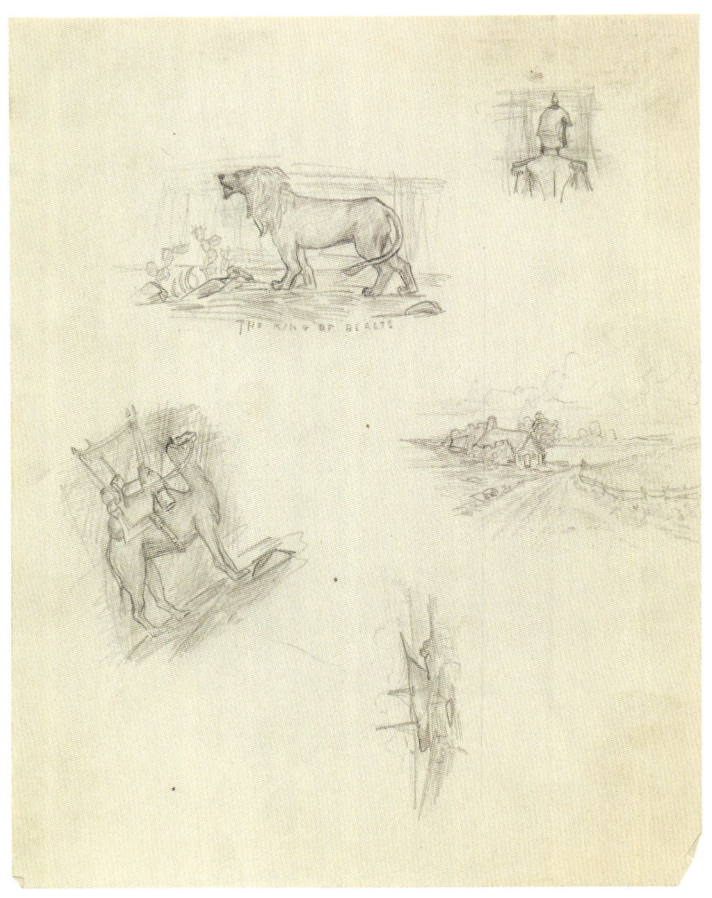

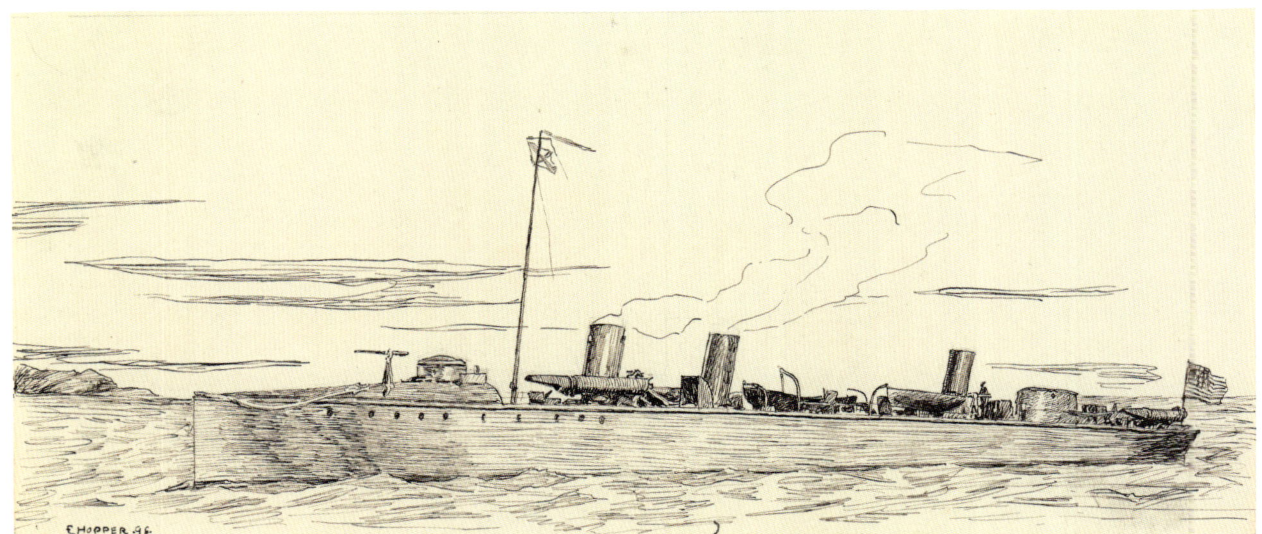

7. *Cylinder*, 1894
Charcoal on paper, $14\frac{15}{16} \times 10\frac{3}{4}$ in. (37.9 × 27.3 cm)
Josephine N. Hopper Bequest 70.1606.7

8. *Lion, Camel with Mount, Country Road with House, Large Sailboat, and Soldier with Spiked Helmet*, 1892–95
Graphite pencil on paper, $9\frac{7}{8} \times 7\frac{7}{8}$ in. (25.1 × 20 cm)
Josephine N. Hopper Bequest 70.1556.83

9. *Large Ship at Sea*, 1898
Pen and ink on paper, $3\frac{3}{4} \times 8\frac{15}{16}$ in. (9.5 × 22.7 cm)
Josephine N. Hopper Bequest 70.1556.26

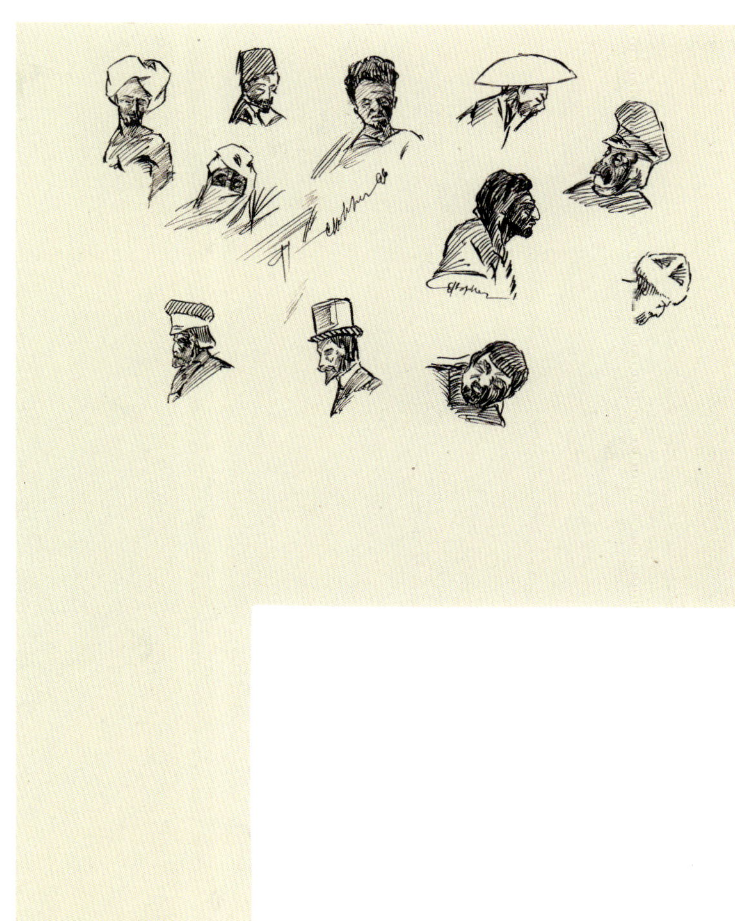

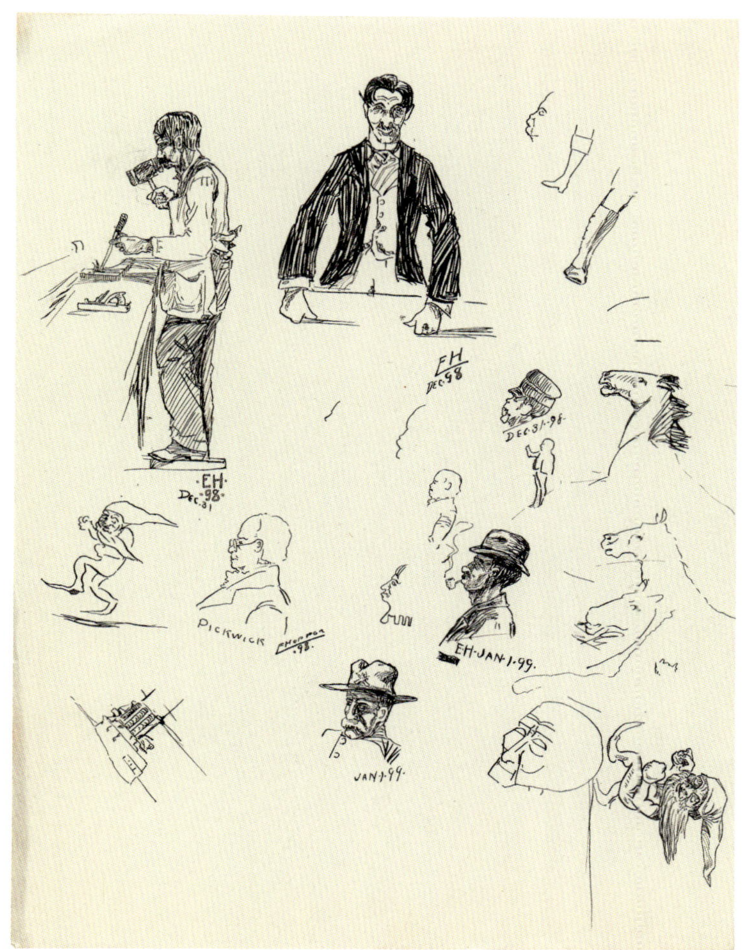

10. *Male Characters*, 1899
Pen and ink on paper, 9 ⅞ × 7 ¹¹⁄₁₆ in. (25.1 × 19.5 cm)
Josephine N. Hopper Bequest 70.1553.17

11. *Carpenter, Elves, Pickwick, and Miscellaneous Sketches*, 1898–99
Pen and ink and graphite pencil on paper, 9 ⅞ × 7 ¹¹⁄₁₆ in. (25.1 × 19.5 cm)
Josephine N. Hopper Bequest 70.1553.201

Student Work, 1899–1906

In 1899, Hopper commuted regularly to New York City to attend classes at the New York School of Illustrating. A number of signed, dated sheets from this year help document his progress. One group is comprised of pen and black ink drawings on a similar type of tan paper and typically featuring multiple small individual studies. They often show a wide variety of character types from history, fiction, and mythology, with heads and figure studies emphasizing facial expression and dress conveying social roles or historical periods (figs 10–12). These drawings are just what one would expect from a young artist studying illustration. A number of the sheets show what a gifted caricaturist and portraitist Hopper could be, fully in command of a graphic tradition that had flourished in Europe at the end of the nineteenth century (figs. 13, 14). In larger studies from the same year, Hopper tried his hand at fuller renderings of a wide variety of costumes and figures, including some in contemporary dress (fig. 15). These drawings display a fluid graphic style using mostly parallel hatching in long strokes—all line and little or no ink wash.

In the fall of 1900, Hopper moved on to the far more sophisticated New York School of Art, founded by the prominent American painter William Merritt Chase (1849–1916). Hopper studied briefly with Chase, but was more influenced by the great teacher, painter, and theorist Robert Henri (1865–1929), as well as with Kenneth Hayes Miller (1876–1952). His fellow students went on to become some of the most prominent artists of his generation, including Rockwell Kent, George Bellows, Guy Pène du Bois, and Patrick Henry Bruce. At first he continued to study illustration, and a number of drawings from this period are character studies in a similar vein to earlier work, albeit with a wider variety of costumes and in more complicated techniques, from deep black ink wash to charcoal and even pastel, all now handled with clear technical mastery (figs. 16–19). Hopper, however, wanted to be a painter. A sketchbook from the transitional period of 1899–1900 is full of confident graphite drawings, some of which foreshadow future subjects (fig. 20) and one of which appears to be a self-portrait featuring the artist very much as a painter, looking content with a huge palette and brush (fig. 21).

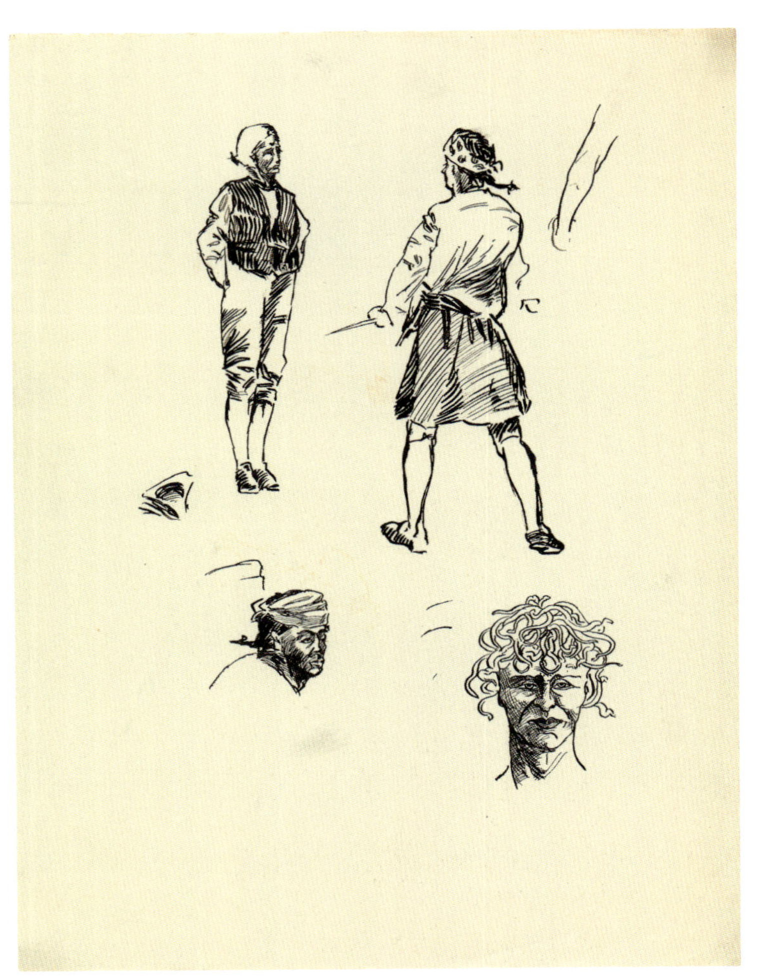

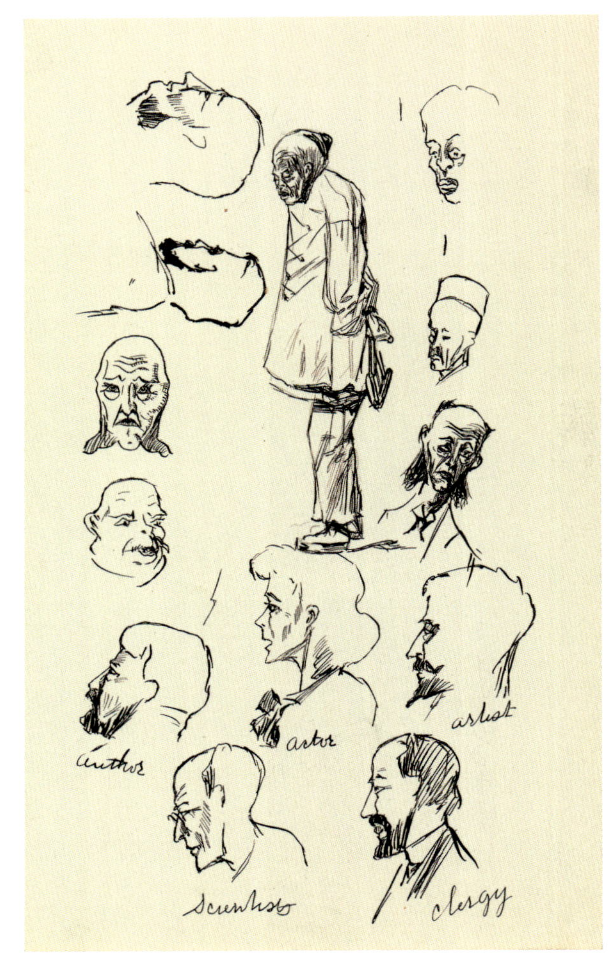
author
actor
artist
scientists
clergy

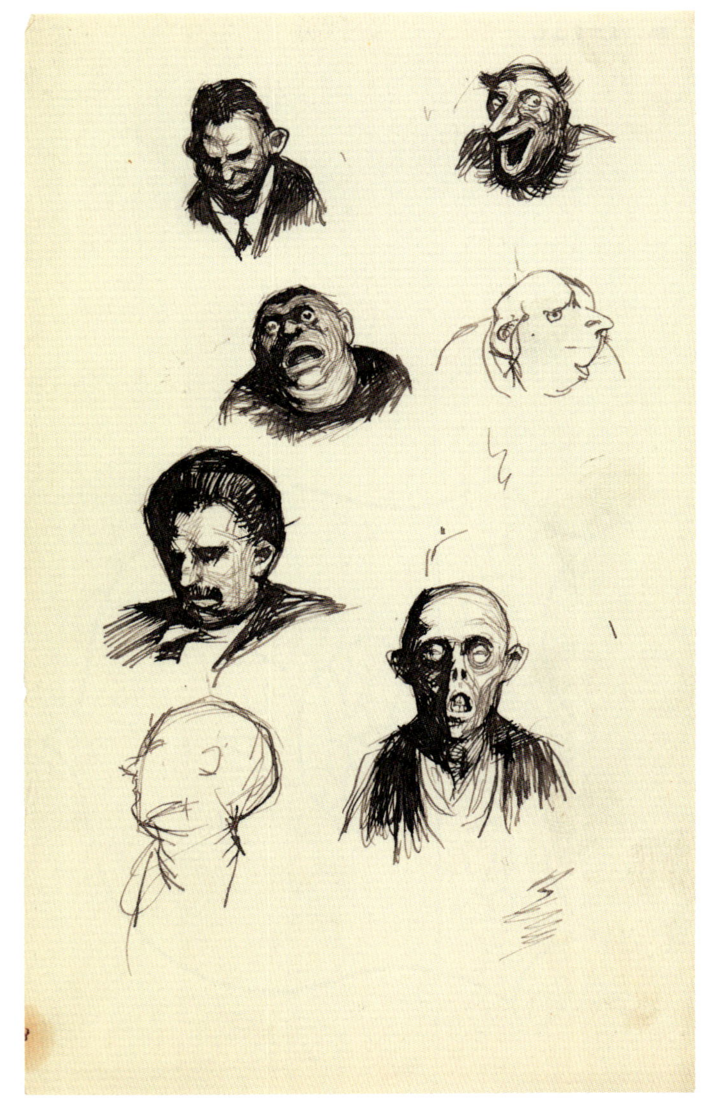

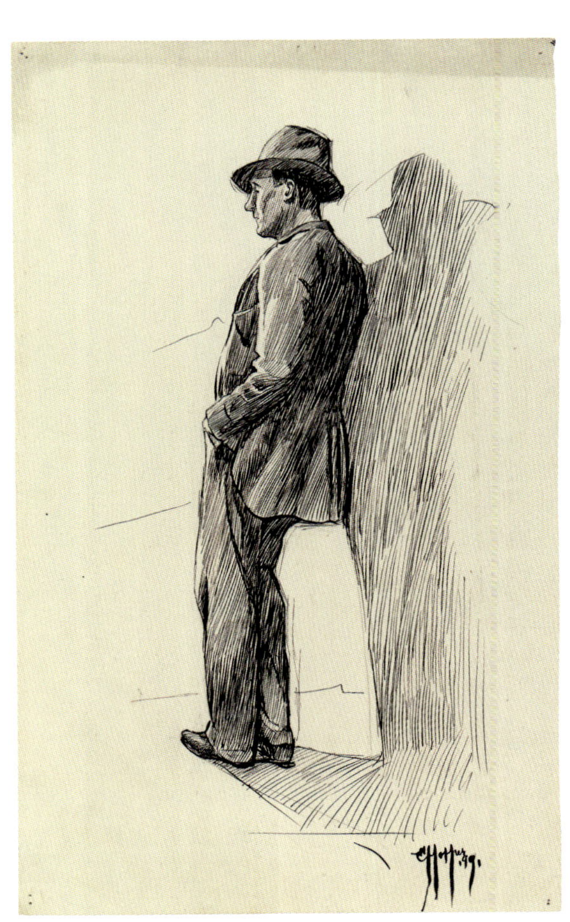

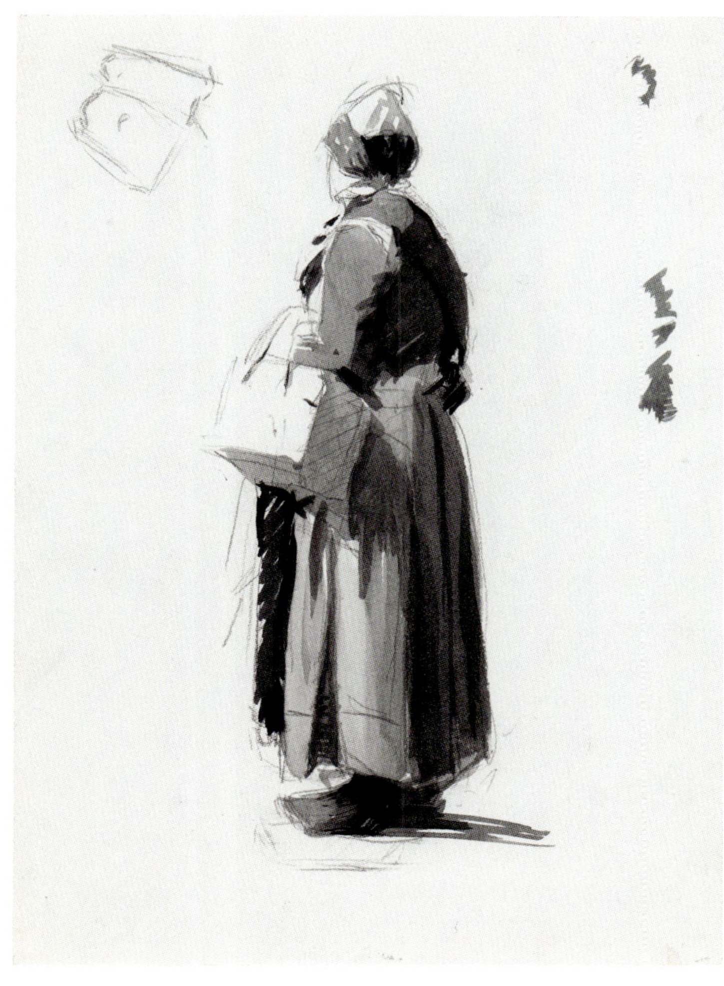

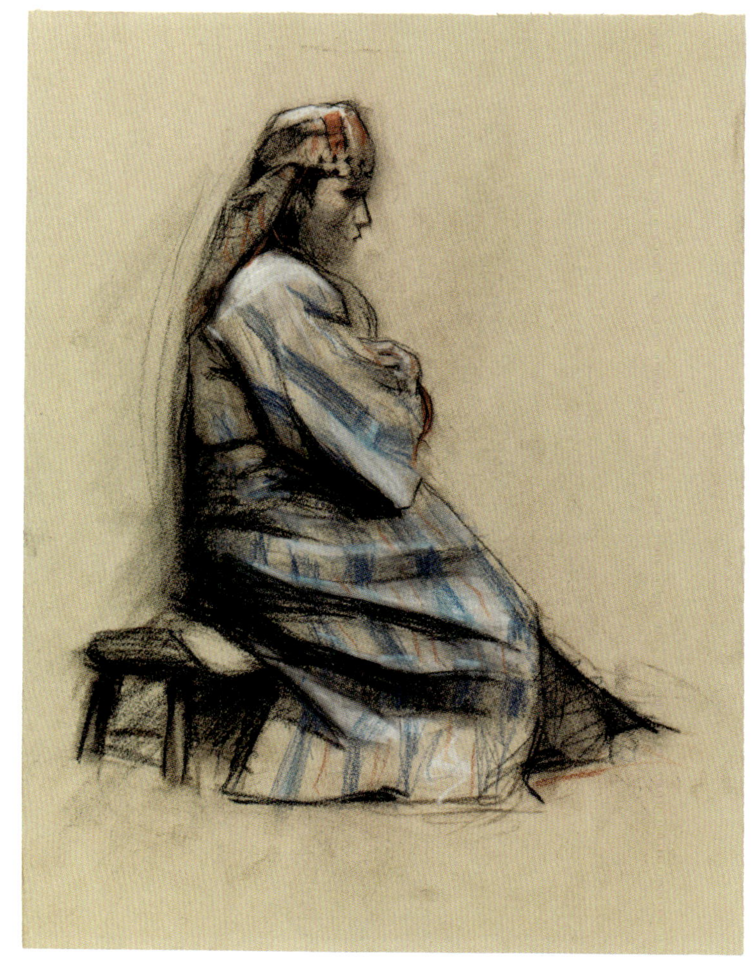

12. (opposite, top left)
Men in Colonial Attire, Man with Head Scarf, Medusa, and Leg, 1895–99
Pen and ink on paper, 9 ⅞ × 7 11⁄16 in. (25.1 × 19.5 cm)
Josephine N. Hopper Bequest 70.1557.90

13. (opposite, top right)
Figure and Character Studies by Occupation, 1899–1906
Pen and ink on paper, 8 × 5 in. (20.3 × 12.7 cm)
Josephine N. Hopper Bequest 70.1605.38

14. (opposite, bottom left)
Caricatured and Grotesque Faces, 1899–1906
Pen and ink on paper, 7 ⅞ × 4 15⁄16 in. (20 × 12.5 cm)
Josephine N. Hopper Bequest 70.1559.26

15. (opposite, bottom right)
Man Leaning Against a Wall, 1899
Pen and ink and graphite pencil on board, 15 ¾ × 9 15⁄16 in. (40 × 25.2 cm)
Josephine N. Hopper Bequest 70.1566.49

16. *Woman with Basket, Profile View*, 1899–1906
Brush and ink and graphite pencil on paper, 11 15⁄16 × 9 in. (30.3 × 22.9 cm)
Josephine N. Hopper Bequest 70.1565.4

17. *Seated Man in Robes and Headdress* (recto), 1899–1906
Fabricated chalk, colored pencil, and charcoal on paper, 12 ⅞ × 9 ⅞ in. (32.7 × 25.1 cm)
Josephine N. Hopper Bequest 70.1566.10a–b

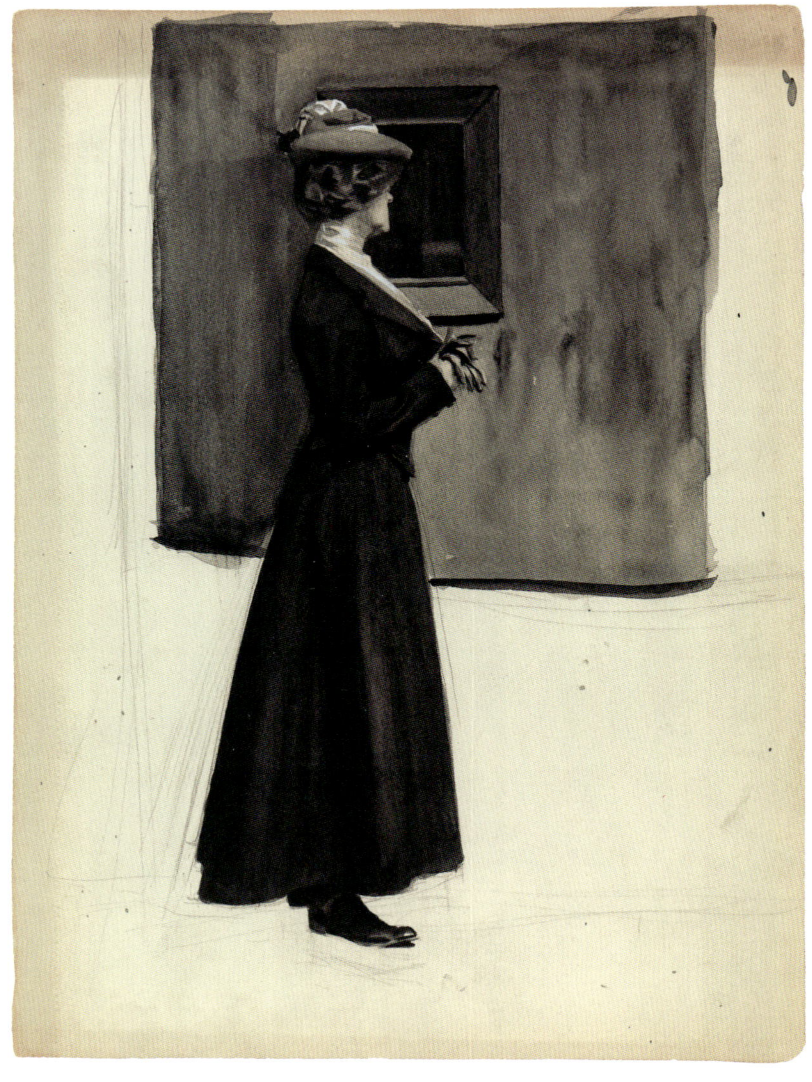

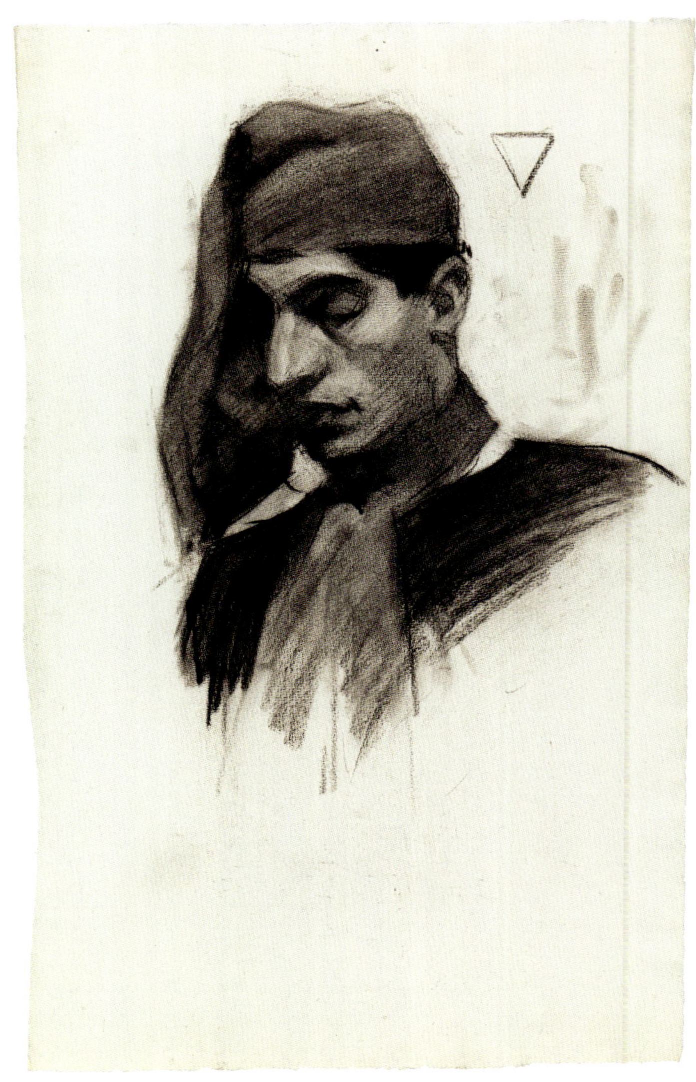

18. *Woman with Gloves Viewing Painting*, 1899–1906
Opaque watercolor and graphite pencil on board
15 × 11 ⅜ in. (38.1 × 28.9 cm)
Josephine N. Hopper Bequest 70.1646

19. *Man in Stocking-like Hat*, 1899–1906
Charcoal on paper, 18 ¾ × 12 5⁄16 in. (47.6 × 31.3 cm)
Josephine N. Hopper Bequest 70.1507

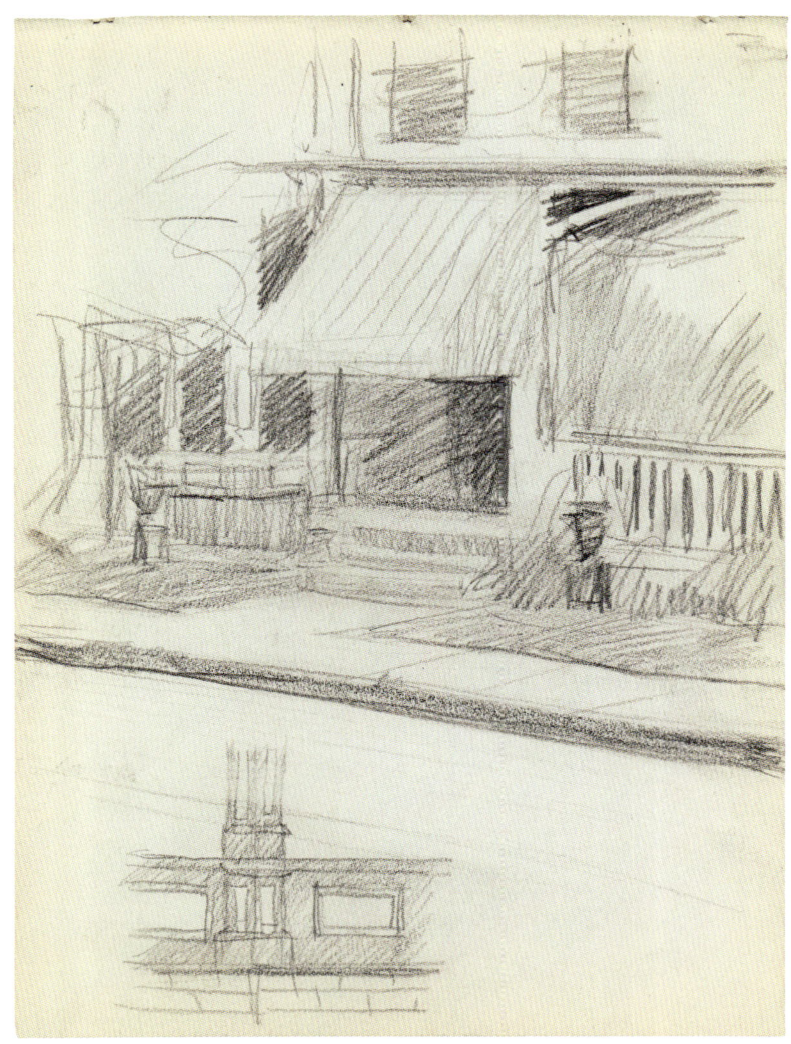

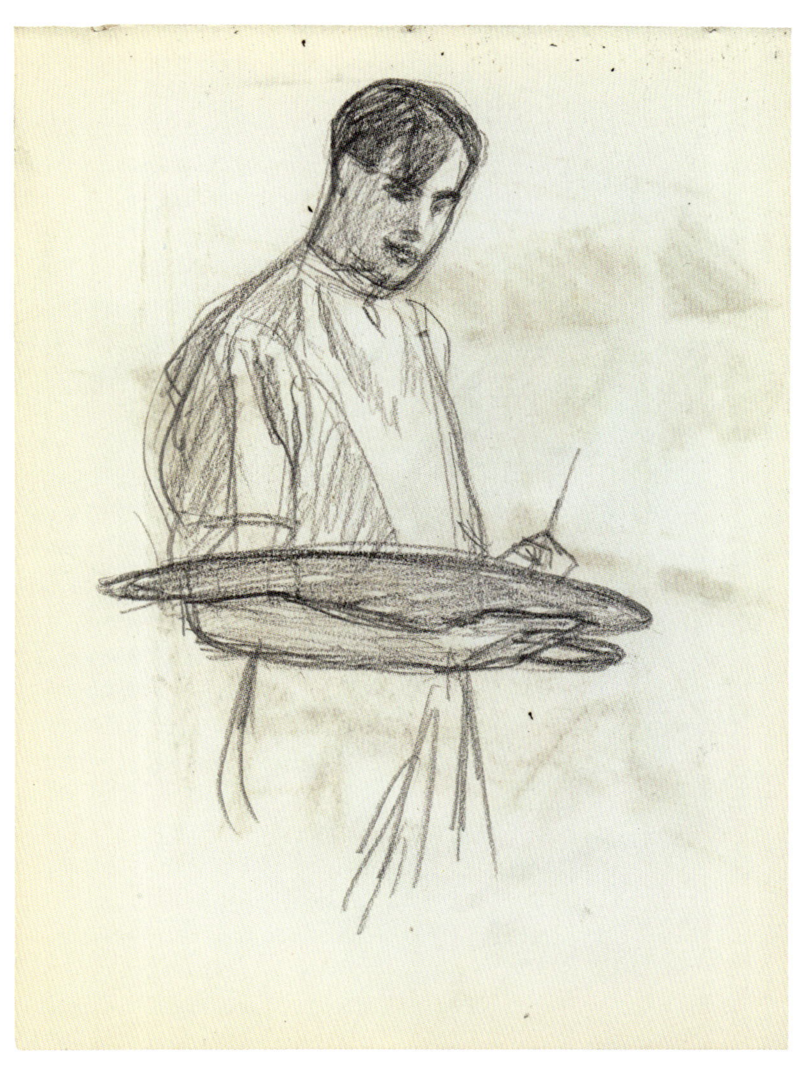

20. *House* (part of a sketchbook), 1899–1900
Graphite pencil on paper, 9⅞ × 7¹¹⁄₁₆ in.
(25.1 × 19.5 cm)
Josephine N. Hopper Bequest 70.1567a–nn

21. *Self-Portrait with Palette* (part of a sketchbook), 1899–1900
Graphite pencil on paper, 9⅞ × 7¹¹⁄₁₆ in.
(25.1 × 19.5 cm)
Josephine N. Hopper Bequest 70.1567a–nn

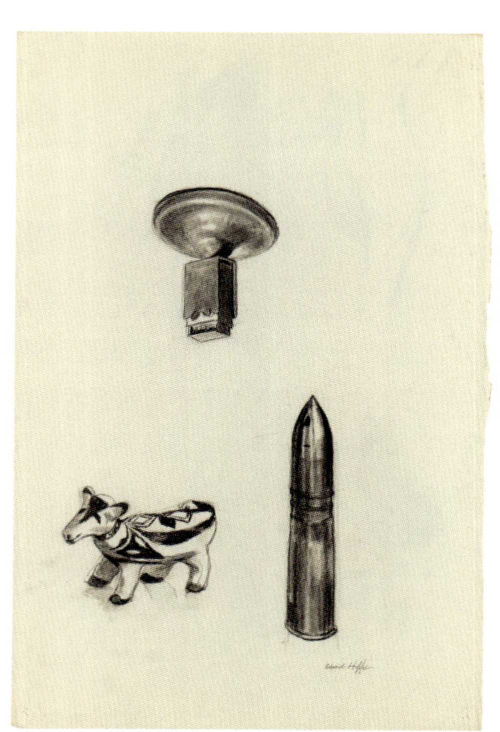

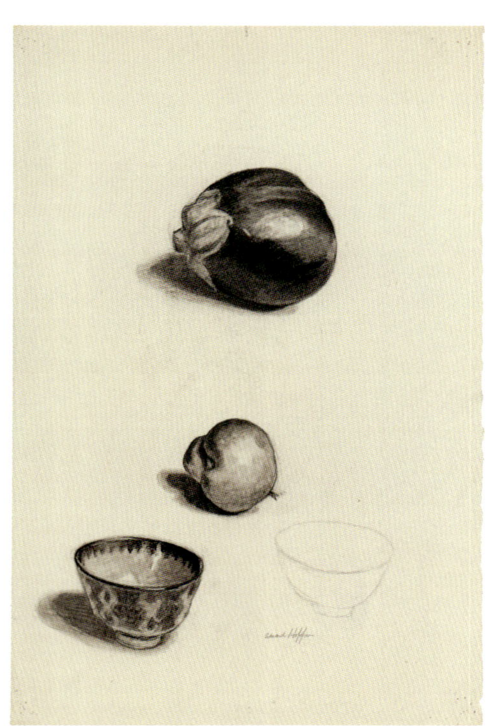

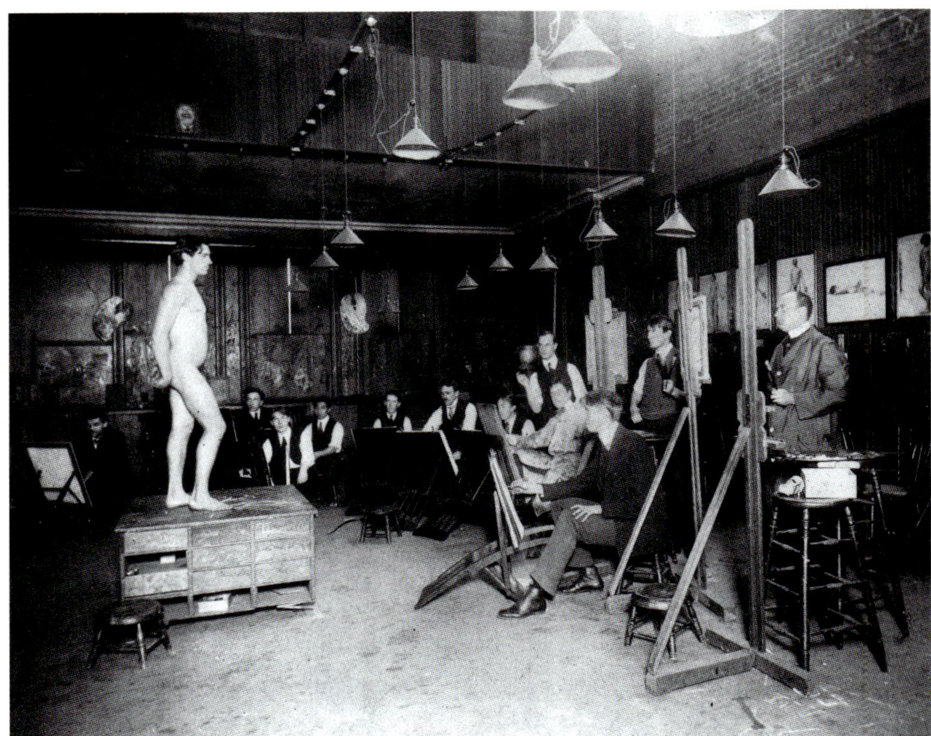

Hopper's gifts were obvious and appreciated at the New York School of Art. Kent noted his accomplished drawing ability and called him the "John Singer Sargent" of the class, high praise at the time.[40] Even mundane academic exercises such as his still life studies of various objects have commanding presence, the artist deftly handling volume, texture, and space even as they are starkly set against a large expanse of paper (figs. 22, 23), giving them an abstract, slightly strange quality consistent with his artistic personality. Life class—the practice of drawing and painting the nude figure from a live model—was a core activity at the school. Hopper excelled at this long-standing pedagogical tradition in the history of art. A wonderfully evocative period photograph shows the serious atmosphere in Henri's life class; Hopper is visible seated third from right (fig. 24). Dozens of Hopper's life drawings, of both male and female models, survive from this period (figs. 25, 26).

Hopper invested the presence, implied presence, and absence of the human being with substantial meaning throughout his career, so it is significant that his mastery of the human form came early. The figure's relationship to its surroundings is at the core of Hopper's art, and this relationship appears early in a group of charcoal drawings featuring the model in a classroom environment. Though some of these sheets, early masterpieces in the handling of tone and the creation of atmosphere and mood in interior spaces, depict the model posing (fig. 27), others strangely show her hugging close to the wall, caught in a private moment even as she remains exposed to the open gaze of students and spectator (fig. 28). We are indeed already in the realm of the "Hopperesque." This series of drawings is part of a larger group in the same technique and materials. Executed with black Conté crayon or charcoal on a fairly heavily textured French paper, they strongly evoke the technique of the French master Georges Seurat as exercises in tonal variation, using the reserve white of the paper and subtle variation of pressure with the crayon to modulate black, white, and gray. One especially appealing drawing shows a group of fellow students looking at paintings, perhaps at the Metropolitan Museum of Art (fig. 29).[41] Hopper was a supremely gifted tonal draftsman, and the young artist's growing self-awareness and intentions of being a presence in the art world are demonstrated both in the subject depicted and in his clear mastery of this difficult technique. Eventually, he came to prefer black mediums almost exclusively, whether chalk, crayon, or charcoal. In this way his drawings are consistent with his concept of painting, where one of his primary stated interests was the rendering of light. We see this interest appear early here in his drawing practice.

Hopper's vocational self-awareness comes through as well in a wonderful series of smaller self-portraits, mostly in pen and brown ink (figs. 30–35), that often show him juxtaposing his face with his expressively posed hands. He thus presents two sides of his profession—the manual and the intellectual—with an engaged, intelligent gaze back at the viewer. These early self-portraits thus state visually with great directness the approach to art he would articulate decades later: the imagination in the artist's mind that is controlled by the concrete limits of technique from the artist's hand.

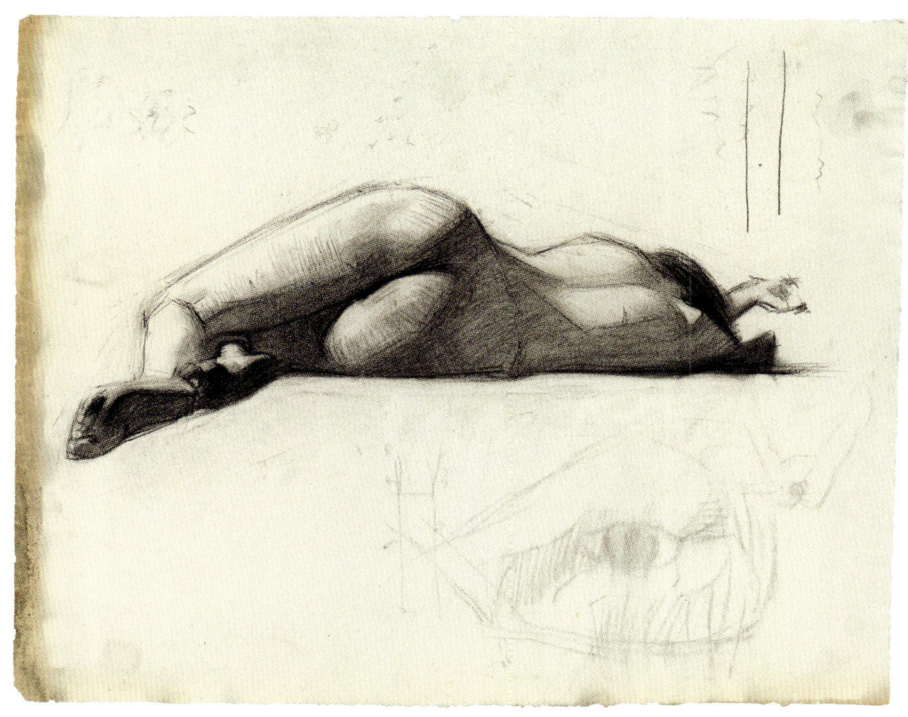

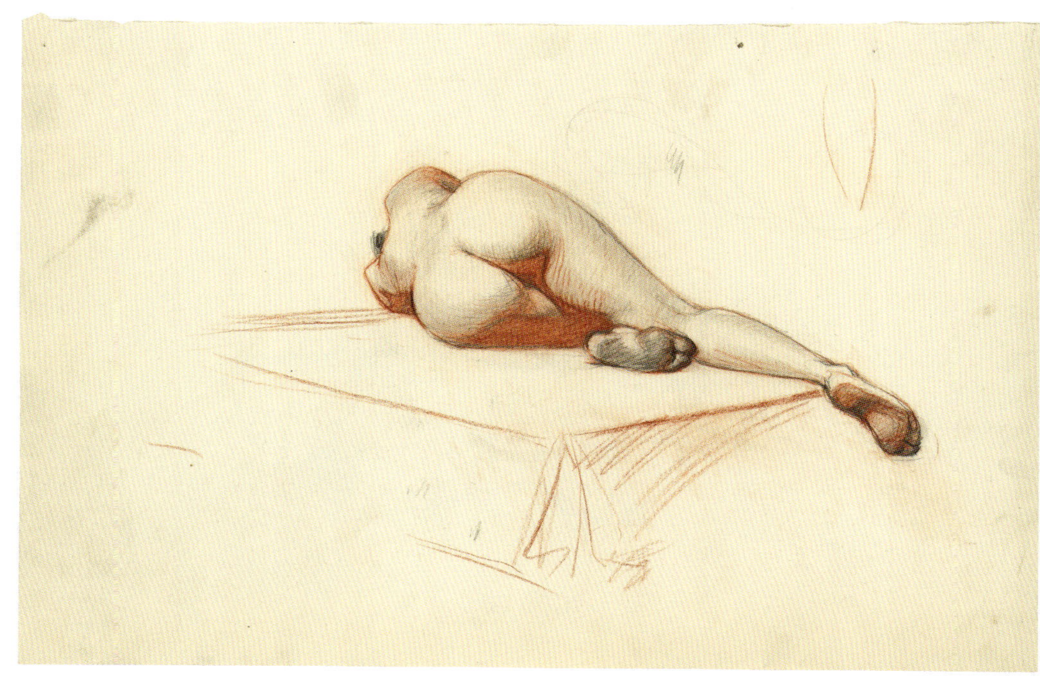

22. (opposite, top left)
Matchbox on Base, Bullet, and Decorative Cow (recto), 1899–1906
Fabricated chalk and charcoal on paper,
22 1/16 × 15 3/16 in. (56 × 38.6 cm)
Josephine N. Hopper Bequest 70.812a–b

23. (opposite, bottom)
Eggplant, Fruit, and Bowl (recto), 1899–1906
Fabricated chalk on paper, 22 1/16 × 15 in. (56 × 38.1 cm)
Josephine N. Hopper Bequest 70.817a–b

24. (opposite, top right)
Robert Henri's life drawing class at the New York School of Art, c. 1903–04. Frances Mulhall Achilles Library, Archives, Whitney Museum of American Art, New York

25. *Reclining Female Nude, Rear View*, 1900–06
Fabricated chalk on paper, 18 3/4 × 24 7/16 in. (47.6 × 62.1 cm)
Josephine N. Hopper Bequest 70.1491

26. *Reclining Female Nude, Rear View* (recto), c. 1902–04
Fabricated chalk and graphite pencil on paper,
12 1/4 × 19 3/16 in. (31.1 × 48.7 cm)
Josephine N. Hopper Bequest 70.1534a–b

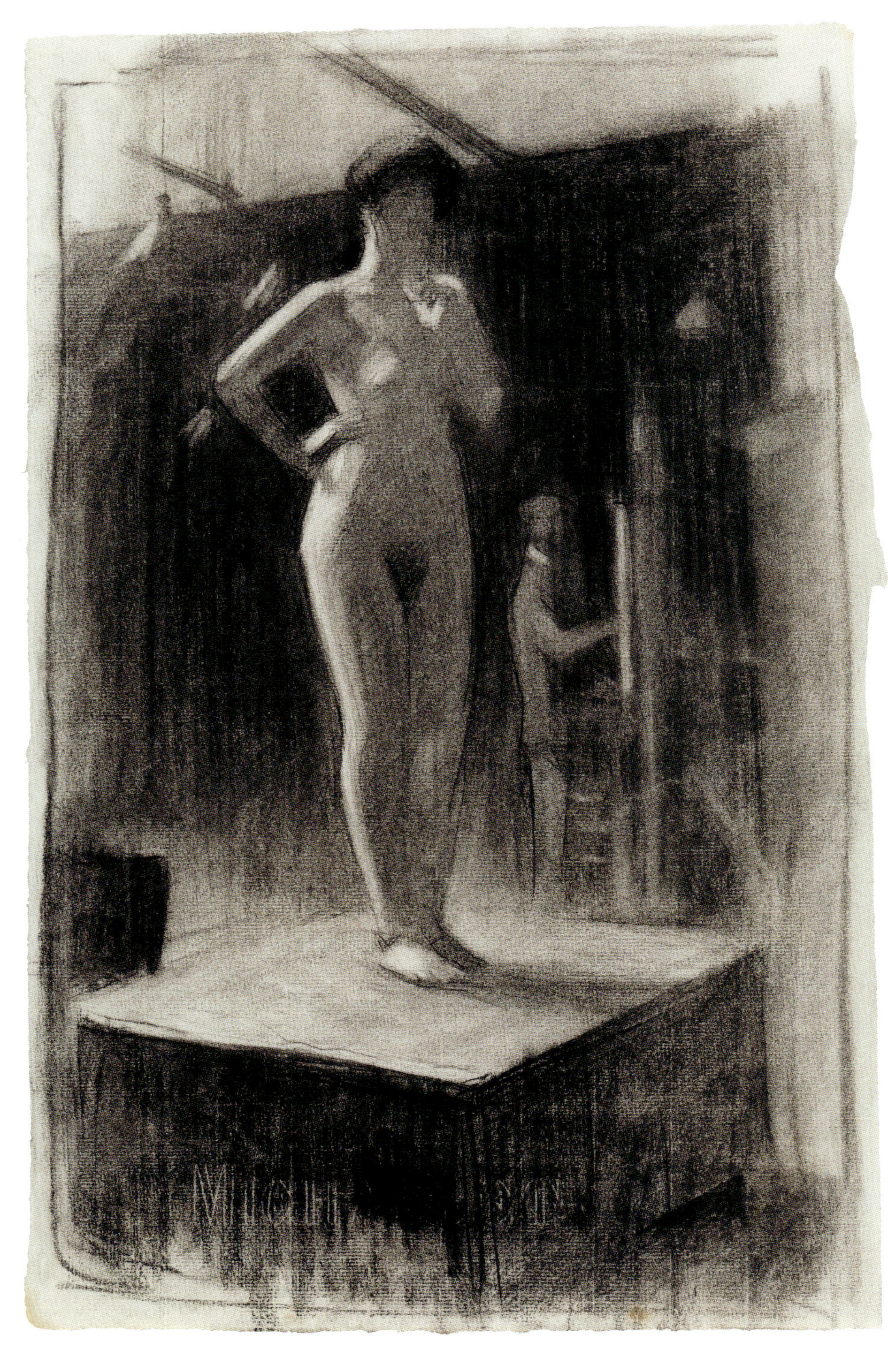

27. *Female Nude on Model's Platform*, c. 1900–03
Charcoal on paper, 19 1⁄16 × 12 3⁄8 in. (48.4 × 31.4 cm)
Josephine N. Hopper Bequest 70.1566.118

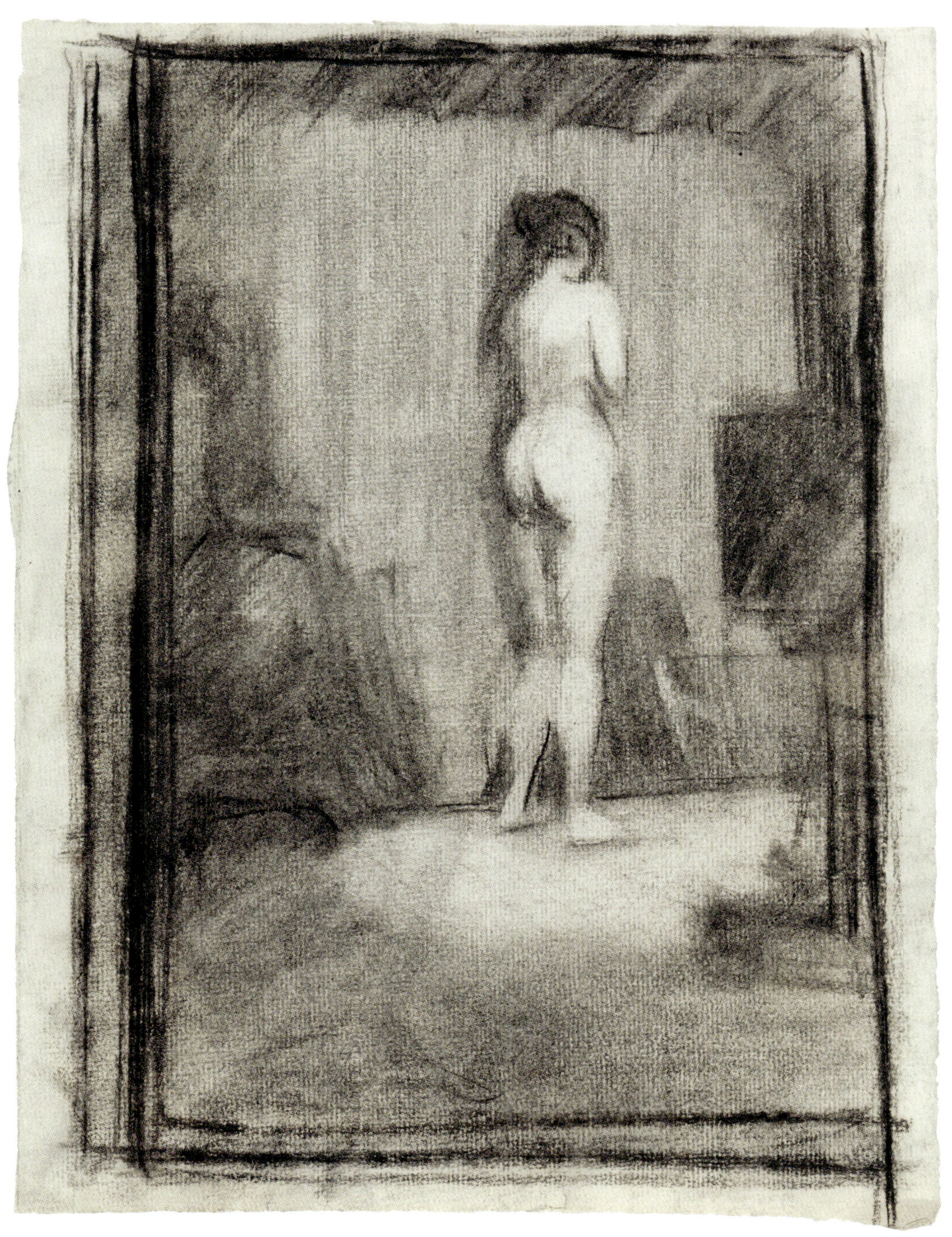

28. *Female Nude in Studio, Rear View*, c. 1900–03
Charcoal on paper, 12 ¼ × 9 9⁄16 in. (31.1 × 24.3 cm)
Josephine N. Hopper Bequest 70.1560.90

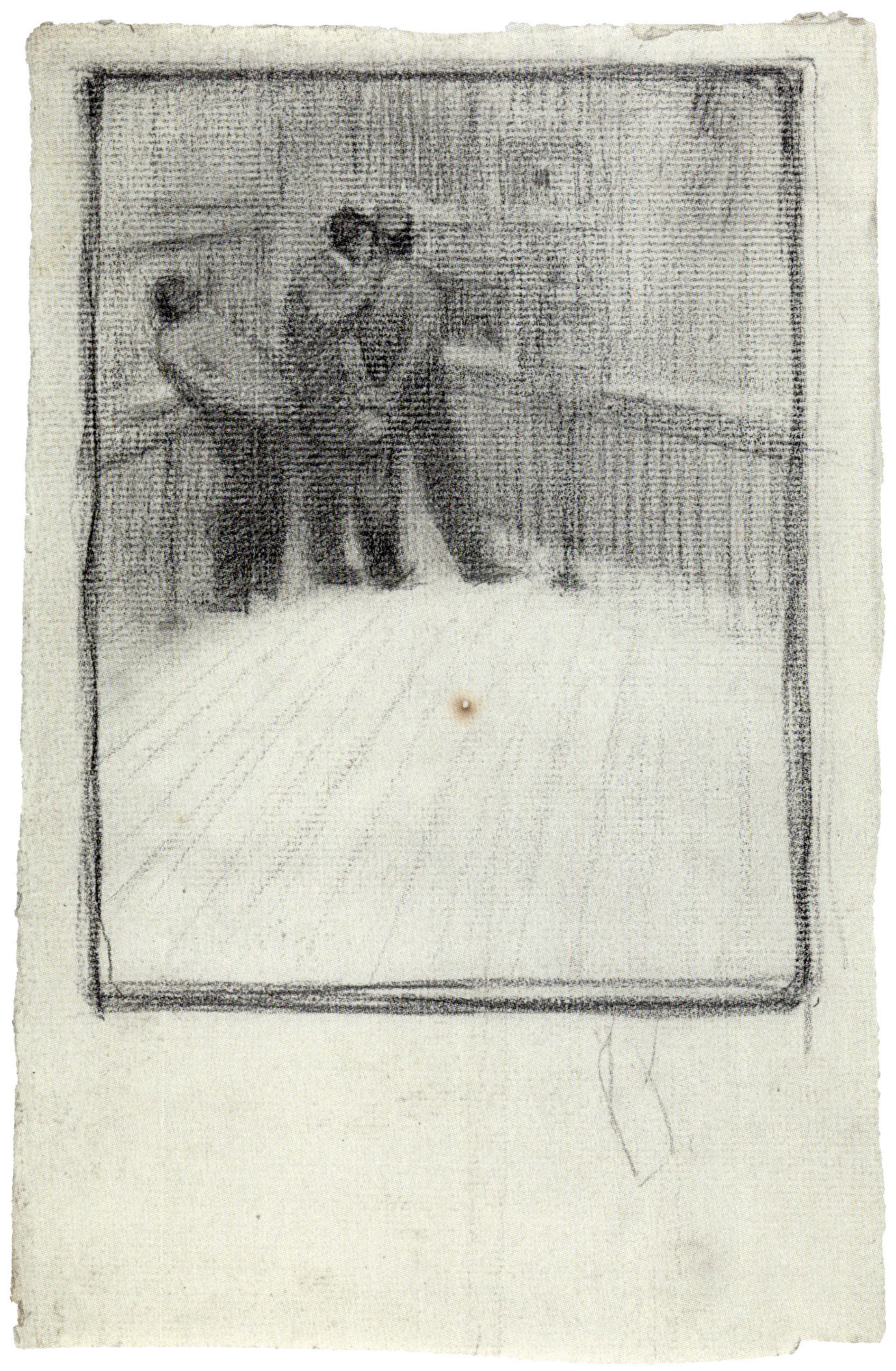

29. *Three Men at Art Exhibition*, c. 1900–03
Graphite pencil on paper, 9 3/8 × 6 1/8 in. (23.8 × 15.6 cm)
Josephine N. Hopper Bequest 70.1560.51

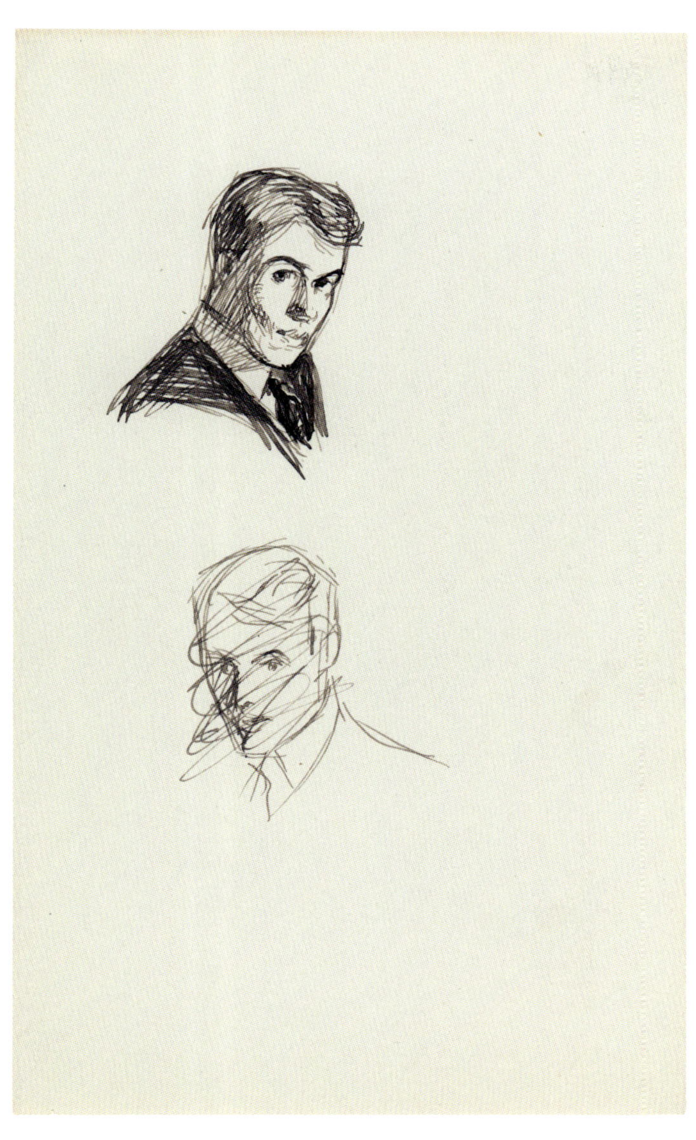

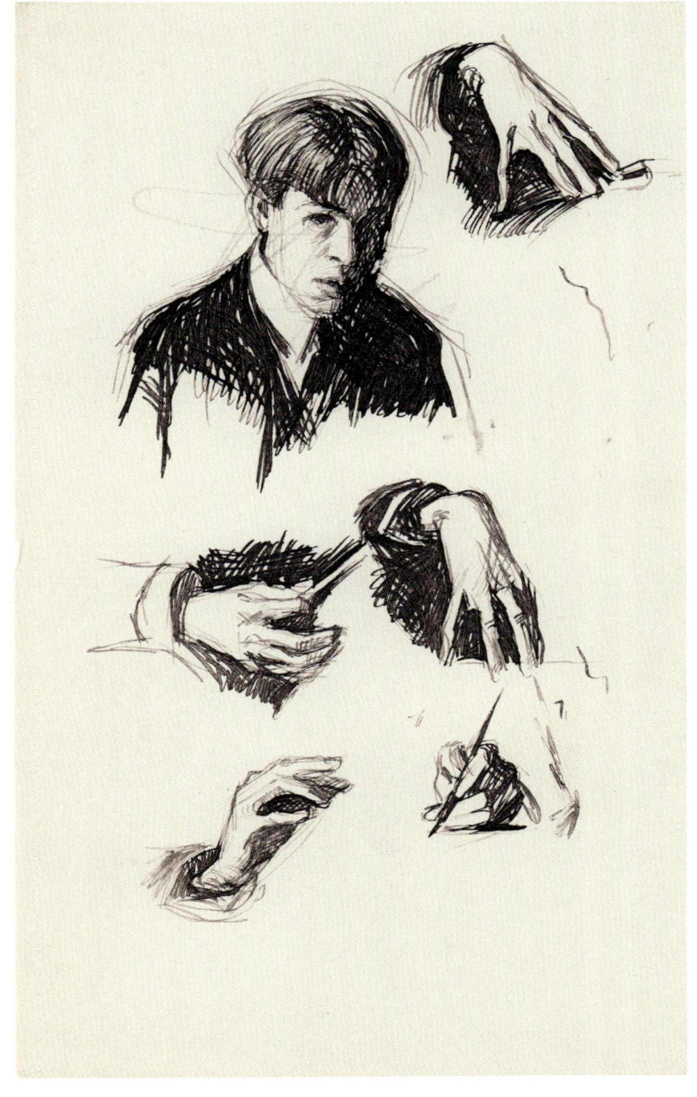

30. *Two Self-Portraits*, c. 1900
Pen and ink on paper, 8 ⅞ × 5 $^{9}/_{16}$ in. (22.5 × 14.1 cm)
Josephine N. Hopper Bequest 70.1561.115

31. *Self-Portrait and Hand Studies*, c. 1900
Pen and ink and graphite pencil on paper,
7 ⅞ × 4 $^{15}/_{16}$ in. (20 × 12.5 cm)
Josephine N. Hopper Bequest 70.1559.28

32. *Two Self-Portraits and Two Hand Studies*, c. 1900
Pen and ink on paper, 7 ⅞ × 4 $^{15}/_{16}$ in. (20 × 12.5 cm)
Josephine N. Hopper Bequest 70.1559.24

33. *Self-Portrait and Hand Studies*, c. 1900
Pen and ink on paper, 8 ⅞ × 5 $^{9}/_{16}$ in. (22.5 × 14.1 cm)
Josephine N. Hopper Bequest 70.1559.21

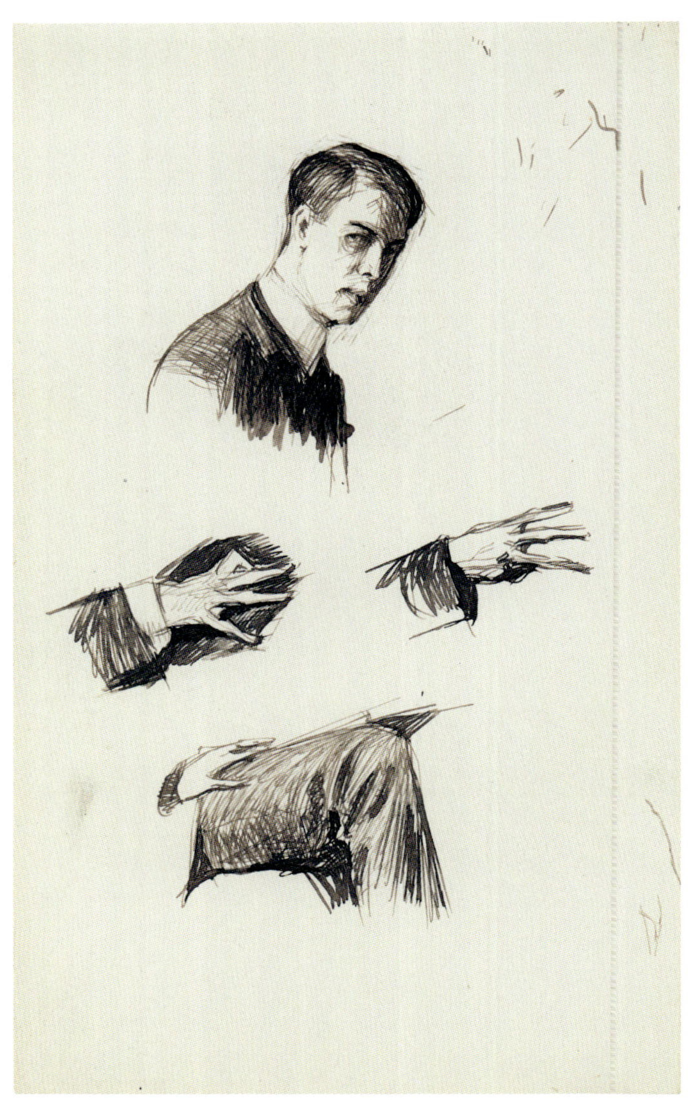

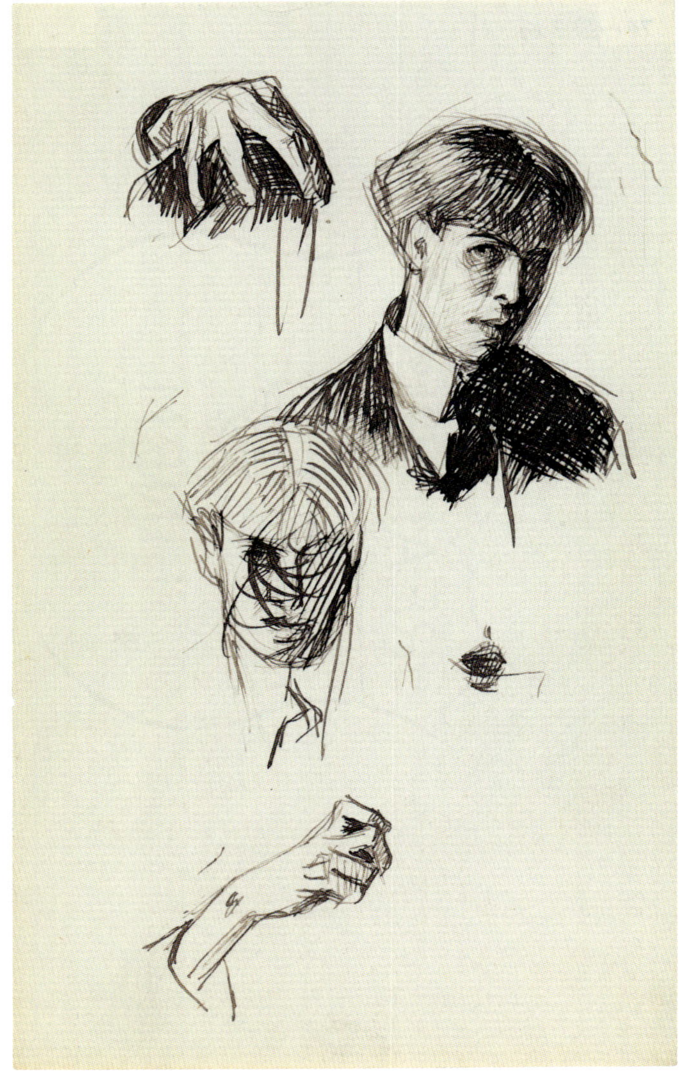

34. *Self-Portrait*, 1899–1906
Charcoal on paper, 18 ⅞ × 12 ⅜ in. (47.9 × 31.4 cm)
Josephine N. Hopper Bequest 70.1536

35. *Two Hand Studies* (recto), c. 1905–06
Charcoal on paper, 18 ⅞ × 12 ¹⁄₁₆ in. (47.9 × 30.6 cm)
Josephine N. Hopper Bequest 70.1535a–b

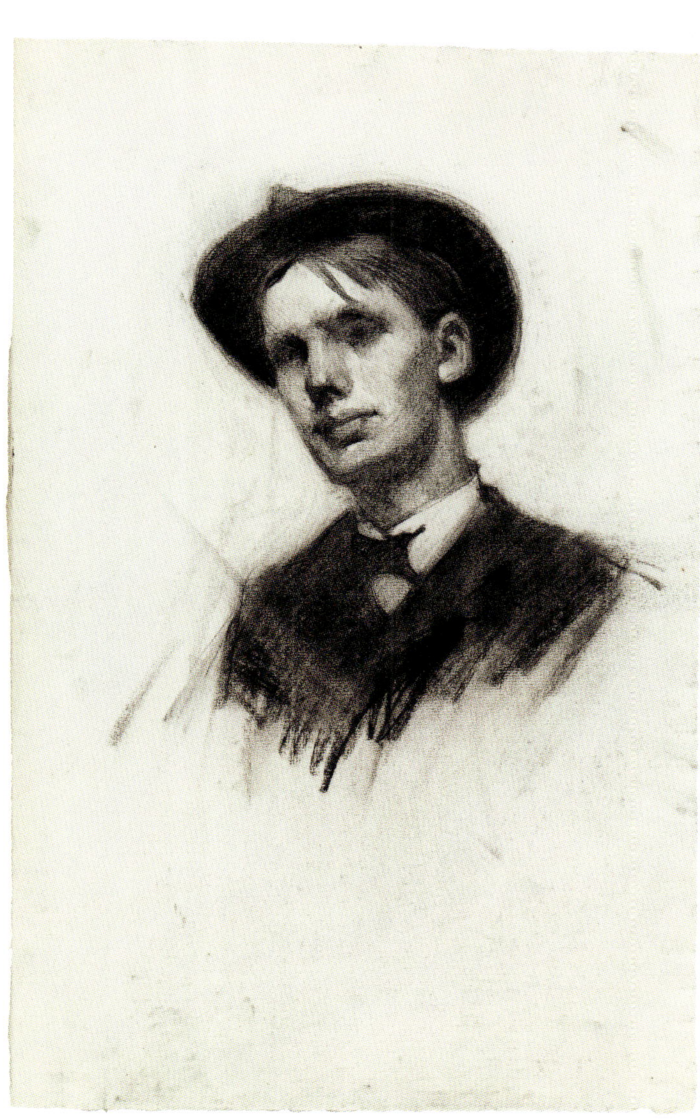

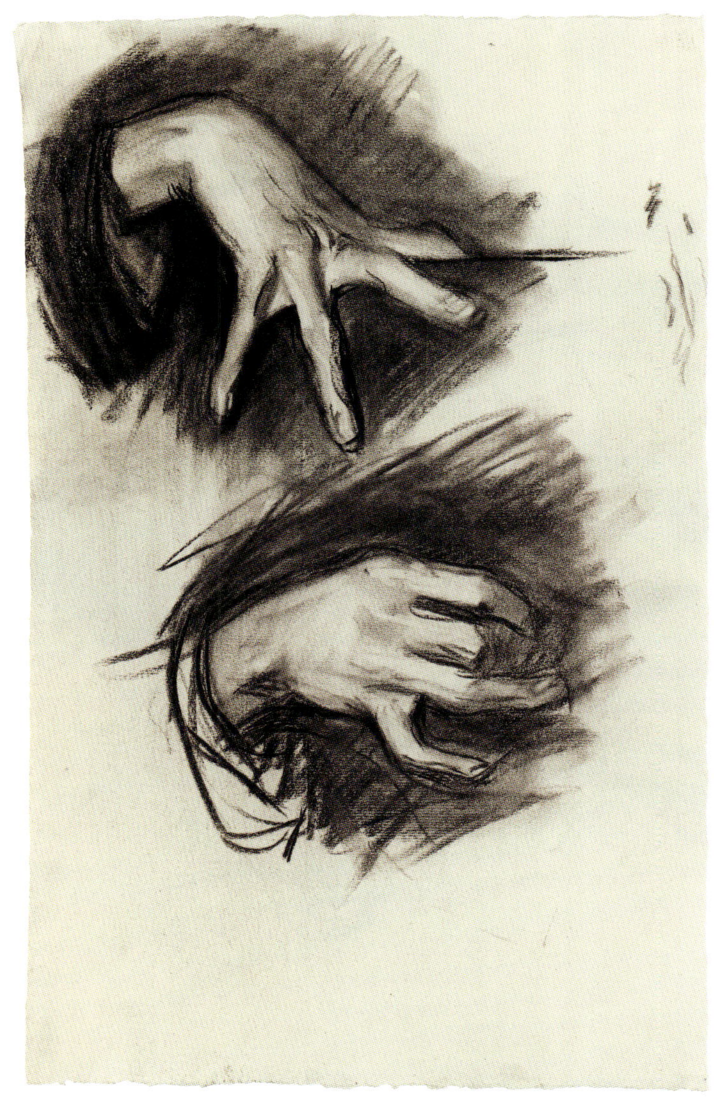

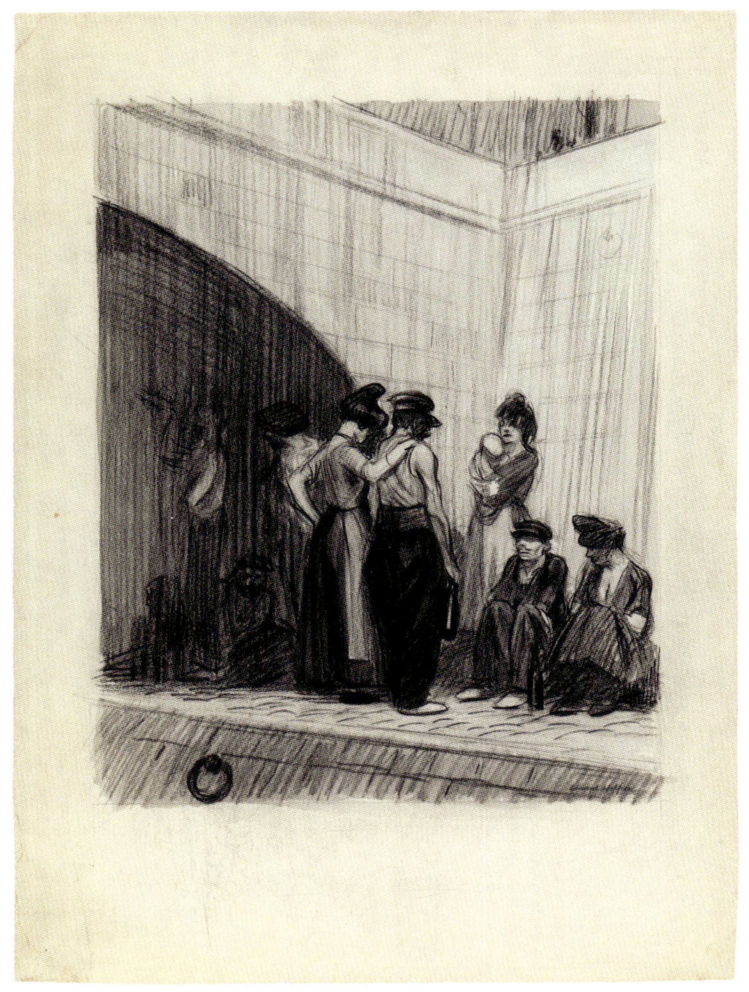

Paris and After, 1906–15

Hopper continued to draw in a variety of modes after leaving school and during his period of travel to Paris and other cities in Europe. He filled two sketchbooks with close but quick observations in pen and brown ink of contemporary Parisian street and café life, subjects he mined for some time to come (see "Hopper in Paris and *Soir Bleu*," in this volume). These drawings correspond to a fruitful, Impressionist mode in his oeuvre and share a common impulse in recording observed reality, but they focus on people rather than empty urban landscapes. Hopper was also creating more carefully constructed subjects that reflected his training in illustration, perhaps in preparation for the work he would seek back in America (fig. 36). An incredibly black, very finished sheet showing the Panthéon from a low point of view is the drawn equivalent of Hopper's Paris paintings (fig. 37). Though similar in subject and composition, the drawing looks totally different from his light-filled canvases of the same moment, as it fully exploits the dark tonal possibilities of the medium by suggesting the fall of night. Drawings of French subjects, inspired by his travels and by French literature and history, remain rooted in a graphic, illustrative style, with thick black lines outlining flat areas of color. There is a significant body of work done in this technique (fig. 38), with the artist occasionally transcending its limitations, as in the magisterial *Boy and Moon* (see fig. 141). Hopper hated illustration work but made a steady living at it for a number of years.[42] His detail-filled, anecdotal drawings done for popular magazines such as *Every Week* (fig. 39) from the 1910s and 1920s nonetheless show some of the close observation of urban life that informs his paintings. Some even hint at the symbolism of his fully mature work, such as in the weight given to interior and exterior spaces through the loaded use of windows and light in an illustration of a beating (fig. 40).

36. *Figures Under a Bridge in Paris*, 1906–07
Fabricated chalk, wash, and graphite pencil on paper, 20 × 15 in. (50.8 × 38.1 cm)
Josephine N. Hopper Bequest 70.1339

37. *Dome*, c. 1907
Fabricated chalk and wash on paper, 21 3/8 × 19 15/16 in. (54.3 × 50.6 cm)
Josephine N. Hopper Bequest 70.1434

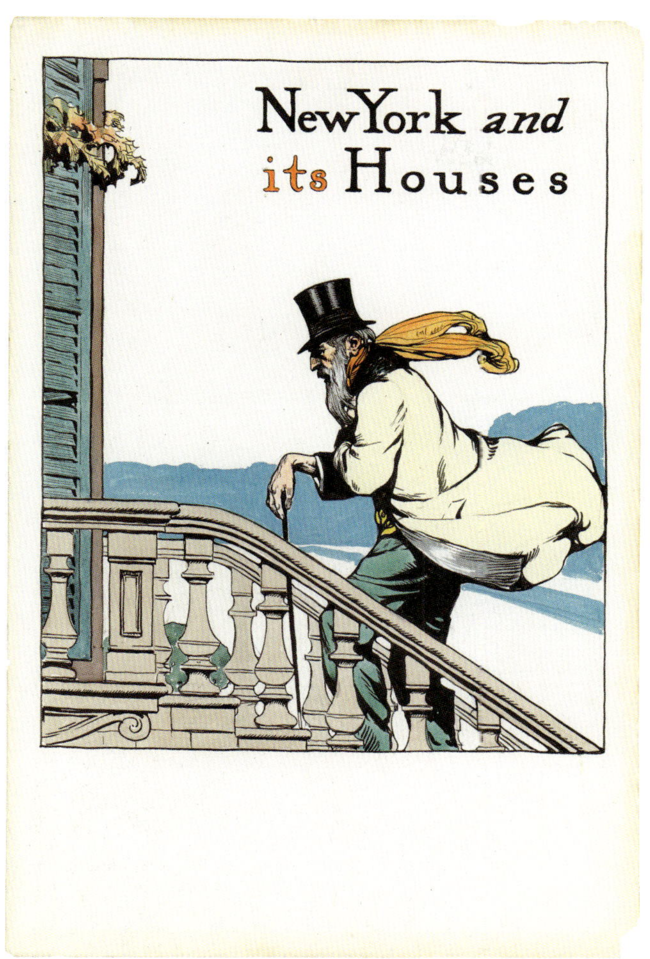

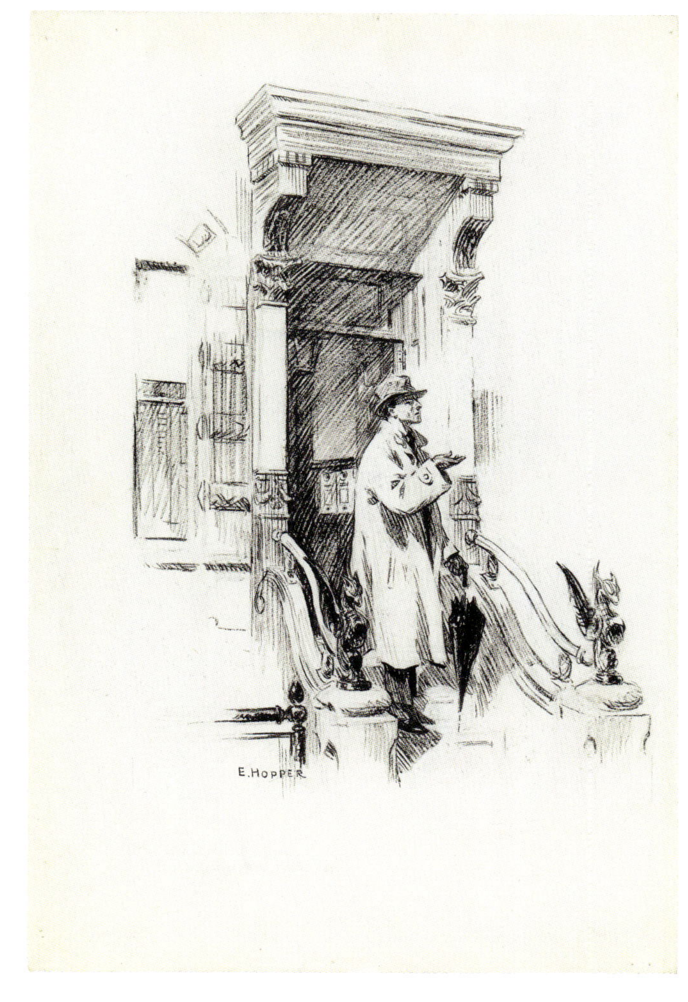

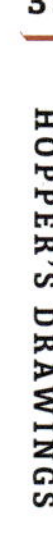

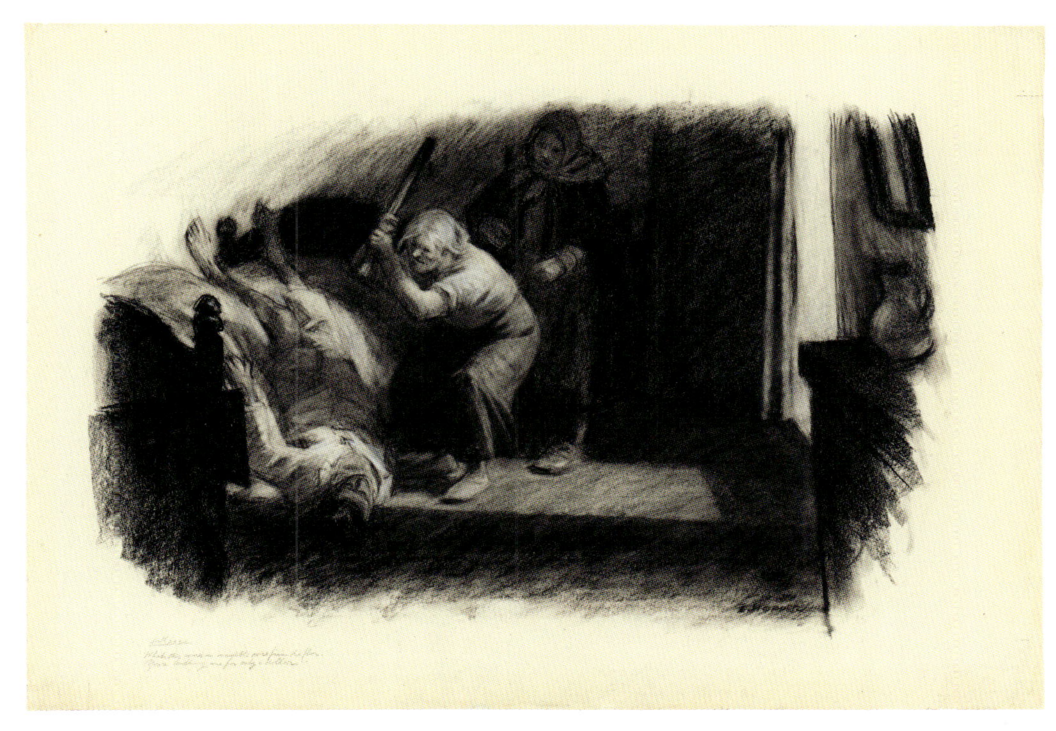

38. *New York and Its Houses*, c. 1906–10
Brush and ink, transparent and opaque watercolor, and graphite pencil on paper, 21 13⁄16 × 14 13⁄16 in. (55.4 × 37.6 cm)
Josephine N. Hopper Bequest 70.1347

39. "*They conjure up visions of possible mistakes in connection with the carrying of an umbrella*," 1917
Illustration for H. Addington Bruce, "What Trivial Doubts Can Do to You," *Every Week* 4 (April 16, 1917)
Brush and ink, graphite pencil, and opaque watercolor on paper, 21 13⁄16 × 14 13⁄16 in. (55.4 × 37.6 cm)
Josephine N. Hopper Bequest 70.1446

40. "*What's this?... Don't, don't—Hannah!*" 1925
Illustration for Emerson Low, "The Man Who Had Been Away," *Scribner's Magazine* 77 (May 1925)
Fabricated chalk and charcoal on paper, 19 7⁄8 × 29 13⁄16 in. (50.5 × 75.7 cm)
Josephine N. Hopper Bequest 70.1450

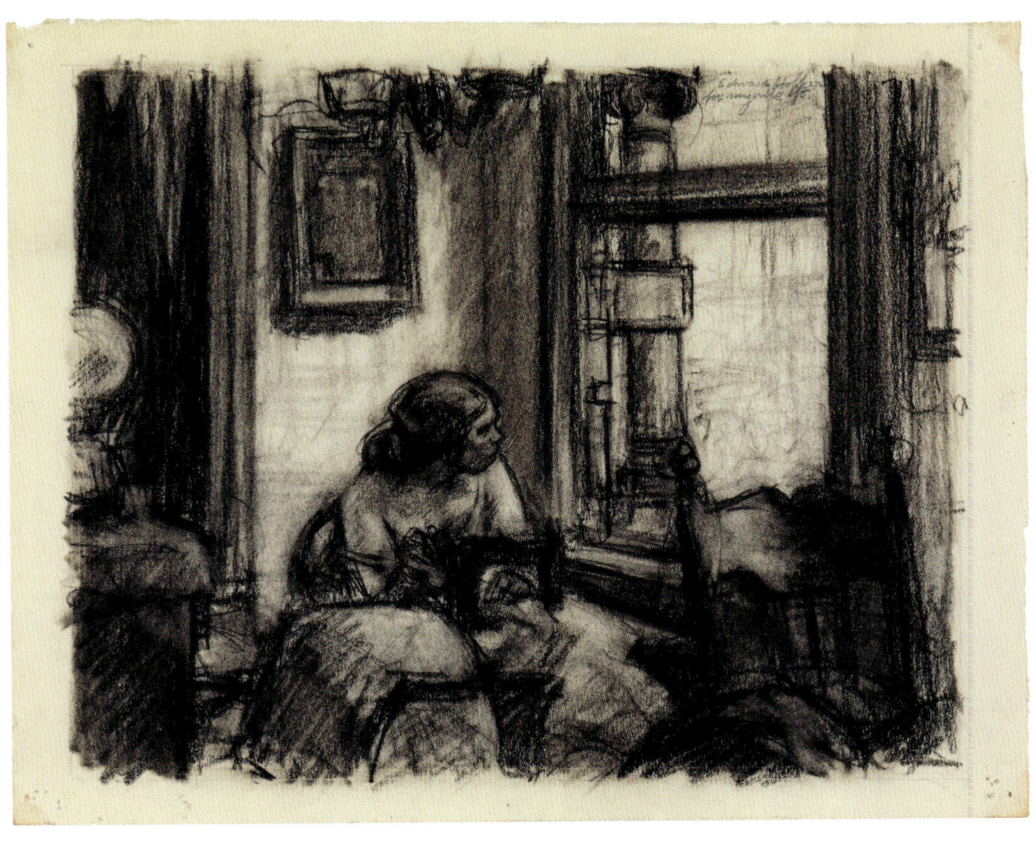

Hopper's Mature Style, circa 1920

Hopper's first significant critical and financial successes came toward middle age, through his prints and watercolors.[43] He had taught himself to etch and bought his own printing press in the mid-1910s, and he won two museum prizes for *East Side Interior* in 1923 (see study, fig. 41). In 1924, after a successful watercolor show at the Frank K. M. Rehn Galleries, he was finally able to support himself exclusively by making the art that interested him, rather than the assignments of commercial illustration. For Hopper, drawing was practical and functional and served as the connective tissue among his diverse activities without being the end product. This is hardly atypical in post-Renaissance art history, and Hopper was, in many ways, a very traditional draftsman. He used drawing as many artists do, as a personal activity to keep his eye honed and as a way to explore ideas.

The 1910s and early 1920s had been a period of artistic searching. While continuing commercial illustration (and no doubt making hundreds of drawings turned over to publishers that have not survived), he created the ambitious, Eurocentric oil painting *Soir Bleu* in 1914, along with paintings of urban views and imagined landscapes. As the 1910s progressed, Hopper began developing his etching practice in earnest and, during the summers, became a fairly prolific plein air oil painter, producing a group of small panels over three summers spent on Monhegan Island, Maine.[44] Fairly straightforward drawings of rocky outcroppings and seascapes correspond to this body of work (figs. 42, 43). In the 1920s he increasingly turned to watercolor and, with summer depictions of spots in Maine and Massachusetts, began to establish his reputation in this medium. Unlike his drawings, Hopper clearly saw his watercolors as potentially finished products worthy of sale. The medium is finicky and difficult, regularly resulting in abandoned or rejected pieces. In drawing there was less pressure, though he approached many of the drawings from this moment in his career much like his watercolors, executing them outdoors, "from the fact," their compositions determined by a specifically chosen view. As personal exercises created in a more easily controlled medium, Hopper could feel free to leave them unfinished, to change and erase them, or to study fragments of views that interested him. Many of them are nonetheless quite resolved and can stand alone as drawn versions of the subjects that also attracted him in watercolor and oil during this period (figs. 44–46, 48–51, 59–63).

By this time, the artist had established fabricated black chalk or crayon as his preferred medium in drawing. He described it to others as Conté crayon, referring to the prominent French brand of fabricated black chalk (this description was used in the two Whitney exhibition catalogues done in consultation with Hopper that included his drawings),[45] but

41. Study for *East Side Interior* (recto), 1922
Fabricated chalk and charcoal on paper,
9 × 11½ in. (22.9 × 29.2 cm)
Josephine N. Hopper Bequest 70.342a–b

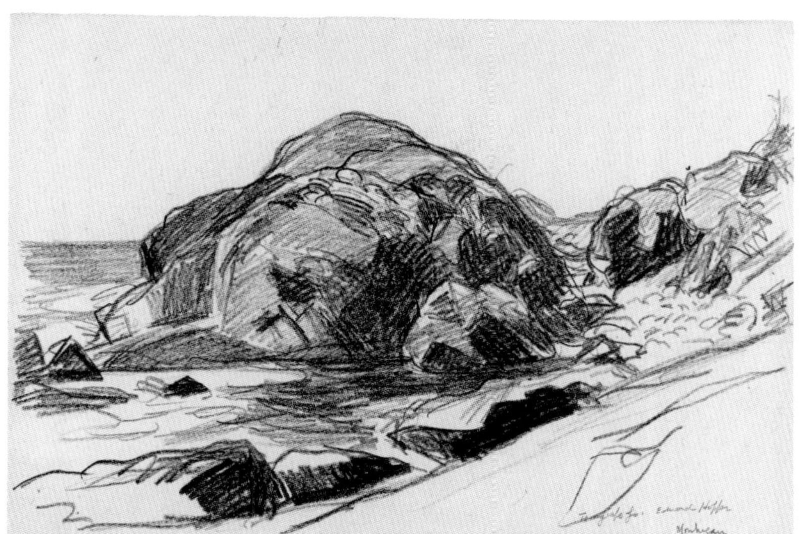

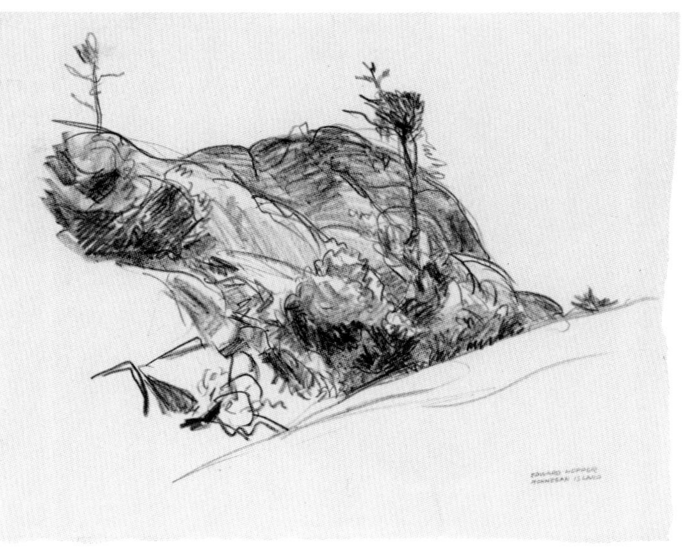

the medium is not consistent in his drawings, being more or less waxy or powdery depending on the amount of binder in it. Such variation is unsurprising over the course of a long career, and the exact type of fabricated chalk (and sometimes charcoal) Hopper actually purchased must have evolved slightly with the decades, if nothing else because of changes in materials and methods used by manufacturers. Whatever the precise makeup and consistency of the chalk or charcoal, Hopper was an absolute master at manipulating black medium, capable of getting a wide variety of effects, textures, and line quality. He achieved deep, rich blacks, pressing the medium firmly into the paper, as well as tonally diverse gradations of various grays with a lighter touch. He could create sharp lines with a narrow point or broad strokes of texture using a stump (a tightly rolled piece of cloth, paper, or leather traditionally used to blend dry drawing mediums) or the broad side of the chalk stick. Hopper could mix these textures and shades with complete virtuosity and to impressive effect, sometimes adding white chalk to modulate light more effectively. He erased or removed medium with equal skill, and often did so in fluid, gestural strokes to create white, "negative" lines using the reserve of the paper.

Scholars typically and quite reasonably see in Hopper's etchings the first rich explorations of the subject matter for which he would become celebrated. While there are very early oil paintings that fully express the aesthetic that made him famous, the etchings established typically Hopperesque subject matter and atmosphere in a consistent and concentrated fashion.[46] Some of the great preparatory studies that exist for Hopper's prints suggest he was searching for material out-of-doors while drawing from life (figs. 52, 53) during New England summers. His most impressive prints, however, moved beyond this; works such as *Night Shadows* (see fig. 284) are among his greatest work in any medium, fully mature expressions of synthetic distillations of memory and observation. *East Side Interior*, whose drawing has many searching pentimenti but comes close to the final etching, is an early masterpiece in his favored black medium, indicating Hopper's growing interest in the symbolic, metaphoric qualities of both light and interior and exterior space (fig. 41).

42. *Monhegan*, 1916–19
Fabricated chalk on paper, 10½ × 16 in. (26.7 × 40.6 cm)
Josephine N. Hopper Bequest 70.679

43. *Monhegan Island*, 1916–19
Fabricated chalk on paper, 12 9/16 × 16⅛ in. (31.9 × 41 cm)
Josephine N. Hopper Bequest 70.363

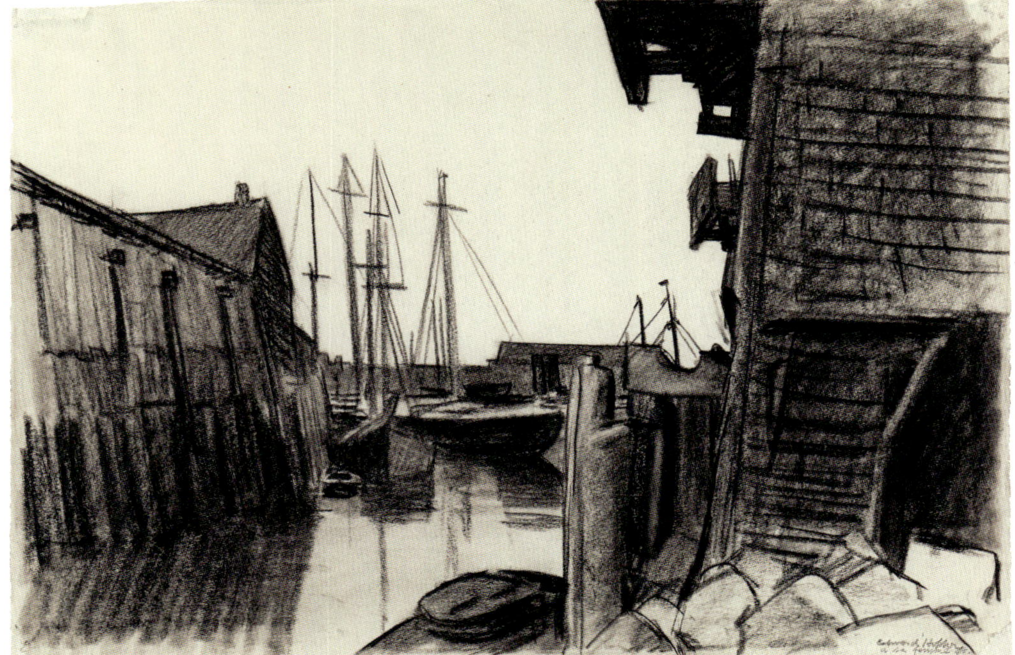

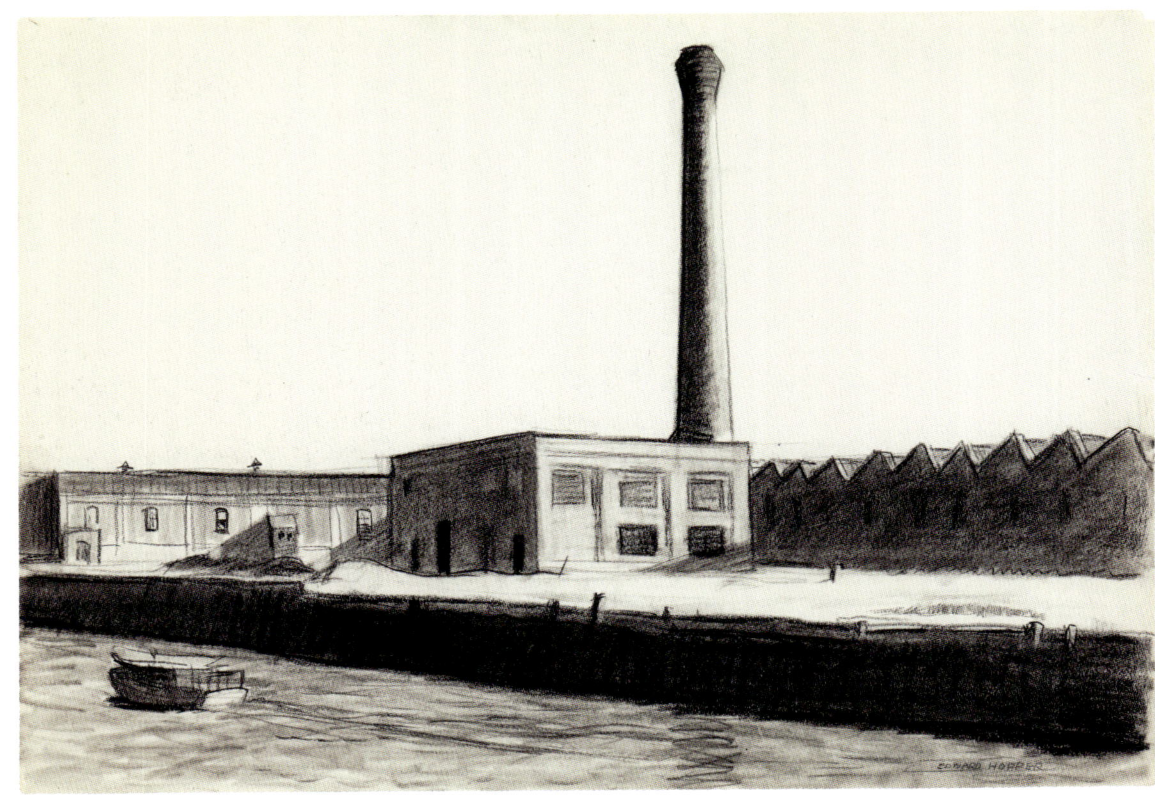

44. *Harbor Landscape with Docks, Boats, and Buildings*, c. 1926
Fabricated chalk on paper, 11 13⁄16 × 18 1⁄16 in. (30 × 45.9 cm)
Josephine N. Hopper Bequest 70.304

45. *Salem*, 1929
Fabricated chalk on paper, 15 × 22 1⁄16 in. (38.1 × 56 cm)
Josephine N. Hopper Bequest 70.307

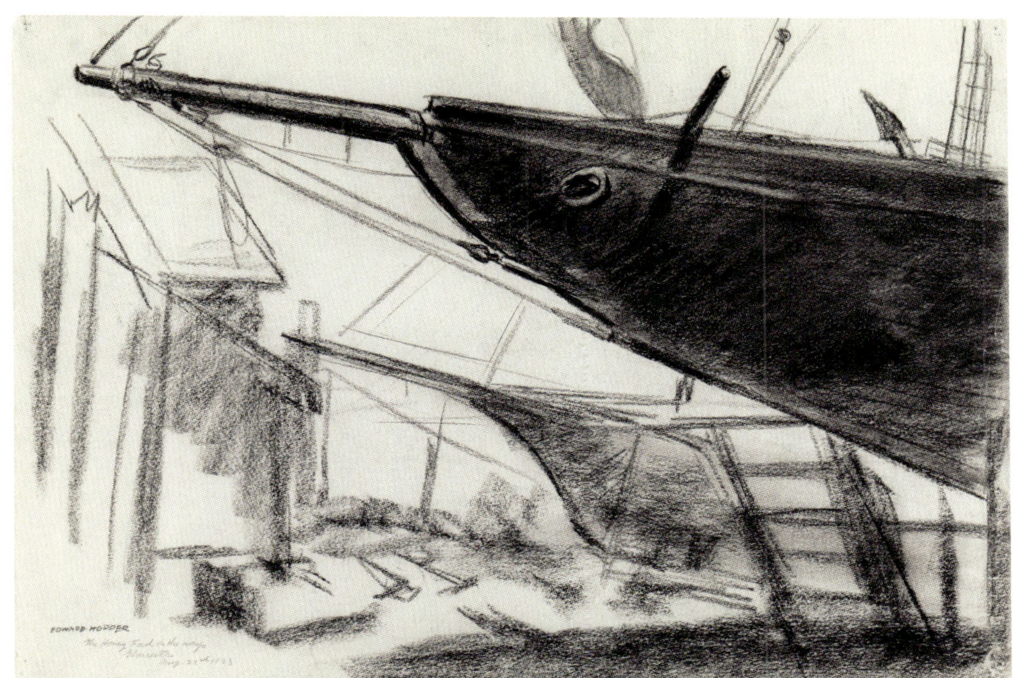

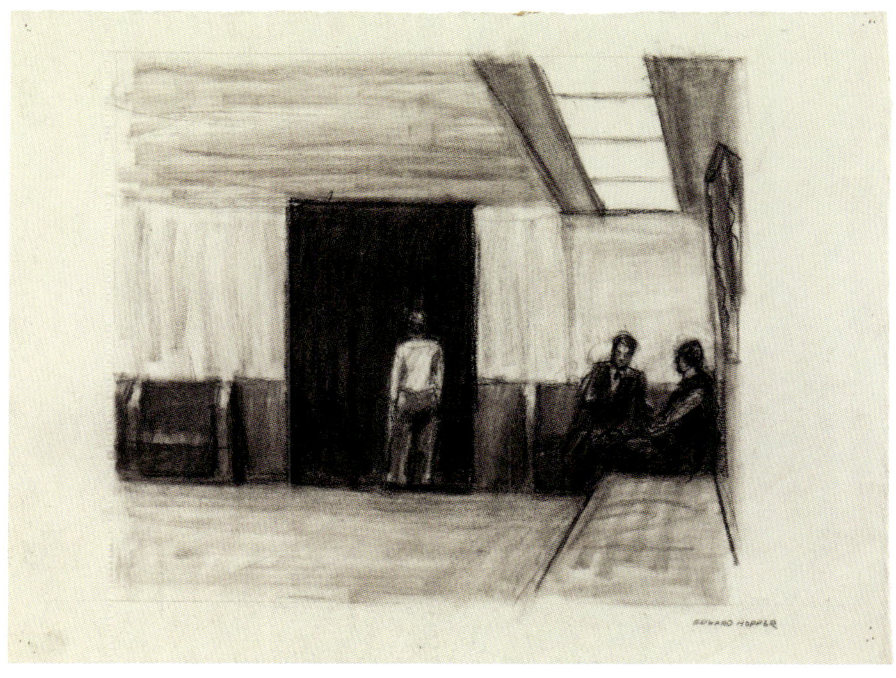

46. *The Henry Ford on the Ways, Gloucester*, 1923
Charcoal on paper, $12 \times 17\frac{15}{16}$ in. (30.5 × 45.6 cm)
Josephine N. Hopper Bequest 70.837

47. *Three Men in an Interior Space*, c. 1925(?)
Fabricated chalk on paper, $11\frac{1}{8} \times 15\frac{1}{8}$ in. (28.3 × 38.4 cm)
Josephine N. Hopper Bequest 70.836

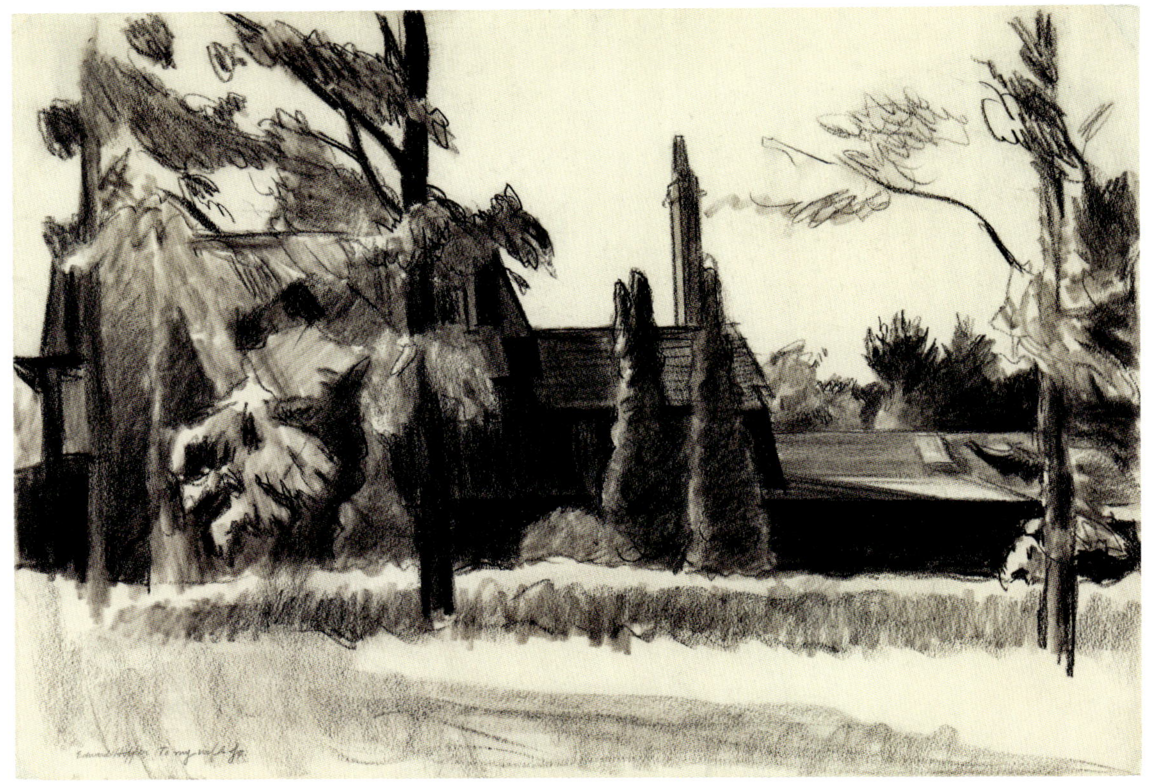

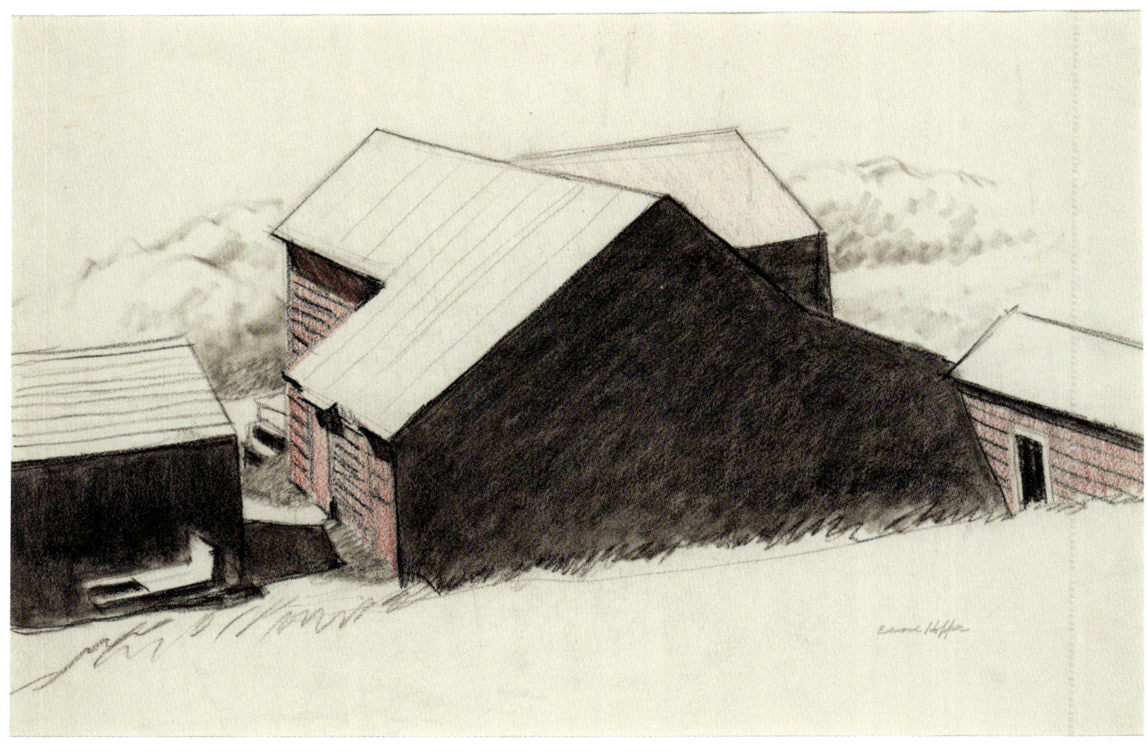

48. *Topsfield*, 1929
Fabricated chalk on paper, 15 × 22 1/16 in. (38.1 × 56 cm)
Josephine N. Hopper Bequest 70.682

49. *Cobb's Barns, South Truro*, 1930–33
Fabricated chalk and wax crayon on paper,
15 1/16 × 22 1/8 in. (38.3 × 56.2 cm)
Josephine N. Hopper Bequest 70.684

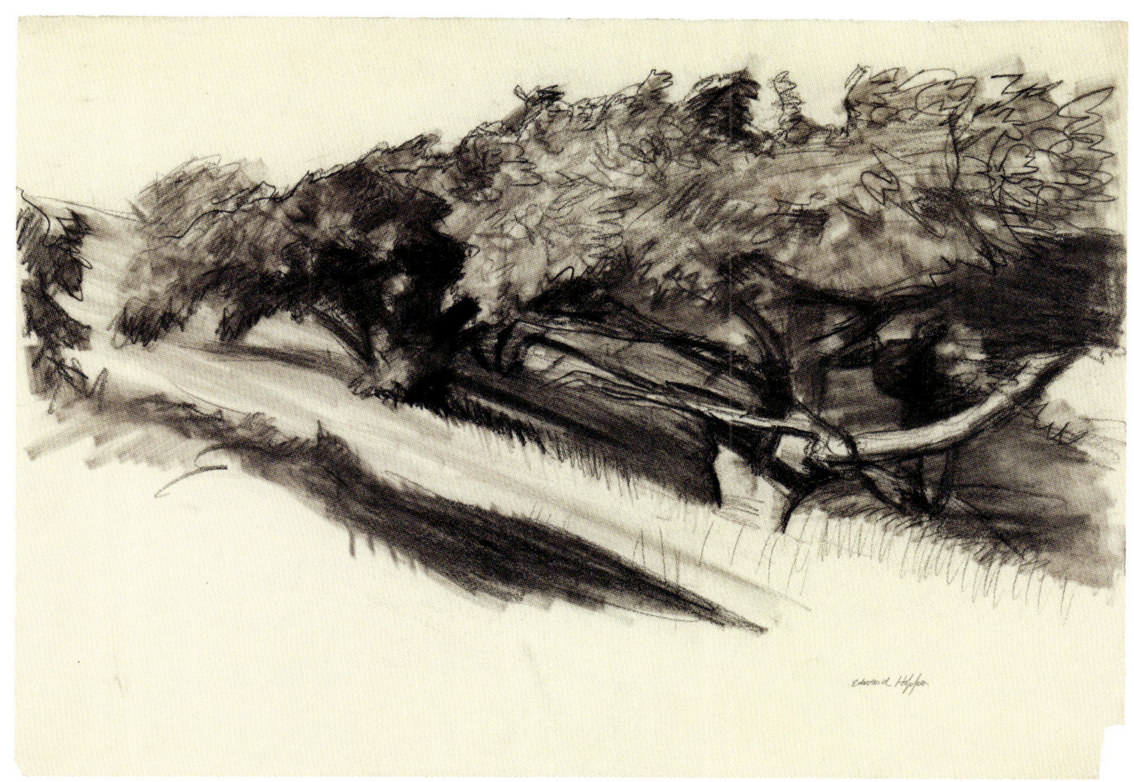

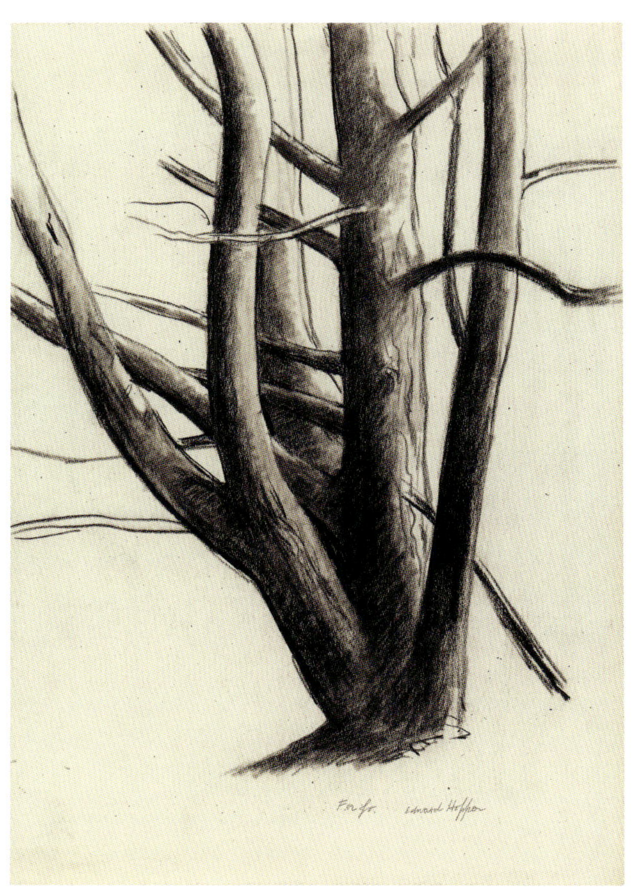

50. *Hillside Landscape with Trees*, c. 1936–38
Fabricated chalk on paper, 15 × 22 ⅛ in. (38.1 × 56.2 cm)
Josephine N. Hopper Bequest 70.305

51. *Tree Trunk*, c. 1920
Fabricated chalk on paper, 14 × 10 in. (35.6 × 25.4 cm)
Josephine N. Hopper Bequest 70.730

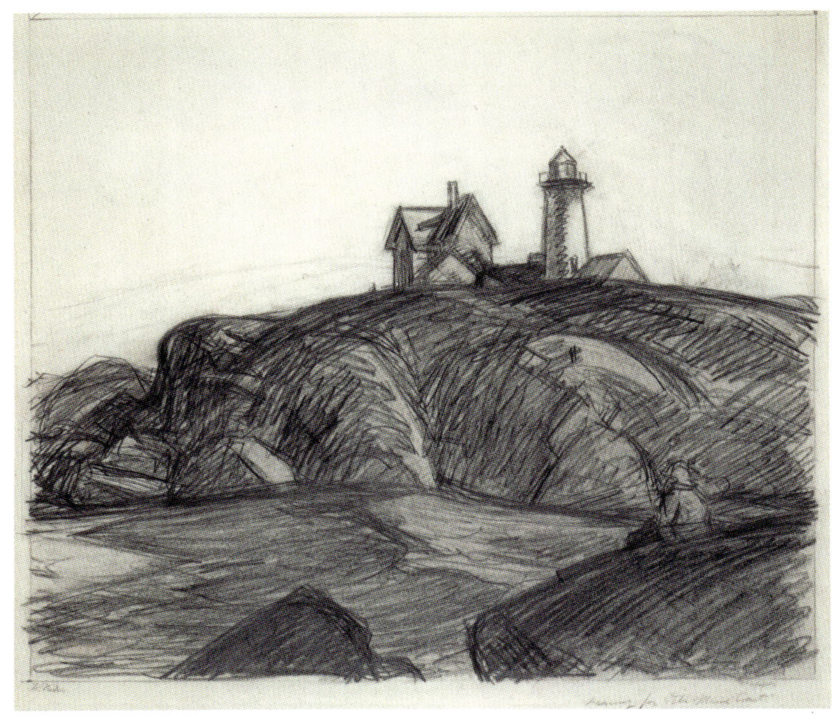

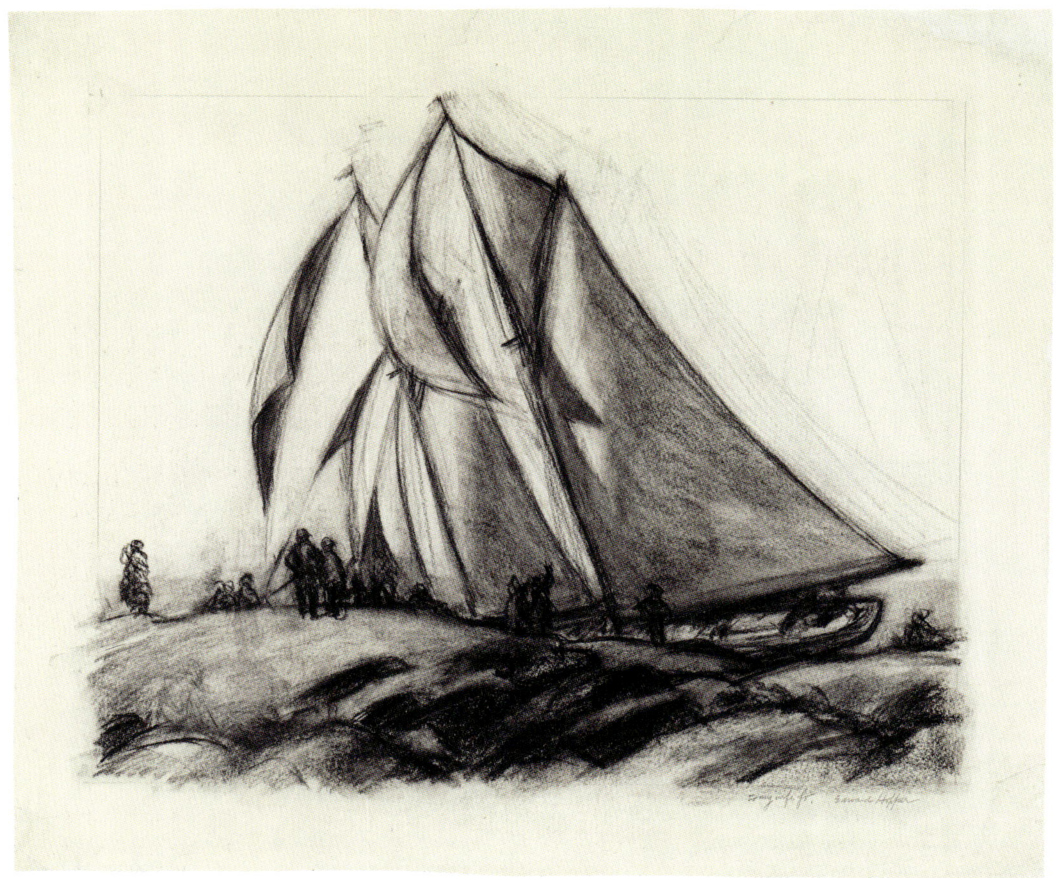

52. *Drawing for The Maine Coast*, 1923
Charcoal on paper, 10¾ × 12½ in. (27.3 × 31.8 cm)
Collection of Aaron I. Fleischman

53. Study for *The Henry Ford*, 1923
Fabricated chalk and charcoal on paper,
15 1/16 × 18 3/16 in. (38.3 × 46.2 cm)
Josephine N. Hopper Bequest 70.680

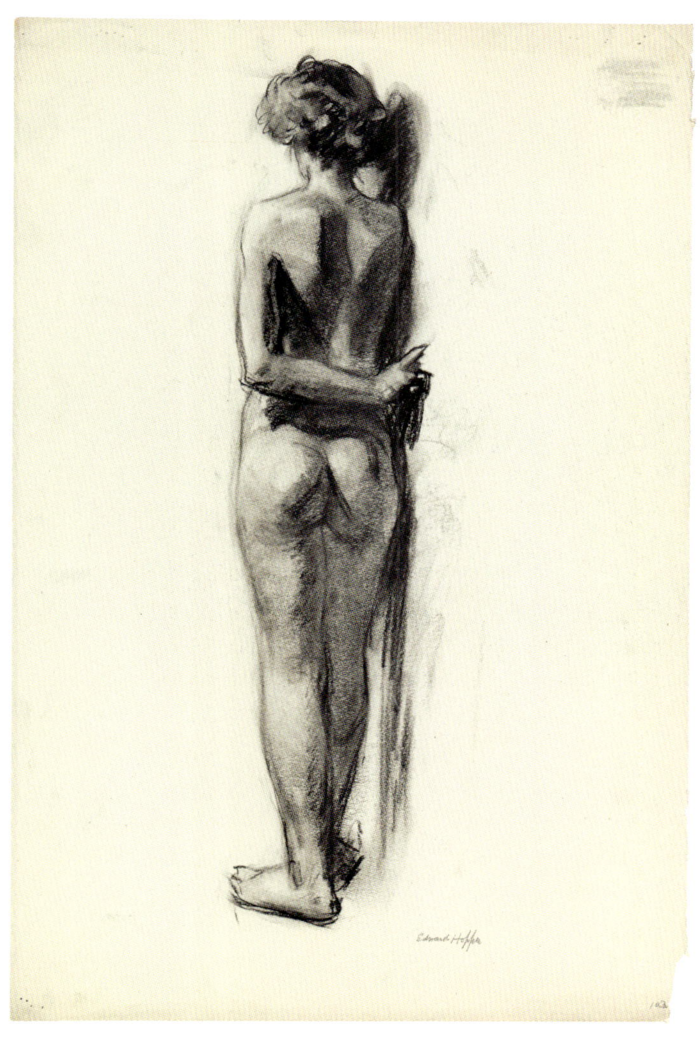

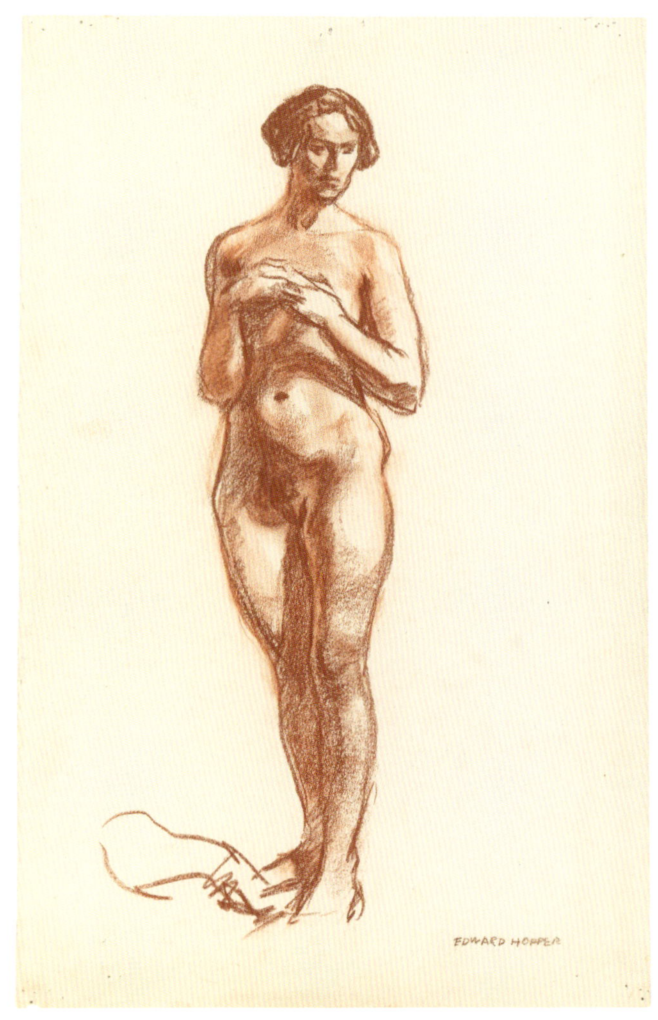

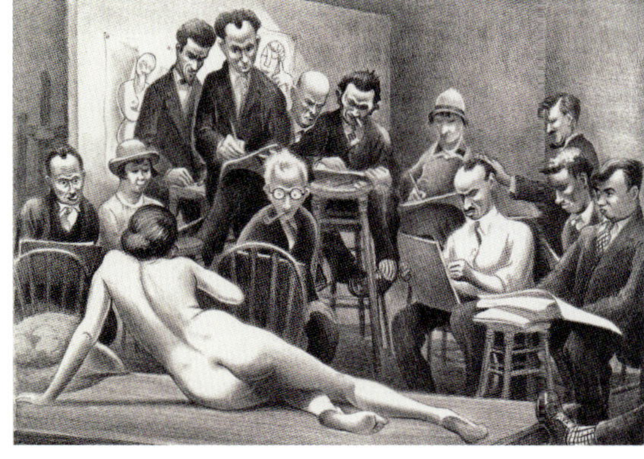

Whitney Studio Club Nudes, 1920–25

In the early 1920s, Hopper regularly attended the life drawing classes organized by the Whitney Studio Club—Mabel Dwight humorously depicted him as part of a class drawing from the female nude in a lithograph from some years later (fig. 56). Another artist, Katherine Schmidt, the wife of Yasuo Kuniyoshi, ran the classes from 1923 to 1925 and recalled that Hopper never missed one during this time.[47] The figure studies he produced from these classes account for a significant portion of his entire drawn output—there are more than 640 in the Whitney collection. Perhaps the artist, honing and developing his mature style even as he approached middle age, enjoyed this narrowly defined activity as a way to keep the manual side of his skills well practiced. Certainly it freed him from having to think of a subject and let him fully focus on the human figure, whose pose and position in a life drawing class were determined by someone else. For an artist who struggled to find subjects, the class freed him from this concern yet also suited his tendency to focus narrowly. Considering the large number of carefully and subtly shaded studies in black and red chalk from this era (figs. 54, 55), this prolonged period of prolific drawing in a single genre may have been a kind of self-imposed master class in the human form that served him for the rest of his life. The figures in the drawings, as in most of his paintings, are nearly all women.

54. *Standing Female Nude with Arm Behind Back, Rear View*, 1920–25
Fabricated chalk on paper, 22 × 15 in. (55.9 × 38.1 cm)
Josephine N. Hopper Bequest 70.315

55. *Standing Female Nude*, 1920–25
Fabricated chalk on paper, 17 15/16 × 11 ½ in. (45.6 × 29.2 cm)
Josephine N. Hopper Bequest 70.320

56. Mabel Dwight (1876–1955)
Life Class, 1931
Lithograph; sheet: 13 11/16 × 18 1/16 in. (34.8 × 45.9 cm), plate: 9 13/16 × 13 9/16 in. (24.9 × 34.4 cm)
Purchase 33.90

Hopper's Record Books

After their marriage in 1924, Edward and Jo Hopper began a series of ledger books recording information about his work.[48] Jo inscribed their purpose inside the cover of Book I: "Recorded by Jo N Hopper (Mrs. Edward Hopper) at time each work is finished, or before it leaves studio. Drawings in the 3 books done by Edward Hopper." Jo created written descriptions—often quite evocative and fanciful, sometimes giving names to Hopper's painted characters—and recorded the sale price and purchaser (see fig. 217). The written entries are accompanied by drawings the artist made in fluid pen and black ink to record the appearance of his paintings; he started small but the renderings become larger and more elaborate as the books progress. He also recorded notes about his materials, including the type of canvas and paint. The books follow a general chronology but are not totally systematic, and also record quite voluminously sales of watercolors, prints, and drawings as well as publications featuring Hopper's work. Books I (96.208), II (96.209), and III (96.210) cover the oil paintings and are usually what people mean when they refer to Hopper's "Record Books" or "Ledger Books." One of the books (96.211, which has been catalogued by the Whitney as "Book IV" but has no number indicated on it) is actually a different size and type than the others and is essentially a financial ledger kept only by Edward that spans his entire career and includes, for example, his numerous illustration commissions. Book V (96.212) primarily records the drawings Hopper began selling through Rehn later in his life. A sixth book (96.213) consists mostly of lists of sales of Hopper's prints. Jo bequeathed Books I, II, III, and V to Lloyd Goodrich, who left them to the Whitney. The other two were purchased by the Museum in 1989 (all of them received successive accession numbers in 1996).

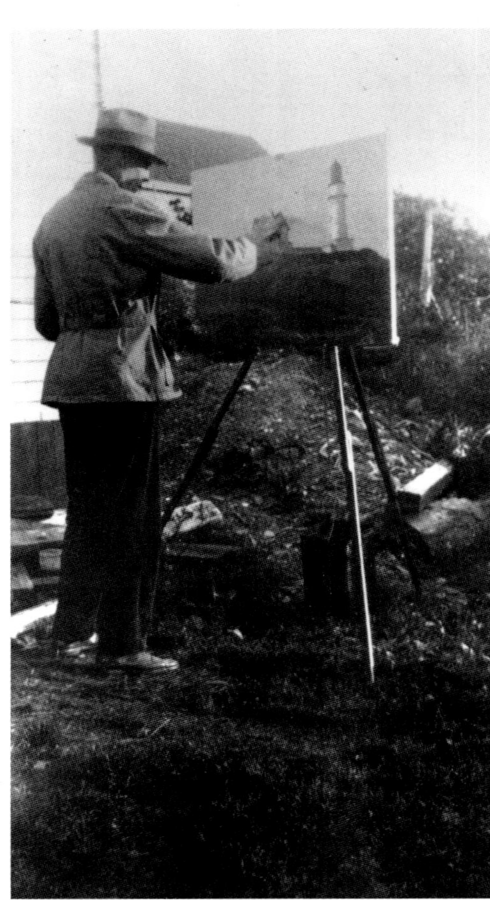

57. Hopper painting *Lighthouse Hill* (1927; Dallas Museum of Art) at Two Lights, near Cape Elizabeth, Portland, Maine, 1927. The Arthayer R. Sanborn Hopper Collection Trust, 2005

Hopper's Studio Practice and Studies for Paintings

A 1927 photograph of Hopper in Cape Elizabeth, Maine, standing outside at his easel painting *Lighthouse Hill* (1927; Dallas Museum of Art), is one of the few documents we have of the artist at work (fig. 57). In a 1946 conversation with Goodrich, he explained that he had painted outdoors more "in the beginning" but had not done so for a number of years; he thought that the last painting done outside was *Cape Cod Afternoon* from 1936 (The Carnegie Museum of Art, Pittsburgh).[49] He further spoke of shifting his practice, as he got older, to a synthetic process of "improvising" rather than working "from the fact." Although Hopper had always invented subject matter, even very early in his career, producing imagined scenes with regularity, his process of synthesis indeed deepened as his style matured into the 1930s. His drawing practice seems to have changed accordingly. The Whitney's collection reflects this, as there are few preparatory studies for paintings from the 1910s and 1920s. *Blackwell's Island* (1928; collection of Soledad and Robert Hurst) is one of the earliest for which there is a significant group of studies, but there are no known drawings for several of his most famous paintings from this era, such as *Chop Suey* (1929; collection of Barney A. Ebsworth), *House by the Railroad* (1925; The Museum of Modern Art, New York[50]), or *Automat* (1927; Des Moines Art Center, Iowa). Occasionally there are single drawings that relate to specific paintings from the late 1920s and early 1930s, such as the wonderfully sketchy sheet (fig. 58) for *Barber Shop* of 1931 (Neuberger Museum of Art, Purchase, New York). Drawings related to *Lighthouse Hill* and *The Camel's Hump* (Munson-Williams-Proctor Arts Institute, Utica, New York), however, are medium-specific versions of these subjects more than preparatory studies (figs. 59, 60), since the artist was still frequently working *en plein air*.

In 1939, Hopper wrote to Charles H. Sawyer at the Addison Gallery of American Art about the process of painting *Manhattan Bridge Loop* (1928; see fig. 153), which had been in the Addison's collection since 1932: "The picture was planned very carefully in my mind before

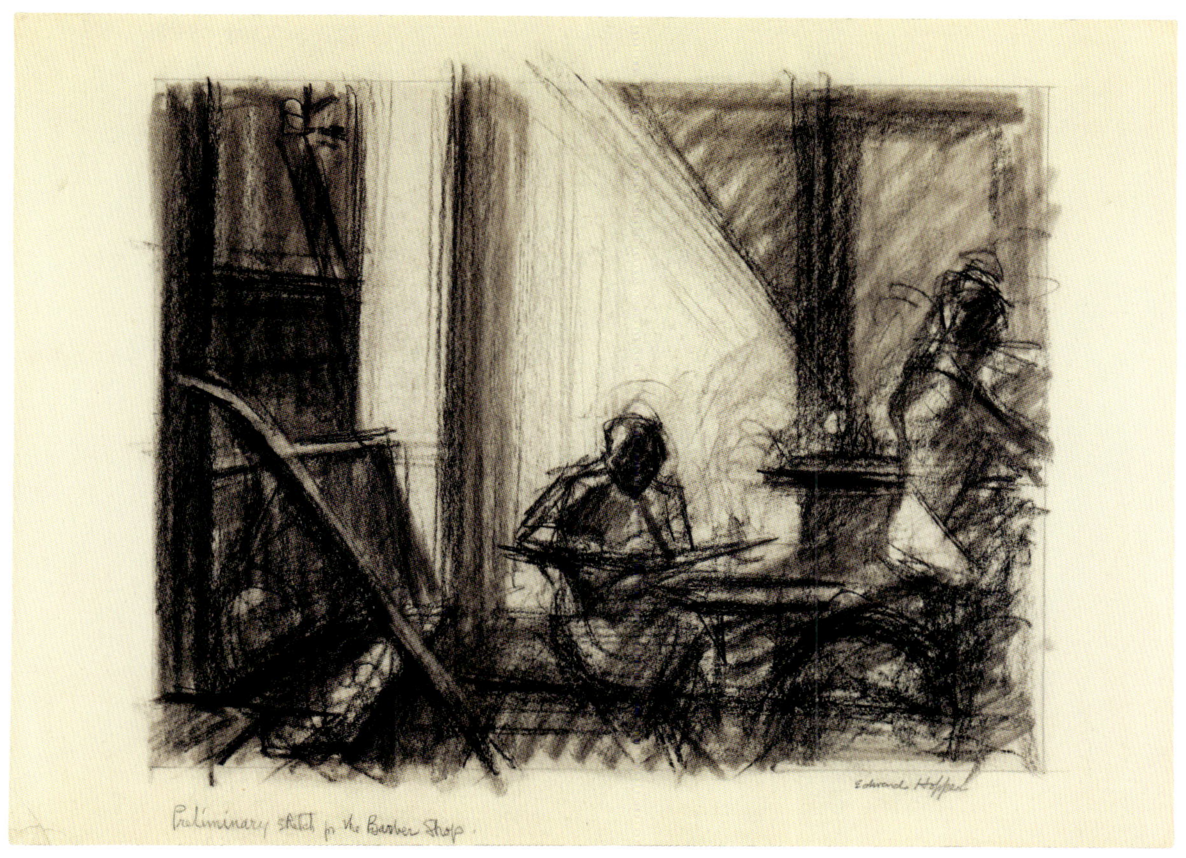

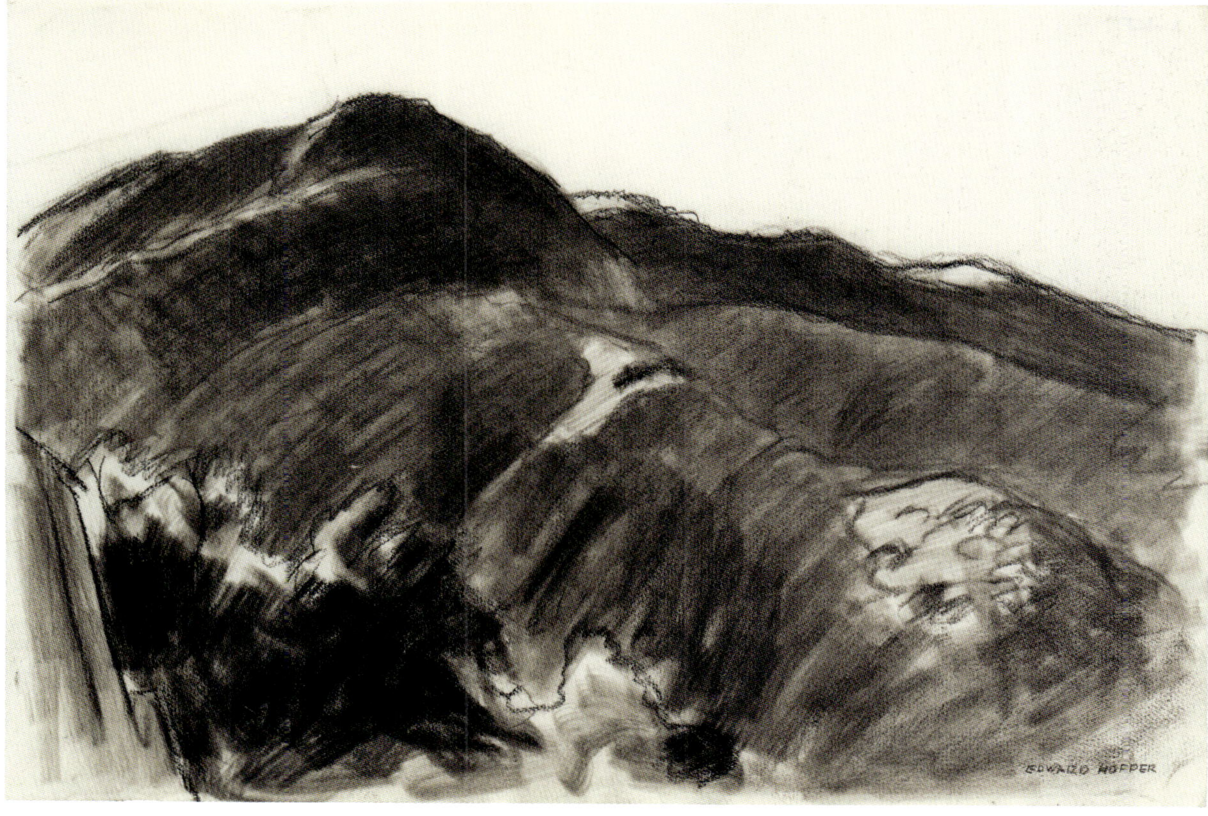

58. Study for *Barber Shop*, 1931
Fabricated chalk and charcoal on paper,
12½ × 17⅝ in. (31.8 × 44.8 cm)
Josephine N. Hopper Bequest 70.853

59. *The Camel's Hump*, 1931
Fabricated chalk on paper, 11⅞ × 17 15⁄16 in.
(30.2 × 45.6 cm)
Josephine N. Hopper Bequest 70.858

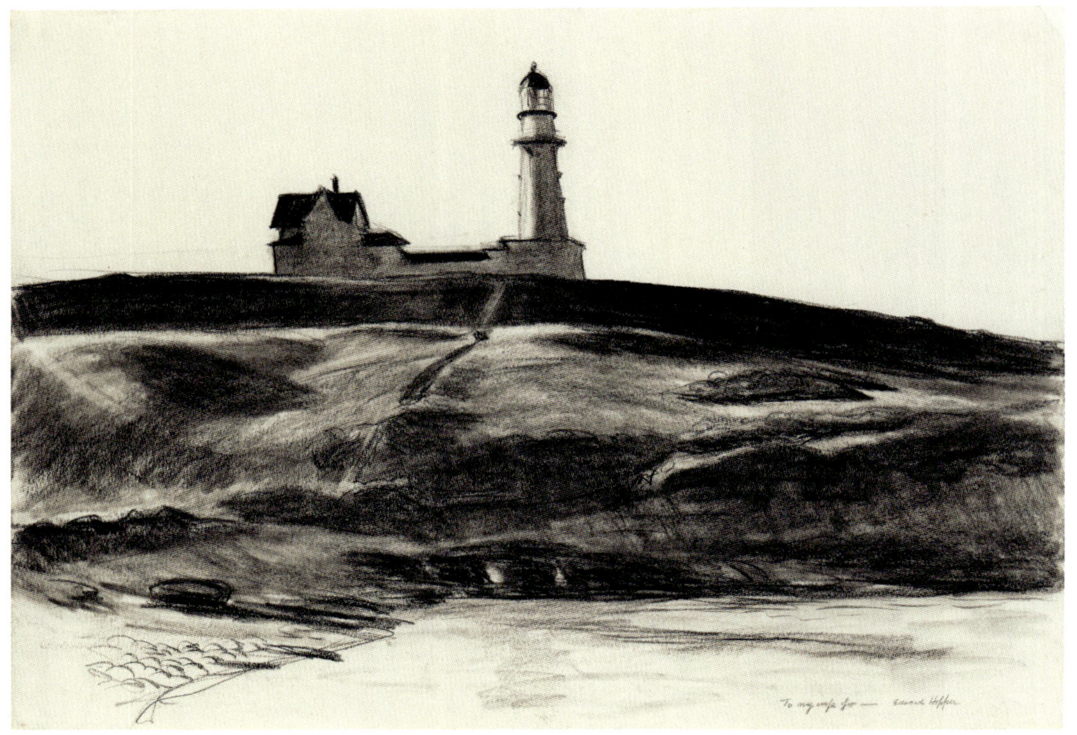

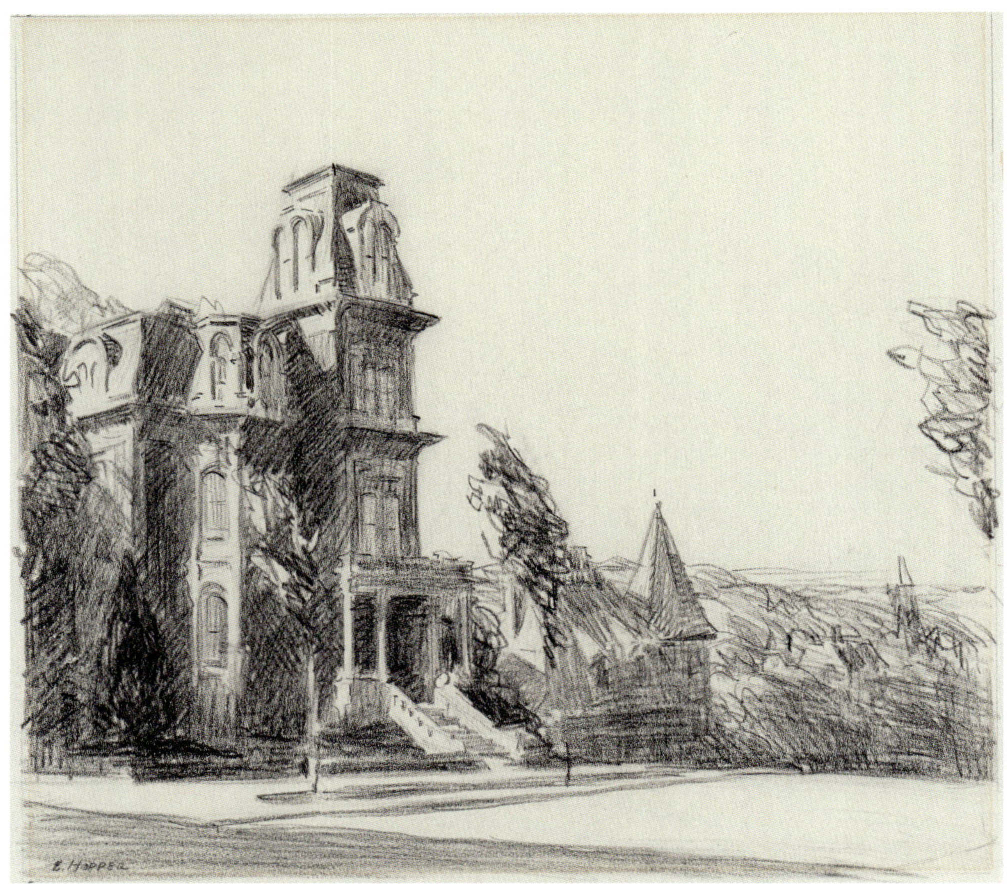

60. *Light at Two Lights*, 1927
Fabricated chalk and charcoal on paper, 15 × 22 1/16 in.
(38.1 × 56 cm)
Josephine N. Hopper Bequest 70.683

61. *Victorian House on a Wooded Street*, c. 1923–25
Fabricated chalk on paper, 16 × 17 ½ in. (40.6 × 44.5 cm)
Josephine N. Hopper Bequest 70.901

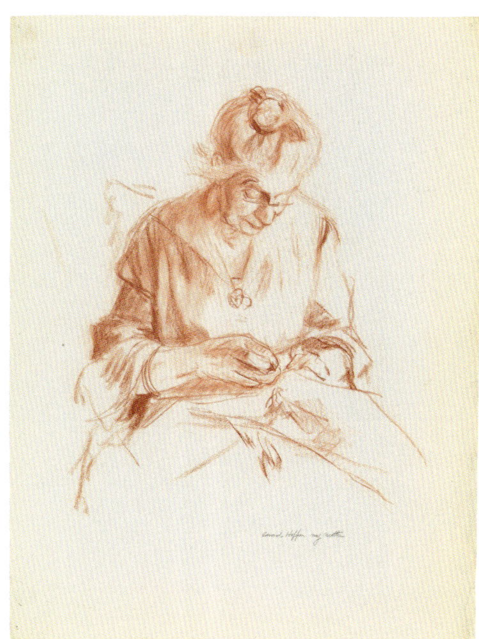

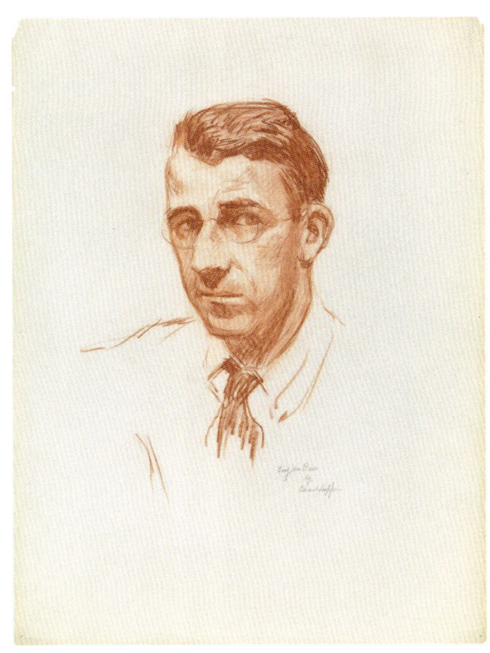

62. *My Mother*, c. 1920
Fabricated chalk on paper, 20 15⁄16 × 15 15⁄16 in. (53.2 × 40.5 cm)
Josephine N. Hopper Bequest 70.298

63. *Guy du Bois*, 1919
Fabricated chalk on paper, 21 × 16 in. (53.3 × 40.6 cm)
Josephine N. Hopper Bequest 70.907

starting it, but except for a few small black and white sketches made from the fact, I had no other concrete data, but relied on refreshing my memory by looking often at the subject"[51] (see figs. 153, 156–158). By the mid-1930s, Hopper was more typically making extensive groups of drawings for a single painting, usually around fifteen to twenty but sometimes more. What we don't know is what Hopper may have destroyed or the degree to which what has survived is a reflection of what he actually made. In 1948, he tantalizingly told *Time* magazine: "Of course I do dozens of sketches for oils—just a few lines on yellow typewriter paper—and then I almost always burn them. If I do one that interests me, I go on and make a painting, but that happens only two or three times a year."[52] Hopper did do many sketches on cheap typewriter paper; some of his drawings, in fact, are on the backs of drafts of typewritten letters. However, he also drew on many other types of paper, from small sketchbook sheets to more expensive, finer grade artist's paper. One thus wonders how seriously to take this statement, which implies that of the drawings he created in order to explore potential subjects for painting, he destroyed those that led him nowhere. And yet this is largely consistent with what has survived.

What, then, was Hopper's studio practice when he was not painting directly "from the fact," but improvising? It is important to understand that he painted in the same two studios almost his entire career. The first was on the top floor of 3 Washington Square North, where he moved in 1913, and where, in 1932, he took over the larger room at the front of this space overlooking the square, which became his studio from then on. The second was at the house that he designed for himself and Jo in Truro, which was finished in 1934; the large and open main room had an oversize factory window where Hopper set up his easel. He thus became settled in the two spaces he would use for the rest of his life around the same time he began to more frequently "improvise" his subjects, composing them in the studio and using drawings more extensively. There are fascinating photographs from various decades of both of these spaces, allowing us to see the immediate surroundings in which the artist made his work.[53] The Hoppers lived simply and frugally. Both were well read and enjoyed theater and film, tendencies consistent with an attraction to experience more than objects. Material goods interested them little, and the images of their dwellings show simple furniture and a generally spartan air. Hopper worked on easels he built himself (one of which sits in his Washington Square space, still owned by New York University; the other is still in the Truro house) and in the company of books and magazines, which are often visible near his work areas in photographs.

Hopper told Goodrich in 1946 that he had never found the perfect method for painting, either "from the fact" or "improvised," that he was "torn between the two."[54] He consistently described the painting process as a difficult one, both in terms of finding a suitable subject and getting it down in paint. (Goodrich recounted: "He said he works a long time on his oils; paints and scrapes and re-paints."[55]) His drawings find him either thoroughly engaged with "the fact" out in the world, drawing from life in the studio (posing himself or, more frequently, Jo), or getting his imaginings down in compositional studies (figs. 58, 64–73, 75–86). From painting to painting, his drawing practice followed no consistent system: the degree to which he needed to search for a subject by going out and drawing versus developing studio improvisations seems to have been specific to each canvas. Subjects in oil that are grounded in real places often have immensely specific drawings, many with extensive color notations. This is the case, for example, with the Truro paintings and their related drawings: *Route 6, Eastham* (see figs. 327 and 330–336), and *Rooms for Tourists* (see figs. 337 and 338–346). Hopper's detailed jottings about color and light, and the fragmentary randomness of multiple spaces and images on these sheets, reflect the fact that they are very much working drawings. The specificity of Hopper's need for "the fact" could lead to drawings that look and feel very precisely observed, sometimes with a wonderful and appealingly conceptual balance between word and image.

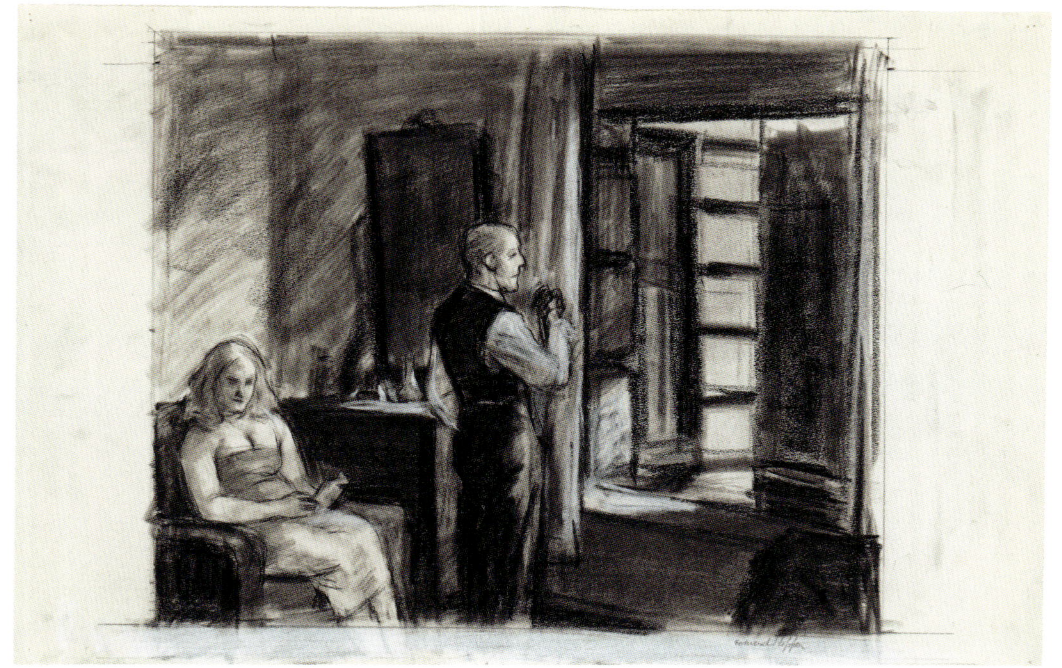

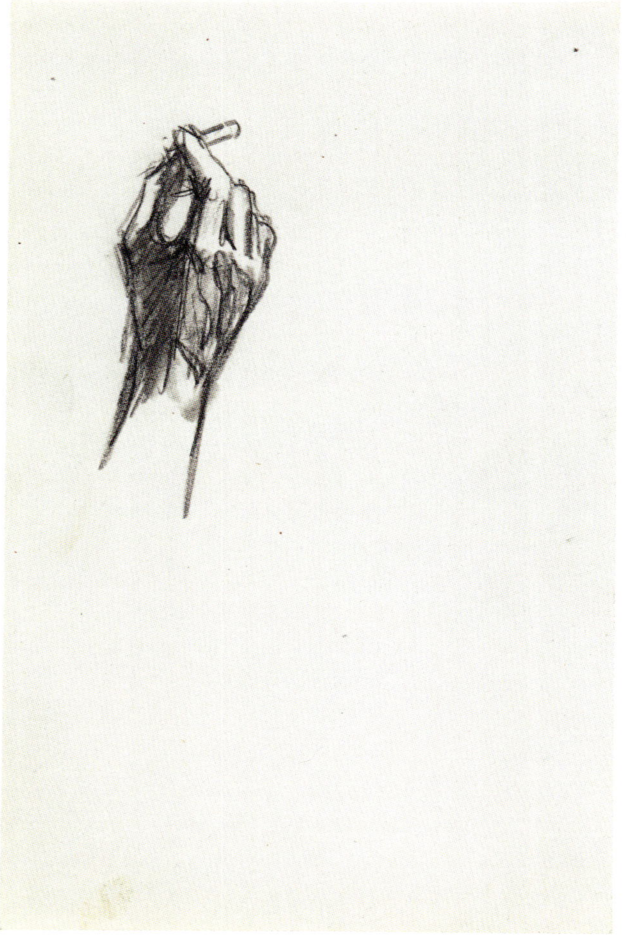

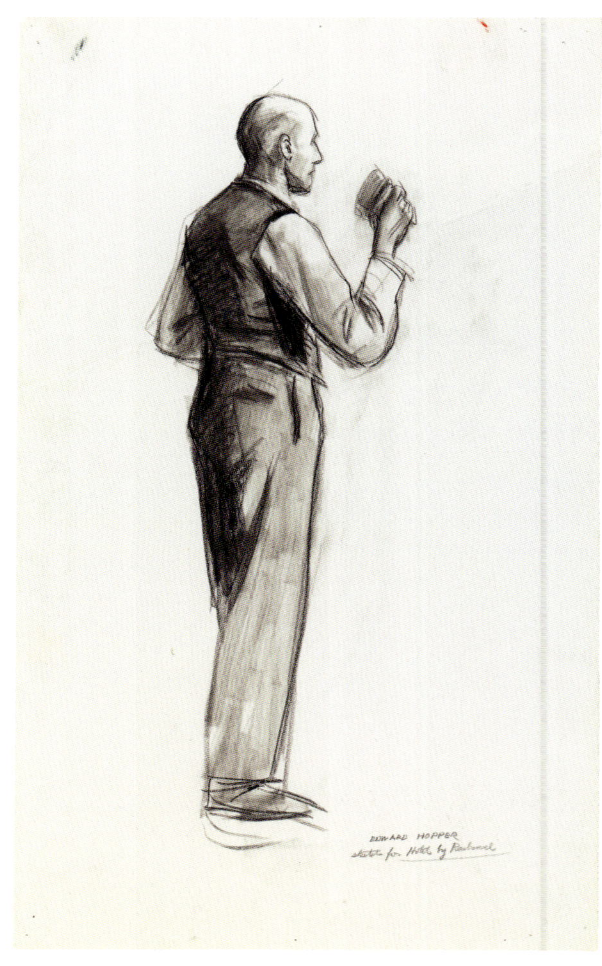

64. Study for *Hotel by a Railroad*, 1952
Fabricated chalk on paper, 12 × 19 in. (30.5 × 48.3 cm)
Josephine N. Hopper Bequest 70.427

65. Study for *Hotel by a Railroad*, 1952
Fabricated chalk on paper, 7 9/16 × 5 in. (19.2 × 12.7 cm)
Josephine N. Hopper Bequest 70.428

66. Study for *Hotel by a Railroad*, 1952
Fabricated chalk on paper, 19 × 12 in. (48.3 × 30.5 cm)
Josephine N. Hopper Bequest 70.874

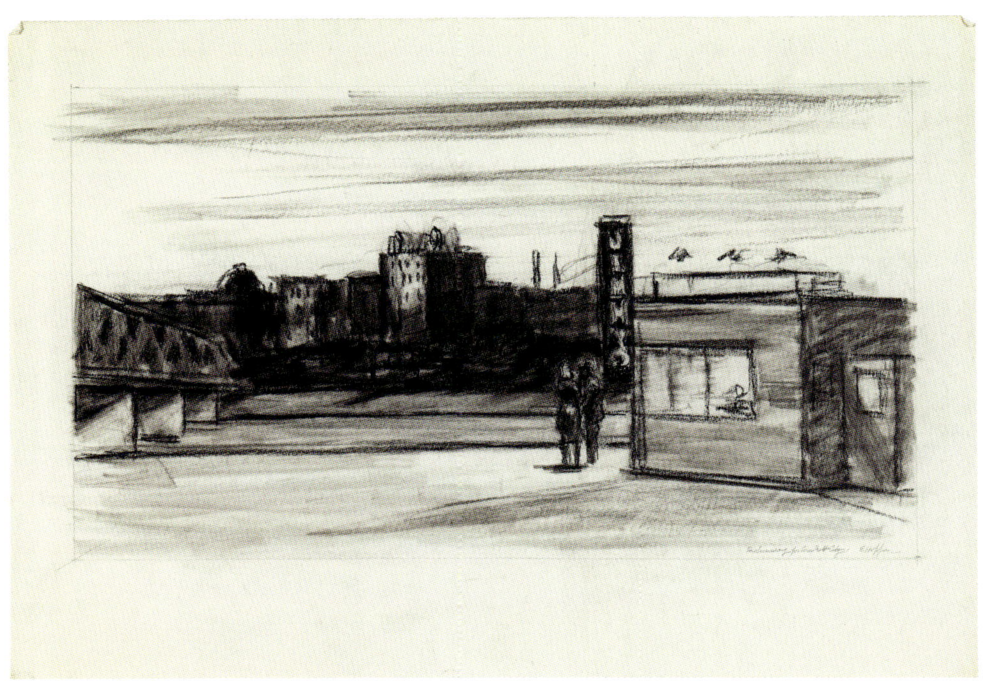

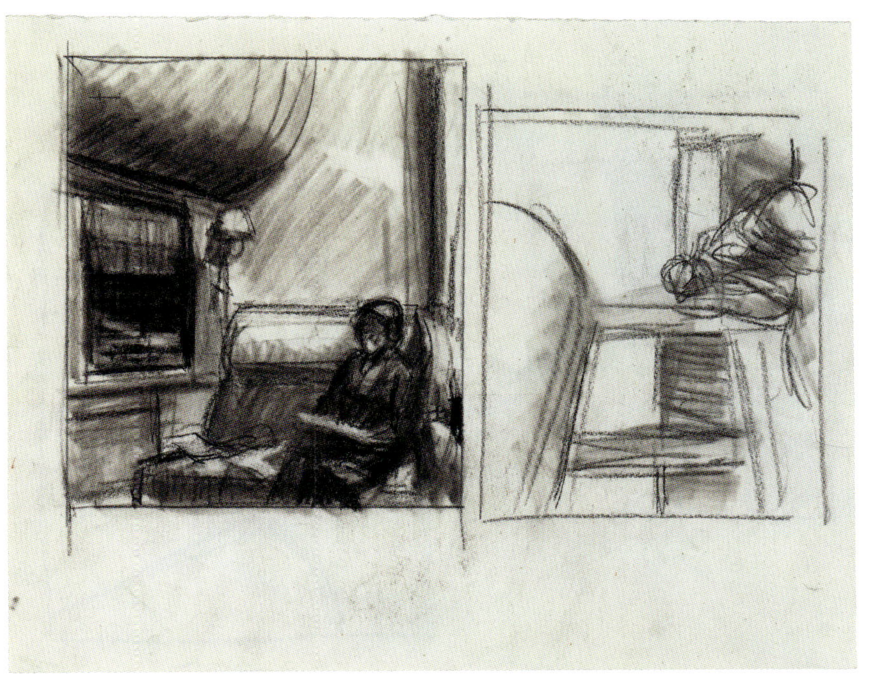

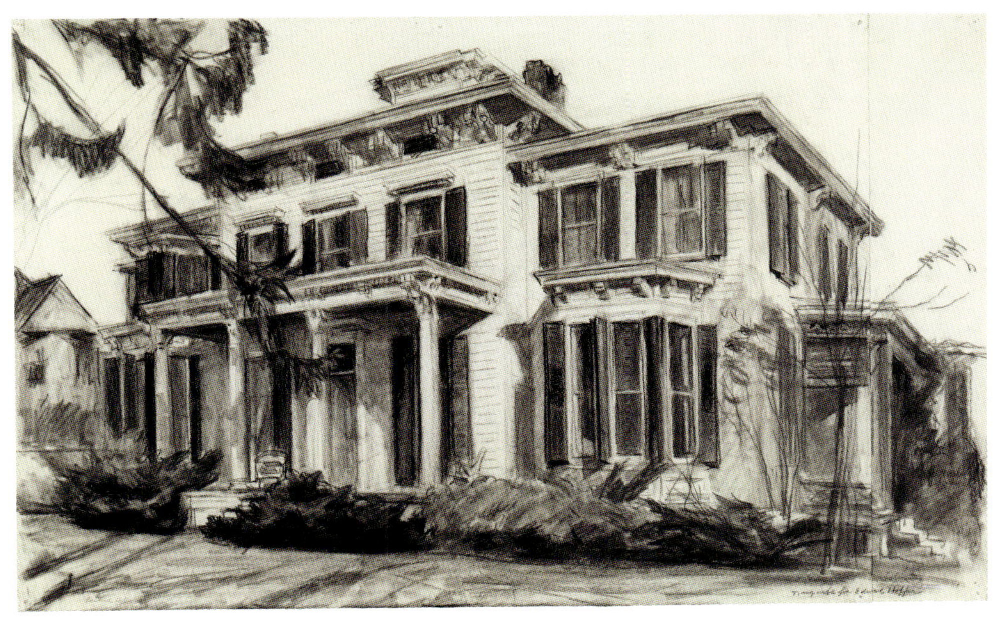

67. Study for *Corn Belt City*, 1946 or 1947
Charcoal on paper, $14\frac{15}{16} \times 22\frac{1}{8}$ in. (37.9 × 56.2 cm)
Josephine N. Hopper Bequest 70.840

68. Study for *Compartment C, Car 293* (recto), 1938
Fabricated chalk and charcoal on paper, $8\frac{1}{16} \times 10\frac{1}{2}$ in. (20.5 × 26.7 cm)
Josephine N. Hopper Bequest 70.431a–b

69. Study for *Pretty Penny*, 1939
Fabricated chalk on paper, $15\frac{1}{16} \times 25\frac{3}{16}$ in. (38.3 × 64 cm)
Josephine N. Hopper Bequest 70.658

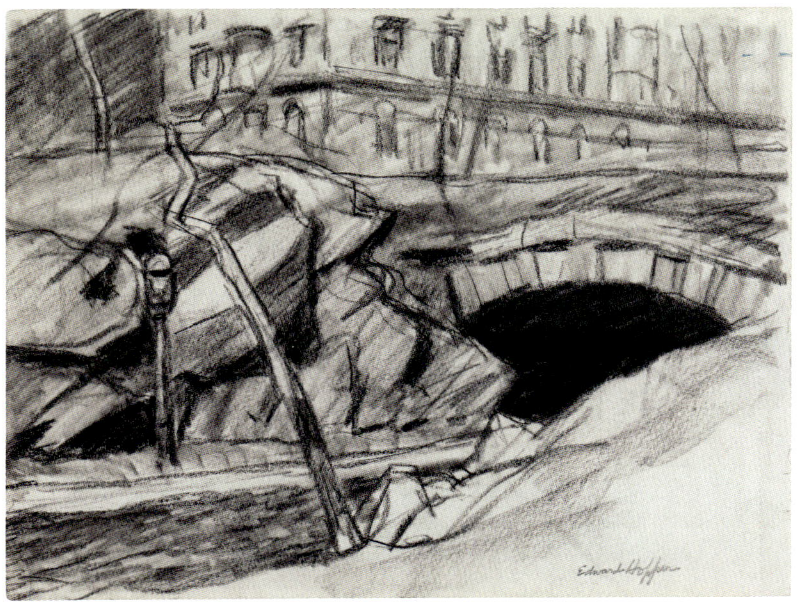

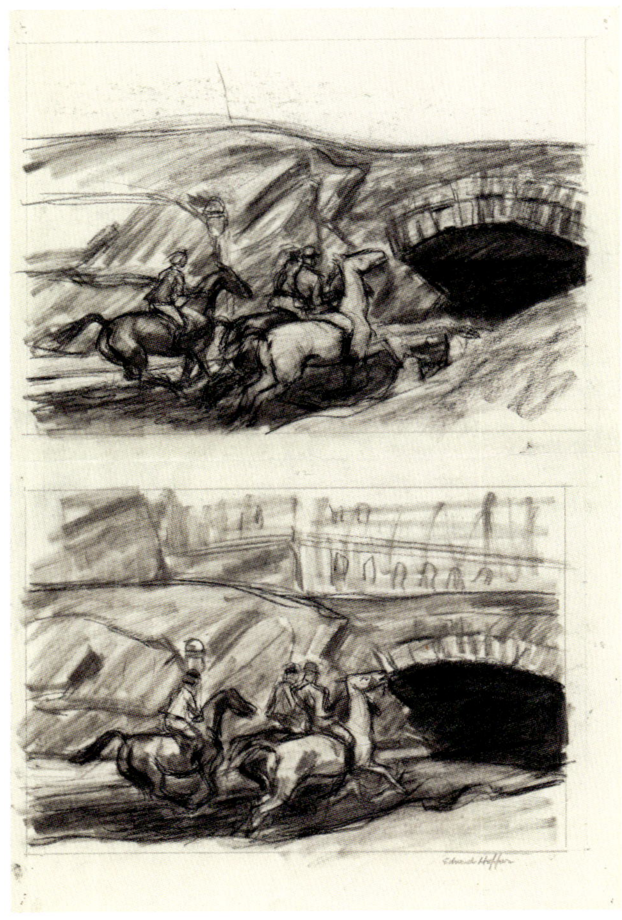

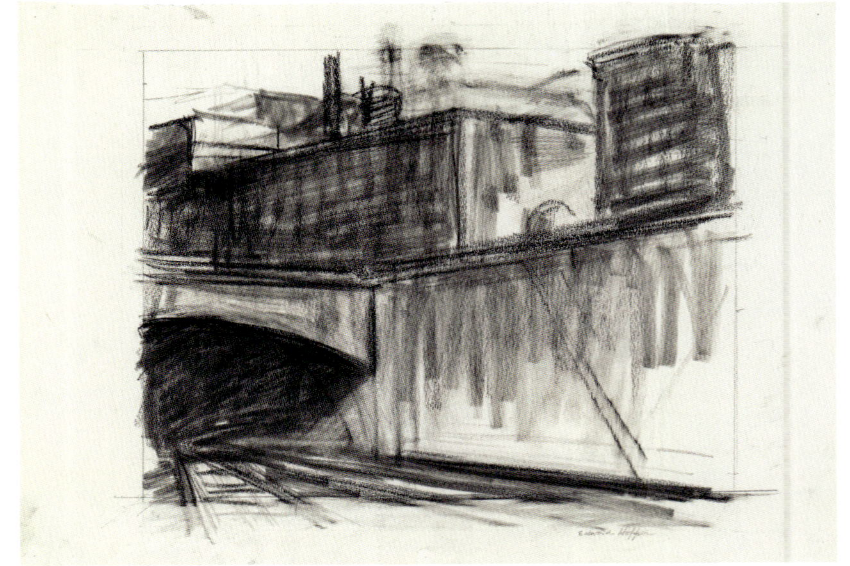

70. Study for *Bridle Path*, 1939
Fabricated chalk on paper, 8 13⁄16 × 11 13⁄16 in. (22.4 × 30 cm)
Josephine N. Hopper Bequest 70.463

71. Study for *Bridle Path* (recto), 1939
Fabricated chalk and charcoal on paper, 22 1⁄16 × 15 in. (56 × 38.1 cm)
Josephine N. Hopper Bequest 70.857a–b

72. Study for *Approaching a City*, 1946
Fabricated chalk and charcoal on paper, 15 3⁄16 × 22 3⁄16 in. (38.6 × 56.4 cm)
Josephine N. Hopper Bequest 70.869

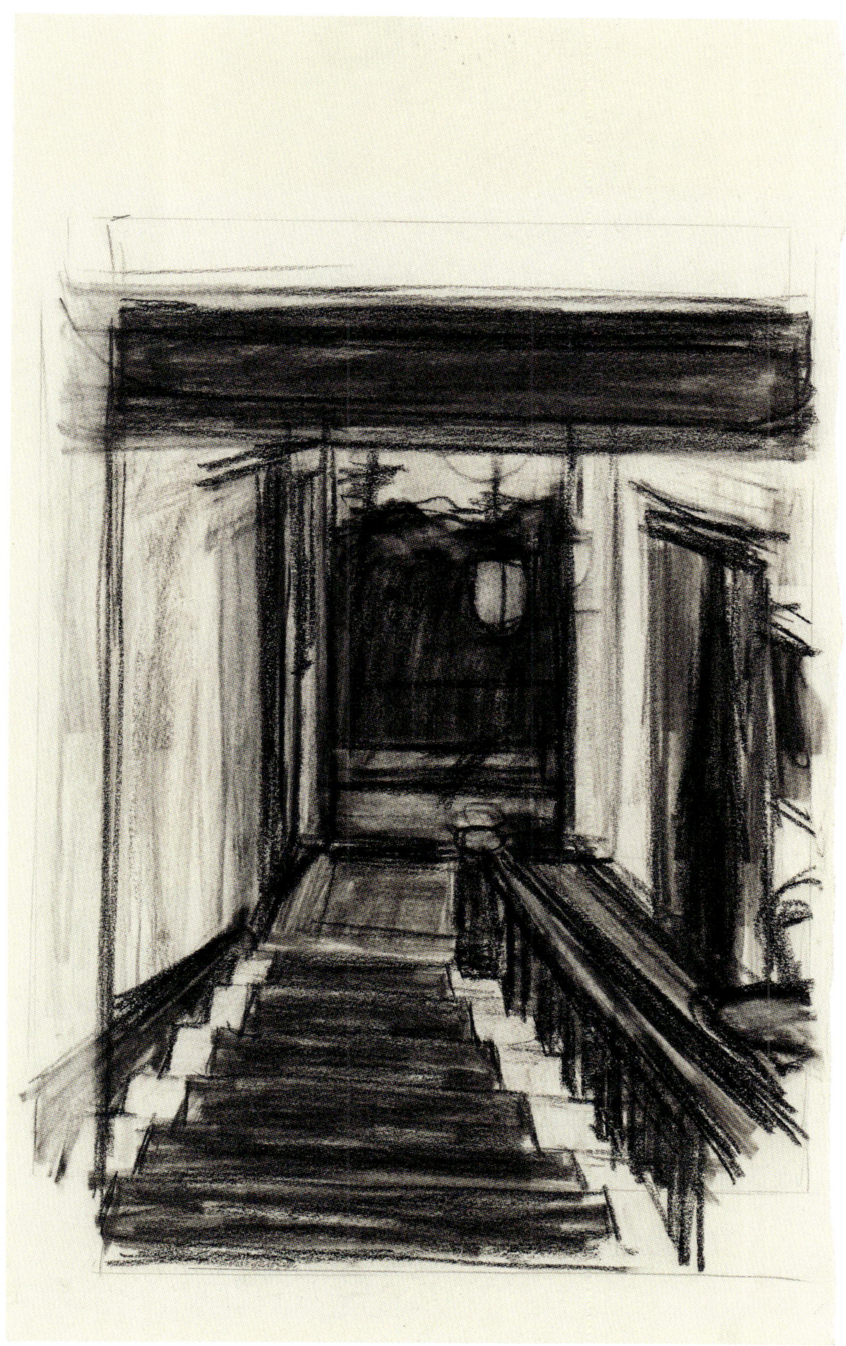

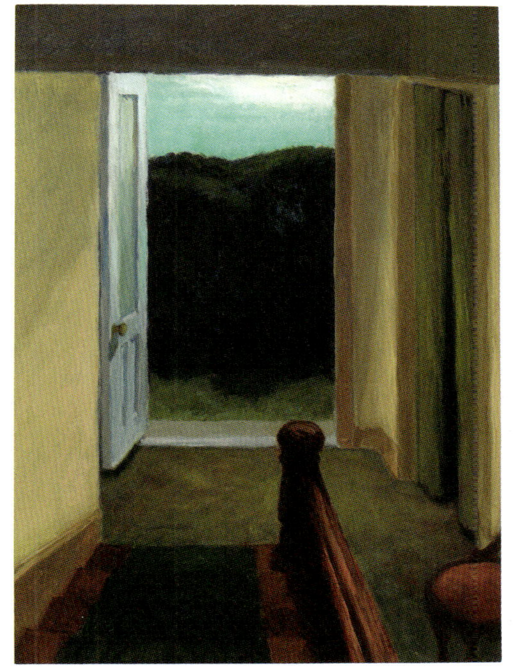

73. Study for *Stairway*, 1949
Fabricated chalk and graphite pencil on paper,
19¼ × 12³⁄₁₆ in. (48.9 × 31 cm)
Josephine N. Hopper Bequest 70.849

74. *Stairway*, 1949
Oil on wood, 16 × 11⅞ in. (40.6 × 30.2 cm)
Josephine N. Hopper Bequest 70.1265

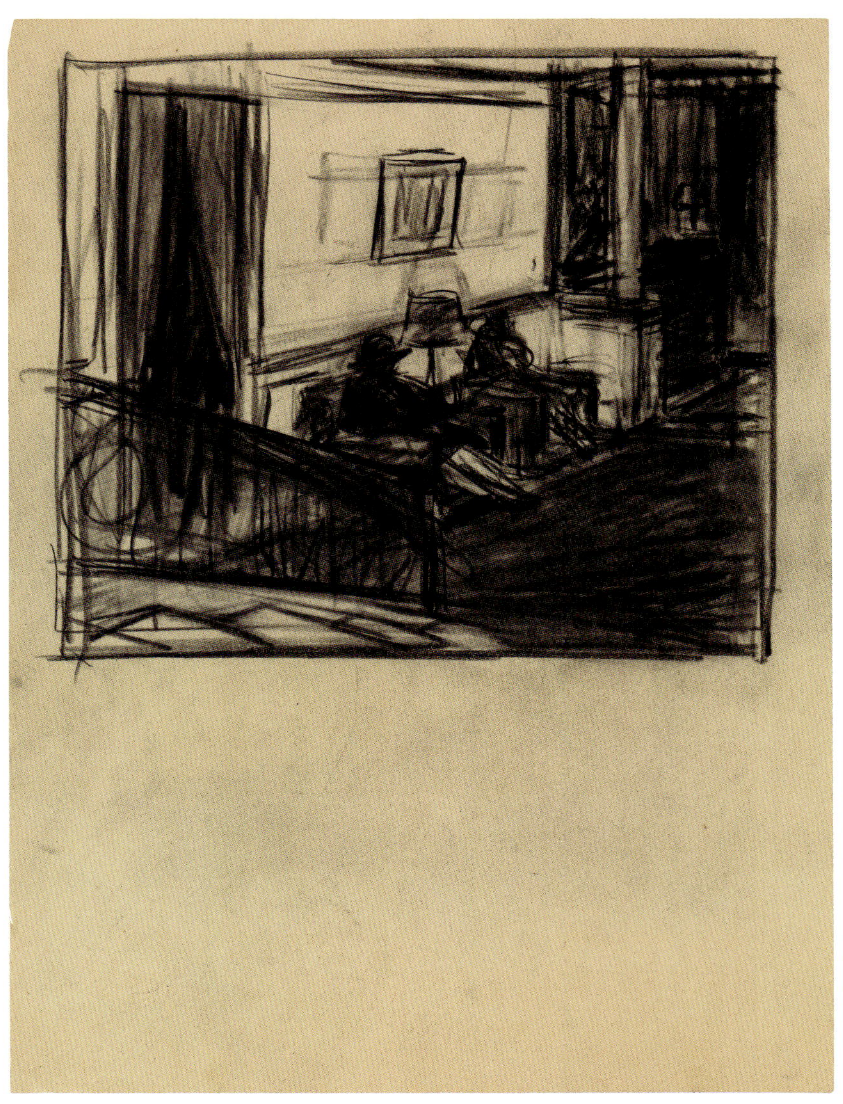

In other cases, however, the artist almost seems to be storyboarding his own paintings. In the great suite of studies for *Hotel Lobby* of 1943 (Indianapolis Museum of Art), his multiple points of view make us feel we are walking through the structure, experiencing it sequentially and spatially (see figs. 75–77).[56] Hopper's compositional tinkering and refinements in this vein often veer from the extreme economy of a few lines to thoroughly worked surfaces with fully rendered effects of light and texture. He also develops, in some cases, extremely nuanced spatial variants with subtle shifts in points of view and the fall of light, as in the studies for *Dawn in Pennsylvania* of 1942 (Terra Foundation for American Art, Chicago; see figs. 78–80) and *Summertime* of the following year (Delaware Art Museum, Wilmington; see figs. 81–83). For *Ground Swell* of 1939 (Corcoran Gallery of Art, Washington, DC) he produced a suite of drawings that are relatively sparse and generalized, developing overall composition rather than detail (fig. 84). In this oil, painted in Truro surrounded by sea, sky, and sailing, Hopper tackled a subject with elements so familiar that he seems to have pulled it almost entirely from his head. This type of sailboat, for example, and even its particular angle catching the wind (which has its artistic roots in Winslow Homer), is one he had been drawing since his youth. For the figures he could depend on his deep life drawing experience, though Jo may have posed for the female.[57] Mostly, though, the studies find him concentrating on compositional variants that he had a firm handle on from the start. This suggests that *Ground Swell* may be one of the artist's most purely imagined pictures, which helps explain the strange and frozen stillness of this weird nautical confrontation between man and object.[58]

The *Ground Swell* studies focus on cropping and framing, a quality of special importance for Hopper and one he mentioned in multiple interviews.[59] A number of Hopper's drawings show ratio calculations in which he is clearly working out how to scale up a drawn composition to a larger, painted one. His compositional studies often have framing lines, either hand-drawn rapidly but assuredly or carefully put down with a straightedge, usually in graphite rather than the medium with which he made the drawing. Occasionally they show an orthogonal line from a corner toward the center, another tool that would have helped him transfer a design. Hopper's drawings were working documents, which is why he never cared to

75. Study for *Hotel Lobby*, 1942
Fabricated chalk on paper, 10 13/16 × 8 7/16 in. (27.5 × 21.4 cm)
Josephine N. Hopper Bequest 70.112

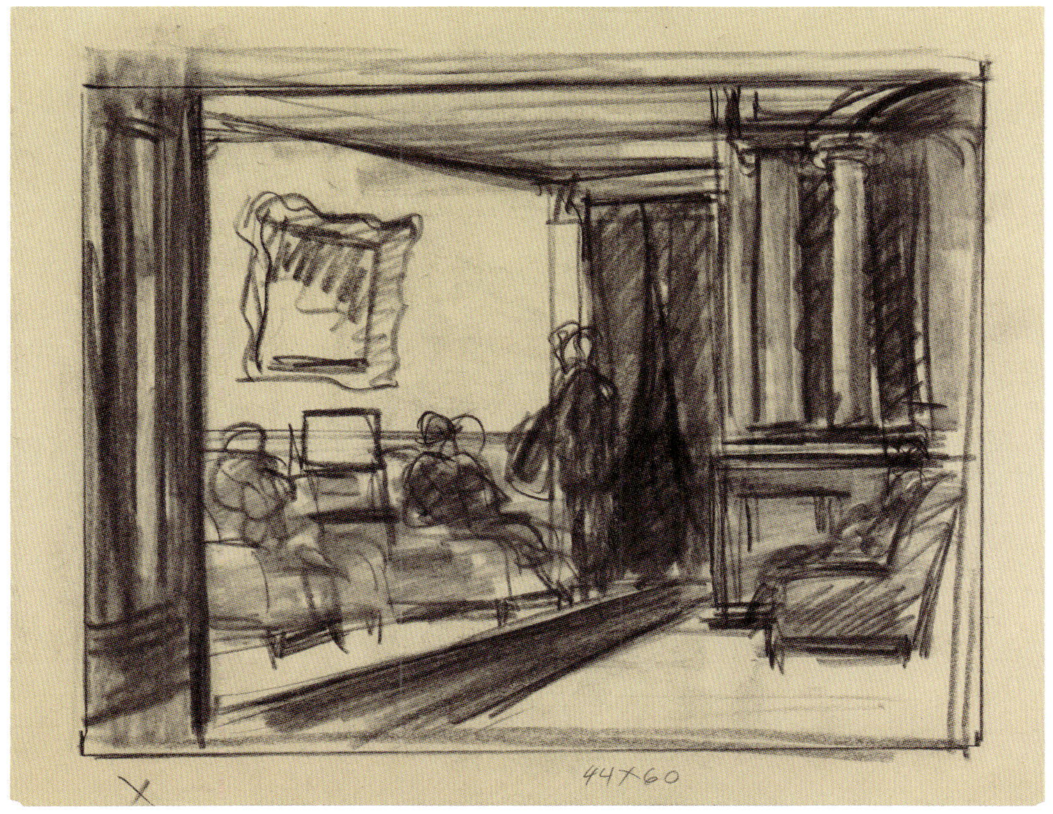

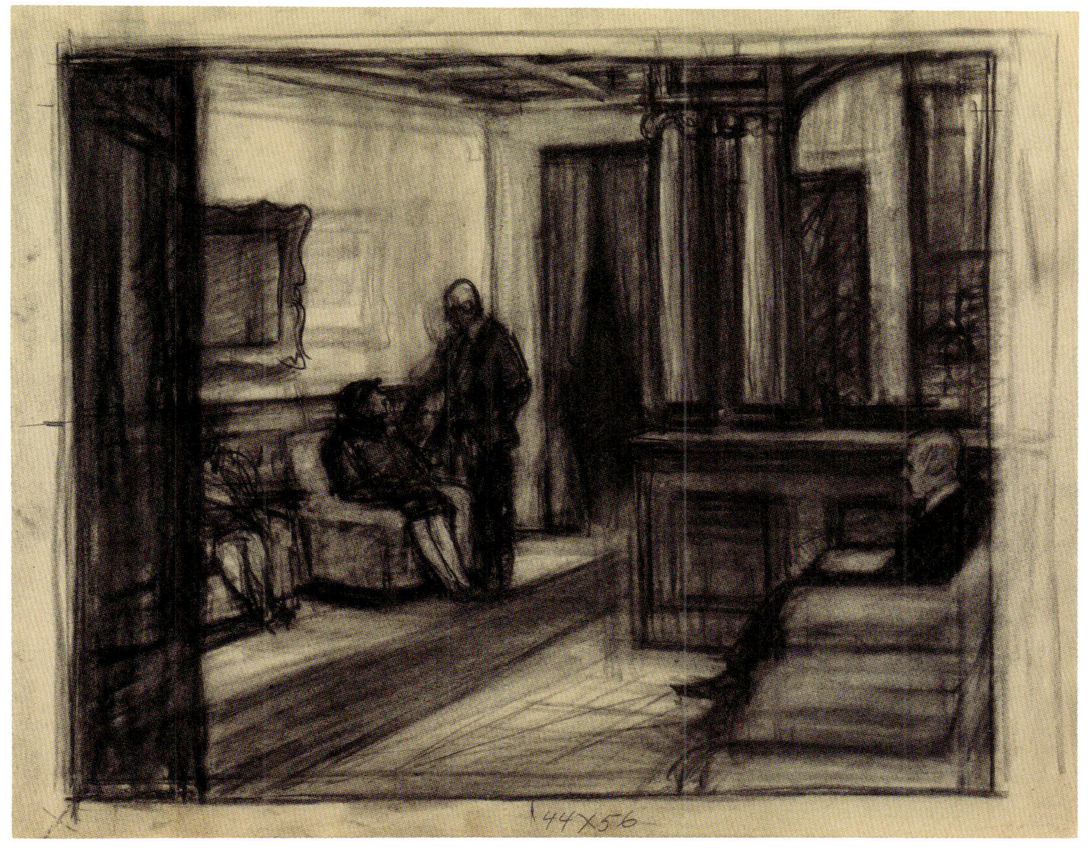

76. Study for *Hotel Lobby* (recto), 1942
Fabricated chalk on paper, $8\frac{1}{2} \times 11$ in. (21.6 × 27.9 cm)
Josephine N. Hopper Bequest 70.114a–b

77. Study for *Hotel Lobby*, 1942
Fabricated chalk and graphite pencil on paper,
$8\frac{7}{16} \times 10\frac{15}{16}$ in. (21.4 × 27.8 cm)
Josephine N. Hopper Bequest 70.117

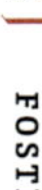

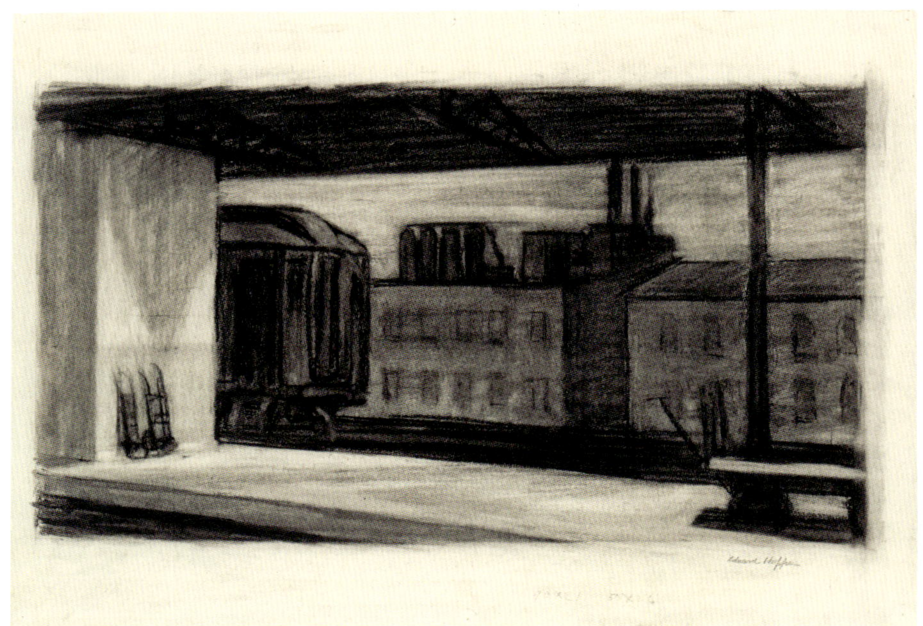

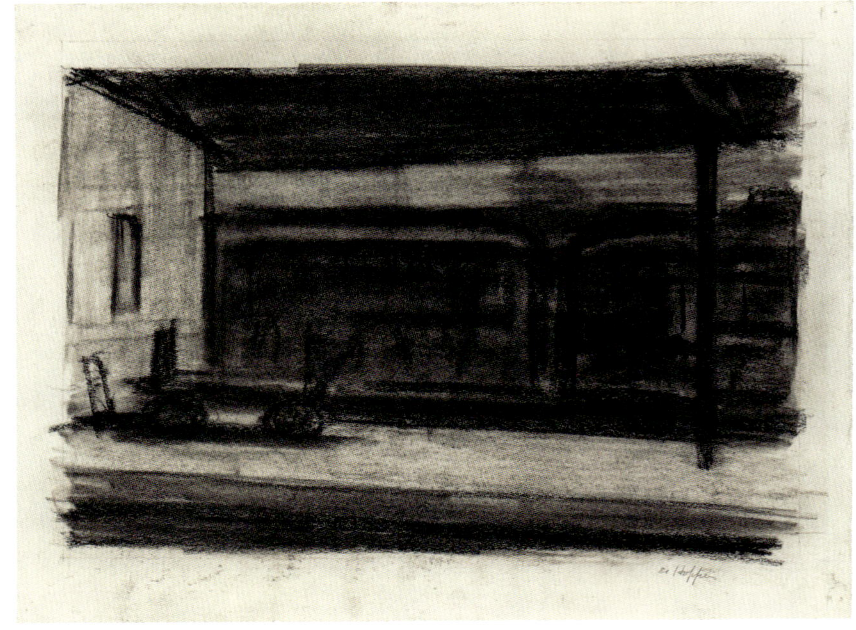

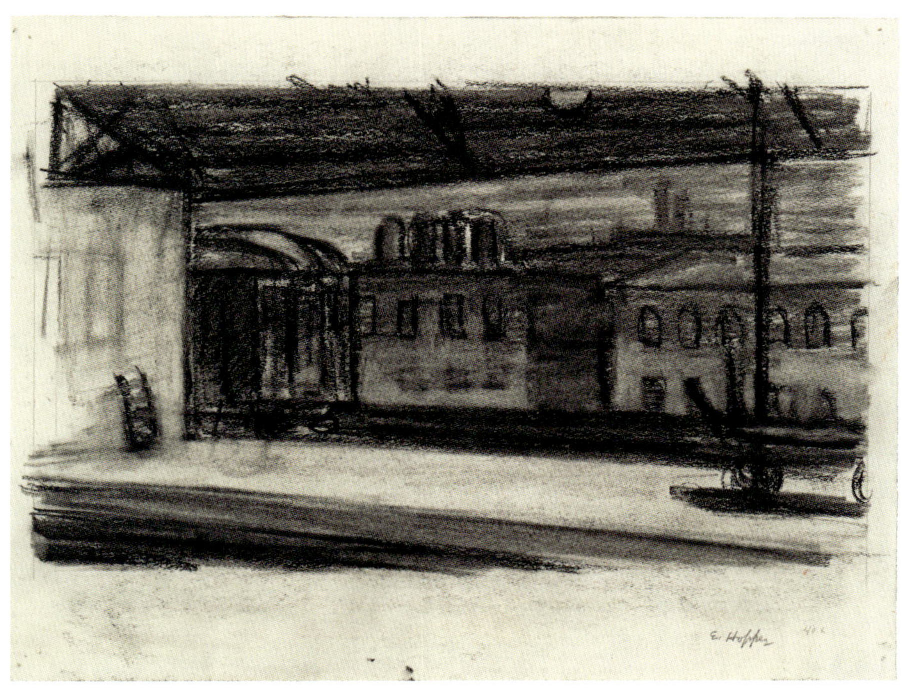

78. Study for *Dawn in Pennsylvania*, 1942
Charcoal, fabricated chalk, and graphite pencil on paper, 15 × 22 ⅛ in. (38.1 × 56.2 cm)
Josephine N. Hopper Bequest 70.850

79. Study for *Dawn in Pennsylvania*, 1942
Charcoal on paper, 11 × 15 in. (27.9 × 38.1 cm)
Josephine N. Hopper Bequest 70.851

80. Study for *Dawn in Pennsylvania*, 1942
Charcoal on paper, 11 1/16 × 15 1/16 in. (28.1 × 38.3 cm)
Josephine N. Hopper Bequest 70.852

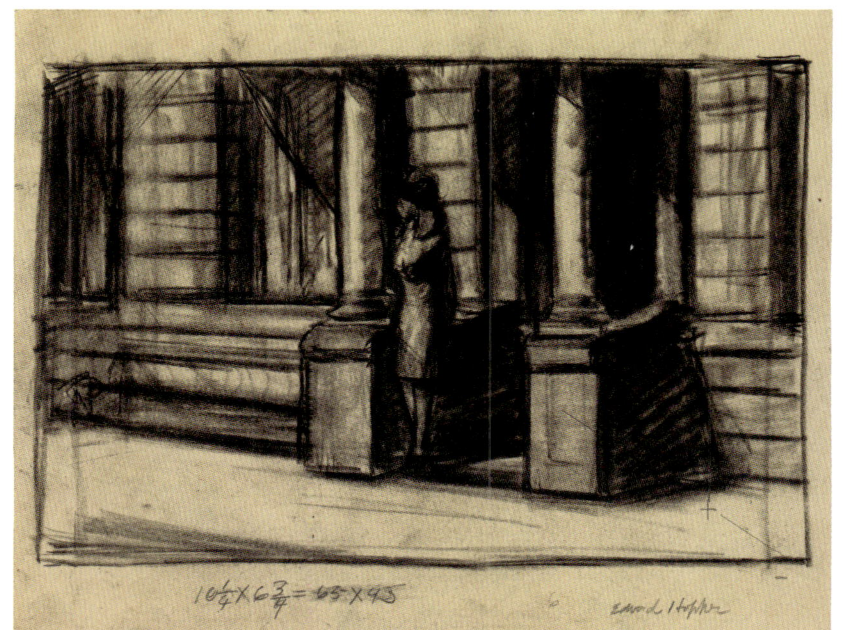

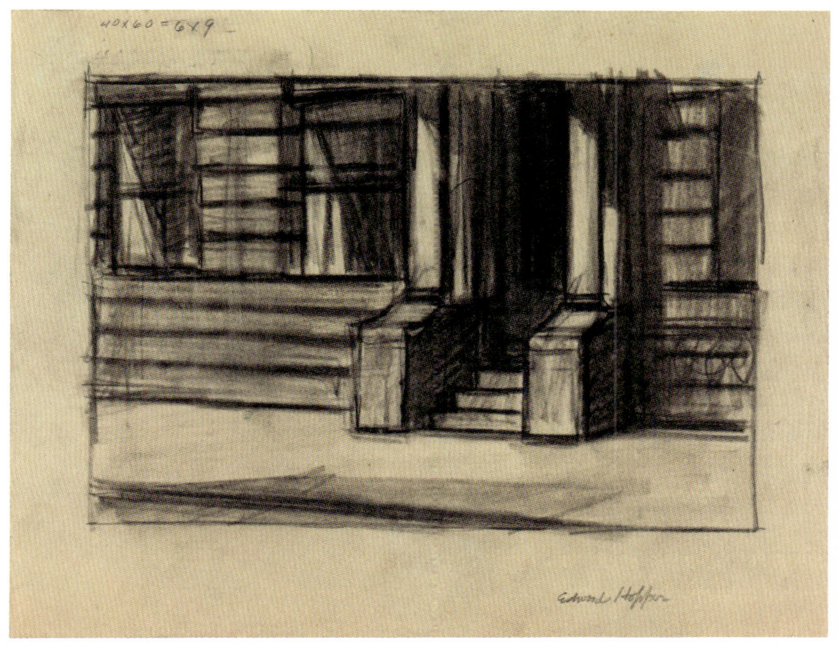

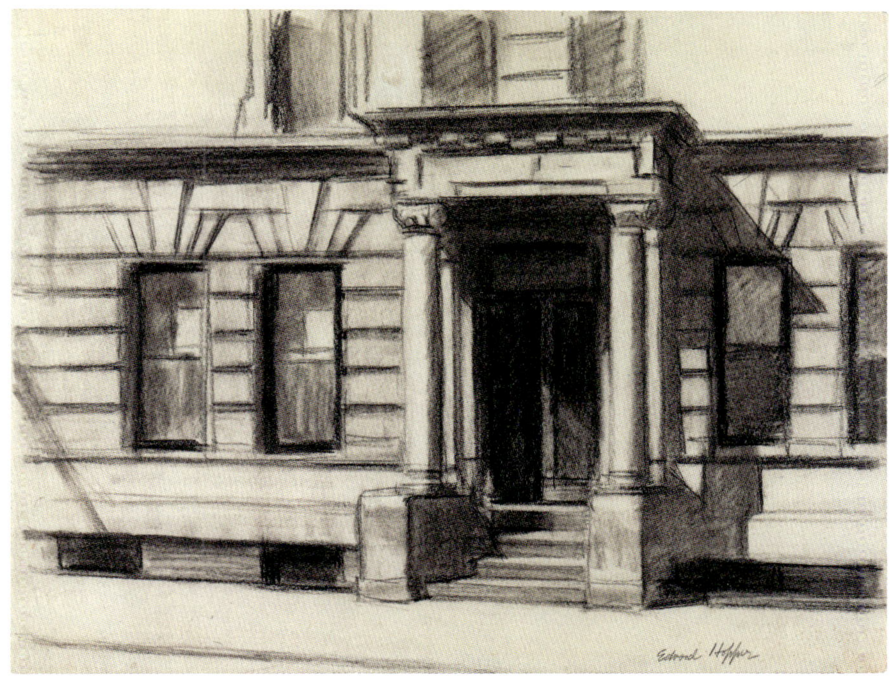

81. Study for *Summertime*, 1943
Fabricated chalk and graphite pencil on paper,
8 3/8 × 10 15/16 in. (21.3 × 27.8 cm)
Josephine N. Hopper Bequest 70.458

82. Study for *Summertime*, 1943
Fabricated chalk on paper, 8 3/8 × 11 in. (21.3 × 27.9 cm)
Josephine N. Hopper Bequest 70.459

83. Study for *Summertime*, 1943
Fabricated chalk on paper, 8 13/16 × 11 13/16 in. (22.4 × 30 cm)
Josephine N. Hopper Bequest 70.460

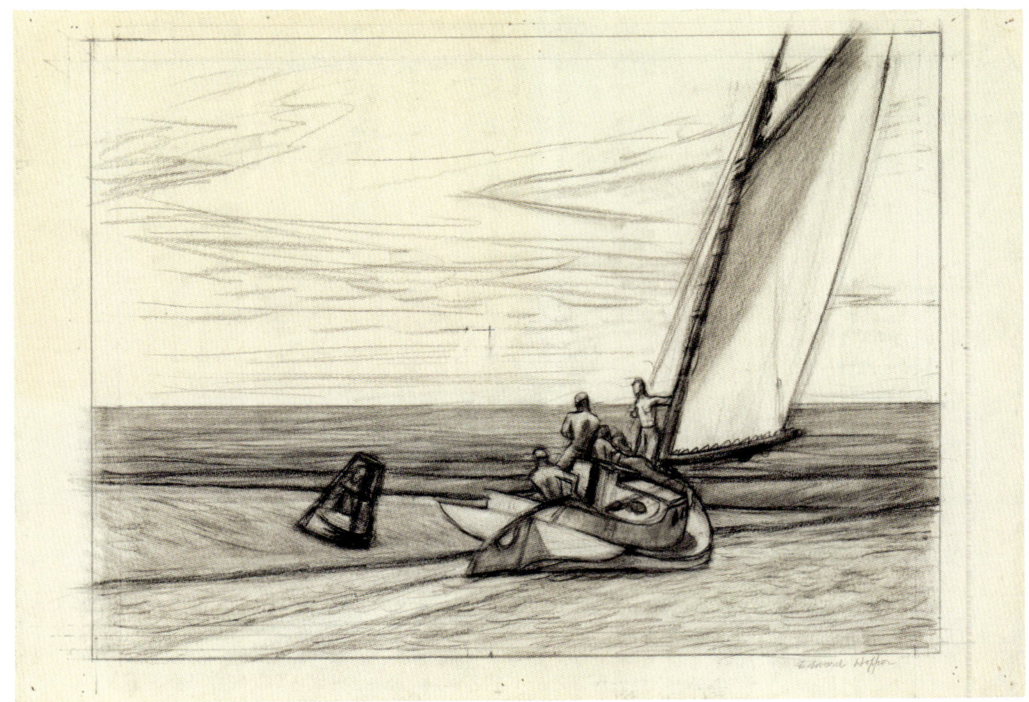

show them. The paint stains and tack holes that exist on many attest to their use in the studio.[60] Hopper either built his own stretchers or had them made to order[61] and the proportions of a canvas were absolutely specific to each subject—the edges being as crucial a part of a composition for Hopper as its painted elements. As a totality his mature paintings follow no consistent size or format (though he generally painted easel-sized works and almost exclusively favored horizontality).[62] Hopper also blocked out the basic elements of a composition with charcoal or chalk on the primed canvas before he started painting. Jo described this in numerous instances in her diaries, and underdrawing has been documented for some of his paintings, including *Nighthawks*. But Hopper also frequently made changes and allowed a painting to evolve even as he was working on it. Very few of his paintings follow his drawings completely, though the latter necessarily served as guides and aide-mémoire. Hopper's tendency was to simplify and empty out, removing elements as a work developed, both in the drawings as the composition developed and on the canvas.

Once Hopper had worked out basic compositional structure in drawing, he would often set up a life session (see fig. 85) with his wife so that he could further develop the pose or better understand a detail of clothing, gesture, facial expression, or the specific fall of light on an object or limb (see fig. 86). He sometimes posed for himself (as in the case of *Office at Night* and *Nighthawks*)[63] using a mirror (there were several in his Washington Square studio, including a long one that hung between the front windows; see fig. 386).

Many friends tenderly attest to the intimacy of his life with Jo and the close living quarters they shared (fig. 87). He drew his wife frequently, often in bust-length portraits that show her absorbed in thought (fig. 88) or in intimate nudes, among the most directly erotic pieces Hopper ever created (fig. 89). At his creative peak, he drew two powerful self-portraits seemingly done one after another, a rare example of the artist depicting himself beyond his youth (figs. 90, 91); together they offer a brilliant example of his interest in exploring the same subject with singular focus and subtle variation. Powerful studies of his hands (figs. 92, 93), one of which is dedicated to Jo, and a commanding surrogate self-portrait showing his hat on his printing press (fig. 94), reflect his use of drawing as an expression of both professional station in life and creative self-awareness.

Drawing was a constant activity for Hopper, even when he was not working on a painting. As with most artists trained following traditions established in Western art during the Renaissance, for Hopper, drawing was the natural default when exploring artistic ideas and working toward a finished, carefully considered artistic statement. For him, this usually meant an oil painting. Despite his generally negative statements about his drawings, he was fully at home in this technique, one he mastered before any other and practiced more thoroughly than oil, watercolor, and etching combined. His accomplishments as a draftsman can reasonably be seen as the most significant constant over his long career, one that stretches across and thus ties together the nearly eight decades during which he made his extraordinary contributions to modern art.

84. Study for *Ground Swell*, 1939
Fabricated chalk, charcoal, and graphite pencil on paper, 15 × 22 ⅛ in. (38.1 × 56.2 cm)
Josephine N. Hopper Bequest 70.339

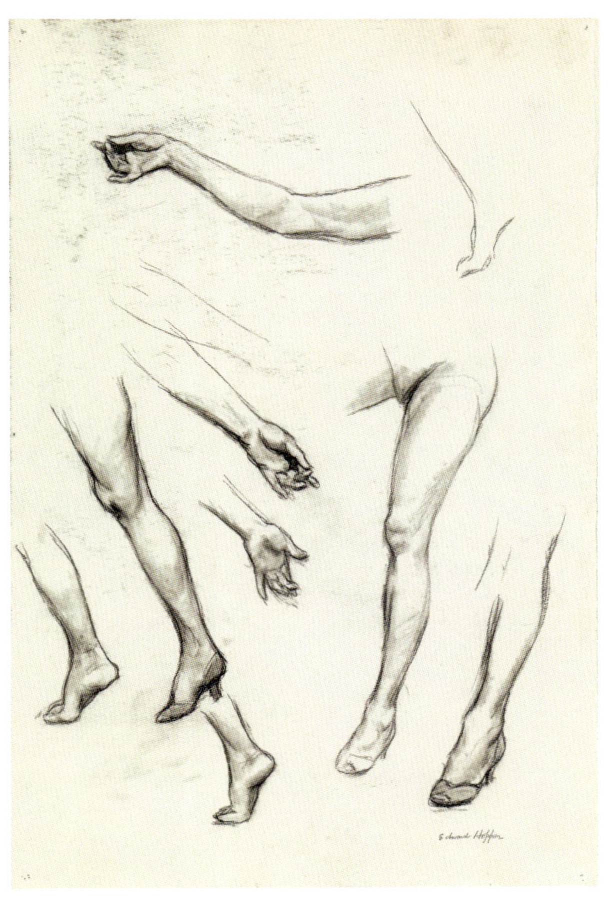

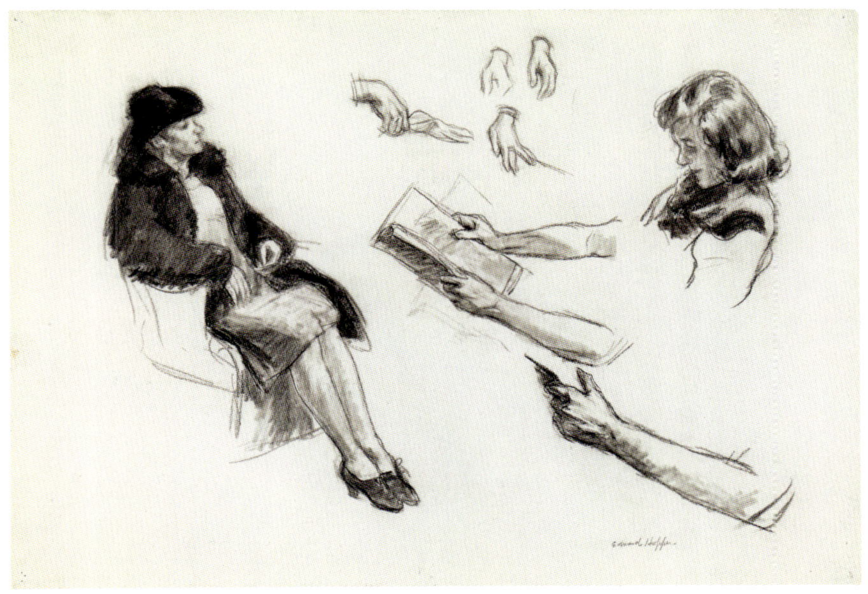

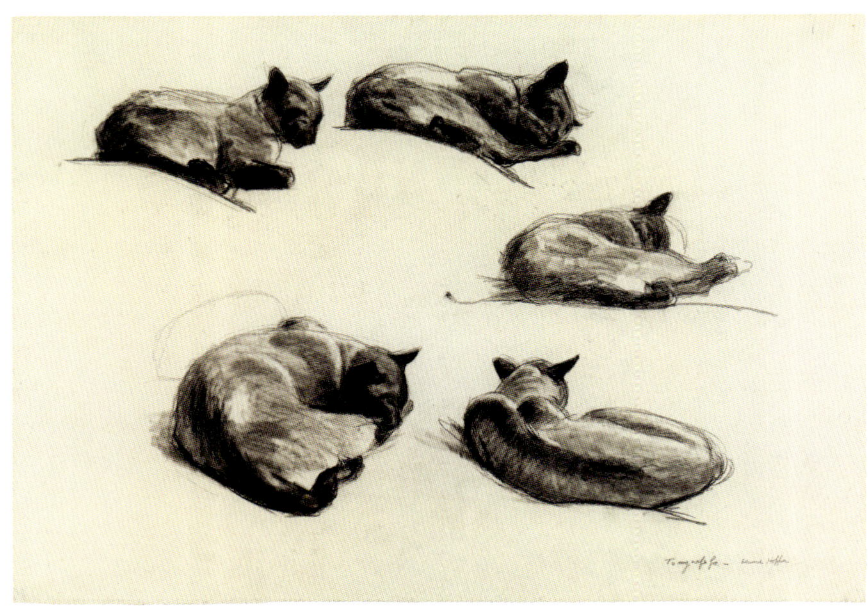

85. Study for *Girlie Show*, 1941
Fabricated chalk and charcoal on paper,
22 1/8 × 15 3/16 in. (56.2 × 38.6 cm)
Josephine N. Hopper Bequest 70.997

86. Study for *Hotel Lobby*, 1942
Fabricated chalk and charcoal on paper,
15 × 22 3/16 in. (38.1 × 56.4 cm)
Josephine N. Hopper Bequest 70.996

87. *Perkins Youngboy Dos Passos*, 1941
Fabricated chalk on paper, 15 × 22 in. (38.1 × 55.9 cm)
Josephine N. Hopper Bequest 70.659

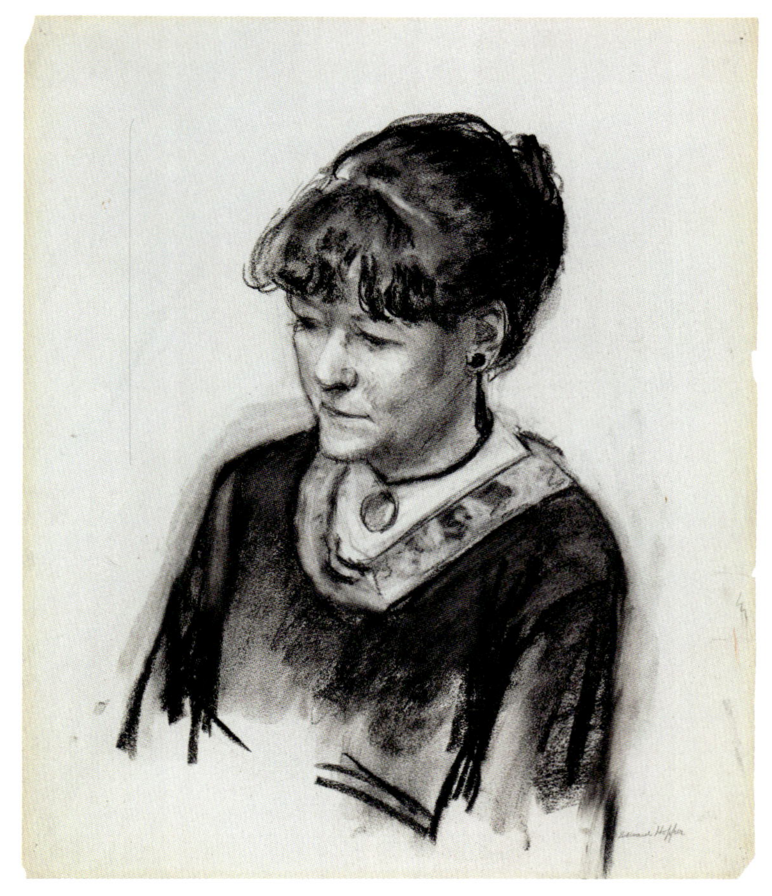

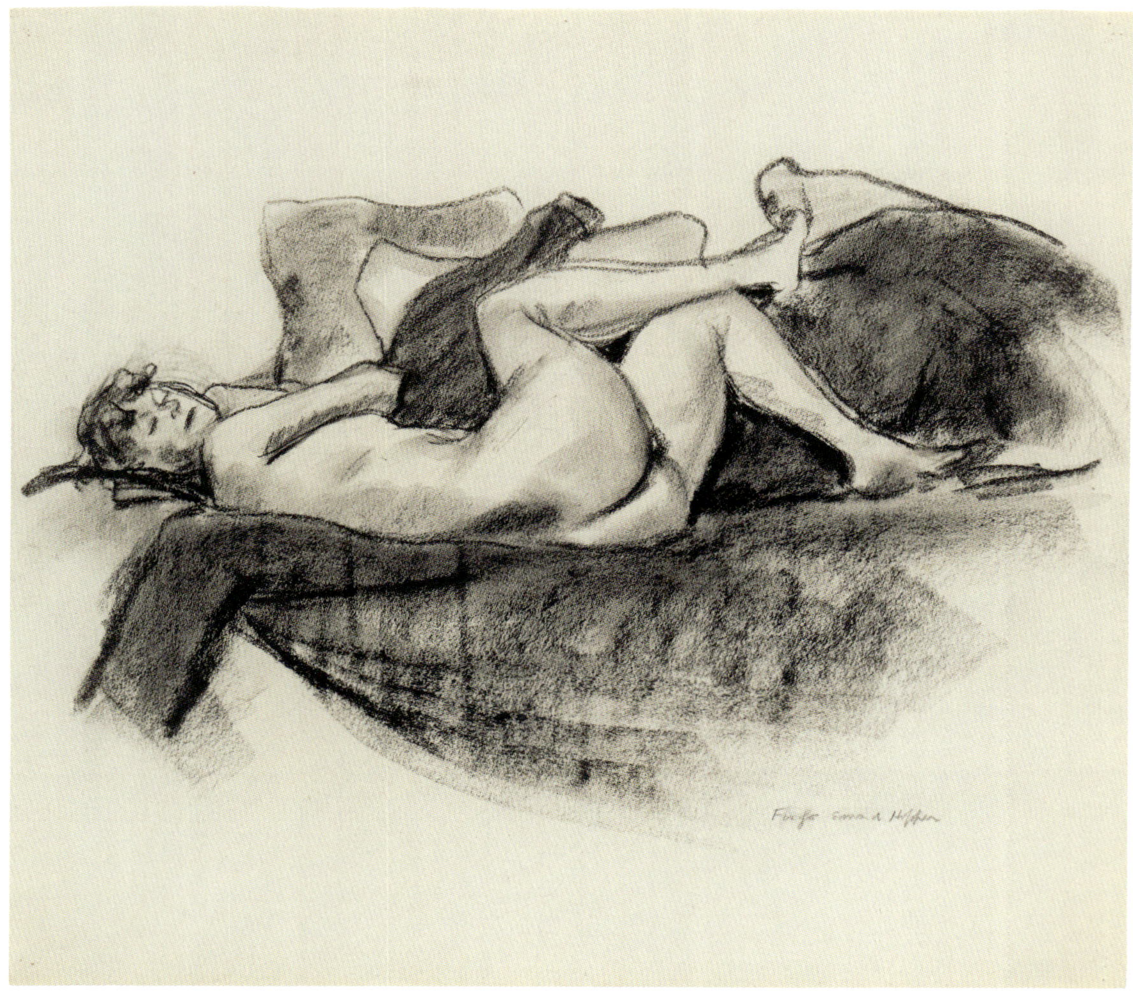

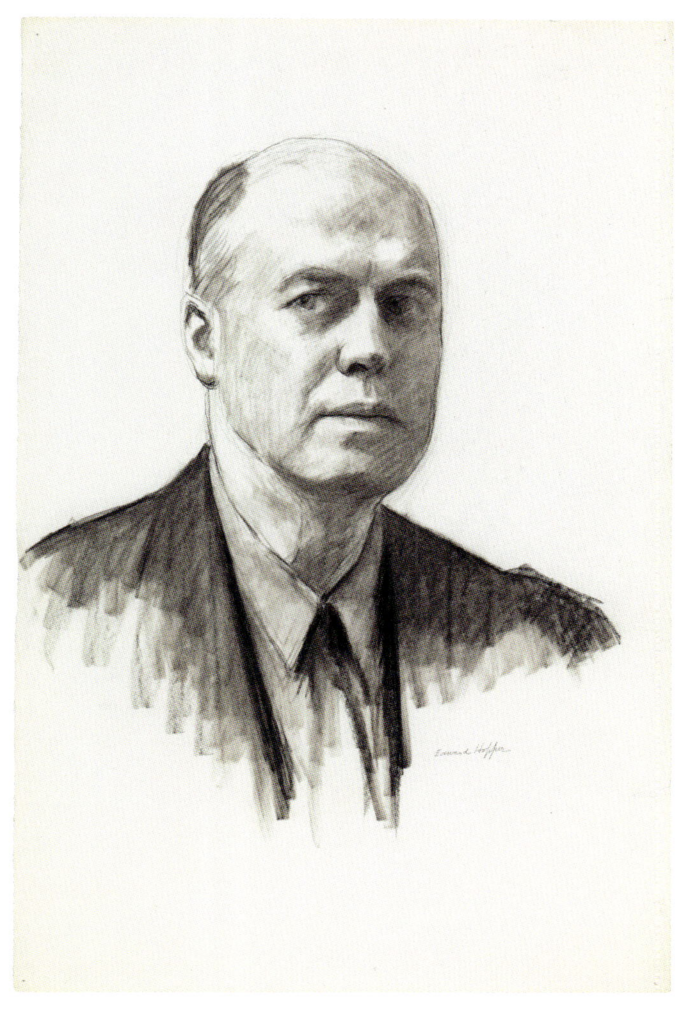

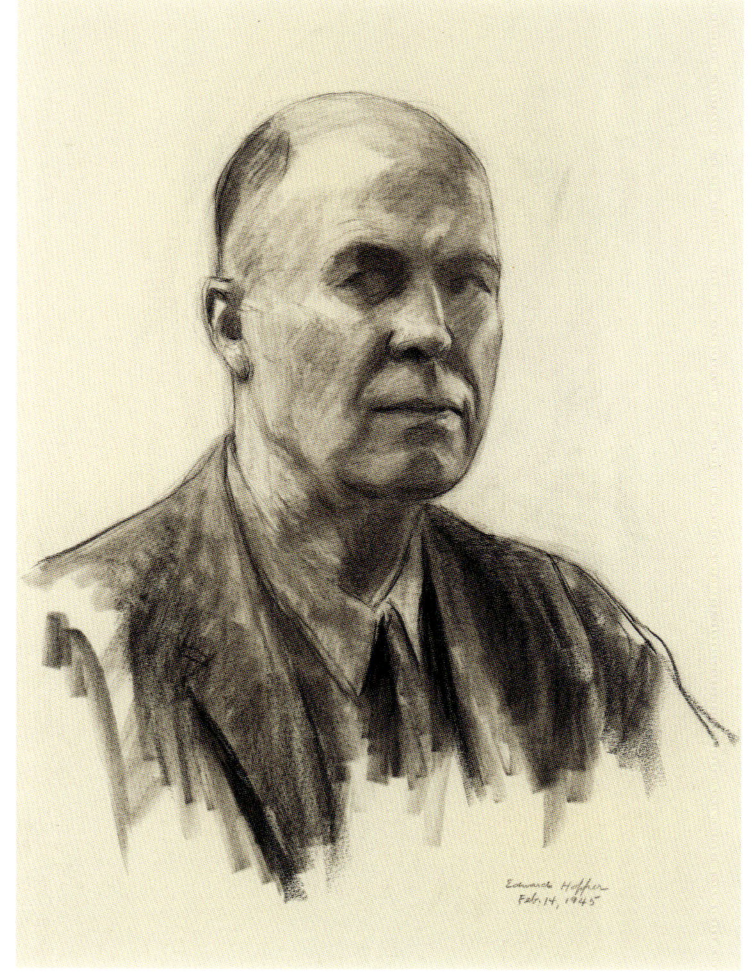

88. *Jo Hopper*, 1945–50
Charcoal on paper, 18 × 15 7/16 in. (45.7 × 39.2 cm)
Josephine N. Hopper Bequest 70.288

89. *Jo Hopper Reclining on a Couch*, 1925–30
Fabricated chalk on paper, 15 9/16 × 18 in. (39.5 × 45.7 cm)
Josephine N. Hopper Bequest 70.296

90. *Self-Portrait*, 1945
Fabricated chalk and charcoal on paper,
22 × 14 15/16 in. (55.9 × 37.9 cm)
Josephine N. Hopper Bequest 70.287

91. *Self-Portrait*, 1945
Fabricated chalk and charcoal on paper,
22 1/8 × 15 in. (56.2 × 38.1 cm)
Josephine N. Hopper Bequest 70.336

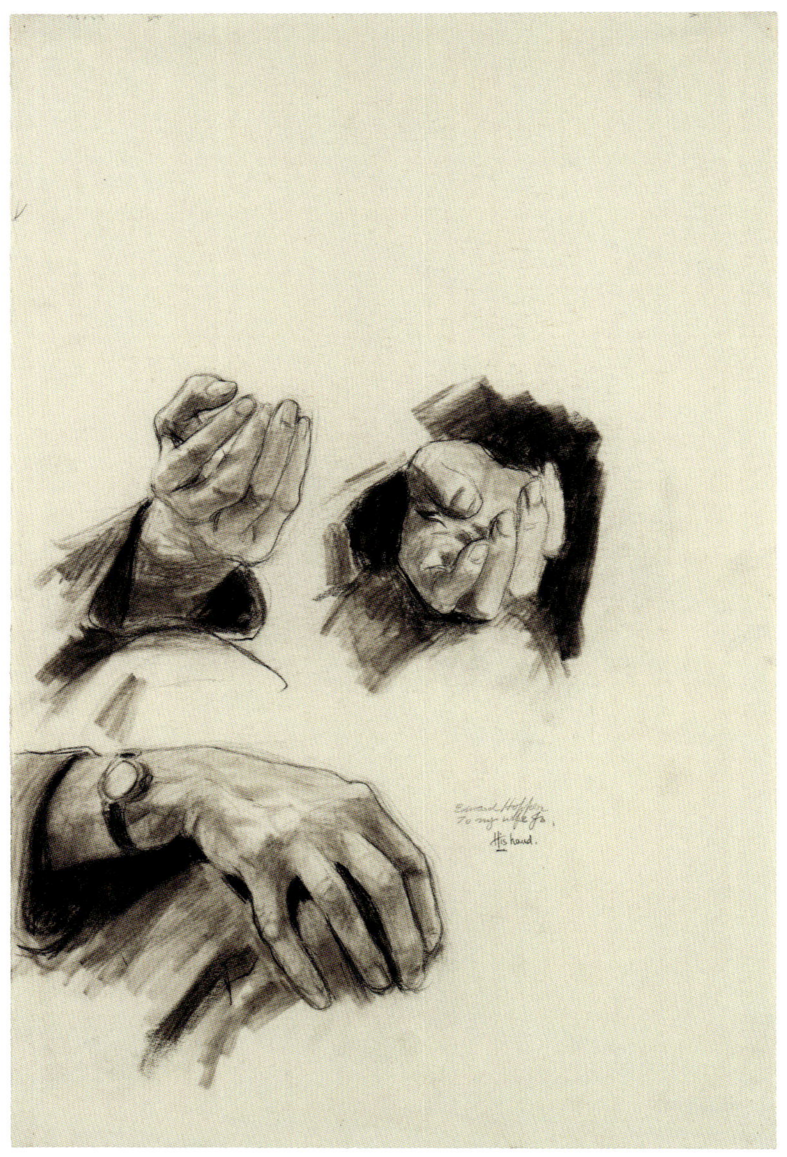

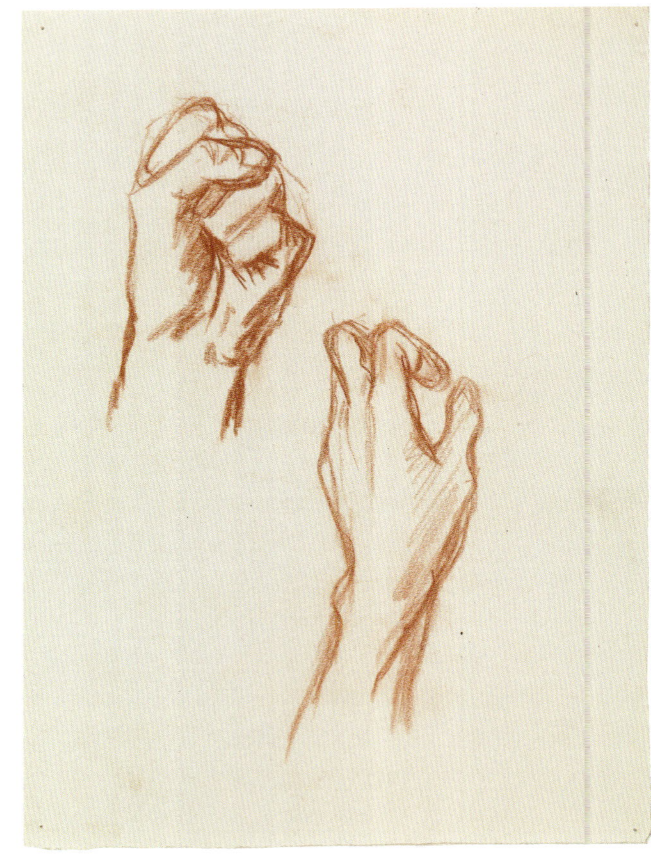

92. *Three Hand Studies* (*Hands* or *The Artist's Hands, Three Views*), 1943
Fabricated chalk, charcoal, and graphite pencil on paper, 22 ⅛ × 15 in. (56.2 × 38.1 cm)
Josephine N. Hopper Bequest 70.337

93. *Two Hand Studies*, c. 1920
Fabricated chalk on paper, 10 ⅝ × 8 in. (27 × 20.3 cm)
Josephine N. Hopper Bequest 70.631

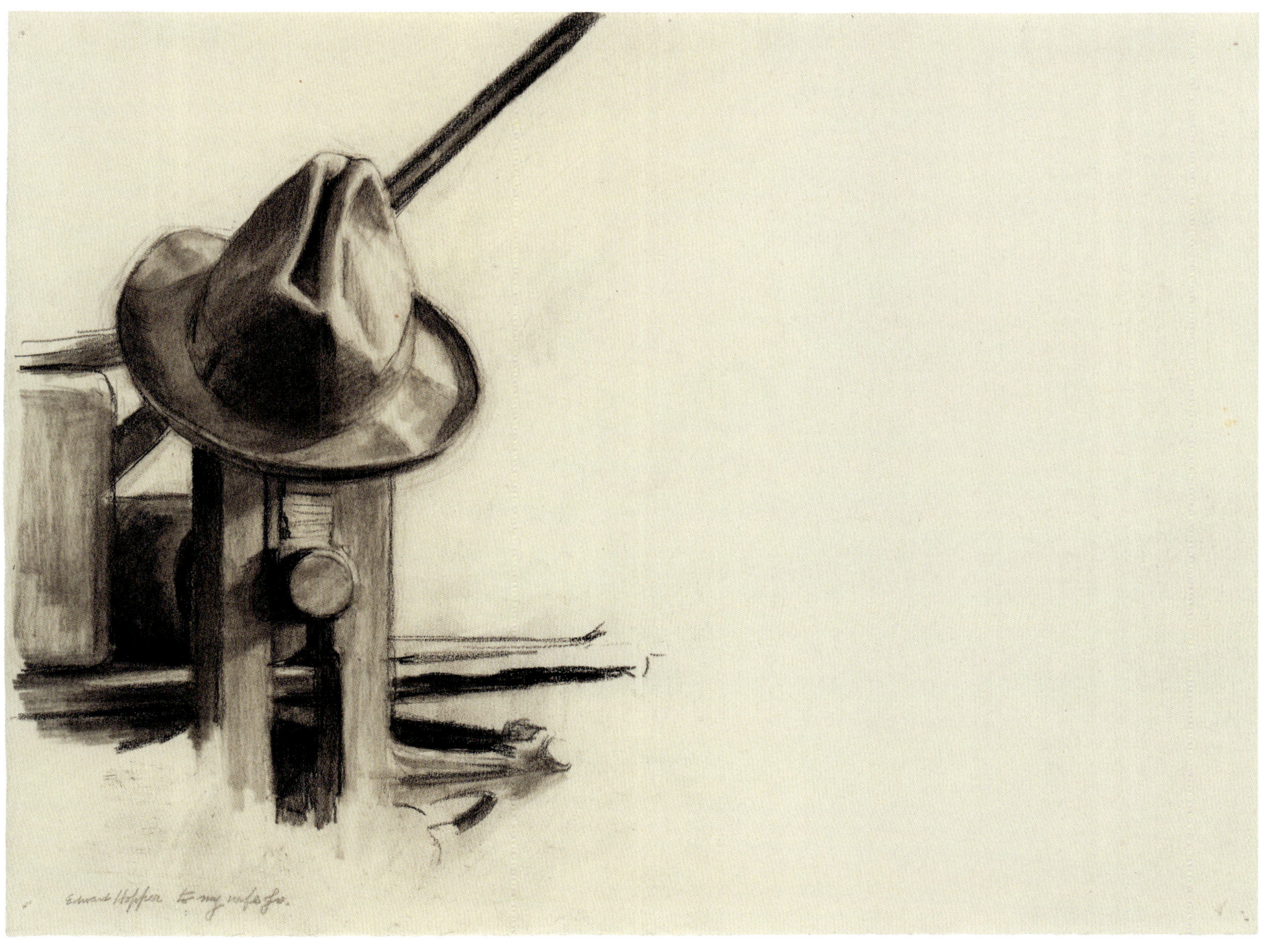

94. *Hopper's Hat on His Etching Press*, after 1924
Fabricated chalk on paper, 11 1/16 × 15 1/8 in. (28.1 × 38.4 cm)
Josephine N. Hopper Bequest 70.344

NOTES

1 Brian O'Doherty describes this quality in Hopper thus: "The window as lens or eye is a persistent metaphor of the vital traffic between inside and outside, object and subject—an image of the processes in which we know ourselves, and discover ourselves. Through the mediumship of the window he rediscovers the primitive, pre-verbal identification of object and feeling through means of extreme honesty and sophistication." Brian O'Doherty, "Portrait: Edward Hopper," *Art in America* 52, no. 6 (December 1964): 78.

2 "I'm after ME," the artist once said. See Brian O'Doherty, "Edward Hopper's Voice," in *American Masters: The Voice and the Myth* (New York: Random House, 1973), 26.

3 Both the painting and a double-sided drawing for it are in the collection of the Yale University Art Gallery, New Haven, Connecticut. See *Edward Hopper: The Capezzera Drawings*, exh. cat. (New York: Peter Findlay Gallery, 2005), 18–19.

4 Artist Philip Koch, who has spent time in the Hoppers' former house making his own work, shared these illuminating thoughts about the difference between the painting and the views from and inside the house: "A comparison of Hopper's inventive vision with the actual 'facts' of the studio's architecture is revealing. Hopper's famous oil contrasts the open waves of Cape Cod Bay directly against the doorway. To heighten the contrast, he places a big blast of sunlight on the empty wall and darkens down the water. It works beautifully. But to get to this, he had to move the wooden dutch [*sic*] door to hinges on the opposite side of the doorframe. Then he widened the white wall. And best of all, he has the sunlight shining on a wall it never hits in reality. The view is looking south, and the empty wall faces due north. In his most daring move, he eliminates the land between the studio and the water, lending the painting a delicious slightly surreal quality. I used to wonder about this lovely but odd placement before I ever had visited the studio. But I found that when one sits in a chair at the far end of the studio away from the water (which is where Hopper usually placed his easel when he worked) that his viewpoint was low enough to the ground he would have seen the doorway seeming to lead directly out into the water. So the oddness of the painting's composition actually stemmed from something he actually saw. He just had the sense to take advantage of it." Email to author, September 12, 2012.

5 For a photograph showing the view from the Hoppers' Cape Cod house, see Gail Levin, *Hopper's Places* (New York: Alfred A. Knopf, 1989), 86. It is useful to compare this with *Rooms by the Sea*, as she does on the facing page.

6 See Lloyd Goodrich, "Notes of Conversation with Hopper" (typescript, April 20, 1946), Edward and Josephine Hopper Research Collection, 4.044, Whitney Museum of American Art Archives, New York (hereafter cited as Hopper Research Collection and reproduced in this volume on pages 221–27); Lloyd Goodrich, "Notes of Conversation with Hopper" (unpublished typescript, April 21, 1947), Hopper Research Collection, 4.044; Lloyd Goodrich, *Edward Hopper* (New York: Harry N. Abrams, 1971); O'Doherty, "Portrait: Edward Hopper," 66–88; O'Doherty, "Hopper's Voice," 10–43; Edward Hopper to Charles H. Sawyer, October 19, 1939, Archives of the Addison Gallery of American Art, Phillips Academy, Andover, Massachusetts; Katharine Kuh, "Edward Hopper," in *The Artist's Voice: Talks with Seventeen Artists* (New York: Harper and Row, 1962), 130–39; "Oral History Interview with Edward Hopper, 1959 June 17," Archives of American Art, Smithsonian Institution, Washington, DC; Arlene Jacobowitz, "Interview with Edward Hopper. 1966," transcript from January 23, 1968, Hopper Research Collection, 4.043; Bill Johnson, "Hopper Cover Research" (unpublished typescript, October 30, 1956), Hopper Research Collection, 4.043; "Art: The Silent Witness," *Time*, December 24, 1956, 28–39; Charles Burchfield, "Hopper: Career of Silent Poetry," *ARTnews* 49, no. 1 (March 1950): 14–17, 62–63; Edward Hopper, "John Sloan and the Philadelphians," *The Arts* 11, no. 4 (April 1927): 169–78; Edward Hopper, review of *The Art and Craft of Drawing*, by Vernon Blake, *The Arts* 11, no. 6 (June 1927): 333–34; Edward Hopper, "Charles Burchfield: American," *The Arts* 14, no. 1 (July 1928): 3–12.

7 Edward Hopper, "Notes on Painting," in Alfred H. Barr, Jr., et al., *Edward Hopper: Retrospective Exhibition, November 1–December 7, 1933*, exh. cat. (New York: Museum of Modern Art, 1933), 17.

8 Hopper to Sawyer, October 19, 1939.

9 O'Doherty, "Portrait: Edward Hopper," 72; O'Doherty, "Hopper's Voice," 14.

10 Although his statements about it are characteristically few, Hopper seems to have felt that the material substance of paint and the manner in which it was applied had much to do with a painting's impact. See O'Doherty, "Portrait: Edward Hopper," 80: "Many Cézanne's [*sic*] are very thin. They don't have weight." Goodrich, "Notes of Conversation with Hopper" (1946), 6: "He admires Courbet very much; spoke of his 'mechanical strength' or some such phrase, meaning the physical force and substance of his work. He seemed to feel that Courbet had this quality more than any other 19th Century painter. He contrasted it with the lack of substance in Cézanne, the papery qualtiy [*sic*]."

11 Goodrich, "Notes of Conversation with Hopper" (1946), 4, 5; O'Doherty, "Hopper's Voice," 19–22.

12 O'Doherty clarified Hopper's use of this term based on conversations with the artist: "When he spoke of the fact he meant a recognizable image from life, as distinct from abstraction." O'Doherty, "Hopper's Voice," 21–22.

13 He first used this term in "Notes on Painting": "I find, in working, always the disturbing intrusion of elements not a part of my most interested vision, and the inevitable obliteration and replacement of this vision by the work itself as it proceeds. The struggle to prevent this decay is, I think, the common lot of all painters to whom the invention of arbitrary forms [i.e., abstraction] has lesser interest." Hopper, "Notes on Painting," 17.

14 O'Doherty, "Portrait: Edward Hopper," 77.

15 O'Doherty asked Hopper when he painted and received this pained response: "When I can force myself to. . . . So many people say painting is fun. I don't find it fun at all. It's hard work for me." O'Doherty, "Hopper's Voice," 41. See also Goodrich, "Notes of Conversation with Hopper" (1946), 4.

16 Johnson, "Hopper Cover Research," 29; "Art: The Silent Witness," 39.

17 Richard R. Brettell and Éric Darragon, *Edward Hopper: Les années parisiennes, 1906–1910*, exh. cat. (Giverny: Musée d'Art Américain, 2004); Kevin Salatino et al., *Edward Hopper's Maine*, exh. cat. (Brunswick, ME: Bowdoin College Museum of Art; Munich: Prestel, 2011); Virginia M. Mecklenburg, *Edward Hopper: The Watercolors*, exh. cat. (Washington, DC: National Museum of American Art; New York: W. W. Norton, 1999).

18 O'Doherty, "Portrait: Edward Hopper," 73; Johnson, "Hopper Cover Research," 1, 28; Goodrich, "Notes of Conversation with Hopper" (1946), 5; Joan Dye, "Luncheon Interview with Hopper and His Wife Jo at Charles French Restaurant in the Village" (transcript, May 19, 1955), Hopper Research Collection, 4.043, 2.

19 On Hopper's watercolors, see Gail Levin, *Edward Hopper: A Catalogue Raisonné*, vol. 2, *Watercolors* (New York: Whitney Museum of American Art in association with W. W. Norton, 1995); Mecklenburg, *Edward Hopper: The Watercolors*; Virginia M. Mecklenburg, "Edward Hopper: The Watercolors," *American Art Review* 12, no. 1 (January–February 2000): 128–39.

20 Hopper to Sawyer, October 19, 1939.

21 The full quote is: "the intimate memory-traces all of us possess, persisting from experiences, often without memory of the experience—which may be what Mr. Hopper means by his repeated use of the word 'intimate.'" O'Doherty, "Portrait: Edward Hopper," 76.

22 In a letter to Bartlett H. Hayes, Jr., thanking him for his book *The Naked Truth and Personal Vision*, Hopper stated, "I do not know what the 'Naked Truth' is, but I know that a 'personal vision' is the most important element in a painter's equipment, but it must be *communicated*." Edward Hopper to Hayes, July 4, 1955, Hopper Research Collection, 4.011.

23 O'Doherty, "Hopper's Voice," 22.

24 O'Doherty, "Portrait: Edward Hopper," 77; O'Doherty, "Hopper's Voice," 21–22.

25 O'Doherty, "Hopper's Voice," 22.

26 Hopper to Sawyer, October 19, 1939.

27 O'Doherty, "Hopper's Voice," 22.

28 Edward Hopper to Alfred H. Barr, Jr., August 24, 1933, Hopper Research Collection, 4.010.

29 Edward Hopper Record Book I, 87. For information on and a partial facsimile of Hopper's Record Books, see Deborah Lyons, *Edward Hopper: A Journal of His Work* (New York: Whitney Museum of American Art in association with W. W. Norton, 1997); Deborah Lyons, "By Necessity or Invention: The Record-Book Sketches of Edward Hopper," *Drawing* 18, no. 4 (Spring 1997): 101–6.

30 Lloyd Goodrich, *Edward Hopper: Retrospective Exhibition*, exh. cat. (New York: Whitney Museum of American Art, 1950), 59.

31 See "A View from the Bridge" in this volume.

32 Edward Hopper Record Book I, 69; Hopper's *Drawing for The Maine Coast* (1923; see fig. 52) is inscribed "To Ned" and, presumably, was a gift to the print dealer Ned Jennings; Frank K. M. Rehn Galleries records, Archives of American Art, Smithsonian Institution, Washington, DC, box 7, reel 5857, frame 1178: invoice for sale of drawing "Houses at Gloucester" to McCurrach in 1944; box 7, reel 5857, frame 1214: invoice for sale of drawing "Landscape" to Santa Barbara Museum of Art in 1949; box 7, reel 5857, frame 1243: Jo Hopper explains to a potential buyer in Houston, Warren Breidenbach, in a letter of 1952 that the Rehn Galleries have for sale for about $100 "drawings—not recent—of houses, trees, boats, barns etc. Some life drawings from some years ago." In the late 1950s and early 1960s, Hopper sent a group of drawings from the 1920s to the Rehn Galleries for sale, perhaps indicating a shift in his attitude toward them near the end of his life. Edward Hopper Record Book V.

33 "Edward Hopper: Drawings from the Artist's Portfolio," *American Artist* 14, no. 5 (May 1950): 28–33 and cover illustration.

34 Lloyd Goodrich, *Edward Hopper*, exh. cat. (New York: Whitney Museum of American Art, 1964), 68.

35 Hopper's rejection of an invitation to show etchings and drawings at the Corcoran Gallery in Washington, DC, demonstrates this: "As to the drawings, I care so little for them to be seen, that they are rarely shown." Edward Hopper to C. Powell Minnigerode, August 8, 1939, copy in Hopper Research Collection, 4.011.

36 In a letter to James Biddle in 1964, Hopper wrote, "I have decided that a book of my drawings reproduced and published would only very inadequately express what I attempt to do in my painting, and I would not be happy with such a project, and do not care to consider it." Edward Hopper to James Biddle, January 21, 1964; copy in Hopper Research Collection, 4.018.

37 O'Doherty, "Hopper's Voice," 26. For the drawing, see Peter Schjeldahl, *Edward Hopper: Light Years*, exh. cat. (New York: Hirschl & Adler Galleries, 1988), no. 104, 56, 58.

38 Two other friends of Jo Hopper acquired some of her husband's drawings. Mary Schiffenhaus was close to Jo at the end of her life and was bequeathed part of the Truro property, including the house and its contents, apparently including drawings Hopper kept in the house. (Some of these drawings she in turn left to Frank M. Capezzera in 1969, and to her sons, J. Anton and Laurence C. Schiffenhaus.) Arthayer Sanborn, a minister from Nyack who helped Hopper's sister, Marion, as well as Edward and Jo in their later years, also acquired a substantial group. According to a letter in the object files of the Yale University Art Gallery related to their Hopper drawings, Sanborn explains that Jo Hopper gave him some of her husband's drawings before she died. Arthayer Sanborn, letter of March 27, 1987, Yale University Art Gallery object files. Many of these drawings were exhibited at commercial galleries in New York in the late 1970s and 1980s and had begun to enter the market then or before. Several publications, among the first to deal in any depth with Hopper's drawings, document these important groups, which tend to be from either early or late in the artist's career. Besides the drawings Hopper sold or gave away during his lifetime, the works bequeathed to the Whitney along with the Schiffenhaus and Sanborn material seem to represent the totality of what the artist kept. For publications on non-Whitney drawings, see *Edward Hopper at Kennedy Galleries*, exh. cat. (New York: Kennedy Galleries, 1977); Douglas Dreishpoon, *Edward Hopper: Early and Late; Drawings, Watercolors, and Paintings, March 14–April 18*, exh. cat. (New York: Hirschl & Adler Galleries, 1987); Gail Levin, *In Black and White: Selected American Drawings and Prints—Part II; Edward Hopper: Selected Drawings*, exh. cat. (Beverly Hills, CA: Louis Newman Galleries, 1989); Schjeldahl, *Edward Hopper: Light Years*; Gail Levin, *The Early Drawings of Edward Hopper*, exh. cat. (New York: Kennedy Galleries, 1995); *Edward Hopper: The Capezzera Drawings*; J. Anton Schiffenhaus, *A Window into the World of Edward and Josephine Hopper*, exh. cat. (Provincetown, MA: privately printed, 1996); *Edward Hopper / John Register: Works on Paper*, exh. cat. (San Francisco: Modernism, 1996); Robert P. Metzer and Bruce C. Loch, *Edward Hopper (1882–1967). "Early Impressions,"* exh. cat. (Provincetown, MA: Thurston Royce Gallery of Fine Art, 2010).

39 John Gordon memorandum to John Baur, Margaret McKellar, and Stephen Weil, May 8, 1969, Hopper Research Collection, 6.1.

40 Rockwell Kent, *It's Me O Lord* (New York: Dodd, Mead, 1955), 84.

41 "Henri encouraged his students to study Manet's *Woman with a Parrot* and *Boy with a Sword* at the Metropolitan Museum, where he, like Chase, often took groups of students." Gail Levin, *Edward Hopper: An Intimate Biography* (New York: Rizzoli, 2007), 40.

42 Gail Levin has thoroughly catalogued this side of his career. See Levin, *Edward Hopper as Illustrator* (New York W. W. Norton in association with the Whitney Museum of American Art, 1979).

43 Although Hopper had sold a painting at the 1913 Armory Show, he made his living by commercial work and selling prints until about 1924. On Hopper's prints, see Virgil Barker, "The Etchings of Edward Hopper," *The Arts* 5, no. 6 (June 1924): 322–27; Guy Pène du Bois, "Edward Hopper, Draughtsman: An Appreciation of the Work of an Etcher Who Does Not Belong to the Rank and File," *Shadowland* 7, no. 2 (October 1922): 22–23; Carl Zigrosser, *The Complete Graphic Work of Edward Hopper* (N.p.: Print Council of America, 1962), excerpted from *Prints: Thirteen Illustrated Essays on the Art of the Print* (New York: Holt, Rinehart and Winston, 1962); Carl Zigrosser, "The Prints of Edward Hopper," *American Artist* 27, no. 9 (November 1963): 38–43, 64–65; Gail Levin, *Edward Hopper: The Complete Prints*, exh. cat. (New York: W. W. Norton in association with the Whitney Museum of American Art, 1979); Levin, *Edward Hopper as Illustrator*. On Hopper's watercolors, see the sources cited in note 19 above.

44 See Salatino et al., *Edward Hopper's Maine*.

45 See Goodrich, *Edward Hopper: Retrospective Exhibition* (1950), 59: "Drawings / All in conte crayon. All lent by the artist, courtesy of Frank K. M. Rehn, Inc."; Goodrich, *Edward Hopper* (1964), 68: "Drawings / All are in conte crayon unless otherwise stated." The only other stated medium is here described as "sanguine."

46 During the artist's lifetime, the Hoppers arranged to donate seven of his preparatory drawings for prints to the Philadelphia Museum of Art to accompany the museum's purchase of a large collection of his prints for a print retrospective. Initiated because of the interest of the print curator, former gallerist, and longtime acquaintance Carl Zigrosser, this was an important example of Hopper showing awareness of the legacy of his drawings for posterity.

47 Avis Berman, *Rebels on Eighth Street: Juliana Force and the Whitney Museum of American Art* (New York: Atheneum, 1990), 159, citing an oral history interview between Katherine Schmidt and Paul Cummings, December 8–15, 1969, Archives of American Art, Smithsonian Institution, Washington, DC.

48 Lyons, *Edward Hopper: A Journal of His Work*; Lyons, "By Necessity or Invention," 101–6.

49 Goodrich, "Notes of Conversation with Hopper" (1946), 4–5.

50 Though there is a drawing of a similar subject in the Whitney; see fig. 61.

51 Hopper to Sawyer, October 19, 1939. See also "A View from the Bridge" in this volume.

52 "Traveling Man," *Time*, January 19, 1948, 60.

53 Reproduced in O'Doherty, "Hopper's Voice," 27–33; Sheena Wagstaff, ed., *Edward Hopper*, exh. cat. (London: Tate Publishing, 2004), 32, 66, 98; Carter E. Foster, ed., *Edward Hopper*, exh. cat. (Milan: Skira, 2009); *São Paulo 9, United States of America: Edward Hopper, Environment U.S.A., 1957–1967*, exh. cat. (Washington, DC: Smithsonian Institution Press, 1967).

54 Goodrich, "Notes of Conversation with Hopper" (1946), 5.

55 Ibid., 4.

56 See Harriet G. Warkel, *Paper to Paint: Edward Hopper's "Hotel Lobby"* (Indianapolis: Indianapolis Museum of Art, 2008).

57 A graphite study for the female figure is in the collection of the Whitney Museum of American Art (70.867).

58 Alexander Nemerov, "Ground Swell: Edward Hopper in 1939," *American Art* 22, no. 3 (Fall 2008): 50–71.

59 O'Doherty, "Hopper's Voice," 24; Goodrich, "Notes of Conversation with Hopper" (1947), 2.

60 When Bill Johnson describes "a rough pencil drawing pinned to the back of a chair next to the easel," he is referring to the drawing for *Four Lane Road* (1956). Johnson, "Hopper Cover Research," 1.

61 See ibid., 15 (describing the Truro house): "there was no sign of the tools of Hopper's craft except for some brushes atop a battered dresser and the beautifully kept box of tools with which he works on stretchers and frames." O'Doherty, "Portrait: Edward Hopper," 80, quotes Jo Hopper as saying: "Eddie always waits . . . and it isn't until it knocks him over that he gets up and stretches a canvas." In a 1959 interview, John Morse asked the artist: "I remember Lloyd Goodrich describing your studio as looking somewhat like a carpenter's shop. Do I imply that you make your own stretchers?" Hopper replied: "No, I do not." "Tape Recorded Interview with Edward Hopper at the Whitney Museum, New York, New York" (unpublished transcript, June 17, 1959), 5, Archives of American Art, Smithsonian Institution, Washington, DC.

62 Hopper's avoidance of vertical compositions is frankly addressed in his 1956 interview in *Time* magazine: "I just never cared for the vertical." "Art: The Silent Witness," 37.

63 See *Office at Night* and *Nighthawks*, in "*Office at Night*, the El Train, and Urban Voyeurism" and "City Pendants: *Early Sunday Morning* and *Nighthawks*," in this volume.

Hopper in Paris and *Soir Bleu*

CARTER E. FOSTER

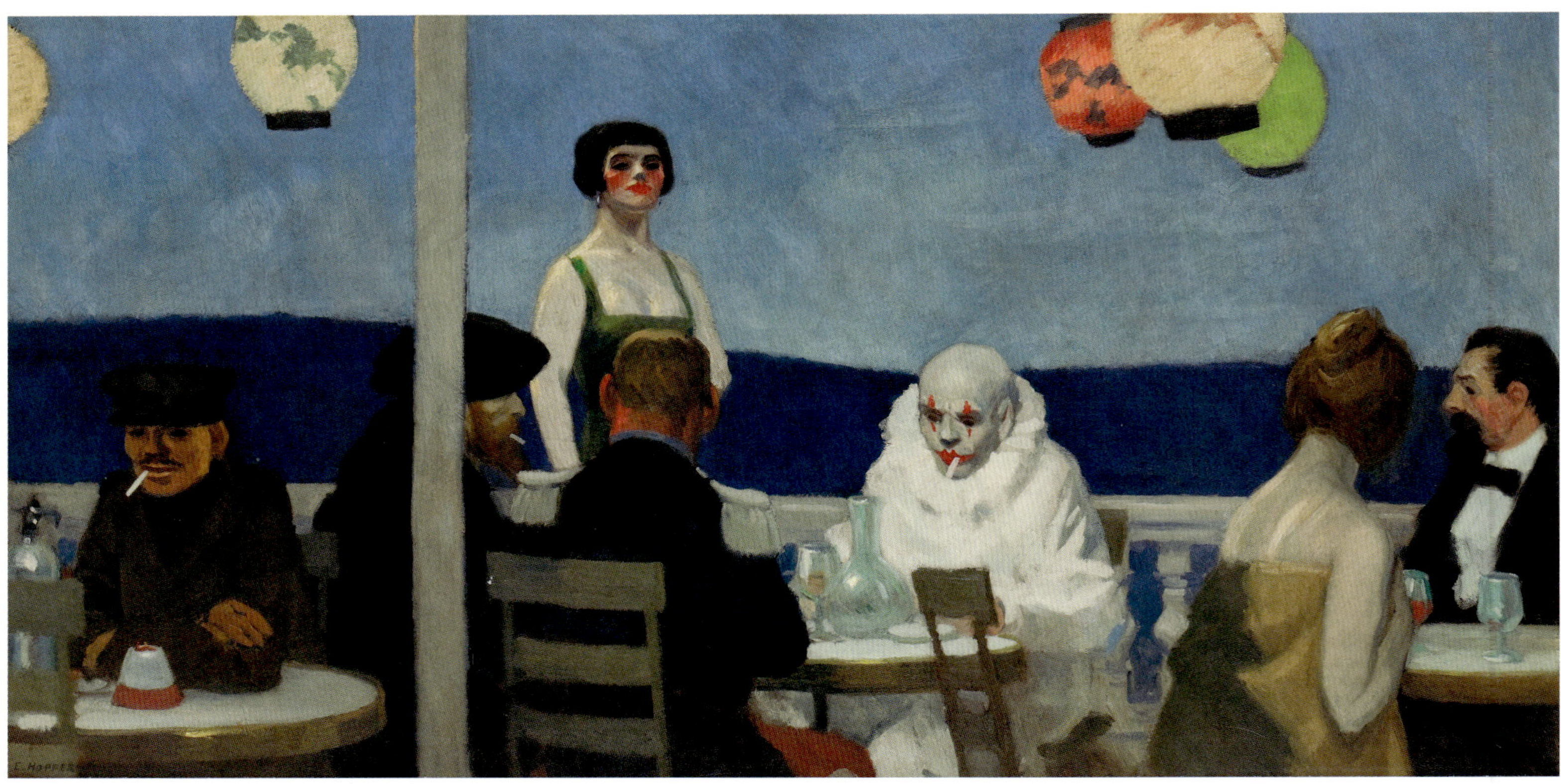

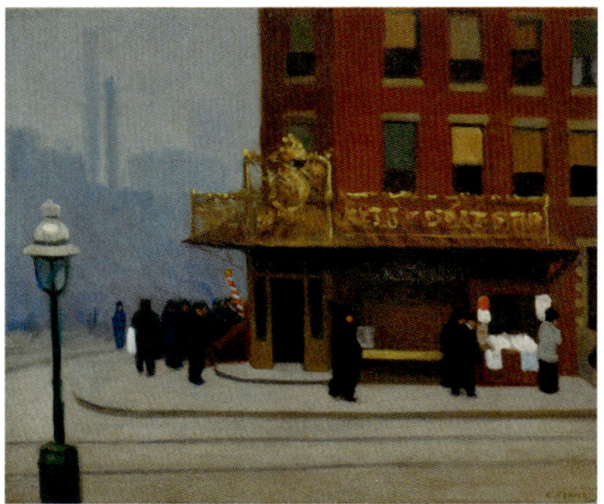

Soir Bleu of 1914 is Edward Hopper's French picture (fig. 95).[1] Painted in New York several years after his last trip to Paris, it is an ambitious summation of the artist's impressions of France and his admiration of its art and culture, which ran deep. It spurred no similar explorations—a true one-off in his career, though it was no doubt an important picture on a personal level. He showed it only once, in 1915, at the MacDowell Club at 108 West Fifty-fifth Street. In that exhibition, critics responded favorably to his humbler, quotidian, and fairly slight street scene *New York Corner* (fig. 96); those who noticed *Soir Bleu* tended to discount it.[2] Nevertheless, its ambition is striking given the directions Hopper had been taking at the time. Back from Europe for the last time after his third trip in 1910, he was searching artistically during those next few years and doing illustration work to foot his bills. Small oils of landscapes and city scenes were his mainstays when he tried *Soir Bleu*, which stands apart in its involved subject and array of art historical references. Its scale alone is telling; it is one of the artist's largest canvases. Whether the relatively negative reaction it received nudged Hopper into fully pursuing the imagery that would make him famous we cannot know. But the visual and cultural sophistication of *Soir Bleu*, which synthesizes a number of sources without being slavish to them, is a reflection of the man who painted it. As Hopper said much later: "It took me ten years to get over Europe."[3] Clearly he painted *Soir Bleu* while fully enamored. Using drawings made years before, Hopper reworked his observations of Paris street life into an almost allegorical depiction of café culture filtered through his understandings of key Impressionist and Post-Impressionist artists (especially Edgar Degas and Henri de Toulouse-Lautrec), Japonisme and Japanese prints, caricature, and the rich traditions of graphic art and illustration in both Europe and America.[4]

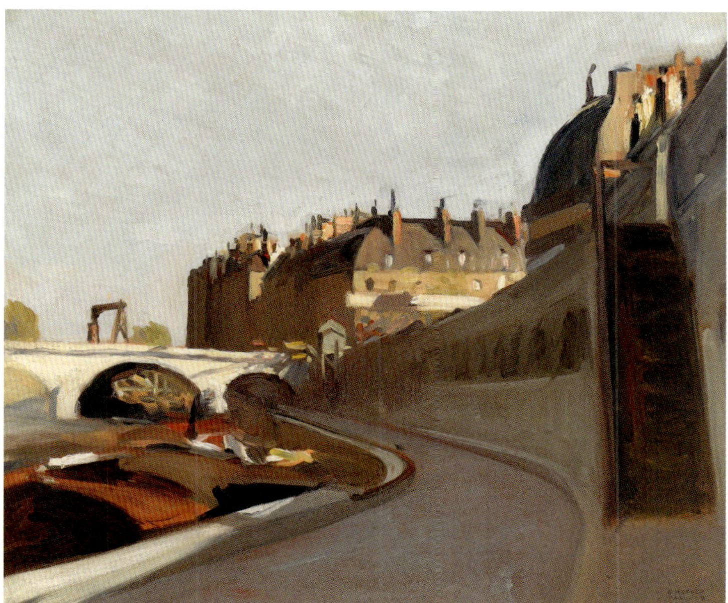

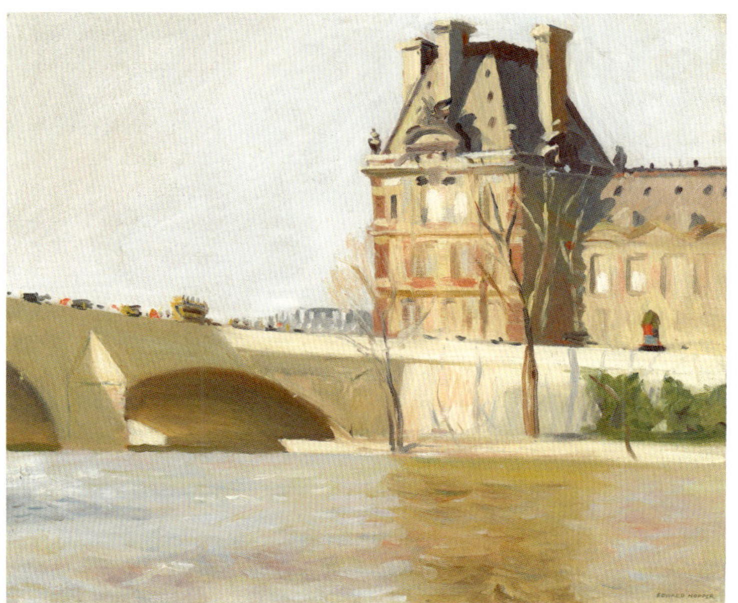

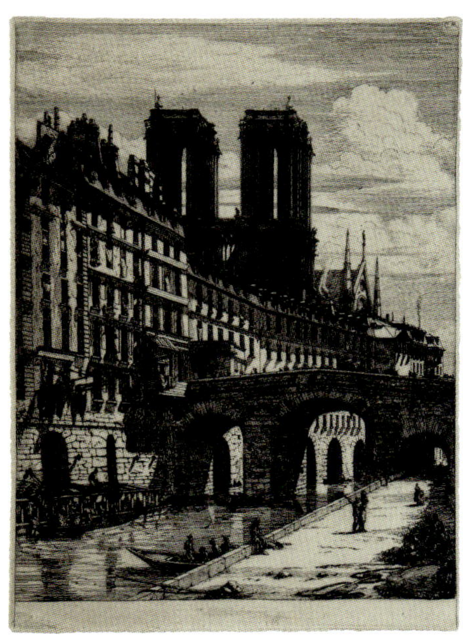

95. (opposite, top)
Soir Bleu, 1914
Oil on canvas, 36 × 72 in. (91.4 × 182.9 cm)
Josephine N. Hopper Bequest 70.1208

96. (opposite, bottom)
New York Corner (Corner Saloon), 1913
Oil on canvas, 24 x 29 in. (61 x 73.7 cm)
Private collection; courtesy Fraenkel Gallery and Pace Gallery, New York

97. (this page, top)
Le Quai des Grands Augustins, 1909
Oil on canvas, 23 11⁄16 × 28 3⁄4 in. (60.2 × 73 cm)
Josephine N. Hopper Bequest 70.1173

98. (this page, bottom left)
Le Pont Royal, 1909
Oil on canvas, 24 × 29 1⁄16 in. (61 × 73.8 cm)
Josephine N. Hopper Bequest 70.1175

99. (this page, bottom right)
Charles Meryon (1821–1868)
Le Petit Pont, Paris, 1850
Etching; sheet: 10 7⁄8 × 8 1⁄16 in. (27.6 × 20.4 cm), plate: 10 1⁄16 × 7 3⁄8 in. (25.6 × 18.7 cm)
Yale University Art Gallery, New Haven; University Purchase, Everett V. Meeks Fund 1963.9.49

Much of Hopper's artistic energies in Paris resulted in a group of small oil paintings executed *en plein air*.[5] These visual explorations of the city reflect the straightforward influence of Impressionist practice and technique, a nod toward Camille Pissarro and others who had celebrated the French capital in paint so often in the previous century. On his first trip, he started small and dark in the winter of 1906, depicting both interiors and outdoor sights, and then lightened his palette and increased scale slightly in the spring of 1907 with light-filled, easel-sized works.[6] His most accomplished pieces were done on his second trip in 1909, during which he continued to explore the low points of view he favored from the quais in and around the Île de la Cité and Île Saint-Louis, in the heart of the city (figs. 97, 98). These vantage points were likely influenced by the etchings of Charles Meryon (fig. 99), whom Hopper admired, an interest indicative of his engagement with nineteenth-century French visual culture. Hopper copied works by Édouard Manet and other artists of the previous century in drawings from this period (figs. 100, 101),[7] while all but ignoring Paris's contemporary burgeoning avant-garde.[8]

The Paris oils were a prolific moment for a painter whose later norm was a struggle to find subjects, and they reveal how he came to use his drawings to absorb the observable world and then make use of these observations (sometimes years later) as a springboard for a painting. This is evident when we fully understand one of Hopper's first great, mature paintings, *Le Bistro*, to which he also gave an English title *The Wine Shop* (fig. 102). He painted

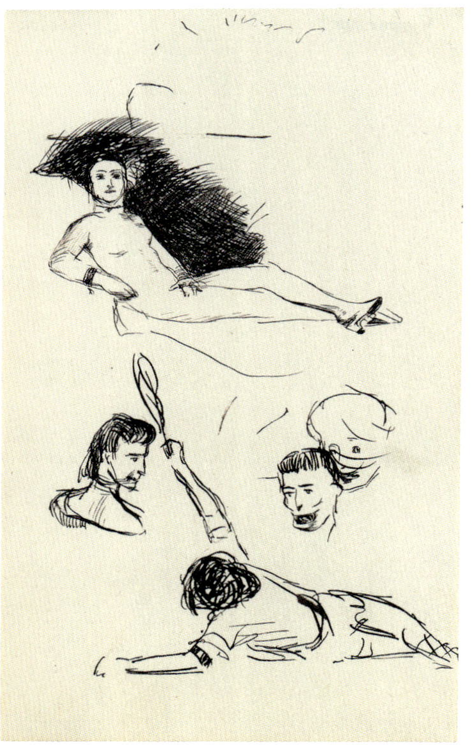

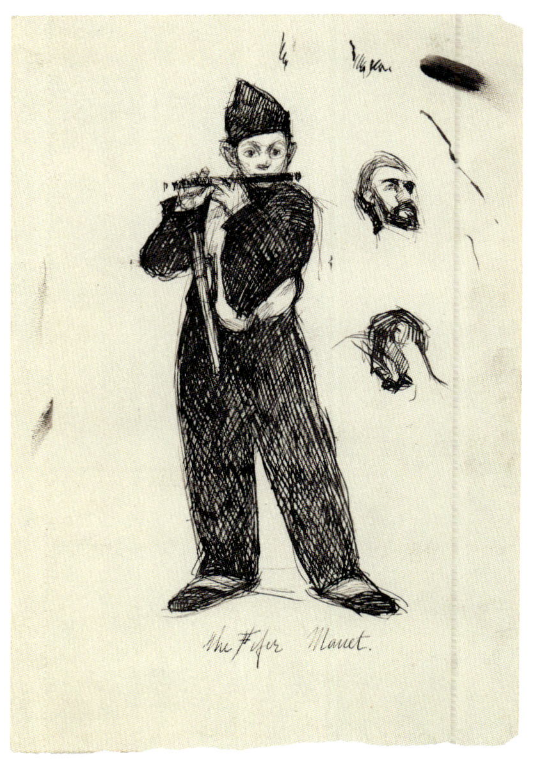

100. *Copy after Edouard Manet's* Olympia *and Heads and Figure*, 1900–07
Pen and ink on paper, 8 7/8 × 5 5/8 in. (22.5 × 14.3 cm)
Josephine N. Hopper Bequest 70.1561.133

101. *Copy after Edouard Manet's* The Fifer *and Two Heads*, 1900–07
Pen and ink on paper, 10 × 7 in. (25.4 × 17.8 cm)
Josephine N. Hopper Bequest 70.1560.96

it in New York in 1909, between his second and third trips to Europe. Paris was on his mind, and that is where the painting came from: it is a memory of Paris, not Paris itself.[9] This is of profound significance since the idea of memory is a unifying trope in Hopper's oeuvre. Memory and the act of remembering are often his implicit subjects; his acute awareness of the relationship between memory and the act of painting is suggested by his own statements about making his art and is one of the keys for us in understanding it.[10]

At first *Le Bistro* seems a straightforward Paris view: we are looking northwest up the Seine from the Quai Voltaire toward the Pont Royal, with its distinctive triangular buttresses between each arch.[11] These structural details are present on the bridge at the right in *Le Bistro*, and the actual view from the Quai Voltaire today is similar, but comparison reveals the painting to be an evocation of it, not an observation. Hopper did paint an accurate view of the Pont Royal (see fig. 98) in the work of that title from the same year, which balances the lateral expanse of the bridge and river with the vertical anchor of the Louvre's Pavillon de Flore. In comparison to *Le Bistro*, this view and his others like it, such as *Le Quai des Grands Augustins* (see fig. 97), are packed with visual information. Though broken up in an Impressionist manner, these other paintings correspond to actual things Hopper saw and represent quite a bit of visual detail closely observed: construction machinery, pockets of shadow articulating architecture, equipment piled on boats. *Le Bistro* is, by contrast, fully Hopperesque in its slightly stretched out, noticeably empty space. With fewer buildings and objects in view, the pale blue sky and the whites, yellows, and grays of the street and bridge create the quality of light that give the work its still atmosphere and mood. Crucially, the artist added human protagonists whose placement transforms this from a pure cityscape to a genre scene. The passages with the most detail are in these two figures seated at a table, but in general there are fewer brushstrokes corresponding to less detail than in his plein air views (as this was an imagined view, not an observed one), a smoother facture, and a more unified vision.[12]

The open spaces to the right are generalized forms with little articulation. The four strange trees on the bridge place this scene firmly in the imagined realm. Their tapering forms (more like cypresses than the plane trees so common in Paris)[13] center the composition and thus have a visual function, but they spring unrealistically from the bridge and lean strangely in unison to the left, as if pressured by the light itself, their tips bowing together like notes in a musical chord. Trees are common in Paris and grow along the banks of the Seine, so it is easy to understand their inclusion here. By putting them in the distance and in the

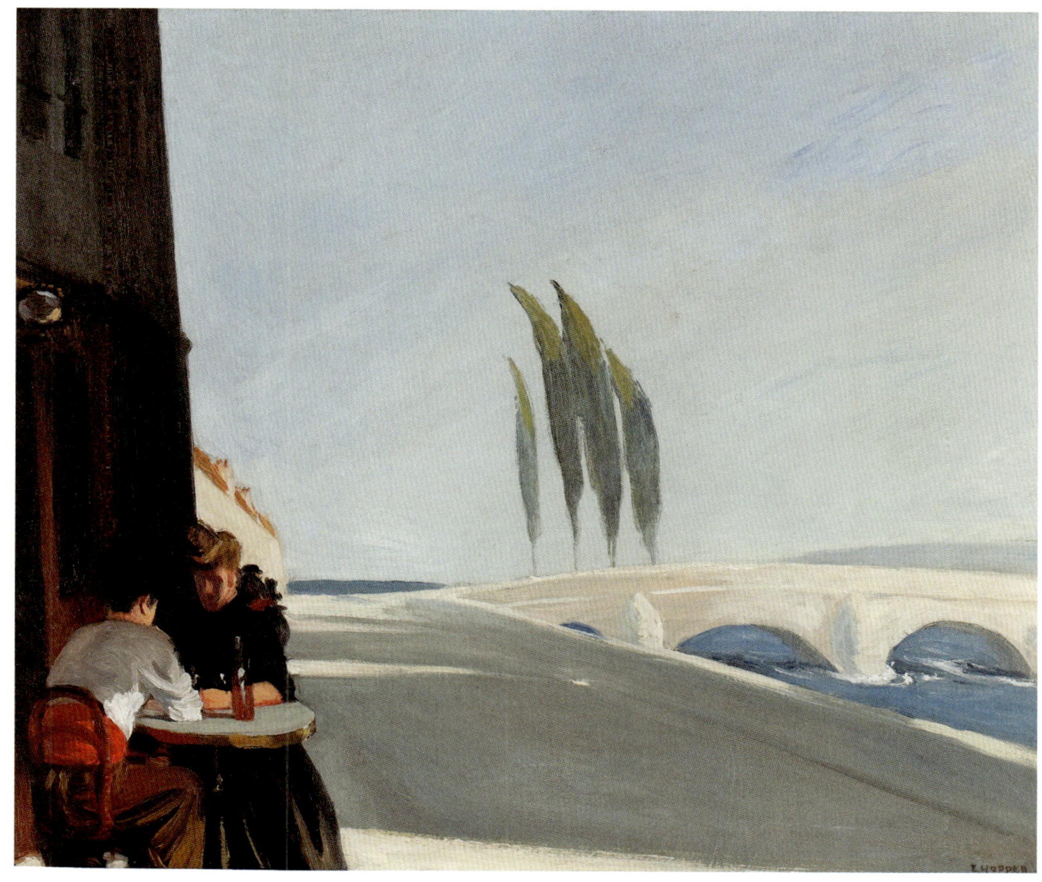

center rather than at the edges of the quai (where they actually grow), Hopper left the right side of the painting relatively empty. Back in his New York studio, he let the painting's logic place these strange tapering cylinders on the bridge. Going further still, he enhanced this shift to unreality with something far more subtle: the play of shadows and light. Large masses of shadows take up much of the surface area to the right of the café and are punctuated by measured rhythms of light; this play of immaterial forms seems symbolically important, as it often is in Hopper's work. His real sleight of hand, though, is something he occasionally did in later paintings (such as *Early Sunday Morning*; see fig. 164) to enhance a sense of the uncanny: he painted as if there were two sources of sunlight. As Richard Brettell noted in his close reading of *Le Bistro*, the large shadows are improbable: the sun seems to be coming from the upper right, as evidenced by the way it hits the tops of the trees, but there is no large mass at right to cast a shadow since we are at the edge of a *quai* giving on to open space over the river.[14] Our own visual instincts in initially viewing *Le Bistro* are to understand the large shadows as cast by the buildings at the left, the obvious source if the sun were coming from behind them. The long, tapering shears of light on the ground must be coming from spaces between buildings along this block. The first of these, which starts just above the elbow of the seated woman, is further emphasized by one or two standing figures barely noticeable over her shoulder (and almost not visible in reproductions of the painting).[15]

The crux of Hopper's mature painting practice is here: its internal visual logic develops from empiricism but trumps it. The unreal light, dictated by Hopper's subjective picture-making rather than his observations of Paris, is only discernible through close secondary viewing. Memory is never real, but always a mediated version of reality based in actual experience, and Hopper shows here that he had found a way to paint it. He would achieve his subtle play between the real and the imagined by delving back into his own mind over and over. Hopper's actual paintings of Paris, careful and reasonably accurate, gave him the foundation to create the dream view we see in *Le Bistro*. This is precisely how his drawings came to function later in life. He worked on them out in the world, the medium through which he developed the motifs and views that interested him, for absorption and reinterpretation back in the studio.

When Hopper started *Soir Bleu* in 1914, his experiences in Europe had had time to gestate. In New York, his career was gaining little traction; perhaps he felt he had nothing to lose by trying something new, ambitious, and "French." Impressionist and Post-Impressionist painting had in fact been prominently exhibited and collected in America since the 1890s, and

102. *Le Bistro* or *The Wine Shop*, 1909
Oil on canvas, 24 × 28 7/8 in. (61 × 73.3 cm)
Josephine N. Hopper Bequest 70.1187

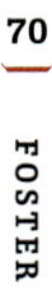

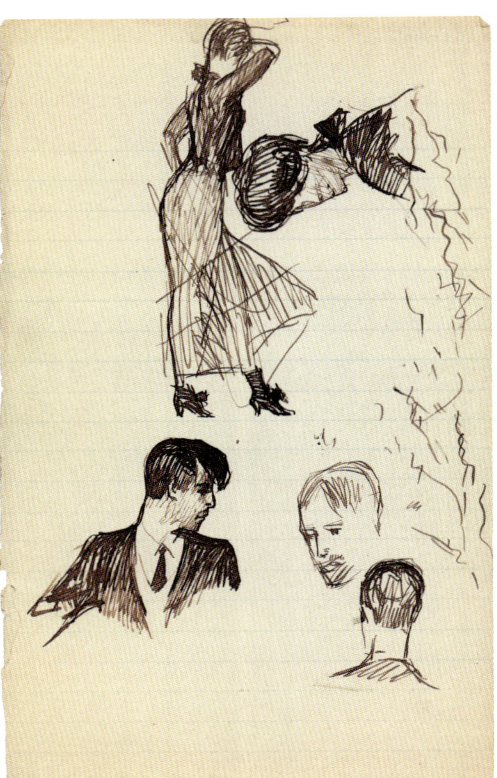

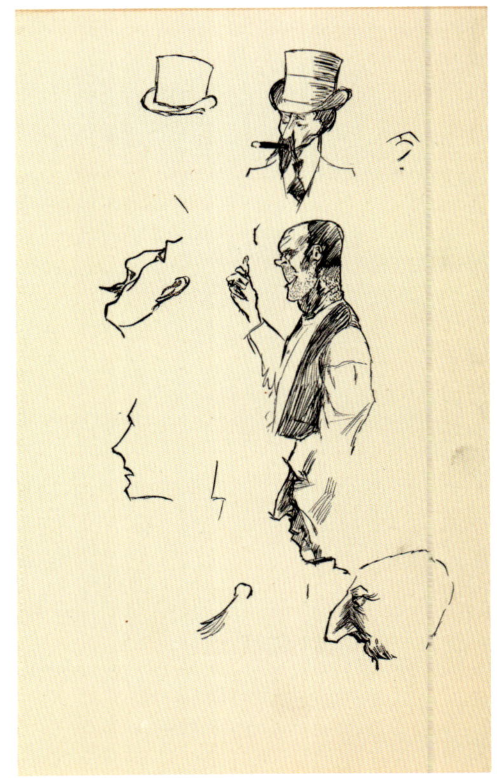

103. *Heads, Woman Dancing, and Man in Suit with Moustache*, 1906–07
Pen and ink on paper, 8 13/16 × 5 3/4 in. (22.4 × 14.6 cm)
Josephine N. Hopper Bequest 70.1555.27

104. *Man Wearing Top Hat with Cigar, Man in Profile, and Hats*, 1895–99
Pen and ink on paper, 8 × 5 in. (20.3 × 12.7 cm)
Josephine N. Hopper Bequest 70.1553.176

the famed Armory Show in New York (which included Hopper's work) had brought European art to the fore in America in 1913.[16]

The roots of *Soir Bleu* lie in the drawings Hopper made of Paris street life. In several letters to his family from France, Hopper described his impressions of the city's physical beauty, as well as its lively inhabitants and the seemingly nonstop public urban culture to which they belonged. He clearly enjoyed observing the French in their capital's streets, cafés, and parks and found their joie de vivre a striking contrast to New Yorkers. The artist's direct visual impressions are preserved in the pages from two dismantled sketchbooks (and a few related sheets) that he probably started in the spring of 1907, during his first trip (fig. 103).[17] He likely used them simultaneously; they often overlap in subject matter and are exactly the same stylistically, with rapid linear drawings in pen and the same brown ink. They focus on people and types that interested Hopper, but which also relate strongly to nineteenth-century graphic traditions and caricature. Hopper was well versed in caricature, as numerous drawings from his student years demonstrate (see fig. 10). Portraiture (of which caricature is a subgenre), including self-portraiture, is ever present in his early work (see figs. 30–34), but a serious rendering of a face turns into a deft caricature on the same sheet in a number of Hopper's early drawings (fig. 104). In Paris, Hopper formalized his caricature skills in a specifically conceived series of finished watercolors, some of which he developed straight out of his Parisian sketchbooks (figs. 105–115). He felt them sufficiently important to include a selection in his 1933 retrospective at the Museum of Modern Art, New York, as well as in two other early exhibitions.[18] They were, in many ways, a practice run for the characters in *Soir Bleu*.

The seven protagonists in *Soir Bleu* have been tempered down from caricatures into identifiable types. Hopper grouped Parisians as such in his own head as soon as he got to Paris: "Every street here is alive with all sorts and conditions of people, priests, nuns, students, and always the little soldiers with wide red pants."[19] He drew them eagerly, paying great attention to the way their demeanor and clothing made them identifiable. Hopper was clearly quite aware of clothing's function in signifying social and occupational status, and while he seems to have had a special fascination with well-dressed, well-to-do women (figs. 116–125), he also enjoyed drawing soldiers, policemen, bourgeois gentlemen, and workers, among others (figs. 126–132). As one would expect in a sketchbook, most pages contain multiple renderings on a single sheet, often with varying degrees of finish, some crossed out, others capturing a face, body part, or item of clothing with just a few quick lines. Hopper, who showed his talents as a draftsman early in life, is in full command here, and the rapidity with which he can shift from careful observation to the interpretive flourish of caricature is impressive in this body of work. The cohesiveness in style and subject of these sketches suggests that they were completed in a relatively short period of time, perhaps with the caricature series

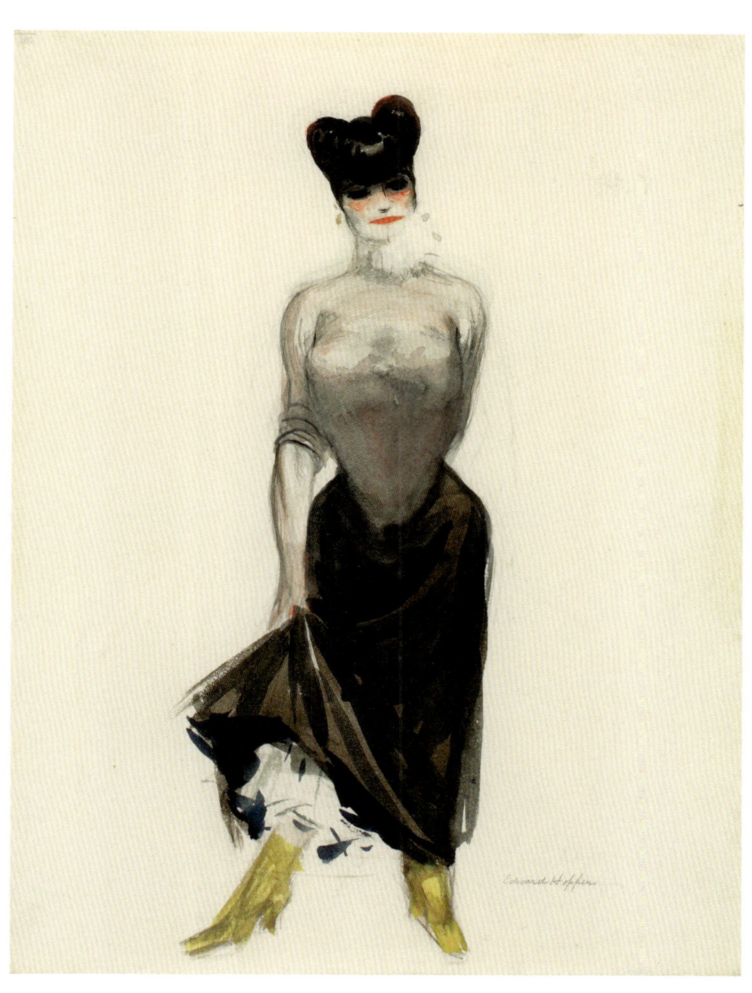

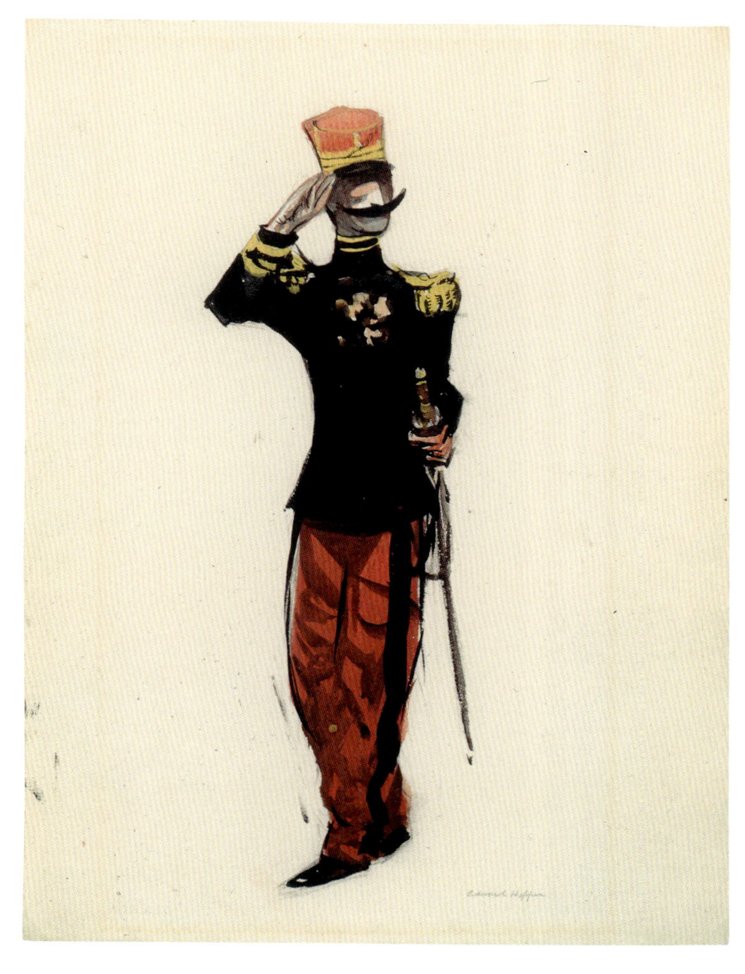

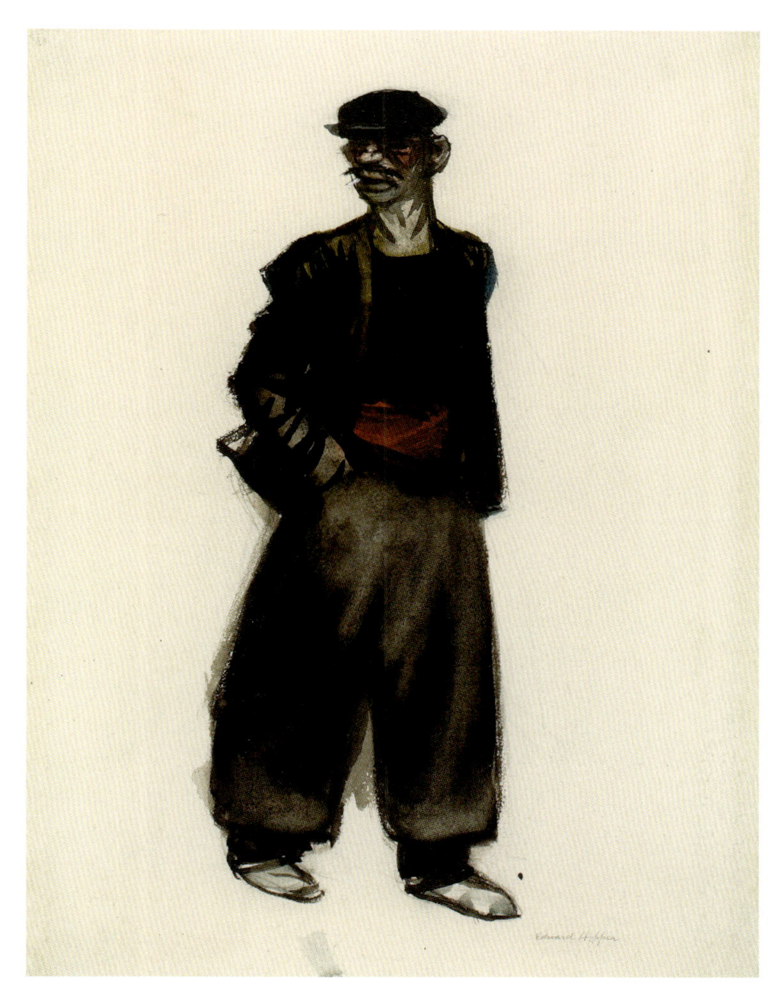

105. *La Pierreuse*, 1906–07
Transparent and opaque watercolor, and graphite pencil on paper, 11 7/8 × 9 5/16 in. (30.2 × 23.6 cm)
The Art Institute of Chicago; Olivia Shaler Swan Memorial Collection, 1933.488

106. *Le Militaire*, 1906–07
Watercolor on paper, 11 3/4 × 9 1/4 in. (30 × 23.5 cm)
The Dayton Art Institute, Ohio; bequest of Virginia Rike Haswell, 1977.51

107. *Le Terrassier*, 1906–07
Transparent and opaque watercolor, and graphite pencil on paper, 11 13/16 × 9 1/4 in. (30 × 23.5 cm)
The Art Institute of Chicago; Olivia Shaler Swan Memorial Collection, 1933.489

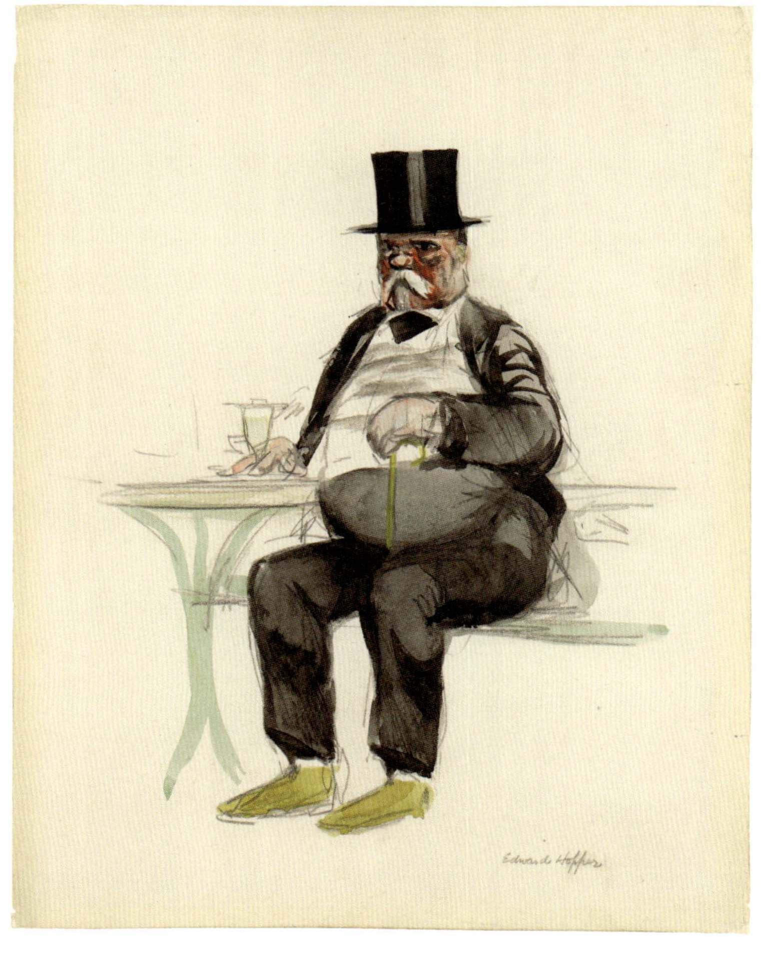

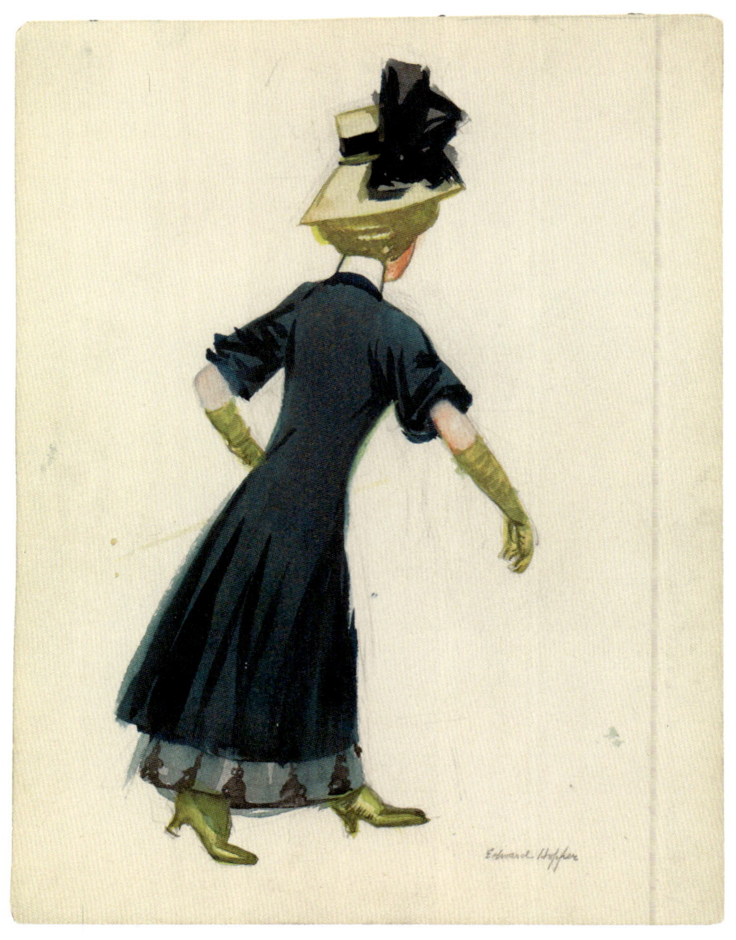

108. *At the Café*, 1906–07
Watercolor and graphite pencil on paper,
11⅞ × 9½ in. (30.2 × 24.1 cm)
Josephine N. Hopper Bequest 70.1321

109. *Parisian Woman Walking*, 1906–07
Watercolor and graphite pencil on board,
11⅞ × 9⅜ in. (30.2 × 23.8 cm)
Josephine N. Hopper Bequest 70.1322

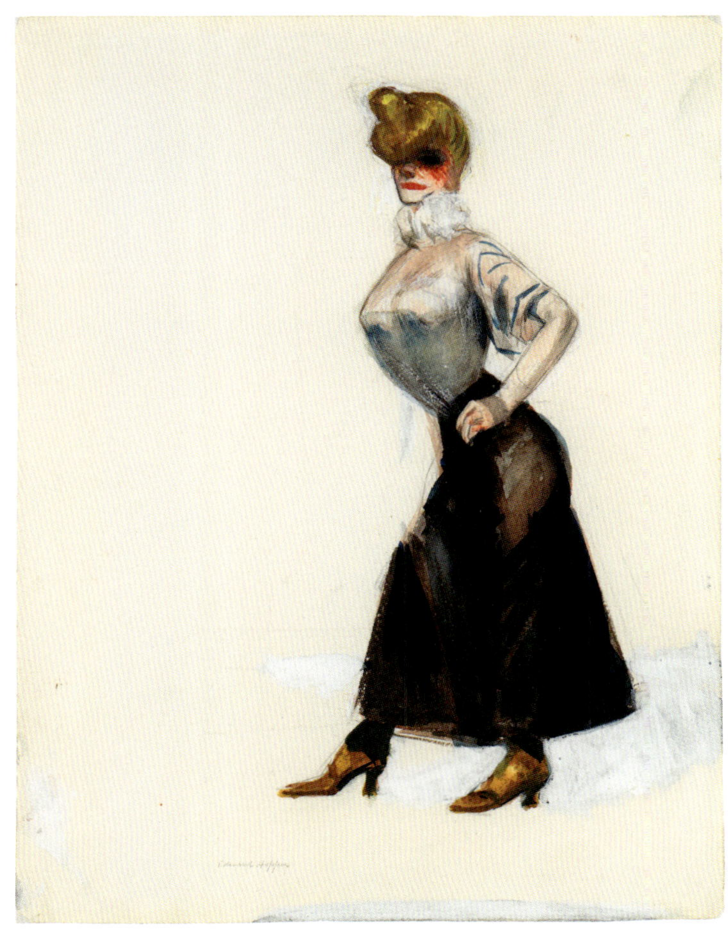

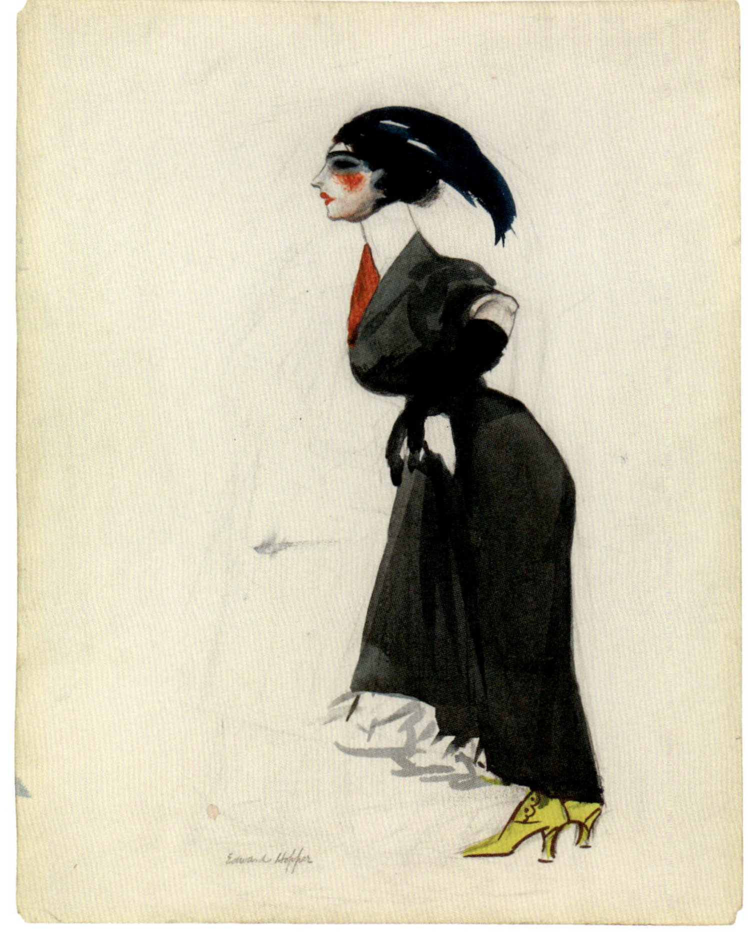

110. *Fille de Joie*, 1906–07
Transparent and opaque watercolor and graphite pencil on paper, 11 13⁄16 × 8 7⁄16 in. (30 × 24 cm)
Josephine N. Hopper Bequest 70.1324

111. *Woman*, 1906–07
Watercolor and graphite pencil on paper, 11 7⁄8 × 9 5⁄16 in. (30.2 × 23.7 cm)
Josephine N. Hopper Bequest 70.1325

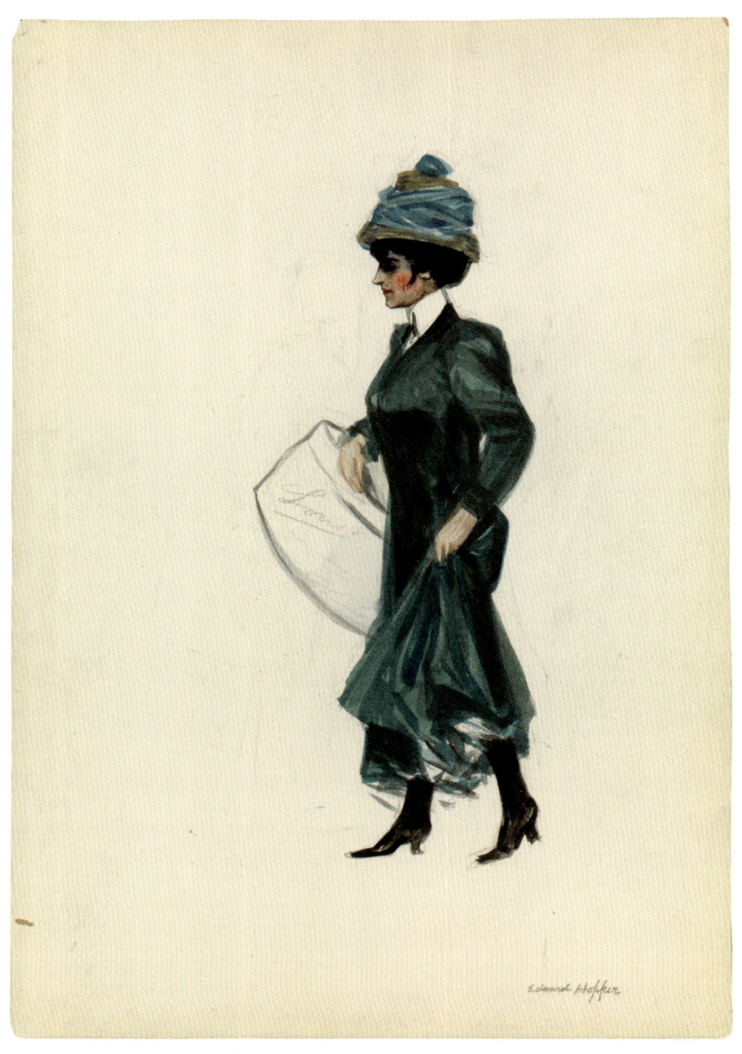

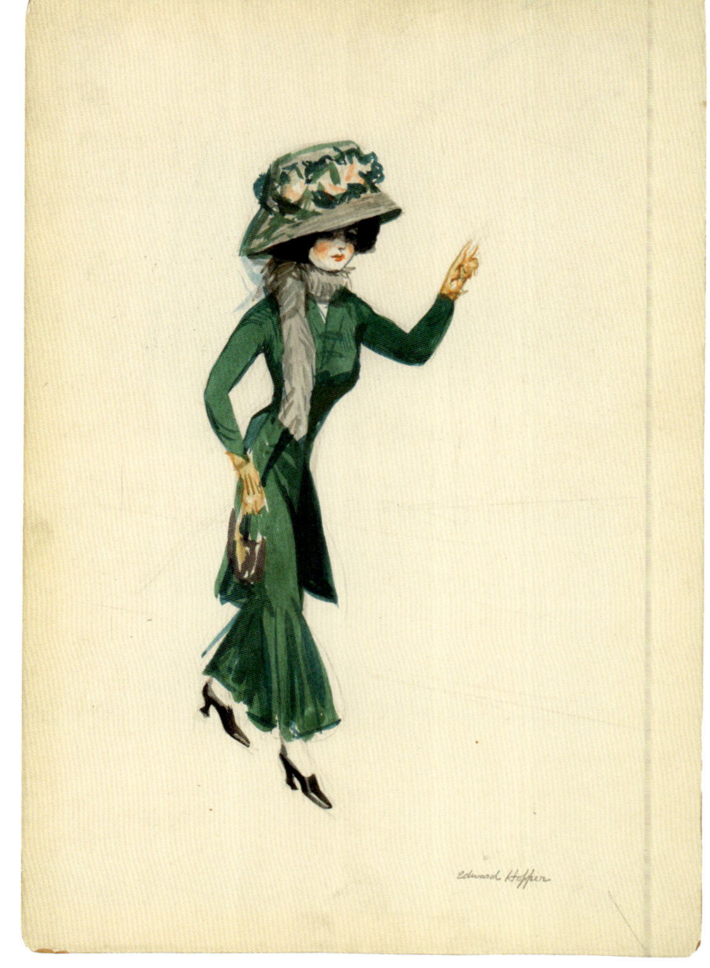

112. *Parisian Woman Dressed in Green*, 1906–07
Watercolor and graphite pencil on board,
15 × 10⅝ in. (38.1 × 27 cm)
Josephine N. Hopper Bequest 70.1332

113. *Parisian Woman Walking*, 1906–07
Watercolor and graphite pencil on paper mounted
on board, 15⅛ × 10¾ in. (38.4 × 27.3 cm)
Josephine N. Hopper Bequest 70.1326

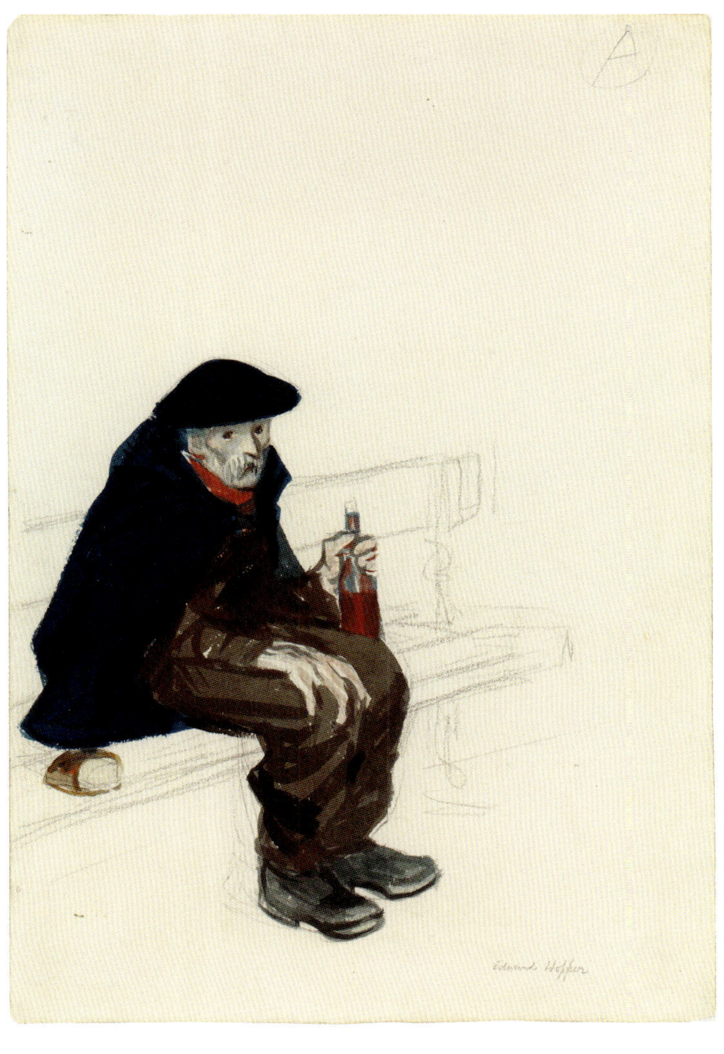

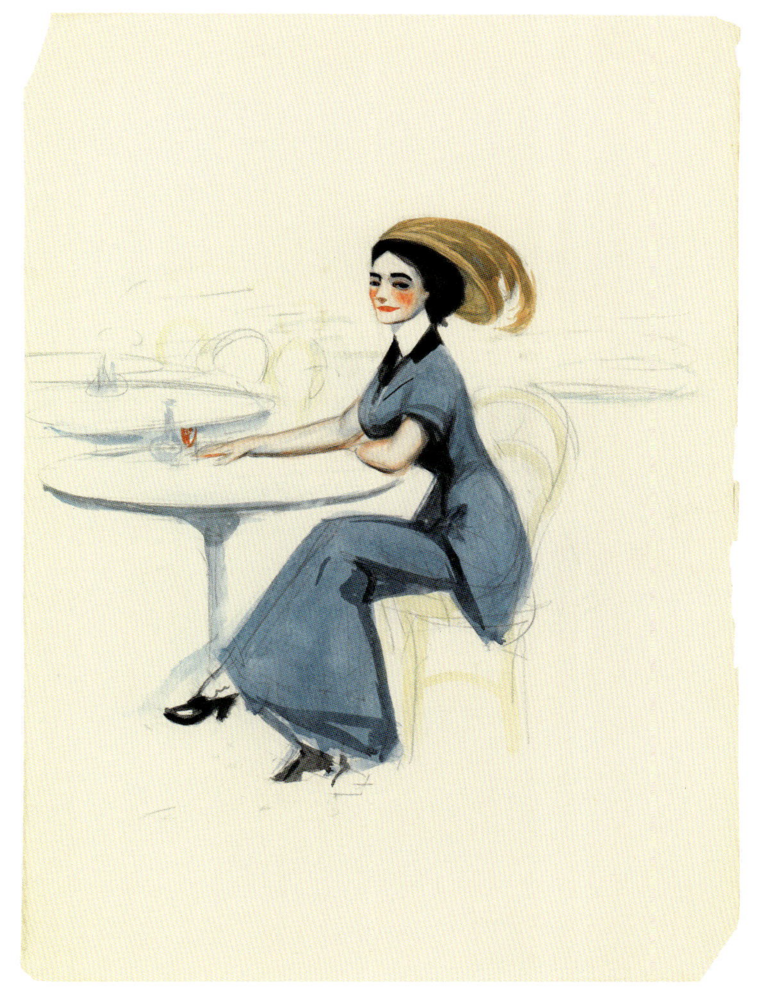

114. *Parisian with Wine Bottle and Loaf of Bread*, 1906–07
Watercolor and graphite pencil on paper,
26 1/8 × 10 1/2 in. (66.4 × 26.7 cm)
Josephine N. Hopper Bequest 70.1329

115. *Woman at Café Table*, 1906–07
Watercolor and graphite pencil on board,
19 15/16 × 14 7/8 in. (50.6 × 37.8 cm)
Josephine N. Hopper Bequest 70.1372

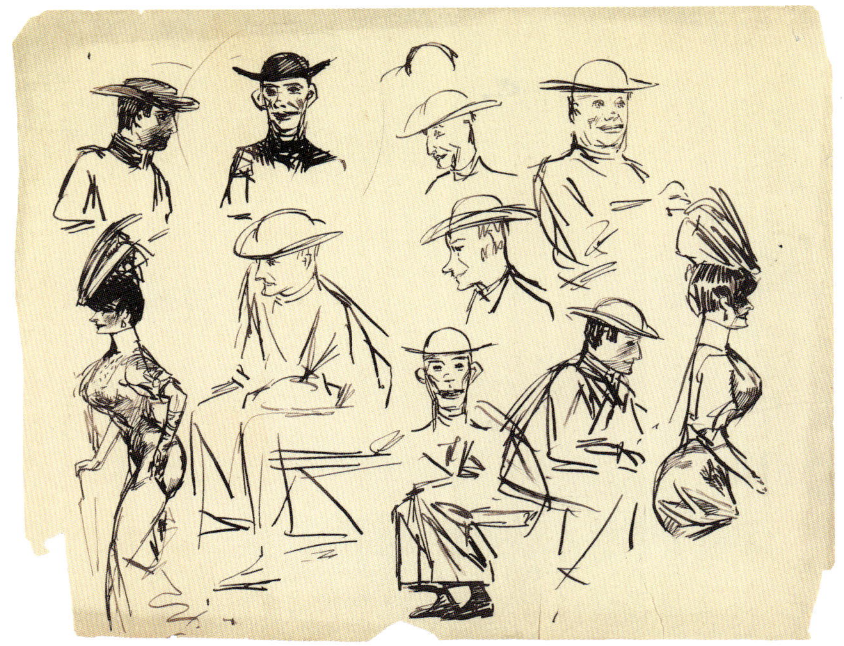

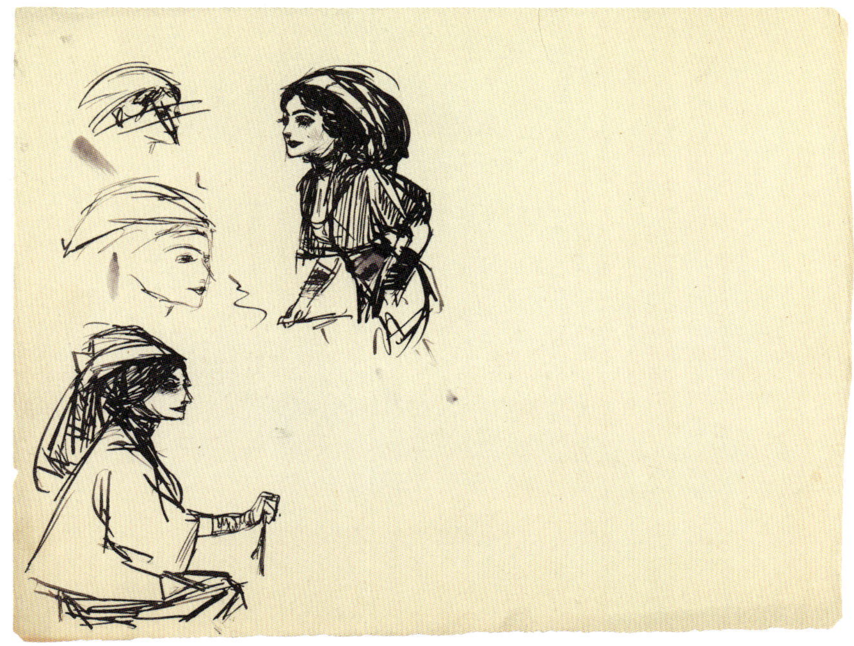

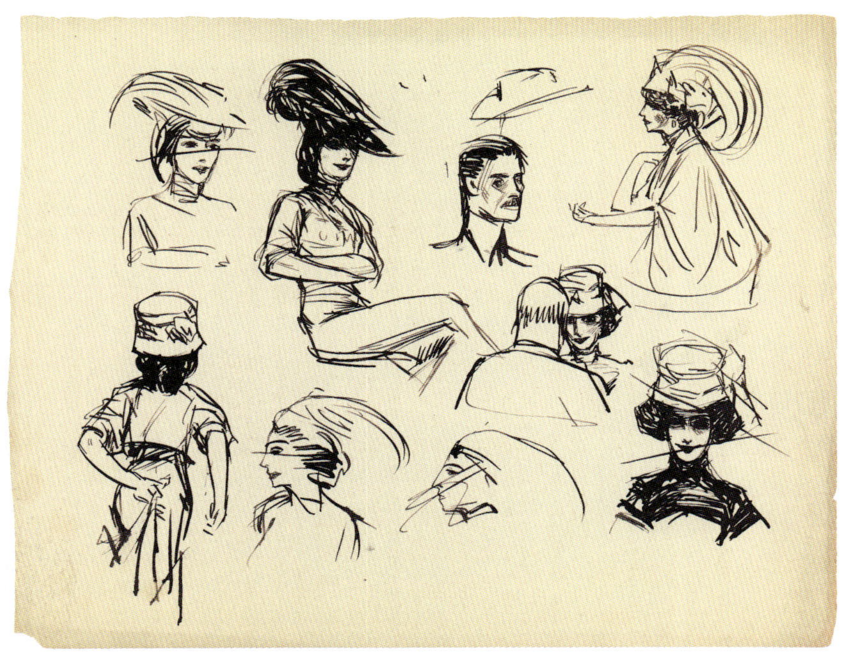

116. *Figures in Hats*, 1906–07
Pen and ink on paper, 9 7/8 × 12 7/8 in. (25.1 × 32.7 cm)
Josephine N. Hopper Bequest 70.1555.2

117. *Four Women in Hats*, 1906–07
Pen and ink on paper, 9 13/16 × 13 1/16 in. (24.9 × 33.2 cm)
Josephine N. Hopper Bequest 70.1555.7

118. *Seated Woman, Women in Hats, Man and Woman in Conversation, and Man with Moustache*, 1906–07
Pen and ink on paper, 9 13/16 × 13 1/16 in. (24.9 × 33.2 cm)
Josephine N. Hopper Bequest 70.1555.11

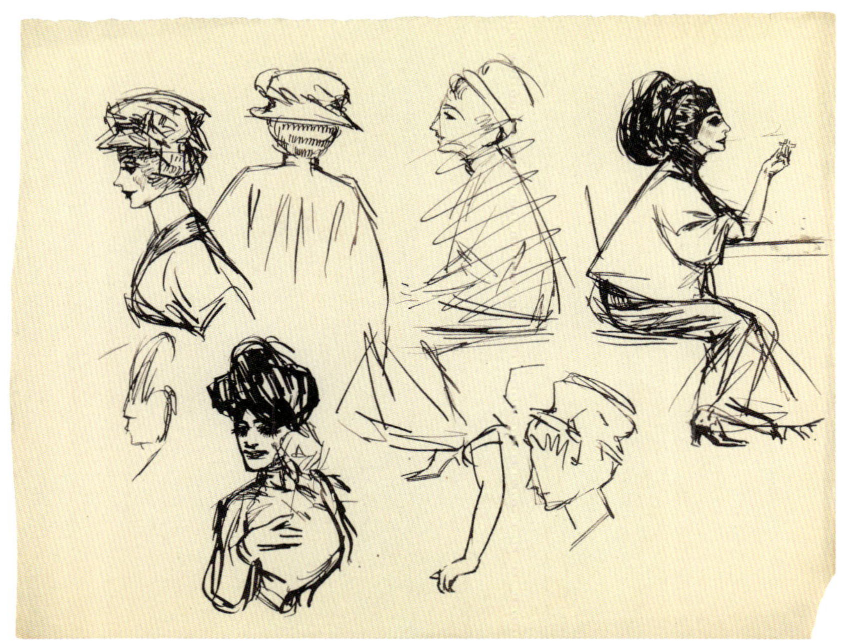

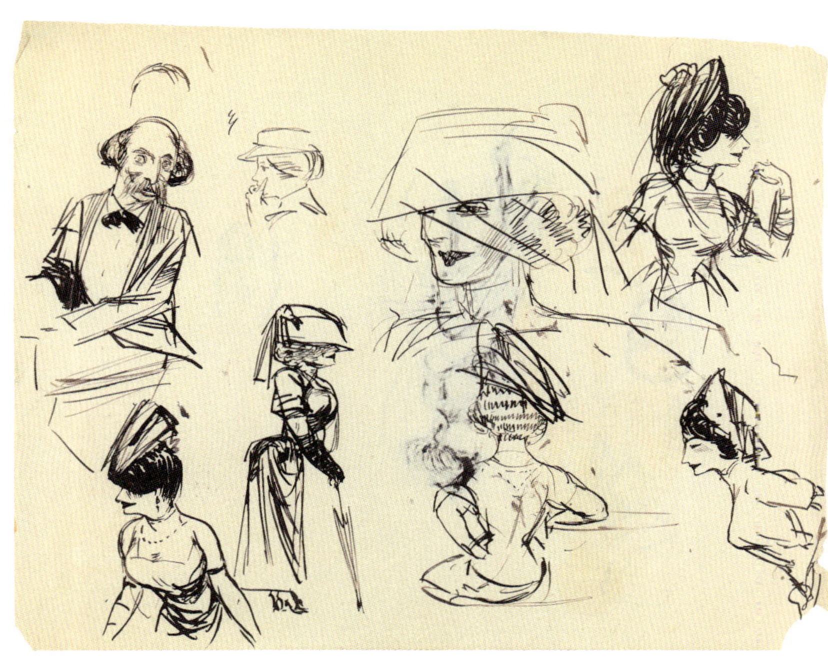

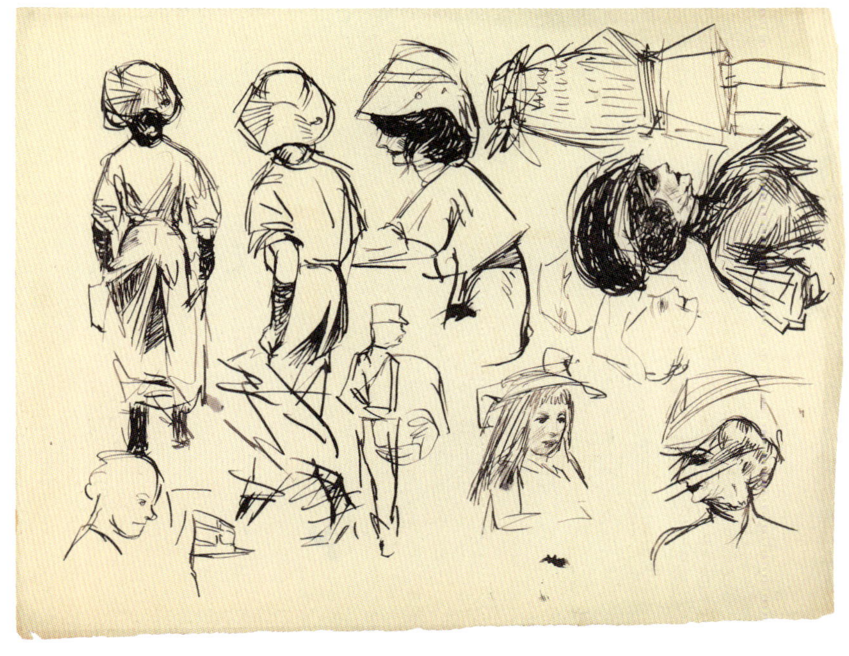

119. *Two Seated Women in Profile and Women's Busts*, 1906–07
Pen and ink on paper, 9 13⁄16 × 13 1⁄16 in. (24.9 × 33.2 cm)
Josephine N. Hopper Bequest 70.1555.12

120. *Man with Moustache and Women in Dresses and Hats* (recto), 1906–07
Pen and ink on paper, 9 7⁄8 × 12 7⁄8 in. (25.1 × 32.7 cm)
Josephine N. Hopper Bequest 70.1555.18a–b

121. *Women and Man in Hats*, 1906–07
Pen and ink on paper, 9 13⁄16 × 13 in. (24.9 × 33 cm)
Josephine N. Hopper Bequest 70.1555.13

122. *Woman Seated at Table with Glass and Woman in Dress* (recto), 1906–07
Pen and ink on paper, 8 11/16 × 6 5/8 in. (22.1 × 16.8 cm)
Josephine N. Hopper Bequest 70.1559.3a–b

123. *Seated Woman with Opera Gloves and Two Women in Hats*, 1906–07
Pen and ink on paper, 8 11/16 × 6 9/16 in. (22.1 × 16.7 cm)
Josephine N. Hopper Bequest 70.1562.4

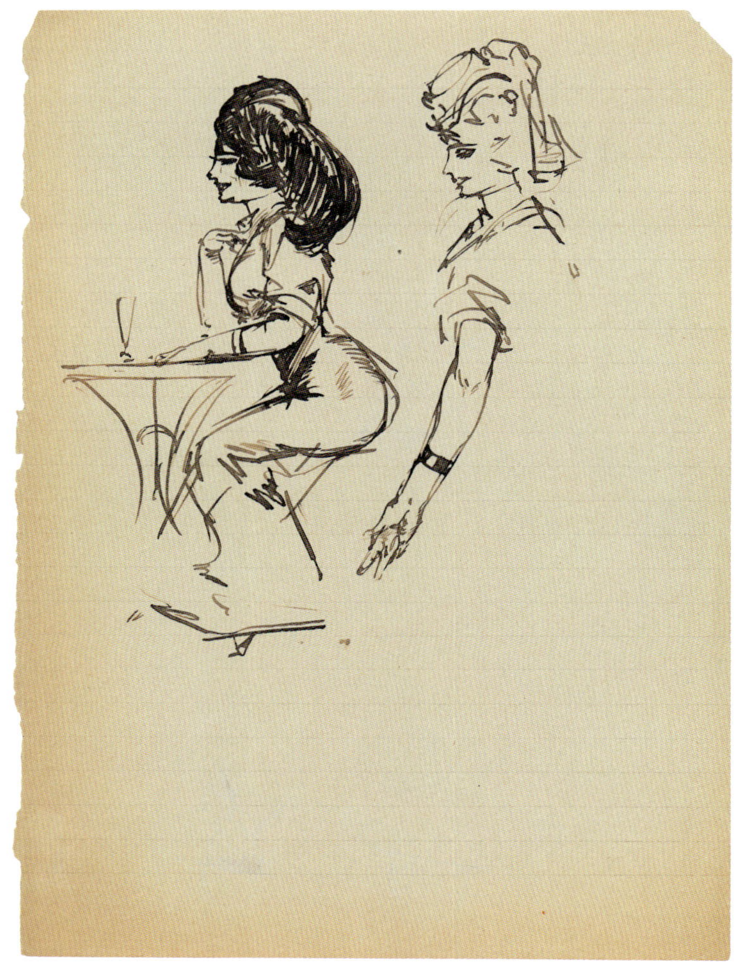

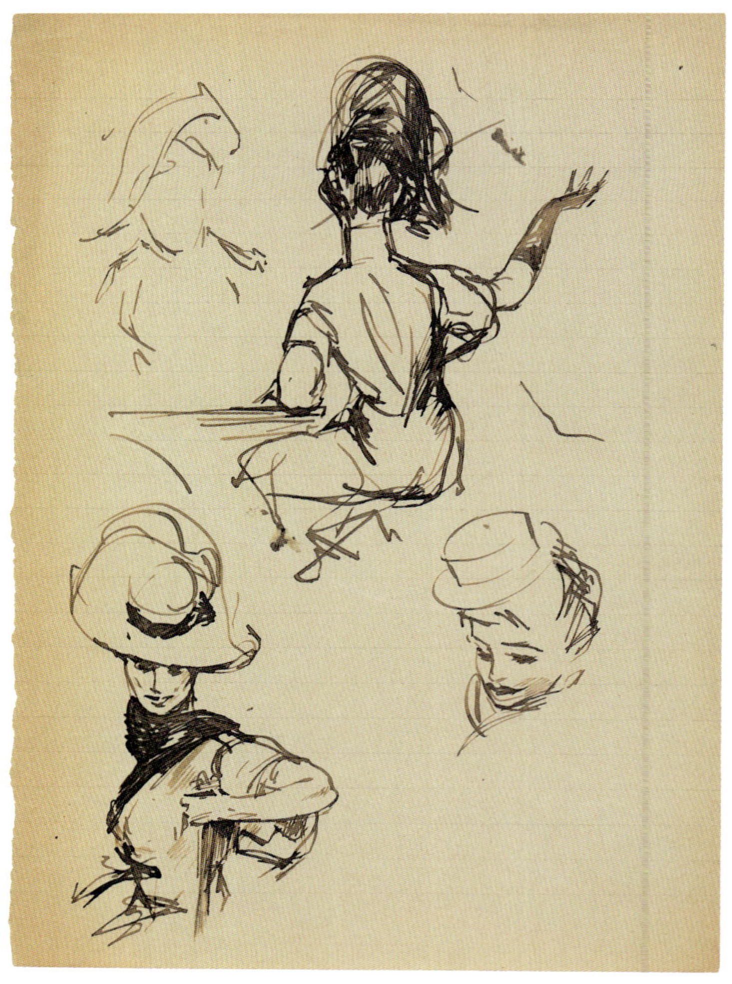

124. *Woman in Hat and Man's Legs*, 1906–07
Pen and ink on paper, 8 11⁄16 × 6 7⁄8 in. (22.1 × 17.5 cm)
Josephine N. Hopper Bequest 70.1559.62

125. *Four Women*, 1906–07
Pen and ink on paper, 8 11⁄16 × 6 9⁄16 in. (22.1 × 16.7 cm)
Josephine N. Hopper Bequest 70.1562.7

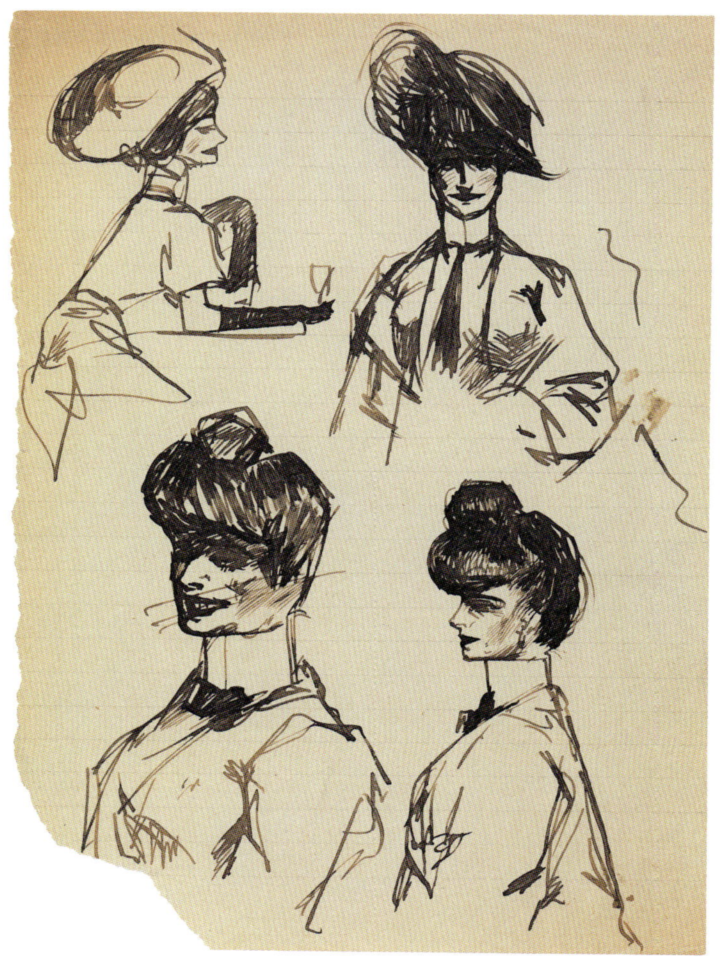

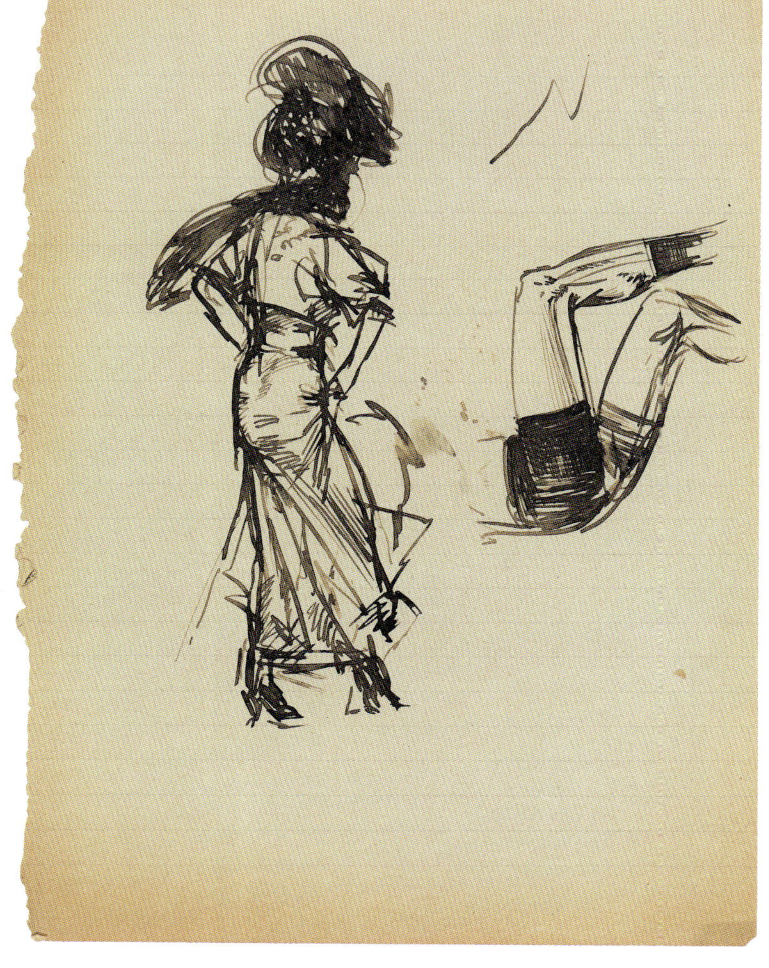

126. *Seated Men, Boats, Pigs, Feet, Arm, and Legs* (recto), 1906–07
Pen and ink on paper, 10 1/16 × 12 3/4 in. (25.6 × 32.4 cm)
Josephine N. Hopper Bequest 70.1555.5a–b

127. *Men in Berets, Sailors, and Man in Pointed Hat* (recto), 1906–07
Pen and ink on paper, 10 1/16 × 12 3/4 in. (25.6 × 32.4 cm)
Josephine N. Hopper Bequest 70.1555.6a–b

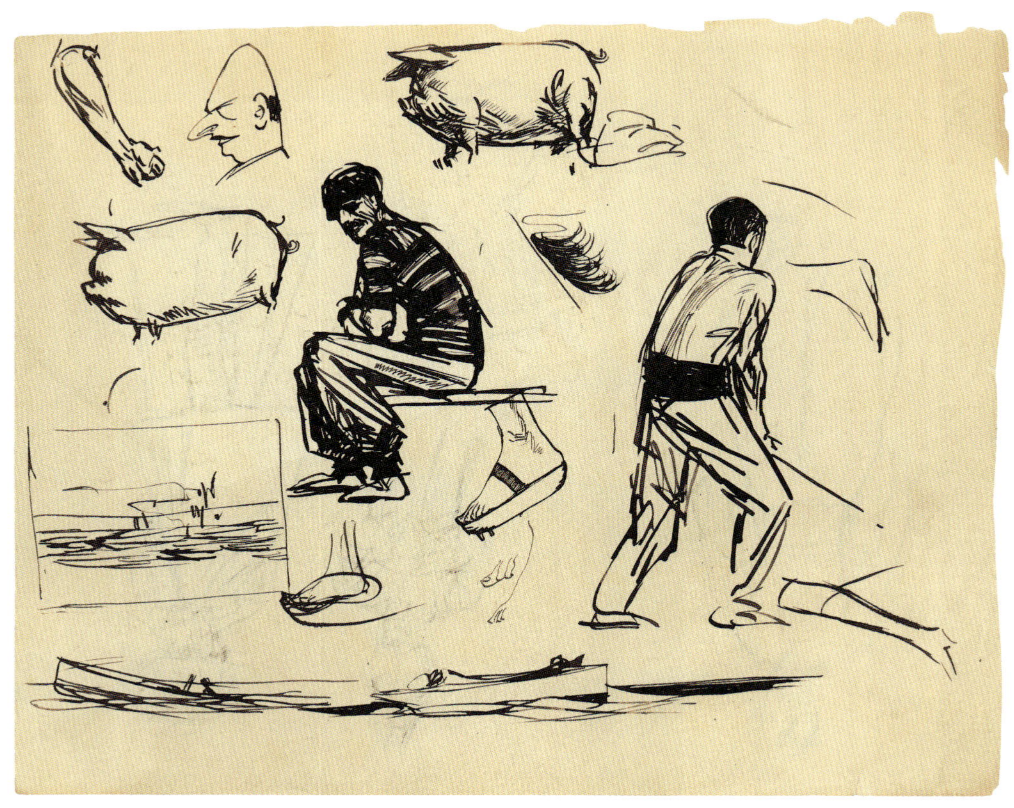

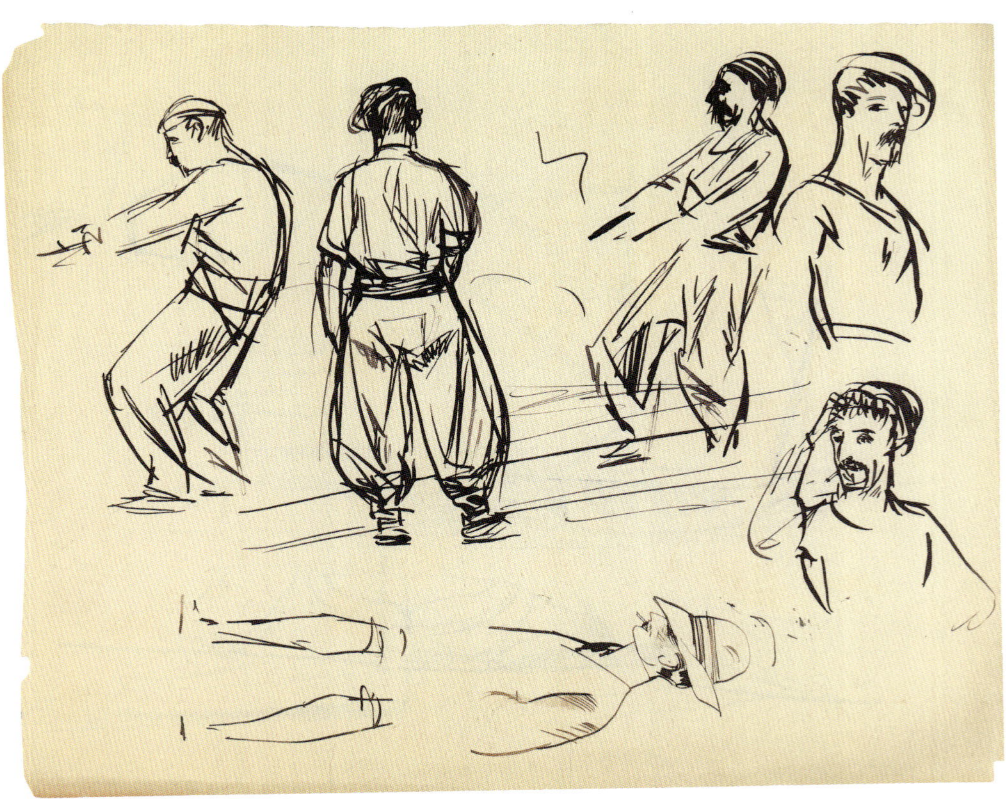

128. *Man in Suit, Male and Female Figures, and Men in Hats* (recto), 1906–07
Pen and ink on paper, 10 ⅛ × 12 ⅞ in. (25.7 × 32.7 cm)
Josephine N. Hopper Bequest 70.1555.17a–b

129. *Diver, Sailors, Male Figure, and Arm*, 1906–07
Pen and ink on paper, 10 ⅛ × 12 ⅞ in.
(25.7 × 32.7 cm)
Josephine N. Hopper Bequest 70.1555.16

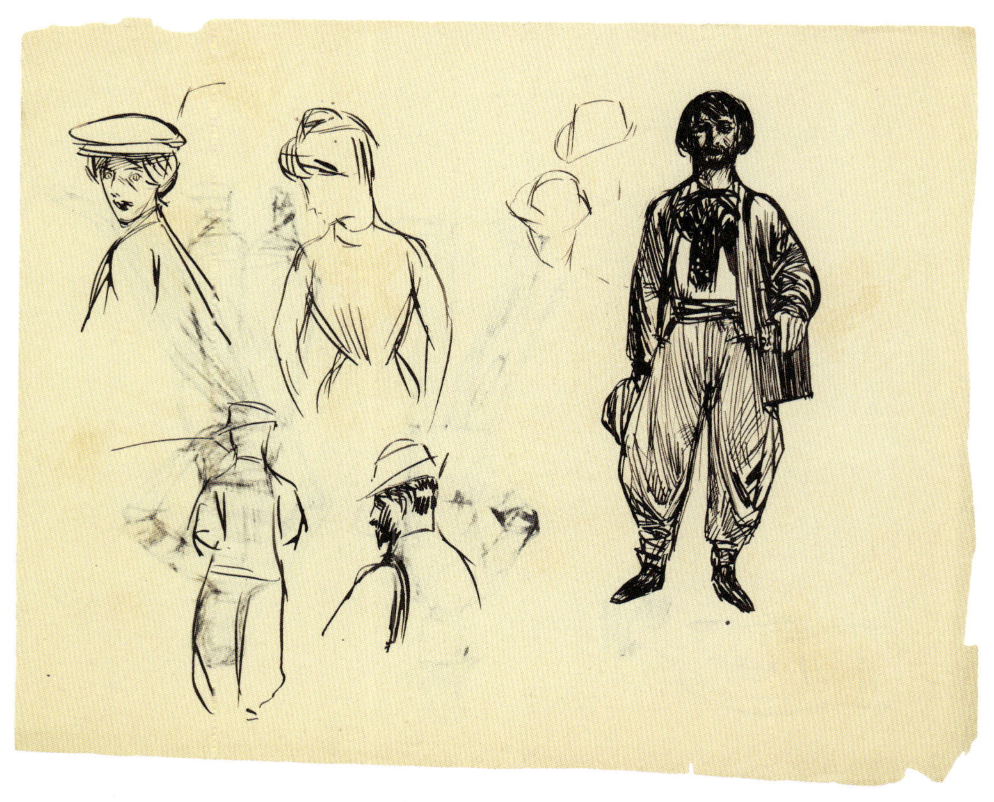

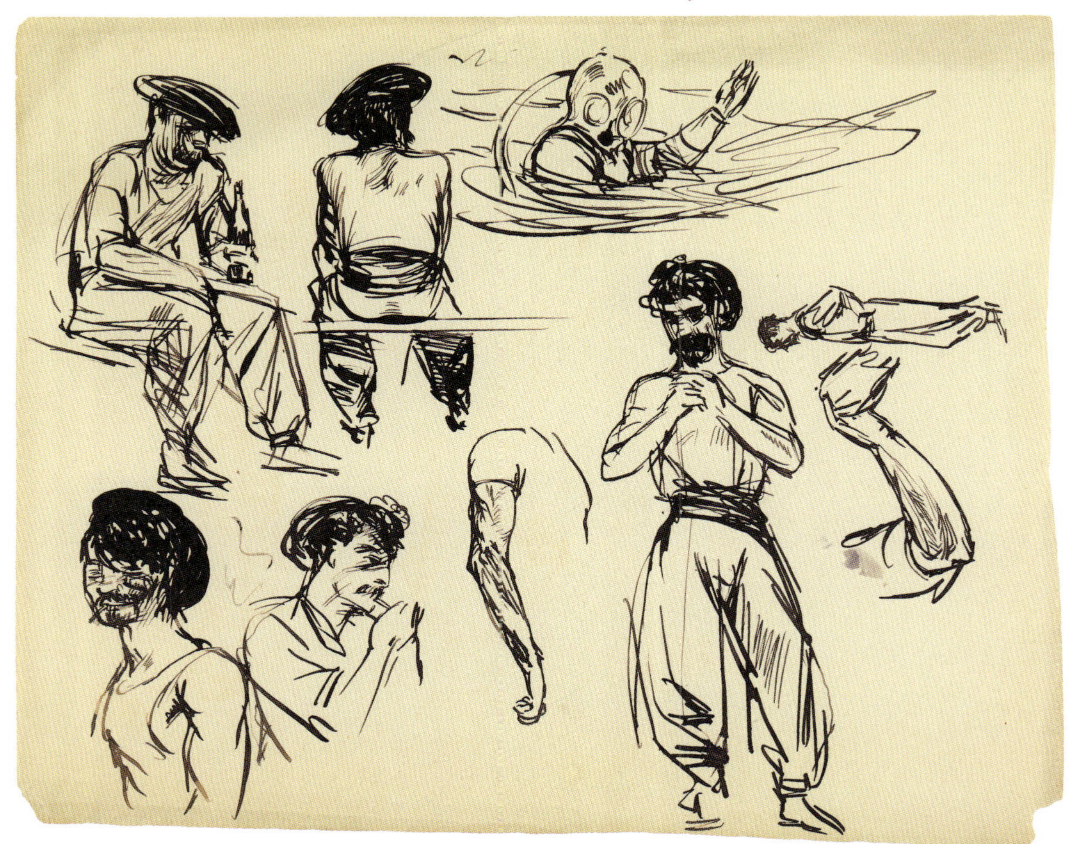

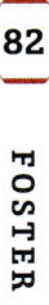

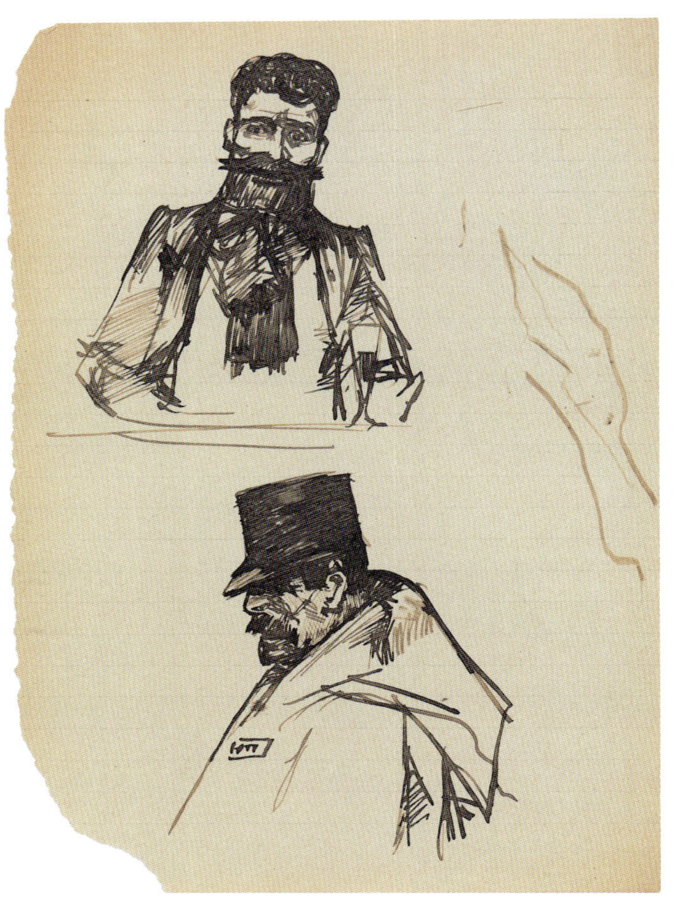

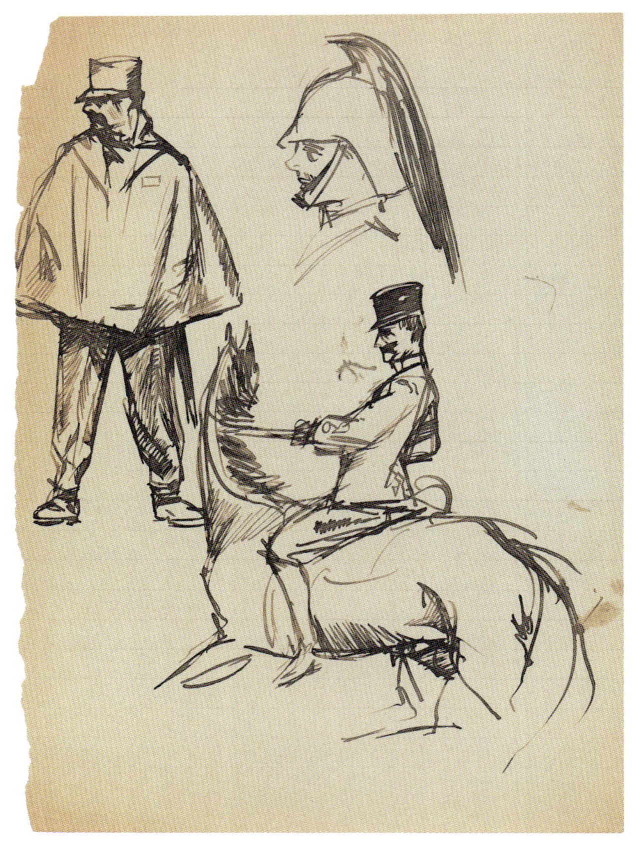

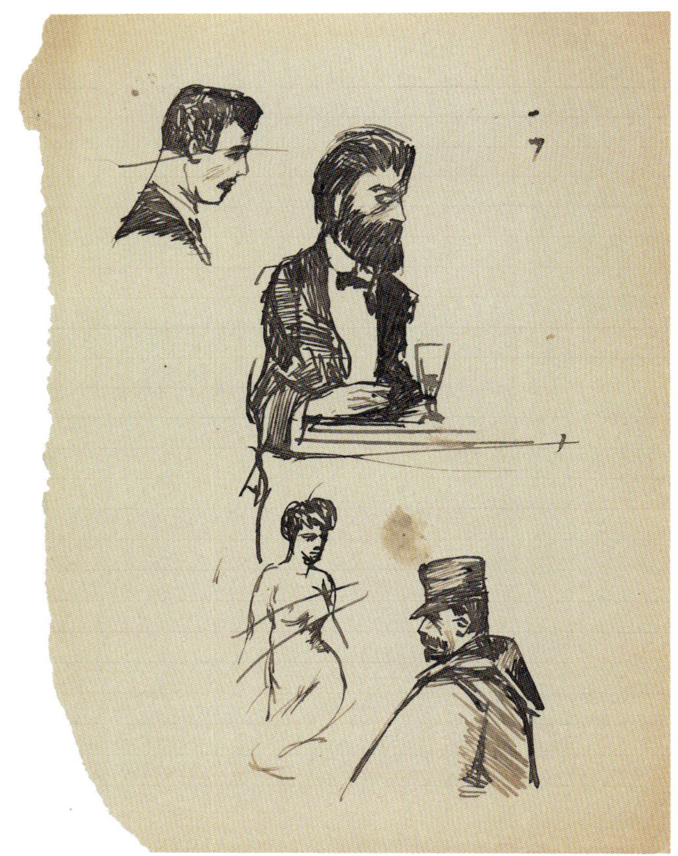

130. *Man with Moustache and Beard and Man in Hat*, 1906–07
Pen and ink on paper, $8\frac{11}{16} \times 6\frac{9}{16}$ in. (22.1 × 16.7 cm)
Josephine N. Hopper Bequest 70.1562.2

131. *Man on Horseback, Gendarme, and Man's Head in Helmet*, 1906–07
Pen and ink on paper, $8\frac{11}{16} \times 6\frac{9}{16}$ in. (22.1 × 16.7 cm)
Josephine N. Hopper Bequest 70.1562.3

132. *Bearded Man with Champagne Glass, Female Nude, Man in Uniform, and Man with Moustache*, 1906–07
Pen and ink on paper, $8\frac{11}{16} \times 6\frac{13}{16}$ in. (22.1 × 17.3 cm)
Josephine N. Hopper Bequest 70.1562.8

133. (bottom)
Henri de Toulouse-Lautrec (1864–1901)
Seated Clowness (La Clownesse assise) from the portfolio *Elles*, 1896
Lithograph; sheet and image: 20½ × 15⅞ in. (52 × 40.3 cm)
The Museum of Modern Art, New York; gift of Abby Aldrich Rockefeller 170.1946.3

134. (right)
Male and Female Figures, 1906–07
Pen and ink on paper, 9⅞ × 12⅞ in. (25.1 × 32.7 cm)
Josephine N. Hopper Bequest 70.1555.9

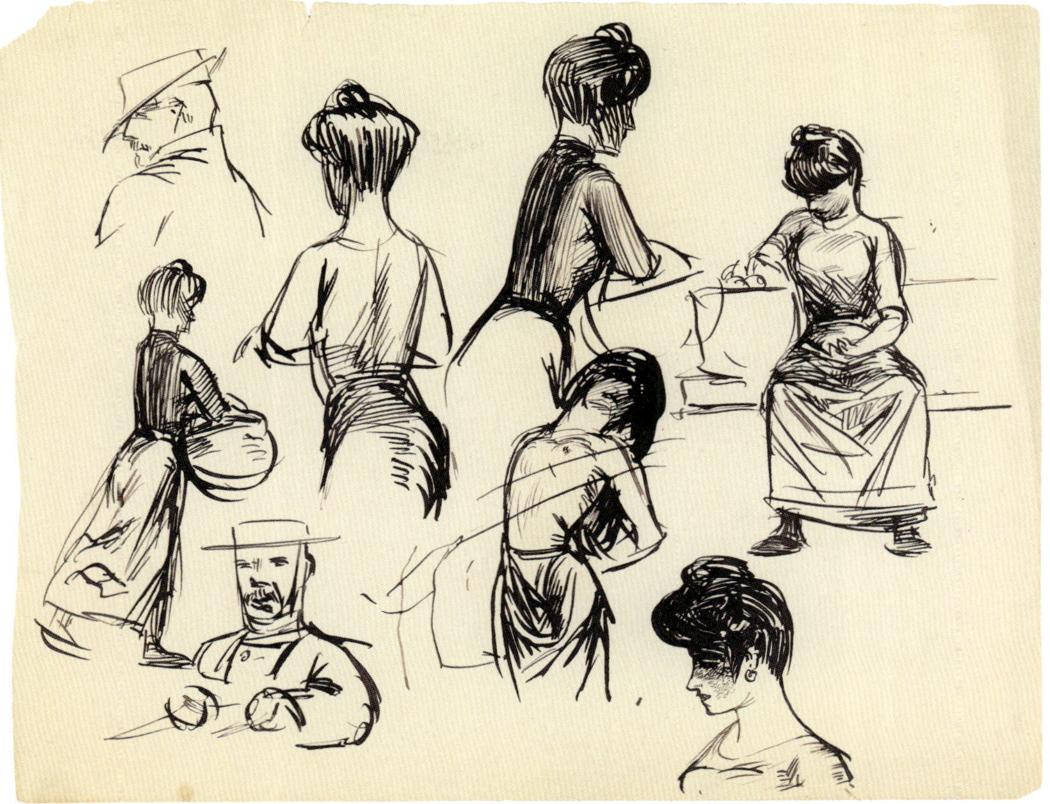

already an end goal in Hopper's mind. The series has a clear relationship to contemporaneous graphic art, with its focus on social types, attendant modes of dress, and, formally, on an overall silhouette whose outlines sit cleanly against a blank background, often with no setting suggested. Toulouse-Lautrec's *Elles* series (fig. 133) and, more directly, Pierre Bonnard's lithograph *La Petite Blanchisseuse* (The Little Laundry Girl) for *La Revue Blanche* (fig. 135) are obvious precedents.[20] Hopper also admired the work of such chroniclers of Parisian life as Constantin Guys, Jean-Louis Forain, Albert Guillaume, and others.[21] Like them, his direct observations of street life fed into other modes, from caricature to illustration and, ultimately, to *Soir Bleu*. The step from life drawing to caricature was easy and quick, as several comparisons attest (see figs. 120, 125, 126, 129).

Some of Hopper's liveliest drawings of women focus on their demeanor, clothes, and, in particular, their hats, as he drew them taking their leisure in cafés, walking on the street, and socializing. Hopper was particularly fascinated with the swept-back profile of a particular hat style, featuring feathers tapering back and down from the head, which he drew several times, at least twice on the same woman (see figs. 115, 117, 118, 122). His full-length views of bourgeois and upper-class women project the S-curve profile typical of stylish dress of the day and common in fashion magazines (see figs. 113, 124); several of these women made it directly into his caricatures. He also drew working-class figures such as the laundress, a type that had been widely depicted in recent decades by Toulouse-Lautrec, Bonnard, and Degas, among others (figs. 134, 136, 137). Hopper's French caricatures also emphasize a different type of working woman, the prostitute. Of the ten watercolor caricatures he chose for early exhibitions, five are women to whom he gave descriptive titles suggesting their profession or station in life—*Fille de Joie*, *Type de Belleville*, *La Pierreuse*, *La Grisette*, *La Concierge*—perhaps as a nod to Toulouse-Lautrec's *Elles* (see figs. 105, 110).

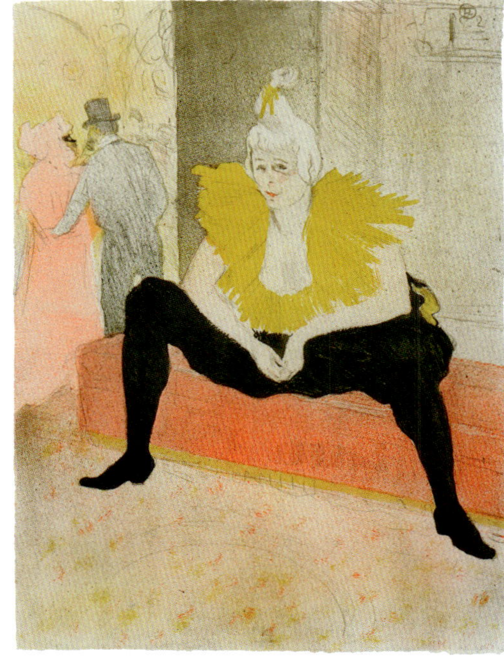

The single surviving preparatory study for the painting is a detailed crayon and charcoal drawing of the head of the man at the far left in a dark visored hat, a cigarette dangling from his mouth (fig. 138). Hopper carefully inscribed the sheet with the French word for mackerel: "un maquereau," slang for a pimp. Gail Levin, among others, has accordingly interpreted the standing female in the painting as a prostitute.[22] When Hopper set to work on *Soir Bleu*, he surely pulled out his old drawings from Paris for inspiration, and figures from them migrated into his oil. On the other hand, *Soir Bleu*'s roots on the streets of Paris were subsumed into one of the most artificial scenes Hopper ever created. We can place ourselves in the scene, seated in the café—Hopper adapted the same point of view familiar from the life studies in his sketchbook (see figs. 119, 130, 132)—that of a café patron seated near the depicted subjects. But the space is abstracted. Its shallow depth begins behind the post at left, which vaguely suggests an architectural support; its form is firmly parallel to the picture

135. (left)
Pierre Bonnard (1867–1947)
The Little Laundry Girl (*La Petite Blanchisseuse*)
from the portfolio *The Album of Painter-Printmakers*
(*L'Album des peintres-graveurs*), 1896
Lithograph; sheet: 22 ½ × 16 ⅝ in. (57.2 × 42.3 cm),
image: 11 ⅝ × 7 ⅞ in. (29.5 × 20 cm)
The Museum of Modern Art, New York; gift of
Victor S. Riesenfeld 315.1948

136. (top right)
Woman with Basket, Woman in Dress, and Man in Beret, 1906–07
Pen and ink on paper, 10 1/16 × 6 ⅝ in. (25.6 × 16.8 cm)
Josephine N. Hopper Bequest 70.1562.11

137. (bottom right)
French Woman with Basket, 1906–07
Watercolor and graphite pencil on paper,
14 13/16 × 10 7/16 in. (37.6 × 26.5 cm)
Josephine N. Hopper Bequest 70.1331

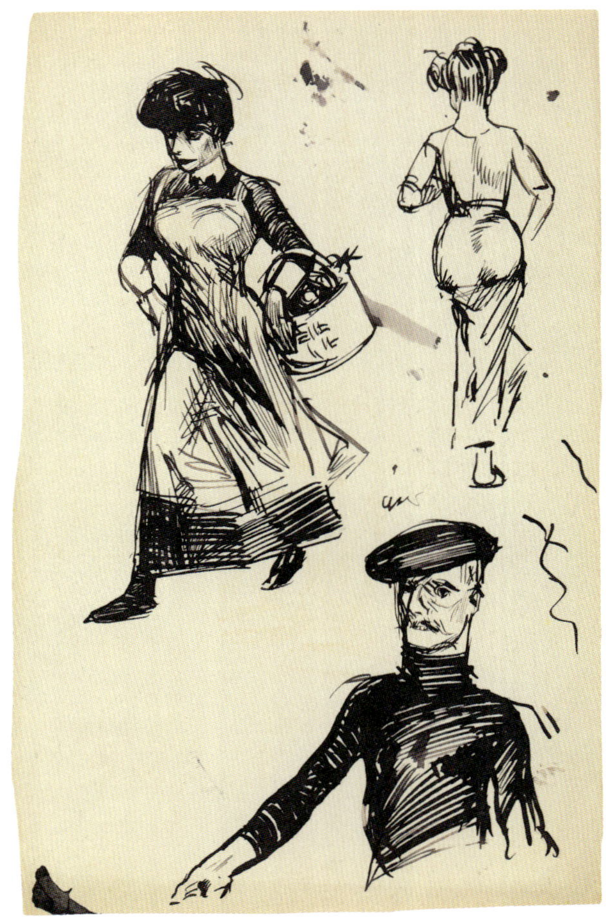

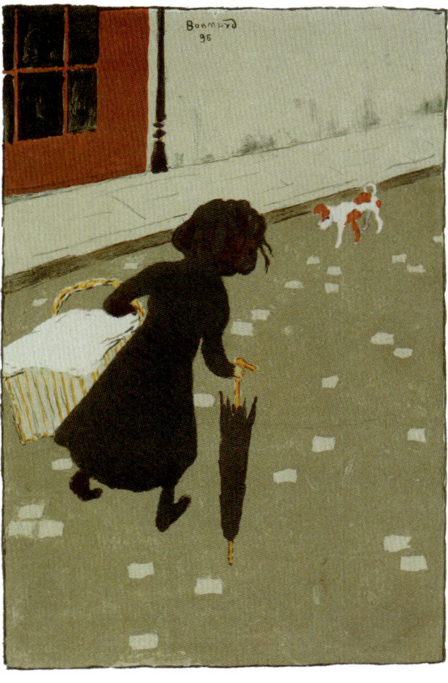

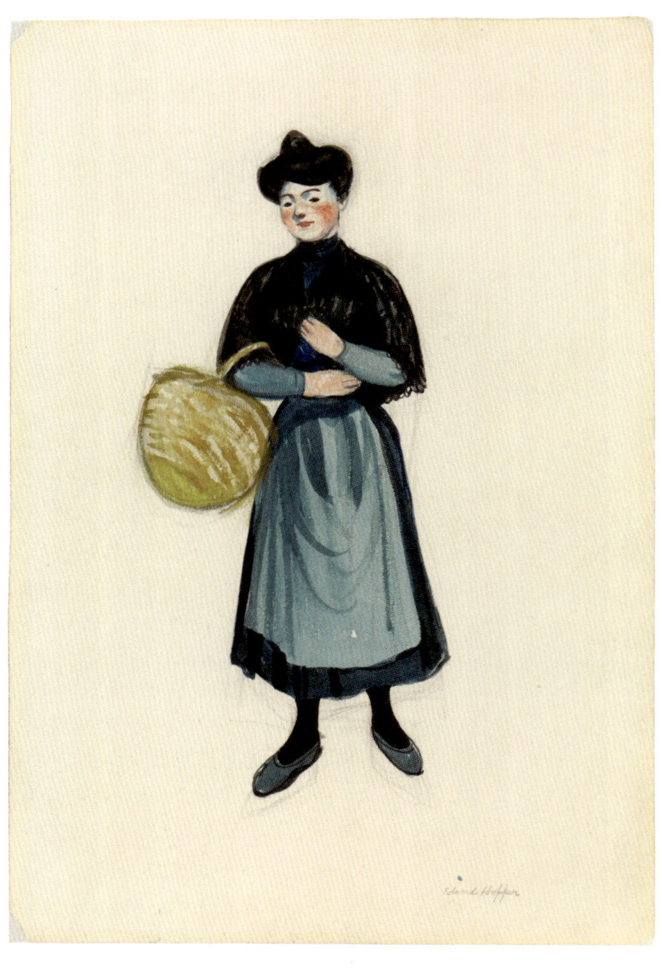

138. *Un Maquereau*, 1914
Fabricated chalk and charcoal on paper, 10 9/16 × 8 3/8 in. (26.8 × 21.3 cm)
Josephine N. Hopper Bequest 70.318

139. Edgar Degas (1834–1917)
Women on the Terrace of a Café in the Evening (Femmes à la terrasse d'un café le soir), 1877
Pastel and monotype on paper, 16 1/8 × 23 5/8 in. (41 × 60 cm)
Musée d'Orsay, Paris RF 12257

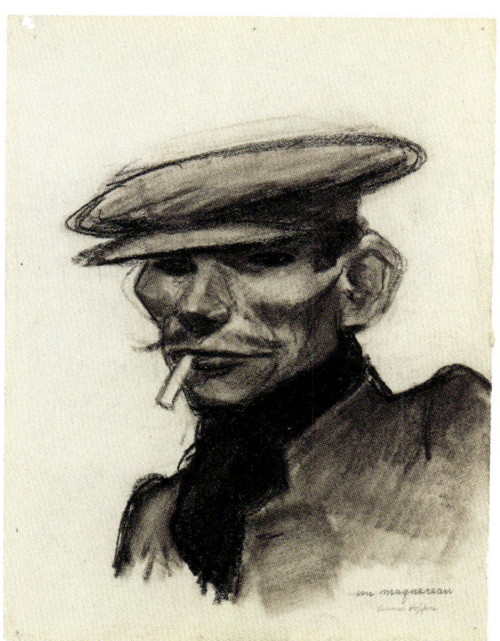

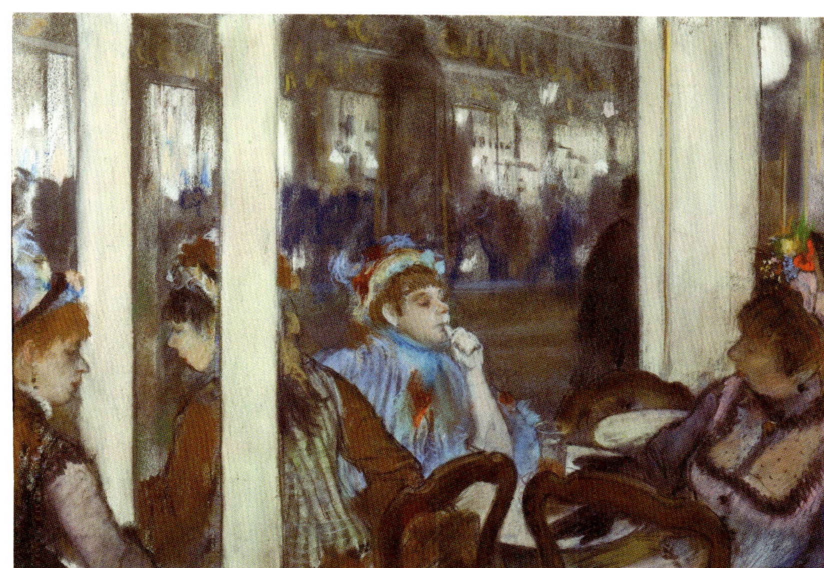

plane, separating the viewer from the scene with flat, unmodulated two-dimensionality. The two-toned background is also fairly flat and reads like a theatrical backdrop, with light and dark blue expanses forming a gently undulating line that suggests a horizon but creates little perspective. Between these two emphatically flat areas of paint Hopper placed his frieze of characters in a rhythmic composition, the various positions of the heads uneven but balanced and unfolding laterally like notes on a musical score (the one-two-one-two dispositions of the seated figures' heads playing off the wavy line behind them). The glowing Japanese lanterns above create a counterpoint of round forms above the heads.

Edgar Degas's well-known pastel over monotype, *Women on the Terrace of a Café in the Evening* (fig. 139), from 1877, no doubt influenced Hopper directly here. We know Hopper admired Degas, and while in Paris he would most certainly have seen the piece in the Gustave Caillebotte collection on view at the Luxembourg Museum.[23] It was also reproduced in early monographs on Degas, so Hopper could have had access to the image back in America as well.[24] Degas's composition is firmly defined by three vertical supports, one of which abuts the picture plane and separates roughly the left quarter of the image, as in *Soir Bleu*. Degas presents a much more defined and recognizable place—clearly a boulevard in Paris at night, visible behind the four seated women, with a gas-lit facade, a blurry crowd of pedestrians, the open boulevard, and a single male figure passing in silhouette closer to the main scene. Degas's café scene was understood from its first showing as representing prostitutes at leisure with one another, recounting tales of the work from which they have temporarily taken respite at café tables, the vulgar gesture of the woman in blue at the center creating the most direct nod to their profession.[25] Hopper's scene shows something of the opposite, for here the prostitute—and it seems reasonable given her appearance to assume she is such—stands next to the balustrade looking vaguely to the viewer's right, as if soliciting someone in our space. But the subject is roughly the same, one of the richest and most popular among the artists of late-nineteenth-century France—evening café culture. Though Hopper's figures are more socially mixed types, they are similarly arrayed at tables under an awning or other shelter (unseen but from which the lanterns hang). The formal similarities with Degas are clear enough—the flattened vertical support was a device the French painter favored, and its frank acknowledgment of the picture plane, as Hopper well understood, marked an important step in modernist painting.

Another clear influence is Japanese prints. Their effect on the generation of artists Hopper admired is difficult to overstate. Hopper would certainly have seen Japanese prints

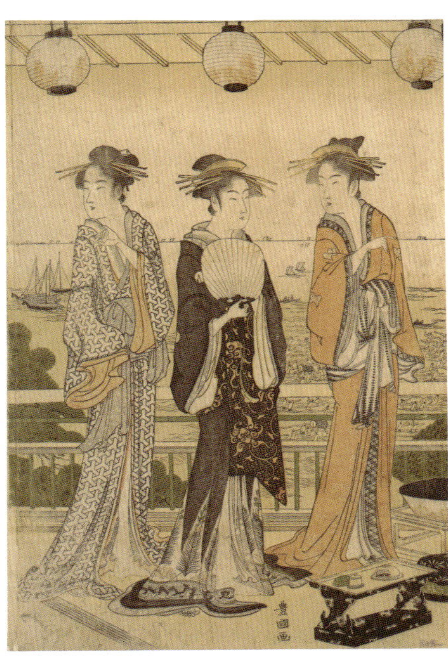
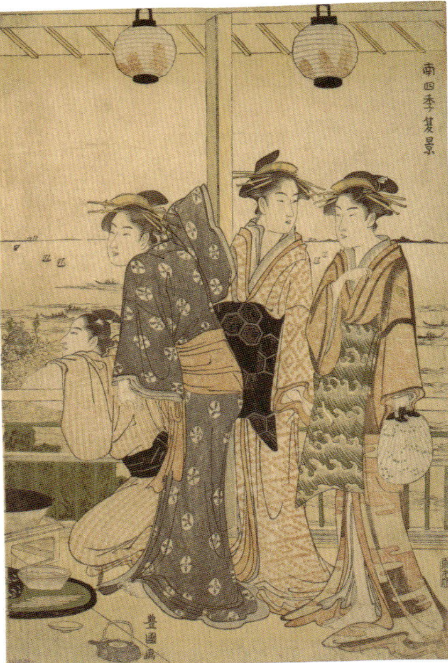
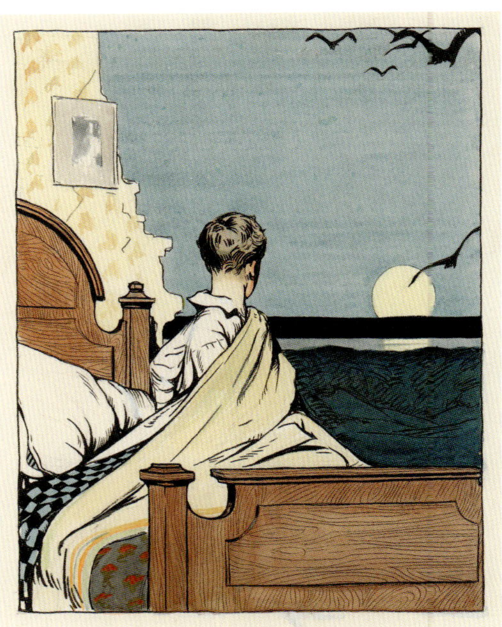

while in Paris—they were sold, for example, at one of the art supply stores he used.[26] By the time he returned to the States, Japonisme was in full force. This aesthetic is manifest in *Soir Bleu* in Hopper's use of Japanese lanterns at the top, as well as in the overall flatness of the background and its use of blue (whose dual tones are not unlike the blue gradients much favored in Japanese ukiyo-e woodblock prints).[27] Even Hopper's flattened pole disrupts the scene in much the same way that the space between separate sheets of Japanese prints breaks up a continuous scene (fig. 140).

An important precedent for *Soir Bleu*, also indebted to Japanese prints, is Hopper's unpublished illustration known as *Boy and Moon* (fig. 141).[28] This descriptive title is not one the artist bestowed. Had he provided one, we could well imagine him calling the piece "La Lune Blanche," from Paul Verlaine's poem. As with Arthur Rimbaud's "Sensation," which inspired the title of *Soir Bleu*, the connection to the Symbolist poetry Hopper admired is significant.[29] Imagery and mood from both poems overlap in *Boy and Moon*, in which Hopper clearly evokes a dream state. A boy sits upright in bed but peers off toward the moon rising in a blue sky with black birds above a dark blue landscape. The walls of his bedroom, indicated by the architectural profile at left, have dissolved and opened up into this blue evening in a wonderful evocation of the imaginative journey being taken. Verlaine's and Rimbaud's phrases well describe Hopper's image: "the hour of dreams"; "the white moon"; "in the blue summer evenings, I will go along the paths . . . Dreaming . . . I will let the wind bathe my bare head."[30] The flat areas of design suitable to this illustrative mode, and so close here to Japanese prints (the moon against blue being a visual standard of the genre), are a clear precedent for *Soir Bleu*.

Hopper expressed his Paris experiences in several pictorial modes, each with a specific aesthetic. They include *Le Bistro*, *Soir Bleu*, the Paris caricatures, a group of finished illustrations, and several early etchings. His Paris sketchbooks are the common link, and we see figures moving from them into these other mediums, which are conceived differently because the artist considered them finished works of art. Thus Hopper's types, rooted in his observations of Parisians on the street, circulate among these modes: policemen, workers, working women and prostitutes, and fashionably dressed men and women are differently deployed in each like characters in a play. The comparison is apt—the artist was an avid theatergoer all his life—as has been noted by several writers in relation to *Soir Bleu*.[31] We see, for instance, a Parisian workman developed from several of the sketches into a figure in a caricature, a watercolor illustration, and later his painting *Le Bistro* (figs. 127, 129, 142–144, 102). A type like the "maquereau" of *Soir Bleu* appears in a few of the caricature watercolors, including one of the most developed compositions, where he sits with a female companion (fig. 145).[32] The bearded, smoking, beret-wearing bohemian behind the pole in *Soir Bleu* is the same figure, reversed, in the illustration *Les Étudiants de Paris* (fig. 146). The bourgeois couple at the right

140. Utagawa Toyokuni I (1769–1825)
The Four Seasons in Southern Edo: A Summer Scene, late 1780s (Edo period, 1615–1868)
Right and middle sheets of a triptych of polychrome woodblock prints, ink on paper; left: 14 3/8 × 10 1/8 in. (36.5 × 25.7 cm), right: 14 1/2 × 9 15/16 in. (36.8 × 25.2 cm)
The Metropolitan Museum of Art, New York; bequest of Mrs. H. O. Havemeyer, 1929 JP1747

141. *Boy and Moon*, c. 1906–10
Pen, brush and ink, and transparent and opaque watercolor on paper, 21 13/16 × 14 13/16 in. (55.4 × 37.6 cm)
Josephine N. Hopper Bequest 70.1349

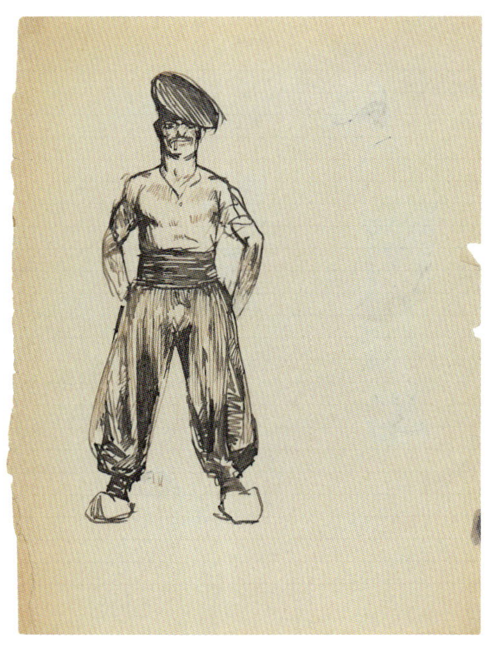

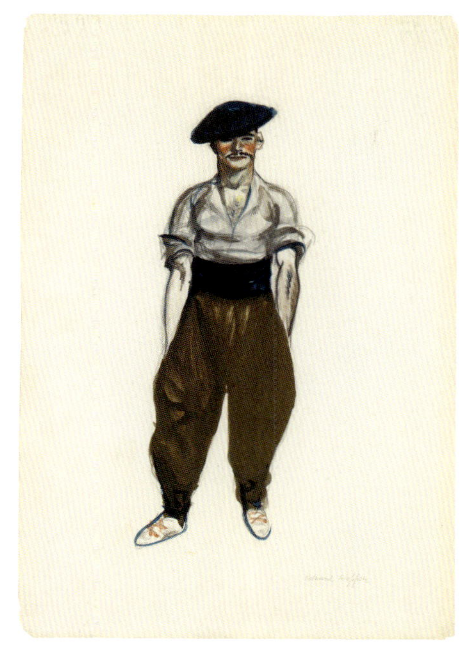

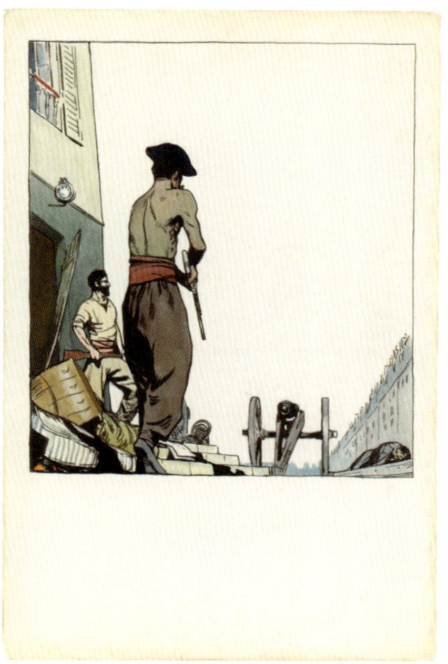

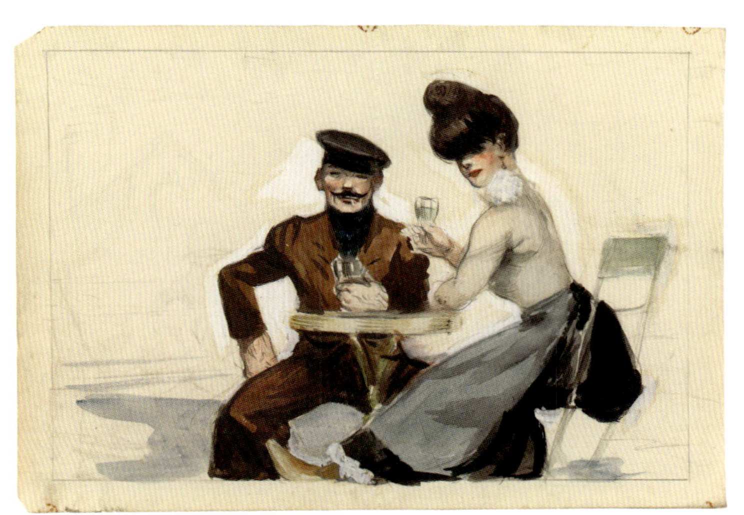

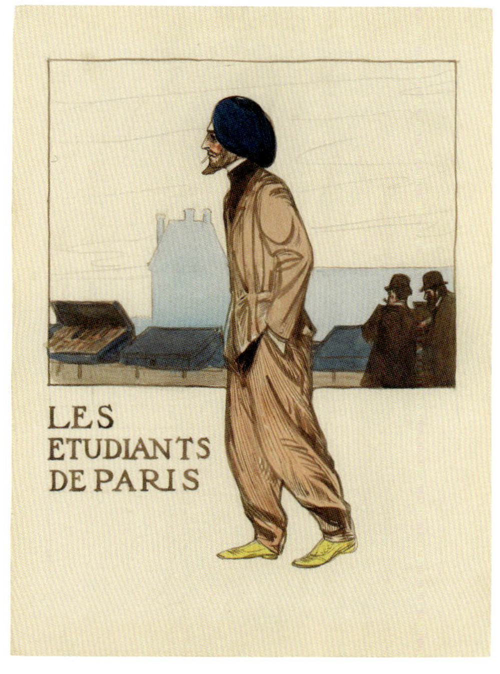

142. *Man in Beret and Clogs* (recto), 1906–07
Pen and ink on paper, 8 11⁄16 × 6 3⁄4 in. (22.1 × 17.1 cm)
Josephine N. Hopper Bequest 70.1561.119a–b

143. *Parisian Workman*, 1906–07
Watercolor and graphite pencil on paper,
15 1⁄16 × 10 5⁄8 in. (38.3 × 27 cm)
Josephine N. Hopper Bequest 70.1333

144. *L'Anneé Terrible: At the Barricade*, c. 1906–10
Transparent and opaque watercolor, brush and ink, and graphite pencil on paper, 21 3⁄4 × 14 3⁄4 in. (55.2 × 37.5 cm)
Josephine N. Hopper Bequest 70.1337

145. *Couple Drinking*, 1906–07
Transparent and opaque watercolor, graphite pencil, and fabricated chalk on paper, 13 1⁄2 × 19 7⁄8 in. (34.3 × 50.5 cm)
Josephine N. Hopper Bequest 70.1340

146. *Les Étudiants de Paris*, c. 1906–10
Watercolor, brush and ink, and graphite pencil on paper, 19 3⁄4 × 14 5⁄8 in. (50.2 × 37.1 cm)
Josephine N. Hopper Bequest 70.1345

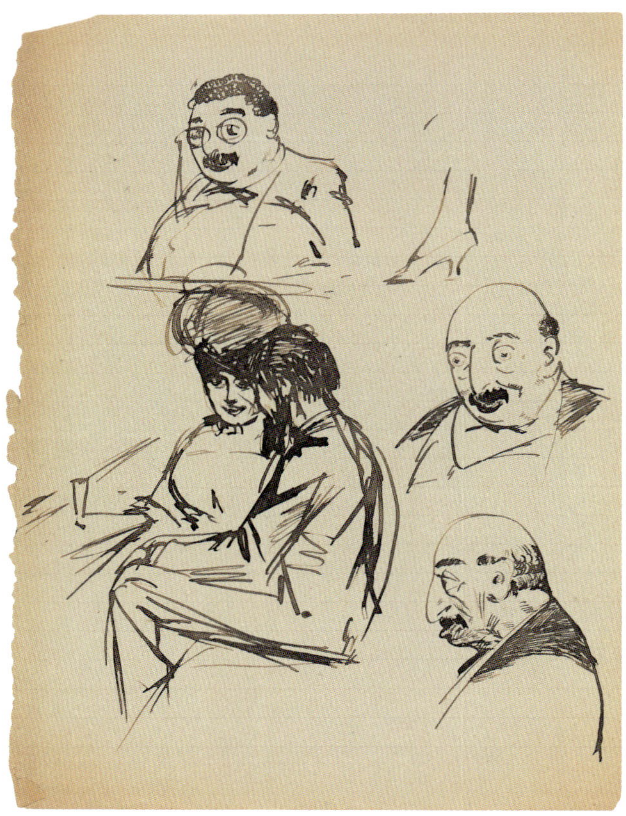

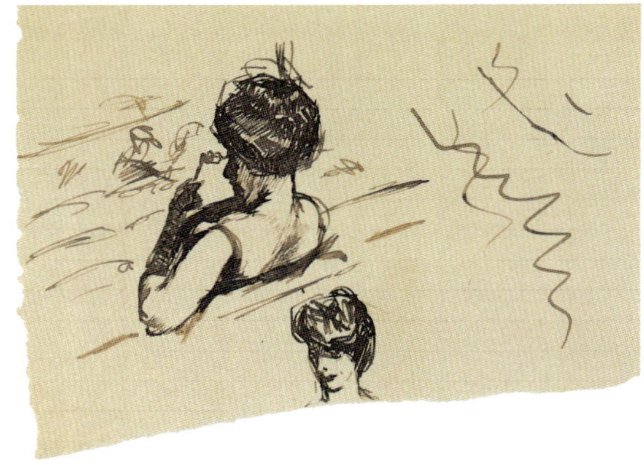

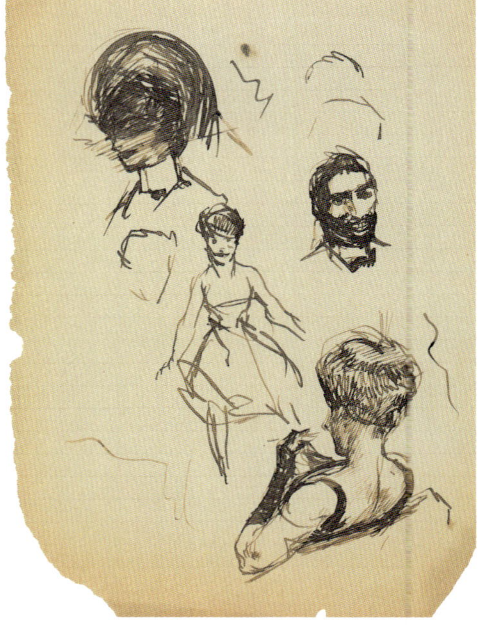

147. *Seated Man and Woman, Bald Men, Man with Glasses, and High Heel* (recto), 1906–07
Pen and ink on paper, 8 11/16 × 6 3/4 in. (22.1 × 17.1 cm)
Josephine N. Hopper Bequest 70.1559.54a–b

148. *Woman with Opera Glasses and Woman's Head*, 1906–07
Pen and ink on paper, 4 11/16 × 6 9/16 in. (11.9 × 16.7 cm)
Josephine N. Hopper Bequest 70.1561.122

149. *Woman with Opera Gloves, Female Figures, and Man with Beard*, 1906–07
Pen and ink on paper, 8 11/16 × 6 9/16 in. (22.1 × 16.7 cm)
Josephine N. Hopper Bequest 70.1562.5

in the painting derives from several sketchbook drawings: the bearded, well-dressed man appears three times in the drawings (figs. 130, 132, 147); and the bare-shouldered woman with her back to us is developed from two sketches of women Hopper observed while sitting behind them in the theater (figs. 148, 149). Though we have scant evidence of how Hopper worked, the artist's Paris sketchbooks came to the Whitney Museum of American Art already dismantled. It seems likely the artist did this himself because he worked from these sheets and had them at hand while he was painting.

Like many artists, Hopper seems to have used drawings this way from the very beginning. His easy adaptation of his Paris sketches into the various genres he tried is evidence of his visual sophistication, but also of the artistic searching he did during the teens. *Soir Bleu*'s roots in close observation and its synthesis of the crosscurrents of French art at the end of the nineteenth century do not, however, make for an unoriginal work, for Hopper infused it with the sense of ambiguity that he developed so beguilingly throughout his career. This ambiguity stands out more when we compare the painting to another of the illustrative watercolors, *Waiter and Diners* (fig. 150), that dates to his French trips or shortly thereafter—it also shows a café scene, but it is far lighter in mood and shows no mingling of disparate social levels, only bourgeois politesse. In the more socially tense *Soir Bleu*, none of the figures interact or make eye contact with one another. It is significant that Hopper left the eye sockets of the figures whose faces we can see dark and blank, with no articulation of reflected light in the pupils to give them the life any painter easily could bestow with a few dabs of white. The abstract setting further adds to the ambiguity. Although *Soir Bleu* reflects the influences of Degas's and Toulouse-Lautrec's images of Parisian café culture, their depictions are far livelier and make much more of the urban context. Hopper may well have meant for *Soir Bleu* to take place on the outskirts of the city, in a setting similar to the one we see in his print *Les Deux Pigeons* (fig. 151), which takes place in a café on a raised terrace that drops off to a distant landscape. If *Soir Bleu* is similarly set, that would in fact explain its vague horizon line and the subtle atmospheric articulation within the light blue of the background, which does dissolve the flatness a bit. Read in this way, the standing woman would necessarily

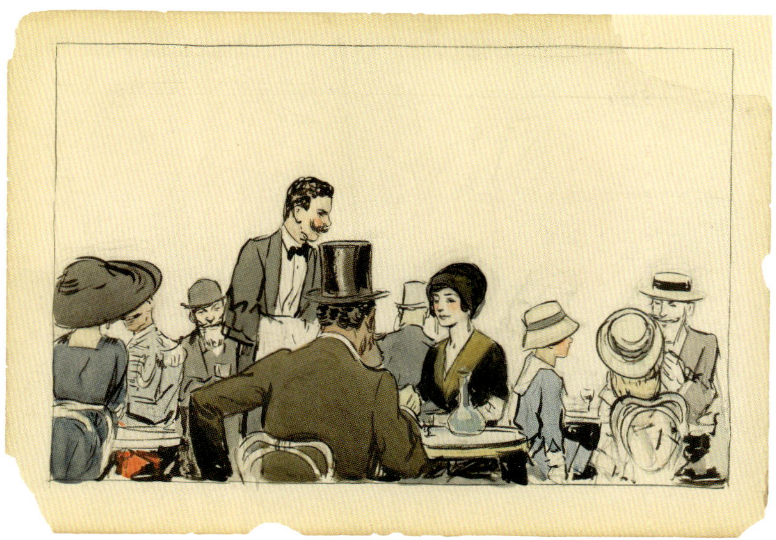

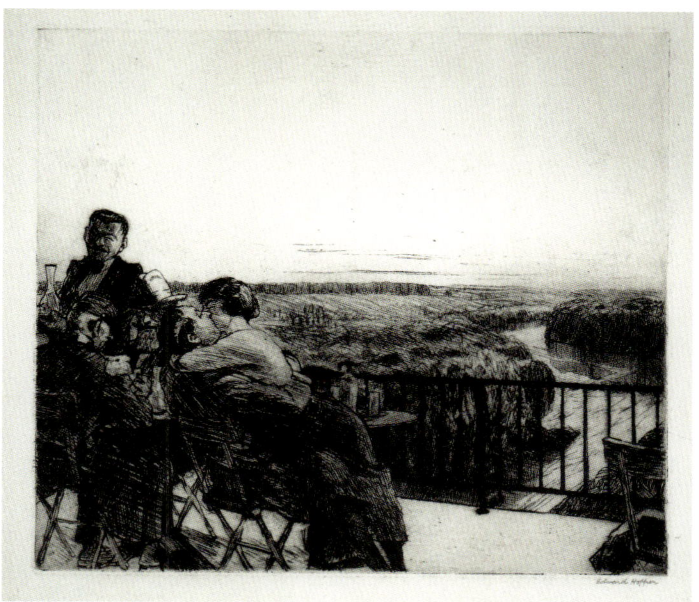

have to be inside the balustrade, not soliciting from the outside, something that changes our understanding of the scene. This lack of specificity in both narrative and setting gives the work its charge.

The most prominent character of all here is perhaps the clown, set apart from the others in full white costume and makeup.[33] Hopper's descriptions of Paris correspond fairly precisely to *Soir Bleu* on several occasions: in one letter he mentions the "cafes where the Demimondaines [*sic*] sit with the silk hatted boulevardiers,"[34] and he also wrote of seeing someone dressed to evoke a clown during the mid-Lent festival of Mi-Carême: "Do not picture these in costume, they are not for the most part, but here and there you will see them, perhaps a clown with a big nose, or two girls with bare necks and short skirts trying to escape the confetti which half a dozen bearded frenchmen are playfully forcing them to eat."[35] It is the clown who most clearly straddles the line between the artificial and the real. His costume is an artifice and belongs to a character and type with a long tradition—Gilles/Pierrot from the commedia dell'arte, painted most famously by Jean-Antoine Watteau (fig. 152) in a work on view in the Louvre when Hopper visited.[36] The commedia dell'arte, an Italian theatrical tradition that was widely performed in France in the seventeenth and eighteenth centuries, features stock characters in improvised scenes and developed a popular following at fairs and street festivals. It enjoyed a revival in the nineteenth century, and the character of Pierrot, with his white costume, became a significant part of visual and literary culture into the early twentieth century and a predecessor to the modern mime. As the Pierrot type evolved, sometimes into a more general "sad clown," artists ranging from the academic traditionalists Jean-Léon Gérôme and Thomas Couture to avant-garde figures such as Paul Cézanne and Pablo Picasso used him in their work. At the 1907 Salon in Paris, one of the paintings even featured a boy dressed Pierrot-like for Mi-Carême.[37] In America, such figures were likewise treated by a wide array of artists, from the illustrator Maxfield Parrish to the realist John Sloan, with whose melancholy *Clown Making Up* of 1910 (The Phillips Collection, Washington, DC) Hopper would have been familiar. Another important precedent for *Soir Bleu* is a literary one: the Belgian poet Albert Giraud's book *Pierrot Lunaire* (Moonstruck Pierrot). Given his interest in the Symbolist movement, Hopper was almost certainly familiar with this cycle of fifty rondels published in 1884, later more famously used as the basis for composer Arnold Schoenberg's seminal 1912 piece of music of the same title.

As much as looking back to the nineteenth century, *Soir Bleu*'s Pierrot thus tapped a contemporary zeitgeist. Two years after Hopper showed the painting in 1915, for example, a production of the French pantomime *Pierrot the Prodigal* appeared in New York at the Booth Theatre, and Schoenberg's composition premiered in the city in 1923. Hopper matured much as an artist in the years after *Soir Bleu*, developing his own imaginative synthesis of observed reality to produce the artifice of his paintings. In the case of *Soir Bleu*, however, that artifice derives from the seamless combination of a diverse and rich trove of sources based in fairly recent French cultural history. The balance Hopper achieved between these multiple, artful references and the concrete reality of Paris street life converge most forcefully in his clown's white cigarette against made-up, bright red lips. This powerful avenue of expression was one to which Hopper would never again return.

150. *Waiter and Diners*, 1906–07
Brush and ink, watercolor, and fabricated chalk on paper, 14 15/16 × 22 1/16 in. (37.9 × 56 cm)
Josephine N. Hopper Bequest 70.1443

151. *Les Deux Pigeons*, 1920
Etching; sheet: 12 3/8 × 13 11/16 in. (31.4 × 34.8 cm), plate: 8 1/2 × 9 7/8 in. (21.6 × 25.1 cm)
Philadelphia Museum of Art; purchased with the Thomas Skelton Harrison Fund, 1962 1962-19-18

NOTES

1 On *Soir Bleu*, see Robert Hobbs, *Edward Hopper*, (New York: Harry N. Abrams in association with the National Museum of American Art, 1987), 38–41; Gail Levin, *Edward Hopper: A Catalogue Raisonné*, vol. 3, *Oils* (New York: Whitney Museum of American Art in association with W. W. Norton, 1995), 118; Gail Levin, *Edward Hopper: An Intimate Biography* (New York: Rizzoli, 2007), 98–101; Gail Levin, "Edward Hopper, Francophile," *Arts Magazine* 53, no. 10 (June 1979): 114–21; Evelyn C. Hankins, "Edward Hopper: The Paris Years," *American Art Review* 15, no. 1 (January–February 2003): 168–73.
2 See Charles H. Caffin, "New and Important Things in Art—Exhibit at MacDowell Club," *New York American*, February 15, 1915, 9; Guy Pène du Bois, "Exhibitions in the Galleries," *Arts & Decoration*, April 1915, 238; James Gordon Bennett, "Art Shows and Sales: Mr. Bellows Paints Cross-Eyed Boy," *New York Herald*, February 13, 1915, 7; "Art Notes," *New York Evening Post*, February 20, 1915, 12; "Strong Men at the MacDowell," *New York Evening Mail*, February 18, 1915, 10.
3 Brian O'Doherty, "Edward Hopper's Voice," in *American Masters: The Voice and the Myth* (New York: Random House, 1973), 16.
4 William C. Seitz discusses Hopper's "fundamental divergence" from Impressionism by contrasting Claude Monet's use of "a specific motif, on a particular day or even during a single half-hour, as his point of departure," to how Hopper conceived his paintings before he executed them, noting that they "are never the record of a single perceptual encounter with a scene or event, even though an existing building or landscape is sometimes re-created with crystal clarity. . . . His compositions arise from a synthesis of observations, impressions and thoughts, are carefully and intellectually planned, and take form within a preconceived pictorial language." William C. Seitz, "Edward Hopper: Realist, Classicist, Existentialist," in *São Paolo 9, United States of America: Edward Hopper, Environment U.S.A., 1957–1967*, exh. cat. (Washington, DC: Smithsonian Institution Press, 1967), 18–19.
5 Hopper kept these paintings, which are now in the collection of the Whitney Museum of American Art.
6 Richard R. Brettell and Éric Darragon, *Edward Hopper: Les années parisiennes, 1906–1910*, exh. cat. (Giverny: Musée d'Art Américain, 2004), 41.
7 John Updike refers to Hopper's works from this period as "a subdued and chunky version of Impressionism." John Updike, "Hopper's Polluted Silence," *New York Review of Books* 42, no. 13 (August 10, 1995): 20. For more on Hopper's French influences, see Levin, "Edward Hopper, Francophile," 114–21; Elliot Bostwick Davis, "Hopper's Foundation," in Carol Troyen et al., *Edward Hopper*, exh. cat. (Boston: Museum of Fine Arts, 2007), 29–52; Anne Coffin Hanson, "Edward Hopper, American Meaning and French Craft," *Art Journal* 41, no. 2 (Summer 1981): 142–49; Jerrold Lanes, "Edward Hopper: French formalist, Ash Can realist, neither, or both?" *Artforum* 7, no. 2 (October 1968): 44–49. On Hopper and Meryon, see Lawrence Campbell, "Edward Hopper and the Melancholy of Robinson Crusoe," *ARTnews* 70, no. 6 (October 1971): 38.
8 "I have just been to the 'Autumn Salon' and found it for the most part very bad, although it is much more liberal in its aims than the shows at home." Edward Hopper to Elizabeth Griffiths Smith Hopper,

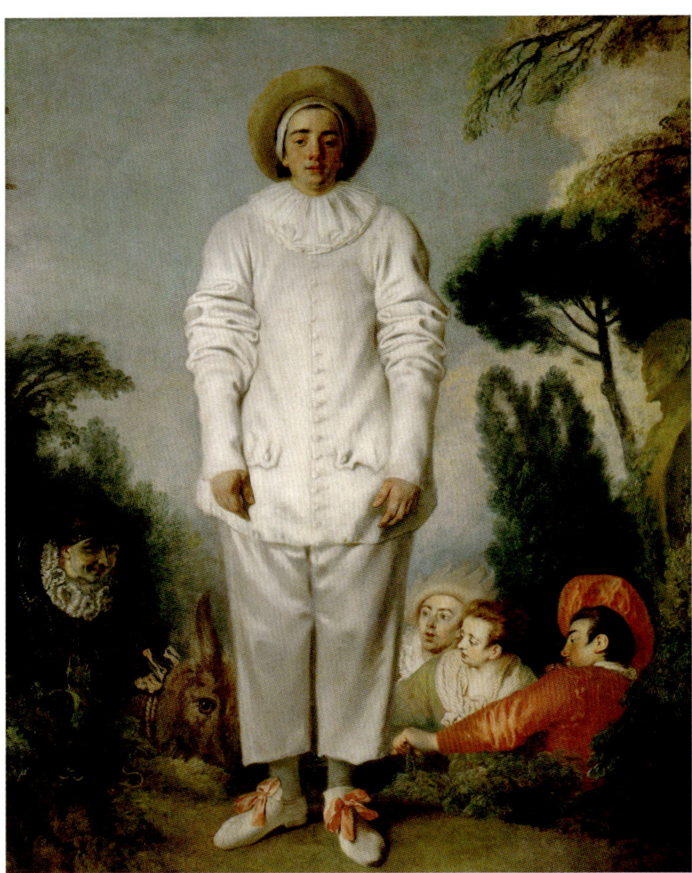

152. Jean-Antoine Watteau (1684–1721)
Pierrot, formerly known as Gilles, c. 1718–19
Oil on canvas, 72 13/16 × 59 1/16 in. (185 × 150 cm)
Musée du Louvre, Paris; bequest of Dr. Louis La Caze, 1869 M.I. 1121

October 30, 1906, Edward and Josephine Hopper Research Collection, 4.1.2, Whitney Museum of American Art Archives, New York (hereafter cited as Hopper Research Collection). "Who did I meet? Nobody. I'd heard of Gertrude Stein but I don't remember having heard of Picasso at all." Hopper, quoted in Brian O'Doherty, "Portrait: Edward Hopper," *Art in America* 52, no. 6 (December 1964): 73.

9 Brettell and Darragon, *Edward Hopper*, 72. Lloyd Goodrich noted that "*Le Bistro* is also a memory of France painted in America. No particular place, but made up from memories. Very broad and without detail." Lloyd Goodrich, "Notes on Paris oils seen at Edward Hoppers [*sic*] studio" (unpublished typescript, April 21, 1947), 2, Hopper Research Collection, 4.044.

10 "It's hard to define how they come about... but it's a long process of gestation in the mind and a rising emotion.... To me that applies to painting from the memory." O'Doherty, "Hopper's Voice," 22.

11 Brettell and Darragon, *Edward Hopper*, 66.

12 Henry Geldzahler describes this phenomenon in Hopper's paintings quite nicely: "His works appear to be 'hard-edge' paintings, but on closer examination we see this is an illusion created by the sureness of his touch. The brushwork is loose, but the placement is so exact, the light portrayed so effectively and with such economy, that the whole becomes sharp and controlled. It is not tightness of technique, but clarity of composition, in the classical tradition of Poussin, David, and Cézanne, that gives such firmness and presence to his work." Henry Geldzahler, "Edward Hopper," *The Metropolitan Museum of Art Bulletin* 21, no. 3 (November 1962): 116.

13 William Robinson, *The Parks and Gardens of Paris: Considered in Relation to the Wants of Other Cities and of Public and Private Gardens* (London: Macmillan, 1878).

14 Brettell and Darragon, *Edward Hopper*, 66–72. On the qualities of light in Paris, Hopper claimed: "The light was different from anything I had known.... The shadows were luminous—more reflected light. Even under the bridges there was a certain luminosity. Maybe it's because the clouds are lower, just over the housetops. I've always been interested in light—more than most contemporary painters, and certainly more than the abstractionists." "Art: The Silent Witness," *Time*, December 24, 1956, 30. On Hopper's "transforming" light sources, see Mark Strand, *Hopper* (New York: Alfred A. Knopf, 2001), 27, 34–36; John Hollander, "Hopper and the Figure of Room," *Art Journal* 41, no. 2 (Summer 1981): 159; Parker Tyler, "Edward Hopper: Alienation by Light," *Magazine of Art* 41, no. 8 (December 1948): 290–95.

15 These figures derive from the workman type Hopper drew in his sketchbooks and from which he created the watercolor *Parisian Workman* (see fig. 143).

16 Ann Dumas, "Degas in America," and Richard Kendall, "Influence in Low Places: Degas and the Ashcan Generation," in *Degas and America: The Early Collectors*, ed. Ann Dumas and David A. Brenneman, exh. cat. (Atlanta: High Museum of Art; New York: Rizzoli, 2001), 13–34, 61–76; Milton W. Brown, *The Story of the Armory Show* (New York: Abbeville Press, 1988).

17 The dismantled sketchbook sheets come from two different sketchbooks, discernible because of different types of paper. Accession numbers 70.1555.1–2 and 70.1555.5–18 comprise the sixteen surviving full sheets from the large Paris sketchbook, which are of a smooth, beige, machine-made wove paper and measure on average approximately 9 7/8 x 12 7/8 inches each; six of the sheets from this sketchbook were cut down to about half that size, about 10 x 6 inches, and include accession numbers 70.1559.7, 70.1561.118, and 70.1562.10–13. The other, small Paris sketchbook was of a cheap, blue-lined, beige-brown machine-made wove paper measuring on average 8 11/16 x 6 11/16 inches; thirty-five sheets survive; its accession numbers include 70.1559.2–6, 70.1559.53–66, 70.1561.119–125, and 70.1562.1–9.

18 The MacDowell Club of New York, *Exhibition of Water Colors, Pastels and Drawings by Four Groups of Artists*, April 22–May 11, 1919; Whitney Studio Club, New York, October 24–November 14, 1922; Alfred H. Barr, Jr., et al., *Edward Hopper: Retrospective Exhibition, November 1–December 7, 1933*, exh. cat. (New York: Museum of Modern Art, 1933). For the exhibition history of individual sheets in the series, see Gail Levin, *Edward Hopper: A Catalogue Raisonné*, vol. 2, *Watercolors* (New York: Whitney Museum of American Art in association with W. W. Norton, 1995), CD-ROM; a selection was also published in "Exhibition of the Work of Walkowitz and Hopper," *Arts and Decoration* 3 (February 1916): 191. On Hopper's watercolors, see Virginia M. Mecklenburg, *Edward Hopper: The Watercolors*, exh. cat. (Washington, DC: National Museum of American Art; New York: W. W. Norton, 1999).

19 Levin, *Edward Hopper: An Intimate Biography*, 50.

20 Riva Castleman and Wolfgang Wittrock, eds., *Henri de Toulouse-Lautrec: Images of the 1890s*, exh. cat. (New York: Museum of Modern Art, 1985), 170–79; Colta Ives, Helen Giambruni, and Sasha M. Newman, *Pierre Bonnard: The Graphic Art*, exh. cat. (New York: Metropolitan Museum of Art, 1989), 118.

21 Hopper based one of his French watercolor illustrations on a Guillaume image, for example: *French Couple on Embankment after Albert Guillaume*, Whitney Museum of American Art, 70.1343. Levin suggests that Hopper developed an interest in popular French illustration: "He saved several of the humor magazines he must have acquired on one of his last two trips to Paris. Of the three issues he saved of *Les Maitres Humoristes*, one was devoted to the cartoons of Albert Guillaume and two to the satirical illustrations of Jean-Louis Forain." Levin, "Edward Hopper, Francophile," 116. The issue of *Les Maîtres Humoristes* featuring Guillaume appeared in October 1908; the two issues devoted to Forain appeared in January and November 1908.

22 John S. Farmer and W. E. Henley, eds., *Slang and Its Analogues: Past and Present* (London, 1902), 5:248; Levin, *Edward Hopper: An Intimate Biography*, 98.

23 Karl Baedeker, *Paris and Its Environs: With Routes from London to Paris; Handbook for Travellers* (New York: Scribner's, 1907), 318.

24 Georges Grappe, *Edgar Degas* (Paris: Librairie Plon, 1908); Paul-André Lemoisne, *Degas et son oeuvre* (Paris: Librairie Plon, 1912), 73–74. Kendall suggests that the latter volume was one of the texts that was "detectable in the histories of the Ashcan circle, and there is reason to believe that they played a wider role in the dissemination of Degas's art to Europe, America, and beyond." Kendall, "Influence in Low Places," 66. See also, later, Paul Jamot, *Degas* (Paris: Éditions de la Gazette des Beaux-Arts, 1924).

25 Hollis Clayson, *Painted Love: Prostitution in French Art of the Impressionist Era* (New Haven: Yale University Press, 1991), 103–8.

26 One of Hopper's Parisian caricatures has a label for the Paris American Art Company, described in a contemporary source as "a very good shop, where artists' materials may be bought, and framing done. There are for sale here, at very reasonable prices, photographs, bronzes, busts and statuettes; also Japanese prints, art publications, and magazines. Everything is of superior quality, and one is not cheated.... 125, boulevard du Montparnasse." Elizabeth Otis Williams, *Sojourning, Shopping & Studying in Paris: A Handbook Particularly for Women* (Chicago: A. C. McClurg, 1907), 161.

27 Colta Feller Ives, *The Great Wave: The Influence of Japanese Woodcuts on French Prints*, exh. cat. (New York: Metropolitan Museum of Art, 1974), 7–21.

28 Levin has dated the piece based on Hopper's Paris trip, though the artist could easily have done it back in New York, perhaps even around the time he painted *Le Bistro*.

29 Pamela N. Koob, "States of Being: Edward Hopper and Symbolist Aesthetics," *American Art* 18, no. 3 (Fall 2004): 52–77. The Hoppers' cat was named "Arthur," presumably after Rimbaud: "The cat, named Arthur, looms sizably in the mythos of the early Hopper household." O'Doherty, "Hopper's Voice," 18.

30 *One Hundred and One Poems by Paul Verlaine: A Bilingual Edition*, trans. Norman R. Shapiro (Chicago: University of Chicago Press, 2010), 68–69; *Rimbaud: Complete Works, Selected Letters; A Bilingual Edition*, trans. Wallace Fowlie (Chicago: University of Chicago Press, 2005), 12.

31 Levin, *Edward Hopper: An Intimate Biography*, 101; Hobbs, *Edward Hopper*, 40. On the sad clown and theater in American Art, see H. Barbara Weinberg, Doreen Bolger, and David Park Curry, *American Impressionism and Realism: The Painting of Modern Life, 1885–1915* (New York: Metropolitan Museum of Art, 1994), 204–5.

32 This figure also appears, with other Parisian types, in an "erased" study—a very faint chalk drawing on the verso of Hopper's study for the etching *La Barrière* (1915–18) in the collection of the Whitney Museum of American Art, 70.886a–b.

33 Linda Nochlin identifies the clown figure as the "alter ego" of the beret-wearing artist figure. Linda Nochlin, "Edward Hopper and the Imagery of Alienation," *Art Journal* 41, no. 2 (Summer 1981): 140.

34 Edward Hopper to Elizabeth Griffiths Smith Hopper, December 8, 1906, Hopper Research Collection, 4.1.2.

35 Edward Hopper to Elizabeth Griffiths Smith Hopper, May 11, 1907, Hopper Research Collection, 4.1.2.

36 Robert F. Storey, *Pierrot: A Critical History of a Mask* (Princeton, NJ: Princeton University Press, 1978); Donald Posner, "Watteau Melancolique: La Formation d'un Mythe," *Bulletin de la Société de l'Histoire de l'Art Français* (1973), 345–61; Francis Haskell, "The Sad Clown: Some Notes on a Nineteenth-Century Myth," in *Past and Present in Art and Taste: Selected Essays* (New Haven: Yale University Press, 1987), 116–28.

37 *Mi-Carême* by P.-C. Chocarne-Moreau. See *Catalogue illustré du Salon Peinture et Sculpture* (Paris: Société des artistes français, 1907), 59.

A View from the Bridge

DANIEL S. PALMER

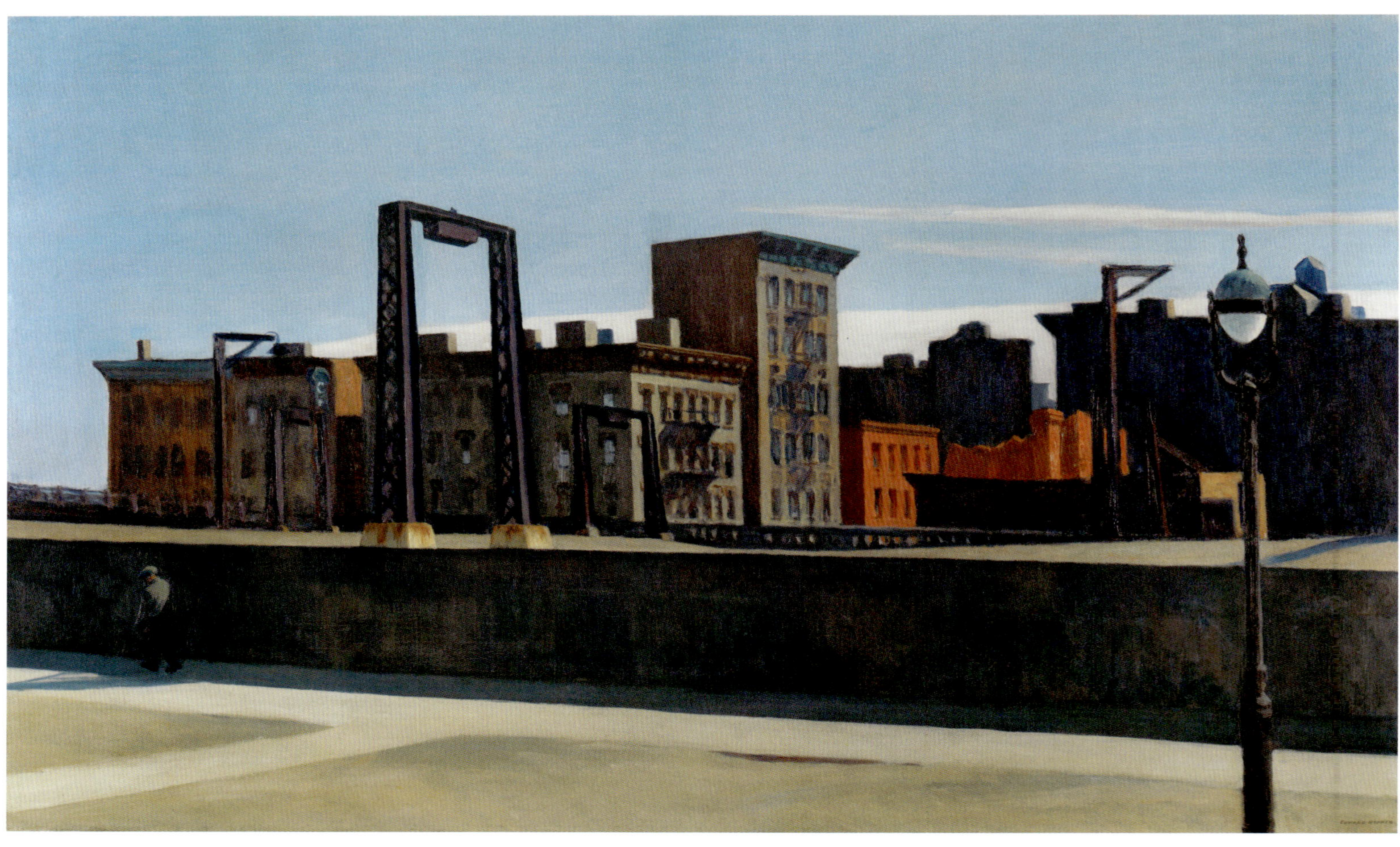

153. *Manhattan Bridge Loop*, 1928
Oil on canvas, 35 × 60 in. (88.9 × 152.4 cm)
Addison Gallery of American Art,
Phillips Academy, Andover, Massachusetts;
gift of Stephen C. Clark, Esq. 1932.17

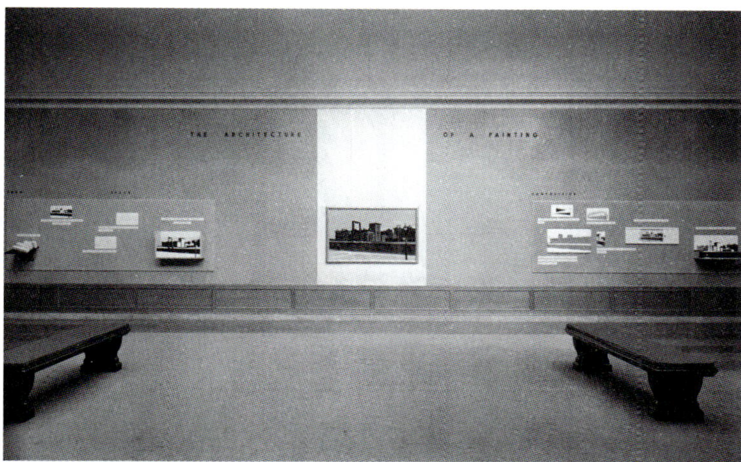

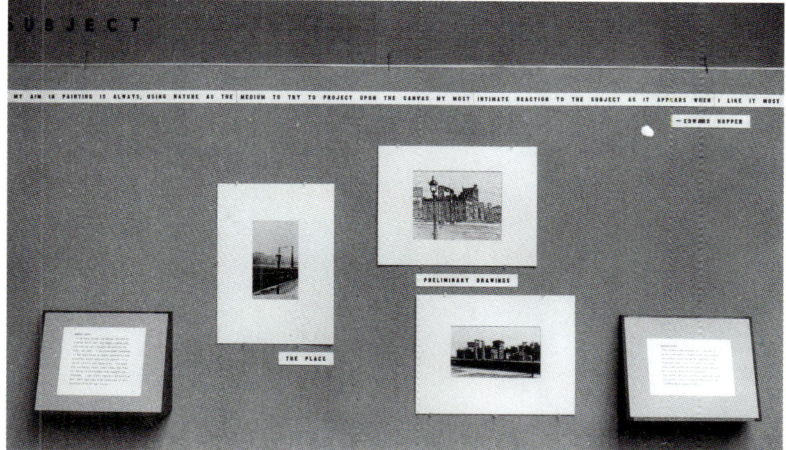

Manhattan Bridge Loop (fig. 153) left Edward Hopper's studio on April 17, 1928, for the Rehn Gallery, where it was purchased by collector Stephen C. Clark.[1] This painting has significant implications for our understanding of Hopper's career because of a request made in 1939 by Charles H. Sawyer, director of Phillips Academy's Addison Gallery of American Art in Andover, Massachusetts, which had acquired the work in 1932. He wrote to the painter, "bothering" him for a statement to be included in an exhibition highlighting the artist's methods.[2] This began an exchange that reveals unique insights into Hopper's creative process and his attentiveness to New York's architecture.

The Architecture of a Painting: Edward Hopper's "Manhattan Bridge Loop" opened at the Addison Gallery on January 13, 1940. Sawyer organized the exhibition with Bartlett H. Hayes, Jr., as an accessible, interpretive study consisting of the painting, ten sections that displayed how the artist combined the elements of design, and an innovative, participatory experience with models of the scene that could be manipulated by visitors in order to "show the different effects which could be given by different arrangements."[3] The exhibition's most significant contribution to posterity, however, is that it elicited a rare and remarkably cogent declaration from Hopper—that was partly excerpted and displayed as wall text—in which the artist addressed his working process and explained how he translated quotidian subjects into paintings.[4]

In his correspondence with Sawyer, Hopper rejected the idea that his drawings would help explain his technique: "The preliminary sketches would do little for you in explaining the making of the picture. The color, design and form have all been subjected, consciously or otherwise to considerable simplification." Nevertheless, the exhibition made it clear that while "the picture was planned very carefully in my mind before starting it, but except for a few small black and white sketches made from the fact," this drawing process was a central step in the evolution of his paintings (figs. 154, 155).[5] Hopper's initial on-site lithographic crayon sketch (fig. 156) was placed next to his photograph of the pedestrian entrance to the Manhattan Bridge.[6] This juxtaposition showed how he faithfully recorded the main elements of the scene: the architectural details of nearby tenement buildings, trolley scaffolds, and a lamppost. He also drew thin horizontal and vertical lines on the page to mark his calculations for the painting's composition.[7] Hopper must have found the scene too square, because in his next drawing (fig. 157) he stretched it horizontally and began to alter the setting, incorporating the bridge's trolley tracks as a solid elevated volume, lowering the heights of the scaffold and the tallest building, and changing the latter's cornice. Another drawing (fig. 158), not included in the Addison exhibition, indicates that Hopper analyzed the lamppost on the bridge with careful scale and color notations. Perhaps the artist executed this study when he adjusted the street lamp's position from one drawing to the next. When compared to the photograph of the scene, these artworks demonstrate how Hopper transformed Lower Manhattan through a method of "selection" and "construction" to meet formal objectives, and how important drawing was in that process.[8]

The show helped elucidate the artist's process and explain the formal qualities of his works. It was so successful that the Museum of Modern Art circulated the exhibition on an eighteen-venue tour across the country.[9] Furthermore, Hopper's statement about his working method has had a widespread influence since it was canonized in Lloyd Goodrich's 1971 monograph on the artist.[10] Both communicate his astute attention to architectural detail and the profound impact of New York's built environment on his oeuvre.[11]

154 and 155. Installation views of *The Architecture of a Painting: Edward Hopper's "Manhattan Bridge Loop,"* January 30–April 4, 1940, Addison Gallery of American Art, Phillips Academy, Andover, Massachusetts; courtesy Addison Gallery Archives

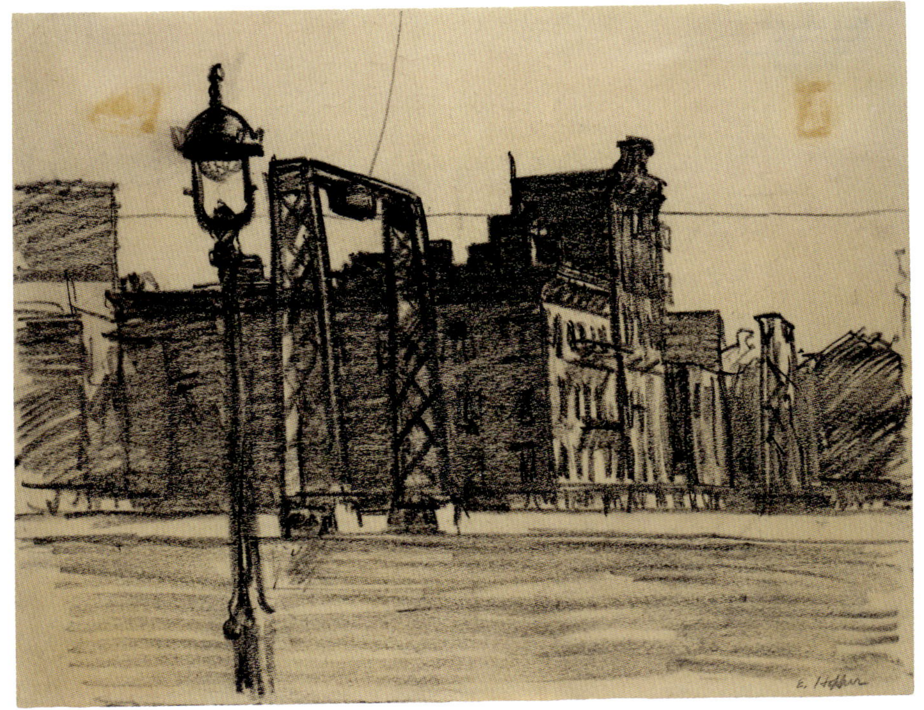

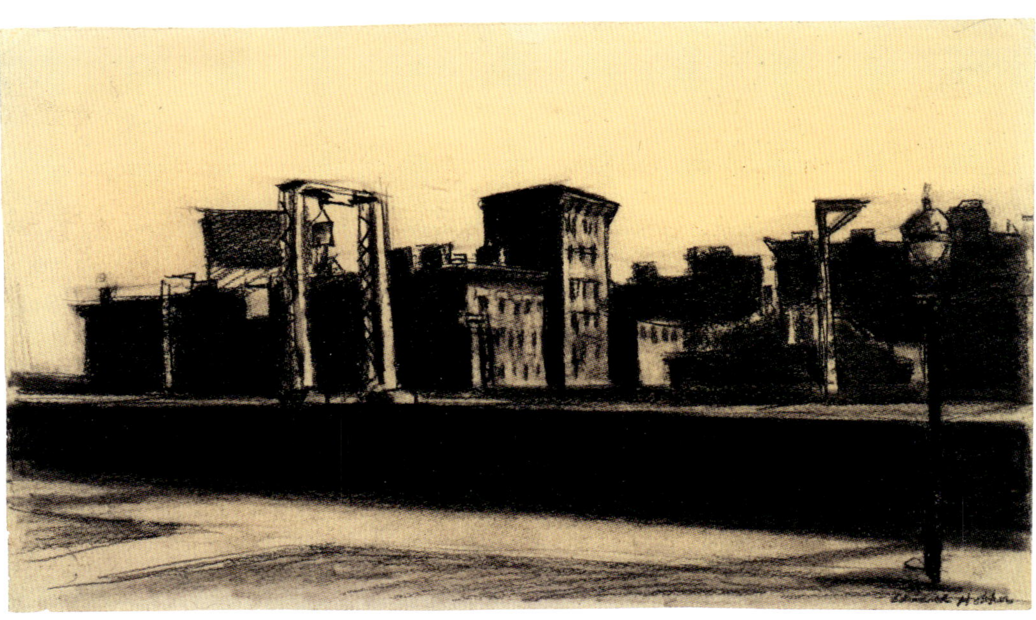

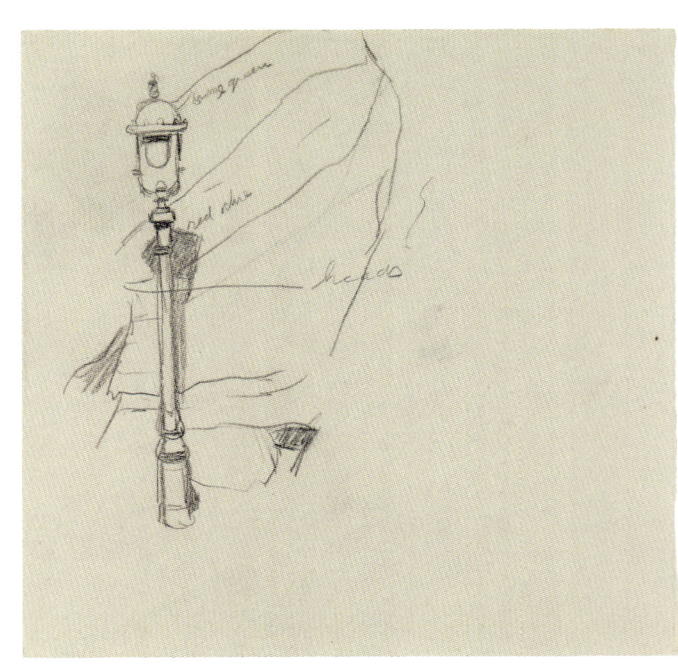

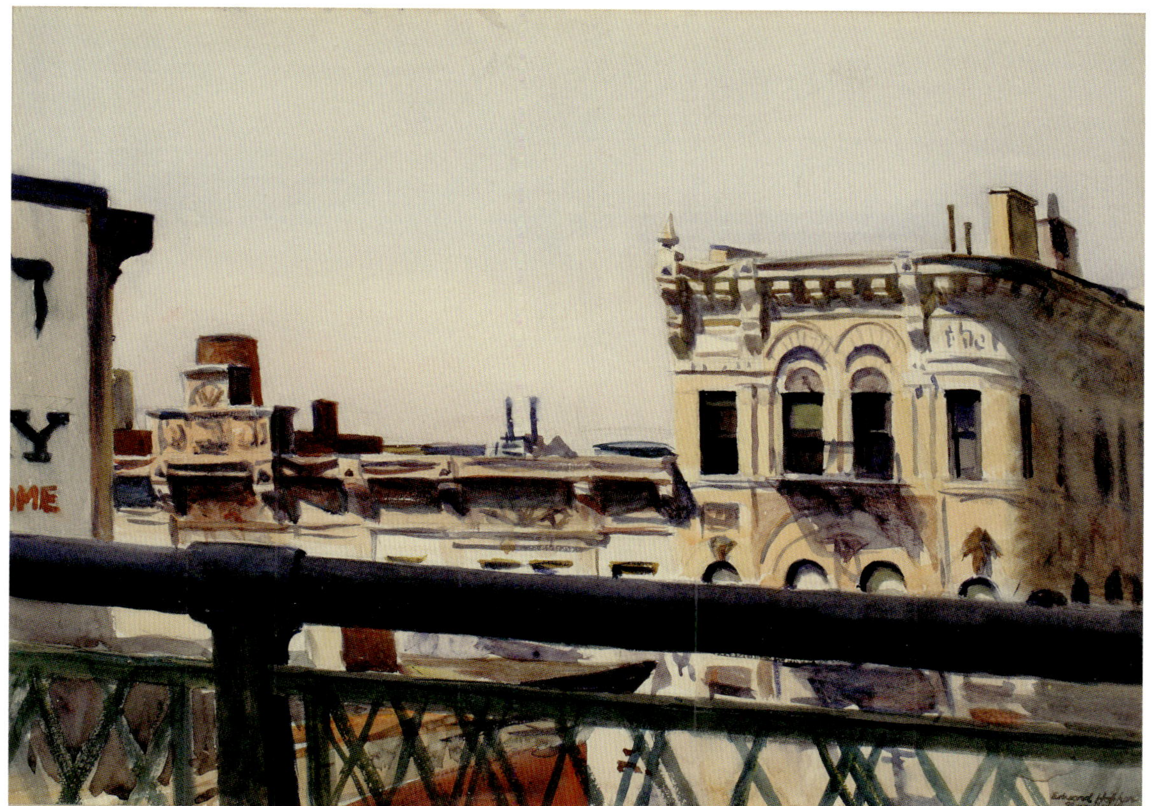

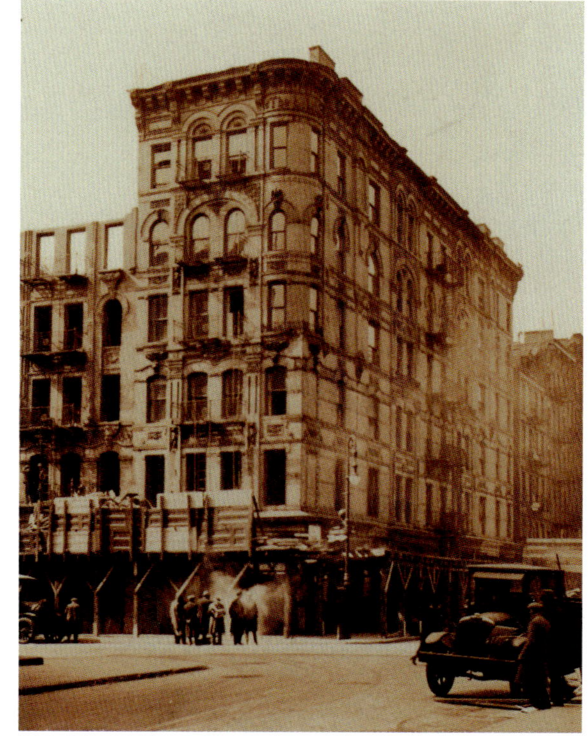

156. Study for *Manhattan Bridge Loop*, 1928
Crayon on paper, 8½ × 11¹⁄₁₆ in. (21.6 × 28.1 cm)
Addison Gallery of American Art, Phillips Academy, Andover, Massachusetts; gift of the artist 1940.71

157. Study for *Manhattan Bridge Loop*, 1928
Fabricated chalk on paper, 6⅜ × 11¼ in. (16.2 × 28.6 cm)
Addison Gallery of American Art, Phillips Academy, Andover, Massachusetts; gift of the artist 1940.72

158. *Street Lamp* (Study for *Manhattan Bridge Loop*), 1928
Fabricated chalk on paper, 8⅞ × 9⁷⁄₁₆ in. (22.5 × 24 cm)
Josephine N. Hopper Bequest 70.235

159. *The Lily Apartments*, 1926
Watercolor on paper, 14 × 20 in. (35.6 × 50.8 cm)
Private collection

160. Market and Henry Streets, prior to the complete demolishment of the buildings on this corner, including The Lilly Apartments, March 9, 1932. Photograph by Percy Loomis Sperr. Irma and Paul Milstein Division of United States History, Local History and Genealogy, The New York Public Library, Astor, Lenox and Tilden Foundations Image ID: 721633F

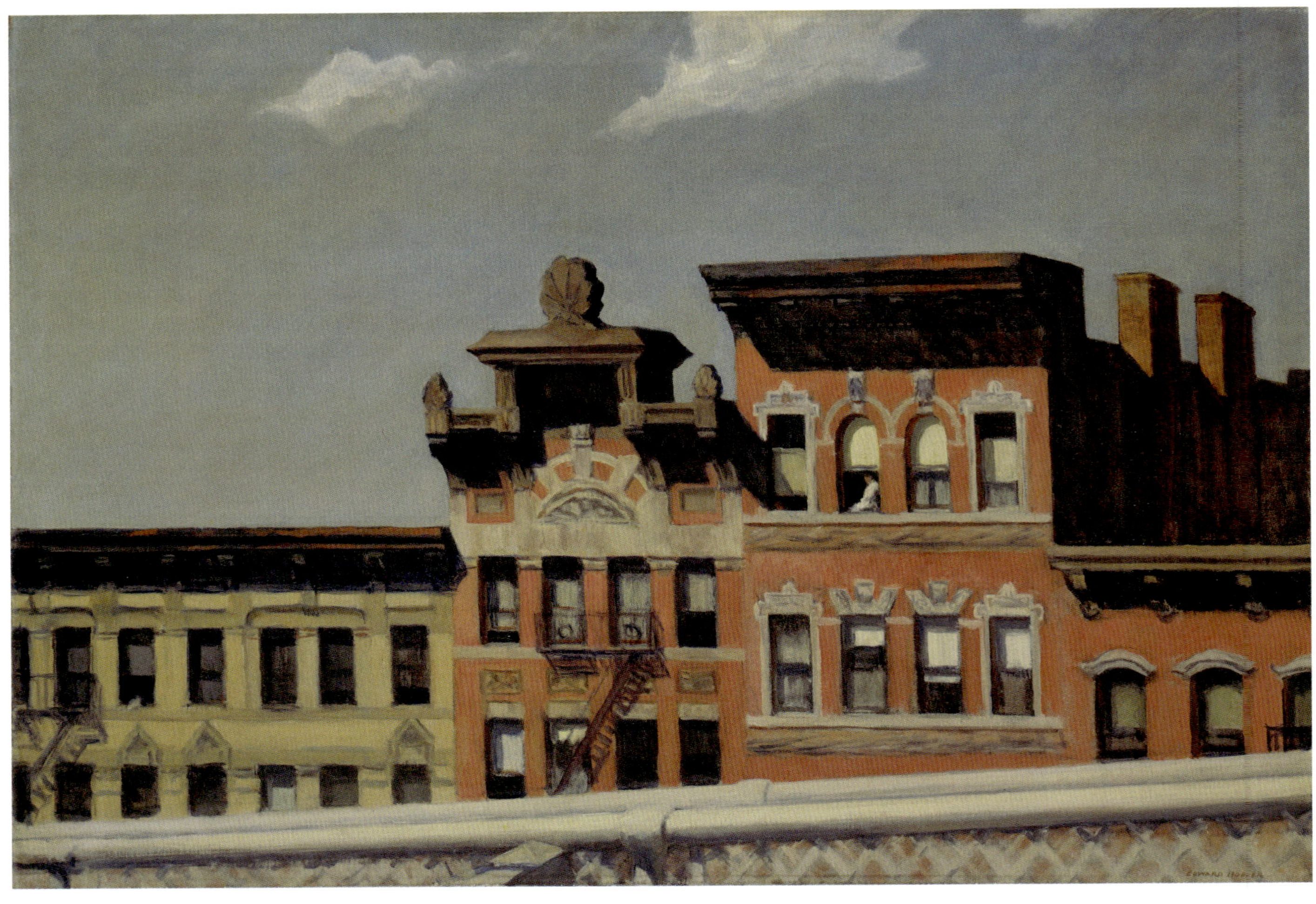

Another of Hopper's notable views from the pedestrian walkway of the Manhattan Bridge, a 1926 watercolor titled *The Lily Apartments* (fig. 159), conveys this perfectly.[12] Here, he depicted the intersection of Market and Henry streets just under the bridge (fig. 160), recording the bridge railing, billboard, and ornate apartment buildings with great accuracy. He even alluded to the inscription on the title building's upper corner, which read "The Lilly" before it was demolished in 1932 (not "Lily," as his wife, Jo, wrote in the Record Book).[13] This level of detail in an inexact medium shows how precisely Hopper observed and recorded his surroundings.

Although Hopper didn't classify these works as a series, the oil painting *From Williamsburg Bridge* (fig. 161) also looks out from an East River bridge's pedestrian walkway to a row of apartment buildings.[14] The preparatory sketch (fig. 162) shows how a momentary impression interested the artist sufficiently for him to record and eventually translate the view into a painting.[15] He seems to have been especially attracted to the formal complexities produced by the shadows on the buildings' facades, and detailed the darkness cast by their partially shaded windows, fire escapes, eaves, palmettes, and other ornamental embellishments. This vista must also have been appealing because the railing created a slanted wedge shape across the scene as the bridge sloped up toward its center, a formal device he used frequently.[16]

In these and other urban scenes (fig. 163), Hopper emphasized the oblique views afforded by bridges, elevated train lines, and the upper stories of buildings. Such raised perspectives offer unique configurations that differ from the typical pedestrian viewpoint, revealing the city to its inhabitants in new ways. This opportunity interested Hopper, and he used the act of drawing as an epistemological tool to mediate and comprehend these experiences. While many artists use drawing as a method for observation and to compose their paintings, Hopper's process and the masterful works that resulted are noteworthy because they demonstrate how finely attuned he was to the intricate dynamics and subtle beauty of New York.

161. *From Williamsburg Bridge*, 1928
Oil on canvas, 29 × 43 in. (73.7 × 109.2 cm)
The Metropolitan Museum of Art, New York; George A. Hearn Fund, 1937 37.44

162. Study for *From Williamsburg Bridge*, 1928
Fabricated chalk on paper, 8 9/16 × 11 1/16 in. (21.7 × 28.1 cm)
Josephine N. Hopper Bequest 70.457

163. *Study of the Upper Stories of 82 Washington Square East*, c. 1928
Fabricated chalk on paper, 8 7/8 × 11 7/8 in. (22.5 × 30.2 cm)
Josephine N. Hopper Bequest 70.234

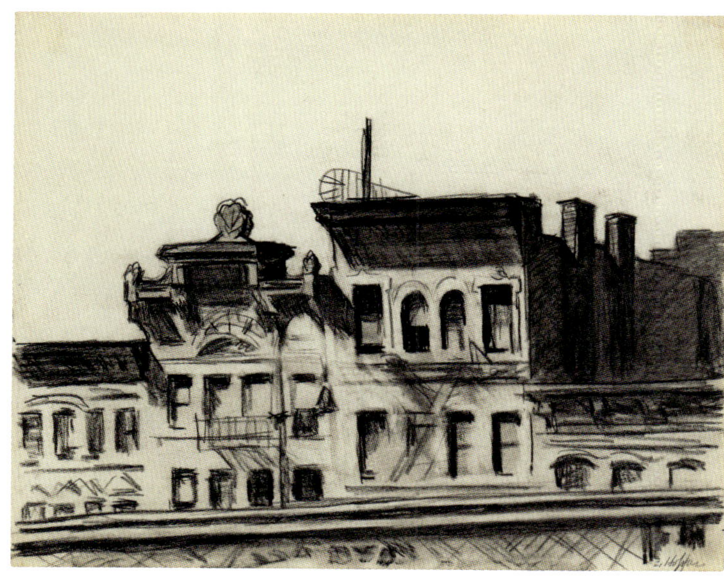

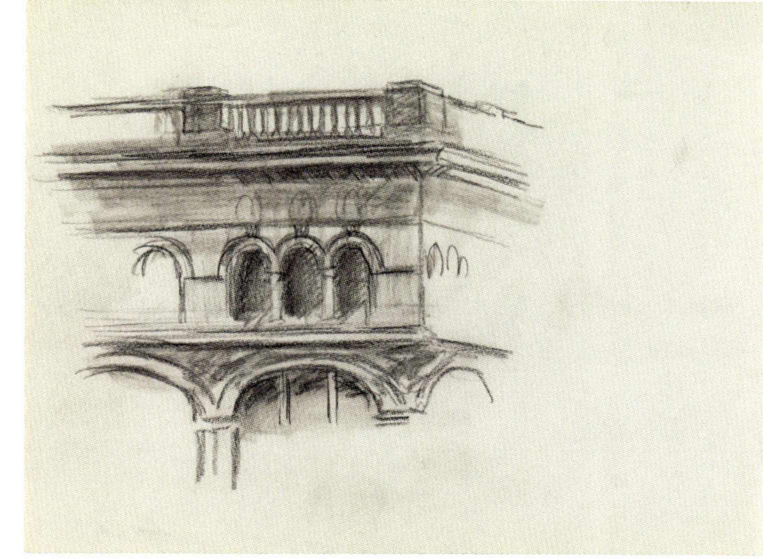

NOTES

1 On *Manhattan Bridge Loop*, see Lloyd Goodrich, *Edward Hopper* (New York: Harry N. Abrams, 1971), 142; Robert Hobbs, *Edward Hopper* (New York: Harry N. Abrams in association with the National Museum of American Art, Smithsonian Institution, 1987), 76–79; Gail Levin, *Edward Hopper: A Catalogue Raisonné*, vol. 3, *Oils* (New York: Whitney Museum of American Art in association with W. W. Norton, 1995), 180; Gail Levin, *Edward Hopper: An Intimate Biography* (New York: Rizzoli, 2007), 215; Avis Berman, *Edward Hopper's New York* (San Francisco: Pomegranate, 2005), 75–81. On the Manhattan Bridge and its construction, see Mark Alan Hewitt et al., *Carrère & Hastings, Architects* (New York: Acanthus Press, 2006), 1:210–20; Robert A. M. Stern, Gregory Gilmartin, and John Massengale, *New York 1900: Metropolitan Architecture and Urbanism, 1890–1915* (New York: Rizzoli, 1983), 50–53.
2 "Our excuse for bothering you with these details is that we sincerely believe that the project itself may be enlightening and worth while.... We shall appreciate very much any help you may be willing to give us." Charles H. Sawyer to Edward Hopper, October 17, 1939, Archives of the Addison Gallery of American Art, Phillips Academy, Andover, Massachusetts (hereafter cited as Addison Gallery Archives).
3 Press release sent to the *Lawrence Tribune* from the Addison Gallery of American Art, January 18, 1940, Addison Gallery Archives.
4 This statement is in the form of his written response to Sawyer's request, dated just two days after the first letter was sent. Hopper to Sawyer, October 19, 1939, Addison Gallery Archives.
5 Hopper to Sawyer, October 19, 1939, Addison Gallery Archives. Hopper later donated the two sketches to the Addison's collection; see Susan C. Faxon, Avis Berman, and Jock Reynolds, eds., *Addison Gallery of American Art: 65 Years; A Selective Catalogue* (Andover, MA: Addison Gallery of American Art, 1996), 146.
6 Whether or not Hopper took this photograph, he included it when he sent the two drawings to Hayes, who replied: "Thank you for your letter of the third and for the drawings and photographs which arrived safely, all of which will help us a great deal." Bartlett H. Hayes, Jr., to Hopper, December 11, 1939, Addison Gallery Archives. In another letter to Hopper, Hayes documents his trip to Truro to take a different set of photographs, "I enjoyed my trip to Truro to take the photographs and found Mrs. Hopper's map most helpful." These photographs showed the settings for three additional watercolors included in the last section of the exhibit (*Railroad Embankment*, 1932; *Cold Storage Plant*, 1933; and *Highland Light, North Truro*, 1930, lent by the Fogg Art Museum, Harvard University, and Mrs. H. C. Bentley of Boston). Hayes to Hopper, February 16, 1940, Addison Gallery Archives.
7 Hopper remarked about the sketches and photograph: "These small sketches were all that I had to work from, except a careful memorizing of color, form, character etc. You can see that the photos were of little use to me. In fact they were perhaps taken after the picture was painted. I do not remember. I know that I returned to the spot many times to refresh my memory while I was working upon the canvas." Hopper to Hayes, November 3, 1939, Addison Gallery Archives.
8 The wall text read: "The painter selects and constructs—the photographer selects and records."
9 The Museum of Modern Art retitled the exhibition *The Plan of a Painting* and charged twenty-five dollars for the show to run three weeks in each venue. It was shipped across America in four boxes, opening on August 1, 1941, at the Chicago Art Institute, and finishing its run on May 16, 1943, at Rollins College in Winter Park, Florida. Significant stops along the way included the Carnegie Art Institute in Pittsburgh, the San Francisco Museum of Art, and various university art galleries, including those at Skidmore, Middlebury, Brown, Cornell, and Swarthmore. Documents pertaining to the exhibition can be found in the Museum of Modern Art Archives, New York.
10 Hopper's statement was first published in Goodrich, *Edward Hopper*, 163–64; it is excerpted in Hobbs, *Edward Hopper*, 79; Levin, *Edward Hopper: A Catalogue Raisonné*, 3:180; Levin, *Edward Hopper: An Intimate Biography*, 215.
11 Hopper had direct architectural experience in 1934 when he designed the house in Truro, Massachusetts, where he and Jo lived and worked during the summer. Levin, *Edward Hopper: An Intimate Biography*, 257–59.
12 In addition to the works discussed here, Hopper depicted the bridge in three other watercolors: *Manhattan Bridge*, 1925 (Harvard Art Museums/Fogg Museum); *Manhattan Bridge*, 1925 or 1926 (Whitney Museum of American Art, New York); and *Manhattan Bridge Entrance*, 1926 (present location unknown). For this last work, Hopper also drew a diagram of the site to explain the composition and included this sketch in a March 19, 1928, letter to its buyer, A. P. Saunders; Hamilton College Library, Clinton, New York, cited in Levin, *Edward Hopper: A Catalogue Raisonné*, 2:105.
13 Edward Hopper Record Book I, 63. Hopper also describes the billboard to the left side of the painting with the same exactitude. He faithfully renders its Hebrew character, which could be a Hey (ה) or Dalet (ד). This makes sense for a view from the Manhattan Bridge; the area was predominantly Jewish from the 1900s through the 1930s, and billboards with Yiddish text were common. Perhaps Hopper depicted an advertisement with the Yiddish word for home, *heym* (היים); note that the last three letters on the bottom line of the billboard are "ome."
14 *From Williamsburg Bridge* was completed February 22, 1928. For more on this painting, see Levin, *Edward Hopper: A Catalogue Raisonné*, 3:179; Levin, *Edward Hopper: An Intimate Biography*, 213. On the Williamsburg Bridge and its construction, see Stern, Gilmartin, and Massengale, *New York 1900*, 50–51.
15 The view from the bridge today has changed significantly. Demolitions and post–World War II public housing construction created the Baruch Houses by Emery Roth & Sons to the north of Delancey Street and Cooperative Village to the south. See Richard Plunz, *A History of Housing in New York City* (New York: Columbia University Press, 1990), 268; Robert A. M. Stern, Thomas Mellins, and David Fishman, *New York 1960: Architecture and Urbanism between the Second World War and the Bicentennial* (New York: Monacelli Press, 1995), 141–43.
16 As the bridge slants down to the left of the frame, Hopper would have been facing north, if in Manhattan. The climactic scene of Jules Dassin's 1948 film *The Naked City* offers excellent views of the Williamsburg Bridge as police chase the villain up the pedestrian walkway. On this wedge form in Hopper's compositions, see Gail Levin, *Hopper's Places* (New York: Alfred A. Knopf, 1989), 12; Jean Gillies, "The Timeless Space of Edward Hopper," *Art Journal* 31, no. 4 (Summer 1972): 404–12.

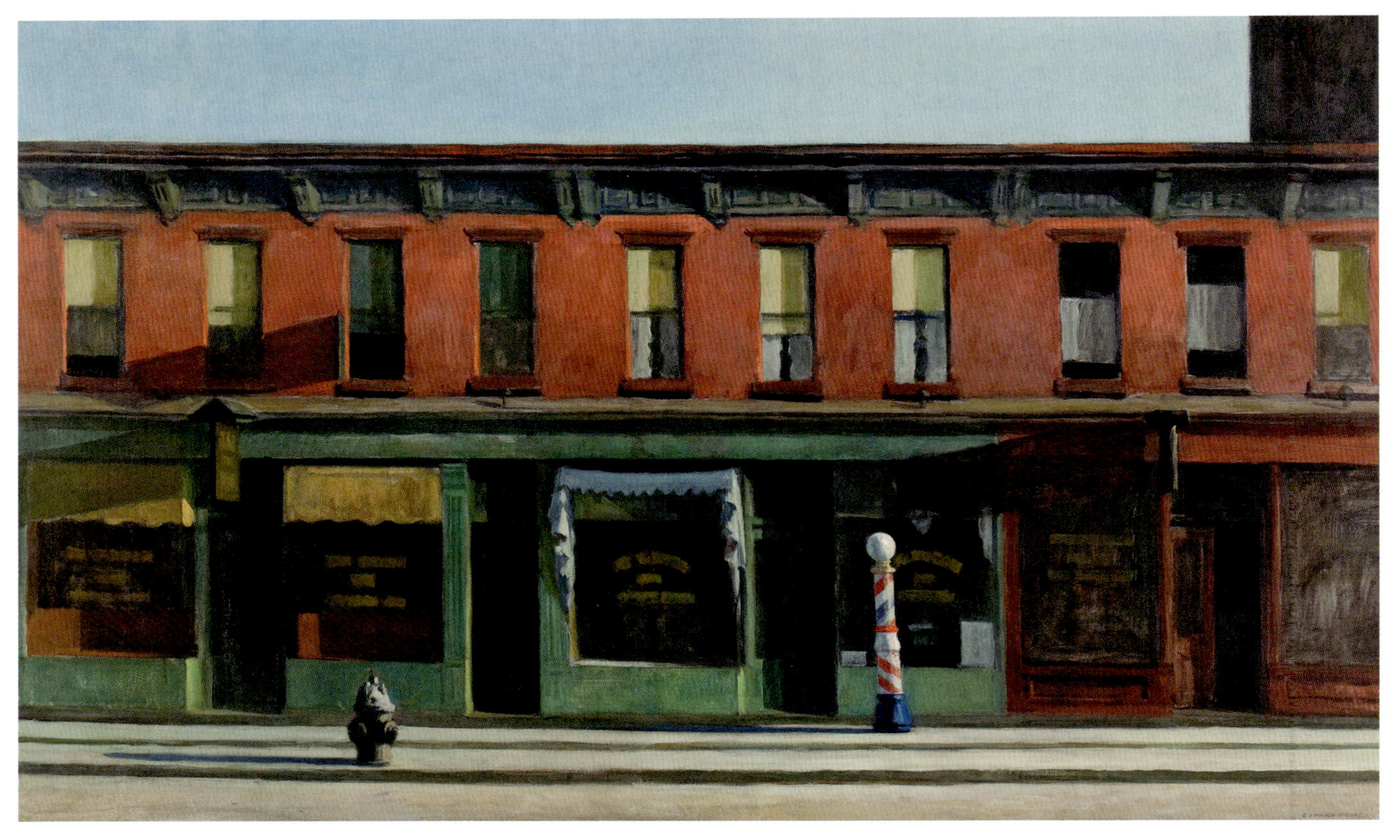

City Pendants: *Early Sunday Morning* and *Nighthawks*

CARTER E. FOSTER

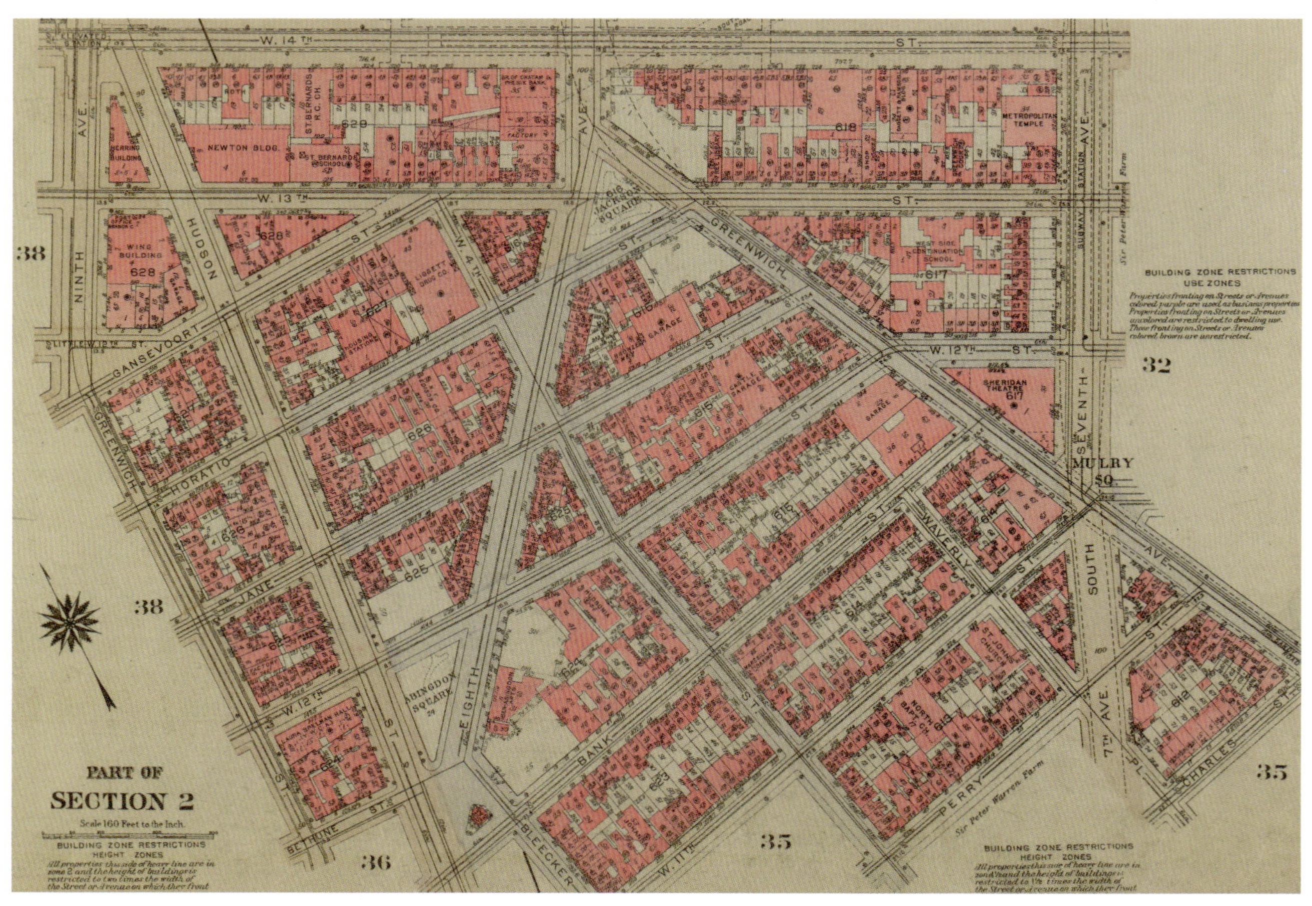

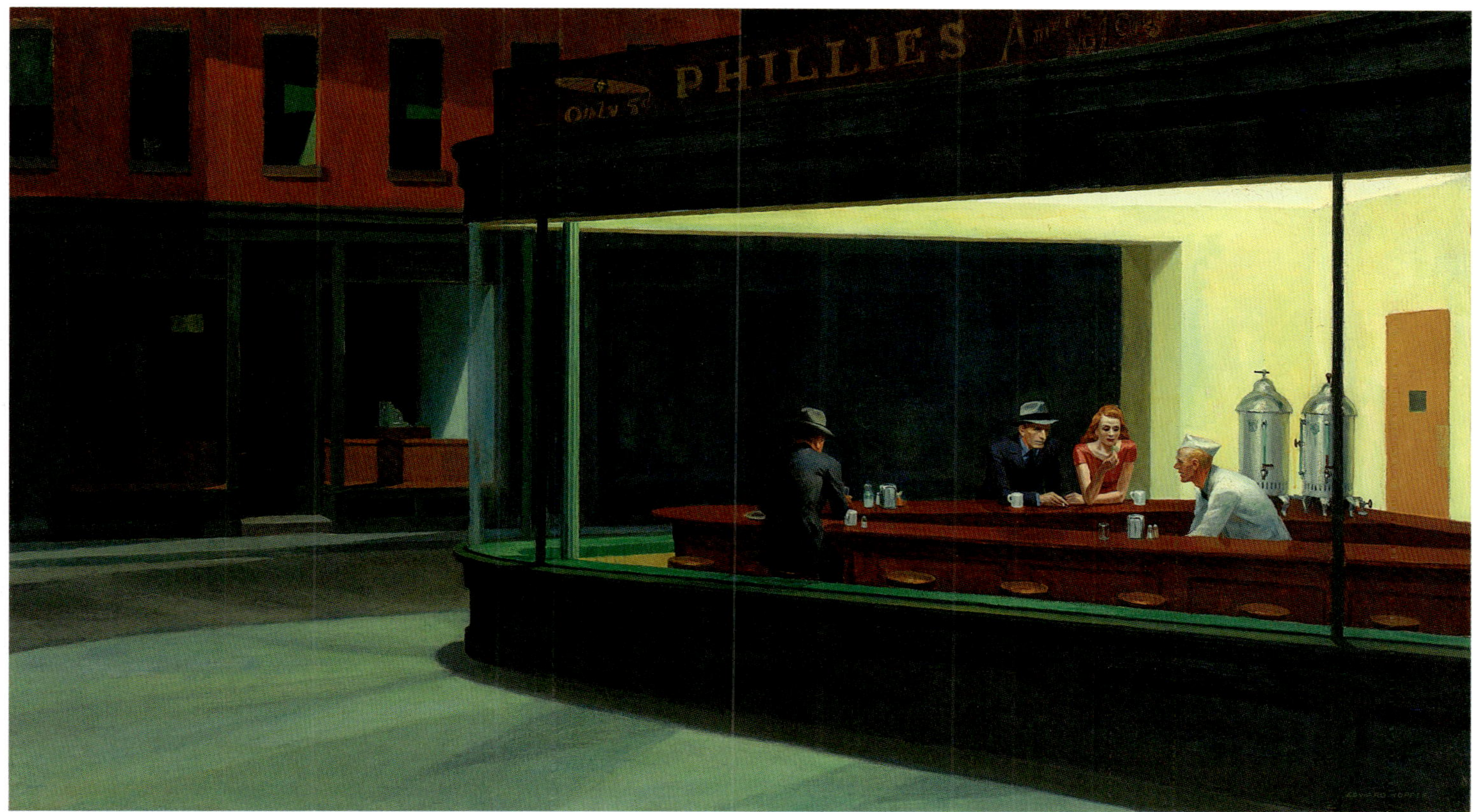

Edward Hopper lived at number 3 Washington Square North in New York's Greenwich Village almost his entire life. When he climbed down the seventy-four steps from his modest top-floor apartment and studio to street level and turned right, toward the west, he would have reached Sixth Avenue in two blocks. Turning right again and heading north for one more block would have brought him to Greenwich Avenue, which cuts diagonally against the regular Manhattan street grid and runs northwest from Sixth to Eighth Avenues. It defines one of the borders that sets apart this loose counter-grid of streets (now known as the West Village) from the rest of Manhattan, retaining an older plan that gives the area its picturesque irregularity (fig. 165). Hopper must have walked Greenwich Avenue often; it was near his home and there was a branch of the New York Public Library he frequented in a building that still stands near where the Avenue hits Jackson Square Park.[1] Greenwich Avenue's diagonal trajectory creates a series of triangular wedges where it intersects Eleventh, Twelfth, and Thirteenth Streets. The buildings conform to these shapes in acute angles, not unlike like the one formed by the wedge of glass that cuts through the dark in his most famous painting, *Nighthawks* of 1942. Hopper himself stated that the painting was inspired by one of these intersections.[2] Just four blocks north of where Greenwich and Seventh Avenues cross, between Fifteenth and Sixteenth Streets, there stood for most of the artist's lifetime a nondescript horizontal brick building that Hopper once called "7th Ave Shops," which had received his concentrated attention in 1930, when he painted *Early Sunday Morning*, arguably his second most famous work.

Early Sunday Morning and *Nighthawks* work beautifully in tandem as expressions of Hopper's experiences of New York on foot (figs. 164, 166).[3] Though painted more than a decade apart, they represent two related views and are almost exactly the same size and emphatically horizontal format.[4] A building very similar to the one in *Early Sunday Morning* forms the background of *Nighthawks*, as if the viewpoint of the former painting has been expanded in the latter to reveal more of its urban context. Taken together, they reflect Hopper's spatial and temporal impressions of the city, and specifically of his immediate neighborhood in New York—"The American city that I know best and like most."[5] And though we can tie them quite specifically to what Hopper saw, they also represent a more generalized urbanity in pre–World War II America. *Nighthawks* is a synthesis of several locales; *Early Sunday Morning* closely followed an actual (no longer extant) building—though the artist certainly took license, generalizing to make his work more universal and more ambiguous. With his evocative titles, the artist also gives the viewer permission to universalize them. Even so, knowing what he saw and which parts of New York inspired him as he conceived each of these key pieces in his career tells us much about how he worked, as well as the subtexts of personal and collective memory that he must have understood when he painted them.[6]

164. *Early Sunday Morning*, 1930
Oil on canvas, 35 3/16 × 60 in. (89.4 × 152.4 cm)
Purchase, with funds from Gertrude Vanderbilt Whitney 31.426

165. Plate 37 from *Land Book of the Borough of Manhattan, City of New York* (New York: G. W. Bromley and Company, 1930). The Lionel Pincus and Princess Firyal Map Division, The New York Public Library, Astor, Lenox and Tilden Foundations. Courtesy The Sanborn Library LLC

166. *Nighthawks*, 1942
Oil on canvas, 33 1/8 × 60 in. (84.1 × 152.4 cm)
The Art Institute of Chicago; Friends of American Art Collection 1942.51

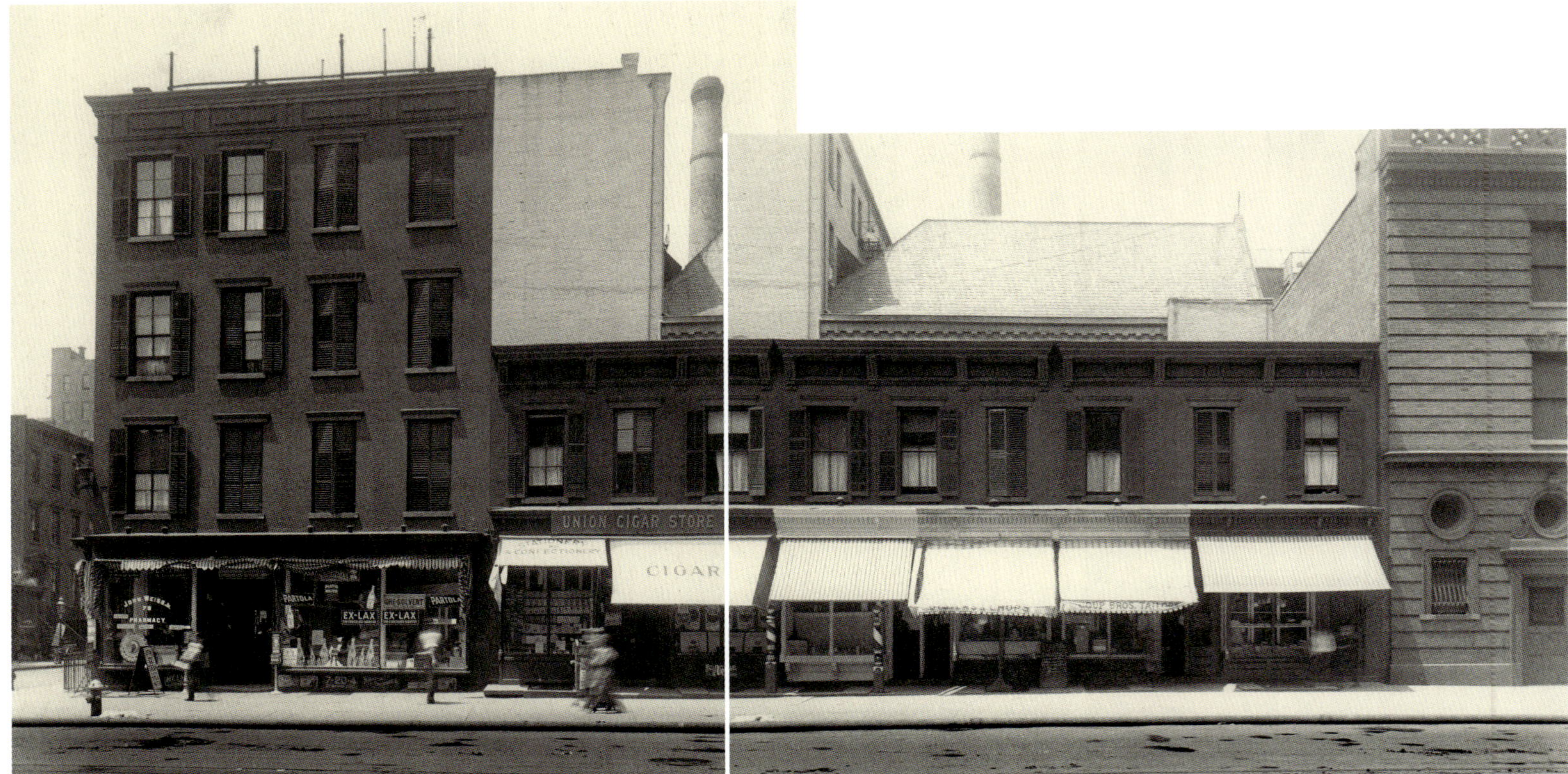

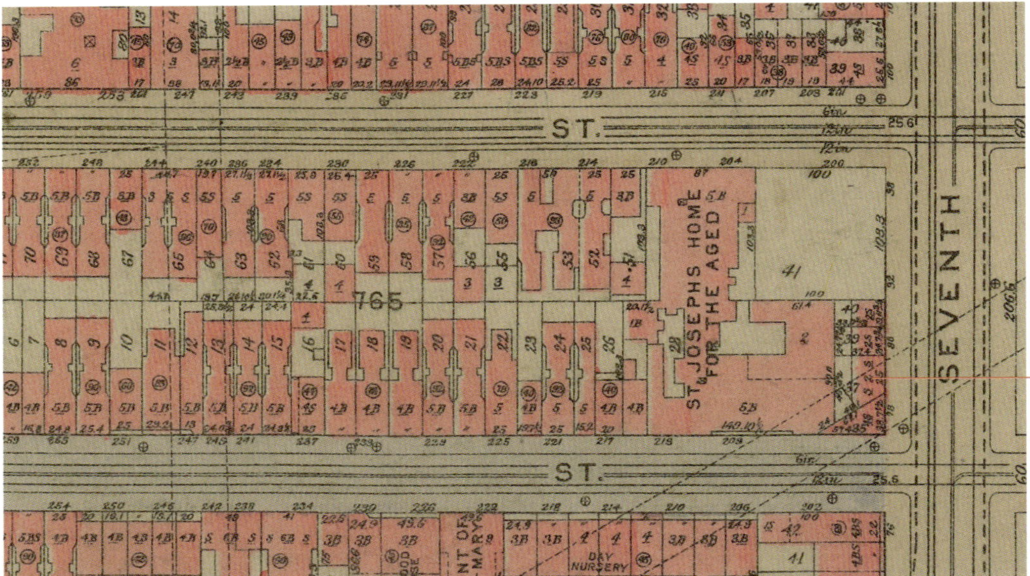

167. Seventh Avenue between Fifteenth and Sixteenth Streets, June 10, 1914. Subway Construction Photograph Collection, composite of Photographs #1003 and #1004. The New-York Historical Society 86450d, 86451d

168. Plate 42 from *Land Book of the Borough of Manhattan, City of New York* (detail) (New York: G. W. Bromley and Company, 1930). The Lionel Pincus and Princess Firyal Map Division, The New York Public Library, Astor, Lenox and Tilden Foundations. Courtesy The Sanborn Library LLC

The original title of *Early Sunday Morning* as recorded by his wife, Jo Hopper, in the artist's Record Books was "7th Ave Shops." Next to this title she wrote: "later changed to Early Sunday Morning."[7] Decades later, Hopper described the painting as "almost a literal translation of Seventh Avenue," adding "these houses are gone now."[8] Jo seems to have suggested titles for, or in fact given them to, many of Hopper's paintings; these titles are often consistent with her somewhat fanciful interpretive descriptions in the Record Books. Shifting the title from *7th Ave Shops* to *Early Sunday Morning*, from the mundane to the evocative, is also consistent with the way in which Hopper transformed the plain building into a poetic, atmospheric scene. The new title did the work justice, though the artist himself dryly challenged it much later when he stated, "It wasn't necessarily Sunday. That word was tacked on later by someone else."[9] In any case, it was not much later, because when the painting was sold to Gertrude Vanderbilt Whitney a few months after it was finished, the invoice (dated May 15, 1930) listed the title as "Early Sunday Morning."[10] The original title was never attached to the piece outside the artist's studio or Record Books. When it was shown at the Museum of Modern Art for Hopper's first retrospective in 1933, the catalogue used the current title and simply stated that it depicted Seventh Avenue in New York.[11]

We now know the exact building that inspired the work (fig. 167), thanks to the historic photographic record of the city, which has left us numerous images of this two-story brick structure.[12] It stood on the west side of Seventh Avenue between Fifteenth and Sixteenth

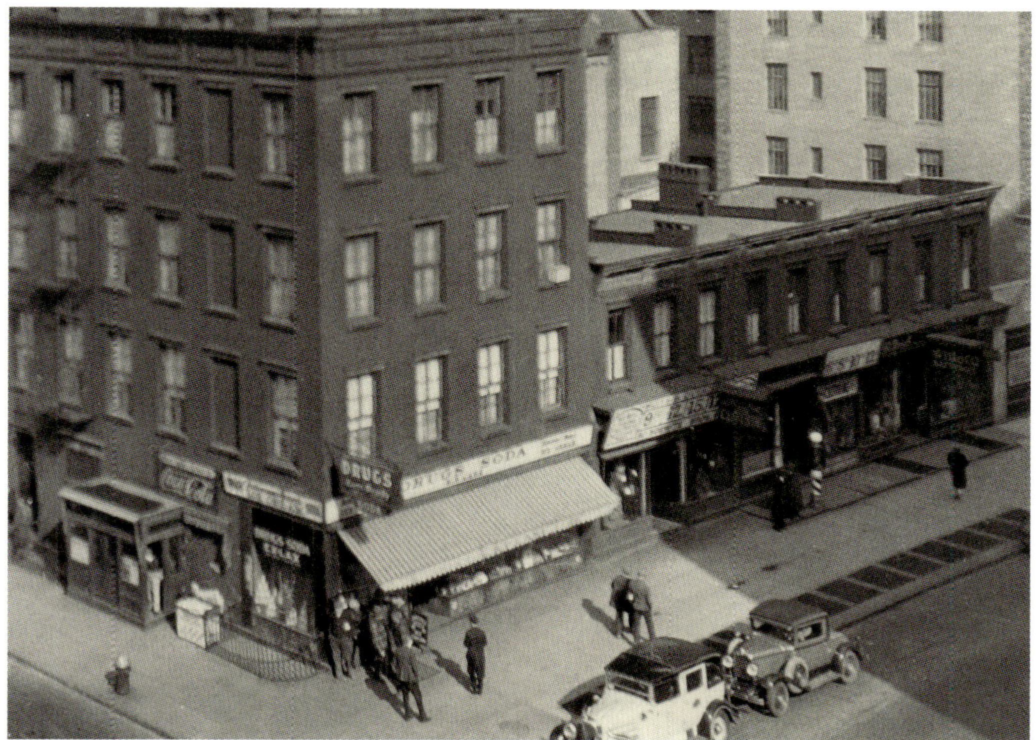

Streets, a "two-part commercial block" type of building[13] (zoned commercial on the first floor, residential on the second) on lots thirty-seven, thirty-nine, and forty, as recorded in the atlases regularly published in the nineteenth and early twentieth centuries (fig. 168). The 1930 and 1934 editions of the Bromley Atlases of Manhattan record the address of one of the shops as 88 Seventh Avenue.[14] A 1931 photograph commissioned by the New York Public Library (and still in their local history collection) taken from across the street and several stories above shows the building, the year after Hopper painted it, at an oblique angle, with a barber pole clearly visible in front (fig. 169).[15] In 1914 and 1918, a series of photographs (taken as part of subway construction projects) recorded the building in a frontal view and from other angles (figs. 167, 170–173).

A comparison between the actual building and *Early Sunday Morning* offers an interesting way into Hopper's thought process.[16] His self-described tendency to synthesize and amalgamate from multiple observed subjects is here distilled more than usual because of the painting's closeness to its source. He did change things, however, and it is telling to consider what "almost" refers to in his description of *Early Sunday Morning* as "almost a literal translation of Seventh Avenue." In the abstract, it refers to Hopper's memory and process: the breaks and mental shifts between the building as an observable object and Hopper's mind's-eye image of it that occurred during the act of painting it. Comparing the photographs with the painting allows us, in fact, to understand more precisely the "decay" the artist wrote about in his 1933 "Notes on Painting."[17]

The painting has a subtle, strange unreality, mostly due to the play of shadows and light. As in *Le Bistro* (see fig. 102), Hopper painted as if there was more than one source of sunlight. The long blue shadows of the fire hydrant and barber pole are roughly parallel with the two long horizontals formed by the curb and the stepped-up elevation of the sidewalk. On the other hand, the long rectilinear shapes cast onto the building by the projecting signs perpendicular to it slant downward. The three small, top-shaped ventilation pipes in the molding just below the second-story windows cast their shadows slightly upward, while the brackets supporting the cornice at the top slant upward more sharply. One notices such inconsistencies only on close looking, but they beautifully elucidate the artist's desire to alter the world, however subtly, when he painted it. Many have also noted that this painting cannot realistically depict Seventh Avenue in New York on any Sunday morning given that street's north-south axes and the fact that the sun rises in the east. Hopper had no problem bending light to his own will.

The building at 88 Seventh Avenue, which went up in 1878, was less than a mile from the studio and apartment where he had lived since 1913, and it would have been a familiar sight when he decided to paint it. The subway construction photographs taken in 1914 and 1918 give us an idea of what the artist saw. Back then, the upper windows all had shutters. In 1914, barber poles stood on either side of the shop's window, in from the sidewalk and close

169. Fifteenth Street at the northwest corner of Seventh Avenue (detail), 1931. Photograph by Percy Loomis Sperr. Irma and Paul Milstein Division of United States History, Local History and Genealogy, The New York Public Library, Astor, Lenox and Tilden Foundations Image ID: 711337F

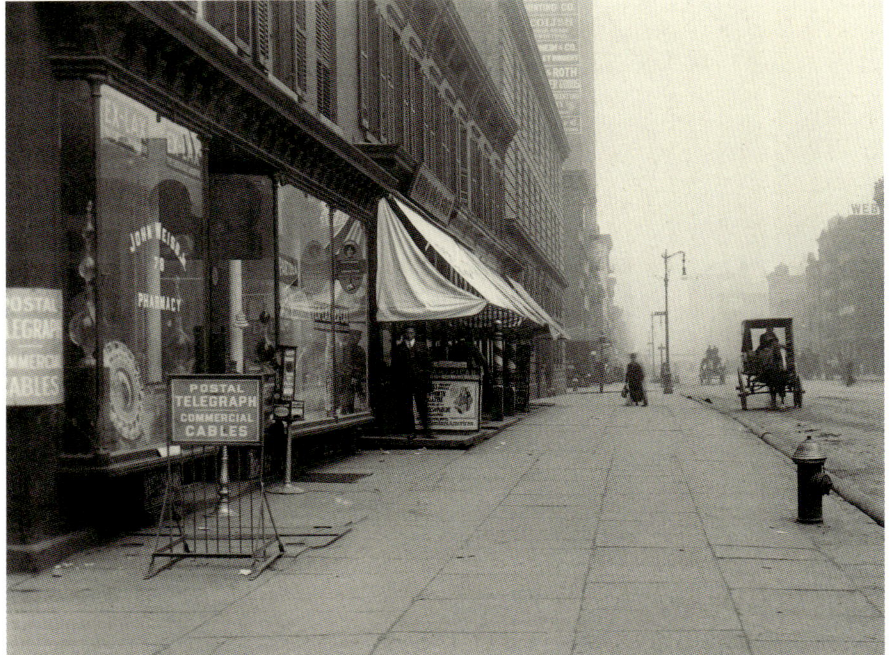

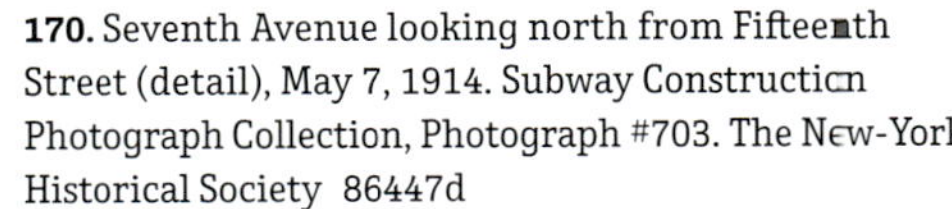
170. Seventh Avenue looking north from Fifteenth Street (detail), May 7, 1914. Subway Construction Photograph Collection, Photograph #703. The New-York Historical Society 86447d

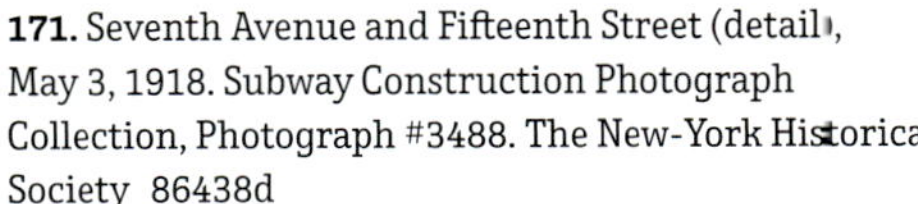
171. Seventh Avenue and Fifteenth Street (detail), May 3, 1918. Subway Construction Photograph Collection, Photograph #3488. The New-York Historical Society 86438d

172. Seventh Avenue and Fifteenth Street (detail), May 3, 1918. Subway Construction Photograph Collection, Photograph #3489. The New-York Historical Society 86439d

173. Seventh Avenue and Fifteenth Street (detail), May 3, 1918. Subway Construction Photograph Collection, Photograph #3489. The New-York Historical Society 86439d

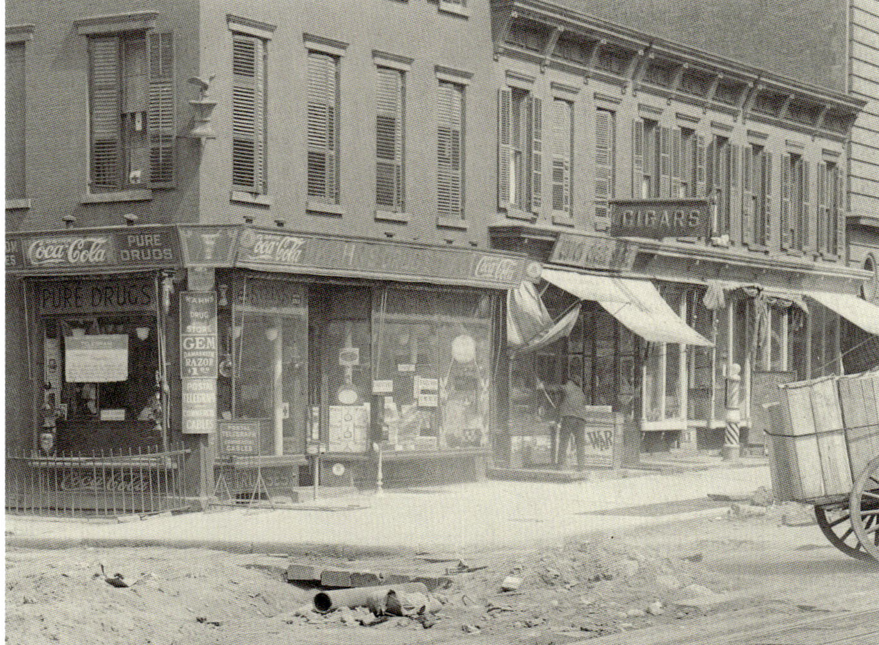

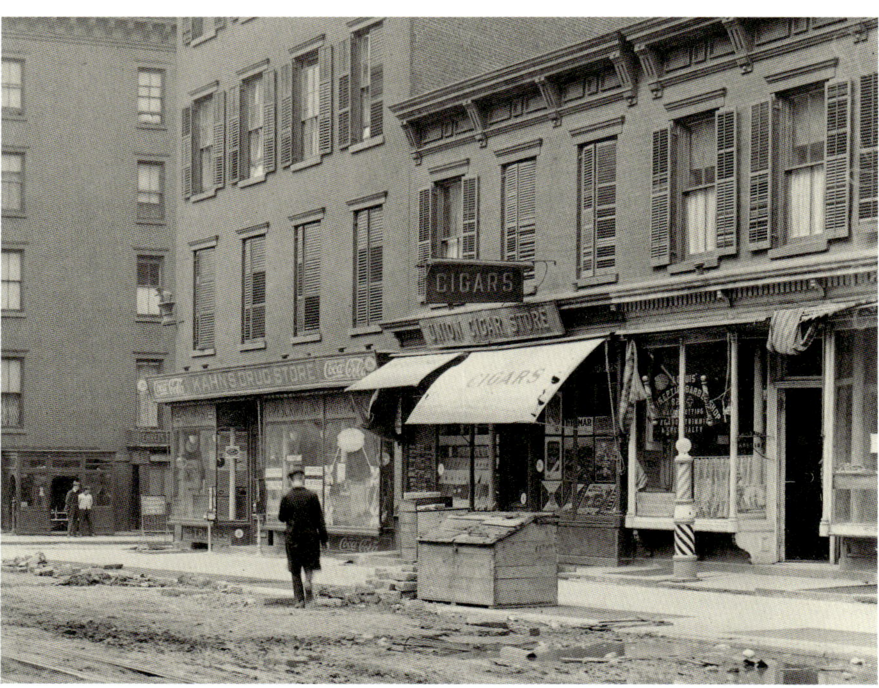

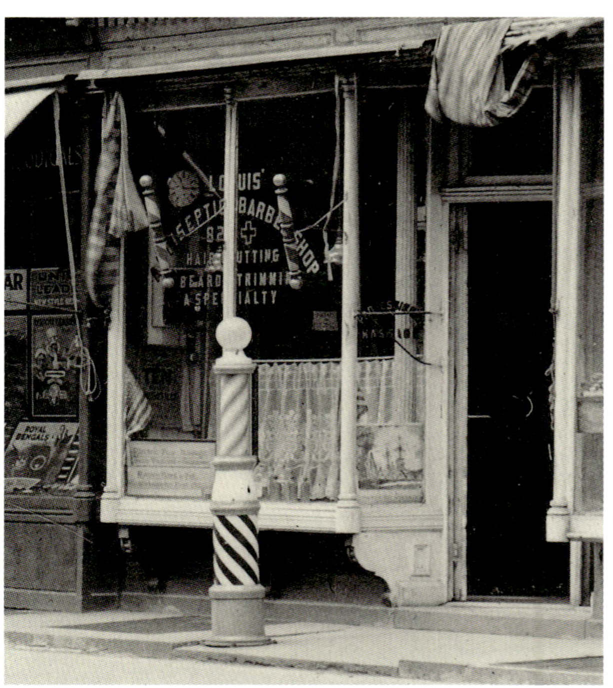

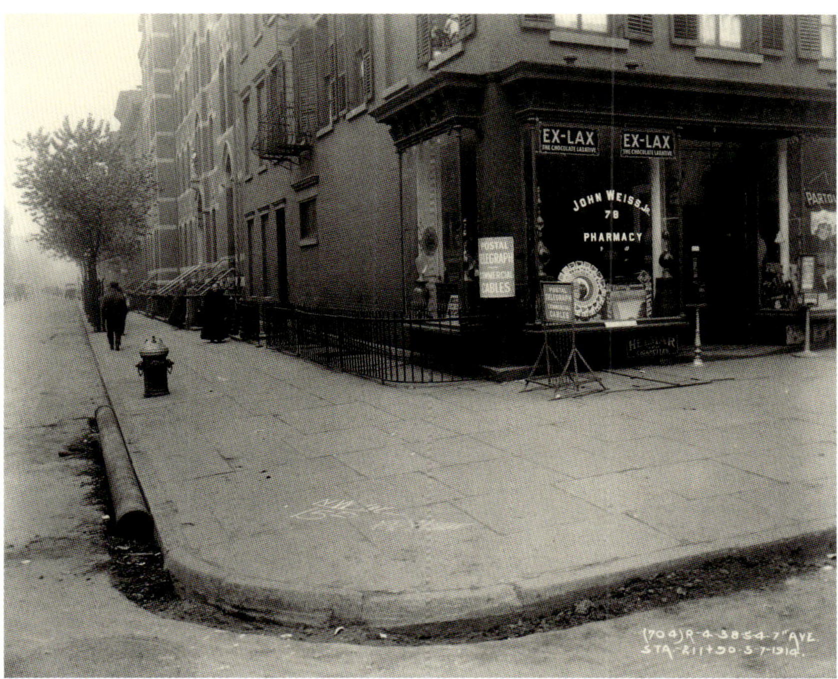

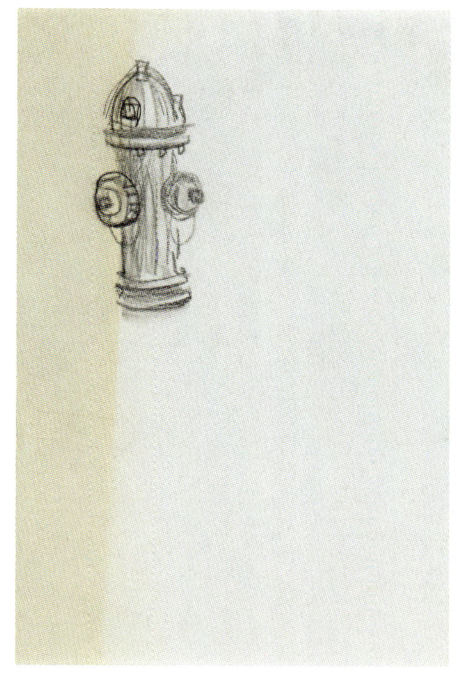

to the building (see fig. 167). In 1918, these were gone and a single pole, set out further on the sidewalk was in place, as well as a projecting, perpendicular sign that had been added to the facade toward the left (see figs. 171, 172). The photographs also record the building's shops, which were, from left to right: the Union Cigar Store; a barbershop (its sign appears to read "LOUIS' ANTISEPTIC BARBER SHOP" in a 1918 image [fig. 173]); a restaurant whose sign reads "Oysters & Chops"; the Coup Bros. Tailors; and possibly a bakery at the north end. In 1931, there was still a barbershop as indicated by the pole in front, but the shutters had been removed, as in the painting. The cigar store had become a clothing store; Coup Bros. was now something called "Willard"; and various other signs had been added to the facade, including another projecting, perpendicular one toward the right (see fig. 169). The shop awnings, so prominent in the earlier photographs, seem to have been mostly removed by 1931. None of the photographs show a fire hydrant directly in front of the building, but there were two on the southwest corner of the intersection of Fifteenth Street and Seventh Avenue—one squat and shorter (fig. 174), as in the painting, and one taller and longer (see fig. 170), as in the only known extant drawing we can associate with this campaign of work by Hopper (fig. 175). Perhaps he made no further studies, as it would have been impractical to stand in the middle of Seventh Avenue or even on the busy sidewalk opposite.[18]

The point of view is crucial to *Early Sunday Morning*'s effect. Hopper made the building emphatically frontal, its facade precisely parallel to the picture plane with almost no sense of receding perspective, and no recessional lines save for the brackets supporting the upper cornice and the corners of the lower center windowsill and doorframe.[19] He painted the structure right up to the lateral edges of the canvas, giving us the sense that the building continues its expanse. Hopper even spoke of this as one of his intentions in his work: to give a sense of continuation beyond the scene.[20] His emphasis on the lateral and horizontal come through in other painted elisions, for example, the elimination of the brackets in the molding between the stories to create an uninterrupted line. Some writers have puzzled over the play of the shadows in the foreground. The first, closest to the bottom edge, clearly represents the curb where the sidewalk meets the Avenue. Between it and the edge of the building is another long horizontal line, less thick, which also runs the length of the canvas. This step up from the sidewalk was in fact in front of the actual shops, but it was irregular and served to level off their entrances from the sidewalk, which sloped slightly downward (see fig. 170). Hopper brushed it into a steady, level line as befitted his painting. He did something similar in the cornice at the top of the structure. The two paired brackets that support the cornice in roughly the middle third of the painting also have a source in reality: the actual building was decorated with three identical pressed-metal cornices of four brackets each, with decorative panels in between, supporting a deeper crown molding that topped off the facade (see fig. 167). These decorations—which were serially produced for generic building types rather than for specific buildings—were probably intended for a single-width brownstone building; it took three of them to cross the facade, so their brackets doubled up twice where the cornices break. Hopper, however, chose to paint the moldings above as a continuous horizontal.

174. Seventh Avenue and Fifteenth Street (with John Weiss Jr. Pharmacy), May 7, 1914. Subway Construction Photograph Collection, Photograph #704. The New-York Historical Society 86448d

175. Study for *Early Sunday Morning*, 1930
Fabricated chalk on paper, 6 × 4 in. (15.2 × 10.2 cm)
Josephine N. Hopper Bequest 70.823

More interesting still is the artist's delicate, complex tinkering with the building's form. Here is a piece of humble architecture whose appeal lay in its simplicity: its windows, doors, signs, and lettering, its vertical and horizontal lines, and the objects around it—namely, the hydrant and the barber pole—come together in a commanding, masterfully painted composition.[21] All of these features were there at 88 Seventh Avenue and observable when Hopper was walking through New York in the teens and twenties. Yet it is Hopper's cumulative manipulation of these elements that quietly transforms these quotidian shops into the powerful *Early Sunday Morning*.[22] The artist's deepest and most subtle changes come from the way he simultaneously elongated and compressed the structure and changed the rhythm and arrangement of its parts. The building was essentially symmetrical, with nine windows evenly distributed across its upper story, each one under a pair of brackets, so that each group of three windows corresponded to one of the three separate cornices and more or less lined up between their brackets (see fig. 167). Hopper unbalanced it by adding a tenth window at the far left and extending the cornice by one bracket.[23] Below, he painted four entrances to the shops, not three as there actually were. In adding one he compressed all the doorways, making the proportions smaller and narrower in relation to the building. The doorways he painted do have two doors, but the doors themselves seem too large for their openings. The reddish brown door visible at the far right seems cut off and too small—strangely thin and narrow, as are the green doors in the next opening. Hopper also dropped down the transoms over each doorway to make the openings lower, adding to the sense of compression. He narrowed the shopwindows, making them single panes without a dividing mullion. And though large barber poles were common on the streets of New York in Hopper's day, this one is certainly larger than the one that stood there. It reaches to the top of the doorway near which it stands, and almost to the top of the shopwindow. As an anthropomorphic stand-in for the lack of human beings in this scene, this pole is a giant. Hopper was an absolute master of this manner of scale disjunction—visual innuendo suggesting alternate reality—and it is often one of the eeriest techniques he deploys. The pole's prominence in the composition, however, paradoxically seems to hide the fact that it is out of scale; its white head fully catching the strong light, it seems too present to be wrong. In contrast, the dark openings of the shop entrances underscore the pole's oversize when one notices that, were it a man, it could not fit through their shadowy space.[24]

Hopper used the subjectivity of his own memory as a filter when painting this scene. The artist knew the building—which was itself a remnant of a vanishing New York when he painted it—but did not need to record it closely. Rather, his changes invested it with content, as he filled the fissures between the thing itself and his memory of it with his own suggestive elisions, making the mundane poetic in the process. The direct comparison of the painting and its real subject allow us to see this. Some changes are incredibly subtle, as discussed above. Some, like the awnings that seem not to have been there when Hopper made his painting, but which were part of the structure's recent history and the artist's memory of it, are more obvious. This filter of memory in Hopper is crucial to the process he developed and used over and over in his mature paintings. A final specific example in *Early Sunday Morning* is the lettering on the glass windows—Hopper represents them and even imitates some of their forms from the shops he knew, such as the curving arc of the letters from the barbershop (see fig. 173). But the photographs we have, taken from the middle of the street and even a bit further back than what we see in *Early Sunday Morning*, show us that these phrases were clearly legible from this distance. Hopper blurred them because such specificity was not what he wanted and not what he remembered, or wanted to remember, when painting.

By focusing tightly in on this building Hopper completely decontextualized it from its dense urban setting, where it was packed into New York's built environment and surrounded by many other types of architecture. He was painting a remnant of another era—the Garfield administration, a different age for America and New York. In this sense, *Early Sunday Morning*

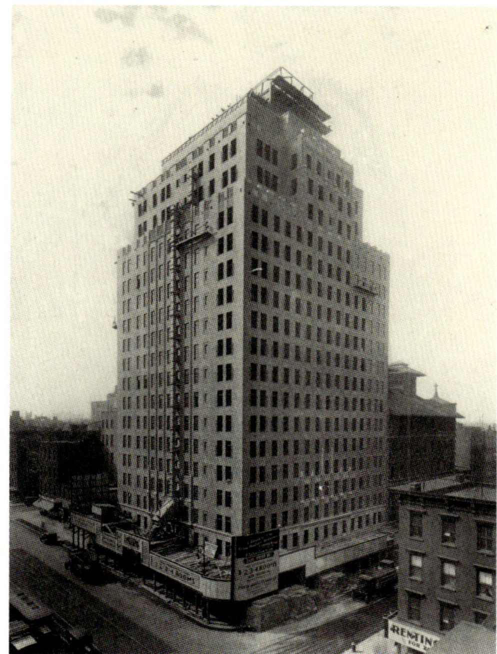

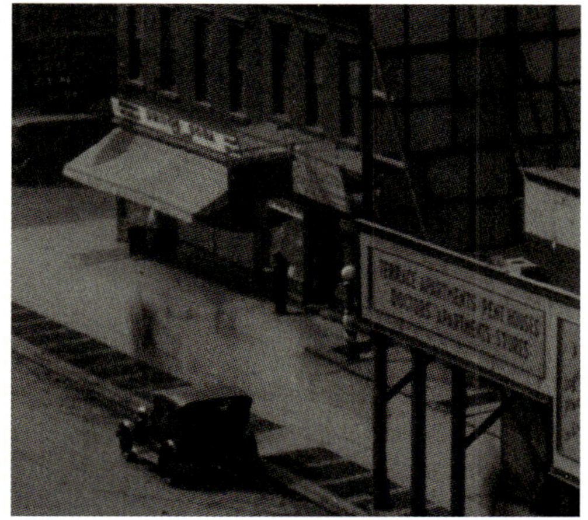

could be compared to Walker Evans's photographs of small-town America, as this building type could be found all over the country and the work beautifully evokes the downtown shops of "Anywhere, USA."[25] Critics often note that the black square in the upper right corner is Hopper's only acknowledgment of the skyscrapers that were taking over the city in which he lived.[26] In fact, we now know that two large apartment buildings were going up around 88 Seventh Avenue at the same time Hopper was painting it—each relatively tall for the time, built in a similar style, and both still there. The one now on the northwest corner of Sixteenth Street and Seventh Avenue was just being finished in 1930 (figs. 176, 177), replacing a much smaller four-story building from the nineteenth century.[27] The changing urban fabric of New York was quite literally surrounding the Seventh Avenue shops that interested Hopper right when he was painting them. One can reasonably speculate here that Hopper chose to paint the structure precisely because of this—its mundane qualities were becoming historic and distinctive, an architectural remnant from the city's past intertwined with Hopper's own personal memory. The building was torn down in 1939 and replaced by the brick apartment house that stands today. Three years later Hopper would begin *Nighthawks* and the building in *Early Sunday Morning* would cede its ground to a modern-looking glass wedge illuminating a triangular slice of nocturnal city.

At the end of 1941 photographer Arnold Newman captured Hopper in front of the stretched canvas on which the painter would soon begin blocking out *Nighthawks* (fig. 178).[28] It stands on the easel he had built years before,[29] a blank horizontal expanse awaiting his brush. Hopper developed the particular space of *Nighthawks* (see fig. 166) with a series of overlapping diagonals stepping back from the picture plane. The wedge of the diner creates two of them, its form beginning beyond the right edge, extending in from it, and receding into the picture's space, while the red facade in the background zags back from left to right to parallel the diner's far window. These planes of architecture carve the pictorial space and set up a rhythm with the plane of the picture. The proportions and the edges of the canvas are thus

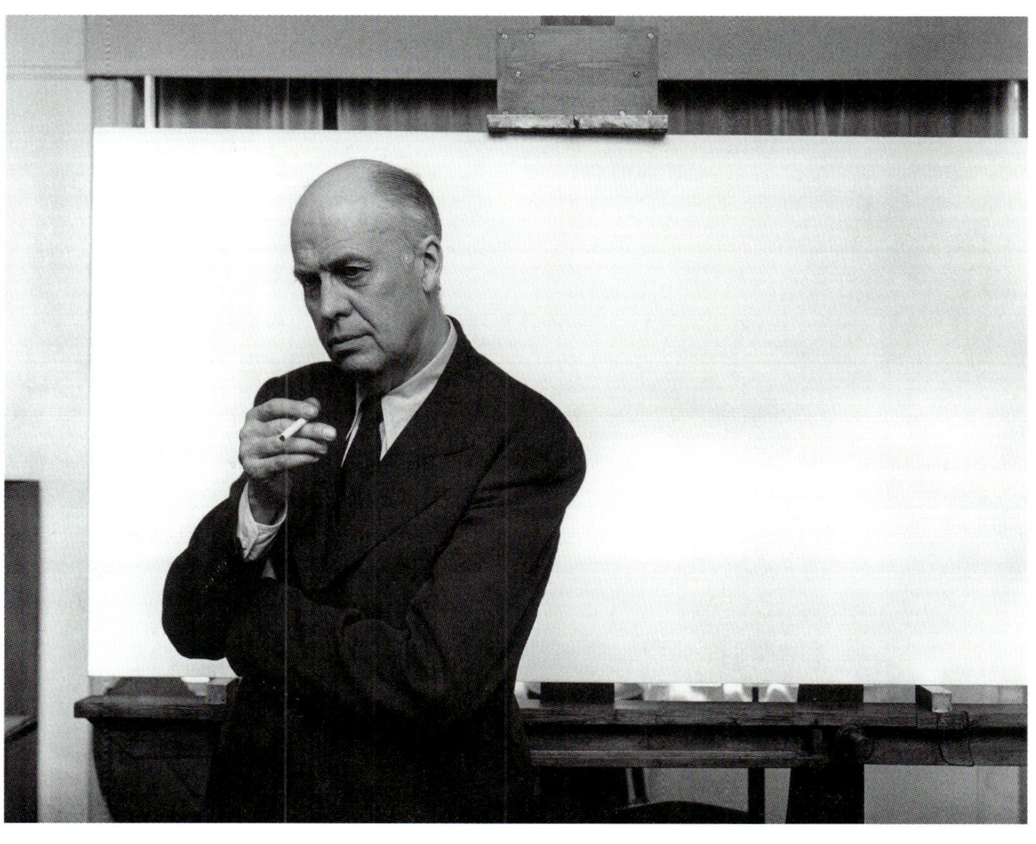

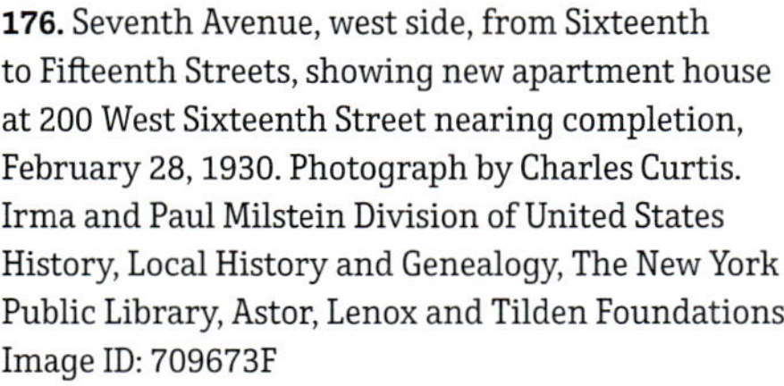

176. Seventh Avenue, west side, from Sixteenth to Fifteenth Streets, showing new apartment house at 200 West Sixteenth Street nearing completion, February 28, 1930. Photograph by Charles Curtis. Irma and Paul Milstein Division of United States History, Local History and Genealogy, The New York Public Library, Astor, Lenox and Tilden Foundations Image ID: 709673F

177. Seventh Avenue, west side, from Sixteenth to Fifteenth Streets, showing new apartment house at 200 West Sixteenth Street nearing completion (detail of fig. 176)

178. Arnold Newman (1918–2006). *Portrait of Edward Hopper*, November 1, 1941. Arnold Newman Collection/ Getty Images

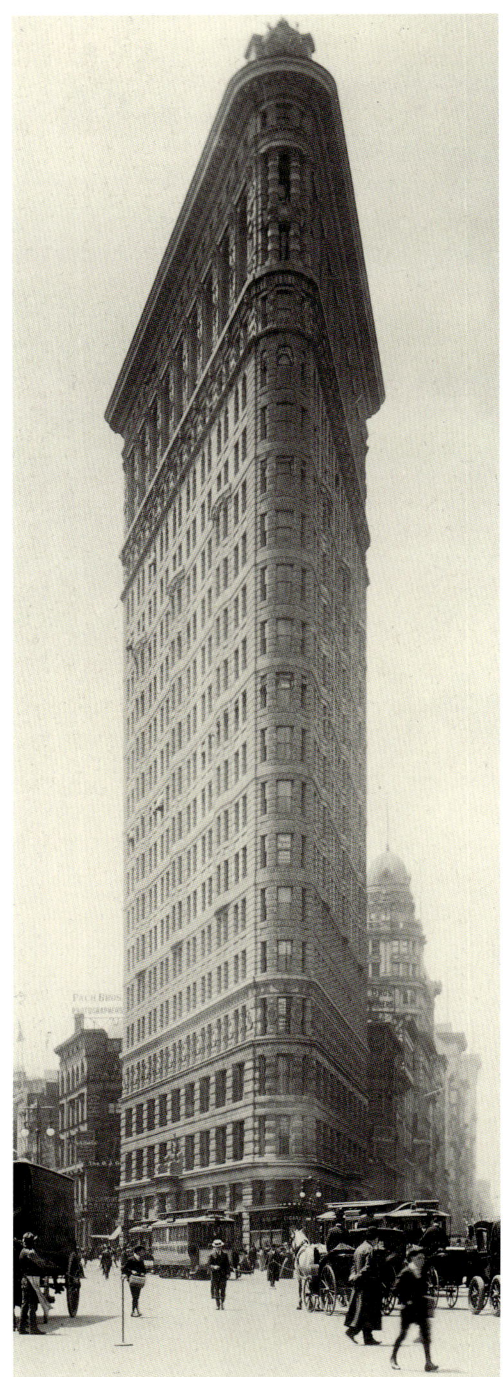

179. Broadway at the corner of Fifth Avenue and Twenty-third Street (Flatiron Building) (detail), c. 1910s. Photograph by Wurts Brothers. Irma and Paul Milstein Division of United States History, Local History and Genealogy, The New York Public Library, Astor, Lenox and Tilden Foundations Image ID: 1509085

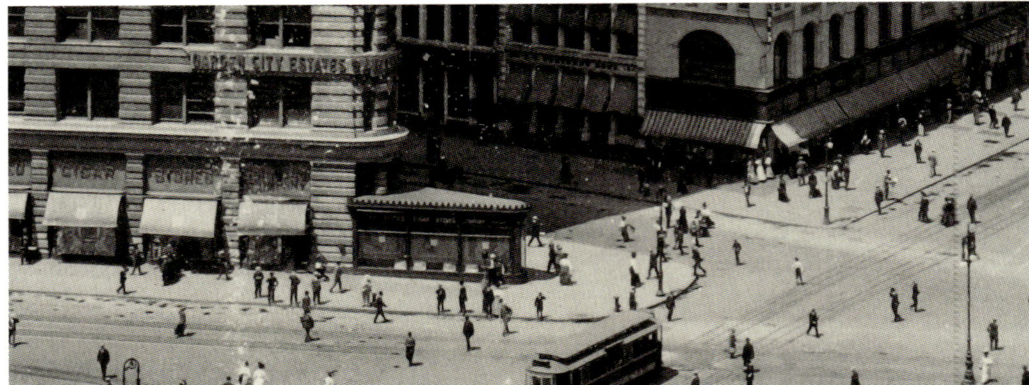

180. Twenty-third Street at Fifth Avenue and Broadway (Flatiron Building) (detail), 1908. Photograph by Brown Brothers. Irma and Paul Milstein Division of United States History, Local History and Genealogy, The New York Public Library, Astor, Lenox and Tilden Foundations Image ID: 711655F

integral to the composition and to the specific urban spatial geometry it depicts. As noted earlier, it was a geometry that Hopper saw at the corners along Greenwich Avenue, his stated inspiration for the work (see figs. 165, 181–189).[30] That Hopper worked out these proportions carefully is borne out by inscriptions on some of the preparatory drawings, which reveal him numerically scaling up his composition (his typical practice), which he had carefully worked out in chalk, to the size he intended.[31] Hopper either built his own stretchers or ordered them specifically for each painting; deciding on its dimensions was the first act toward the final composition.[32] By the time he posed for Newman he had completed at least some of his chalk studies, figured out his ratios, and must have had much of the idea for the painting in his head.

The streamlined simplicity of the *Nighthawks* diner, with its curved form, expanses of glass, and lack of ornament, relates to the Art Deco and machine-age aesthetics that flowered in New York in the 1920s and 1930s, and which were widely expressed in the architecture of the 1939 World's Fair.[33] Set against the nineteenth-century red-brick building behind it, the diner wins this face-off between old and new and implies a developing, changing city.[34] Its brightness, likely referencing newly available fluorescent lighting, further underscores its modernism. On the other hand, Hopper seems to have been at least partly inspired by an older structure, the "prow" at the tip of the Flatiron Building (1902) at Twenty-third Street and Broadway, a form he would have known for decades by the time he painted *Nighthawks* (fig. 179). Though set in a busy intersection rather than a dark side street, the Flatiron's prow is remarkably similar to Hopper's diner[35] despite its Beaux-Arts ornamentation; it is the same shape, made mostly of glass, and includes a curved glass panel at its apex. It even contained a cigar store at one point (fig. 180), echoed by the "Phillies 5¢" sign in the painting.[36]

The striking voyeurism of *Nighthawks* comes from the brightly lit, aquarium-like view we have of the protagonists sandwiched between large plate glass windows; the viewer is distanced from the scene by darkness and glass, but it is very much a pedestrian's viewpoint.[37] The intersections along Greenwich Avenue indeed contained many of the painting's elements. At both Eleventh and Twelfth Streets, low triangular wedges extended out in acute angles from corners of taller buildings. The narrower of these, at Eleventh, still stands. As seen in photographs from 1914 and 1918 it was a tailor and dry cleaning establishment (figs. 181, 182); by 1926 it had become a newsstand, with a sign above advertising tobacco products (figs. 183–185). At Twelfth Street, just up from the Sheridan Theatre (which Hopper frequented and made the subject of a 1937 painting; see fig. 213) and continuing out from it in the same brick was a wider triangular building with large plate-glass windows (figs. 186–189). In 1926 it was called "Crawford Lunch," and this is most likely the establishment to which Hopper referred when he stated that *Nighthawks* "was suggested by a restaurant on Greenwich Avenue where two streets meet."[38] One photograph shows a view through its largest window to the inside (figs. 188, 189), where we see a man seated with his hat silhouetted against the back window, through

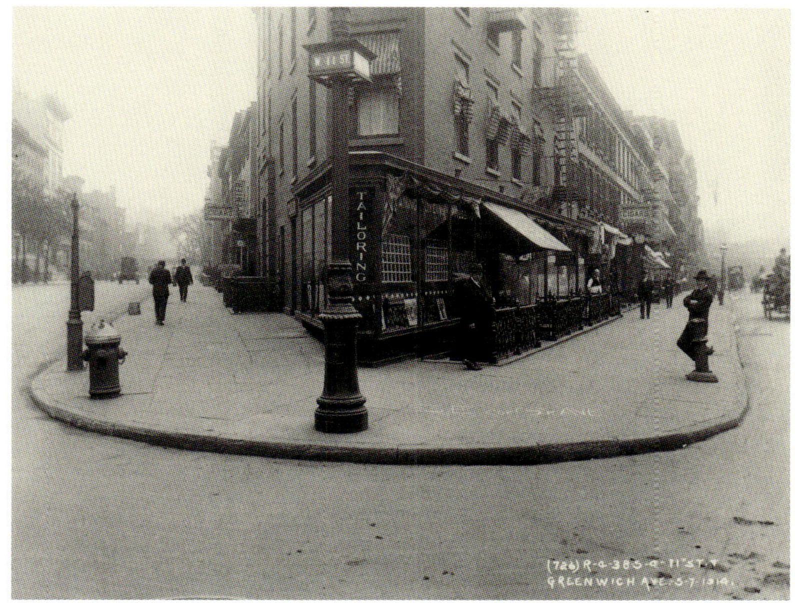

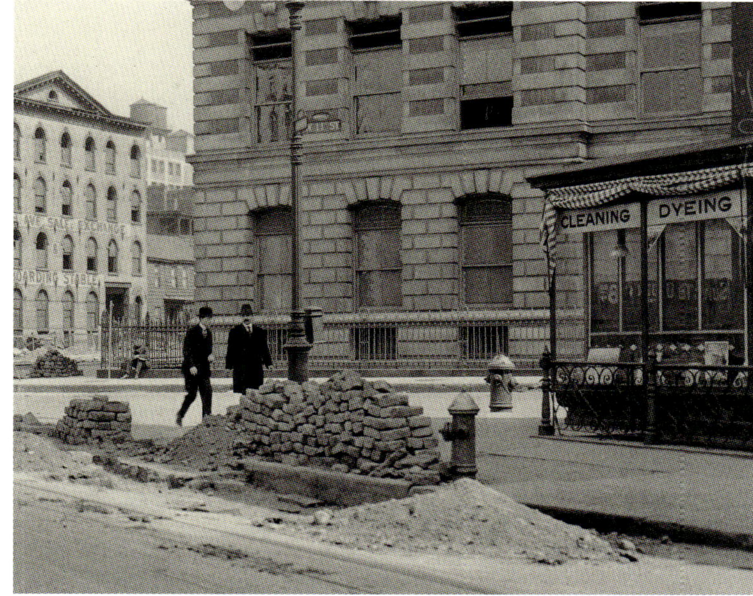

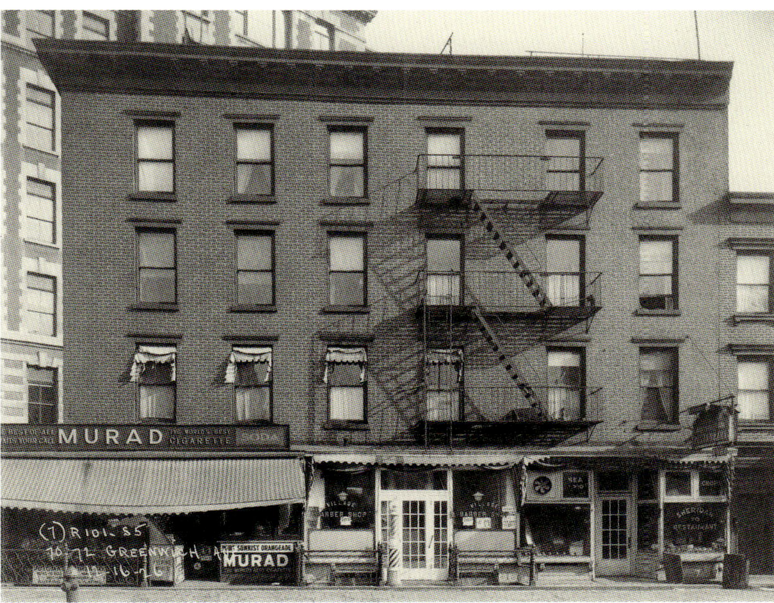

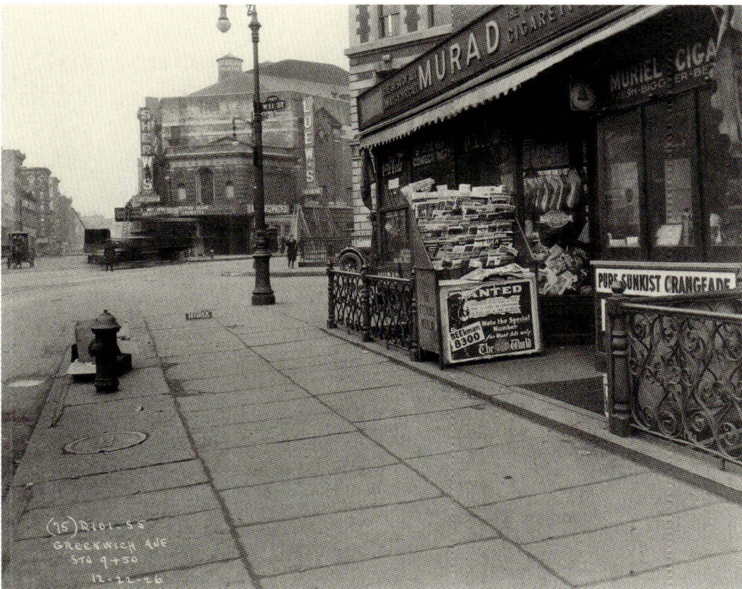

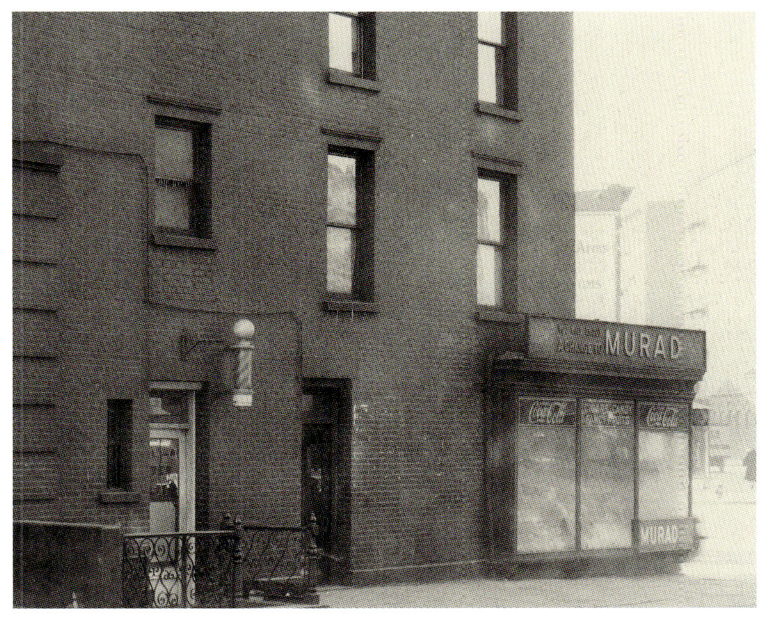

181. (top left)
Eleventh Street and Greenwich Avenue, May 7, 1914. Subway Construction Photograph Collection, Photograph #726. The New-York Historical Society 86449d

182. (top right)
70 Greenwich Avenue at Eleventh Street (detail), May 3, 1918. Subway Construction Photograph Collection, Photograph #3480. The New-York Historical Society 86440d

183. (middle left)
70–72 Greenwich Avenue at Eleventh Street, December 16, 1926. Subway Construction Photograph Collection, Photograph #7. The New-York Historical Society 86441d

184. (middle right)
Eleventh Street and Greenwich Avenue, December 16, 1926. Subway Construction Photograph Collection, Photograph #75. The New-York Historical Society 86443d

185. (bottom right)
70–72 Greenwich Avenue at Eleventh Street (detail), December 16, 1926. Subway Construction Photograph Collection, Photograph #9. The New-York Historical Society 86442d

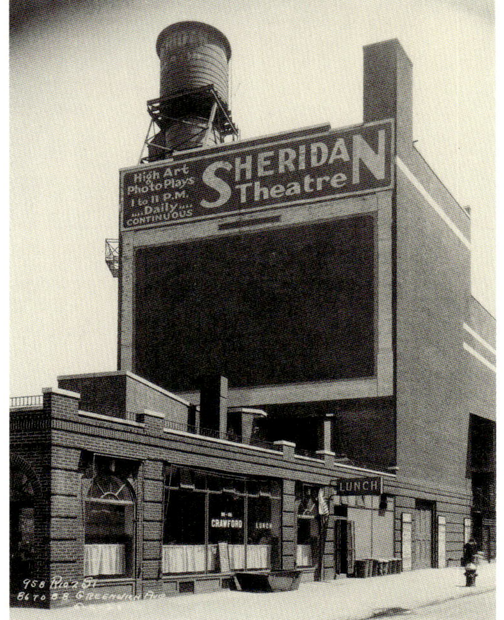

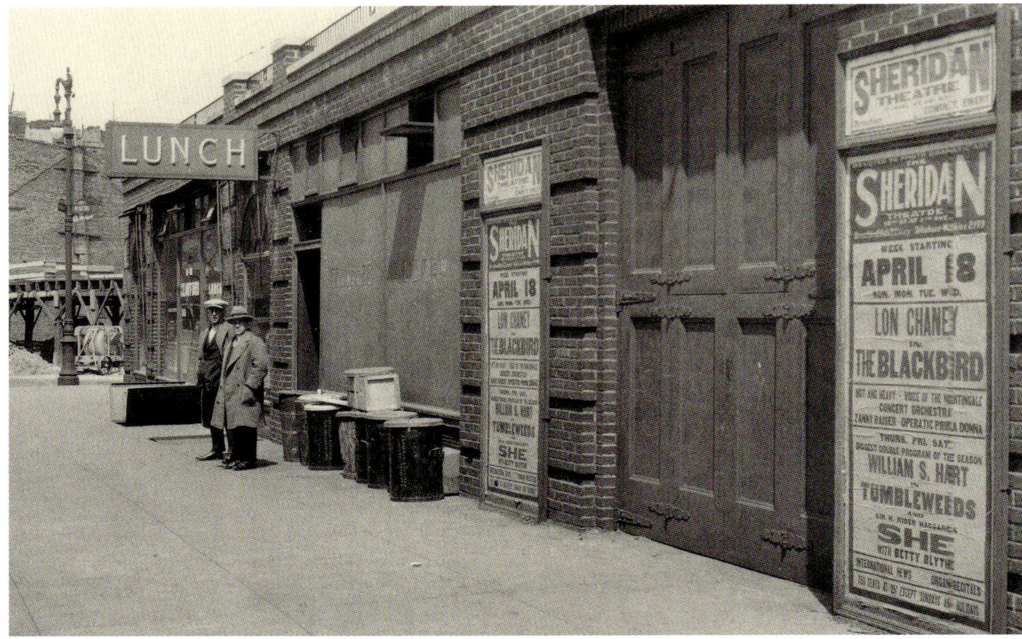

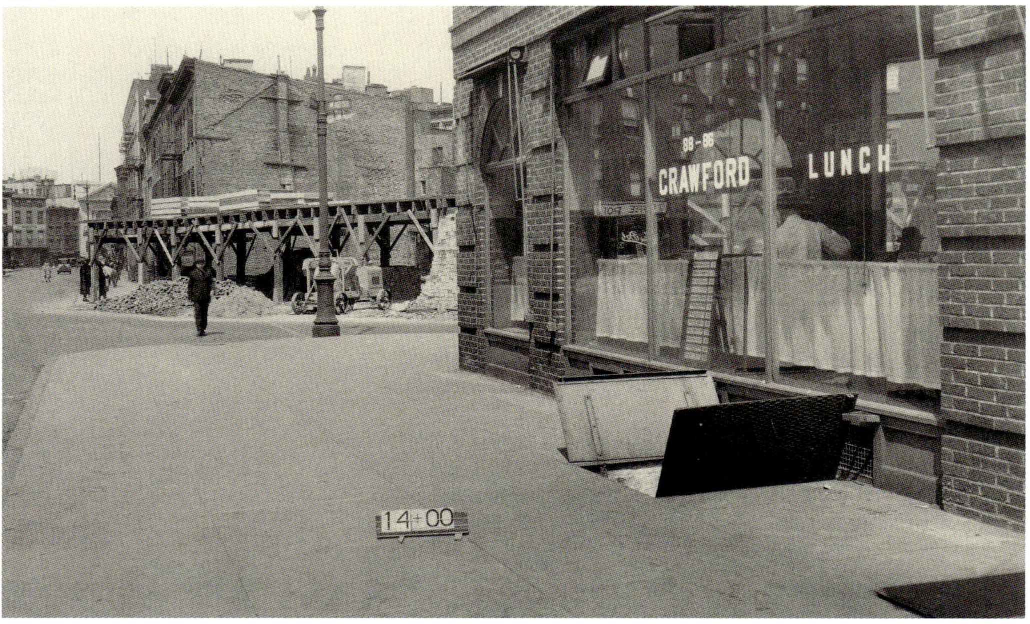

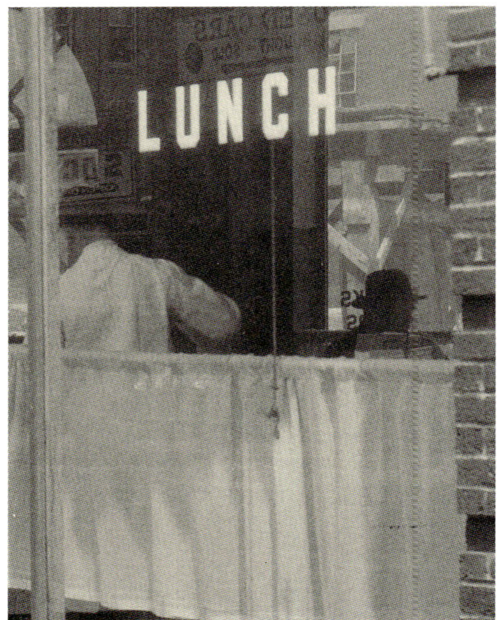

186. 86–88 Greenwich Avenue at Twelfth Street (with Crawford Lunch), May 4, 1926. Subway Construction Photograph Collection, Photograph #958. The New-York Historical Society 86446d

187. 86–88 Greenwich Avenue at Twelfth Street (with Crawford Lunch) (detail), April 18, 1926. Subway Construction Photograph Collection, Photograph #915. The New-York Historical Society 86444d

188. 86–88 Greenwich Avenue at Twelfth Street (with Crawford Lunch) (detail), April 18, 1926. Subway Construction Photograph Collection, Photograph #916. The New-York Historical Society 86445d

189. 86–88 Greenwich Avenue at Twelfth Street (with Crawford Lunch) (detail), April 18, 1926. Subway Construction Photograph Collection, Photograph #916. The New-York Historical Society 86445d

which we can view beyond to Twelfth Street—a scene no doubt similar to what Hopper observed countless times on walks past Crawford Lunch, and one not unrelated to what he ended up painting.

The nineteen extant studies show how Hopper, inspired by the wedge-shaped intersections along Greenwich Avenue and by the Flatiron Building, worked out different aspects in suites of related drawings that fall into three categories: sketchbook pages, compositional studies, and detailed figure/drapery studies. The order of their execution, though perhaps impossible to determine with precision, is nonetheless interesting to consider.

The sketchbook sheets record Hopper's observations from life, and their details and poses ended up, more or less, in his painting. These drawings are small in size, about four by seven inches each; the book would easily have fit in one hand, perfect for use out in the world. They have qualities of rapid execution, with outlines and zigzag hatching put down relatively sparely in the waxy crayon Hopper often used, with little manipulation or blending of the medium. His wife later stated that he went to the Dixie Kitchen, a diner in Midtown, to draw the coffee urns (fig. 190).[39] Details drawn from life of a saltshaker, a creamer, and a cruet also made it into the painting (see fig. 195). Two of the sheets record three-quarter views of the upper half of a man seated at a counter and wearing a suit and a fedora (figs. 191, 192). The poses are similar in both, but they seem drawn from different people, as the hats and faces are not the same. Four other sheets contain studies of a similarly dressed figure from behind (figs. 193–196). Two of these seem to have been made in succession, depicting the same man; one can imagine the artist quickly flipping his page over to capture the subject's slight shift in posture (see figs. 193, 194). Perhaps Hopper made these sketches in Crawford Lunch—

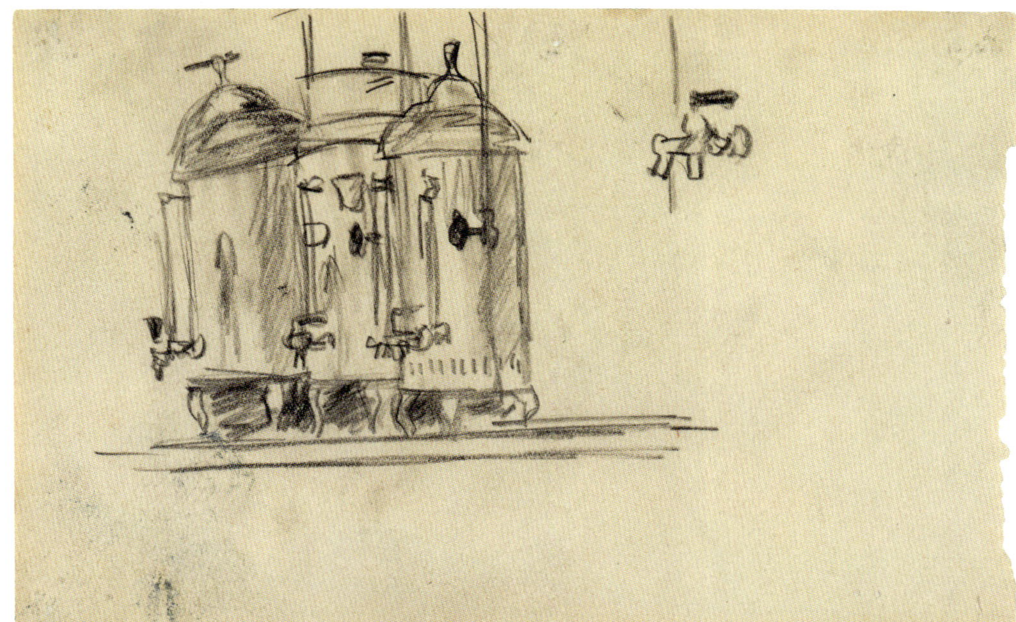

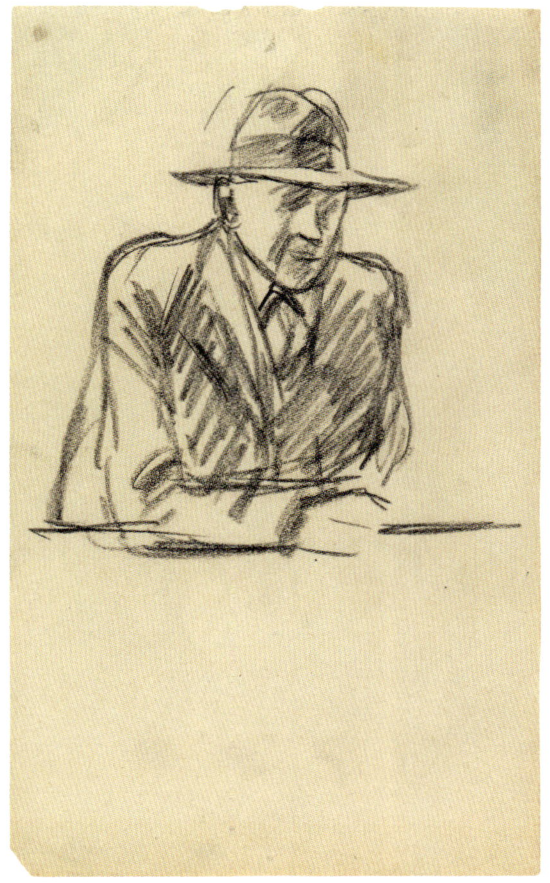

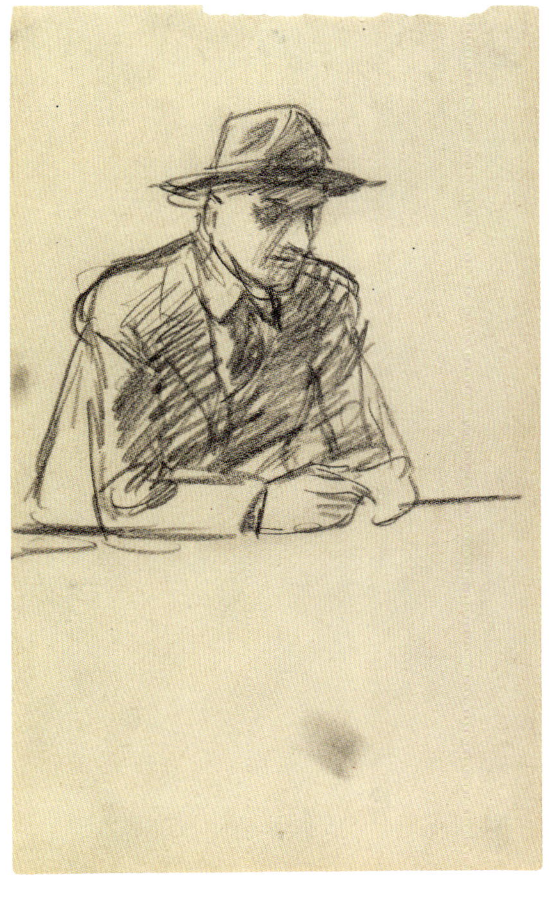

190. Study for *Nighthawks*, 1941 or 1942
Fabricated chalk on paper, 4 7/16 × 7 3/16 in. (11.3 × 18.3 cm)
Josephine N. Hopper Bequest 70.192

191. Study for *Nighthawks*, 1941 or 1942
Fabricated chalk on paper, 7 3/16 × 4 7/16 in. (18.3 × 11.3 cm)
Josephine N. Hopper Bequest 70.188

192. Study for *Nighthawks*, 1941 or 1942
Fabricated chalk on paper, 7 1/4 × 4 7/16 in. (18.4 × 11.3 cm)
Josephine N. Hopper Bequest 70.189

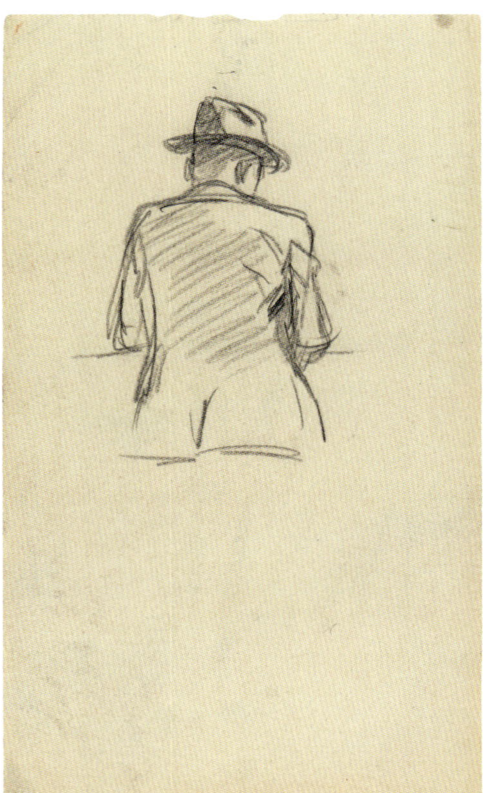

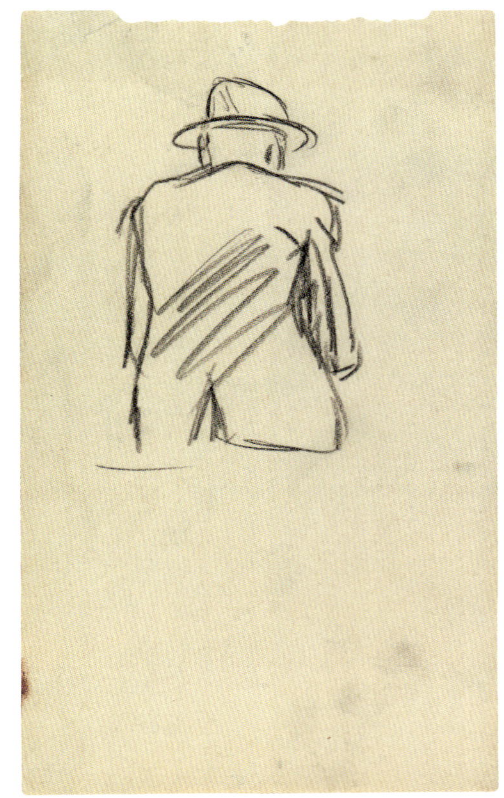

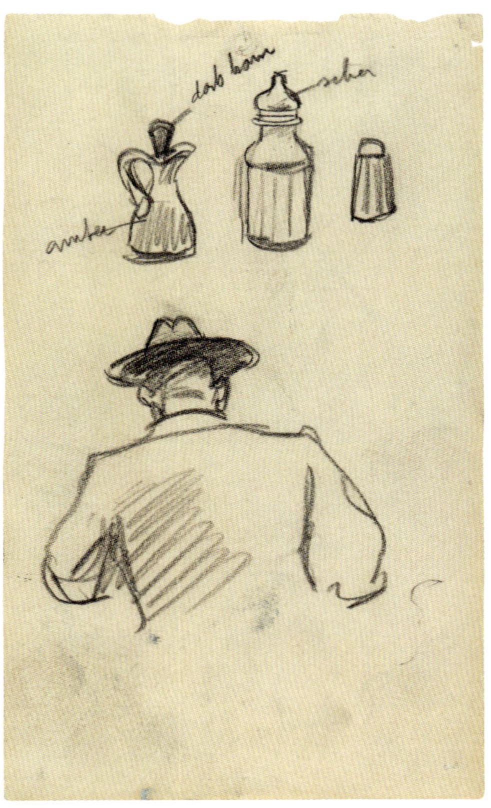

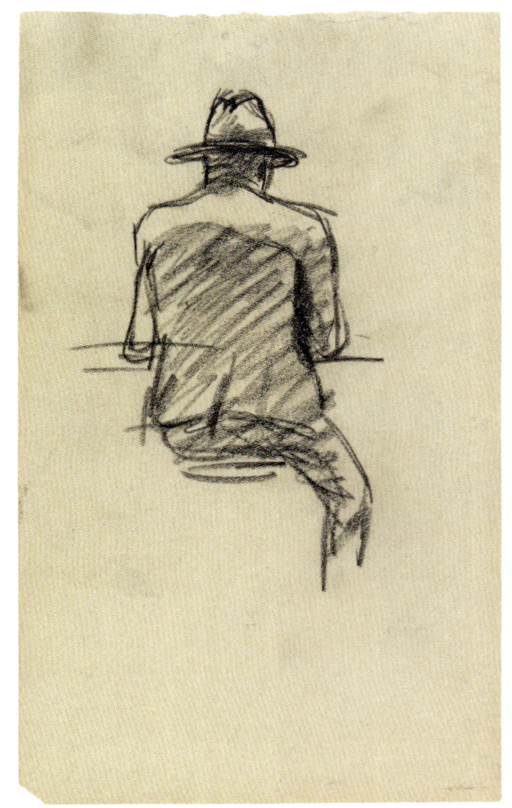

193. (top left)
Study for *Nighthawks*, 1941 or 1942
Fabricated chalk on paper, $7\frac{1}{4} \times 4\frac{7}{16}$ in. (18.4 × 11.3 cm)
Josephine N. Hopper Bequest 70.186

194. (top right)
Study for *Nighthawks*, 1941 or 1942
Fabricated chalk on paper, $7\frac{1}{4} \times 4\frac{7}{16}$ in. (18.4 × 11.3 cm)
Josephine N. Hopper Bequest 70.187

195. (bottom left)
Study for *Nighthawks*, 1941 or 1942
Fabricated chalk on paper, $7\frac{3}{16} \times 4\frac{7}{16}$ in. (18.3 × 11.3 cm)
Josephine N. Hopper Bequest 70.190

196. (bottom right)
Study for *Nighthawks*, 1941 or 1942
Fabricated chalk on paper, $7\frac{3}{16} \times 4\frac{7}{16}$ in. (18.3 × 11.3 cm)
Josephine N. Hopper Bequest 70.191

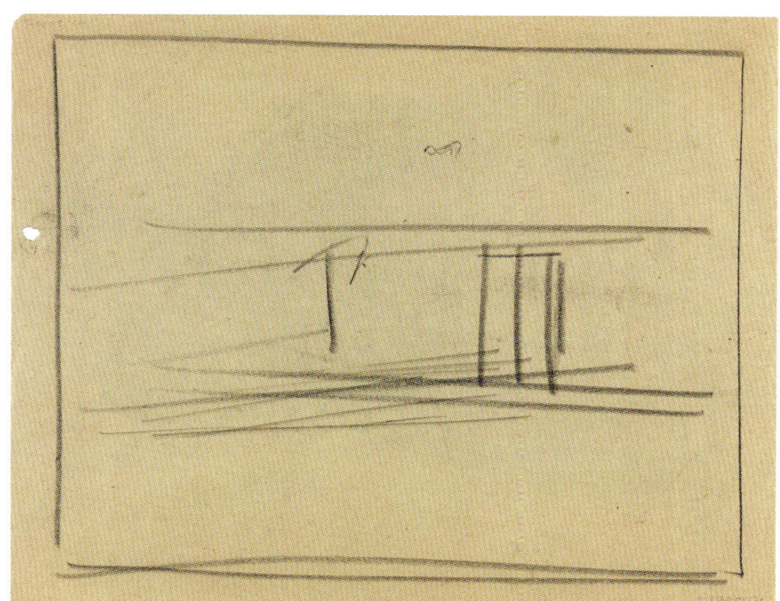

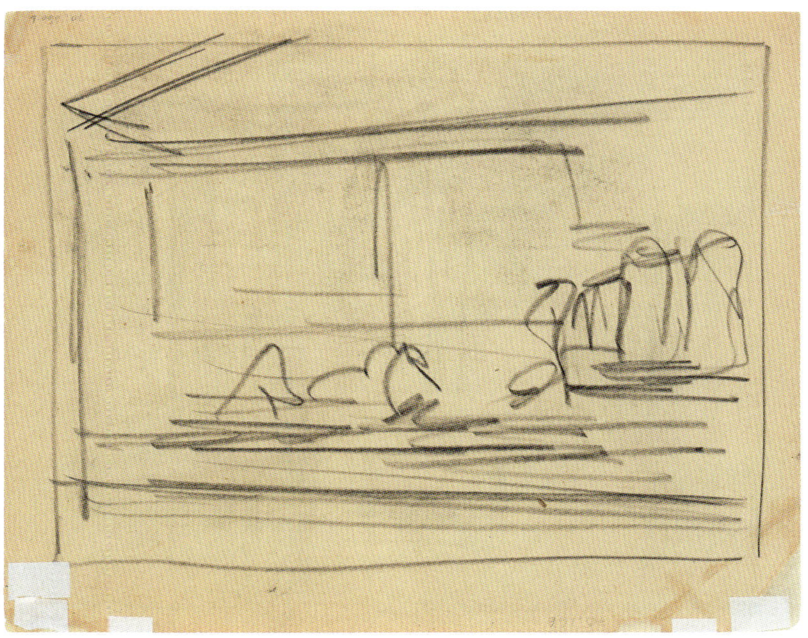

the photo records of Greenwich Avenue show it full of men dressed like his male nighthawks (see fig. 187). Were these sketchbook drawings at the beginning of his concept for *Nighthawks* and thus the real-world seeds for its content, or did the artist seek them out after he knew what subject he wanted to paint? Hopper stated later (in 1955) that his idea for a painting evolved first and that he subsequently made drawings,[40] but perhaps the poses he found in real life nudged him toward the complex give-and-take between the real and the imagined as it operates in this particular work. None of the known drawings for *Nighthawks* stray far from the painting; as a whole, they reflect the artist's nuanced refinement of its elements, which he continued to do as he painted.

Hopper's process is easier to track in the compositional studies. Five of them are on the same size and type of cheap paper (see figs. 197–201). Two of these contain early ideas for the work, done rapidly and very summarily, their subject unrecognizable without knowing the painting (see figs. 197, 198). One has a few slightly diagonal lines punctuated with short verticals to suggest structure and streets (fig. 197); it reflects the essence of the painting's spatial conception and play of angled planes, but little more. Without the serpentine leg of one of the coffee urns in the upper center it would be difficult to relate this sheet to *Nighthawks*. This marvelous demonstration of both extreme specificity and near abstract compositional summation on the same surface beguilingly reflects how empirical observation and imagination coexisted in Hopper's head. In another early study (fig. 198), he zooms in toward the window to just outside the scene, with double rectangles indicating another window parallel to the picture plane but behind the scene. There is little here to indicate the play of diagonals to come. Instead, Hopper focused on the interior, not the street or background, drawing light

197. Study for *Nighthawks* (verso), 1941 or 1942
Fabricated chalk on paper, 8 7/16 × 11 in. (21.4 × 27.9 cm)
Josephine N. Hopper Bequest 70.200a–b

198. Study for *Nighthawks* (verso), 1941 or 1942
Fabricated chalk on paper, 8 1/2 × 10 15/16 in. (21.6 × 27.8 cm)
Josephine N. Hopper Bequest 70.166a–b

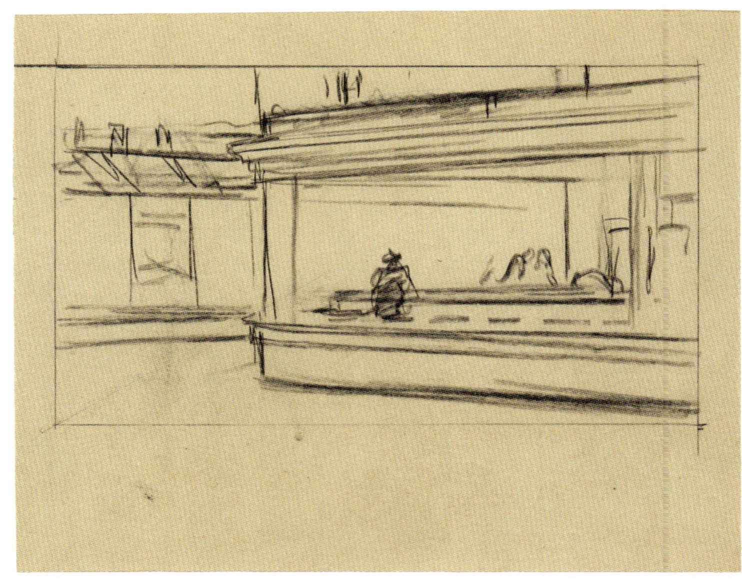

curvilinear squiggles suggesting figures, jumpy horizontal lines for the counter, and rough indications of the silos of coffee urns at the right. Framing lines around the nascent composition in both these drawings indicate a more vertical format for *Nighthawks* that was soon abandoned. Despite their raw simplicity—and they really amount to a kind of personal shorthand—they clearly had their use for the artist.

In the next three studies (see figs. 199–201), Hopper got to the heart of the painting's structure. Clearly he knew what he was after, for despite being fairly minimal, these works are extremely assured. Whether there was another step in arriving at the composition we cannot know, but it is fully formed in each, with the configuration of the space and the placement of the diner's form in relation to the background and the street set much as it would be. By this time he had also changed the proportions from the earlier sketches into the strong horizontal format he would keep.[41] One of these studies brings the entire composition together, including the figures and their placement (fig. 199). All four figures are sketchy but present: the man with his back to us, the couple across the counter, and the stooped-over server. The other two sheets work beautifully as a pair, with one as the skeleton of the structure (fig. 200), the other an essay on light and dark (fig. 201). The economy of means in the former is astonishing: with less than forty strokes of chalk, Hopper renders a composition of great solidity, the complex interaction between the window of the diner, the window of the picture plane, and the space of the street fully realized despite the sheet being mostly blank. In the companion to this study, the artist tackled, perhaps for the first time, the way in which light and dark would play out to underscore the dichotomy of inside and out. Perhaps this was even when he decided to make the painting a night scene, for the swath of chalk that shades the upper left corner—applied broadly with the side of the stick—adds that extra bit of darkness, effectively turning on the interior light in the diner (actually nothing but the reserve of the paper) seen through the large window. The tonal blending of the medium with the chalk stump combined with harder lines beautifully shows here his mastery of monochrome gradation, a great hallmark of his ability as a draftsman.

In three more finished compositional studies, we can see *Nighthawks* coming into sharper focus. Two are small and sketchy (see figs. 203, 204); the third is larger and as finished a drawing as the artist ever made (see fig. 211). None is exactly like the painting: in Hopper's practice in general the process of change (however minute) kept going; the final resolution always occurred on canvas.[42] We can see tinkering, for example, with the background: in one of the small sheets (see fig. 204), he sketched a brownstone-type building with steps similar to those off of Greenwich Avenue behind Crawford Lunch at Twelfth Street (fig. 202), but he finally decided on the storefront building type that echoes *Early Sunday Morning*. We can track a progression from the first of the smaller studies (see fig. 203) to the second (see fig. 204), and finally to the larger sheet (see fig. 211). Hopper refined the relationship of the diner to the picture's edges and opened up the space both inside and out. He made more room for the figures and showed more of the street (see figs. 204, 211), and he elongated the diner and tilted it in from the picture plane.[43]

199. Study for *Nighthawks*, 1941 or 1942
Fabricated chalk on paper, 8 7/16 × 10 15/16 in. (21.4 × 27.8 cm)
Josephine N. Hopper Bequest 70.193

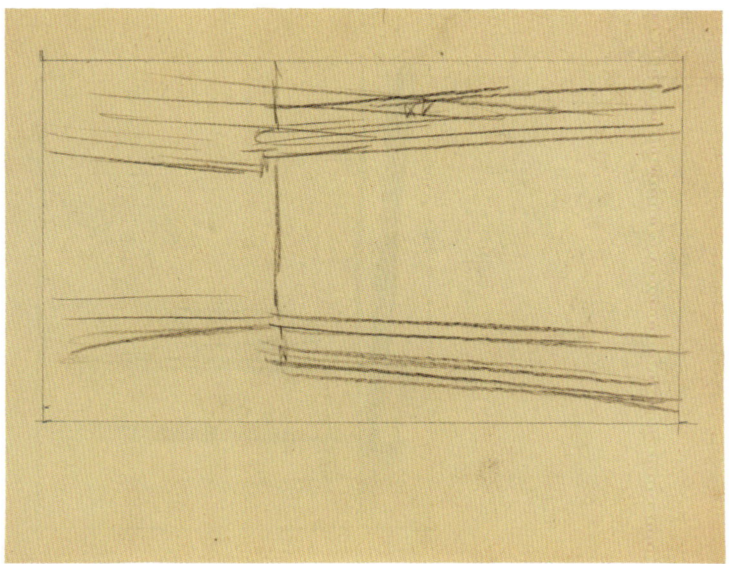

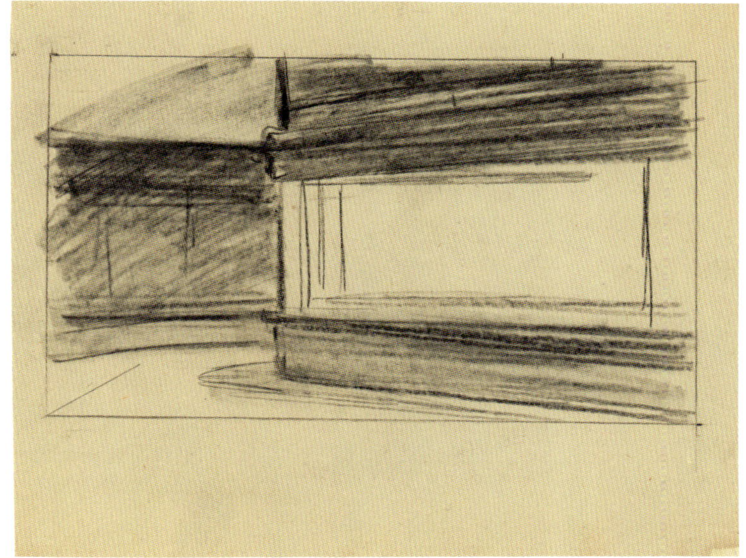

Hopper also honed in on the relationships among his protagonists. In the sketchiest of the three late studies (see fig. 203), the artist blocked his four characters into position following his earlier idea (see fig. 199): the couple faces us across the counter, the male diner has his back to us, and the server is leaning over. But we cannot see their heads or the more precise positions of their bodies; these are rendered more clearly in the next step (see fig. 204): the couple is closer together and the man's head is turned toward the other patron opposite, whose back and shoulders are square and mostly parallel to the picture plane. The server's head is down. In the final drawing (see fig. 211), the couple seems even closer together, their heads now turned toward each other, and the server has come up slightly. At this point Hopper began to refine these positions even more in another group of drawings (see figs. 205–209). These precise bodily positions are crucial to the mood of the painting because they set how we can interpret the characters' interactions. If Hopper's paintings are an art of silence, much is told through nuance of gesture and body.[44]

Jo Hopper reported that the painter himself posed for the male figures in *Nighthawks* using a mirror,[45] and that she posed for the woman.The four extant drawings we can connect to her descriptions (see figs. 205–209) are on larger, better-quality sheets than the others, concentrating on specific aspects of the various poses and especially on the fall of light on both skin and clothing. Working in fabricated black chalk, the artist used the combination of application methods at which he excelled in this medium: firm, linear strokes with the tip of the chalk and nuanced shading achieved with stumping and blending. In the study for the server (fig. 205), he focused on the crook formed where the arm and shoulder meet the body and the play of angles in the drapery at this precise joint below the curve of the back. In two studies of the male diner with his back to us (presumably executed using double mirrors so he could see himself in this pose), Hopper carefully evolved this position from the earlier sketchbook sheets. Using one of these found poses as his starting point (see fig. 196), he then drew himself from behind (see figs. 206, 207). But knowing now where this figure would actually be in the composition, he developed this rear three-quarter view as in the painting, with the right leg partially visible, the left shoulder turning into shadow, light falling on the right shoulder, and the right side of the face just barely visible in almost-lost profile (fig. 206). We can see his progression: after drawing himself in his safari jacket[46] (fig. 207) he adjusted to create the lost profile (see fig. 206), turning the figure more to the right, necessitating a change in the fall of light on the shoulder and making the figure's cheek just visible. A light sketch in the bottom half of the first of these studies also shows this transition; when viewed in the right orientation (it is upside-down to the main image on the sheet; fig. 208), it shows the change in the tilt of the head—a slight difference but one Hopper considered carefully.

When Hopper set about painting this composition, his subtle alterations of the space must have led him to adjust his figures, and these last figure drawings reflect his changes in the setting. In comparing the final study to the painting, we see that he elongated the facade in the background by two bays of windows to increase the composition's lateral sweep. Less obvious are the changes he made to space inside the diner. He opened up the perspective, making

200. Study for *Nighthawks* (recto), 1941 or 1942
Fabricated chalk on paper, 8½ × 11 in. (21.6 × 27.9 cm)
Josephine N. Hopper Bequest 70.194a–b

201. Study for *Nighthawks*, 1941 or 1942
Fabricated chalk on paper, 8½ × 11¹⁄₁₆ in. (21.6 × 28.1 cm)
Josephine N. Hopper Bequest 70.195

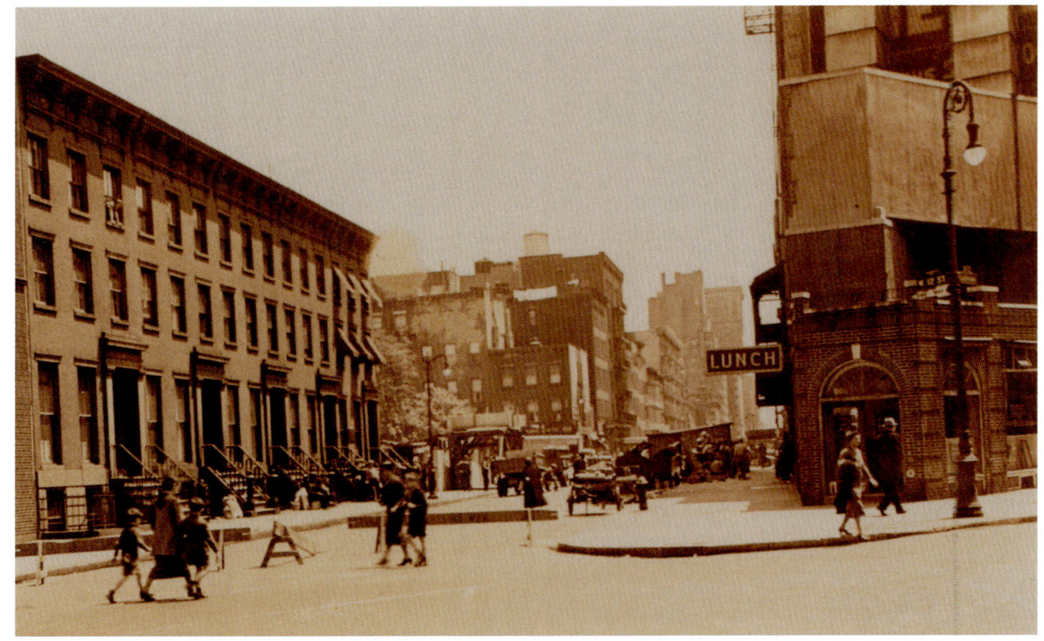

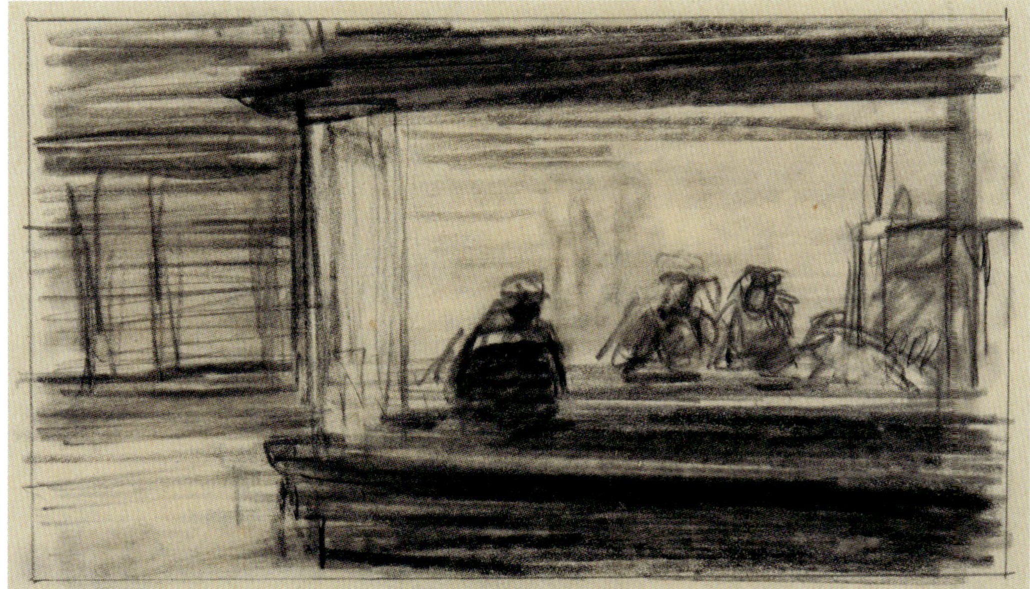

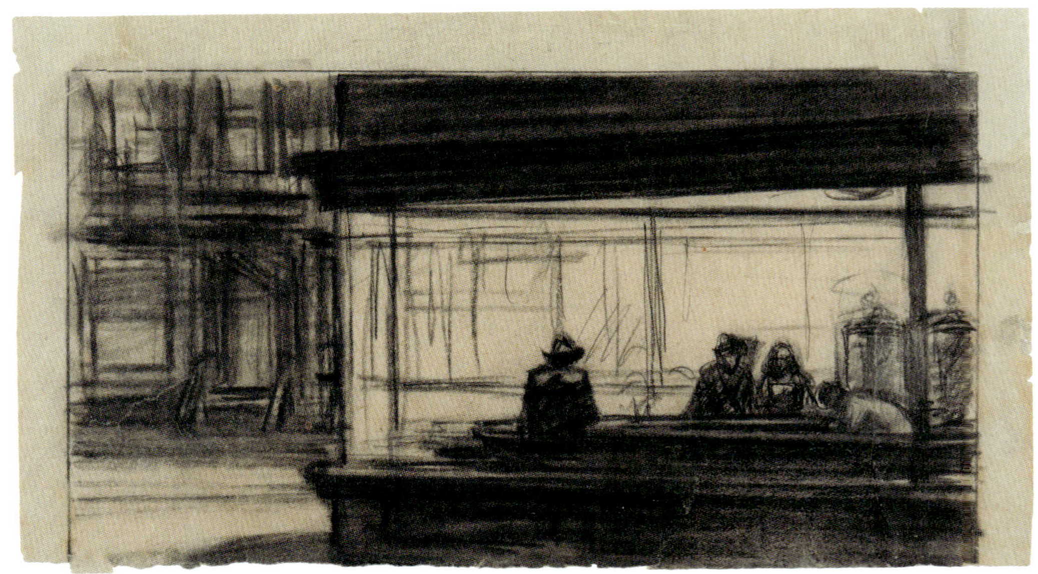

202. Twelfth Street at Greenwich Avenue (detail), May 21, 1937. Photograph by Percy Loomis Sperr. Irma and Paul Milstein Division of United States History, Local History and Genealogy, The New York Public Library, Astor, Lenox and Tilden Foundations Image ID: 711139F

203. Study for *Nighthawks*, 1941 or 1942
Charcoal and white chalk on paper, 5 × 8 ½ in. (12.7 × 21.6 cm)
Collection of Mr. and Mrs. Larry Magid

204. Study for *Nighthawks*, 1941 or 1942
Charcoal on paper, 4 ½ × 8 ½ in. (11.4 × 21.6 cm)
Collection of Mr. and Mrs. Larry Magid

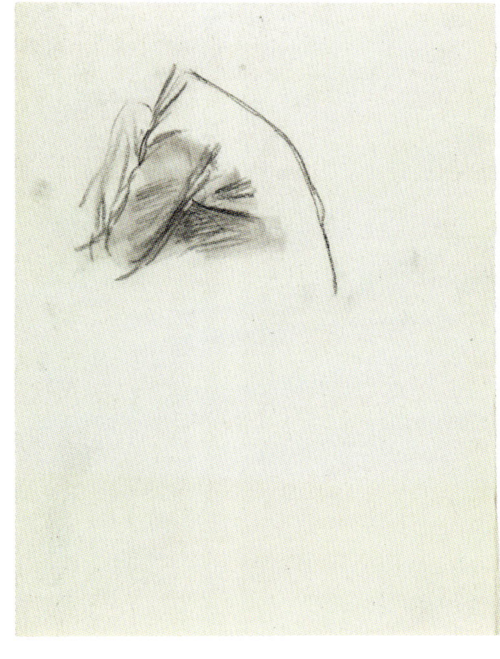

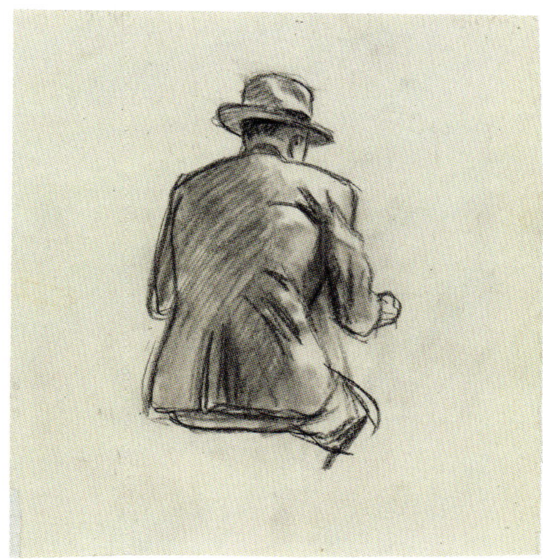

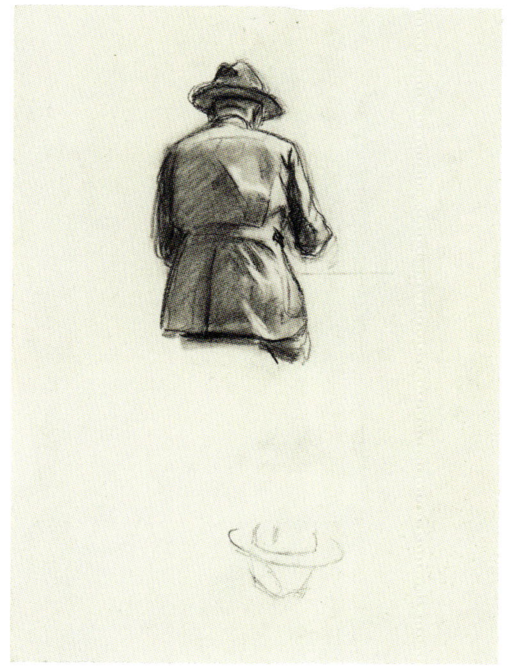

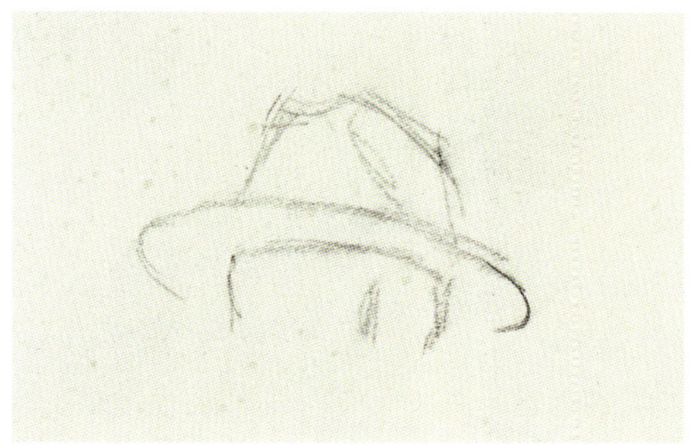

205. Study for *Nighthawks*, 1941 or 1942
Fabricated chalk on paper, 10 7/16 × 8 in. (26.5 × 20.3 cm)
Josephine N. Hopper Bequest 70.255

206. Study for *Nighthawks*, 1941 or 1942
Fabricated chalk and charcoal on paper, 8 1/8 × 8 in.
(20.6 × 20.3 cm)
Josephine N. Hopper Bequest 70.253

207. Study for *Nighthawks*, 1941 or 1942
Fabricated chalk and charcoal on paper, 11 13/16 × 8 7/8 in.
(30 × 22.5 cm)
Josephine N. Hopper Bequest 70.254

208. Study for *Nighthawks* (detail), 1941 or 1942
Fabricated chalk and charcoal on paper, 11 13/16 × 8 7/8 in.
(30 × 22.5 cm)
Josephine N. Hopper Bequest 70.254

visible a small area of the ceiling, which he painted a paler yellow than the walls to form a triangle that echoes the shape of the counter below. Much more of this countertop is now visible as well. In the final drawing, it forms more of a barrier among the diners and server. In the painting its continuous surface now connects the characters, bringing them together visually and physically in a way they were not before. We can also see the tops of the row of stools just inside the window; they were more or less level with the spectator's viewpoint in the related drawings (see figs. 199, 211). Hopper executed these changes in the underdrawing on the canvas (visible through infrared reflectography), in which he blocked out some of the major compositional elements, as was his practice.[47] This shift in point of view necessarily affected the poses and is probably what spurred him to make the last four drawings. The gestures between the couple becomes especially significant since we see their hands and arms against the countertop now, from slightly above. They are still close together, but not as close as they were in the final study, and despite their proximity they do not touch: the man's proper right hand overlaps but is clearly in front of his companion's.

Hopper's study of Jo posed as the female protagonist pays close attention to her arms and hands (fig. 209). He drew her overall position first—which he followed in the painting—leaning on the counter with her proper right arm bent and her hand holding a square object, her left forearm resting on the countertop. Then he did more careful studies of each of her arms separately, and of her right hand holding a cigarette. Considered by itself, this hand study with cigarette looks as if it could reflect an alternate position Hopper considered for the woman, and it makes one want to read the object she holds in one of the arm studies as a pack of cigarettes. Yet it became the man's hand in the painting, where it is also the closest point of physical proximity among anyone in *Nighthawks*—a spot with a tense undercurrent of suggestion. What she is actually holding in the painting is unclear—Jo described it as a

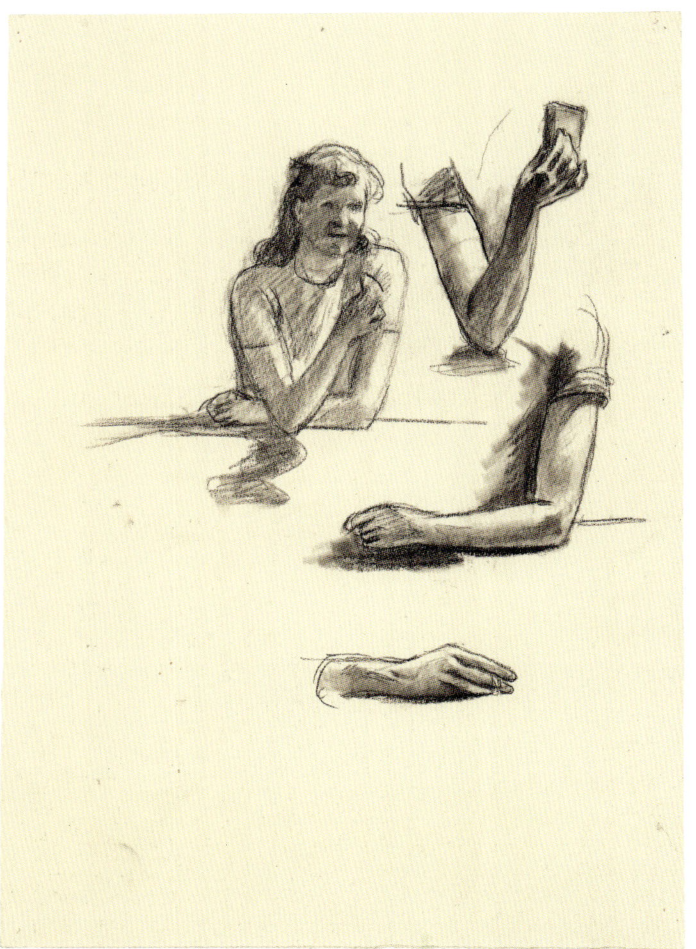

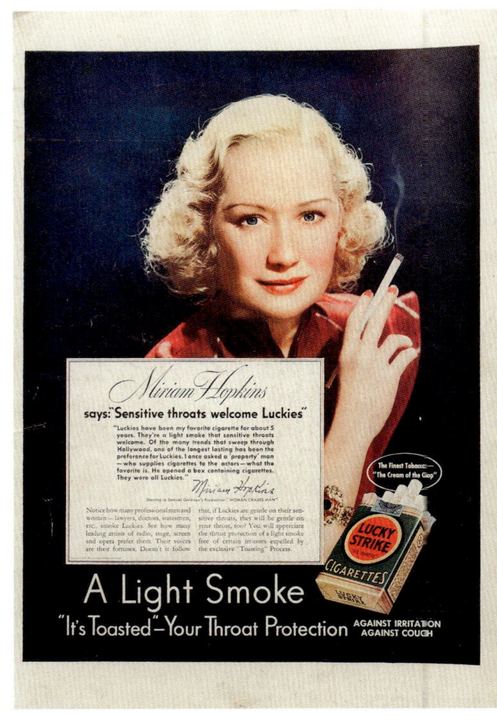

sandwich in the Record Books, though there is no plate nearby.[48] A wad of cash is also a good suggestion, since it is green.[49] But packs of Lucky Strike cigarettes were also green in Hopper's day, and an ad for them on the back cover of a 1937 *Life* magazine (which the artist enjoyed reading) features a woman with striking similarities to the painting's inscrutable redhead (fig. 210). Her holding the pack of cigarettes from which he smokes certainly gives the work an interesting Freudian twist, should one wish to interpret the couple that way.

Early Sunday Morning and *Nighthawks* are distinctly different in atmosphere and mood, yet their formal and conceptual links make the latter like a continuation or a revisiting of the former. Knowing better what Hopper experienced and used as his sources and inspiration for these works, we can see how, especially when taken as a pair, they reflect the changing face of New York City and modernizing America. Hopper returned again and again to the themes that interested him, serially exploring variations over years and decades. Even if they never actually hung side by side, *Early Sunday Morning* and *Nighthawks* do fall perfectly within the tradition of pendant paintings—works of the same size and format with related compositions meant to hang together (in this case conceptually if not actually), which complement one another through oppositional subjects within related categories. These cityscapes inspired by Hopper's immediate neighborhood in New York, nearly identical in size and format, represent day and night, old and new, and more broadly, history, memory, and the passing of time. They are all the more compelling when we understand how the artist used his own memory as part of his technique in order to create their fictions and formal tensions, which were thoroughly grounded in his experiences of Greenwich Avenue, Seventh Avenue, and downtown New York over several decades of his life and the life of the city.

209. Study for *Nighthawks*, 1941 or 1942
Fabricated chalk and charcoal on paper, 15 1/16 × 11 1/16 in. (38.3 × 28.1 cm)
Josephine N. Hopper Bequest 70.256

210. Lucky Strike advertisement on the back cover of *Life* magazine, May 31, 1937

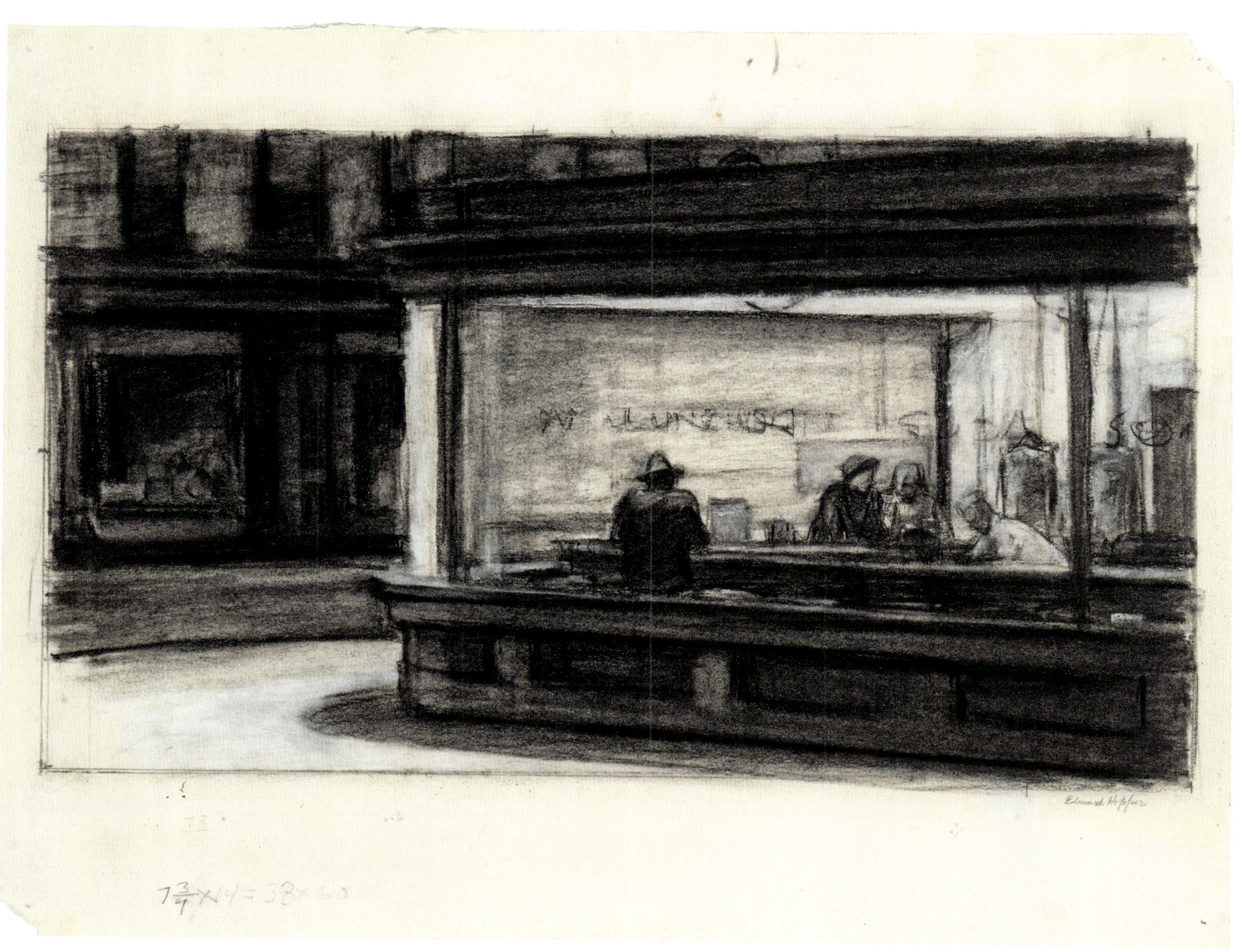

211. Study for *Nighthawks*, 1941 or 1942
Fabricated chalk and charcoal on paper,
11 1/8 × 15 in. (28.3 × 38.1 cm)
Purchase and gift of Josephine N. Hopper by
exchange 2011.65

NOTES

1 The building, designed by Richard Morris Hunt for George W. Vanderbilt in 1887, is located at 251 West Thirteenth Street and was later repurposed as the Jackson Square Branch of the New York Public Library. New York Landmarks Preservation Commission, *Greenwich Village Historic District Designation Report* (1969), 199. Hopper told Bill Johnson in 1956 regarding *Nighthawks*: "It was suggested by a restaurant just at the juncture of Greenwich Avenue and Tenth Street, I think. I used to pass it at night going to the Jackson Square library or the Sheridan Square movie theater." Bill Johnson, "Hopper Cover Research" (unpublished typescript, October 30, 1956), 28, Edward and Josephine Hopper Research Collection, 4.043, Whitney Museum of American Art Archives, New York (hereafter cited as Hopper Research Collection).
2 Katharine Kuh, *The Artist's Voice: Talks with Seventeen Modern Artists* (New York: Harper and Row, 1962), 134.
3 On *Early Sunday Morning*, see Lloyd Goodrich, *Edward Hopper* (New York: Harry N. Abrams, 1971), 103–4, 142; Robert Hobbs, *Edward Hopper* (New York: Harry N. Abrams in association with the National Museum of American Art, 1987), 83; Gail Levin, *Edward Hopper: A Catalogue Raisonné*, vol. 3, *Oils* (New York: Whitney Museum of American Art in association with W. W. Norton, 1995), 198; Gail Levin, *Edward Hopper: An Intimate Biography* (New York: Rizzoli, 2007), 227–30; Karal Ann Marling, "*Early Sunday Morning*," *Smithsonian Studies in American Art* 2, no. 3 (Fall 1988): 22–53; John Updike, "*Early Sunday Morning*," in *Still Looking: Essays on American Art* (New York: Alfred A. Knopf, 2005), 195–98; John Updike, Robert Adams, and Brian O'Doherty, "Edward Hopper: *Early Sunday Morning*," in *Frames of Reference: Looking at American Art, 1900–1950*, ed. Beth Venn and Adam D. Weinberg (New York: Whitney Museum of American Art, 1999), 177–85. On *Nighthawks*, see Goodrich, *Edward Hopper*, 105, 113, 122, 142; Hobbs, *Edward Hopper*, 129–31; Levin, *Edward Hopper: A Catalogue Raisonné*, 3:288; Levin, *Edward Hopper: An Intimate Biography*, 348–59; Judith Barter et al., eds., *American Modernism at the Art Institute of Chicago: From World War I to 1955* (Chicago: Art Institute of Chicago; New Haven: Yale University Press, 2009), 273–75.
4 Each painting is five feet wide; at thirty-three inches high, *Nighthawks* is two inches shorter than *Early Sunday Morning*. Edward Hopper Record Book I, 58, and II, 59. For information on and a partial facsimile of Hopper's Record Books, see Deborah Lyons, *Edward Hopper: A Journal of His Work* (New York: Whitney Museum of American Art in association with W. W. Norton, 1997); Deborah Lyons, "By Necessity or Invention: The Record-Book Sketches of Edward Hopper," *Drawing* 18, no. 4 (Spring 1997): 101–6.
5 Arlene Jacobowitz, "Interview with Edward Hopper. 1966," transcript from January 23, 1968, 1, Hopper Research Collection, 4.043. See also Lloyd Goodrich, "The Paintings of Edward Hopper," *The Arts* 11, no. 3 (March 1927): 134–38; Lawrence Campbell, "Hopper: Painter of 'Thou Shalt Not,'" *ARTnews* 63 (October 1964): 44; Alfred Kazin, "Hopper's Vision of New York," *New York Times Magazine*, September 7, 1980, 112.
6 "In retrospect, I believe that Edward Hopper belongs in the company of those great creative figures in American art, such as Copley, Homer, Eakins, and Ryder, who by expressing with complete integrity their individual visions of the world, both outer and inner, transformed the personal into the universal, and made enduring contributions to the long history of art." Lloyd Goodrich, "Edward Hopper," in *São Paulo 9, United States of America: Edward Hopper, Environment U.S.A., 1957–1967*, exh. cat. (Washington, DC: Smithsonian Institution Press, 1967), 16. Carol Troyen notes that Hopper's contemporary commentators also discussed "his ability to wring beauty out of the most unexceptional of subjects, especially the forgotten corners of America's past." Carol Troyen, "Edward Hopper and *Ryder's House*," *American Art* 20, no. 2 (Summer 2006): 4. One such commentator, Guy Pène du Bois, related this to the artist's youth: "His New York City... is one that people with their restless need for change have overlooked: it is a part of its backwaters untouched by the swift current of the main tide.... His realities are in the past of his youth." Guy Pène du Bois, "The American Paintings of Edward Hopper," *Creative Art* 8, no. 3 (March 1931): 190–91. See also Brian O'Doherty, "Edward Hopper's Voice," in *American Masters: The Voice and the Myth* (New York: Random House, 1973), 14.
7 Edward Hopper Record Book I, 58; Lyons, *Edward Hopper: A Journal of His Work*, 30. Lyons also discusses the collaborative nature of these records in two statements: "Though the prose in Hopper's ledgers is almost entirely Jo's, it is clear, as has been often noted, that naming these works and telling stories about them was often a joint enterprise" (12); and "How much of this is purely in the mind of Jo can only be a matter for speculation" (14).
8 Kuh, *The Artist's Voice*, 131. Hopper also spoke about the painting in a 1955 interview by Joan Dye: "'Early Sunday Morning' was, Hopper says, done from life. 'It was a string of shops on Seventh Avenue—or was it Eighth—Seventh, I guess. They aren't there anymore.'" Dye, "Luncheon Interview with Hopper and his wife Jo at Charles French Restaurant in the Village," (unpublished transcript, May 19, 1955), 2, Hopper Research Collection, 4.043.
9 Presumably that "someone" was Jo Hopper. Kuh, *The Artist's Voice*, 134. John Hollander discusses the "retitling" of the painting as a distraction from its abstract qualities and suggests that the "original" title of *7th Ave Shops* had been applied to the work for some time, which was not the case. John Hollander, "Hopper and the Figure of Room," *Art Journal* 41, no. 2 (Summer 1981): 156. Margaret Iversen repeats this misconception, stating that the painting "left Hopper's studio called simply Seventh Avenue Shops." Iversen, "In the Blind Field: Hopper and the Uncanny," *Art History* 21, no. 3 (September 1998): 414.
10 The invoice is in the object file on the painting at the Whitney Museum of American Art.
11 Alfred H. Barr, Jr., et al., *Edward Hopper: Retrospective Exhibition, November 1–December 7, 1933*, exh. cat. (New York: Museum of Modern Art, 1933), 14, 26.
12 Irma and Paul Milstein Division of United States History, Local History and Genealogy, New York Public Library, Astor, Lenox and Tilden Foundations; Subway Construction Photograph Collection at the New-York Historical Society.
13 For more on the two-part commercial block building type, see Richard Longstreth, *The Buildings of Main Street: A Guide to American Commercial Architecture* (Walnut Creek, CA: AltaMira Press, 2000), 24.
14 *Land Book of the Borough of Manhattan, City of New York* (New York: G. W. Bromley and Company, 1930), pl. 42.
15 The typescript on the back of the photograph reads: "15th Street at N.W. corner of Seventh Avenue, and west to the middle of the block. St. Joseph's Home for the Aged (1873), which is maintained by the Society of St. Vincent De Paul, adjoins the corner. The construction work on the S.W. corner of Seventh Avenue is for a new apartment house. / 1931. / P. L. Sperr."
16 The building shown in the photographs here is surely the one he had in mind as he painted. Although this type of simple two-story brick commercial structure was and still is common in New York (and indeed the rest of America), photographs commissioned by the New York Public Library document Seventh Avenue almost block by block in the 1930s; using these sources, no other building resembling *Early Sunday Morning* is identifiable on Seventh Avenue in the area below Twentieth Street.
17 "I find, in working, always the disturbing intrusion of elements not a part of my most interested vision, and the inevitable obliteration and replacement of this vision by the work itself as it proceeds. The struggle to prevent this decay is, I think, the common lot of all painters to whom the invention of arbitrary forms has lesser interest." Edward Hopper, "Notes on Painting," in Barr, et al., *Edward Hopper: Retrospective Exhibition*, 17. See also Mark Strand, *Hopper* (Hopewell, NJ: Ecco Press, 1994), 31.
18 "You can't go out and look up at an apartment and stand in the street and paint but many things have been suggested by the city." Jacobowitz, "Interview with Edward Hopper," 5.
19 And possibly in the sign at the far left, though it could be its projecting angle; it is difficult to say what Hopper's intent was here. For an analysis of Hopper's use of perspective in *Early Sunday Morning* and other works, see Jean Gillies, "The Timeless Space of Edward Hopper," *Art Journal* 31, no. 4 (Summer 1972): 404–12.
20 In a letter to Charles H. Sawyer, Hopper states: "The very long horizontal shape of this picture, "Manhattan Bridge Loop" is an effort to give a sensation of great lateral extent. Carrying the main horizontal lines of the design with little interruption to the edges of the picture, is to enforce this idea and to make one conscious of the spaces and elements beyond the limits of the scene itself. The consciousness of these spaces is always carried by the artist to the very limited space of the subject that he intends to paint, though I believe all painters are not aware of this." Hopper to Charles H. Sawyer, October 19, 1939, Archives of the Addison Gallery of American Art, Phillips Academy, Andover, Massachusetts; quoted in Levin, *Edward Hopper: An Intimate Biography*, 215. Goodrich also discusses this in his notes (referring to *Pennsylvania Coal Town* [1947; Butler Institute of American Art, Youngstown, OH], which the artist had just finished): "He said that he had wanted to give the feeling that the subject did not stop at the edge of the canvas, that there were more houses of the same kind on each side. But he felt that he had been defeated in trying to convey this. He said that he often wanted to give this feeling in his paintings." Goodrich, "Notes of Conversation with Hopper" (typescript, April 21, 1947), 2, Hopper Research Collection, 4.044. See also Robert Silberman, "Edward Hopper and the Implied Observer," *Art in America* 69, no. 7 (September 1981): 150; Gillies, "The Timeless Space of Edward Hopper," 410–11.
21 Hilton Kramer puts it nicely: "Hopper had a wonderful eye for detail. One could almost write a history

of native American architecture and interior décor based on the visual evidence of his pictures. Yet he absorbed this painstaking observation into a vision entirely his own." Kramer, "Hopper: An Integrity in Realism," *New York Times*, March 19, 1971, 28. Goodrich states that one of Hopper's strongest qualities is his ability to capture "the stark angularity and hardness of American architecture.... The cheap little frame houses that stick up uncompromisingly in the desolate wastes of the outskirts of cities, the pretentious suburban residences of the 'nineties, with their mansard roofs and turrets and jigsaw decorations, the drab monotony of rows of identical red brick tenements, the faded splendors of demodé apartment houses—all these characteristic features of the background of our modern American life appear in his pictures, and are painted with an intense realism that spares us none of their ugliness." Goodrich, "The Paintings of Edward Hopper," 36. Hopper himself, in his article on Charles Burchfield, illustrates his connoisseurship of American architectural styles when he writes of "our native architecture with its hideous beauty, its fantastic roofs, pseudo-Gothic, French Mansard, Colonial, mongrel or what not." Hopper, "Charles Burchfield: American," *The Arts* 14, no. 1 (July 1928): 7.

22 On Hopper's manipulation of what he observed, Bryan Robertson writes: "As a painter with some Dutch forebears, Hopper had an unsentimental respect for physical reality with an acute and deliberate sense of time and place. You are continually aware in his paintings that it is early morning, or exactly noon, or evening or very late at night. The respect, of course, went only so far. Hopper was ruthless in the way he manipulated the scene structurally as well as the degree to which he fixed the lighting. Saying often that he had painted something 'after the fact,' Hopper also made no bones about putting together separate sections of different studies to get the interior or the buildings that he wanted. In this, he exercised his freedom as an artist, broke free from mere topography and behaved as autocratically as the way in which he cast people, alone or together, as personages in some imagined play." Robertson, "Hopper's Theater," *New York Review of Books* 17, no. 10 (December 16, 1971): 39.

23 O'Doherty described the facade of the building in Hopper's painting as "slightly out of register." Brian O'Doherty, "Edward Hopper: Early Sunday Morning," in Venn and Weinberg, *Frames of Reference*, 184.

24 In a letter addressing a request from a physician who wished to use the painting to illustrate a medical journal, the artist shared his awareness of the mood these dark doorways helped create: "I can not imagine how 'Early Sunday Morning' could be used to further the cause of medicine, unless the supposition is that disease must lurk behind that red brick facade." Edward Hopper, letter to Hermon More, January 20, 1951, Hopper Research Collection, 4.014.

25 On Hopper and Evans, see Peter Galassi, *Walker Evans and Company*, exh. cat. (New York: Museum of Modern Art, 2000); Georg-W. Költzsch and Heinz Liesbrock, *Edward Hopper und die Fotografie: Die Wahrheit des Sichtbaren*, exh. cat. (Essen: Museum Folkwang, 1992); Robert Flynn Johnson, *America Observed: Etchings by Edward Hopper, Photographs by Walker Evans*, exh. cat. (San Francisco: Fine Arts Museums of San Francisco, 1976). According to Evans biographer James R. Mellow, Evans himself "discouraged any inference that Hopper had had a direct influence upon his photographic work: 'This is a case of parallel,' he claimed. 'I didn't know Hopper or what he was doing. I was doing very similar things. It just happens. It's one of the wonders of the art world.'" See James R. Mellow, *Walker Evans* (New York: Basic Books, 1999), 217. Eric de Chassey helpfully dissects the misperceptions about the relationship between the two in "Les photographies d'architecture victorienne de Walker Evans et l'invention du style documentaire," *Les Cahiers du Musée National d'Art Moderne* 92 (Summer 2005): 76–78.

26 See Erika L. Doss, "Edward Hopper, Nighthawks, and Film Noir," *Post Script: Essays in Film and the Humanities* 2, no. 2 (Winter 1983): 22.

27 The older building is listed as "Arnold Constable and Co. Storage of Carpets" in *Insurance Maps of the City of New York: Borough of Manhattan* (New York: Sanborn Map Co., 1904), vol. 3, pl. 32.

28 Hopper's underdrawing for *Nighthawks* is visible in infrared photography carried out by the conservation department at the Art Institute of Chicago.

29 The easel is still in situ at Hopper's former studio, now part of New York University's Silver School of Social Work.

30 Kuh, *The Artist's Voice*, 134. A profile of Hopper in *Vogue* describes *Nighthawks*, apparently based on an interview with the artist: "It is based partly on an all-night coffee stand Hopper saw on Greenwich Avenue in downtown New York, 'only more so.'" "People: The America of Edward Hopper," *Vogue* 123, no. 10 (1954): 49.

31 In the lower left of the final *Nighthawks* study (fig. 211), Hopper worked out a ratio for scaling up the drawing for the painting, which reads: "$7^3/4 \times 14 = 33 \times 60$."

32 John Morse, "Tape Recorded Interview with Edward Hopper at the Whitney Museum of American Art, New York, New York" (unpublished transcript, June 17, 1959), Archives of American Art, Smithsonian Institution, Washington, DC. Here Hopper states he does not stretch his own canvases (in answer to a direct question posed by Morse) and states that he uses prepared canvas: "I get the best Winsor and Newton linen I can acquire.... I use the ground of the already prepared canvas.... I trust Winsor and Newton and I paint directly upon it." Others suggest he constructed his own stretchers at times; see "Hopper's Drawings," page 65, note 61, in this volume.

33 Hopper exhibited work at the 1939 World's Fair and presumably visited. Richard Longstreth's description of the second phase of Art Deco design is apt for *Nighthawks*: "The second, or streamlined, phase of Art Deco design was introduced during the 1930s and 1940s. Its slick, machine-inspired imagery became a popular means to create a new appearance for businesses during and after the Depression. In contrast to examples from the earlier phase, these buildings emphasize the facade's horizontality with such devices as decorative banding, long stretches of windows, smooth wall surfaces and rounded corners. New materials such as Vitrolite and Carrara Glass are widely used, often in bold color combinations. Applied ornament is seldom found; however, signs may be treated as an integral part of the whole scheme." Longstreth, *The Buildings of Main Street*, 46, 49. See also Gabrielle M. Esperdy, *Modernizing Main Street: Architecture and Consumer Culture in the New Deal* (Chicago: University of Chicago Press, 2008); David A. Hanks and Anne H. Hoy, *American Streamlined Design: The World of Tomorrow* (Paris: Flammarion, 2005). Erika L. Doss mentions this aspect of the structure in Hopper's painting in "Edward Hopper, Nighthawks, and Film Noir."

34 Doss identifies the architecture from the earlier painting tucked into the background of *Nighthawks*: "In the background of the picture is a red and green building, a specimen of old American commercial architecture. It is clearly the same building which is the subject of Hopper's definitive 1930's painting, *Early Sunday Morning*." Doss, "Edward Hopper, Nighthawks, and Film Noir," 22.

35 As noted in Christopher Gray, "Shop Till You Drop, 19th Century Style," *New York Times*, April 19, 2012, RE7.

36 The store was called the United Cigar Store. Alice Sparberg Alexiou, *The Flatiron: The New York Landmark and the Incomparable City That Arose with It* (New York: St. Martin's Press, 2010), 139.

37 Strand, *Hopper*, 5–7; "Art: The Silent Witness," *Time*, December 24, 1956, 39.

38 Kuh, *The Artist's Voice*, 134.

39 Levin, *Edward Hopper: An Intimate Biography*, 349. The Dixie Kitchen was located at 1 East Forty-eighth Street, according to advertisements in the *New York Times* from the 1930s. See also George Ross, *Tips on Tables: Being a Guide to Dining and Wining in New York* (New York: Covici Friede, 1934), 245.

40 Dye reported after a 1955 lunch with the artist that "he doesn't use his sketches to get an idea, rather an idea evolves and then he does a lot of sketches." Dye, "Luncheon Interview with Hopper and his wife Jo," 2.

41 The proportions and size of this format, as indicated by framing lines applied with a straightedge, are the same in each of these three drawings.

42 This is consistent with his claim that painting was never easy for him, that he scraped down and repainted often as he worked.

43 Since he developed some of these spatial qualities in the two sheets discussed above (figs. 200, 201), it makes one wonder what give and take there was among his various ideas as recorded in the drawings. It is easy to interpret the more finished drawings as coming later in the process, but we can question whether this is always true with Hopper.

44 Joseph Anthony Ward, *American Silences: The Realism of James Agee, Walker Evans, and Edward Hopper* (Baton Rouge: Lousiana State University Press, 1985).

45 Jo Hopper to Marion Hopper, letter of January 22, 1942, cited in Levin, *Edward Hopper: An Intimate Biography*, 349. "When he began painting in oil (after mastering etching and watercolor) Hopper and Jo served as his only models with the help of a full-length mirror at 3 Washington Square North." R. Stark, "Edward Hopper and Research" (unpublished typescript, n.d.), 4, Hopper Research Collection, 10.002. A full-length mirror is visible in one of Hans Namuth's photographs of Hopper taken in 1963–64. See *São Paulo 9*, 4, and fig. 386.

46 See Levin, *Edward Hopper: An Intimate Biography*, 349, on Hopper's safari jacket bought from Abercrombie and Fitch. He may be wearing the jacket in the Hans Namuth photograph taken in 1964 (see note 45).

47 I am grateful to the conservation department at the Art Institute of Chicago for sharing information on Hopper's underdrawing for *Nighthawks*, and to Matthew Skopek for helping me interpret it.

48 Edward Hopper Record Book II, 95; Lyons, *Edward Hopper: A Journal of His Work*, 63.

49 Judith A. Barter, "Nighthawks: Transcending Reality," in Carol Troyen et al., *Edward Hopper*, exh. cat. (Boston: Museum of Fine Arts, 2007), 196.

New York Movie

CARTER E. FOSTER

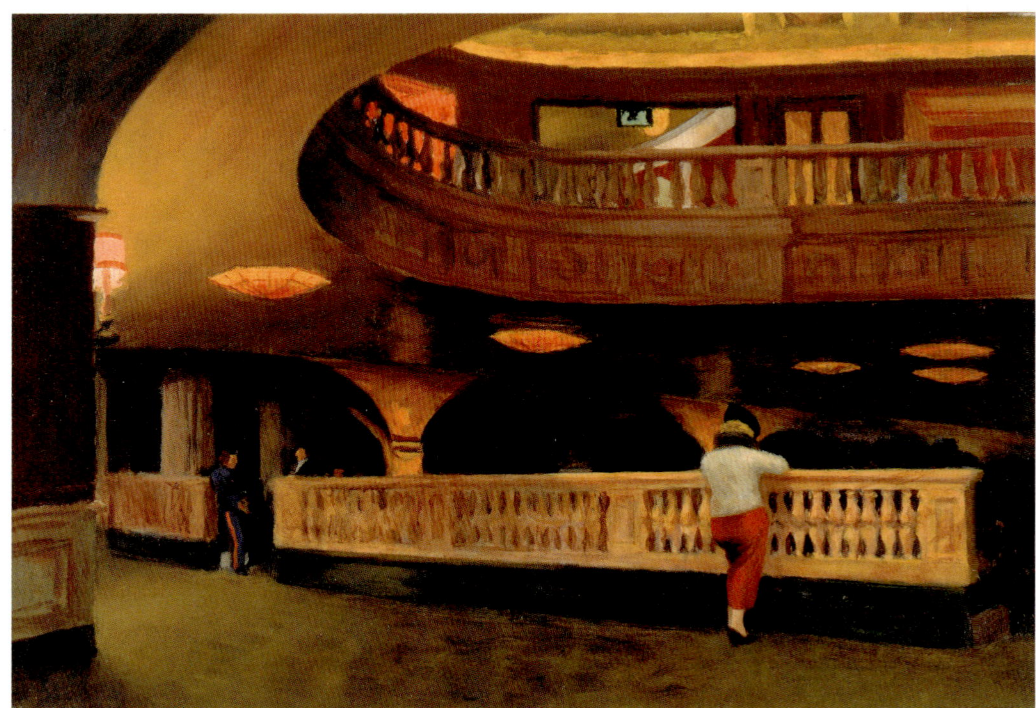

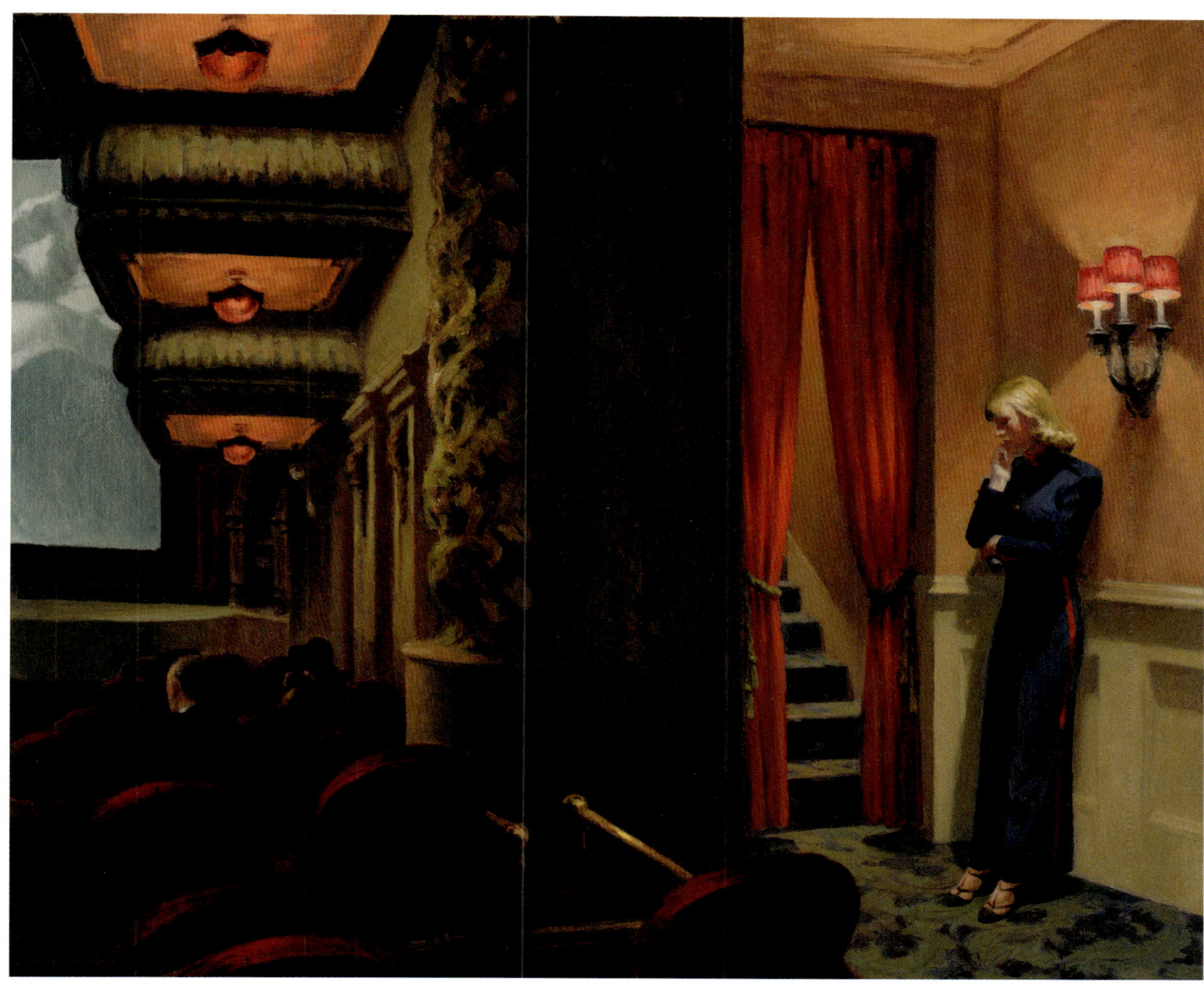

212. *Solitary Figure in a Theater*, c. 1902–04
Oil on board, 12 ½ × 9 $^{5}/_{16}$ in. (31.8 × 23.7 cm)
Josephine N. Hopper Bequest 70.1418

213. *The Sheridan Theatre*, 1937
Oil on canvas, 17 ⅛ × 25 ¼ in. (43.5 × 64.1 cm)
The Newark Museum; purchase 1940 Felix Fuld Bequest Fund 40.118

214. *New York Movie*, 1939
Oil on canvas, 32 ¼ × 40 ⅛ in. (81.9 × 101.9 cm)
The Museum of Modern Art, New York; given anonymously 396.1941

By 1904 the young Edward Hopper had completed *Solitary Figure in a Theater* (c. 1902–04), an absorbing grisaille panel that presciently demonstrated both his interest in this subject and his natural inclination toward a certain atmosphere and mood (fig. 212). More than three decades later he again focused on theater interiors—specifically movie houses—with the small, beautifully rendered *The Sheridan Theatre* (fig. 213) and the magisterial *New York Movie* (fig. 214), one of his single greatest artistic statements.[1] Hopper depicted theaters and theatergoers throughout his career in all modes and mediums, from illustration to etching, ending with his haunting last testament, *Two Comedians* in 1966 (private collection). For an artist whose work is so often and understandably tied to cinema and filmmaking, it is significant that he treated moviegoing as a subject in one of his most important paintings. Hopper's complex relationship with the art of film is fascinating and not easy to categorize. The connections, especially in the first part of his career, have less to do with influence than with parallel development—Hopper matured as an artist just as filmmaking was developing into an art form. He often composed his paintings in ways analogous to the cinematic shot, and filmmakers took note of this crucial intersection between his aesthetic and theirs. As the German director Wim Wenders has beautifully articulated, in a Hopper "you always know where the camera is."[2]

In *New York Movie*, Hopper painted an attractive blonde usherette, absorbed in her own thoughts in a quiet corner of one of New York's opulent movie palaces. A faint black-and-white image, described by Jo Hopper as "snowy mountain tops"[3]—takes up the screen at left while a man and woman each watch in an otherwise empty-looking auditorium. A number of writers have well described the painting's atmosphere and subject, its nod to the rising popularity of this modern form of public entertainment, and its connection to Hopper's own appreciation of cinema.[4] Moviegoing experienced a great surge in the 1920s and 1930s, and 1939,

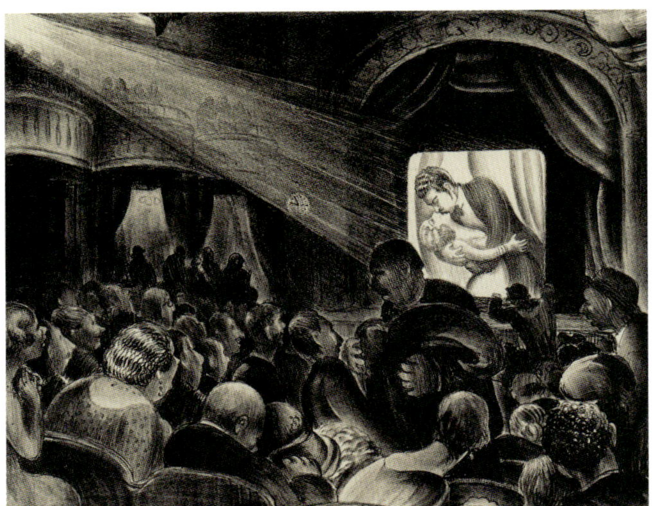

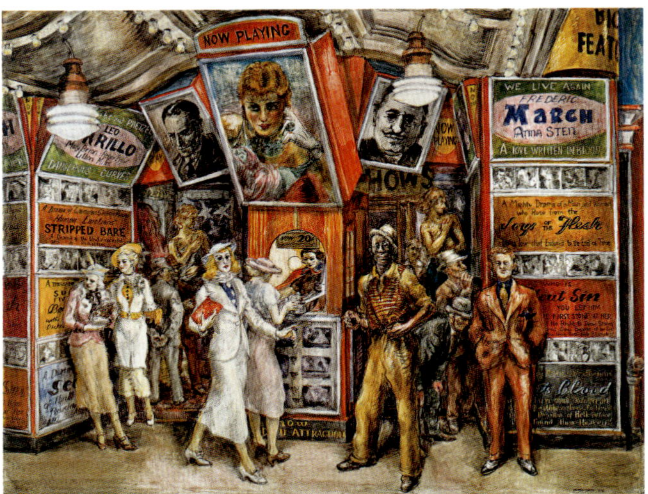

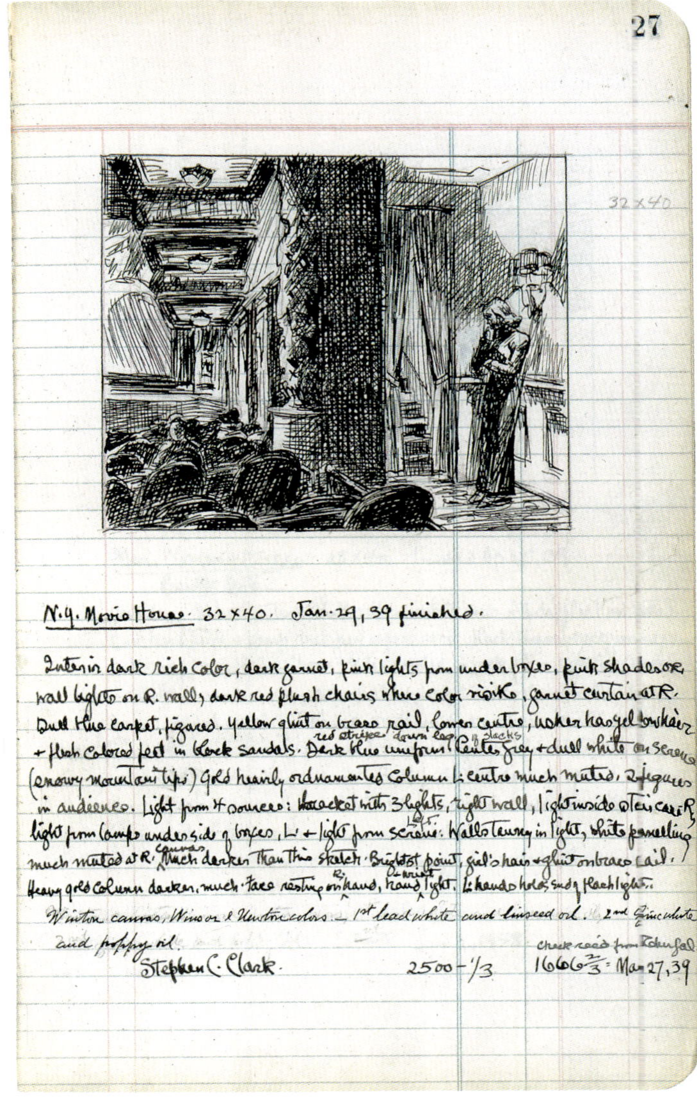
27

32 x 40

N.Y. Movie House. 32 x 40. Jan. 29, 39 finished.

Interior dark rich color, dark garnet, pink lights from under boxes, pink shades on wall lights on R. wall; dark red plush chairs where color visible, garnet curtain at R. Dull blue carpet, figured. Yellow glint on brass rail, lower centre, usher has yel hair + flesh colored feet in black sandals. Dark blue uniform (red stripes down leg of slacks). Center grey + dull white on screen (snowy mountain tips) Gold heavily ornamented column L. centre much muted. 2 figures in audience. Light from 4 sources: bracket with 3 lights, right wall, light inside stairs case R, light from lamps underside of boxes, L. + light from screen. Left walls in light, white panelling much muted at R. Canvas much darker than this sketch. Brightest point, girl's hair + glint on brass rail. Heavy gold column darker, much. Face resting on R. hand, hand + wrist light. L. hand holds end of flashlight.

Winton canvas, Winsor & Newton colors — 1st lead white and linseed oil. 2nd zinc white and poppy oil.

Stephen C. Clark. 2500 – 1/3

check rec'd from Rehn gal 1666 2/3 = Mar 27, 39

215. (top left)
Mabel Dwight (1876–1955)
The Clinch, Movie Theatre, 1928
Lithograph; sheet: 11 9/16 × 15 7/8 in. (29.4 × 40.3 cm), plate: 9 1/8 × 11 3/4 in. (23.2 × 29.8 cm)
Gift of Gertrude Vanderbilt Whitney 31.720

216. (bottom left)
Reginald Marsh (1898–1954)
Twenty Cent Movie (recto), 1936
Carbon pencil, ink, and oil on composition board, 30 × 40 in. (76.2 × 101.6 cm)
Purchase 37.43a–b

217. (right)
Artist's Ledger — Book II (page 27, entry for *New York Movie*, 1939), 1907–62
Pen and ink and graphite pencil on paper, 11 13/16 × 7 1/2 in. (30 × 19.1 cm)
Drawing by Edward Hopper. Text and inscriptions by Edward Hopper and Josephine Nivison Hopper (1883–1968)
Gift of Lloyd Goodrich 96.209

the year Hopper painted *New York Movie*, was a significant one for Hollywood with the release of *Gone with the Wind* and *The Wizard of Oz*. Hopper stated succinctly, "When I don't feel in the mood for painting I go on a regular movie binge!"[5] He was quite familiar with the cinematic experience in New York and typically approached the subject his own way, in contrast to earlier depictions by artists such as Mabel Dwight (fig. 215) and Reginald Marsh (fig. 216).[6] Rather than the spectacle and bustle of the theatergoing public that interested his contemporaries, Hopper found the theater's subdued light and relatively empty, interstitial spaces of more interest, producing one of his most striking and unusual compositions. A dark wall separates the scene into distinct halves—the auditorium on the left and the aisle on the right, where the usherette has found a moment of repose. Hopper's exploration of the quality of light here finds one of its most subtle arenas, and he must have been attracted to the challenge of rendering the variegated softness and dimness inherent in the subject.[7] His wife, Jo Hopper, remarked on the difficulty of painting this dark scene and carefully noted the four sources of light in the Record Books: from the fixture on the wall, from the staircase behind the curtain, from the lights below the balcony, and from the projected film (fig. 217).[8]

Two years earlier, in *The Sheridan Theatre*, Hopper had also displayed a mastery of semidarkness. Despite a distinctly different composition, this painting has important parallels to *New York Movie*—a similar subject, featuring a solitary female figure, and a red-gold color scheme with subtle modulations of low light—but the artist's attention here was also on the vast and complicated interior spaces. This was the golden age of the movie palace in America, a time in which the fantasy of the films themselves was enhanced and extended by costumed

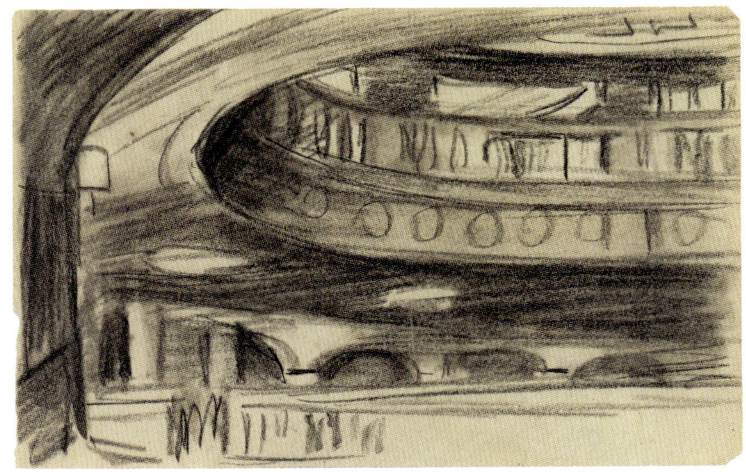

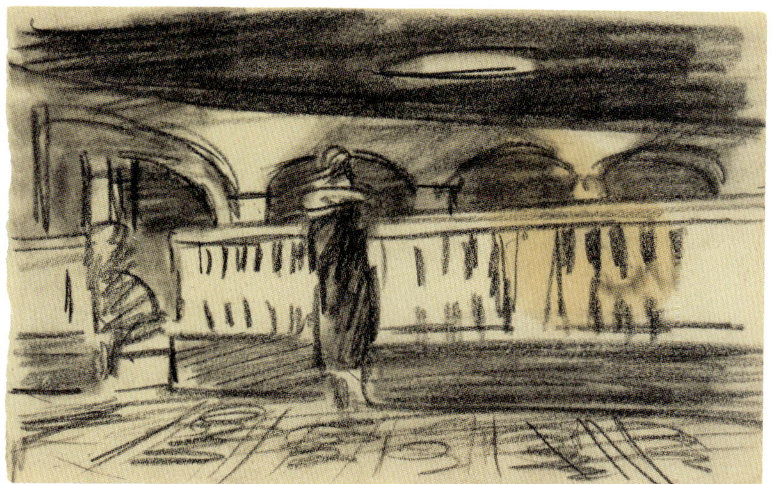

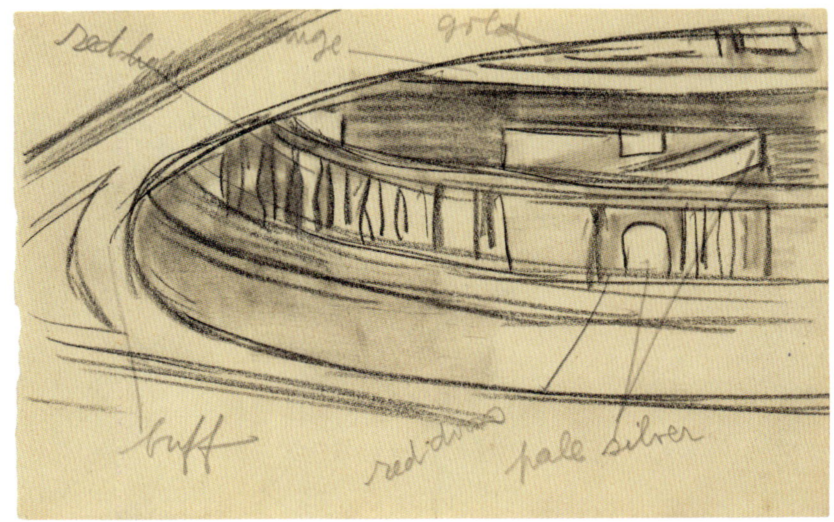

218. Study for *The Sheridan Theatre*, 1936 or 1937
Fabricated chalk on paper, 4 ½ × 7 ⅛ in. (11.4 × 18.1 cm)
Josephine N. Hopper Bequest 70.958

219. Study for *The Sheridan Theatre*, 1936 or 1937
Fabricated chalk on paper, 4 ½ × 7 ⅛ in. (11.4 × 18.1 cm)
Josephine N. Hopper Bequest 70.963

220. Study for *The Sheridan Theatre*, 1936 or 1937
Fabricated chalk and graphite pencil on paper,
4 7/16 × 7 ⅛ in. (11.3 × 18.1 cm)
Josephine N. Hopper Bequest 70.960

attendants and the opulent, often thematic settings that provided a complex spatial experience and appealed to the senses using materials, textures, and lighting.[9] The artist clearly wanted to capture this aspect of the architecture, which he depicted in a sweeping view.[10] The arches, the balcony, and the spaces around them present curves and countercurves typical of the neo-baroque interiors of such theaters. In this view worthy of Piranesi, Hopper clearly appreciated the way in which a multitude of spaces interpenetrated and opened up onto one another, as well as the way light filled each space differently.[11] With sketchbook in hand, Hopper walked the short distance from his apartment to the Sheridan Theatre on Greenwich Avenue in order to develop his composition. He made fourteen preparatory drawings (figs. 218, 219) which reflect how this vantage point interested him from the beginning.[12] They also show the importance of color notations for Hopper, and those inscribed on the drawings record how he perceived the surfaces in variegated light (fig. 220). He followed these notations closely in the painting, demonstrating his wish to be true to what he saw: a grounding in empirical experience was always crucial to his process.

When Hopper decided to revisit the subject two years later, he was somehow more stuck than usual. For an artist who never found it easy to paint, *New York Movie* proved a special challenge, though why it did so is unclear. Jo described his difficulty,[13] which is also evidenced by the large number of preparatory drawings—more than twice as many as was usual for the artist.[14] Hopper's creative block allows us unparalleled insight into the details of his process, and his tendency to parse narrowly and explore nuance applies exquisitely to the totality of the sketches.

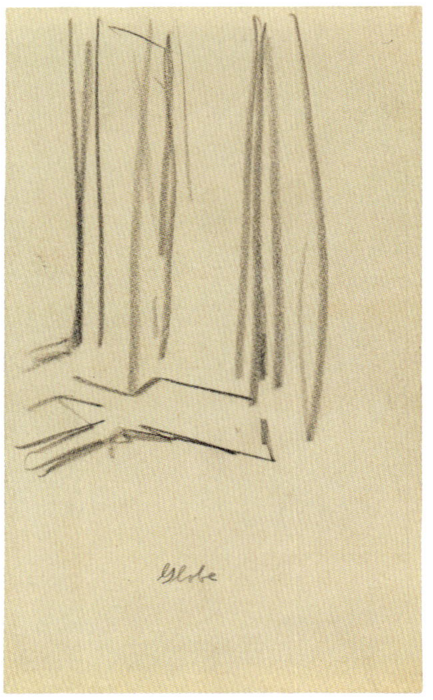

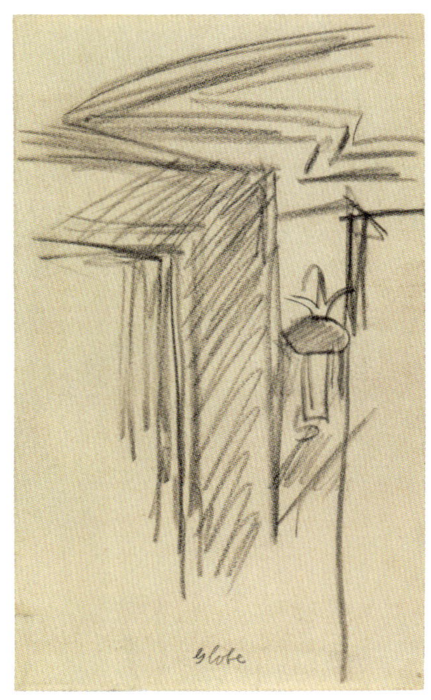

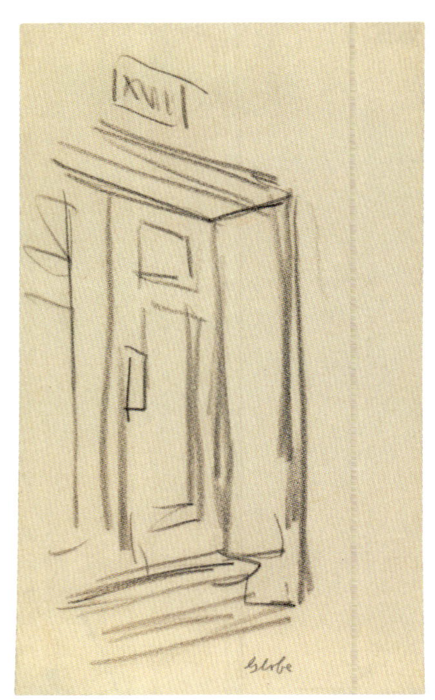

The drawings fall into four basic groups: small sketchbook sheets from trips to several New York theaters (figs. 221–231, 233–244); ten studies from a larger sketchbook, all apparently executed at the Palace Theatre (figs. 245, 250–258); compositional studies (figs. 259–272); and figure studies for which Jo modeled (figs. 275–280).[15] The first two categories were products of the artist's excursions out into the world; the latter two reflect his studio practice and his imagination. While it is difficult to know the exact sequence, the small sketchbook sheets were most likely done first (perhaps in just one or two trips), when the artist was seeking ideas and probably before he started to paint; some or all of the figure studies were made toward the end of the painting process, as Jo's diaries describe.[16] The crux of Hopper's creative process lies, however, in the relationship between the compositional studies and the large Palace Theatre sketchbook sheets, for in comparing these groups we can see in multiple examples the interpenetration of observed reality and Hopper's imaginative alterations of it.

On or around December 13, 1938, Hopper picked up his small sketchbook and set out for several of New York's large entertainment palaces near Times Square and the heart of the Broadway theater district.[17] We know which ones because he inscribed their names on a number of the sheets—the Palace, the Globe, the Strand, and the Republic (see figs. 221–231, 237–244). Clearly he wanted to keep track of what he saw, probably so he would know where to return if he wished to further study a motif or detail. Except for the Strand, these theaters still exist, though extensive interior renovations over the years make it difficult for us to see now just what Hopper saw.[18] They were built as vaudeville houses in the 1910s or earlier but with the rise of film's popularity had converted to showing movies either exclusively or between live acts.[19] An avid theater- and moviegoer all his life, Hopper must have been familiar with these venues well before he decided to paint *New York Movie*. Because they were relatively close to one another, it would have been easy for Hopper to visit all of them during one or two sketching expeditions, combining moviegoing with drawing while he thought about what to paint.

Some or all of the twenty-three small sketchbook pages related to *New York Movie* now in the Whitney must have been made during such a sketching trip—as suggested in Jo's diaries—and they reflect the nascence of the painting.[20] Three of these sheets are inscribed "Globe" (see figs. 221–223) and four "Republic" (see figs. 224–227). Hopper found more of what he wanted at the Strand (see figs. 228–231) and particularly at the Palace (see figs. 237–244), which became the main source for *New York Movie*. These drawings often focus on very

221. Study for *New York Movie* (Globe Theatre), 1938
Fabricated chalk on paper, 7 1/4 × 4 7/16 in. (18.4 × 11.3 cm)
Josephine N. Hopper Bequest 70.77

222. Study for *New York Movie* (Globe Theatre), 1938
Fabricated chalk on paper, 7 1/4 × 4 7/16 in. (18.4 × 11.3 cm)
Josephine N. Hopper Bequest 70.79

223. Study for *New York Movie* (Globe Theatre), 1938
Fabricated chalk on paper, 7 9/16 × 4 7/16 in. (19.2 × 11.3 cm)
Josephine N. Hopper Bequest 70.86

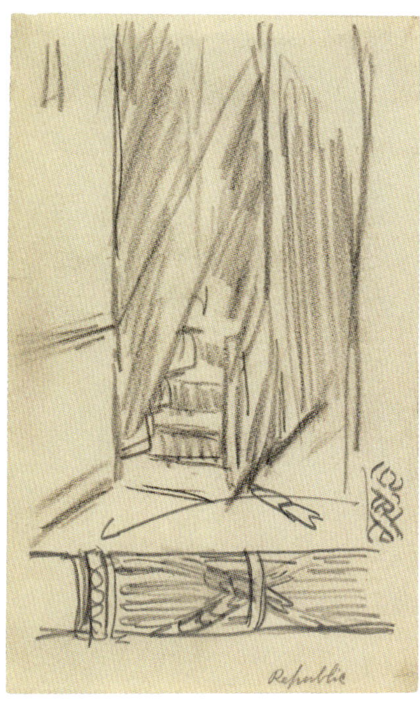

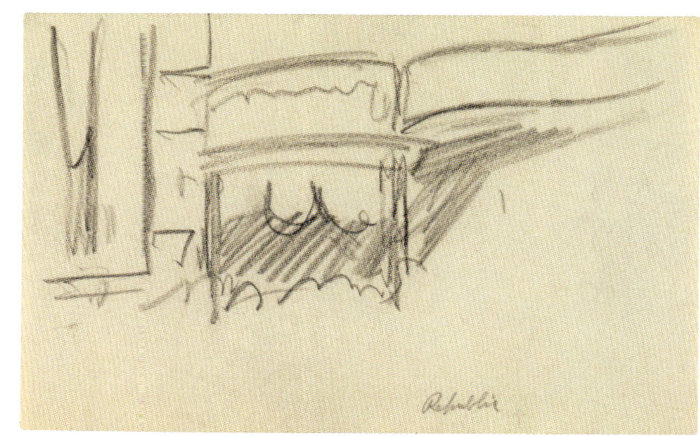

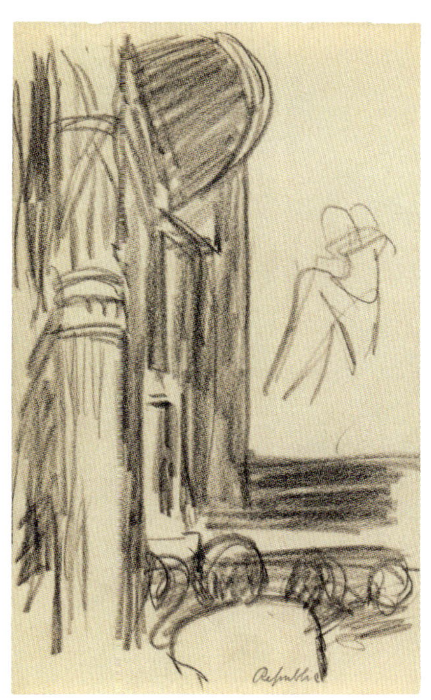

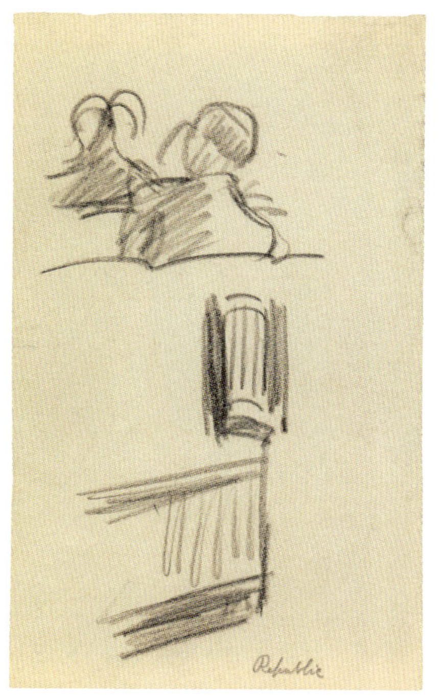

224. Study for *New York Movie* (Republic Theatre), 1938
Fabricated chalk and graphite pencil on paper, 7 1/4 × 4 7/16 in. (18.4 × 11.3 cm)
Josephine N. Hopper Bequest 70.92

225. Study for *New York Movie* (Republic Theatre), 1938
Fabricated chalk on paper, 4 7/16 × 7 1/4 in. (11.3 × 18.4 cm)
Josephine N. Hopper Bequest 70.91

226. Study for *New York Movie* (Republic Theatre), 1938
Fabricated chalk on paper, 7 1/4 × 4 7/16 in. (18.4 × 11.3 cm)
Josephine N. Hopper Bequest 70.147

227. Study for *New York Movie* (Republic Theatre), 1938
Fabricated chalk on paper, 7 1/4 × 4 7/16 in. (18.4 × 11.3 cm)
Josephine N. Hopper Bequest 70.150

particular architectural and decorative details, showing how closely Hopper looked at the world—indeed he seemed to need to cull such specificity from it in order for a subject to cohere in his mind. The three Globe drawings apparently depict framing elements around window and door jambs and did not lead him further. At the Republic (also known as Minsky's Burlesque), Hopper honed in on the X-shaped motifs and the guilloche pattern on the columns, which are still visible in the theater today (now known as the New Victory; see figs. 224, 226).[21] He also studied one of the staircases, which would become an important feature of *New York Movie*. The Republic and Globe drawings, along with two others of decorative elements not inscribed with a theater name (see figs. 233, 234), relate less directly to the painting.[22] Hopper's main interest became the views near the side aisles and under the balcony boxes (see fig. 226), which he ended up developing further at the Palace and the Strand. These two theaters were similar: large, ornate, and heavily decorated, with side orchestra box seats and overhanging balcony boxes (figs. 232, 247). The view from the side box seats in the orchestra captured Hopper's attention and led to the bisected composition that stayed with him and ended up defining the painting. Two sketchbook sheets from the Palace and one from the Strand show the essence of this type of space (see figs. 231, 238, 244), which was similar in the two theaters. In other studies made in both theaters, he focused on the three-tier overhang of the balcony boxes and the stairways (see figs. 228–230, 237, 239–243).

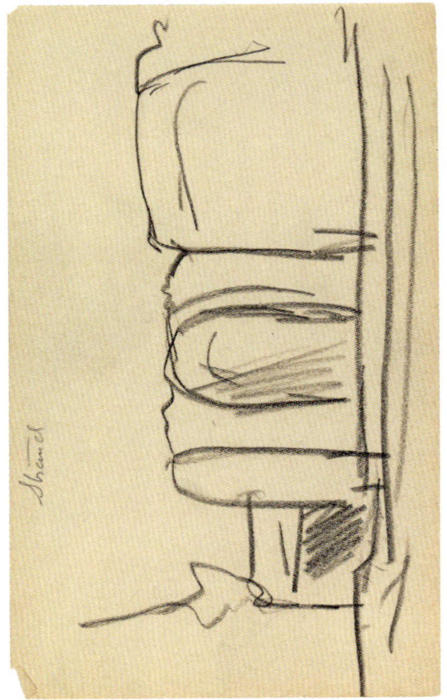

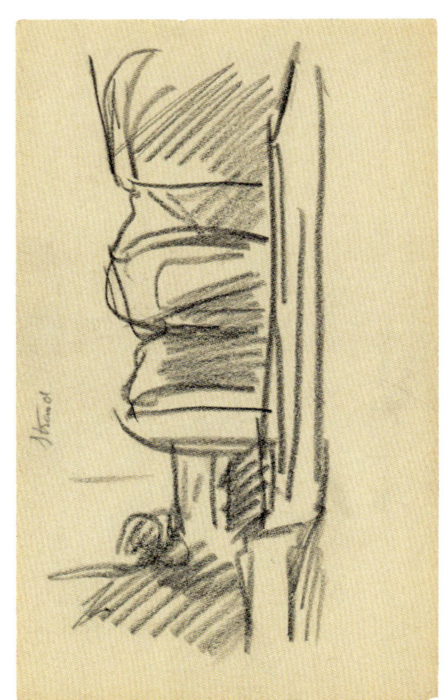

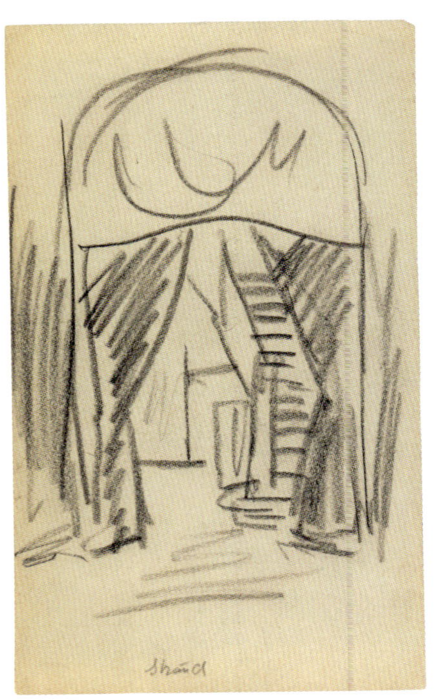

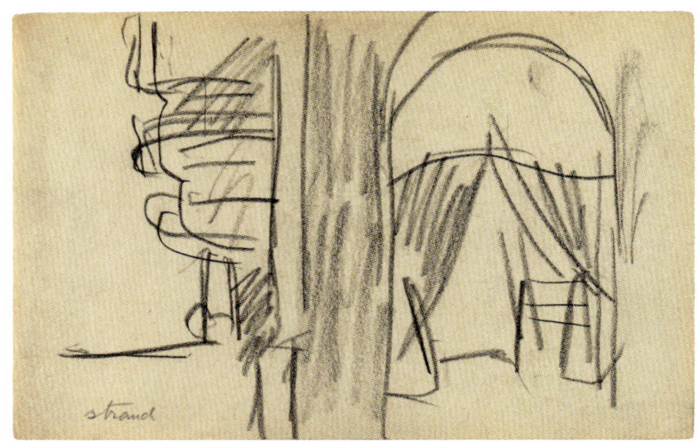

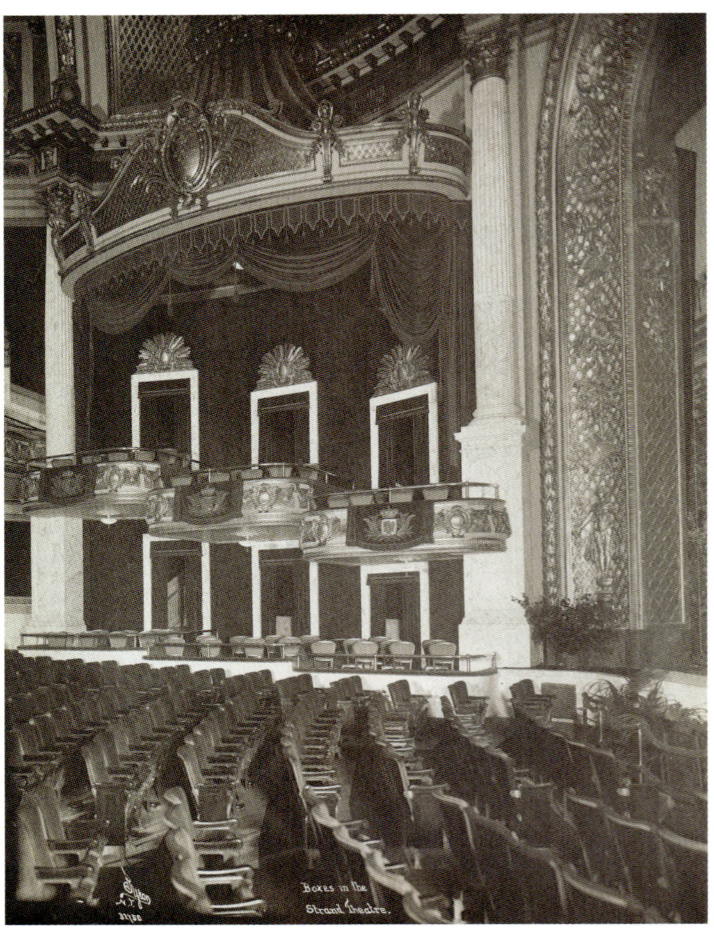

Top, left to right:

228. Study for *New York Movie* (Strand Theatre), 1938
Fabricated chalk on paper, $7\frac{1}{8} \times 4\frac{1}{2}$ in. (18.1×11.4 cm)
Josephine N. Hopper Bequest 70.81

229. Study for *New York Movie* (Strand Theatre), 1938
Fabricated chalk on paper, $7\frac{1}{8} \times 4\frac{1}{2}$ in. (18.1×11.4 cm)
Josephine N. Hopper Bequest 70.82

230. Study for *New York Movie* (Strand Theatre), 1938
Fabricated chalk on paper, $7\frac{1}{4} \times 4\frac{1}{2}$ in. (18.4×11.4 cm)
Josephine N. Hopper Bequest 70.83

Bottom, left to right:

231. Study for *New York Movie* (Strand Theatre), 1938
Fabricated chalk on paper, $4\frac{1}{2} \times 7\frac{3}{16}$ in. (11.4×18.3 cm)
Josephine N. Hopper Bequest 70.87

232. Boxes in the Strand Theatre, c. 1914. Museum of the City of New York 93.1.1.15662

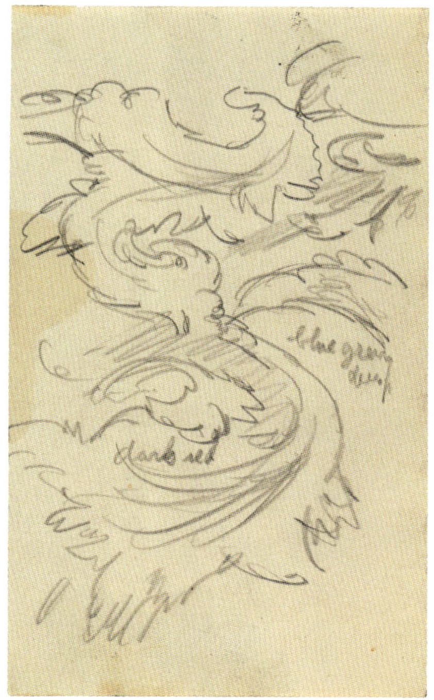

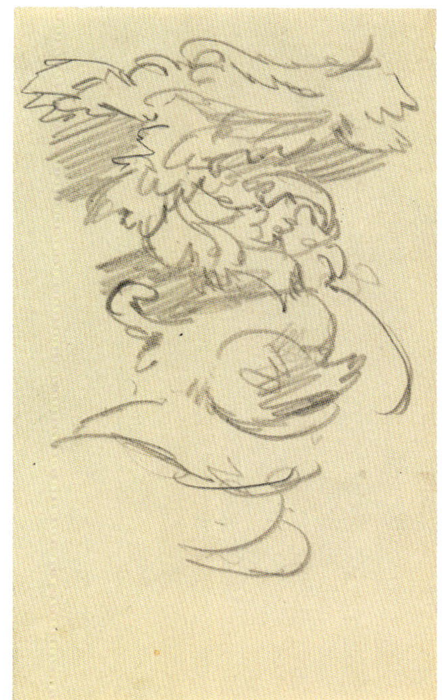

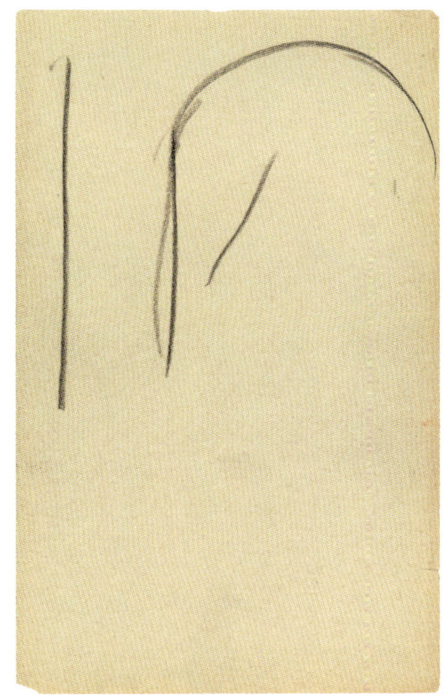

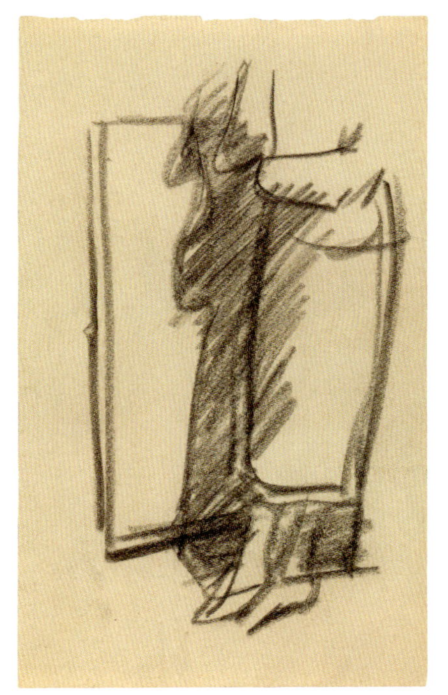

233. (top left)
Study for *New York Movie*, 1938
Graphite pencil on paper, 7 ¼ × 4 7/16 in. (18.4 × 11.3 cm)
Josephine N. Hopper Bequest 70.84

234. (top right)
Study for *New York Movie*, 1938
Graphite pencil on paper, 7 ¼ × 4 7/16 in. (18.4 × 11.3 cm)
Josephine N. Hopper Bequest 70.85

235. (bottom left)
Study for *New York Movie*, 1938
Fabricated chalk on paper, 7 ⅛ × 4 ½ in. (18.1 × 11.4 cm)
Josephine N. Hopper Bequest 70.80

236. (bottom right)
Study for *New York Movie*, 1938
Fabricated chalk on paper, 7 ¼ × 4 7/16 in. (18.4 × 11.3 cm)
Josephine N. Hopper Bequest 70.88

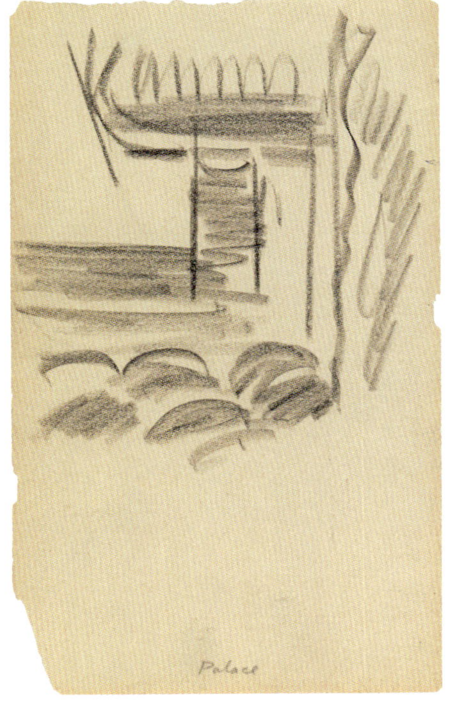

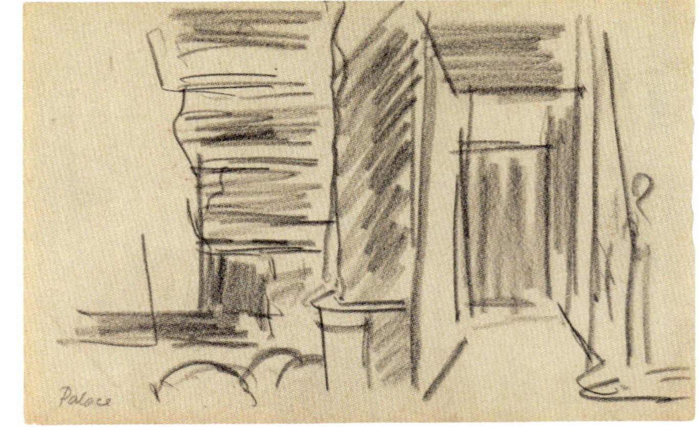

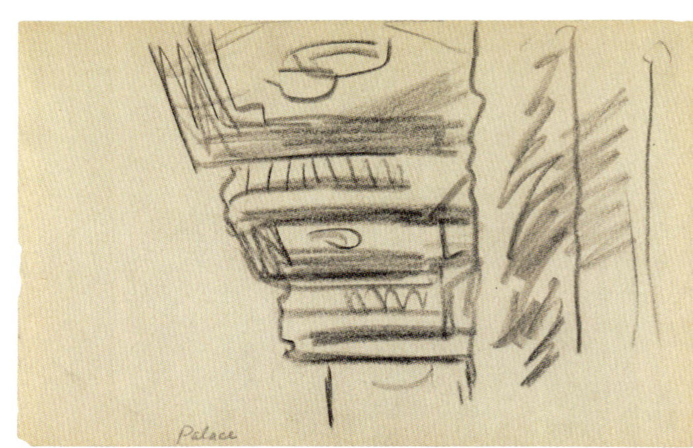

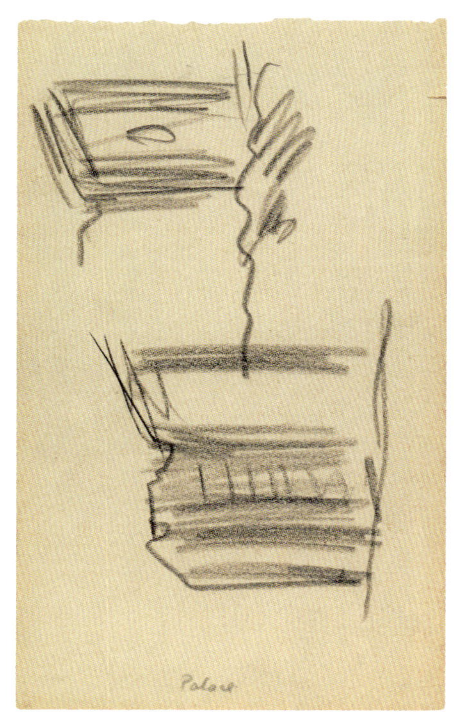

Clockwise, from top left:

237. Study for *New York Movie* (Palace Theatre), 1938
Fabricated chalk on paper, 7 1/8 × 4 7/16 in. (18.1 × 11.3 cm)
Josephine N. Hopper Bequest 70.152

238. Study for *New York Movie* (Palace Theatre), 1938
Charcoal on paper, 4 7/16 × 7 1/8 in. (11.3 × 18.1 cm)
Josephine N. Hopper Bequest 70.78

239. Study for *New York Movie* (Palace Theatre), 1938
Fabricated chalk on paper, 4 7/16 × 7 1/8 in. (11.3 × 18.1 cm)
Josephine N. Hopper Bequest 70.148

240. Study for *New York Movie* (Palace Theatre), 1938
Fabricated chalk on paper, 7 1/8 × 4 1/2 in. (18.1 × 11.4 cm)
Josephine N. Hopper Bequest 70.90

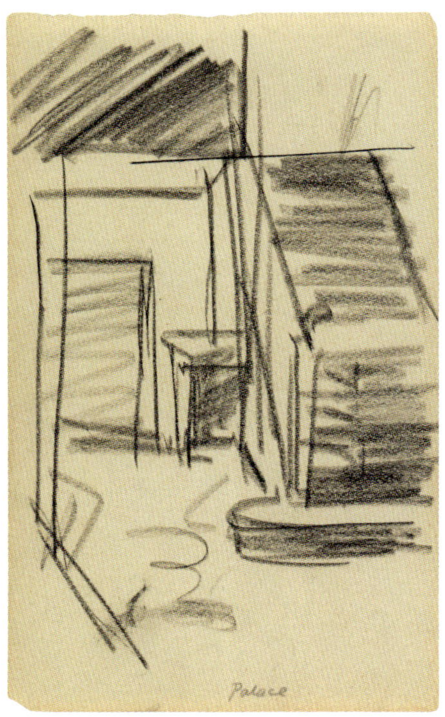

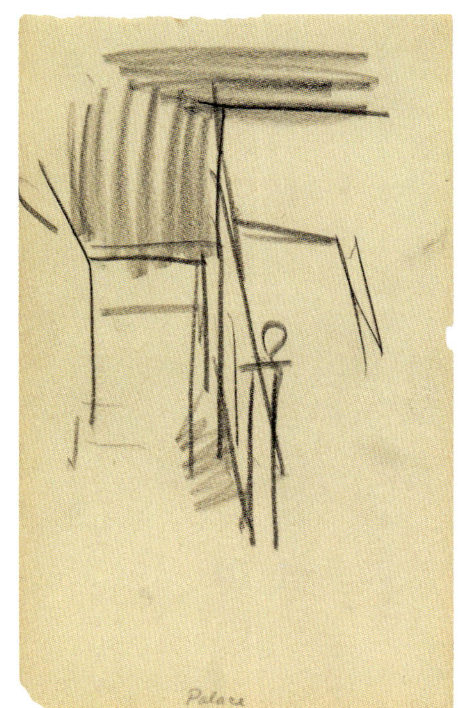

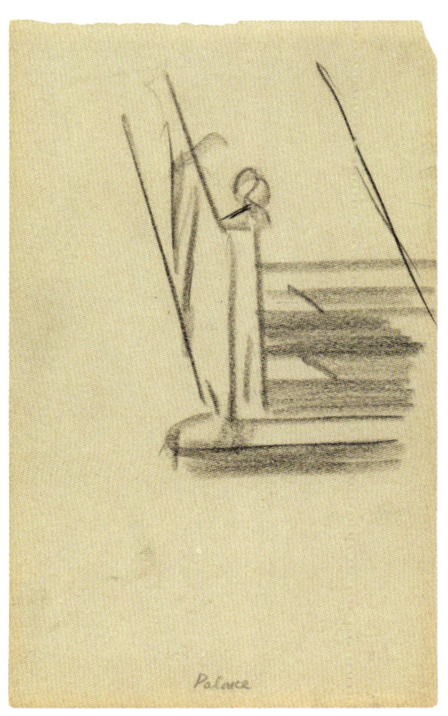

Left to right:

241. Study for *New York Movie* (Palace Theatre), 1938
Fabricated chalk on paper, 7 1/8 × 4 7/16 in. (18.1 × 11.3 cm)
Josephine N. Hopper Bequest 70.149

242. Study for *New York Movie* (Palace Theatre), 1938
Fabricated chalk on paper, 7 1/8 × 4 7/16 in. (18.1 × 11.3 cm)
Josephine N. Hopper Bequest 70.151

243. Study for *New York Movie* (Palace Theatre), 1938
Fabricated chalk on paper, 7 1/8 × 4 1/2 in. (18.1 × 11.4 cm)
Josephine N. Hopper Bequest 70.76

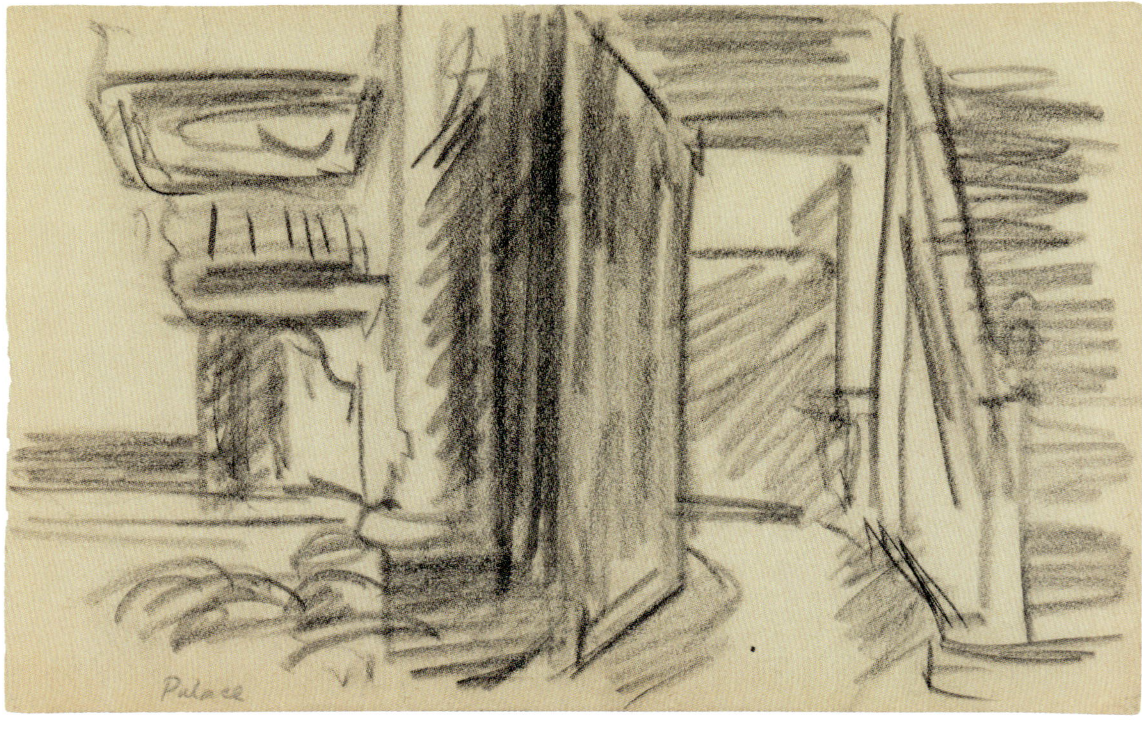

244. Study for *New York Movie* (Palace Theatre), 1938
Fabricated chalk on paper, 4 ½ × 7 ¼ in. (11.4 × 18.4 cm)
Josephine N. Hopper Bequest 70.89

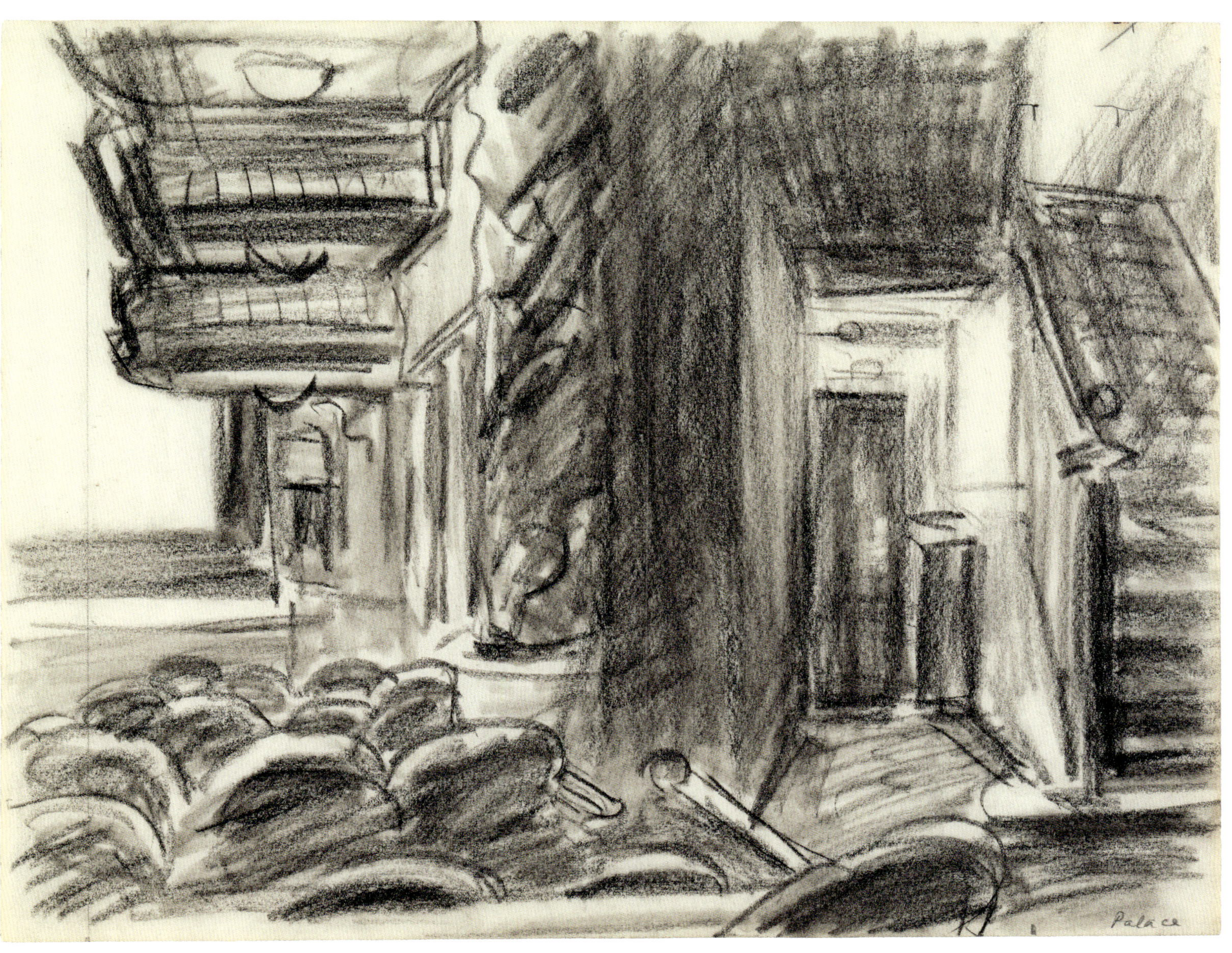

245. Study for *New York Movie* (Palace Theatre), 1938
Fabricated chalk on paper, 8 13/16 × 11 13/16 in. (22.4 × 30 cm)
Josephine N. Hopper Bequest 70.110

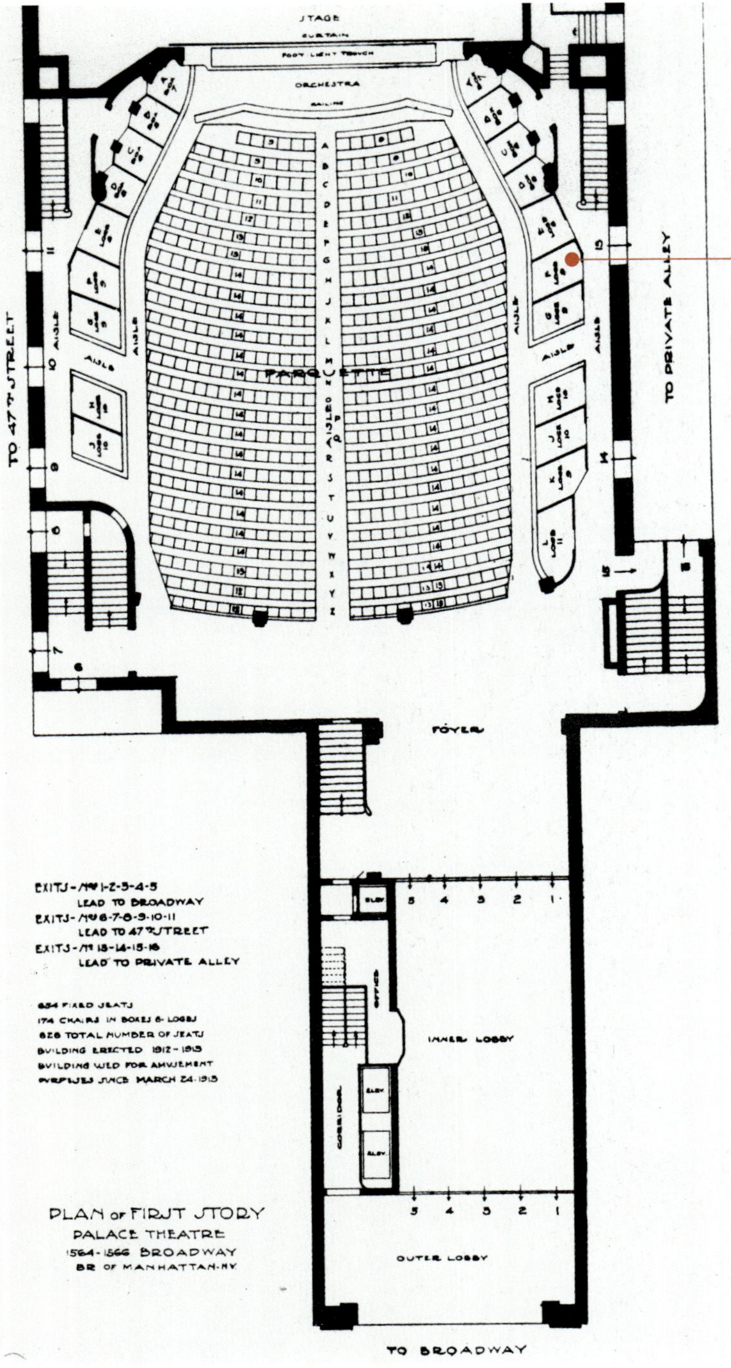

246. Orchestra seating plan, Palace Theatre, c. 1913–30. Terry Hegelson Collection, Theatre Historical Society, Elmhurst, Illinois. The dot indicates the approximate place where Hopper drew the sheets in figs. 244, 245.

247. Side wall and box, Palace Theatre, c. 1913. Terry Hegelson Collection, Theatre Historical Society, Elmhurst, Illinois

248. Proscenium from first balcony, Palace Theatre, 1913. Terry Hegelson Collection, Theatre Historical Society, Elmhurst, Illinois

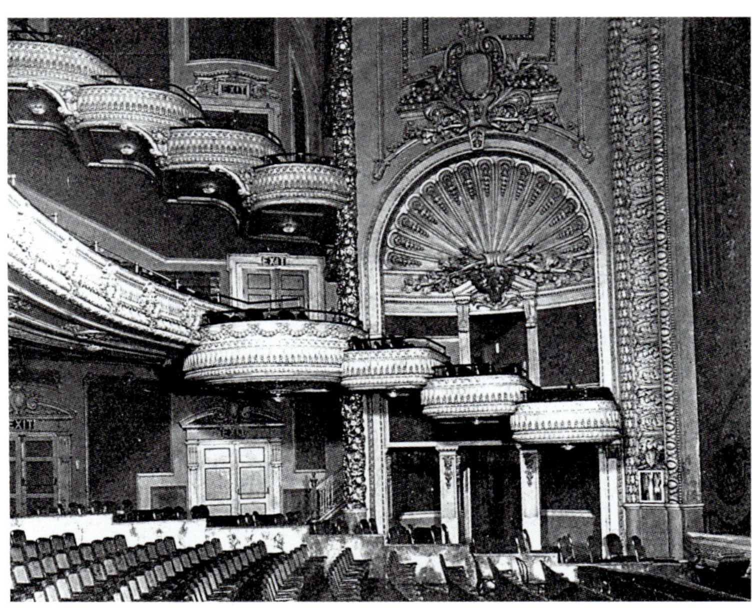

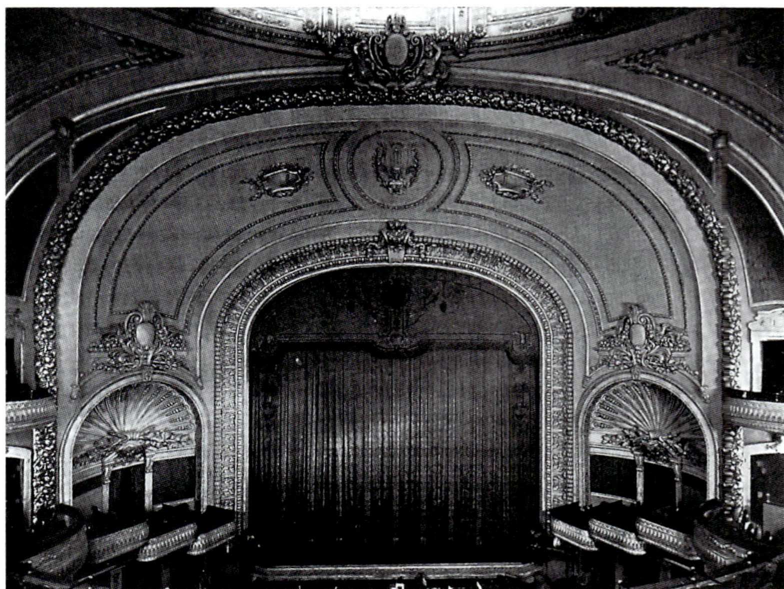

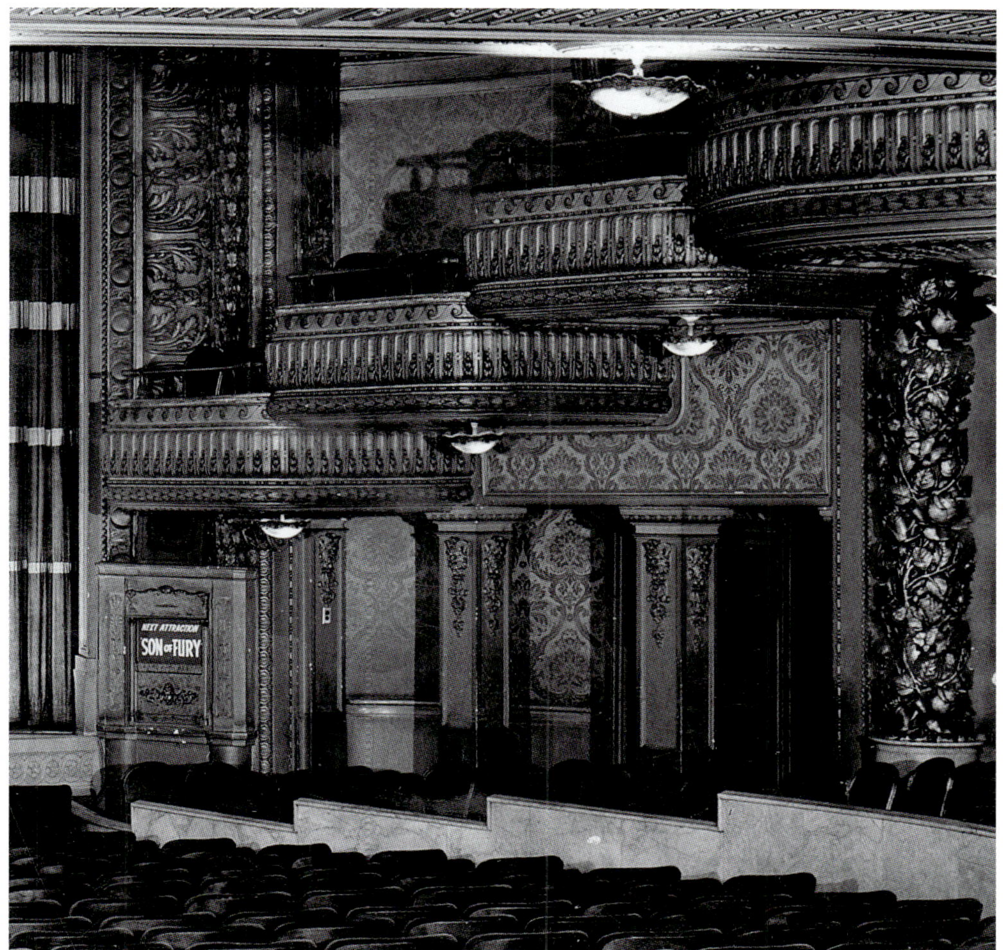

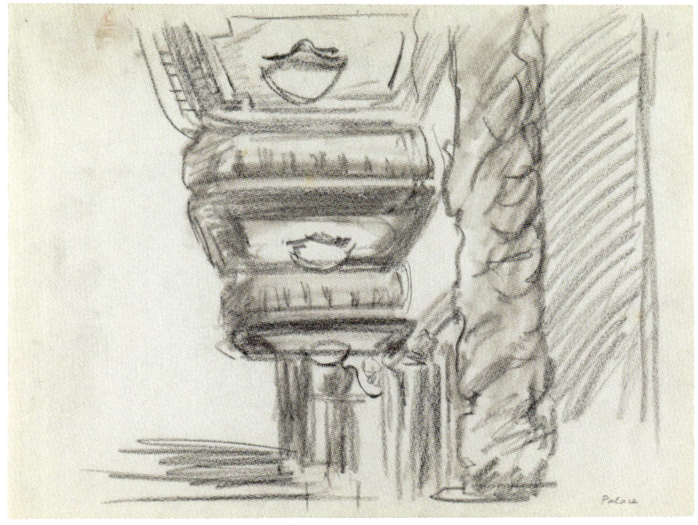

249. Orchestra of Palace Theatre (detail), 1942.
Terry Hegelson Collection, Theatre Historical Society, Elmhurst, Illinois

250. Study for *New York Movie* (Palace Theatre), 1938
Fabricated chalk on paper, 8 7/8 × 11 13/16 in. (22.5 × 30 cm)
Josephine N. Hopper Bequest 70.106

The space that Hopper had found appealing at the Palace was an in-between one, with a view that showed part of the main auditorium and the side aisle, with the end of a wall creating a vertical in the middle. He drew this area in a cohesive larger study (fig. 245), presumably on a return trip to the Palace as described by Jo.[23] We can identify the location on a floor plan of the Palace Theatre that is undated but probably from the 1910s or 1920s[24] (fig. 246), and even find the spot where Hopper drew by correlating his drawing with the plan and contemporary photographs showing where the ornate gilt column met the floor (figs. 247, 249). This column was actually the bottom part of the huge arch framing the balcony boxes, one that echoed the proscenium arch around the stage (fig. 248). To the right of the column's juncture with the orchestra floor, a staircase to the first balcony came down next to a hallway leading backstage (see fig. 246); next to this staircase was an exit, which Hopper focused on in another sheet (see fig. 257). The rest of the drawings from the large Palace sketchbook feature multiple points of view or various details separated out for specific study, many of which can be identified in the photographs illustrated here. While using this large sketchbook, Hopper clearly had the main elements of the composition in mind and focused

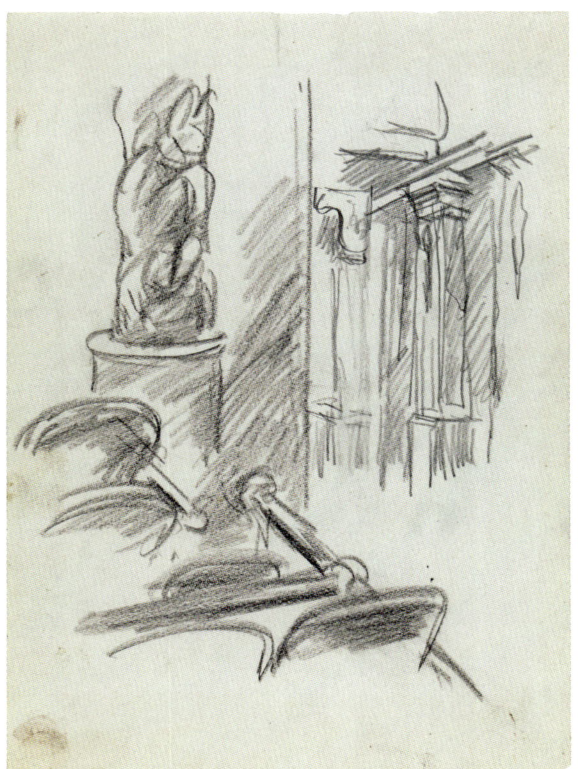

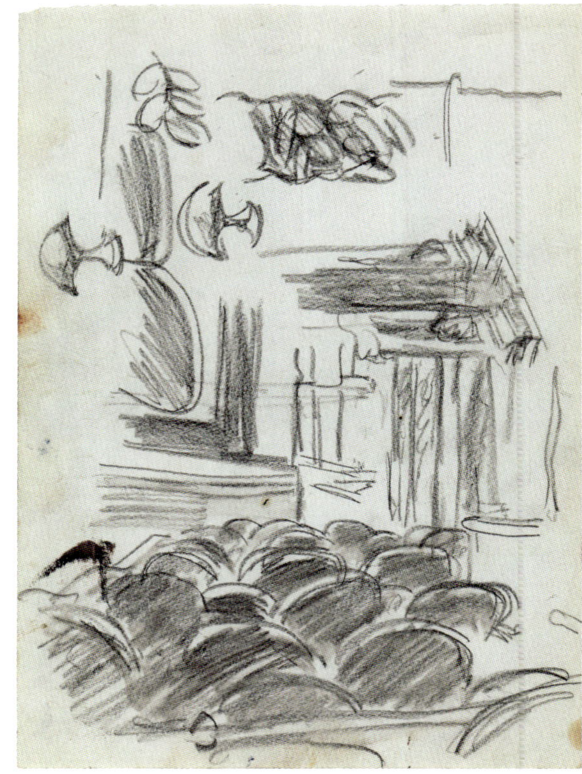

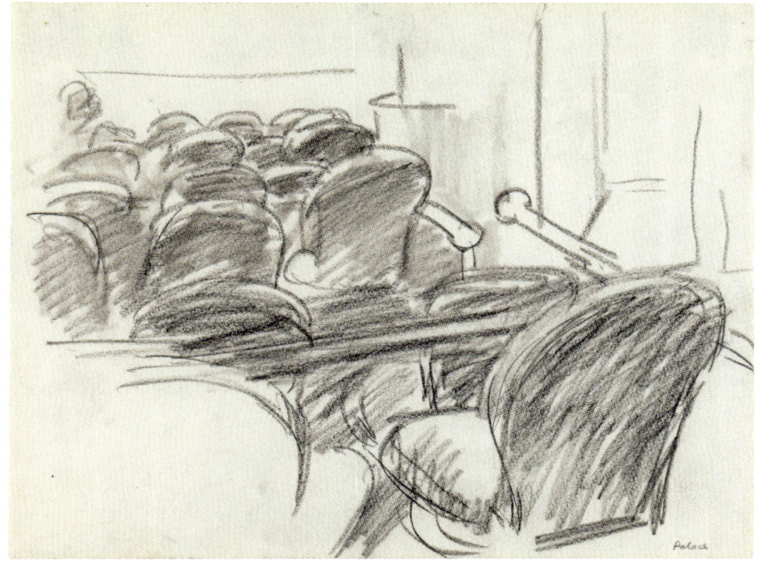

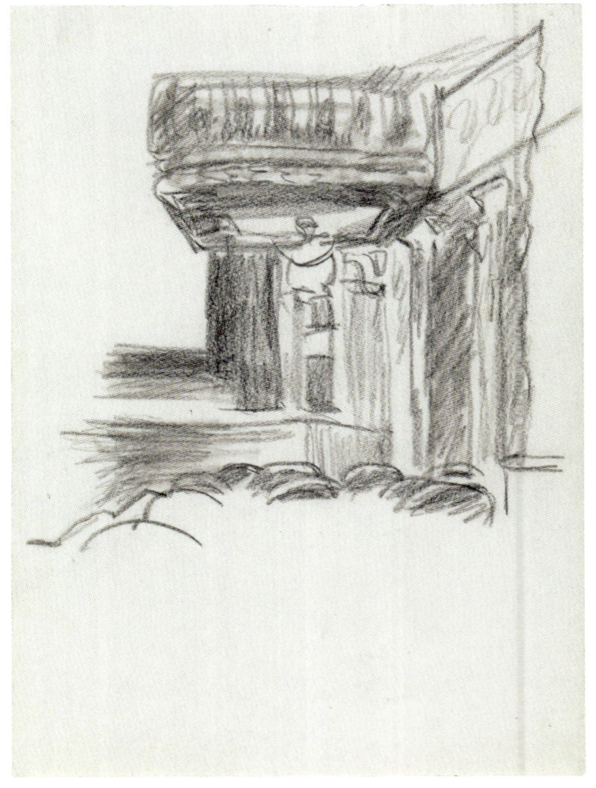

251. (top left)
Study for *New York Movie* (Palace Theatre), 1938
Fabricated chalk and graphite pencil on paper,
$11\frac{7}{8} \times 8\frac{7}{8}$ in. (30.2 × 22.5 cm)
Josephine N. Hopper Bequest 70.105

252. (top right)
Study for *New York Movie* (Palace Theatre), 1938
Fabricated chalk on paper, $11\frac{13}{16} \times 8\frac{13}{16}$ in. (30 × 22.4 cm)
Josephine N. Hopper Bequest 70.103

253. (bottom left)
Study for *New York Movie* (Palace Theatre), 1938
Fabricated chalk on paper, $8\frac{13}{16} \times 11\frac{7}{8}$ in. (22.4 × 30.2 cm)
Josephine N. Hopper Bequest 70.108

254. (bottom right)
Study for *New York Movie* (Palace Theatre), 1938
Fabricated chalk on paper, $11\frac{13}{16} \times 8\frac{13}{16}$ in. (30 × 22.4 cm)
Josephine N. Hopper Bequest 70.102

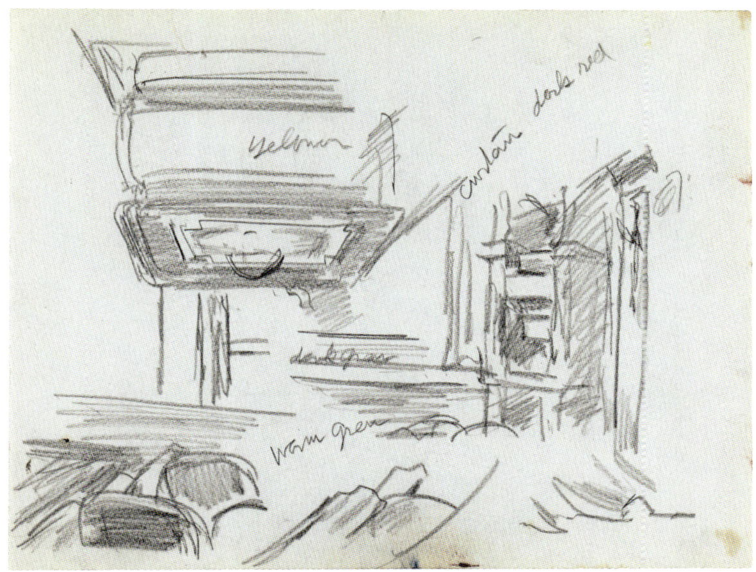

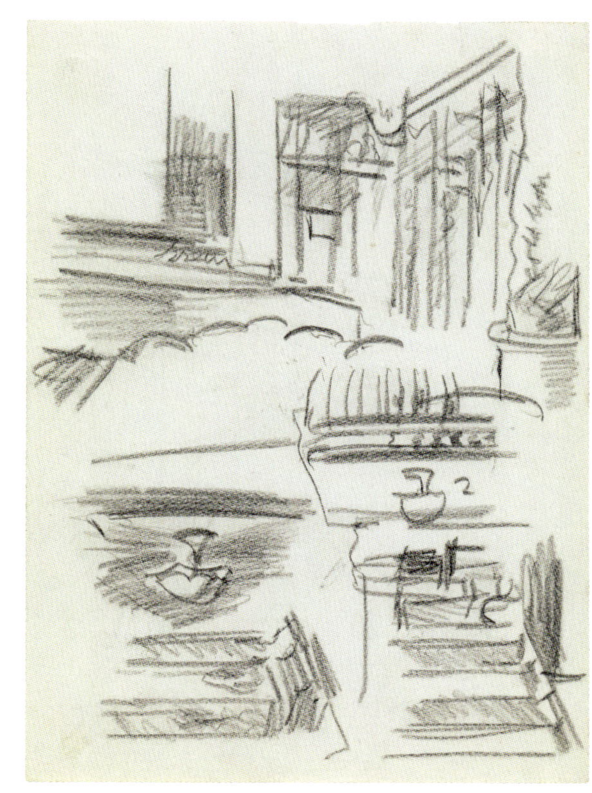

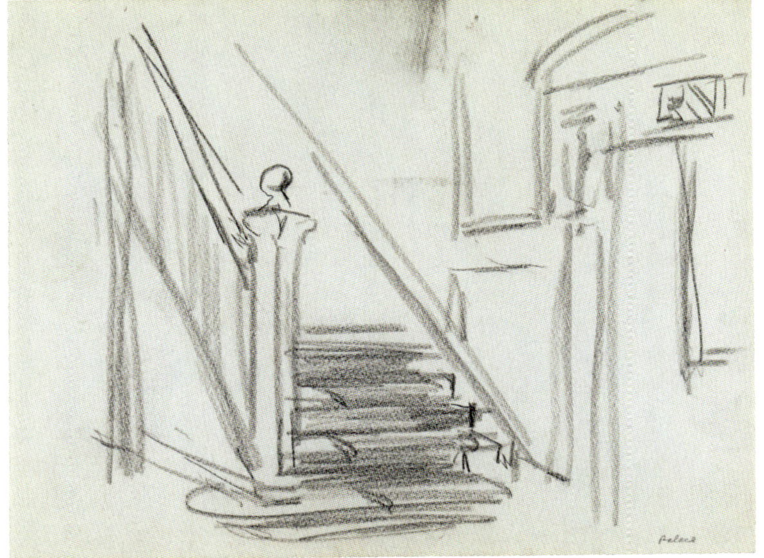

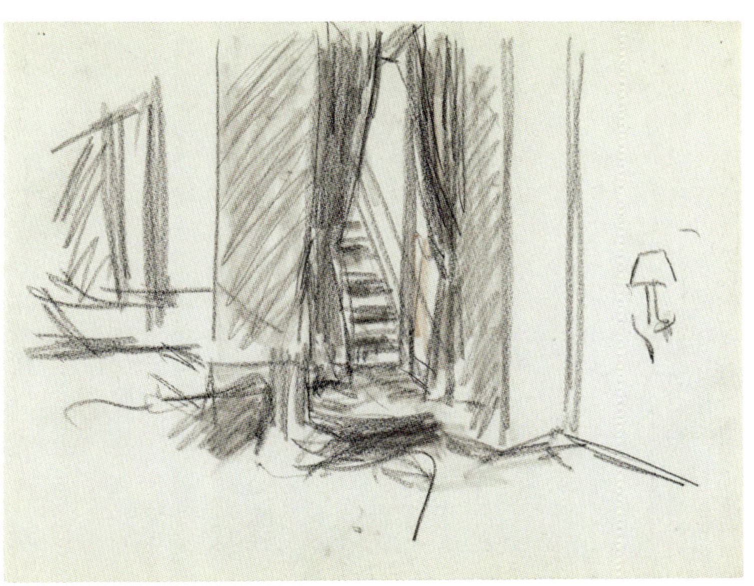

255. (top left)
Study for *New York Movie* (Palace Theatre), 1938
Fabricated chalk on paper, 8 7/8 × 11 7/8 in. (22.5 × 30.2 cm)
Josephine N. Hopper Bequest 70.107

256. (top right)
Study for *New York Movie* (Palace Theatre), 1938
Fabricated chalk on paper, 11 7/8 × 8 13/16 in. (30.2 × 22.4 cm)
Josephine N. Hopper Bequest 70.104

257. (middle)
Study for *New York Movie* (Palace Theatre), 1938
Fabricated chalk on paper, 8 7/8 × 11 7/8 in. (22.5 × 30.2 cm)
Josephine N. Hopper Bequest 70.111

258. (bottom)
Study for *New York Movie* (Palace Theatre), 1938
Fabricated chalk on paper, 8 13/16 × 11 13/16 in. (22.4 × 30 cm)
Josephine N. Hopper Bequest 70.109

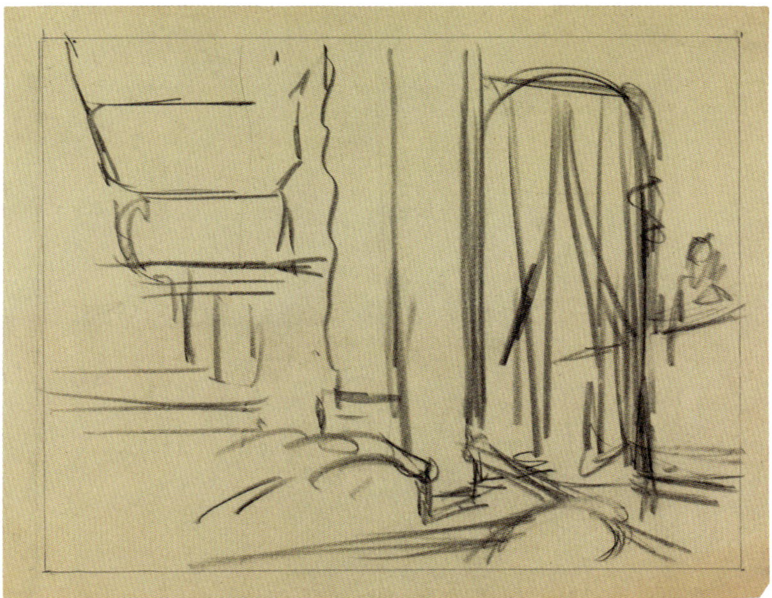

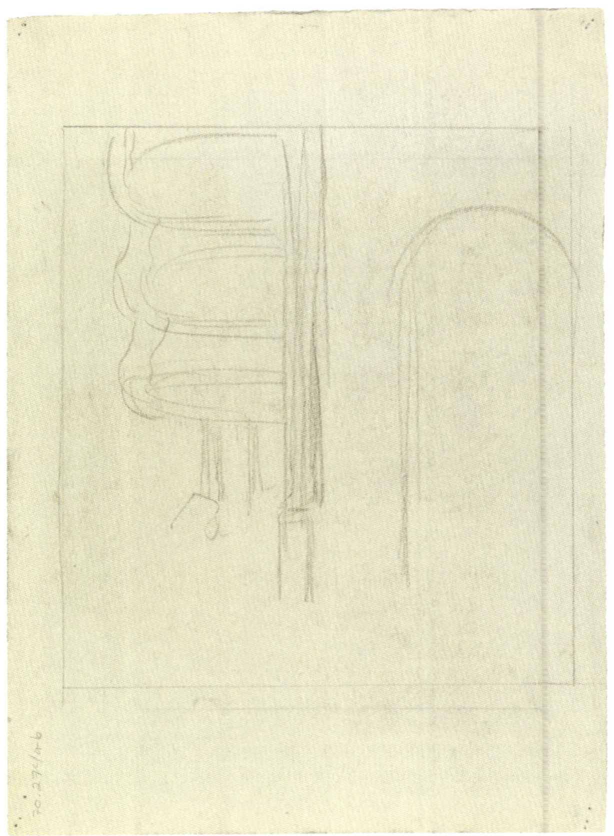

on them: the backs of seats, the stairs, the twisting column, the tiered balcony overhang (figs. 250–258). Some sheets reflect the attention to minute detail so typical of the artist: foliage patterns from the column, the shapes of the light fixtures under the balcony, architectural moldings, and color notations (see figs. 252, 255, 256).

Gail Levin quotes a series of Jo's diary entries that suggest that Hopper began his sketching expeditions by December 13 and continued going to theaters to draw until at least December 26. By that date he had also started to block out the composition in charcoal on canvas, as was his habit. But the diary also implies that he had been making drawings in the studio as early as December 15: "E. busy making crayon drawings—all-dark—of curtained entrance to a box at the theatre."[25] This description may correspond to one or more of the compositional studies (figs. 259, 261–272) in which the curtain is a prominent feature. Presumably he did some of these as he was working out the proportions and dimensions of the painting. All of them have framing lines, and as a group they show that he tried variations on the format and cropping of the scene. The studies got him at least close enough to what he wanted so that he could stretch and prepare his canvas. Comparing one of the most finished of these studies (see fig. 272) to the large sketchbook sheet made at the Palace (see fig. 245), we see how he used much of what was there in the theater but compressed its spaces at the right, collapsing the staircase into the single curtained opening in order to create the small corner for his usherette.[26]

The compositional studies range from skeletal outlines (see figs. 259, 260) to deeply tonal, richly blended dark renderings that are among his finest drawings (see figs. 265–272). Some were executed quickly, with only the point of his chalk stick (see figs. 259, 261–263)—Hopper, who was brilliant at combining stumping and blending with directly applied medium, put this technique to especially good use in seven of these drawings, where he deftly manipulated the texture of the chalk or charcoal in order to explore tonal and light effects (see figs. 265–270, 272). In one, he used red chalk, a rarity for him, which allowed him to grapple in drawing with the reddish ranges of color that became significant in the painting (see fig. 271). More than any other group of drawings in his oeuvre, these fourteen compositional studies reflect just how carefully Hopper needed to orchestrate nuance to get what he wanted. Their variations shift the relational balance of the image in fairly minor ways—subtleties that are as good an indication as any of why Hopper found it difficult to paint, and also why drawing was crucial to his practice.

Hopper used these compositional studies to develop the spectator's point of view—the placement of the "camera," following Wenders's metaphor. For a Hopper painting, *New York Movie* has a fairly rational perspective, with a vanishing point in the area near the lower

259. Study for *New York Movie*, 1938 or 1939
Fabricated chalk on paper, 8¾ × 10⅞ in. (22.2 × 27.6 cm)
Josephine N. Hopper Bequest 70.93

260. Study for *New York Movie* (verso), 1938 or 1939
Fabricated chalk on paper, 15 1/16 × 11⅛ in. (38.3 × 28.3 cm)
Josephine N. Hopper Bequest 70.274a–b

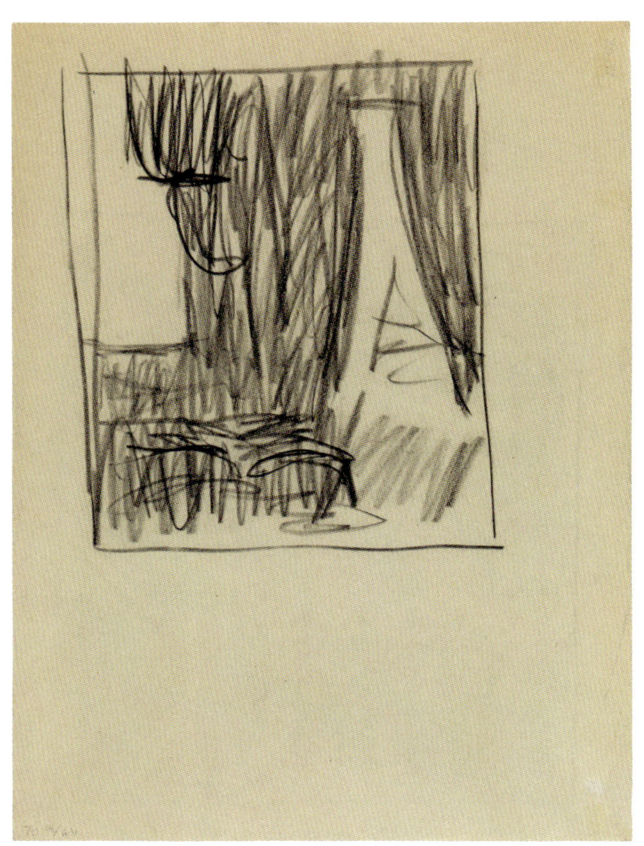

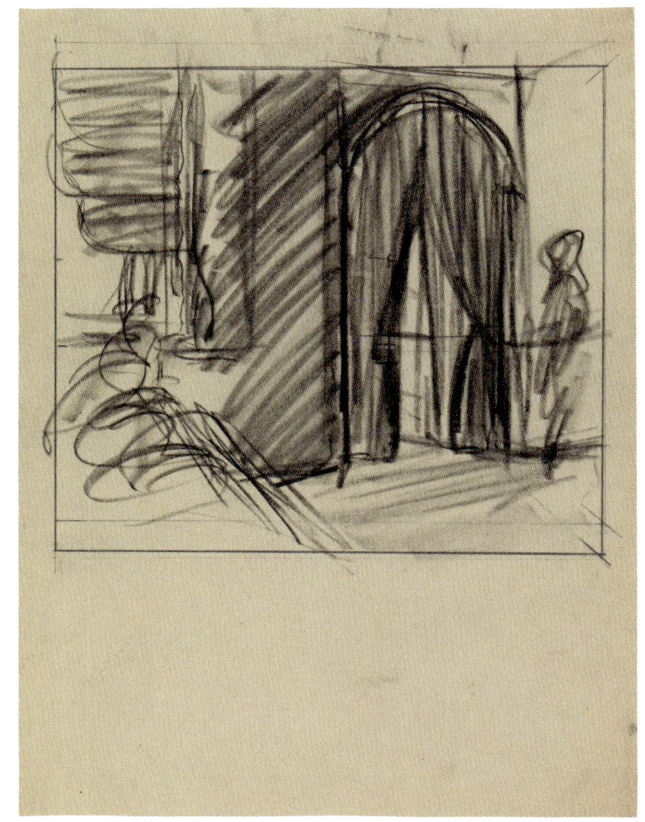

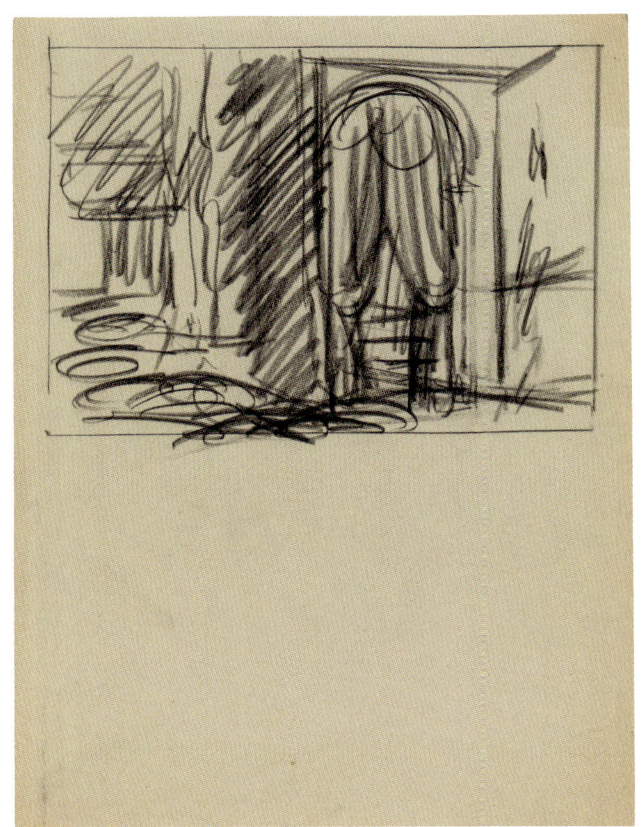

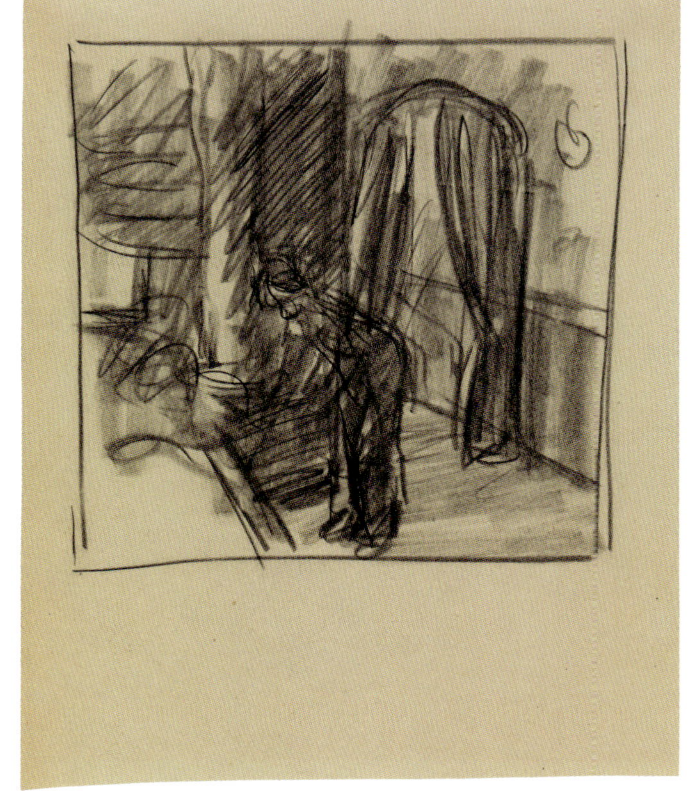

261. (top left)
Study for *New York Movie* (verso), 1938 or 1939
Fabricated chalk on paper, 10 7/8 × 8 3/8 in. (27.6 × 21.3 cm)
Josephine N. Hopper Bequest 70.94a–b

262. (top right)
Study for *New York Movie*, 1938 or 1939
Fabricated chalk and graphite pencil on paper,
10 7/8 × 8 3/8 in. (27.6 × 21.3 cm)
Josephine N. Hopper Bequest 70.98

263. (bottom left)
Study for *New York Movie*, 1938 or 1939
Fabricated chalk on paper, 10 7/8 × 8 3/8 in. (27.6 × 21.3 cm)
Josephine N. Hopper Bequest 70.99

264. (bottom right)
Study for *New York Movie*, 1938 or 1939
Fabricated chalk on paper, 10 3/16 × 8 7/16 in. (25.9 × 21.4 cm)
Josephine N. Hopper Bequest 70.96

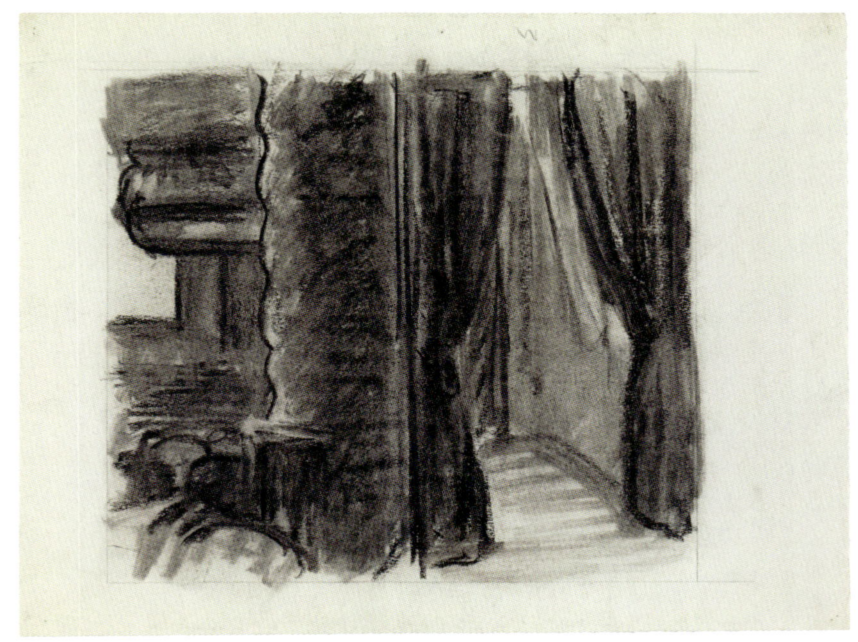

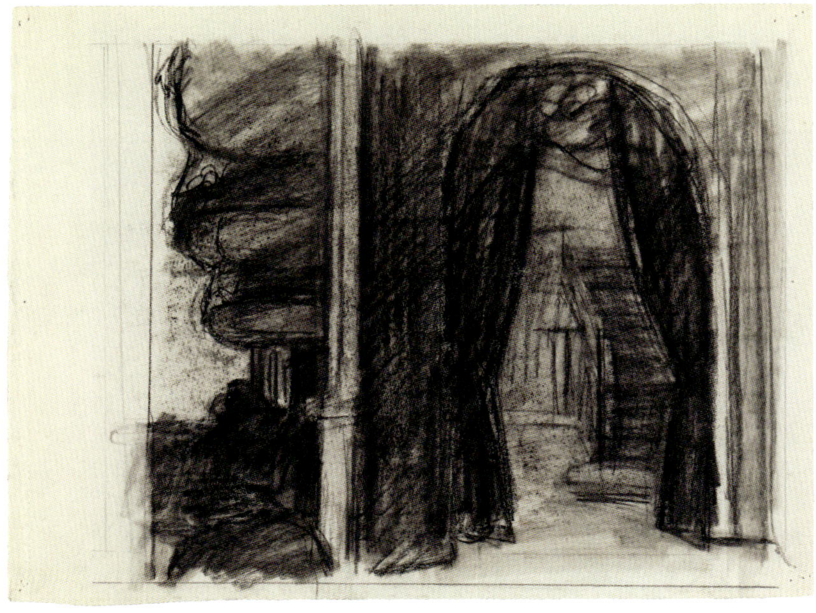

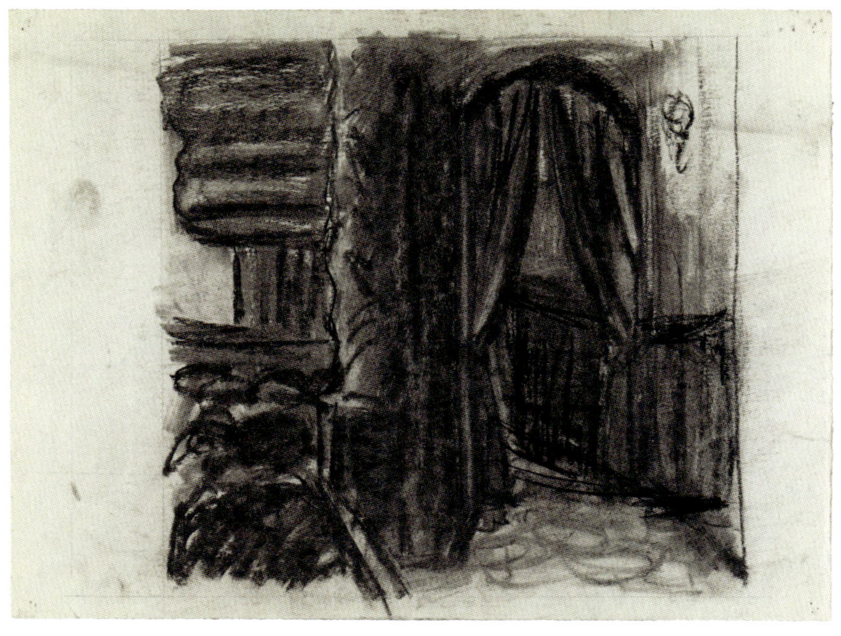

265. Study for *New York Movie*, 1938 or 1939
Fabricated chalk on paper, 11 1/8 × 15 in. (28.3 × 38.1 cm)
Josephine N. Hopper Bequest 70.276

266. Study for *New York Movie* (recto), 1938 or 1939
Fabricated chalk and charcoal on paper, 11 1/8 × 15 1/16 in. (28.3 × 38.3 cm)
Josephine N. Hopper Bequest 70.274a–b

267. Study for *New York Movie*, 1938 or 1939
Charcoal on paper, 11 1/16 × 15 in. (28.1 × 38.1 cm)
Josephine N. Hopper Bequest 70.275

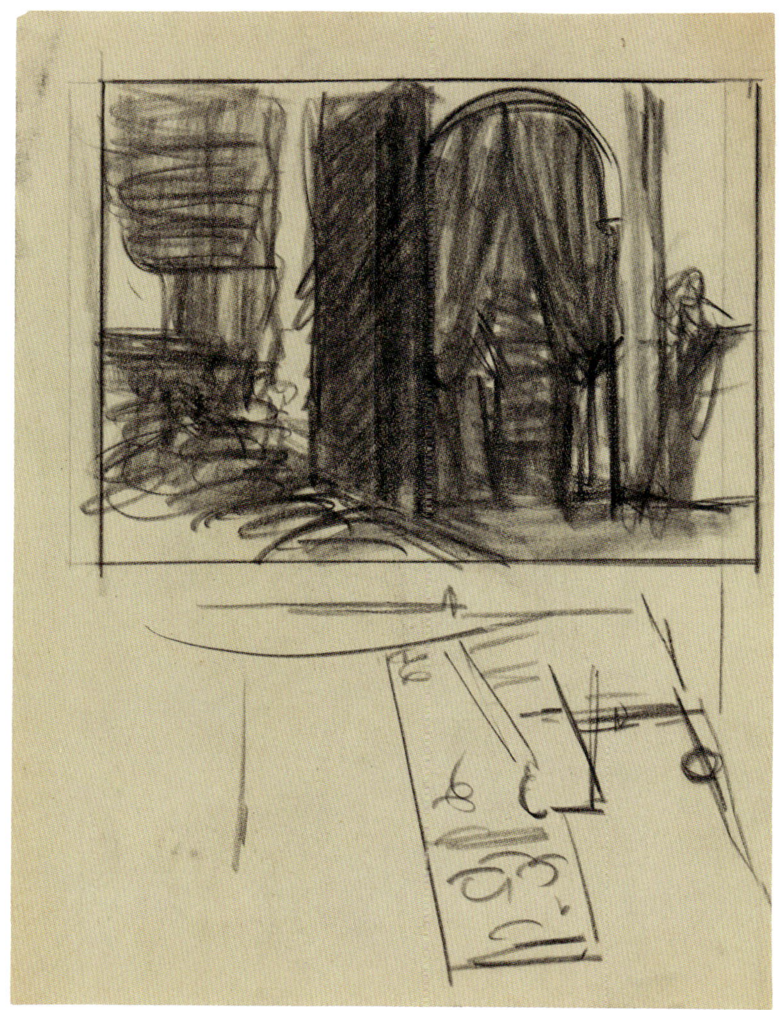

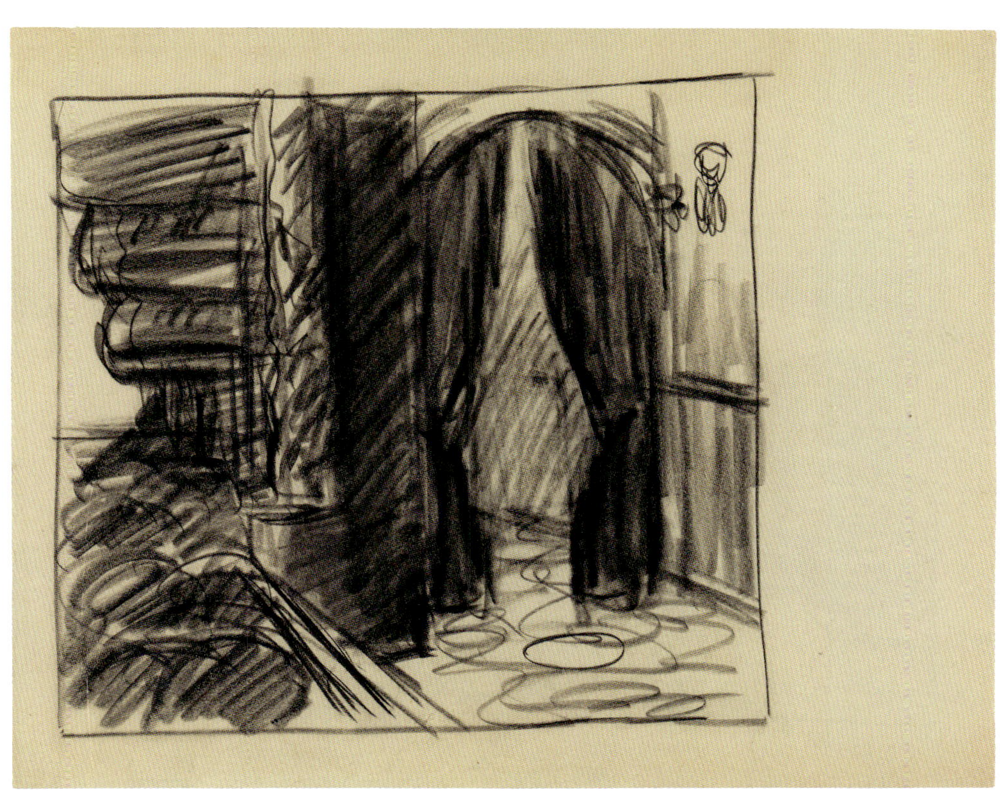

268. Study for *New York Movie*, 1938 or 1939
Fabricated chalk on paper, 10 ⅞ × 8 ⅜ in. (27.6 × 21.3 cm)
Josephine N. Hopper Bequest 70.95

269. Study for *New York Movie* (recto), 1938 or 1939
Fabricated chalk on paper, 8 ⅜ × 10 ⅞ in. (21.3 × 27.6 cm)
Josephine N. Hopper Bequest 70.94a–b

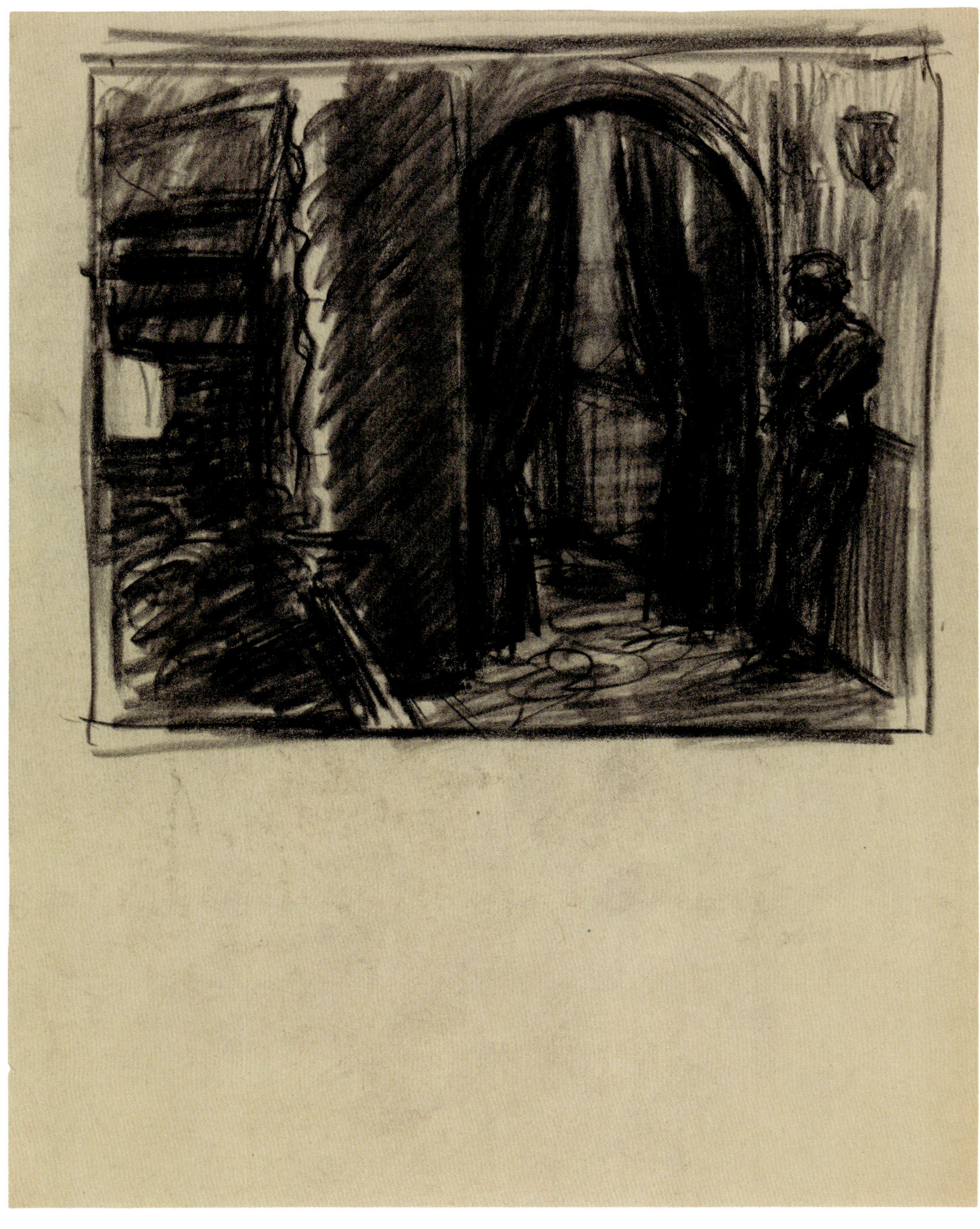

270. Study for *New York Movie*, 1938 or 1939
Fabricated chalk on paper, 10 5/16 × 8 3/8 in. (26.2 × 21.3 cm)
Josephine N. Hopper Bequest 70.97

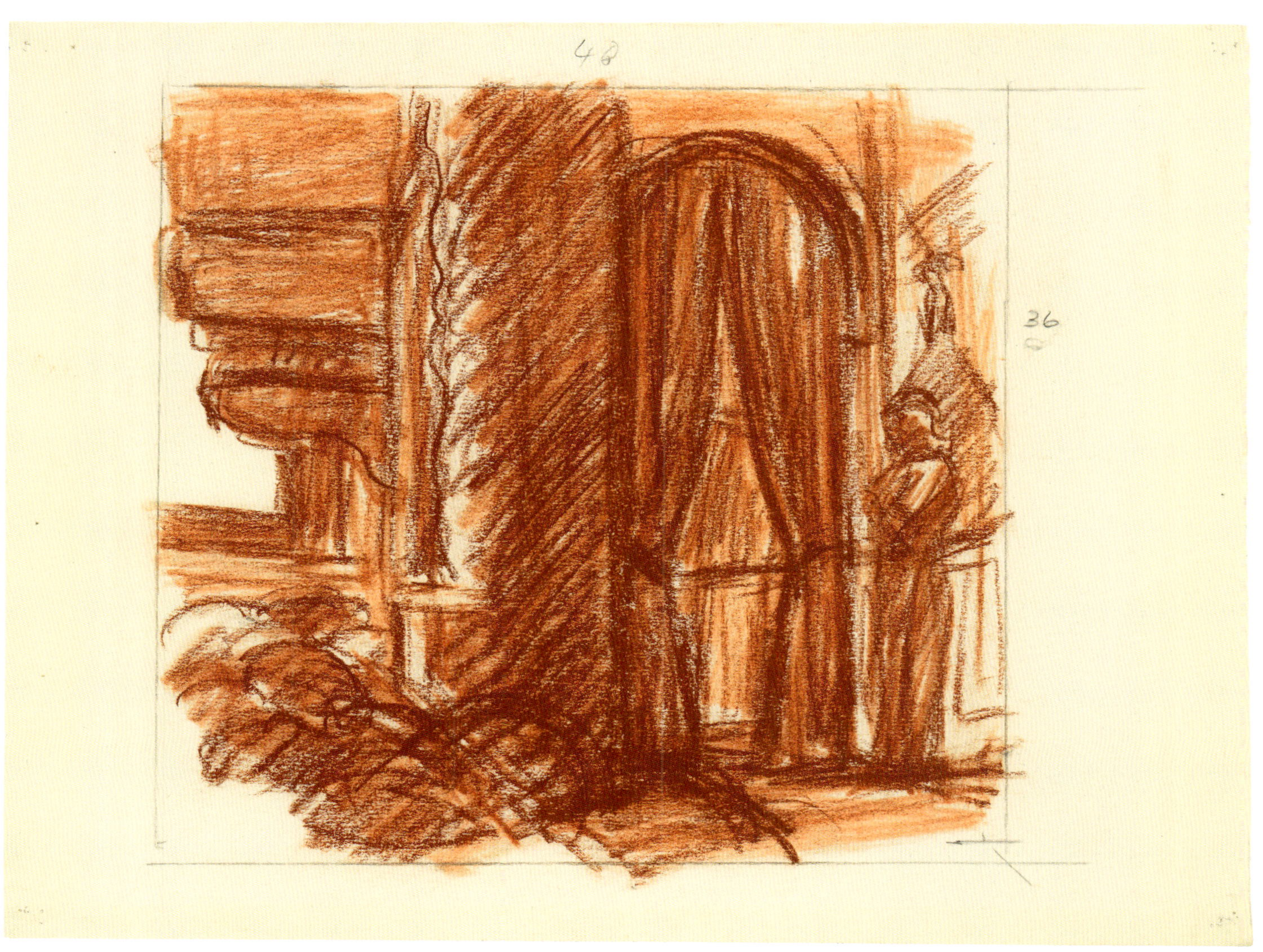

271. Study for *New York Movie*, 1938 or 1939
Fabricated chalk on paper, 11 ⅛ × 15 in. (28.3 × 38.1 cm)
Josephine N. Hopper Bequest 70.277

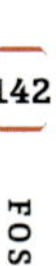

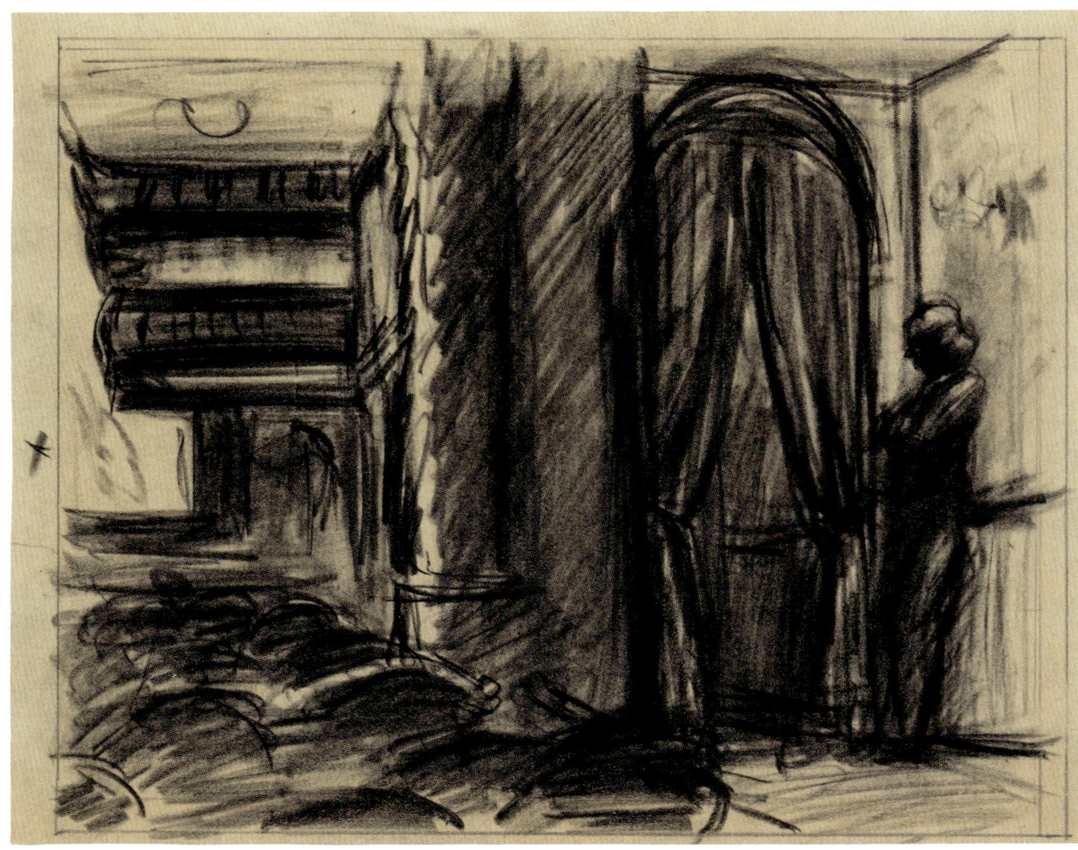

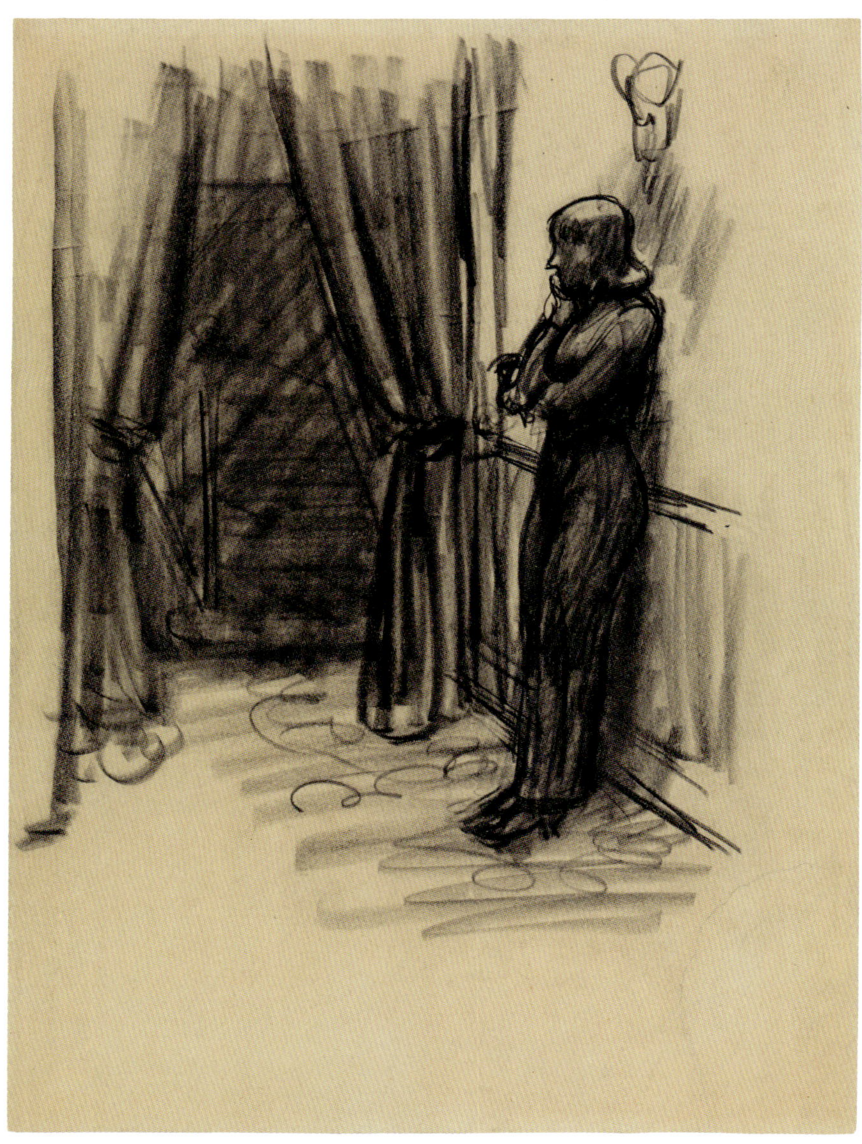

272. Study for *New York Movie*, 1938 or 1939
Fabricated chalk on paper, 8 ³⁄₈ × 10 ¹⁵⁄₁₆ in. (21.3 × 27.8 cm)
Josephine N. Hopper Bequest 70.100

273. Study for *New York Movie*, 1938 or 1939
Fabricated chalk on paper, 10 ⁷⁄₈ × 8 ³⁄₈ in. (27.6 × 21 3 cm)
Josephine N. Hopper Bequest 70.101

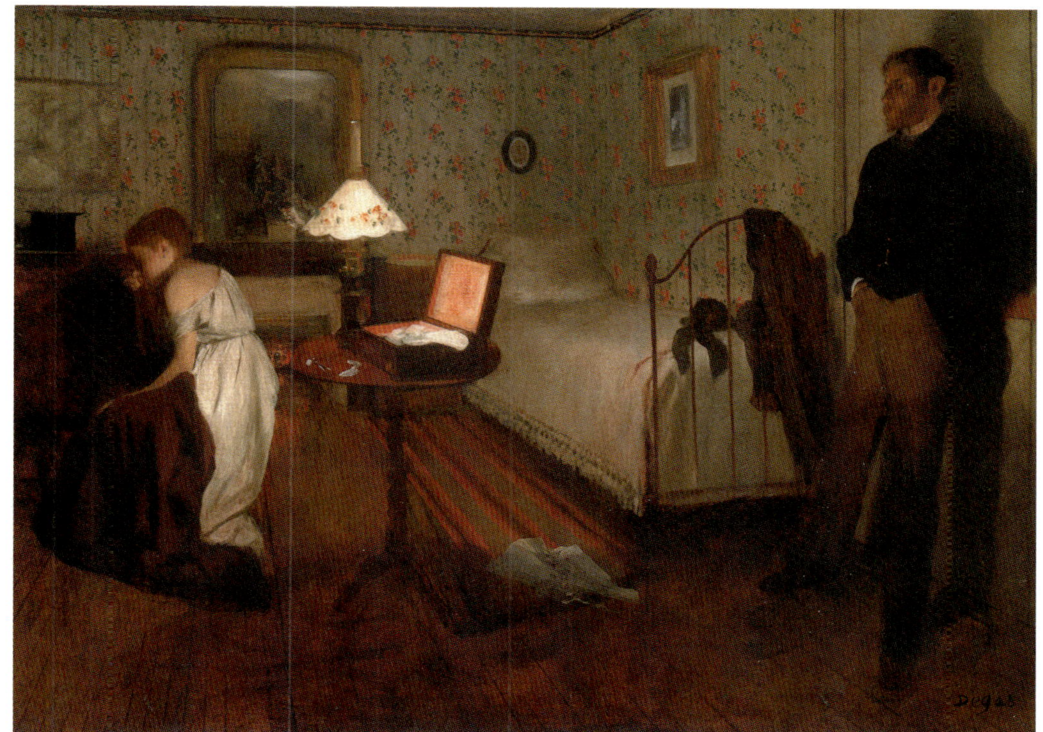

corner of the movie screen, if one follows recessional lines in the architecture and the prominent brass railing in the foreground. Levin and others have written on the similarities of the composition with Edgar Degas's *Interior* of 1868 or 1869 (fig. 274).[27] Hopper greatly admired Degas, and the painting's dim lighting and compositional parallels—Degas's leaning figure, plunging perspective at left, and silvery mirror (a view into another world, like a movie screen or a painting) all have echoes in *New York Movie*—suggest that he may have had *Interior* in mind when working on his own canvas. But crucial to how we, the spectator, ultimately partake in this scene is the viewpoint Hopper developed. If we follow the painting's space and our relationship to it, we understand that the artist is representing the position of a body in transition; the seats in front of us indicate that we are inside a row, not in the aisle, and that we are standing, not seated. In other words, we are either about to take our seat or have just gotten up. We are also in transition between two types of spaces, a large open auditorium and a small alcove in the aisle.[28] The artist only solidified this quality of *New York Movie* when he painted it. In the compositional studies, he played with shifting viewpoints. Three of them, executed in a similar technique (with the chalk and/or charcoal smeared and rubbed into the surface) and on the same paper type, position us more in the side aisle and closer to the curtained opening (see figs. 265–267). These studies lack the figure of the woman and emphasize the theater's varied spaces, including one beyond the curtain. In the five drawings likely done next (see figs. 268–272), the final composition starts to gel. As a group they reveal the artist's cropping of the scene and trying out slightly different viewpoints, including lower ones, until he gets one that comes close to the final composition (see fig. 272). In another study he focuses in on the alcove area with the usherette (fig. 273).

Hopper experimented with the usherette's position in several of these compositional studies. One shows a different idea for the painting, as she leans over one of the seats while helping a patron (see fig. 264). He roughly indicated her form in some of the sketchier renderings (see figs. 262, 263, 268); on the more finished sheets he developed her pose, with crossed arms leaning against the wall, hips meeting it at the top of the wainscoting. He finally settled on the one he liked (see fig. 273), with her left hand holding the flashlight, her right cradling her chin. This slight change, from arms simply crossed to head resting in hand, shifted the tenor of the work significantly because the gesture now emphasized her pensiveness.

The final series of *New York Movie* drawings are studies of the usherette, and Jo's diary entries allow us to date some or all of them to the very end of his campaign on *New York Movie*. On January 12 she recounted posing in two different hats (fig. 275), thus dating one of the sheets to that day. The fact that Hopper posed her in two ways suggests that, even at this late stage, he was still thinking about whom to put in the audience. On January 21,

274. Edgar Degas (1834–1917)
Interior, 1868 or 1869
Oil on canvas, 32 × 45 in. (81.3 × 114.3 cm)
Philadelphia Museum of Art; The Henry P. McIlhenny Collection in memory of Frances P. McIlhenny, 1986
1986-26-10

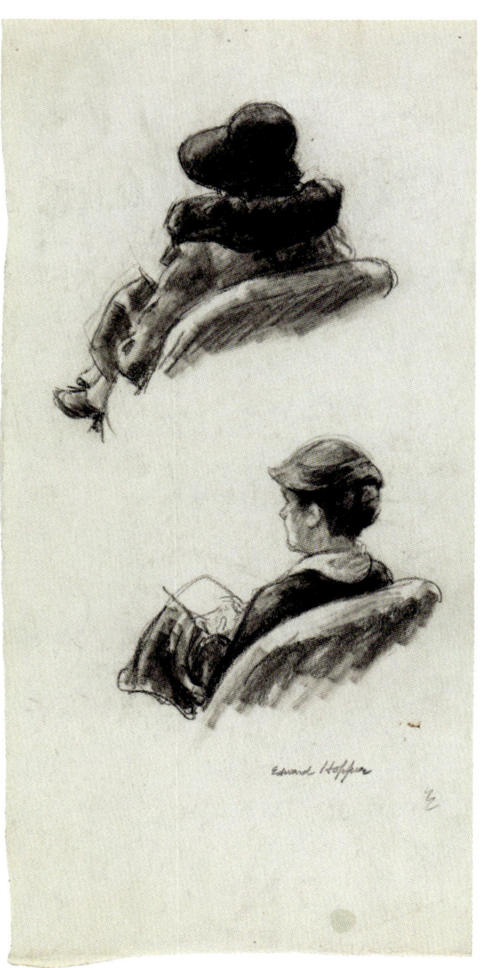

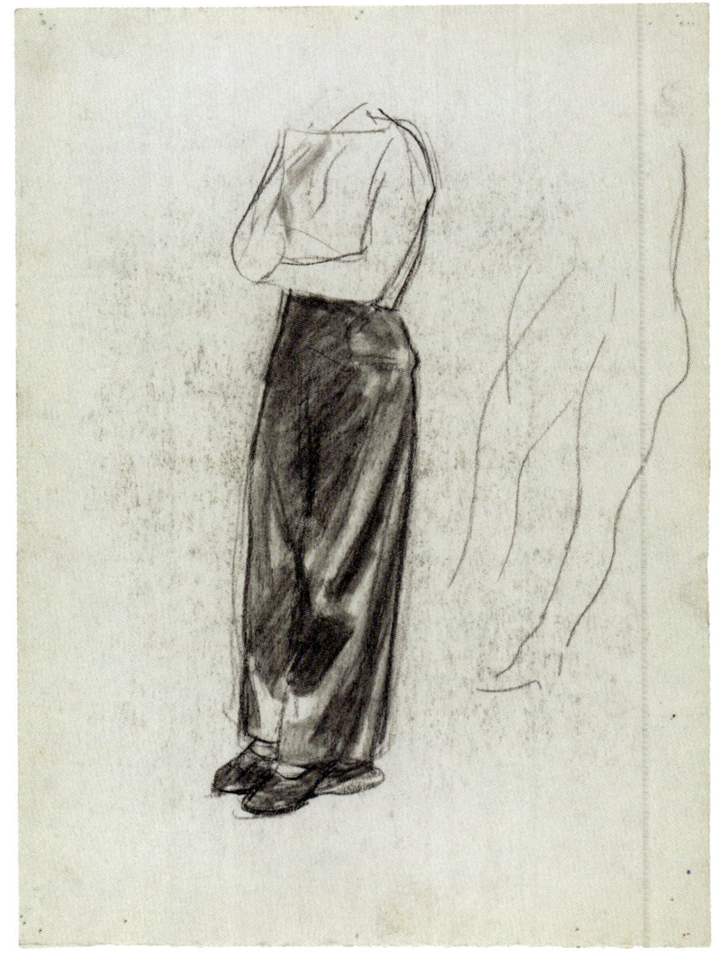

Jo reported that her husband was discouraged and having doubts about the painting, and as late as January 26 she again posed "out in their cold hall for the figure of an usherette holding a flashlight."[29] The usherette studies explore the fall of light on her body and clothes (figs. 236, 276–280); Hopper also refined the position precisely, from the placement of her feet on the floor and the angle of her legs to her arms and head. By now he had transitioned his wife into another person; unlike some of Hopper's studies using Jo as a model for female characters, we really cannot recognize her features here. Perhaps the last drawing Hopper made for *New York Movie* was the bust-length close-up of the usherette (see fig. 280). It is a marvel of technical finesse, especially in such passages as the breasts, where the angled strokes of Hopper's stump cleave together in a series of jagged diagonals. He displays especially focused sensitivity in her face and hair and the way light undulates across them, illuminating her cheek and nose and leaving her eyes and mouth in shadow. We can still tell, however, that she has a very slight smile—an extraordinary rarity for a Hopper character—and that her eyes are closed or nearly so. Her expression is tantalizingly subtle and inscrutable, but it is as genuine a rendering of a person lost in themselves as anything Hopper ever drew or painted.

The young and attractive blonde usherette in *New York Movie* bears a more serious expression than her drawn counterpart; Hopper kept her eyes closed or downcast and eliminated any hint of a smile. The figure studies modeled on Jo depict her wearing a blouse and skirt. In the painting she wears a militaristic blue uniform with epaulets, brass buttons, and a red stripe down the side of her pants. This was in fact quite close to what Palace Theatre usherettes wore in the 1930s, as illustrated in a 1937 *New York Post* article about their work (fig. 281).[30] Ushers and usherettes were very much part of the spectacle in movie palace culture from the 1920s through the 1940s.[31] More typically male, they were chosen for youth and good looks and their training stressed service. Management carefully watched over and regulated their manners, grooming, and solicitousness toward patrons. A military hierarchy

275. Study for *New York Movie*, 1939
Fabricated chalk on paper, 15 ½ × 7 ¾ in. (39.4 × 19.7 cm)
Josephine N. Hopper Bequest 70.447

276. Study for *New York Movie*, 1939
Fabricated chalk on paper, 15 × 11 ⅛ in. (38.1 × 28.3 cm)
Josephine N. Hopper Bequest 70.278

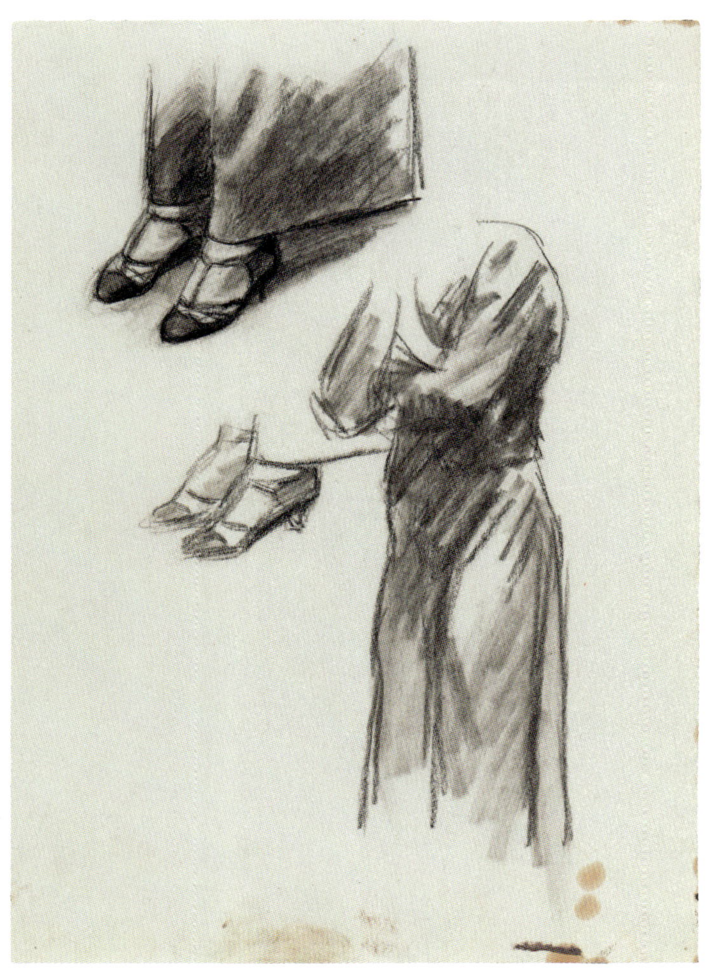

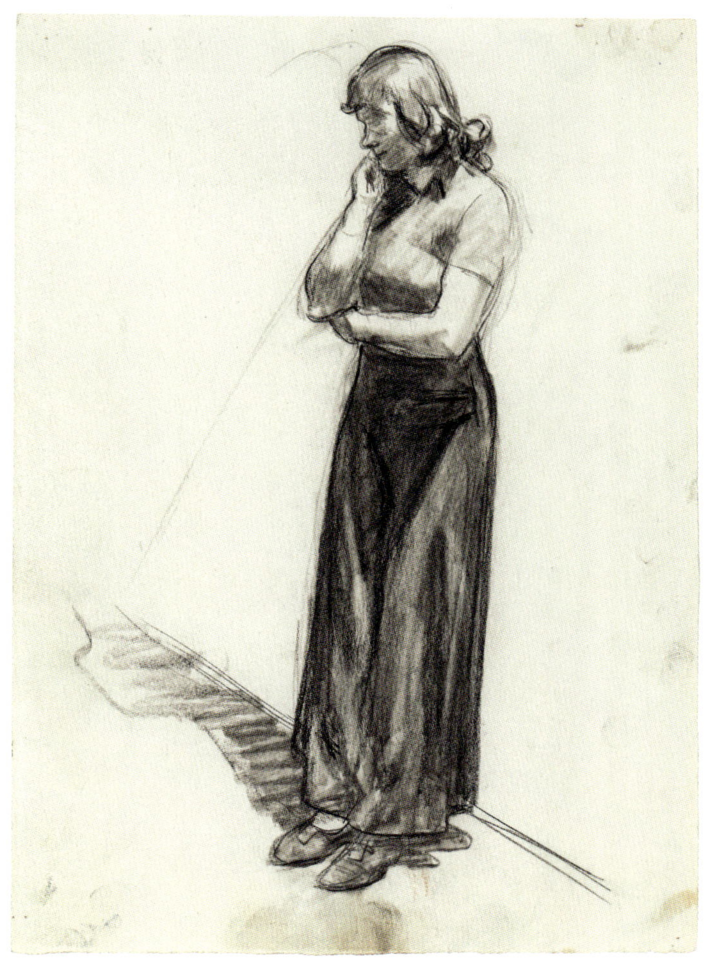

277. Study for *New York Movie*, 1939
Fabricated chalk on paper, 15 × 11 3/16 in. (38.1 × 28.4 cm)
Josephine N. Hopper Bequest 70.273

278. Study for *New York Movie*, 1939
Fabricated chalk and charcoal on paper,
15 × 11 1/16 in. (38.1 × 28.1 cm)
Josephine N. Hopper Bequest 70.272

regimented their work, and their status in this hierarchy was often indicated through the markings and stripes of their uniform. In some prominent theaters, the ushers were even managed by former armed services officers, and they typically performed military-like drills in theater lobbies, stairways, and other areas to entertain and impress moviegoers.[32] Each theater utilized an elaborate system of hand signals so that employees could communicate seat availability and move people efficiently. An usher's flashlight was an important tool, used to signal others and guide patrons in a carefully orchestrated fashion.[33] Contemporary accounts suggest that usherettes were often aspiring actresses, and that the perceived glamour of Hollywood extended, at least partially, to the realm they inhabited, one of the job's attractions.

Many writers have interpreted Hopper's *New York Movie* usherette as bored from having seen the film too many times. In fact, usherettes were forbidden to watch the movie on view while in uniform.[34] If the job had its appeal, it was still work in long shifts, for relatively low wages, in a deeply regulated environment.[35] Not allowed to view the film, Hopper's usherette is restricted to the aisle and adjacent areas of circulation continuing up the stairs, while the flashlight and uniform define her very specific role within this palace of escapism. Comparison to Hopper's *Sheridan Theatre* of two years earlier is telling. In that painting, a male usher wearing similar militaristic garb leans back on the balustrade at the far left. His pose and prominent, red-striped trousers foreshadow *New York Movie*, as does the pinkish light of the wall sconce at left, very similar to the one in the later painting. But rather than illuminating a confined area, its light spreads out into the large auditorium where a female patron sports her own fashion and is at leisure rather than working, free to inhabit its vast space and enjoy her escape into the world of cinema. Hopper compressed the generous spaces of the Palace Theatre into a more confined domain for his usherette, who closes her eyes in the dim light that surrounds her. Presenting her this way, Hopper invites us to imagine what sights she conjures for herself even as the theater provides spectacle for others within it.

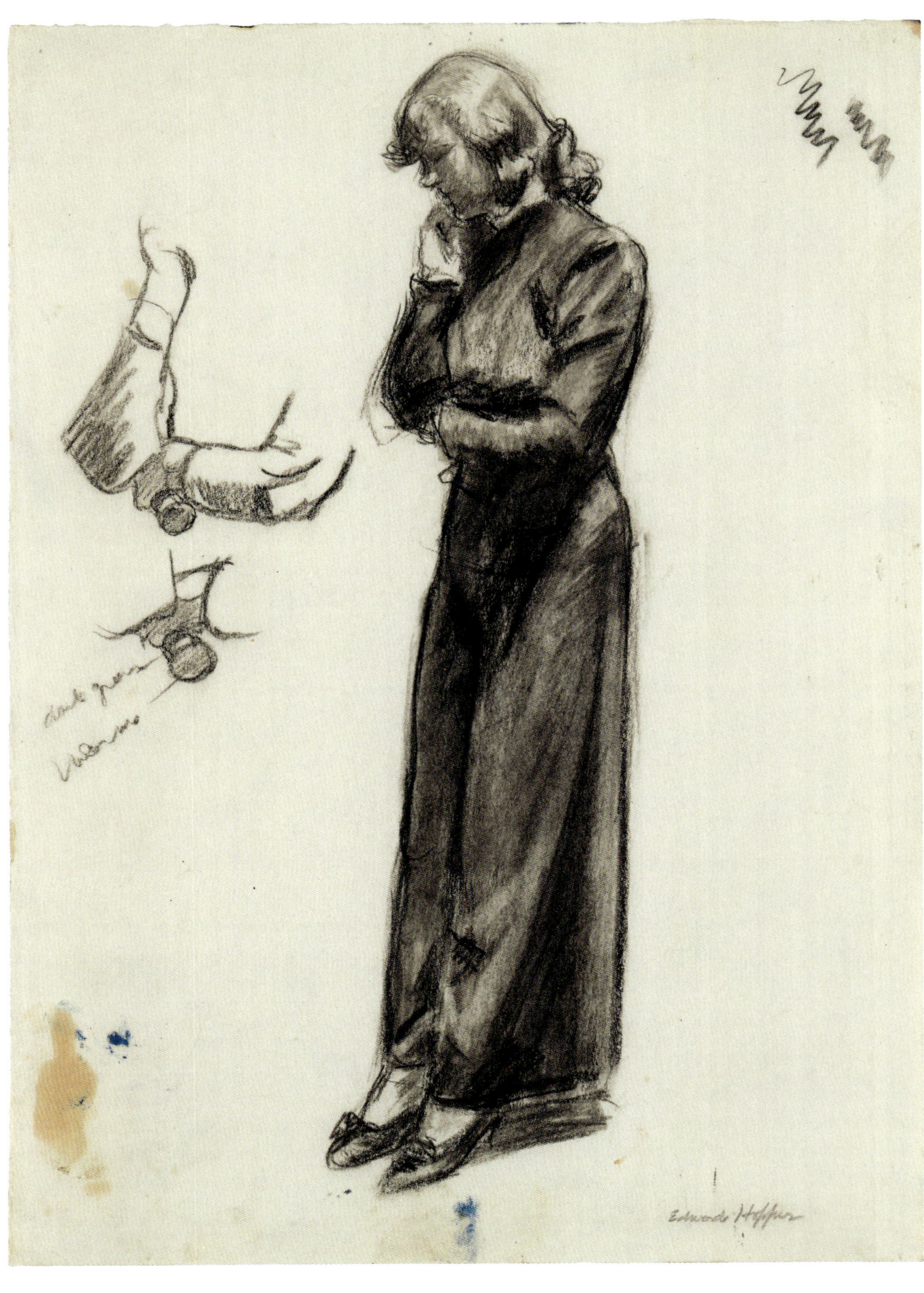

279. Study for *New York Movie*, 1939
Fabricated chalk and charcoal on paper,
14 15/16 × 11 1/8 in. (37.9 × 28.3 cm)
Josephine N. Hopper Bequest 70.452

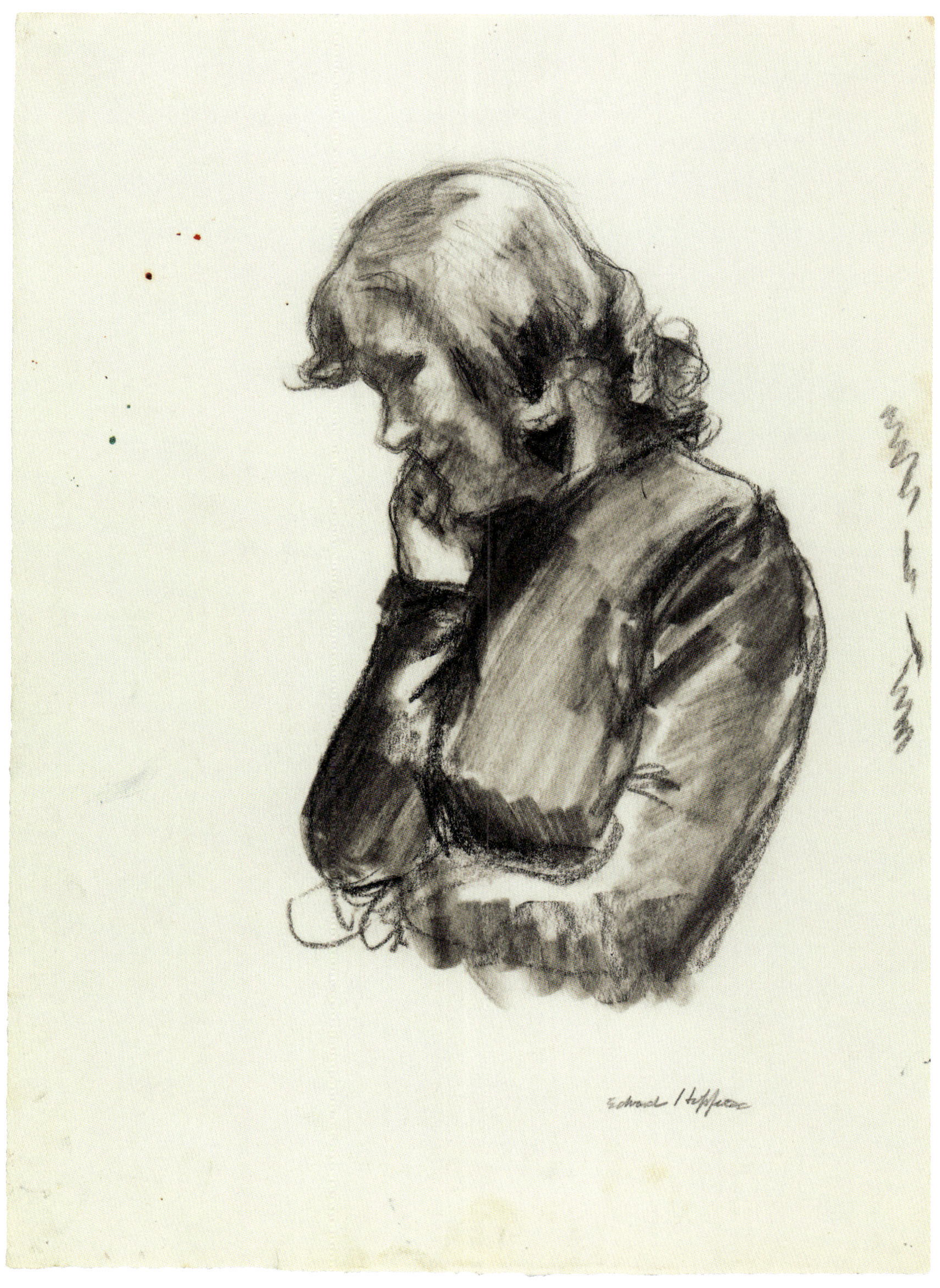

280. Study for *New York Movie*, 1939
Fabricated chalk and charcoal on paper,
15 × 11 ⅛ in. (38.1 × 28.3 cm)
Josephine N. Hopper Bequest 70.455

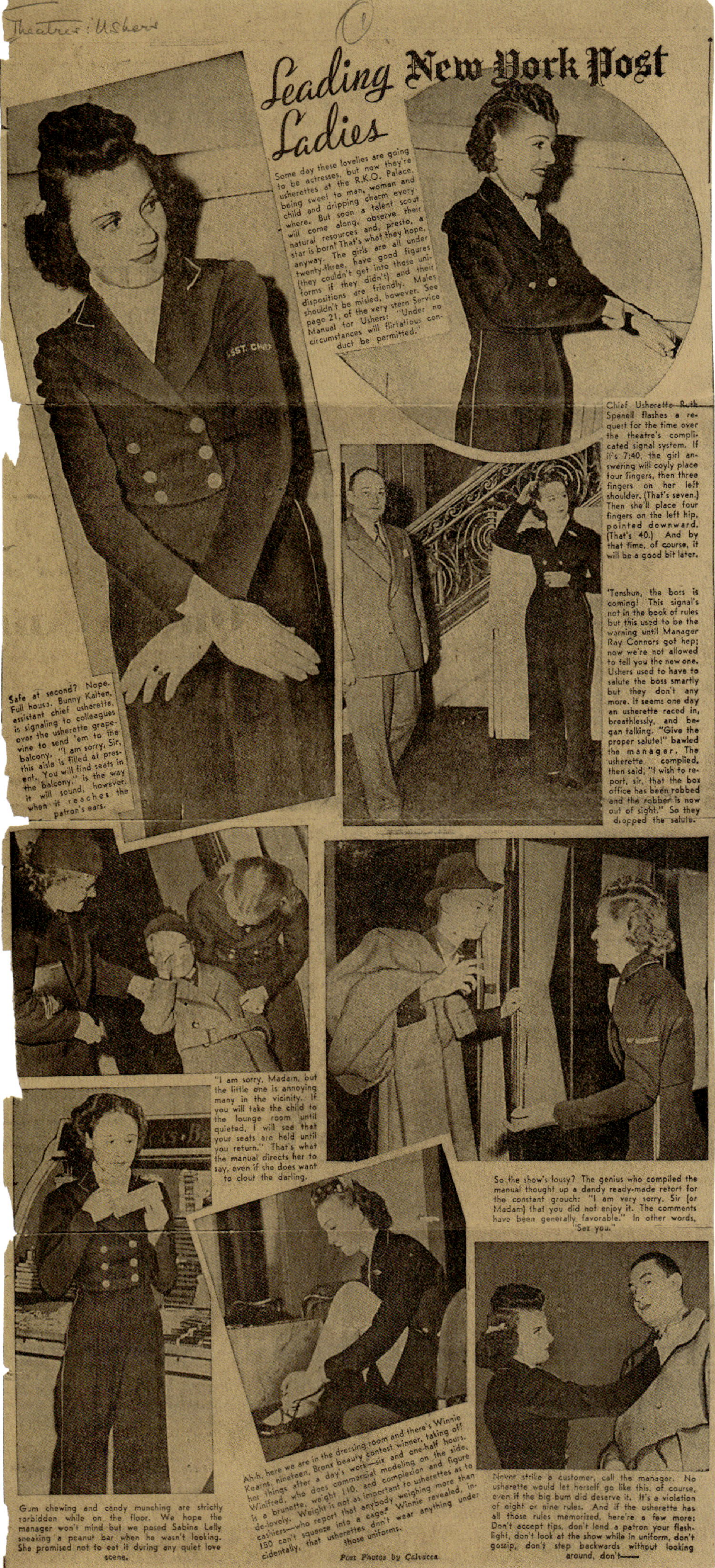

Leading Ladies

New York Post

Some day these lovelies are going to be actresses, but now they're usherettes at the R.K.O. Palace, being sweet to man, woman and child and dripping charm everywhere. But soon a talent scout will come along, observe their natural resources and, presto, a star is born! That's what they hope, anyway. The girls are all under twenty-three, have good figures (they couldn't get into those uniforms if they didn't) and their dispositions are friendly. Males shouldn't be misled, however. See page 21, of the very stern Service Manual for Ushers: "Under no circumstances will flirtatious conduct be permitted."

Chief Usherette Ruth Spenell flashes a request for the time over the theatre's complicated signal system. If it's 7:40, the girl answering will coyly place four fingers, then three fingers on her left shoulder. (That's seven.) Then she'll place four fingers on the left hip, pointed downward. (That's 40.) And by that time, of course, it will be a good bit later.

Safe at second? Nope. Full house. Bunny Kalten, assistant chief usherette, is signaling to colleagues over the usherette grapevine to send 'em to the balcony. "I am sorry, Sir, this aisle is filled at present. You will find seats in the balcony," is the way it will sound, however, when it reaches the patron's ears.

'Tenshun, the boss is coming! This signal's not in the book of rules but this used to be the warning until Manager Ray Connors got hep; now we're not allowed to tell you the new one. Ushers used to have to salute the boss smartly but they don't any more. It seems one day an usherette raced in, breathlessly, and began talking. "Give the proper salute!" bawled the manager. The usherette complied, then said, "I wish to report, sir, that the box office has been robbed and the robber is now out of sight." So they dropped the salute.

"I am sorry, Madam, but the little one is annoying many in the vicinity. If you will take the child to the lounge room until quieted, I will see that your seats are held until you return." That's what the manual directs her to say, even if she does want to clout the darling.

So the show's lousy? The genius who compiled the manual thought up a dandy ready-made retort for the constant grouch: "I am very sorry, Sir (or Madam) that you did not enjoy it. The comments have been generally favorable." In other words, "Sez you."

Gum chewing and candy munching are strictly forbidden while on the floor. We hope the manager won't mind but we posed Sabina Lally sneaking a peanut bar when he wasn't looking. She promised not to eat it during any quiet love scene.

Ah-h, here we are in the dressing room and there's Winnie Kearns, nineteen, Bronx beauty contest winner, taking off her things after a day's work—six and one-half hours. Winifred, who does commercial modeling on the side, is a brunette, weight 110, and complexion and figure de-lovely. Weight is not as important to usherettes as to cashiers—who report that anybody weighing more than 150 can't squeeze into a cage! Winnie revealed, incidentally, that usherettes don't wear anything under those uniforms.

Never strike a customer, call the manager. No usherette would let herself go like this, of course, even if the big bum did deserve it. It's a violation of eight or nine rules. And if the usherette has all those rules memorized, here're a few more: Don't accept tips, don't lend a patron your flashlight, don't look at the show while in uniform, don't gossip, don't step backwards without looking around, don't——

Post Photos by Calvacca

281. "Leading Ladies," *New York Post*, November 18, 1937. Billy Rose Theatre Division, The New York Public Library for the Performing Arts, Astor, Lenox and Tilden Foundations; courtesy the *New York Post*

NOTES

1 On *The Sheridan Theatre*, see Gail Levin, *Edward Hopper: A Catalogue Raisonné*, vol. 3, *Oils* (New York: Whitney Museum of American Art in association with W. W. Norton, 1995), 252; Gail Levin, *Edward Hopper: An Intimate Biography* (New York: Rizzoli, 2007), 291–92. On *New York Movie*, see Lloyd Goodrich, *Edward Hopper* (New York: Harry N. Abrams, 1971), 133; Robert Hobbs, *Edward Hopper*, exh. cat. (New York: Harry N. Abrams in association with the National Museum of American Art, 1987), 110–13; Pamela N. Koob, *Edward Hopper's "New York Movie,"* exh. cat. (New York: Bertha and Karl Leubsdorf Art Gallery, Hunter College, 1998); Levin, *Edward Hopper: A Catalogue Raisonné*, 3:260–61; Levin, *Edward Hopper: An Intimate Biography*, 307–9; Gail Levin, "Edward Hopper: The Influence of Theater and Film," *Arts Magazine* 55, no. 2 (October 1980): 123–27; Leonard Michaels, "The Nothing That Is Not There," in Deborah Lyons and Adam D. Weinberg, *Edward Hopper and the American Imagination*, exh. cat. (New York: Whitney Museum of American Art in association with W. W. Norton, 1995), 1–8; Rolf Günter Renner, *Edward Hopper, 1882–1967: Transformation of the Real* (San Diego: Thunder Bay, 1997), 45–46; Frank Seiberling, Jr., "Movie Scene Subject of Oil Painting: Loneliness of Big City Stressed by Artist," *Toledo Sunday Times*, July 14, 1940, 8; Carol Troyen, "Hopper's Women," in Troyen et al., *Edward Hopper*, exh. cat. (Boston: Museum of Fine Arts, 2007), 177–93.

2 Wim Wenders, conversation with author, November 2006. Walter Wells has also discussed how Wenders and other directors have been influenced by Hopper and how the elevated vantage points of the artist's compositions "resemble cinematic crane shots, or views from the uppermost gallery." Wells, *Silent Theater: The Art of Edward Hopper* (New York: Phaidon, 2007), 224. Bryan Robertson notes that "Hopper was a compulsive dramatist, and a stage director who loaded the structure of his scenes and packed the tension tighter by using light as a dramatic agency to emphasize darkness." Robertson also connects Hopper's views to John Dos Passos's cinematic "camera eye" from his *U.S.A. Trilogy*. Robertson, "Hopper's Theater," *New York Review of Books* 17, no. 10 (December 16, 1971): 38, 40.

3 Edward Hopper Record Book II, 27, in Deborah Lyons, *Edward Hopper: A Journal of His Work* (New York: Whitney Museum of American Art in associataion with W. W. Norton, 1997), 50. It is interesting to note that the famous snowcapped mountains of the Paramount Pictures logo could have been a source here; I am indebted to Daniel S. Palmer, curatorial research assistant at the Whitney, for this suggestion.

4 Levin, "Edward Hopper: The Influence of Theater and Film"; Troyen, "Hopper's Women"; Robert Silberman, "Edward Hopper and the Theater of the Mind: Vision, Spectacle, and the Spectator," in *On the Edge of Your Seat: Popular Theater and Film in Early Twentieth-Century American Art*, ed. Patricia McDonnell, exh. cat. (New Haven: Yale University Press in association with Frederick R. Weisman Art Museum, University of Minnesota, 2002), 138–55; Lucy Fischer, "The Savage Eye: Edward Hopper and the Cinema," in *A Modern Mosaic: Art and Modernism in the United States*, ed. Townsend Ludington (Chapel Hill: University of North Carolina Press, 2000), 334–56; Wells, *Silent Theater*, 224–40; Hobbs, *Edward Hopper*, 110–13; Erika L. Doss, "Edward

Hopper, Nighthawks, and Film Noir," *Post Script: Essays in Film and the Humanities* 2, no. 2 (Winter 1983): 14–36.

5 Reported by Richard Lahey, "Artists I Have Known," Archives of American Art, Smithsonian Institution, Washington, DC; quoted in Levin, "Edward Hopper: The Influence of Theater and Film," 126.

6 For a discussion of Hopper, Dwight, Marsh, and cinema, see Troyen, "Hopper's Women"; Erika L. Doss, "Images of American Women in the 1930s: Reginald Marsh and 'Paramount Picture,'" *Woman's Art Journal* 4, no. 2 (Autumn 1983–Winter 1984): 1–4.

7 Parker Tyler, "Edward Hopper: Alienation by Light," *Magazine of Art* 41, no. 8 (December 1948): 293.

8 Edward Hopper Record Book II, 27, in Lyons, *Edward Hopper: A Journal of His Work*, 50; Levin, *Edward Hopper: An Intimate Biography*, 307–9. Wells also discusses Hopper's obfuscation of light sources, often by placing them outside the frame; Wells, *Silent Theater*, 229.

9 Douglas Gomery, *Shared Pleasures: A History of Movie Presentation in the United States* (Madison: University of Wisconsin Press, 1992), 34–82; Ben M. Hall, *The Best Remaining Seats: The Story of the Golden Age of the Movie Palace* (New York: Clarkson N. Potter, 1961); Patricia McDonnell, "American Early Modern Artists, Vaudeville, and Film," in McDonnell, *On the Edge of Your Seat*, 1–43; David Nasaw, "It Begins with the Lights: Electrification and the Rise of Public Entertainment," in McDonnell, *On the Edge of Your Seat*, 45–59; Robert C. Allen, "'A Decided Sensation': Cinema, Vaudeville, and Burlesque," in McDonnell, *On the Edge of Your Seat*, 61–89; David Nasaw, *Going Out: The Rise and Fall of Public Amusements* (New York: Basic Books, 1993), 221–56; David Naylor, *Great American Movie Theaters* (Washington, DC: National Historic Trust, 1987), 70–78; Robert A. M. Stern, Gregory Gilmartin, and Thomas Mellins, *New York 1930: Architecture and Urbanism between the Two World Wars* (New York: Rizzoli, 1987), 244–68.

10 This is interestingly at odds with the diminutive scale of the actual piece, which is one of his smallest mature paintings.

11 Goodrich, *Edward Hopper*, 108.

12 These drawings are all on the same type of sketchpad paper, perhaps even the same pad, as some of the *New York Movie* drawings. All of the studies are reproduced in Carter E. Foster, ed., *Edward Hopper*, exh. cat. (Milan: Skira, 2009), 182–85.

13 Levin, *Edward Hopper: An Intimate Biography*, 307–9.

14 Hopper seems typically to have made around twelve to fifteen drawings for a painting.

15 The sketchbook pages (70.76–70.92 and 70.147–70.152) are all on beige/brown machine-wove paper and average 7 ¼ by 4 7⁄16 inches; the Palace sketchbook sheets (70.102–70.111) are on cream wove paper and measure approximately 11 13⁄16 x 8 13⁄16 inches each.

16 Levin, *Edward Hopper: An Intimate Biography*, 309: "Five days later [January 26, 1939], he once again had Jo pose out in their cold hall for the figure of an usherette holding a flashlight."

17 Jo Hopper's diary entry for December 14, 1938, states: "E. gone off to look at Palace Theatre to see if it would do for something he has in his mind. Where he went yesterday, not so good." Levin, *Edward Hopper: A Catalogue Raisonné*, 3:260.

18 The Globe, designed by the firm of Carrère and Hastings, opened on January 10, 1910. Located at 205 West Forty-sixth Street, it is now the Lunt-Fontanne Theatre and was designated a New York City Landmark in 1987. The Strand, built by Thomas W. Lamb in 1914, was a massive theater with a capacity of nearly 3,500, located at 1579 Broadway (on the corner of Forty-seventh Street); it was torn down on February 8, 1987. The Republic, located at 209 West Forty-second Street, was in a building designed by Albert Westover that opened September 27, 1900, and became the Belasco Theatre in 1902; the name reverted back to the Republic in 1910 but was changed to Minsky's Burlesque in 1931, the Victory in 1942, and the New Victory in 1995, the name under which it now operates. The Palace, located at 1564 Broadway (also on the corner of Forty-seventh Street), was designed by the firm of Kirchoff and Rose and opened in 1913. Although its exterior has been altered, the interior of the theater was designated a New York City Landmark in 1987. See Nicholas van Hoogstraten, *Lost Broadway Theatres* (New York: Princeton Architectural Press, 1991); Mary C. Henderson, *The City and the Theater* (New York: Back Stage Books, 2004).

19 "The Screen Calendar" cinema schedule in the *New York Times* tells us which films were playing at these theaters during the time Hopper was working on *New York Movie* (except for the Republic / Minsky's Burlesque, which did show films between burlesque acts, but seems not to have left a record of which ones). At the Globe, the cinema schedule lists: 12/4/1938: *Sharpshooters*; 12/11/1938: *Secrets of a Nurse*; 12/18/1938: *Adventure in Sahara*; 12/25/1938: *The Lady Vanishes*. At the Strand: 12/4/1938–12/18/1938: *Angels with Dirty Faces*; 12/25/1938: *Dawn Patrol*. At the Palace: 12/4/1938: *The Mad Miss Manton* and *Next Time I Marry*; 12/11/1938: *Submarine Patrol* and *Service De Luxe*; 12/18/1938: *Hard to Get* and *Comet over Broadway*; 12/25/1938: *Brother Rat* and *While New York Sleeps*. Of special note is the Warner Brothers film *Brother Rat*, directed by William Keighley, which depicts the humorous side of military academy life at Virginia Military Institute and features actresses Priscilla Lane, Jane Bryan, and Jane Wyman in hairstyles similar to that of *New York Movie*'s usherette. The climactic scene centers around an officer searching the cadets' room with a flashlight, and the film's poster also showcases two of these women dressed in military uniform and high heels.

20 Levin, *Edward Hopper: A Catalogue Raisonné*, 3:260. The diary entries quoted by Levin suggest that Hopper was going to the theaters to draw starting on or before December 13 and until at least December 26.

21 Hopper's inscriptions seem to reflect the theater's older name; it was called Minsky's Burlesque in 1939, but showed films in between live striptease. It is possible these sheets were done in connection with the painting *Girlie Show* from 1941 (private collection); there are seventeen sketchbook sheets of the same type of paper for that painting in the Whitney (70.130–70.146): each measures on average 7 ¼ x 4 7⁄16 inches and is on a beige/brown machine-made wove paper. Two other drawings in the Whitney of theater interiors, drawn in an upper balcony (70.128 and 70.129), could be for either *New York Movie* or *Girlie Show*. Another drawing related to this group, *Burlesque Theatre, Times Square*, is in the collection of the Corcoran Gallery of Art, Washington, DC.

22 Perhaps these were the sketches he made on December 13, as Jo's diary entry for the next day implies a dead end: "Where he went yesterday, not so good." See Levin, *Edward Hopper: A Catalogue Raisonné*, 3:260.

23 Jo's diary for December 26 describes "another early trip to movie house—Palace," implying that he'd been going before that date as well. Ibid.

24 The plan essentially matches other floor plans from a theatre program dated 1916; see *B.F. Keith's Palace Theatre* 1, no. 7 (June 1916), in "Theatres: US: NY Palace: Programmes" folder in the Billy Rose Theatre Division, New York Public Library for the Performing Arts, Astor, Lenox and Tilden Foundations.

25 Jo Hopper, diary entry of December 15, 1938, cited in Levin, *Edward Hopper: A Catalogue Raisonné*, 3:260.

26 John Updike describes these manipulations: "The painting *New York Movie*—one of his most telling and beloved pieces of pictorial theater—swallows in its shadows several fine pencil studies of movie-viewers seen from behind, and gives us a golden-haired usherette, in strapped high heels and a pseudo-military uniform, much more glamorous than the dowdy girl he carefully sketched." John Updike, "Hopper's Polluted Silence," *New York Review of Books* 42, no. 13 (August 10, 1995): 21.

27 Levin, *Edward Hopper: A Catalogue Raisonné*, 3:261; Robert Gordon and Andrew Forge, *Degas* (New York: Harry N. Abrams, 1988), 118–19. The painting was on view at Durand-Ruel New York for a brief period in 1909 before it sold to M. Jaccaci, and later in 1921 and 1924–26 at The Metropolitan Museum of Art. Jean Sutherland Boggs et al., *Degas*, exh. cat. (New York: Metropolitan Museum of Art, 1988), 146.

28 Brian O'Doherty describes this quality in Hopper's work in general: "Everything seems massively stable but, if you look closer, is transient or in transit." Brian O'Doherty, "Hopper's Look," in Sheena Wagstaff, ed., *Edward Hopper*, exh. cat. (London: Tate Publishing, 2004), 89.

29 Levin, *Edward Hopper: An Intimate Biography*, 309.

30 "Leading Ladies," *New York Post*, November 18, 1937.

31 John L. Marsh, "Chin Up! Smile! Keep 'Em Happy: The Epitaph of the Movie House Usher," *Marquee: The Journal of the Theatre Historical Society of America* 23, no. 4 (1991): 9; Gomery, *Shared Pleasures*, 49–50; Nasaw, *Going Out*, 235–36; Hall, *The Best Remaining Seats*, 166–73.

32 Marsh, "Chin Up!" 6–7.

33 Ibid., 7–8.

34 "Leading Ladies."

35 Marsh, "Chin Up!" 7–8.

Office at Night, the El Train, and Urban Voyeurism

CARTER E. FOSTER

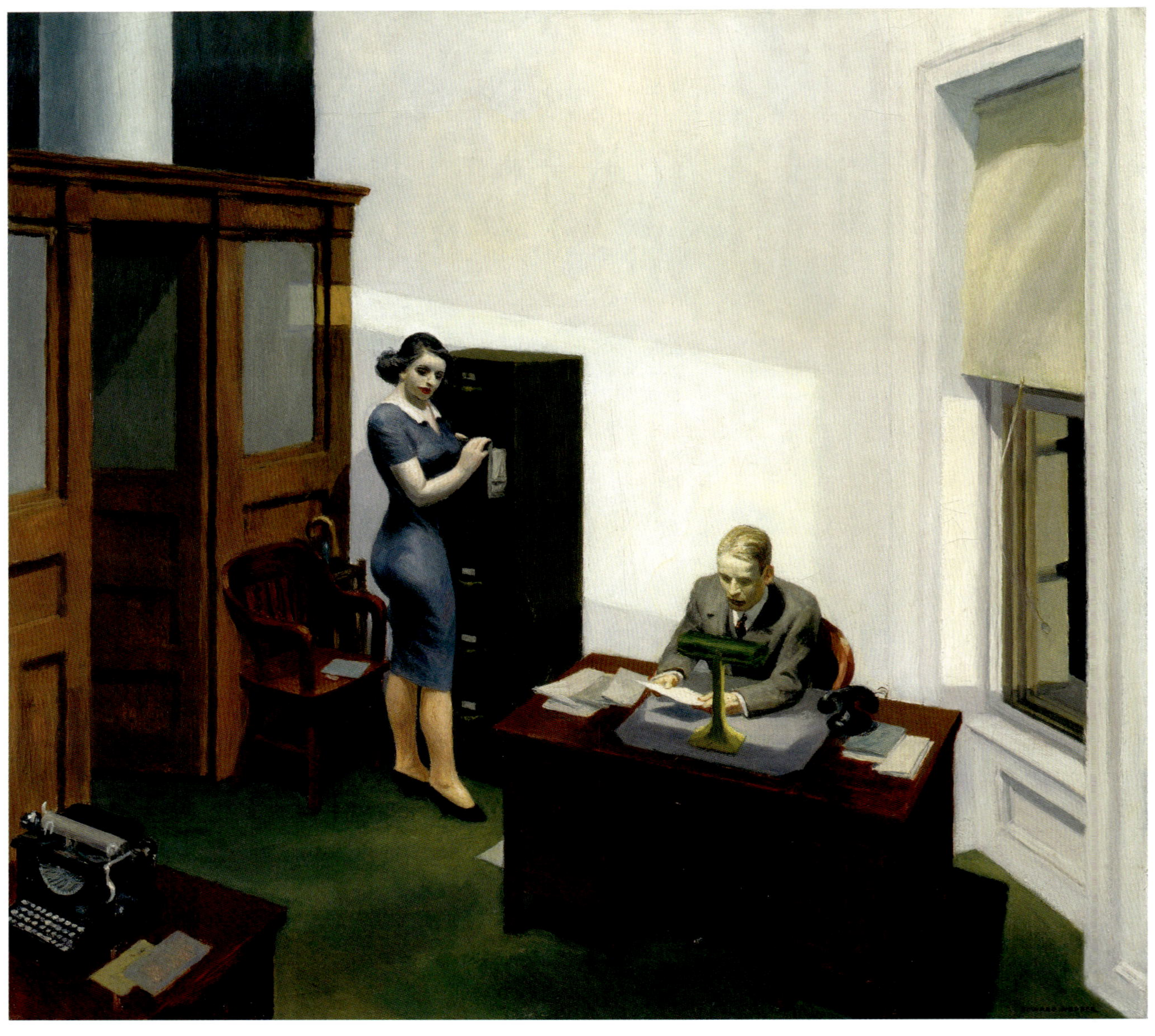

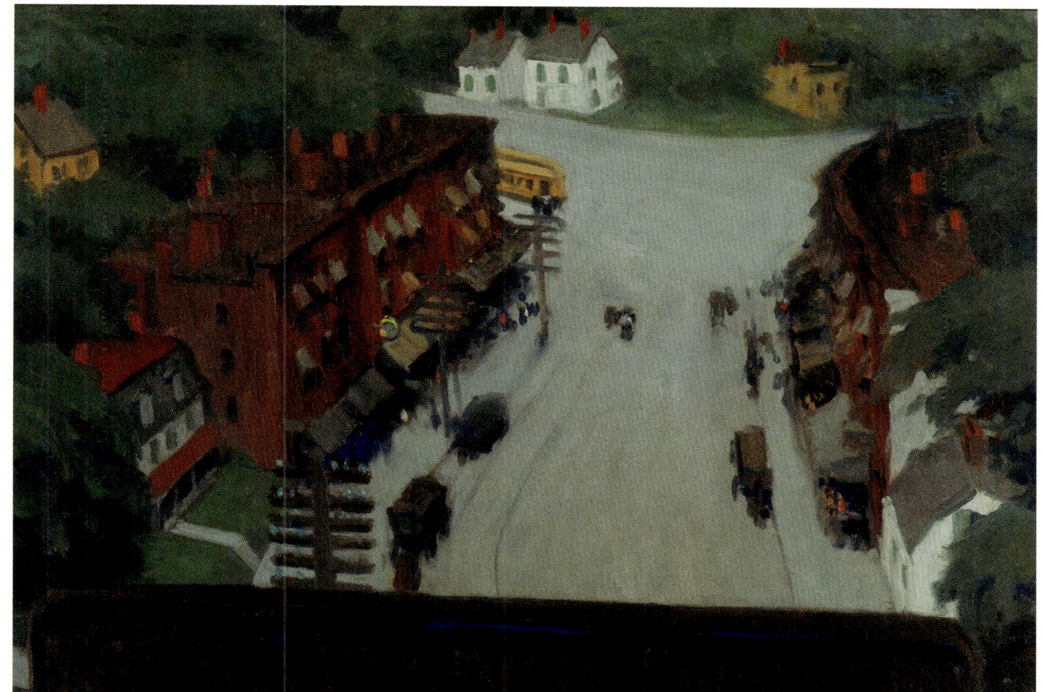

Edward Hopper once stated that it was difficult to depict interior and exterior space simultaneously, implying that this was one of his goals.[1] The two often interpenetrate when he focuses on rooms, with windows or doorways providing the passage between them, usually for the gaze of one of Hopper's protagonists. In some works, he creates a tenuous and nuanced separation between the subject in one space (often a person in an interior) and the implied position of the spectator in relation to that subject. By distancing us slightly from the main action of a scene, Hopper implicates the viewer as voyeur. Indeed, he innovated a formal language of voyeurism for twentieth-century pictorial art that was intimately tied to the densely built environment of the modern city—in Hopper's case, New York. He acknowledged his own voyeuristic viewpoint as a source for one of his masterpieces, *Office at Night* (fig. 282),[2] in a 1948 letter to Norman Geske of the Walker Art Center, which had recently acquired the painting: "The picture was probably first suggested by many rides on the 'L' train in New York after dark, and glimpses of office interiors that were so fleeting as to leave fresh and vivid impressions on my mind."[3]

Completed in 1940, *Office at Night* extends Hopper's earlier explorations of certain kinds of spaces and spatial experiences common in New York that result from being physically close to others but separated from them by a variety of factors, including movement, structures, windows, walls, and light or darkness. Hopper had used the viewpoint from the city's elevated trains in a number of works of the 1910s and 1920s. His 1912 painting *American Village* (fig. 283), for example, adapts the floating, angled sight lines from the elevated train tracks, exploiting the guardrail as a foreground framing device for the scene beyond. By removing the guardrail and any indication of track, he created one of his most haunting compositions in the 1921 etching *Night Shadows* (fig. 284). Here the spectator hovers mysteriously above a fedora-wearing male figure whose foreshortened body casts one of the eponymous shadows; the other shadow, a long diagonal across the picture plane, comes from an unseen lamppost. This print finds Hopper revisiting his 1913 painting *New York Corner* (see fig. 96) from an elevated point of view and at night. Because the sources of both lights and shadows are just out of view, Hopper achieved the sense of continuity beyond the scene that he loved to create, as well as a sense of foreboding, as if the dark, thick line is daring the man to cross it.

Riding the elevated train lines was once a common experience for New Yorkers, as well as a rich source of subject matter for artists in the first half of the century, including John Sloan, Reginald Marsh, Ralston Crawford, and Stuart Davis. The "El" placed the rider in proximity to a wide variety of ever-shifting spaces in the dense urban environment. It can still be experienced today on certain New York subway lines or, for example, on Chicago's downtown Loop. Riding the El almost automatically positioned the spectator as voyeur, especially when looking down from above at unaware pedestrians or through the windows of very close buildings. In such situations, we can choose the degree to which we engage in voyeuristic activity; in Hopper's etching, we have little choice. In his other prints of this subject, such as the 1918 etching *Night on the El Train*, the spectator is implicated in a more mundane fashion—

282. *Office at Night*, 1940
Oil on canvas, 22 3/16 × 25 1/8 in. (56.4 × 63.8 cm)
Walker Art Center, Minneapolis; gift of the T. B. Walker Foundation, Gilbert M. Walker Fund, 1948 1948.21

283. *American Village*, 1912
Oil on canvas, 26 × 38 1/8 in. (66 × 96.8 cm)
Josephine N. Hopper Bequest 70.1185

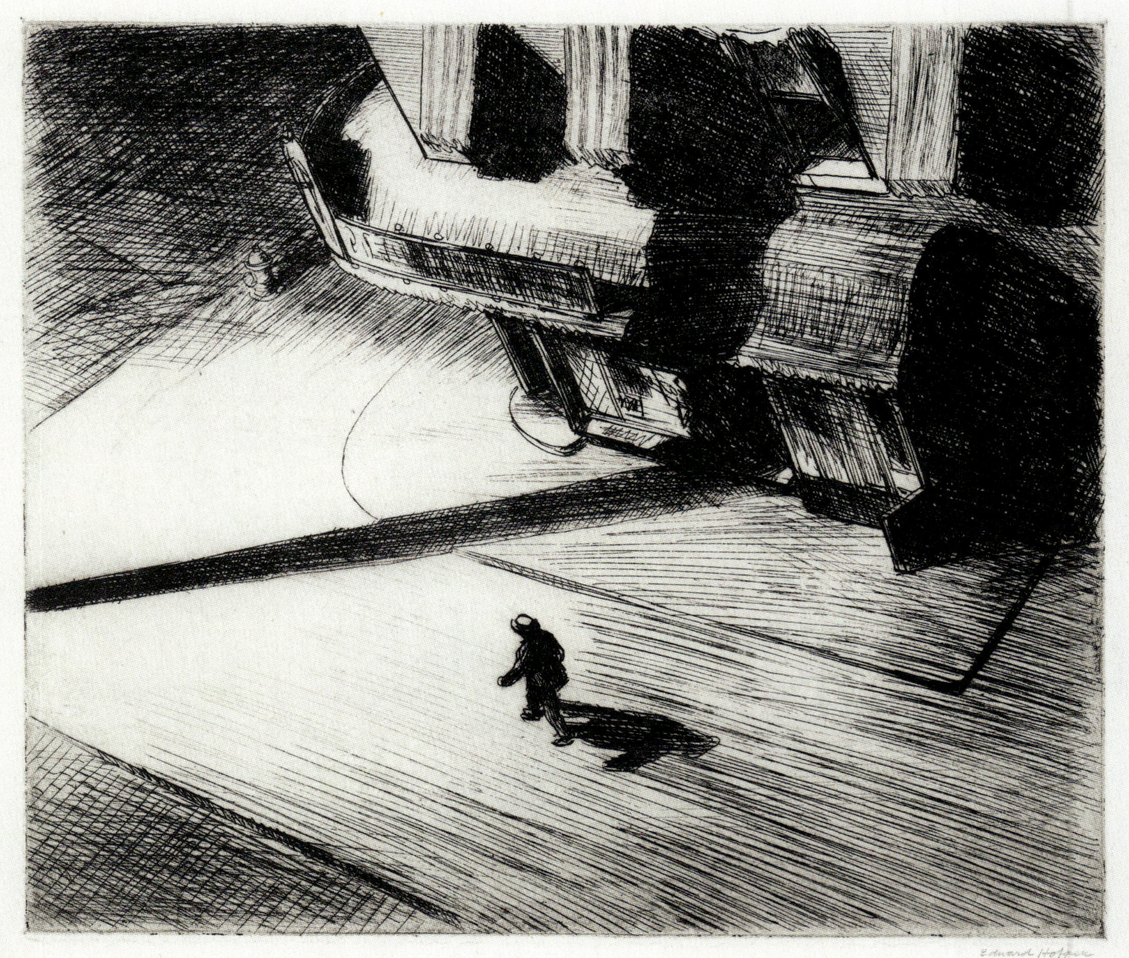

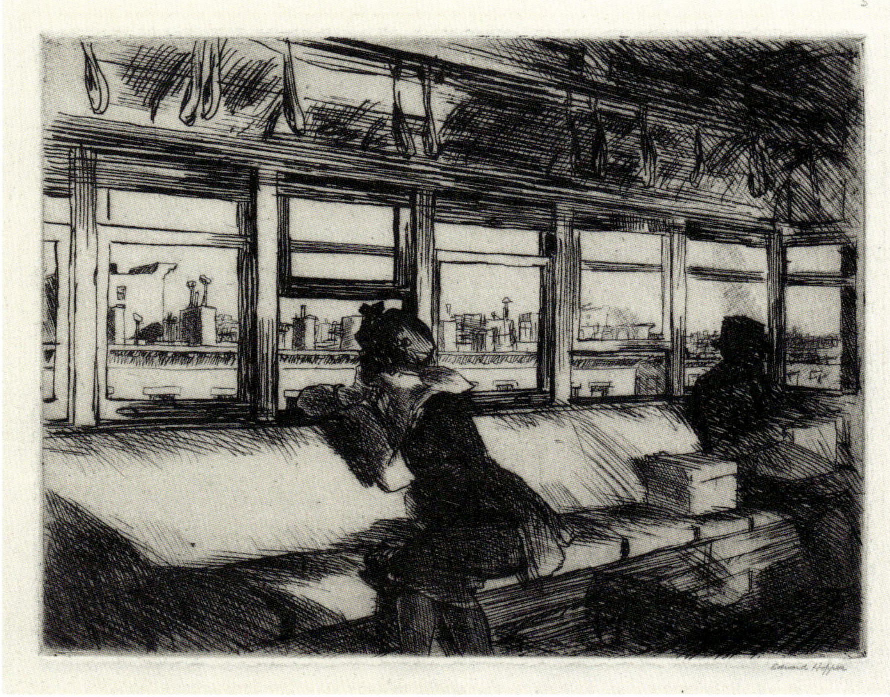

284. *Night Shadows*, 1921
Etching; sheet: 9 5⁄8 × 11 in. (24.4 × 27.9 cm), plate: 6 7⁄8 × 8 3⁄16 in. (17.5 × 20.8 cm)
Gift of Gertrude Vanderbilt Whitney 31.691

285. *House Tops*, 1921
Etching; sheet: 9 15⁄16 × 11 9⁄16 in. (25.2 × 29.3 cm), plate: 5 7⁄8 × 7 7⁄16 in. (14.9 × 20 cm)
Print Collection, Miriam and Ira D. Wallach Division of Art, Prints and Photographs, The New York Public Library, Astor, Lenox and Tilden Foundations

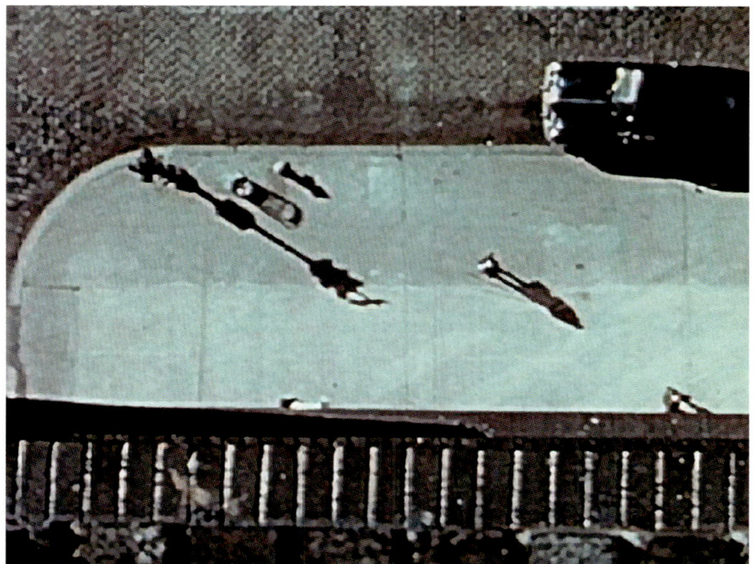

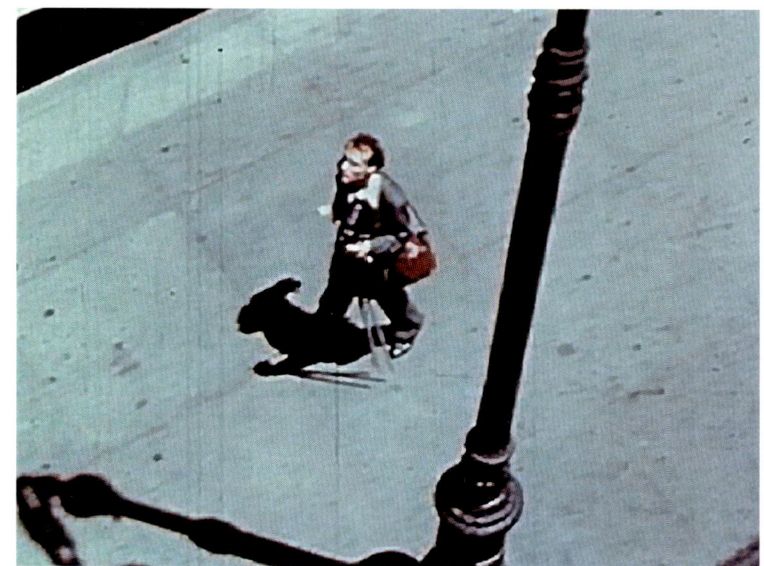

286 and 287. Stills from *3rd Ave. El*, 1955. 35mm film, color, sound; 11 min. Produced and directed by Carson Davidson. Image courtesy the Academic Film Archive of North America and Carson Davidson

as another rider. In *House Tops* of 1921 (fig. 285), Hopper depicts the stratum on elevated train lines that corresponds to the upper stories of buildings, allowing for the type of viewing he cites as the inspiration for *Office at Night.* These earlier works demonstrate that Hopper had already thoroughly investigated the experience of riding the El train before he started the painting in 1939.

New York's last elevated train lines in Manhattan were dismantled in the 1950s, so an experience once common in collective memory is slowly being lost. Indeed, contemporary spectators from 1920s New York must have easily recognized Hopper's experiential source for *Night Shadows*—though, surprisingly, few or none commented about it in print. Fortunately for posterity, Carson Davidson's short film *3rd Ave. El* records the experience of riding the line just before it was torn down.[4] Indeed, certain stills from the film (figs. 286, 287) are striking in their similarity to *Night Shadows*; one segment even includes the same two types of shadows—a man and a lamppost—and reflects how the elevated point of view turns up the ground toward the picture plane, flattening and distorting normal perspective the way Hopper does in the print. Other frames also make illuminating comparisons to the way in which Hopper developed his voyeuristic point of view in other works from the 1920s (figs. 288, 289).

A crucial work in this regard is *New York Interior* (fig. 290). Hopper made this important painting the same year as *Night Shadows*, and though they look quite different, both experiment with the kind of "distanced proximity" possible on the El, where one could inhabit a very different spatial realm and be separated by movement and physical barriers, and yet remain in close proximity to an observed subject. *New York Interior* finds the viewer just outside a well-lit domestic space—as one could be when riding the El, with direct if quickly changing sight lines into the windows of buildings level with the train (see fig. 289). Again, Davidson's film demonstrates this point perfectly, recording how the train moved the rider near and through all manner of built structures, allowing a passing glimpse into other spaces, lives, and worlds. Hopper negotiates the membrane between exterior and interior beautifully in *New York Interior* by eliding elements belonging to both into shapes that serve as framing devices for the brightly lit room and the woman inside it. As is typical and essential to his art throughout his career, Hopper does not acknowledge with paint or render in any way the presumed glass barrier of the exterior window.[5] At left is a long, dark vertical suggesting the structure of the building and marking the passage between outside and inside. At right, Hopper similarly renders dark areas of massed shapes; some, such as the hat sitting on the table in the lower right corner, clearly belong to the interior, but these shapes merge with architectural forms at right which could be inside or out—the exact part of the building to which they belong is ambiguous. By framing the scene this way, Hopper places the viewer on a cusp—just outside the woman's space, seemingly close enough to reach in and touch her—in a tense position that straddles the boundary separating the interior she inhabits from the

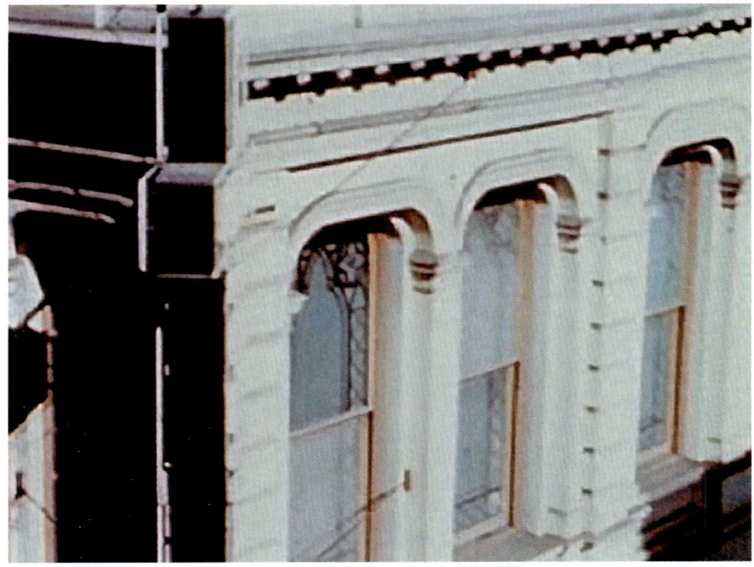

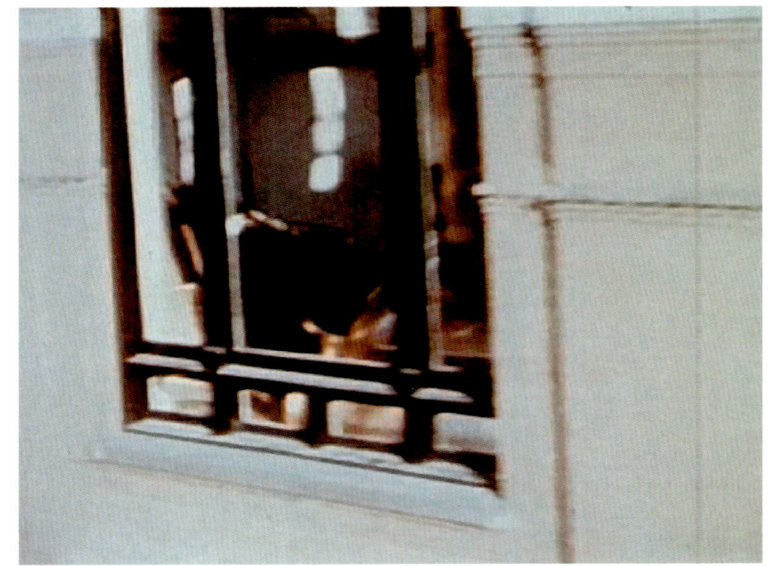

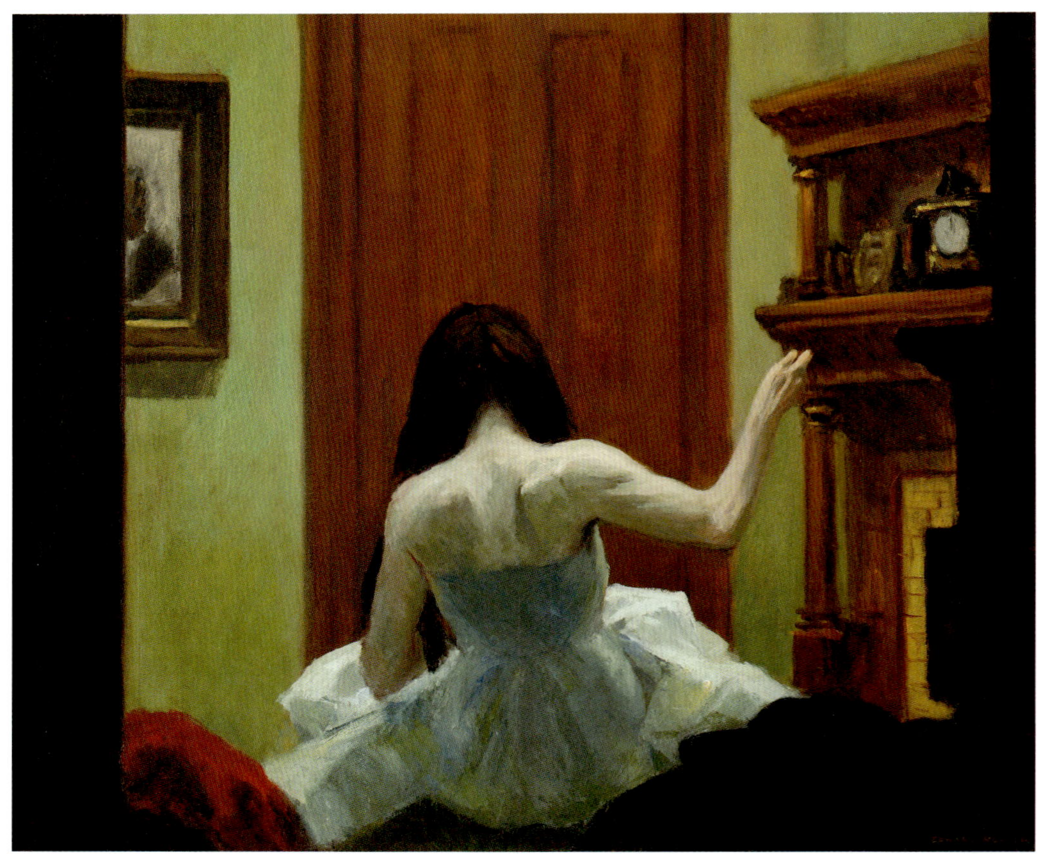

288 and 289. Stills from *3rd Ave. El*, 1955. 35mm film, color, sound; 11 min. Produced and directed by Carson Davidson. Image courtesy the Academic Film Archive of North America and Carson Davidson

290. *New York Interior*, c. 1921
Oil on canvas, 24 5/16 × 29 3/8 in. (61.8 × 74.6 cm)
Josephine N. Hopper Bequest 70.1200

world beyond. In his 1928 painting *Night Windows* (The Museum of Modern Art, New York), a more overtly erotic work, Hopper has pulled back, giving us the kind of glimpse more common on a passing elevated train, catching a private moment quickly while passing a building. *Night Windows* plays with less subtlety on a voyeuristic point of view, and it lacks the unsettling charge of *New York Interior*.

Had Hopper not clued us in, *Office at Night* is not a painting we would easily associate with the El train. It has one of the strangest points of view in his oeuvre—as spectators we are suspended and floating in this space, like an insect hovering in the air.[6] The room itself contains very odd geometry when we look carefully. The back wall is not perpendicular to the window wall but splays away from it at a pronounced obtuse angle. The green floor tilts up toward the picture plane and seems to slope, spilling down toward the lower edge. It is as if we

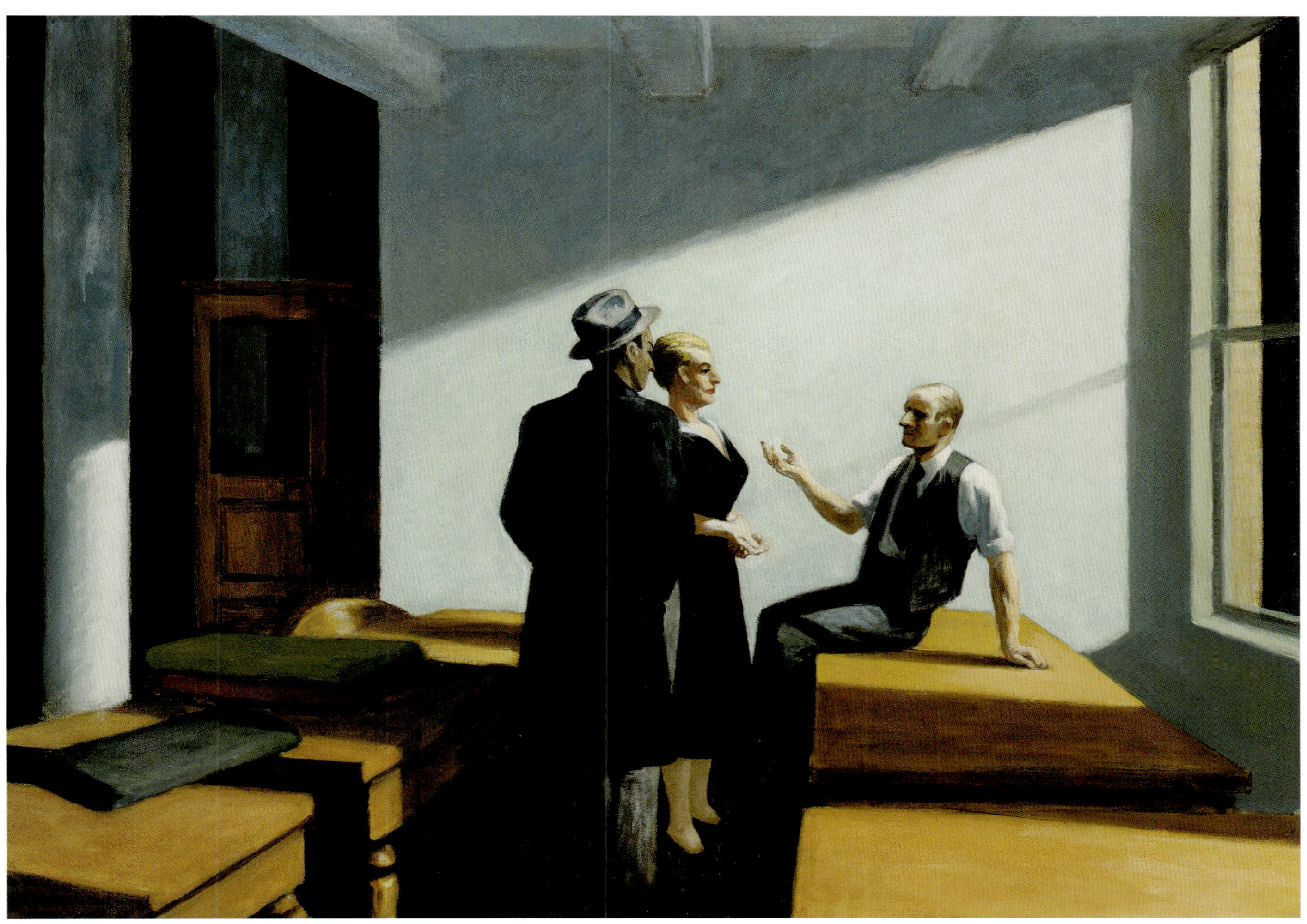

are standing on a piece of furniture across from the desk, on whose top we can look down—a camera's point of view, not that of a person standing in the room. Inhabiting a different spatial realm than the protagonists separates us from them, creating the work's effective and striking voyeuristic tension. Though we are inside, the point of view is in a similar realm to *Night Shadows*. Hopper could compose a scene with disembodied eye, and he does so here to pointed effect. The painting is similar, in this regard, to *New York Interior*, a scene in which Hopper pulled in just close enough to charge the spectator's connection to the subject. In *Office at Night*, our position in space and its relation to the outside—we may be just inside an unseen window—similarly treads a tenuous, though more unmoored, boundary.

Comparison with the thematically related *Conference at Night* (fig. 291) and its associated drawings from ten years later shows how differently the artist could conceive of pictorial space in tandem with the mood and atmosphere he sought. In the later campaign, the geometry is rigid, as close to actual linear one point perspective as Hopper ever got. The eerie blue lighting punctuated by dark shadows helps create the sense that perhaps illicit dealings are being discussed. The strangely arrayed tables emphasize zooming spatial compression and seem to hem the figures into this bizarre interior, with its oddly placed partition and totally open left wall. The receding lines of the tabletops and ceiling beams coalesce around the hands and gestures of the man and woman, making them a focal point of the composition.[7] We can follow the progression of the composition in the drawings (figs. 292–297), where the artist went from a view close in to the figural group, with framing lines suggesting a window, to a strong emphasis on a recessional space that almost seems to trap its inhabitants (figs. 298–301). For an artist whose revisiting of familiar subjects more often involved subtle and nuanced variations, the contrast with *Office at Night* is striking.

The six compositional drawings for *Office at Night* show how the architecture of this room and the point of view evolved as the idea for the space crystallized. Four are on the

291. *Conference at Night*, 1949
Oil on canvas, 28 ¼ × 40 5/16 in. (72.8 × 102.4 cm)
Wichita Art Museum; Roland P. Murdock Collection
M100.52

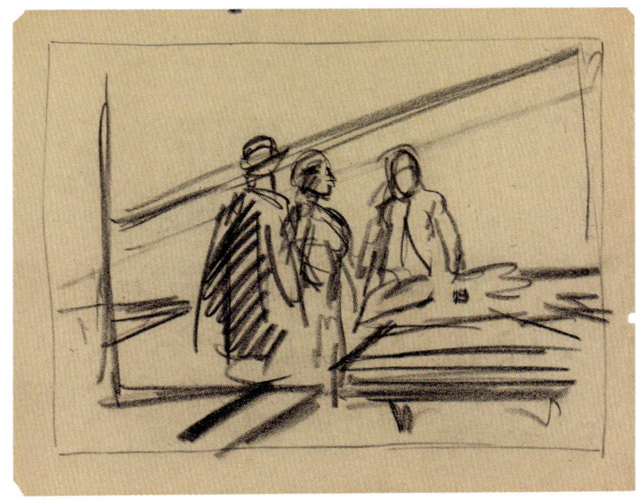

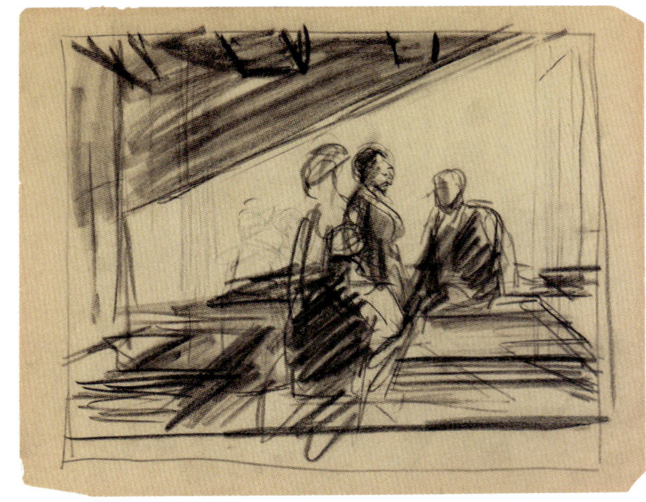

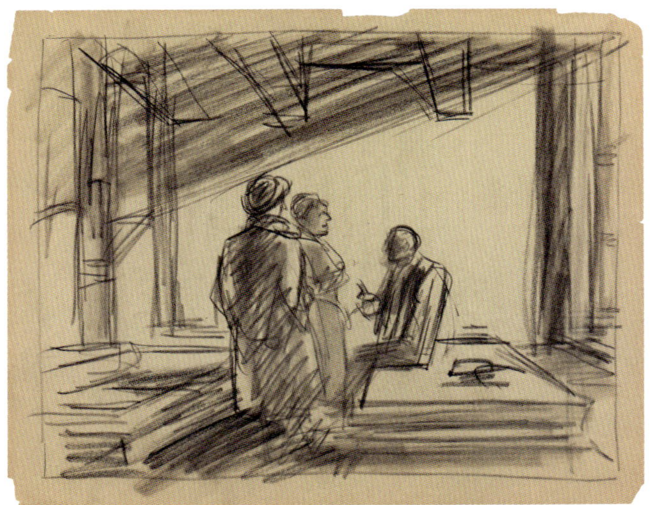

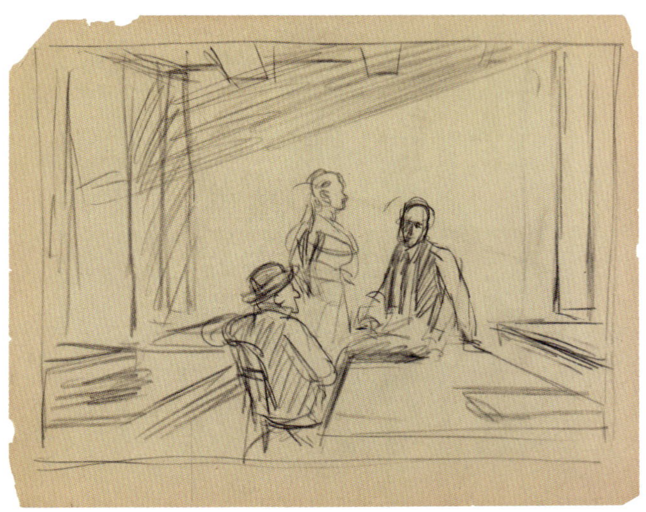

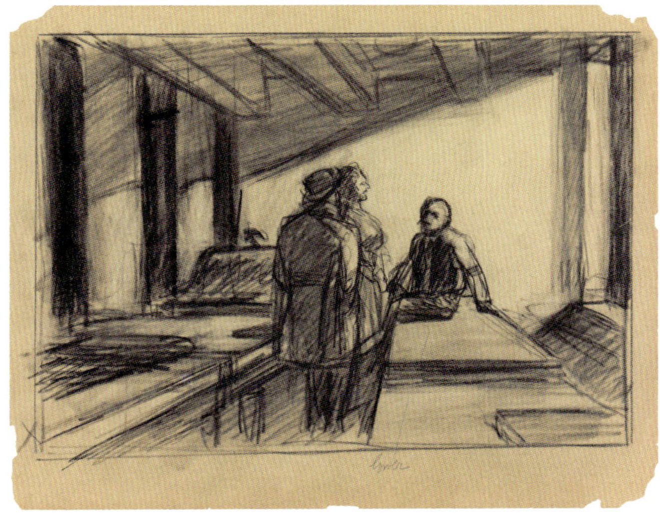

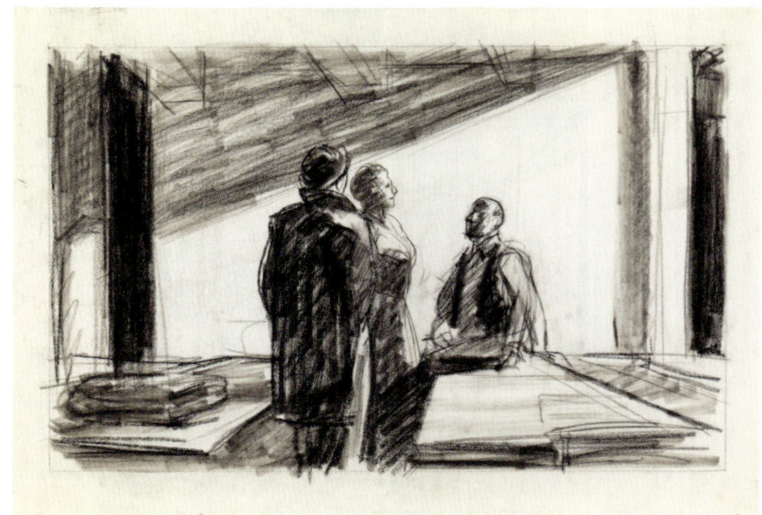

292. (top left)
Study for *Conference at Night*, 1948 or 1949
Fabricated chalk on paper, 8 ½ × 11 in. (21.6 × 27.9 cm)
Josephine N. Hopper Bequest 70.172

293. (top right)
Study for *Conference at Night*, 1948 or 1949
Fabricated chalk on paper, 8 ½ × 10 15⁄16 in. (21.6 × 27.8 cm)
Josephine N. Hopper Bequest 70.173

294. (middle left)
Study for *Conference at Night*, 1948 or 1949
Fabricated chalk on paper, 8 ½ × 10 15⁄16 in. (21.6 × 27.8 cm)
Josephine N. Hopper Bequest 70.174

295. (middle right)
Study for *Conference at Night*, 1948 or 1949
Fabricated chalk on paper, 8 ½ × 10 15⁄16 in. (21.6 × 27.8 cm)
Josephine N. Hopper Bequest 70.170

296. (bottom left)
Study for *Conference at Night*, 1948 or 1949
Fabricated chalk on paper, 8 ½ × 10 15⁄16 in. (21.6 × 27.8 cm)
Josephine N. Hopper Bequest 70.171

297. (bottom right)
Study for *Conference at Night* (recto), 1949
Fabricated chalk and charcoal on paper,
15 1⁄16 × 22 1⁄16 in. (38.3 × 56 cm)
Josephine N. Hopper Bequest 70.842a–b

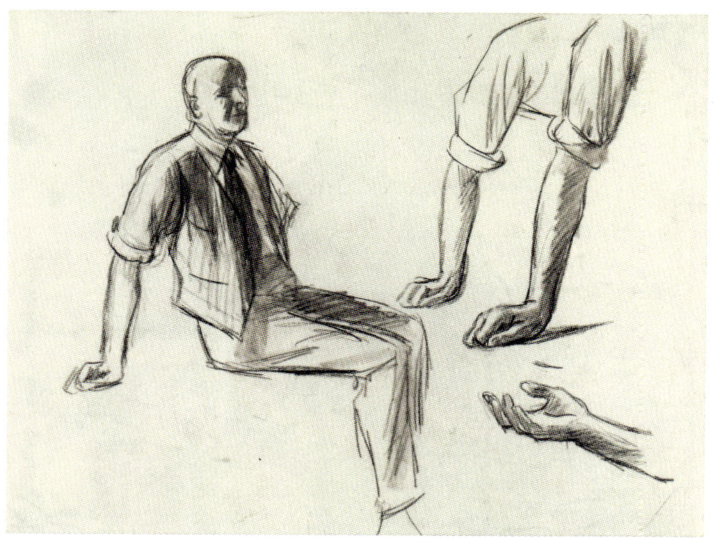

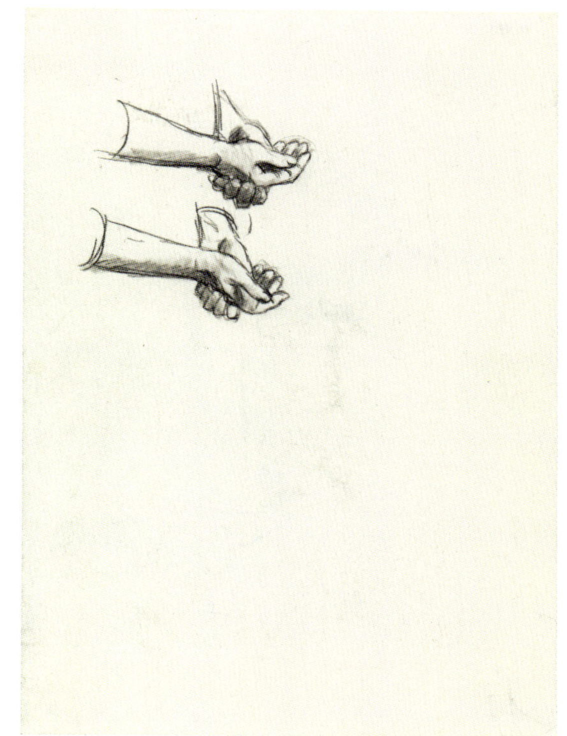

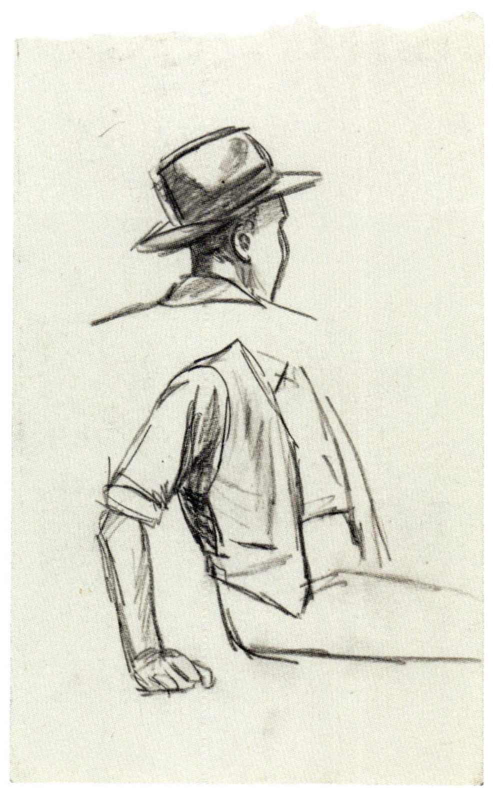

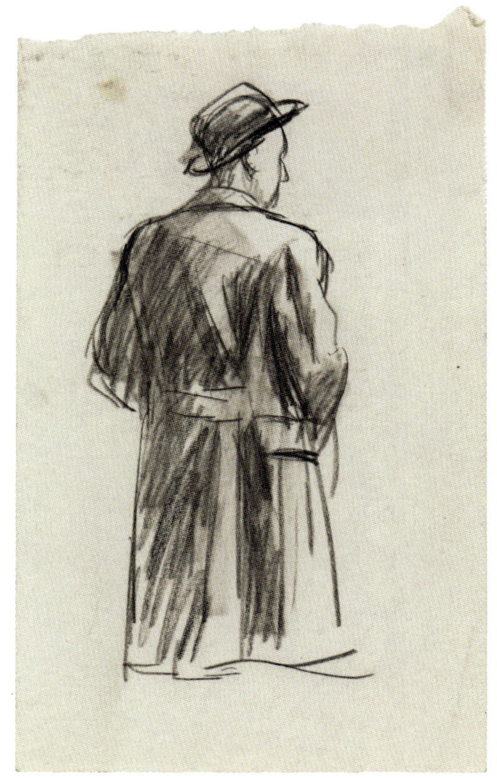

298. (top left)
Study for *Conference at Night*, 1948 or 1949
Fabricated chalk on paper, 8 5/8 × 11 5/8 in. (21.9 × 29.5 cm)
Josephine N. Hopper Bequest 70.844

299. (top right)
Study for *Conference at Night*, 1948 or 1949
Fabricated chalk on paper, 11 5/8 × 8 5/8 in. (29.5 × 21.9 cm)
Josephine N. Hopper Bequest 70.843

300. (bottom left)
Study for *Conference at Night*, 1948 or 1949
Fabricated chalk and charcoal on paper, 8 1/8 × 5 in. (20.6 × 12.7 cm)
Josephine N. Hopper Bequest 70.845

301. (bottom right)
Study for *Conference at Night*, 1948 or 1949
Fabricated chalk and charcoal on paper, 8 1/8 × 5 in. (20.6 × 12.7 cm)
Josephine N. Hopper Bequest 70.846

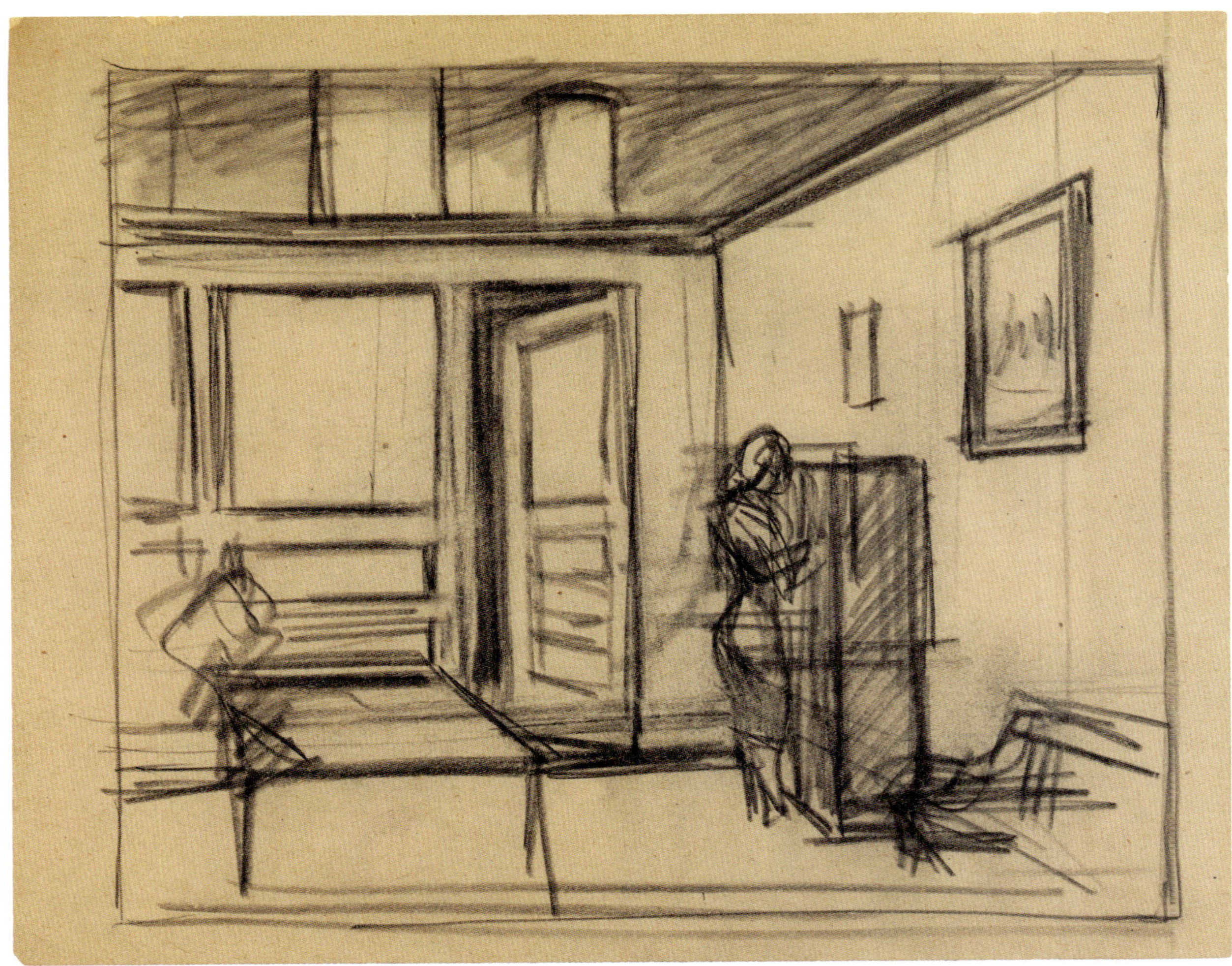

302. Study for *Office at Night*, 1940
Fabricated chalk on paper, 8½ × 11 in. (21.6 × 27.9 cm)
Josephine N. Hopper Bequest 70.169

cheap typing paper Hopper often used for quick preliminary sketches (figs. 302–305). The two quite finished studies, on finer artist's paper, serve as fascinating alternate versions of the painting and are among the most nuanced and materially worked drawings Hopper ever made (figs. 306, 307). As a series, the six sheets are beautifully distilled examples of how the artist tinkered with space, manipulating it as the subject developed. The first sketch (see fig. 302) displays a convincing, rational perspective in which the office is a rectilinear box seen at a different angle than the final painting, with the wood and glass dividing wall roughly parallel to the picture plane and opening up onto the larger space beyond. The male figure has not yet been introduced—the secretary stands next to the filing cabinet, and we see the space from a low perspective, perhaps as if we are the male office worker seated at his desk. Hopper then starts to rotate the viewer's position to create diagonals where walls and floors meet, as well as the beginnings of an elevated point of view and a willful perspective (see fig. 303). In the next sheet, Hopper introduced most of the elements present in the final canvas: the man sits at his desk; there is a window behind him, though not yet a third wall; most of the furniture is in place (see fig. 304). The narrative implications are here different than in the painting, however, since the man is turned toward the woman, reading from a sheet of paper—presumably one she has just handed him from the filing cabinet. The artist altered this close exchange between the two figures in a subsequent sheet (see fig. 305) by turning the man away from the woman, making them less connected and thus heightening the tension as he worked toward the painted composition.[8]

From these two sketchy explorations of alternate compositions Hopper worked up the pair of more finished versions on larger sheets (see figs. 306, 307). One of the latter studies corresponds more closely to the painting (see fig. 307), though the care and attention with which he executed both sheets suggests that he wished to explore the different versions of the scene equally. The one he did not end up following (see fig. 306) focuses on the various qualities of light, giving this drawing a striking materiality in the way he applied white chalk, especially in the angled passage streaked across the floor and doorframe at lower left. The white

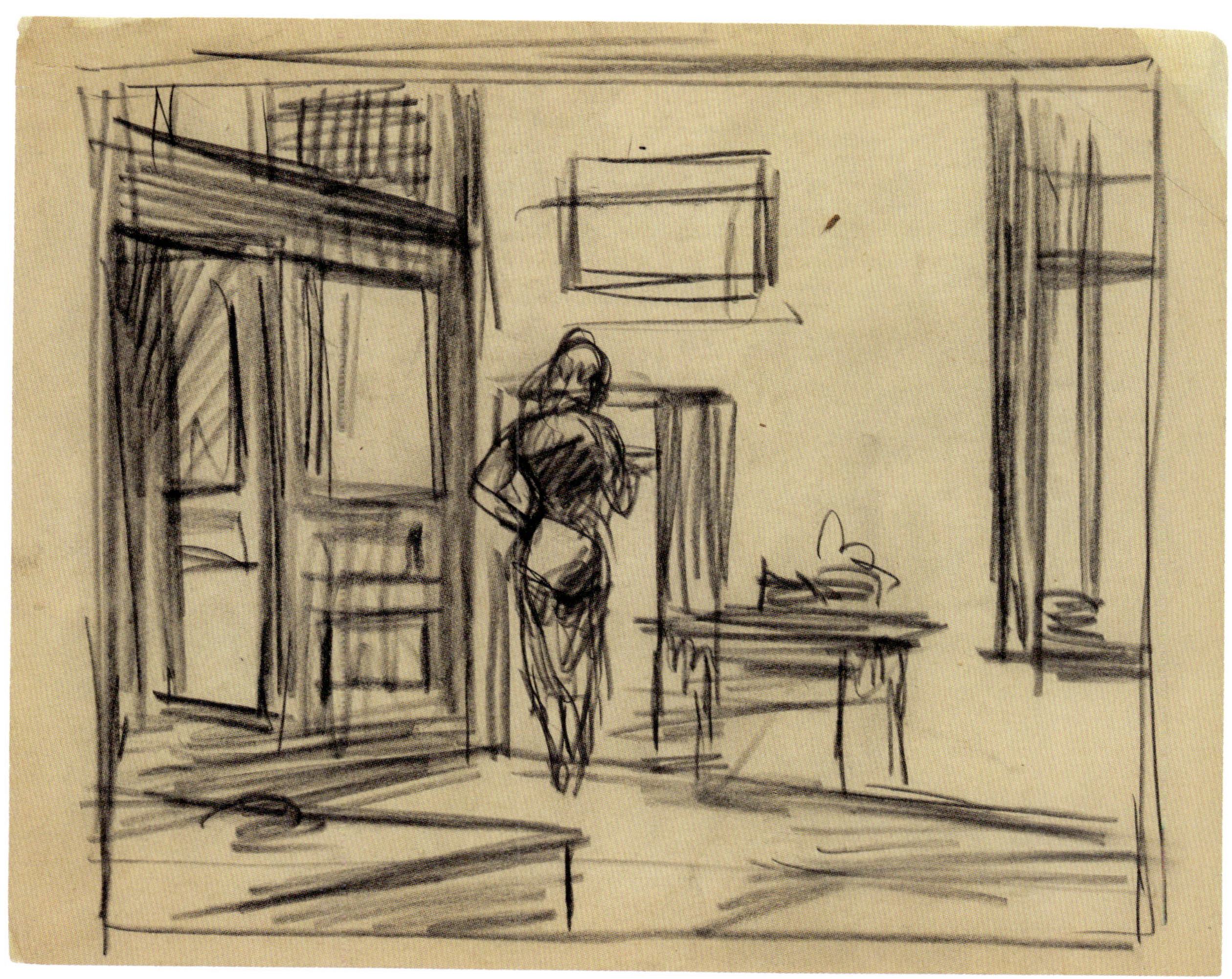

trapezoid of light expanding from right to left across the back wall modulates in intensity as it interacts with various surfaces, shadows, and objects. The sheet offers a virtuoso display of Hopper's love of light, one nearly unique in his drawn oeuvre, especially in the combined use of white and black chalk. The companion sheet has more atmospheric, less contrasting tonalities Here Hopper seems more interested in refining the implications of the story. He developed the woman's strange pose, which became even more pronounced in the painting: impossibly taut, her lower and upper body torque in opposite directions in a position worthy of Italian Mannerism.[9]

As others have noted, the crux of the tension in the painting turns on the sheet of paper just visible on the floor as a white triangle next to the edge of the desk—an out-of-place piece of information whose importance is uncertain, its position between the two figures suggests a next step in the unresolved narrative.[10] Interestingly, it is not present in any of the drawings, so Hopper decided to add this crucial piece of the composition and story late in the work's conception. One of the striking differences between the two very finished large drawings is the slight adjustments made to the space; the upward tilt of the floor in the painting, which the artist changed between these two drawings, is the crucial formal underpinning for the "dropped" piece of paper. In angling up the plane of the floor, Hopper also had to adjust the surfaces parallel to it, namely the desktop (the difference between this surface in the two drawings is pronounced) and the astray sheet. This change is especially notable if we look at the woman's feet, which stand solidly on the ground and exhibit some spatial recession in one sheet (see fig. 306), but turn into side-view profiles in the other (see fig. 307), their relationship to the floor now necessarily different to accommodate its pronounced downward slope. Hopper created this space in impressive tandem with the implied narrative, inextricably interlocking space, figures, and story.

Although *Office at Night* is an interior scene, it uses the same upward-tilted, hovering perspective we see in *Night Shadows* and other El train–inspired Hopper works. The artist's combination of El train experiences, from the voyeuristic window views to the compression

303. Study for *Office at Night* (recto), 1940
Fabricated chalk on paper, 8 ½ × 10 15⁄16 in. (21.6 × 27.8 cm)
Josephine N. Hopper Bequest 70.166a–b

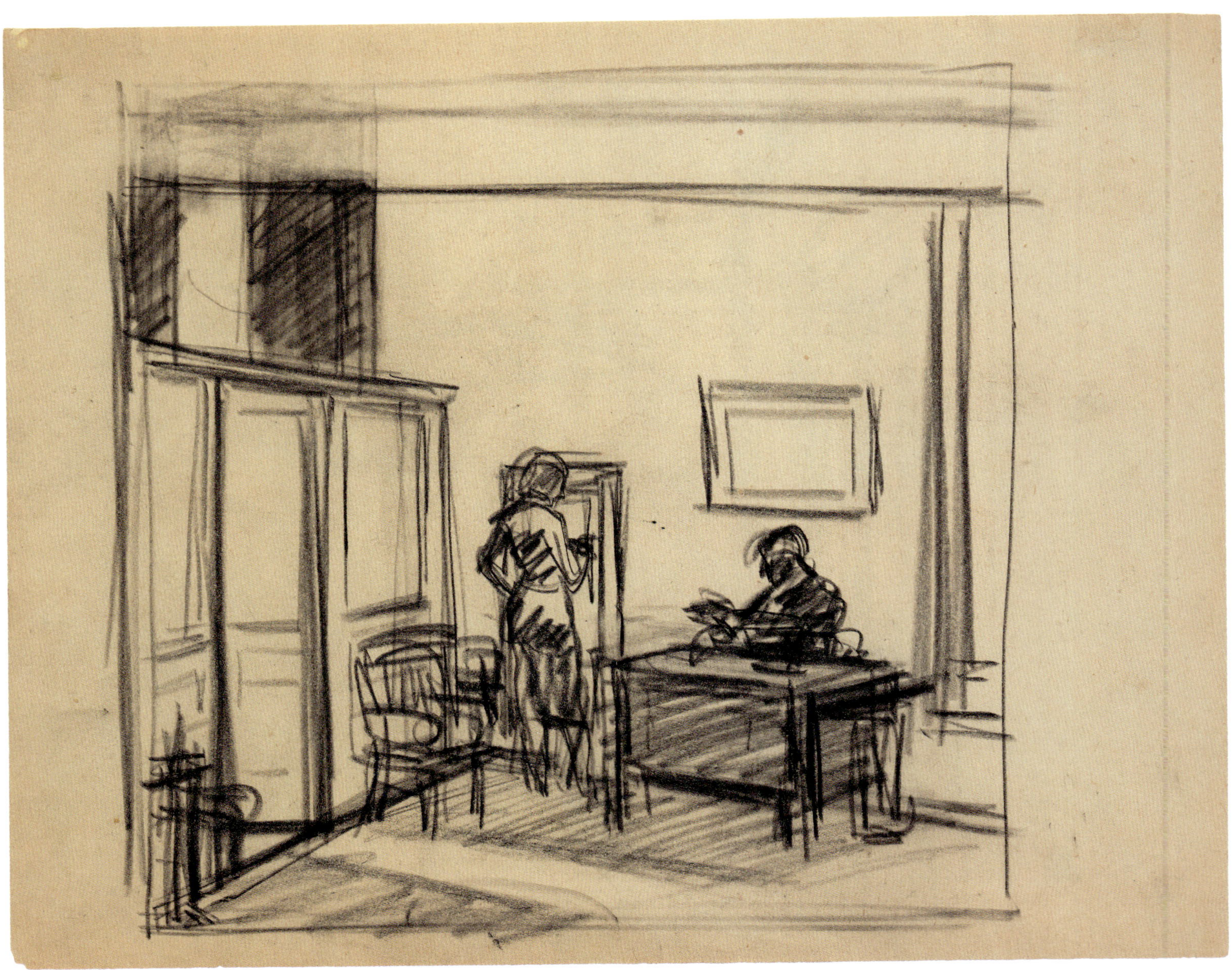

304. Study for *Office at Night* (recto), 1940
Fabricated chalk on paper, 8 ½ × 11 in. (21.6 × 27.9 cm)
Josephine N. Hopper Bequest 70.167a–b

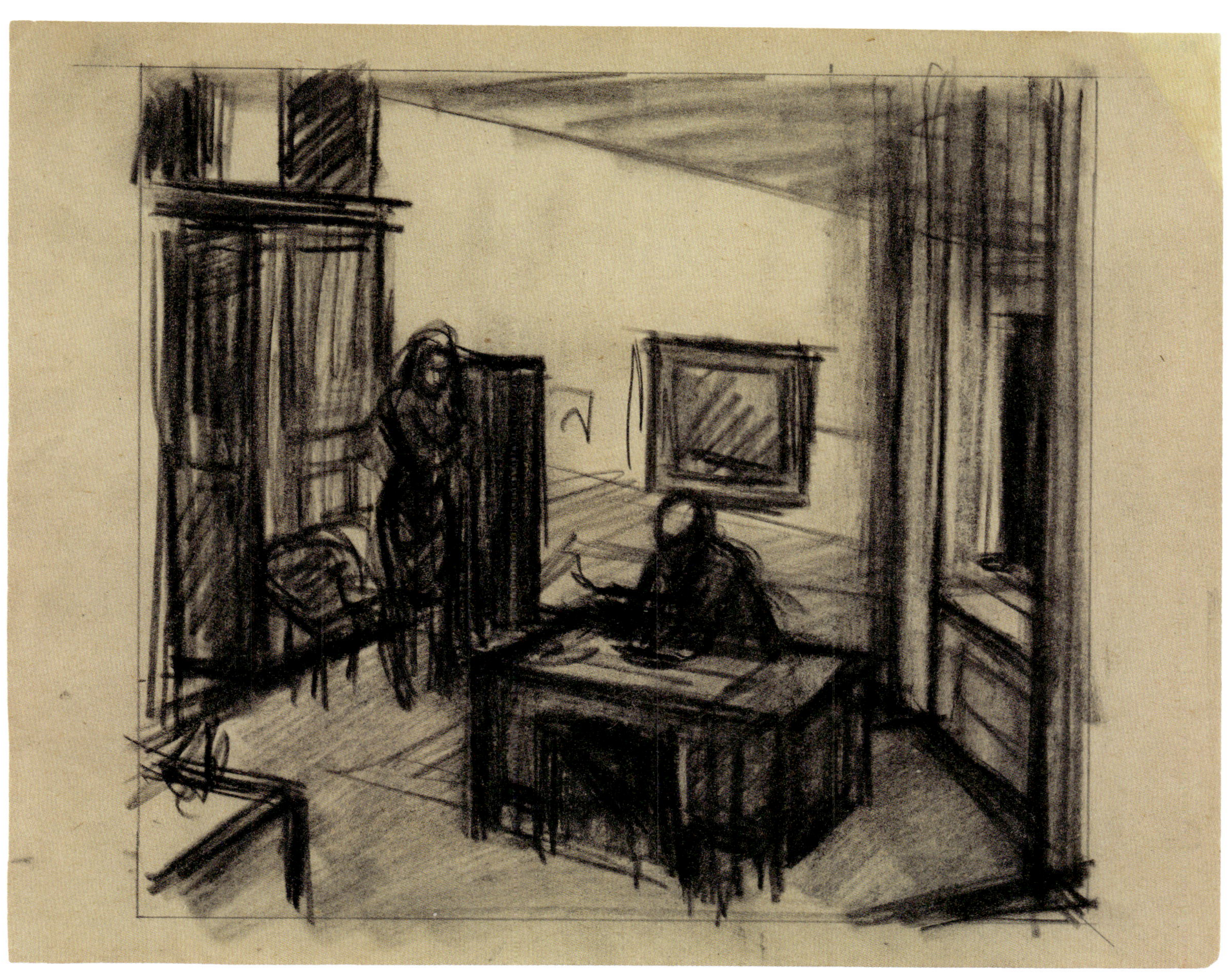

305. Study for *Office at Night*, 1940
Fabricated chalk on paper, 8 7⁄16 × 10 15⁄16 in. (21.4 × 27.8 cm)
Josephine N. Hopper Bequest 70.168

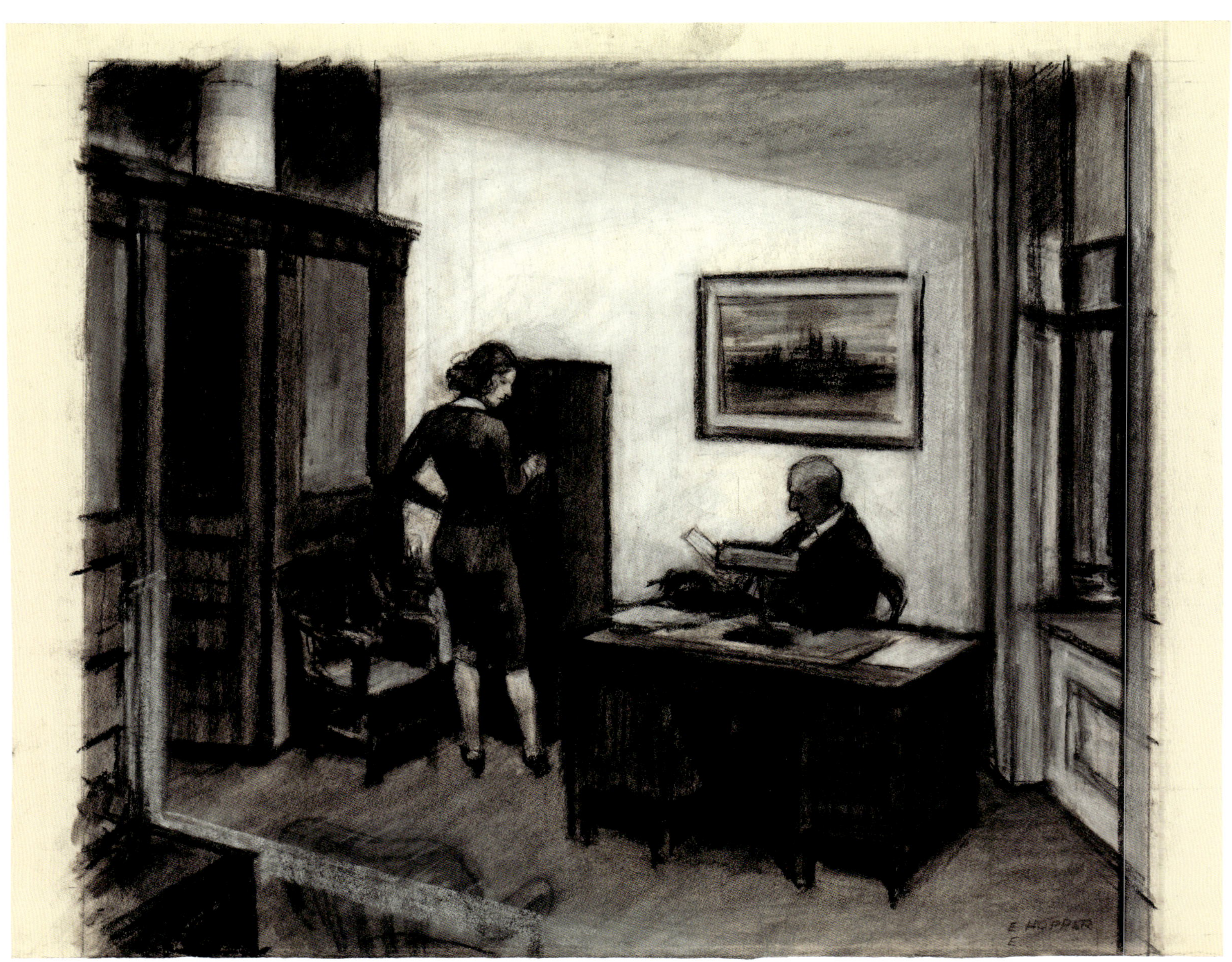

306. Study for *Office at Night*, 1940
Fabricated chalk and charcoal on paper,
15 1/16 × 19 5/8 in. (38.3 × 49.8 cm)
Josephine N. Hopper Bequest 70.340

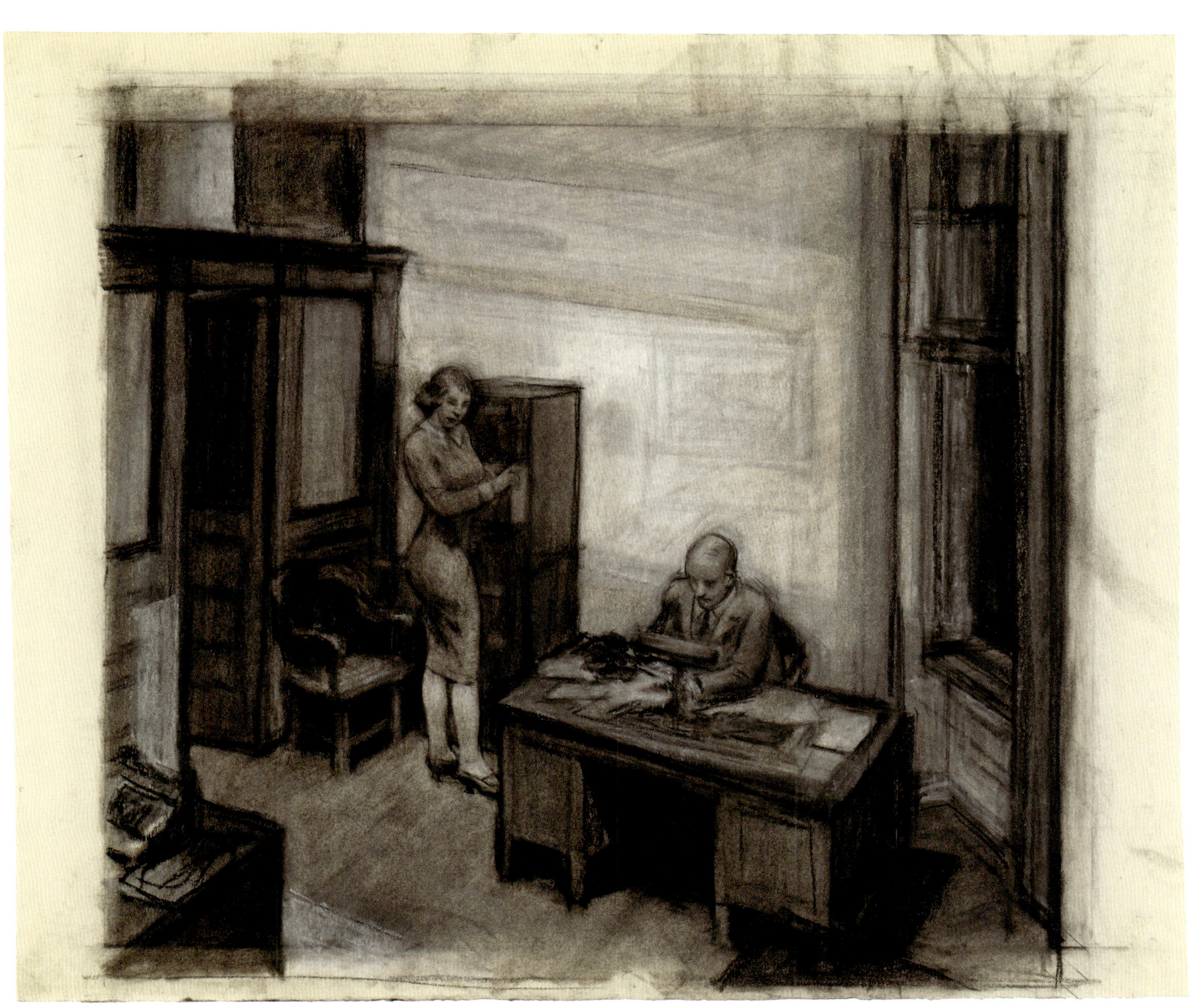

307. Study for *Office at Night*, 1940
Fabricated chalk and graphite pencil on paper,
15 1/16 × 18 3/8 in. (38.3 × 46.7 cm)
Josephine N. Hopper Bequest 70.341

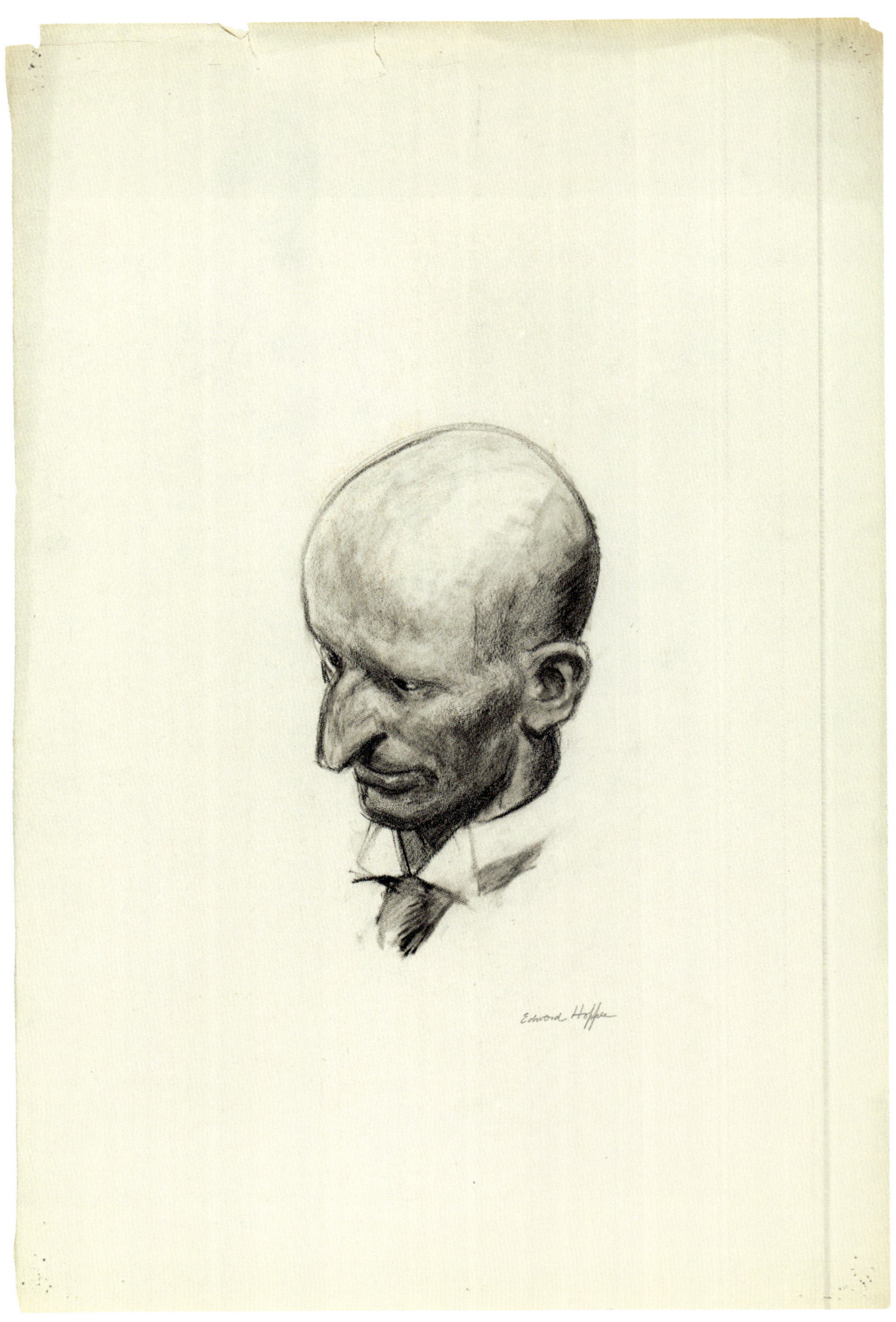

of space, comes together in a seamless whole in his last drawing for *Office at Night*, which he further refined in the painting. One other drawing that seems to relate to this painting also reflects the peculiar spatiality Hopper developed for this work (fig. 308). Its solidly rendered head study of a bald, beak-nosed figure bears some resemblance to *Office at Night*'s male protagonist, especially in two of the compositional studies (see figs. 304, 306). The extremely odd perspective here is completely out of the normal realm of portraiture or any sort of traditional figure study, but it is well explained by the painting and offers a perfect example of the way in which Hopper could disembody his vision and paint or draw things from such imagined, off-kilter angles. It is not, for that reason, a life drawing, but it may have been a crucial step in helping Hopper understand how the odd viewpoint he developed could add to the tension and enhance the narrative implications. Studying the progression of drawings reveals clearly Hopper's mastery in manipulating point of view to heighten the uncertain atmosphere and create what one could call spatial anxiety. We can see, step-by-step, how the space and the subject go hand in hand, and it is fascinating to consider that the process began years before with rides on the El train.

308. Study for *Office at Night* (recto), 1940
Fabricated chalk on paper, 22 × 15 1/16 in. (55.9 × 38.3 cm)
Josephine N. Hopper Bequest 70.815a–b

NOTES

1 Referring to *Sun in an Empty Room* (see fig. 385), on which he was working at the time, Hopper stated: "There're problems of positive and negative areas here on the right that I have to think about. A negative window with a positive tree outside. They're opposed to each other right there.... It's hard to counteract each other.... It's hard to paint outside and inside at the same time." Brian O'Doherty, "Edward Hopper's Voice," in *American Masters: The Voice and the Myth* (New York: Random House, 1973), 26. Hopper's analysis of a painting by Charles Burchfield also shows this interest: "In the Country Blacksmith Shop, he has attempted, and succeeded with, the difficult problem of giving the sensation for which so few try, of the interior and exterior of a building seen simultaneously. A common visual sensation." Hopper, "Charles Burchfield: American," *The Arts* 14, no. 1 (July 1928): 8.

2 On the painting, see Gail Levin, "Edward Hopper's 'Office at Night,'" *Arts Magazine* 52, no. 5 (January 1978): 134–37; Ellen Wiley Todd, "Will (S)he Stoop to Conquer? Preliminaries toward a Reading of Edward Hopper's *Office at Night*," in *Visual Theory: Painting and Interpretation*, ed. Norman Bryson, Michael Ann Holly, and Keith Moxey (New York: HarperCollins, 1991), 47–53; Gail Levin, *Edward Hopper: A Catalogue Raisonné*, vol. 3, *Oils* (New York: Whitney Museum of American Art in association with W. W. Norton, 1995), 270–73.

3 Edward Hopper, letter to Norman Geske and statement about *Office at Night*, August 25, 1948; photocopy in Edward and Josephine Hopper Research Collection, 4.013, Whitney Museum of American Art Archives, New York.

4 *3rd Ave. El*, directed by Carson Davidson (Ardee Films, Carson Davidson Productions, 1955). The film, which was nominated for an Academy Award for best short feature, is part of the Prelinger Archives in the Library of Congress, Washington, DC, and is viewable on the website www.archive.org.

5 The only acknowledgment in Hopper's entire body of work of a reflection on glass or the play of light on an exterior window is on the curved glass in *Nighthawks* (see fig. 166). Otherwise, Hopper never rendered with paint the physical fact of glass in exterior windows.

6 This was noted by Jean Gillies, who also discusses the room's strange shape, in "The Timeless Space of Edward Hopper," *Art Journal* 31, no. 4 (Summer 1972) 409.

7 The figure studies Hopper made for this painting include renderings of the woman's crossed hands and drawings of the seated male figure, including his gesturing right hand (see figs. 298–301). The studies for the seated male are consistent with a mirror point of view, suggesting Hopper posed for the drawings himself and then reversed the figure in the painting. The focus on these hand gestures brings to mind Nicolas Poussin's celebrated painting *Arcadian Shepherds* of 1638–39, which Hopper could certainly have seen in the Louvre or known in reproduction. It is interesting to note that Poussin used wax figures and a kind of shadow box device to compose his paintings. Hopper similarly made a model for his painting *High Noon* (1950; The Dayton Art Institute, Ohio) in order to study the effects of light. The rectilinear geometry and boxy effect of *Conference at Night* suggest that he may have employed this technique here as well.

8 Todd, "Will (S)he Stoop to Conquer?" 49, notes this change in the narrative implications from the earlier studies as well.

9 Two other drawings for this painting are known, both in private collections. One is a figure study for the secretary that tries variations on her pose (reproduced in Douglas Dreishpoon, *Edward Hopper at Kennedy Galleries*, exh. cat. [New York: Kennedy Galleries, 1977], n.p., no. 44). The other is a fascinating study of the man seated at the desk (reproduced in *Edward Hopper: Early and Late; Drawings, Watercolors, and Paintings, March 14–April 18*, exh. cat. [New York: Hirschl & Adler Galleries, 1987], 29, no. 53). The latter drawing was likely done by Hopper using himself posing in a mirror, and is, in that sense, an interesting self-portrait.

10 Linda Nochlin, "Edward Hopper and the Imagery of Alienation," *Art Journal* 41, no. 2 (Summer 1981): 138; Todd, "Will (S)he Stoop to Conquer?" 49.

Hopper's Walls

MARK W. TURNER

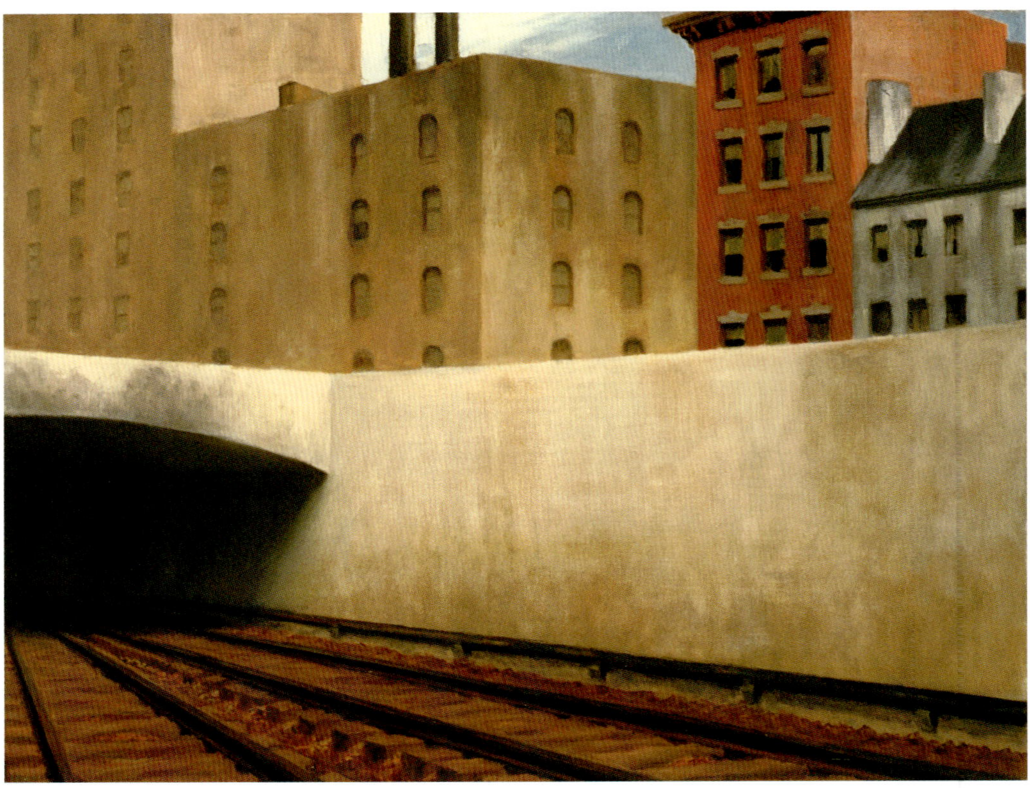

Edward Hopper wasn't one to explain his paintings. Frequently tight-lipped when asked to interpret his work, he preferred not to elaborate about the meaning of particular scenes or figures. Part of the allure of Hopper's work, as viewers have long appreciated, is a state of unknowing for the spectator who suddenly interrupts or halts an ongoing narrative. Hopper leads us into the act of interpretation, only to have the limits of interpretability gradually revealed. Drawing on realist techniques, his paintings capture the weighty banality and allusive moods of everyday life, even as his subjects remain distant, ambiguous, and even unknowable.[1] Off-center and uncannily unsettling,[2] Hopper's world is built around a wall of inscrutability that is both figural and metaphorical.

Hopper's inscrutability derives in part from his lifelong experiences of the city.[3] Like so many of the most poignant artists of urban modernity, Hopper has a particularly acute ability to capture the relationship between individuals (alienated and otherwise) and the built environments they inhabit—hotels, theaters, apartments, office buildings. Further, he is almost instinctual in understanding that the experience of the transient, fleeting moment constitutes what it means to be modern.[4] The city is a place of fragments, in which memory, history, and the self are in continual and uncertain flux; that much we learn from Charles Baudelaire and his French disciples, and from urbanists as distinct as Walt Whitman and James McNeill Whistler. For these writers and artists, among many others, there can never be a completely forthcoming representation. The snatches of everyday life—the glimpses we have of others' lives when we pass them on the street or overhear them on a subway train—prevent anything like a total picture, so that representation is always contingent and partial.

In one of the artist's few written statements about his work, sent to Norman Geske at the Walker Art Center in Minneapolis in 1948, Hopper explains that the idea for *Office at Night* (1940; see fig. 282) "was probably first suggested by many rides on the 'L' train in New York City after dark, and glimpses of office interiors that were so fleeting as to leave fresh and vivid impressions on my mind."[5] One of Hopper's mature paintings, *Office at Night* is in many ways exemplary of his depictions of urban modernity—a captured moment, voyeuristically

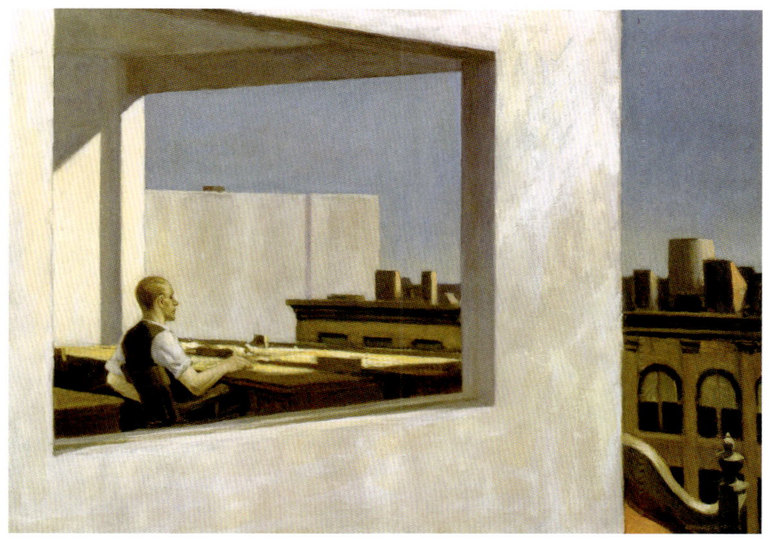

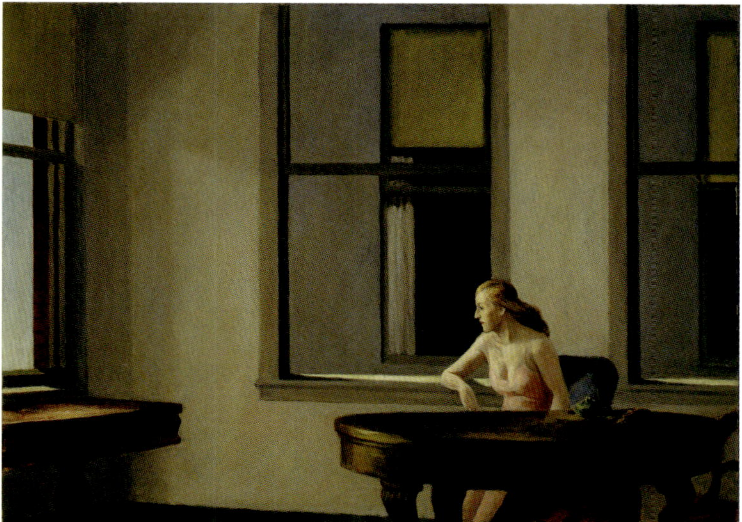

overseen—but his early work is similarly concerned with the fleeting moment and fragmented image. His sketchbook drawings and watercolors of street characters made in Paris in 1906–07 (see figs. 105–132, 134, 136, 137, 142–150) hark back to the nineteenth century in seeking to represent the variety of the urban multitude, but they also speak forward to the kind of conceptual, even existential problem that he returns to throughout his career—for example, the conflicting feelings of distance amid proximity that derive from people's experience of the city's built environment, with its unexpected points of view. As many of his drawings suggest, Hopper's work began with real-world observations—the built environment that he saw around him, in particular—but unlike other, more emphatic contemporary realists (some of the Ashcan artists, for example), he transformed the streets and buildings around him into pictures that speak to the real while suggesting much more than can be uttered. Sometimes his work generalizes and simplifies reality; sometimes he seems to provide a very specific, intimate moment. It is the distance or gap between an engagement with the "real" and our inability ever to pin down that depiction that seems particularly to coalesce in Hopper's walls.

Walls are important features in much of Hopper's work, and once we begin to look for them, we find them everywhere—perhaps unsurprisingly, since he is so much an artist of buildings. *Approaching a City* (1946) is typical of Hopper's use of walls. In both the study (see fig. 72) and the painting (fig. 309) a high wall divides the planes of the picture, with the train tracks where the viewer is positioned on one side, and the city, with the upper floors of its buildings hovering above, on the other. In an interview, Hopper said of this painting:

> I've always been interested in approaching a big city by train; and I can't exactly describe the sensations. But they're entirely human and perhaps have nothing to do with esthetics. There is a certain fear and anxiety, and a great visual interest in the things that one sees coming into the city.[6]

Hopper's interest in the painting is to capture the human sensations of arriving in the city by train, but he does so, strikingly, without depicting any humans. Fear and anxiety are conveyed spatially through the imposing wall that separates us from the city itself. Such stark, usually bare walls can be found throughout Hopper's work: *Rooms by the Sea* (1951; see fig. 1), in which a wall leads us, surreally, to a door and the sea; *Morning Sun* (1952; see fig. 381), with its brightly lit interior wall juxtaposing the built-up city facade outside; *Office in a Small City* (fig. 310), in which glaringly stark walls triangulate out into the city; *City Sunlight* (fig. 311), the composition of which relies on a play between walls and windows; and, the most pensive of them all, *Sun in an Empty Room* (1963; see fig. 385), in which the scene is cleared of all human presence, leaving only light on walls and a glimpse of the natural world beyond. The presentation of natural and artificial light was, of course, a constant preoccupation for Hopper,

309. *Approaching a City*, 1946
Oil on canvas, 27 ⅛ × 36 in. (68.9 × 91.4 cm)
The Phillips Collection, Washington, DC; acquired 1947 0923

310. *Office in a Small City*, 1953
Oil on canvas, 28 × 40 in. (71.1 × 101.6 cm)
The Metropolitan Museum of Art, New York; George A. Hearn Fund, 1953 53.183

311. *City Sunlight*, 1954
Oil on canvas, 28 3⁄16 × 40 ⅛ in. (71.6 × 101.9 cm)
Hirshhorn Museum and Sculpture Garden, Smithsonian Institution, Washington, DC; gift of the Joseph H. Hirshhorn Foundation, 1966 66.2505

and part of the challenge in painting his walls was capturing the play of various light sources. Of the wall in *Office at Night*, he commented:

> The light coming from outside and falling on the wall in back made a difficult problem, as it is almost painting white on white, it also made a strong accent of the edge of the filing cabinet which was difficult to subordinate to the figure of the girl.
>
> I was also interested in the sombre richness of the furniture against the white walls. Any more than this, the picture will have to tell, but I hope it will not tell any obvious anecdote, for none is intended.[7]

Here, Hopper cautions against what he knows will be our instinct to narrate and to create meaning through anecdote. The wall is the place where that inscrutability is felt both visually and symbolically.

The six compositional studies for *Office at Night* (see figs. 302–307) point to the details he focused on as he arrived at his final idea for the painting.[8] Objects are added, bodies reconfigured, perspective altered. In all the compositional drawings, a painting hangs on the wall; tellingly, however, that detail is erased in the final drawing (though its outline remains ghostly visible), leaving the undecorated, blank wall that is so prominent in the painting. This is typical of Hopper's "process of reduction,"[9] partly revealed in studying the drawings alongside the paintings, but it is also typical of his treatment of walls (figs. 312–314). For him, walls were frequently blank—not completely without meaning, not empty, but blank. *Conference at Night* (1949; see fig. 291), a revisiting nearly a decade later of the same subject as *Office at Night*, similarly presents us with an office interior dominated by a blank wall lit from external, artificial sources. As with the earlier painting, *Conference at Night* derives from a remembered, but reconfigured, urban glimpse. Hopper wrote to Elizabeth Navas, "The idea of a loft of business building with the artificial light of the street coming into the room at night had been in my mind for some years before I attempted it. And had been suggested by things I had seen on Broadway in walking there at night."[10] The light from the window and the murky doors and pillars at the left of the painting echo those of *Office at Night*, and there's a similarly impenetrable scenario depicted. We cannot know what the three figures in *Conference at Night* are doing any more than we can fully understand the relationship between the secretary and boss in *Office at Night*. These big, blank walls are not quite abstract in their resistance to mimetic meaning, but they are very nearly so.

Hopper learned a great deal about glimpses of urban life from his ongoing engagement with French writers—Baudelaire, Paul Verlaine, and Marcel Proust, in particular—but it was through the American Herman Melville that he may have come to appreciate the significance of walls. Hopper spent the summer of 1938 on Cape Cod reading the complete works of Melville, as well as criticism of the author by Van Wyck Brooks, who promoted Melville's work in a series of books about nineteenth-century New England writers. Gail Levin notes that Melville was important to Hopper because of the artist's "love of nautical life and his concern with American themes in art," and that Hopper borrowed the title for his painting *The Lee Shore* (1941; private collection) from a chapter in *Moby-Dick*.[11] But Melville was also a great writer about the city, and his short story "Bartleby, the Scrivener" (1853) encapsulates many of the qualities that come to define Hopper's work—urban melancholy, existential tension, and the inability to communicate with those around you.[12]

"Bartleby" is among the first, and remains one of the finest, depictions of an office in American culture. The story recounts how Bartleby, a young employee in a firm of legal scriveners (copyists), decides to stop working, stating simply and confoundingly that he would "prefer not to," which becomes his refrain. He is described variously as "pallid," "pale," and "silent," and "like a very ghost," and we're told that he "was one of those beings of whom nothing was

312. Study for *Office at Night* (detail), 1940
Fabricated chalk and charcoal on paper,
15 1/16 × 19 5/8 in. (38.3 × 49.8 cm)
Josephine N. Hopper Bequest 70.340

313. Study for *Office at Night* (detail), 1940
Fabricated chalk and graphite pencil on paper,
15 1/16 × 18 3/8 in. (38.3 × 46.7 cm)
Josephine N. Hopper Bequest 70.341

314. *Office at Night* (detail), 1940
Oil on canvas, 22 3/16 × 25 1/8 in. (56.4 × 63.8 cm)
Walker Art Center, Minneapolis; gift of the T. B. Walker Foundation, Gilbert M. Walker Fund, 1948 1948.21

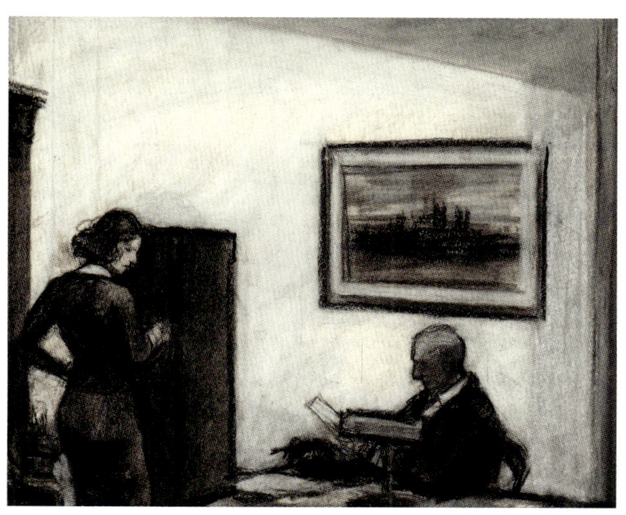
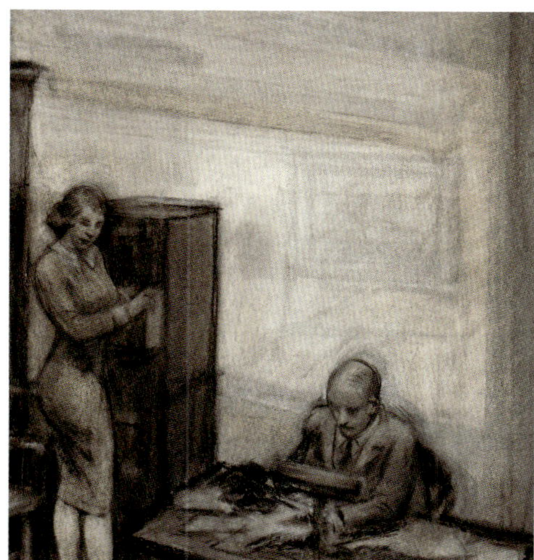
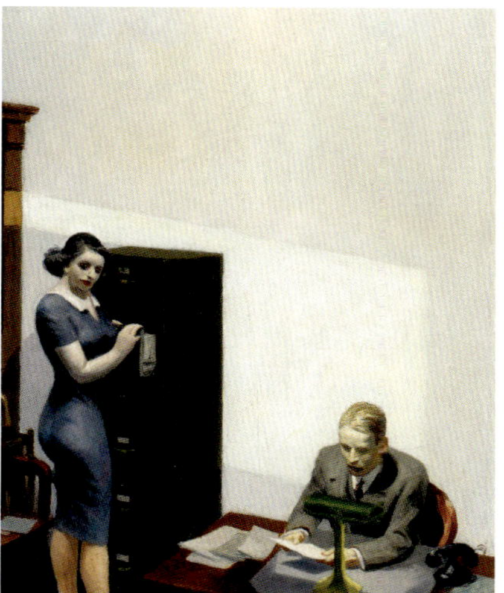

ascertainable."[13] Indeed, the narrator, Bartleby's employer, spends most of the story frustrated in his inability to understand who Bartleby is and what he represents, and readers have followed in the narrator's frustrated footsteps ever since. As Robert Milder suggests,

> interpretations of the character Bartleby are almost as numerous as interpretations of Moby Dick. He has been read (among other things) as Melville the discontented marketplace writer, as Marx's oppressed or alienated labourer, as a proto-existentialist, a nihilist, a schizophrenic, or an anorexic, as a Hindu or Buddhist ascetic, as a Christ figure, and as a precursor of Kafka's "hunger artist."[14]

Our desire to interpret and "know" Bartleby is as overdetermined as our desire to define the narratives in Hopper's paintings. Bartleby, like Melville's great white whale, appears to signify just about everything while simultaneously resisting any specific signification.

The punning subtitle to "Bartleby"—"A Story of Wall-Street"—makes clear that this is a tale about walls.[15] With great precision, Melville describes the office in which the scriveners are doing their copying:

> My chambers were up stairs at No. —Wall-street. At one end they looked upon the white wall of the interior of a spacious sky-light shaft, penetrating the building from top to bottom. This view might have been considered rather tame than otherwise, deficient in what landscape painters call "life." But if so, the view from the other end of my chambers offered, at least, a contrast, if nothing more. In that direction my windows commanded an unobstructed view of a lofty brick wall, black by age and everlasting shade; which wall required no spy-glass to bring out its lurking beauties, but for the benefit of all near-sighted spectators, was pushed up to within ten feet of my window panes. Owing to the great height of the surrounding buildings, and my chambers being on the second floor, the interval between this wall and mine not a little resembled a huge square cistern.[16]

The chamber has high white walls inside and, through a window, offers an immediate and "unobstructed view" of a high black wall outside. Translucent, ground-glass folding doors, we're later told, separate the spaces within the office, allowing some light to pass through. Some pages later, the narrator describes the office in meticulous detail and locates Bartleby within it:

> I placed his desk close up to a small side-window in that part of the room, a window which originally had afforded a lateral view of certain grimy backyards and bricks, but which, owing to subsequent erections, commanded at present no view at all, though it gave some light. Within three feet of the

315. Hammermill Bond advertisement in *Life* magazine, May 3, 1937, page 91

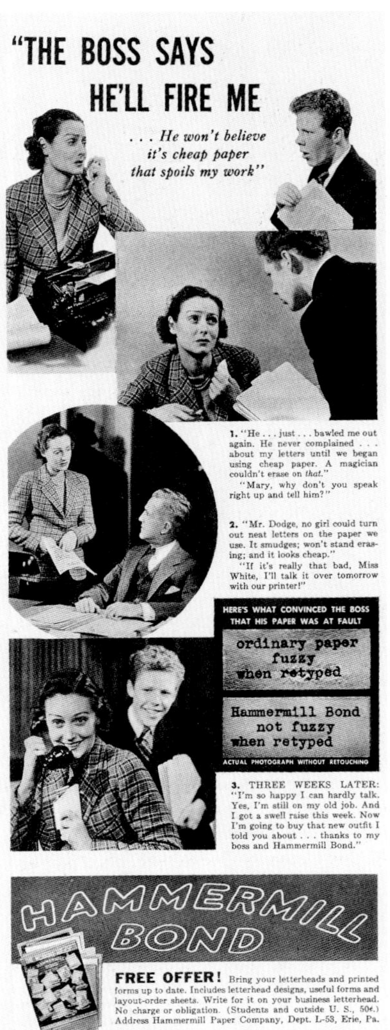

> panes was a wall, and the light came down from far above, between two lofty buildings, as from a very small opening in a dome. Still further to a satisfactory arrangement, I procured a high green folding screen, which might entirely isolate Bartleby from my sight, though not remove him from my voice. And thus, in a manner, privacy and society were conjoined.[17]

The narrator-boss is separated from Bartleby by a folding screen, akin to the glass partition wall that separates Hopper's boss and his private office from the more public world of work beyond in *Office at Night*. As Melville's story unfolds, and as the young scrivener continues to "prefer not to" do what is asked of him, "for long periods [Bartleby] would stand looking out, at his pale window behind the screen, upon the dead brick wall." Near the end of the story, when Bartleby is in prison and about to die, he stands "all alone in the quietest of the yards, his face towards a high wall."[18] In a clever twist, after Bartleby's death we learn that he used to work in the Dead Letter Office in Washington, DC, where undeliverable mail ends up. If we are to make sense of Bartleby, we must make sense of his always coming up against a wall, but the difficulty is that walls are barriers to absolute knowledge, not conduits to greater understanding. As the Dead Letter Office suggests, there are messages that simply cannot be conveyed, texts that do not signify.

Although Hopper read Melville two summers before he painted *Office at Night*, my point is not that there is a simple connection between Melville's tale of a New York office and its walls and the artist's later depiction of a stolen glimpse of an office in a New York loft building. Direct influence is of limited interest here. More suggestive is the way both of these urbanists use the wall to bring us up against the limits of knowledge. Melville was writing at the birth of the modern office,[19] while Hopper was painting during a period when it had already been firmly established at the center of middle-class American life, a recognizable part of popular culture in films and advertising (fig. 315). At the heart of Hopper's *Office at Night* is a telling irony, for while offices were invented as places for the transmission of information, this painting points us to a gap in communication. Technologies of modern communication (typewriter and telephone) are on display, as are the systems of information and knowledge management (the filing cabinet, its letters and documents) that keep the workplace organized; however, there is a distinct lack of communication between the two figures in the picture, where eyes do not meet and paperwork ends up on the floor. This communication gap extends to the viewer's understanding of the picture, in which we cannot be certain of what is going on. Other paintings depict a similar and very modern lack of communication. The employee in *Office in a Small City* sits, Bartleby-like, facing a window, which itself looks on to the walls outside. Perhaps Hopper captures the man in a simple moment of pausing or waiting, or perhaps in a daydreaming reverie—we cannot know. Tellingly, *Office in a Small City* was used as the cover image for a recent edition of "Bartleby" published in France (fig. 316), clearly suggesting the imaginative connection between Melville's office worker and Hopper's. Melville's Bartleby seems both strikingly modern and almost out of time, while Hopper's man sitting in an office in a small city, surrounded by walls, seems both to look back to the nineteenth century and forward to the silence, containment, and communication breakdowns we find a decade later in the work of writers such as Samuel Beckett.[20]

If offices are there for the purpose of communication, what are Hopper's pictures of offices trying to tell us? The composition of *Office at Night* offers us one way out, the open door in the partition wall on the left of the painting. Similarly, in *Conference at Night*, the beam of light on the wall leads the eye to a corner beyond the partition wall. As suggested by the darkness seen beyond the partition glass and through the door, these somber spaces are murky and even more unforthcoming than the offices themselves. If we cannot know what is taking place within the office, we have no idea what lurks in the dark, undefined, and ambiguous spaces beyond. In Hopper's offices, only uncertain realities exist beyond the walls.

316. Cover of 1989 Flammarion edition of Herman Melville's "Bartleby" and "Les Iles enchantées" ("The Encantadas") featuring Hopper's *Office in a Small City* (1953; see fig. 310). Courtesy Groupe Flammarion, Paris, and The Metropolitan Museum of Art, New York

NOTES

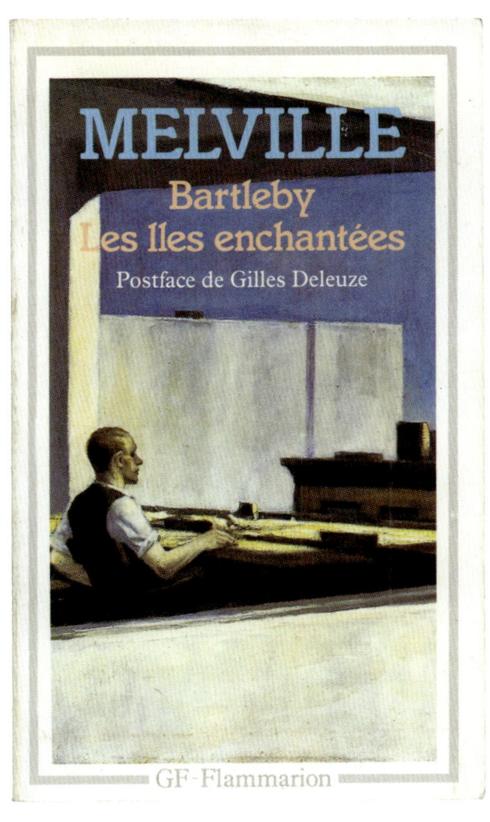

1 A number of critics make this general point about Hopper. See, for example, Joseph Anthony Ward, who writes that Hopper "defamiliarizes the commonplace by, among other things, requiring us to observe the most banal features of a society at a time or in a situation when they are rarely observed; hence they become unfamiliar, as they also become curiously quiet." Ward, *American Silences: The Realism of James Agee, Walker Evans, and Edward Hopper* (Baton Rouge: Louisiana State University Press, 1985), 170.
2 Victor Burgin discusses the uncanny sense of "parallel worlds" in Hopper's paintings, which capture "a latent presence in the interstices of the present." See Burgin, "The Separateness of Things," *Tate Papers* (Spring 2005), http://www.tate.org.uk/download/file/fid/7360.
3 Brian O'Doherty writes: "The city and its anonymity, which Hopper welcomed, was the text for what I believe are his greatest pictures. (Hopper as *flâneur* is a mildly surprising thought.) The city seemed to have provided him with his most intimate sensations." O'Doherty, "Hopper's Look," in Sheena Wagstaff, ed., *Edward Hopper*, exh. cat. (London: Tate Publishing, 2004). For an alternative view that reads Hopper's work in relation to a long history of American anti-urbanism, see Tom Slater, "Fear of the City 1882–1967: Edward Hopper and the Discourse of Anti-Urbanism," *Social and Cultural Geography* 3, no. 2 (2002): 135–54.
4 For Charles Baudelaire, it is the figure of the urban flâneur, the "hero of modern life" who must "distil the eternal from the transitory," that is the essence of what he calls modernity. See Baudelaire, "The Painter of Modern Life," in *Selected Writings on Art and Literature*, trans. P. E. Charvet (London: Penguin Books, 1992), 402.
5 Edward Hopper, letter to Norman Geske and statement about *Office at Night*, August 25, 1948; photocopy in Edward and Josephine Hopper Research Collection, 4.013, Whitney Museum of American Art Archives, New York.
6 Quoted in Gail Levin, *Edward Hopper: A Catalogue Raisonné*, vol. 3, *Oils* (New York: Whitney Museum of American Art in association with W. W. Norton, 1995), 312.
7 Edward Hopper, letter to Norman Geske and statement about *Office at Night*, August 25, 1948.
8 Six are compositional studies owned by the Whitney (see figs. 302–307) and two others—a study of the woman at the filing cabinet and the man at the desk—are in private collections.
9 Ward, *American Silences*, 174. See also Gail Levin, "The Office Image in the Visual Arts," *Arts Magazine* 59, no. 1 (September 1984): 98–103.
10 Levin, *Edward Hopper: A Catalogue Raisonné*, 3:324.
11 Gail Levin, *Edward Hopper: An Intimate Biography* (New York: Rizzoli, 2007), 305.
12 Among Melville's other important urban tales was the New York–based novel *Pierre: or The Ambiguities* (New York: Harper and Bros., 1852), published a year before "Bartleby."
13 Herman Melville, "Bartleby, the Scrivener: A Story of Wall-Street," in *Billy Budd, Sailor and Selected Tales*, ed. Robert Milder, World's Classics (Oxford: Oxford University Press, 1997), 10–11, 15, 3.
14 See Milder's textual notes in ibid., 375–76. More recent significant interpretations have focused on philosophical questions related to ethics and language. See Giorgio Agamben, "Bartleby, or On Contingency," in *Potentialities: Collected Essays in Philosophy*, ed. and trans. D. Heller-Roazen (Stanford: Stanford University Press, 1999), 243–74; Gilles Deleuze, "Bartleby; or, The Formula," in *Essays: Critical and Clinical*, trans. Daniel W. Smith and Michael A. Greco (Minneapolis: University of Minnesota Press, 1997), 68–90.
15 For a classic reading of the walls in "Bartleby," though one that reads the story biographically in relation to Melville's own frustrations in the literary marketplace, see Leo Marx, "Melville's Parable of the Walls," *Sewanee Review* 61, no. 4 (Autumn 1953): 602–27.
16 Melville, "Bartleby," 4.
17 Ibid., 10.
18 Ibid., 21, 38.
19 Peter Cowan writes of the development of the office in the nineteenth century: "The jobs that people do in offices have always been concerned with writing or transcribing messages of one kind or another, and with relaying information," and "the separation of the office function at the level of the industrial firm is repeated on a city-wide scale during the nineteenth century. The need to support and sustain the process of industrialisation called new institutions into being, and changed old ones into new forms." See Cowan et al., *The Office: A Facet of Urban Growth* (London: Heinemann, 1969), 27, 28. On "Bartleby" and the history of the office and communications, see Graham Thompson, *Male Sexuality under Surveillance: The Office in American Literature* (Iowa City: University of Iowa Press, 2003); John Durham Peters, *Speaking into the Air: A History of the Idea of Communication* (Chicago: University of Chicago Press, 1999).
20 See, for example, Samuel Beckett, *Endgame* (1958; London: Faber and Faber, 2009), 11:
CLOV: . . . I'll leave you, I have things to do.
HAMM: In your kitchen?
CLOV: Yes.
HAMM: What, I'd like to know.
CLOV: I look at the wall.
HAMM: The wall! And what do you see on your wall? Mene, mene? Naked bodies?
CLOV: I see my light dying.
The writing on Beckett's walls is more caustic and unremitting than Hopper's, though *Endgame* is similarly about the inability to make meaning.

The Road

NICHOLAS ROBBINS

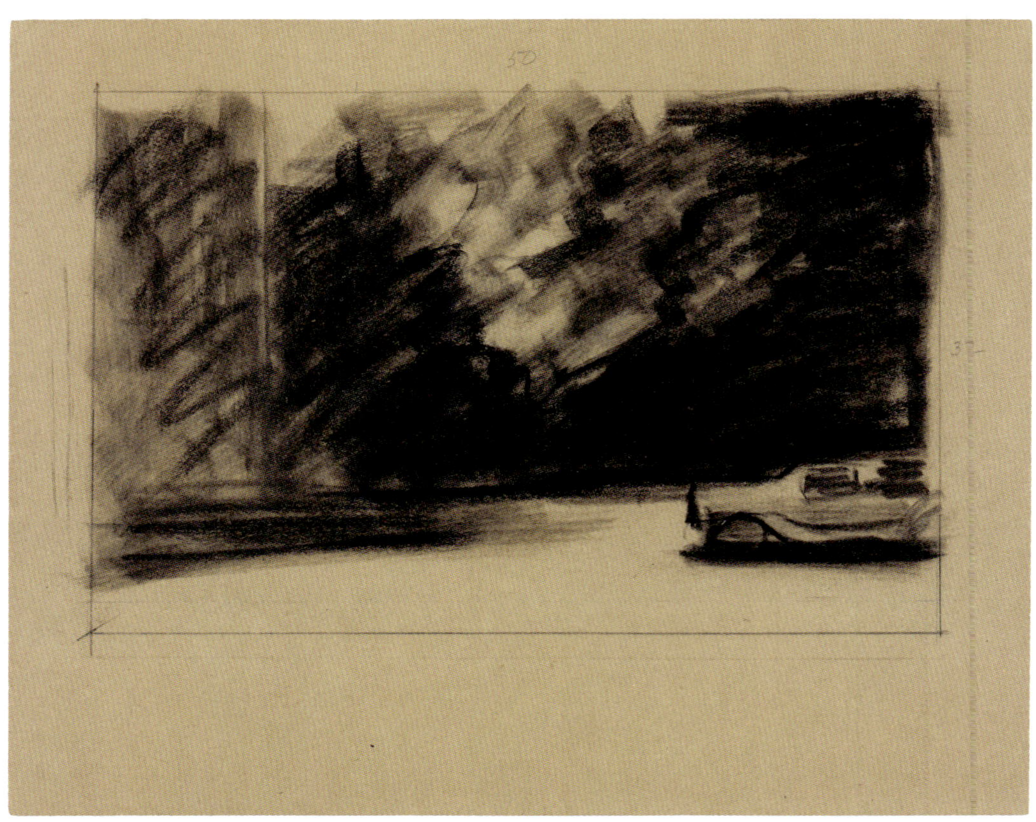

Edward Hopper's small charcoal drawing *Landscape with Automobile* (fig. 317) has a measure of velocity uncommon in the artist's body of work, which is so often marked by a deliberate stillness. Dashed, hurried marks record a screen of roadside trees, forms that approach abstraction—as if the scene was in the process of disappearing even as it was being recorded. The deftly but cursorily delineated sedan in front of this screen of foliage is cut off by the drawn frame of the work, an interruption and incompleteness that implies the car's movement, as well as the moving eye of the viewer.[1] In its speed and fugitive quality, the process of making the drawing matches the landscape it records: the side of road seen in an instant out of the window of an automobile. This drawing has been interpreted as a study for Hopper's late painting *Road and Trees* of 1962 (see fig. 351), a canvas that stills the seemingly moving world into taut, vital composition and is the culmination of a long series of works Hopper made of the road and the roadside landscape.[2]

Earlier in his life, Hopper described seeing Manhattan from an elevated train—a series of "glimpses ... so fleeting as to leave fresh and vivid impressions on my mind."[3] Modernity and fleeting experience have been linked at least since Charles Baudelaire's odes to the encounters of the pedestrian flâneur absorbed in the life of Paris's streets; more than a few writers have even considered Hopper in the mode of the flâneur-observer.[4] Hopper's records of the world seen from an automobile can be considered extensions of his representations of urban life, inspired by his walks through Greenwich Village, his rides on the El train, and his time spent in the public spaces of the movie theater and cafeteria—his records of an urbanized vision.[5] Hopper recognized that the automobile changed the way the American landscape was organized, accessed, and observed, and his art is marked by his response to this and other shifts in visual experience.[6] Lloyd Goodrich, Hopper's most steadfast supporter, understood this aspect of the artist's modernity very early on. In 1927, Goodrich wrote: "Hopper's painting is not modern in the narrow sense in which that word is sometimes used to describe those artists who abjure the representational side of art. The vision expressed in his pictures is very much that of the average man, transformed into something more significant by the vision of the artist."[7] Hopper's realism was always concerned not with the description of facts

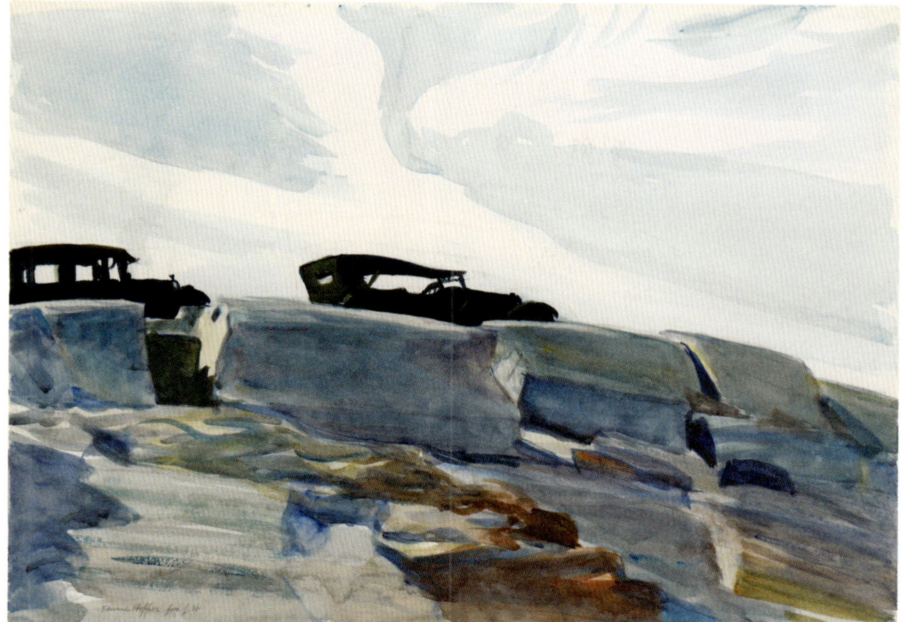

in the world, but rather with the particular way in which those facts impress themselves on the mind and later resurface. In the span of Hopper's lifetime, the "vision . . . of the average man" expanded to include the experience of viewing the world from the road, an experience Hopper internalized as he used his car to travel, to draw and paint, and to seek out subjects for his work. Hopper was one of the first artists to recognize the particular visual experiences linked to the automobile and to the roadside landscape as significant subjects addressing outward modernity and change, yet his depictions of those experiences are also personal, interiorized, and often lyrical. "To me, the important thing is the sense of going on," Hopper said in 1948. "You know how beautiful things are when you're traveling."[8]

Studio on the Road

Hopper drew a sharp distinction between works that were made "from the fact," that is, from life, and those he made in his studio. After the 1920s, the latter category included the majority of his oil paintings, while he continued to paint his watercolors directly in front of his subjects.[9] Yet despite the increasingly "improvised" and synthetic nature of Hopper's oils, the importance of observation, and of undergoing specific modes of seeing and looking, remained an integral part of Hopper's working process throughout his life. From the time that Hopper and his wife, Jo, purchased their first car, a used Dodge, in 1927, his process of observation and the experience of driving were often linked: the automobile served both as a means of developing subjects for his pictures and as a mobile studio for drawing and making watercolors.[10] The Hoppers first traveled in their car to paint in Maine and Gloucester, Massachusetts, popular summer destinations for artists where both had painted before.[11] A watercolor from 1927 (fig. 318), probably made on a trip to Portland, Maine, records a pair of automobiles perched on a rock outcropping, in the place a human observer might occupy, inscribing the increasing centrality of the car to scenic tourism and the pursuit of artistic motifs.[12] Edward and Jo also began to make long journeys throughout the United States and Mexico, taking advantage of improved roads and a burgeoning tourist infrastructure that served millions of new automotive tourists who, no longer bound to train schedules, could choose their own destinations and pace of travel.[13] As Gail Levin has shown through her study of Jo's diaries, driving (and Hopper's unwillingness to let Jo drive) was also a great source of tension and conflict in their relationship, despite the freedom and break from the routine activities and scenes of their daily life it afforded them.[14] In April 1929, they set out on a month-long trip to the South; they would also take two tours of the West, first through Colorado, Utah, California, Oregon, and Idaho in 1941, and then an extended stay in California in 1956–57. The Hoppers also took numerous journeys to Mexico between 1943 and 1955, though they avoided the cities and sights popular with other artists.[15] These long, rambling travels through unfamiliar landscapes were different from the artist's more focused circulation in the familiar landscapes of New England and Cape Cod, though both often left him dissatisfied in his search for subjects.[16]

317. *Landscape with Automobile* (Study for *Road and Trees*), c. 1962
Charcoal on paper, 8 15/16 × 11 in. (22.7 × 27.9 cm)
Peter Findlay Gallery, New York

318. *Cars and Rocks*, 1927
Watercolor and graphite pencil on paper, 13 7/8 × 20 in. (35.2 × 50.8 cm)
Josephine N. Hopper Bequest 70.1104

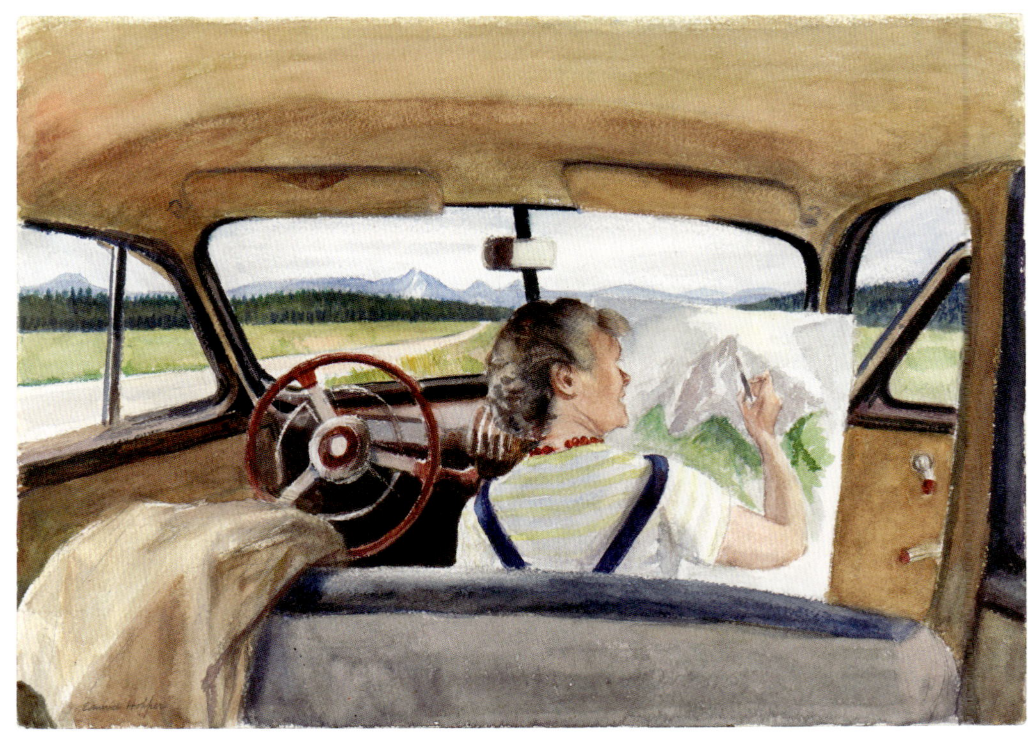

In postcards and letters to Peggy Rehn, the wife of Hopper's dealer, Frank Rehn, Jo described their 1941 automobile tour in the West, during which they visited Yosemite and the Grand Canyon before traveling through California. Jo was enthusiastic about their travels: "These tourist camps are a joy—a little house, plenty of plumbing... & your own garage.... It certainly is a smart thing to pack up and sail off to parts unknown. I'm so glad we made the effort."[17] However, she noted with frustration that despite Hopper's strong reaction to California's Spanish missions, "he won't stay to paint them."[18] A few days later, on the road from Los Angeles to San Francisco, she wrote that Hopper would not stop so she could paint a watercolor of Carmel: "But on he would go. Always on-on-on. Not one lick of work—paints not unpacked, stretchers, canvas etc. packed on top of suitcase."[19] Jo's descriptions characterize the seeking quality of these rambling journeys, and reveal Hopper's desire to find suitable places or subjects to paint, which so often eluded him. The lack of overt productivity, though, was consistent with the long periods of observation and reflection that characterized the artist's process. "He looks a long time for his subjects," Goodrich noted in 1946. "Looks and looks and looks."[20]

Hopper did, however, produce a volume of watercolors during their trips to the South, West, and Mexico; he saw these as "factual" records of places, though as Jo noted he would not often choose to paint the more obviously interesting landscapes or monuments they encountered.[21] Yet, the relatively scant record of Hopper's travels within his work does not preclude his incorporation of the roadside landscapes he experienced; they resurfaced again and again in his later, "improvised" paintings, which draw on his memories of these travels and experiences of seeing the world from the car. His 1946 watercolor *Jo in Wyoming* (fig. 319) is a record of their process of art-making on the road, whether in the Grand Tetons or in Cape Cod; Jo would sit in the front, Hopper in the back seat.[22] The pictorial rectangle of the watercolor that Jo paints is multiplied by the frames of the car's windows and windshield, the road stretching ahead with the more obviously scenic mountains at the edge of the picture.[23] As in this picture, the automobile provided Hopper with just one of many structures for looking, akin to his interest in the sequences of cinema or the pages of image-heavy magazines such as *Life*[24]—although the apparatus itself would remain invisible in most of his works.[25]

319. *Jo in Wyoming*, 1946
Watercolor and graphite pencil on paper, 13 15/16 × 19 15/16 in. (35.4 × 50.6 cm)
Josephine N. Hopper Bequest 70.1159

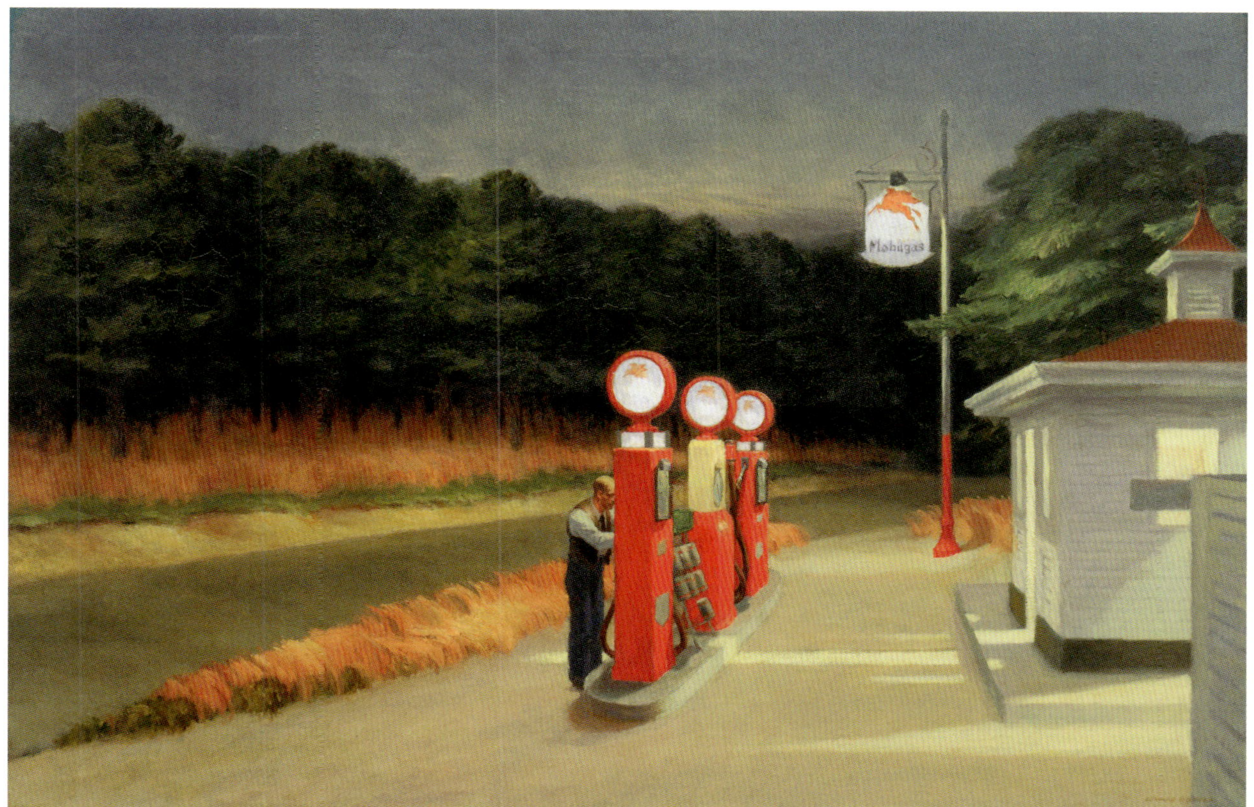

320. *Gas*, 1940
Oil on canvas, 26¼ × 40¼ in. (66.7 × 102.2 cm)
The Museum of Modern Art, New York; Mrs. Simon Guggenheim Fund 577.1943

On the Roadside

Hopper's 1940 painting *Gas* (fig. 320) offers one idea about an experience of seeing and gives paradigmatic evidence of his interest in the built environment and commercial spaces that developed around the road. He told Goodrich that he had "made it up from memories of different places," synthesizing from impressions and experiences.[26] In the painting, Hopper establishes a stark apposition between the visual blare of the station's red filling pumps and the dense surrounding woods, emerging and receding in one plane of shifting deep green tones and expressing a strong feeling of remoteness. As Brian O'Doherty wrote of Hopper's "always impenetrable" woods: "[Hopper] makes 'the wood' a single idea. . . . The wood's silence is formidable, frequently accenting the sensations provoked by the manmade components: the gas stations, the houses, the road itself."[27] The roadside landscape was a particular site of meeting between the changes in the built environment that the road engendered—motels, gas stations, signage—and the natural environment that remained. *Gas* is Hopper's strongest statement about the roadside mixture of mundane human activity—the station attendant at work—and the expressive symbolism of nature, locked together in a strange and mutually transforming glow.[28]

Drawing on his memory of many such encounters, Hopper here addresses the particular quality of a nighttime encounter with the lit landscape of the filling station. As with most of his "improvised" works, Hopper made a number of detailed studies for the painting at filling stations near his Cape Cod studio to aid his development of the composition (see figs. 321–324).[29] Jo's diary entries record his disappointment that the gas pumps were not lit until late in the evening, making it difficult to study them, and their nighttime glow, for his picture.[30] In two of these drawings (figs. 321, 322), Hopper studied the form of the filling pumps and the receding perspective that parallels the trajectory of the road as it disappears into the forest. One of the drawings Hopper made for *Gas* (fig. 324)—comprised mostly of foliage studies—is only identifiable as such by the study of the filigreed bracket on which the station's Mobilgas sign hangs. The foliage studies are curiously abstracted and fragmented, yet, done on-site, they are clearly particular to the visual idea of the surrounding woods that Hopper was in the process of constructing. In the two masterful charcoal studies that Hopper produced for the painting (figs. 325, 326), which would have been made in his studio, the woods emerge in bravura strokes that blend into a mottled dark texture as they recede, as if blurred in movement.[31] The viewpoint developed in the studies, though ambiguous, seems to be that of a motorist pulling into the filling station.[32] The more dutifully rendered forms of the three gas pumps are set against the dark, expressive forms of the woods, and the lower half of their forms are overlaid with white chalk, which Hopper used to denote artificial light in his work.

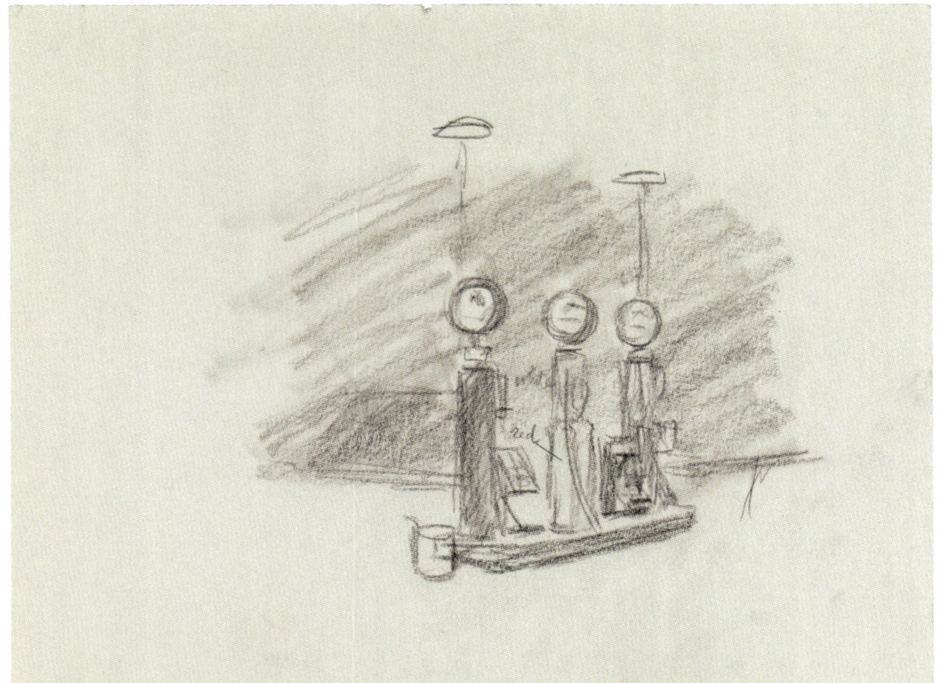

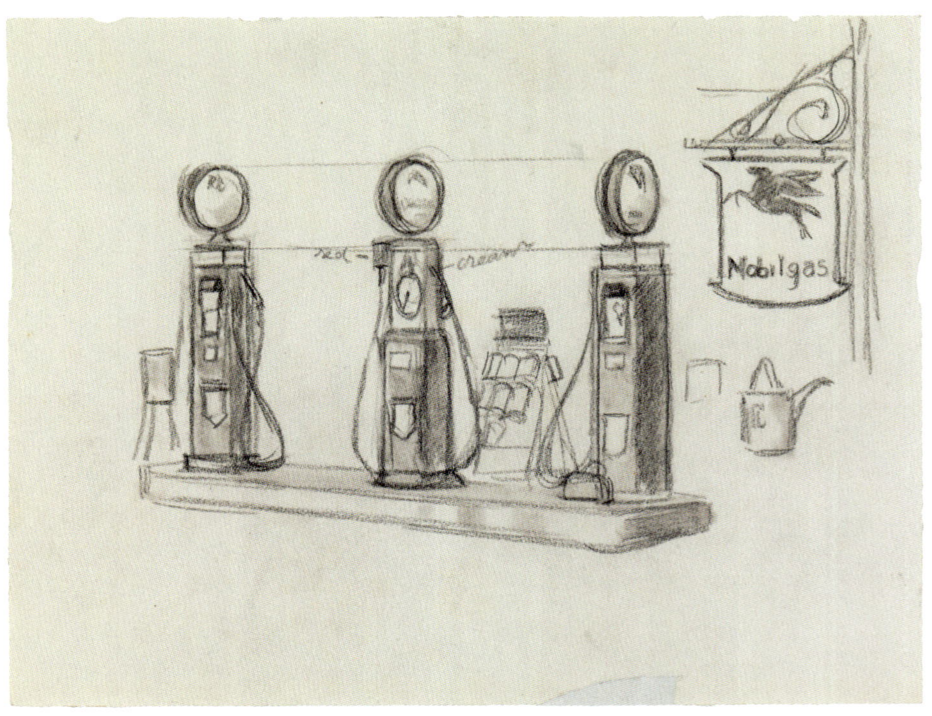

321. Study for *Gas*, 1940
Fabricated chalk on paper, 8 ⅞ × 11 13⁄16 in. (22.5 × 30 cm)
Josephine N. Hopper Bequest 70.224

322. Study for *Gas*, 1940
Fabricated chalk on paper, 8 ⅞ × 11 ⅞ in. (22.5 × 30.2 cm)
Josephine N. Hopper Bequest 70.225

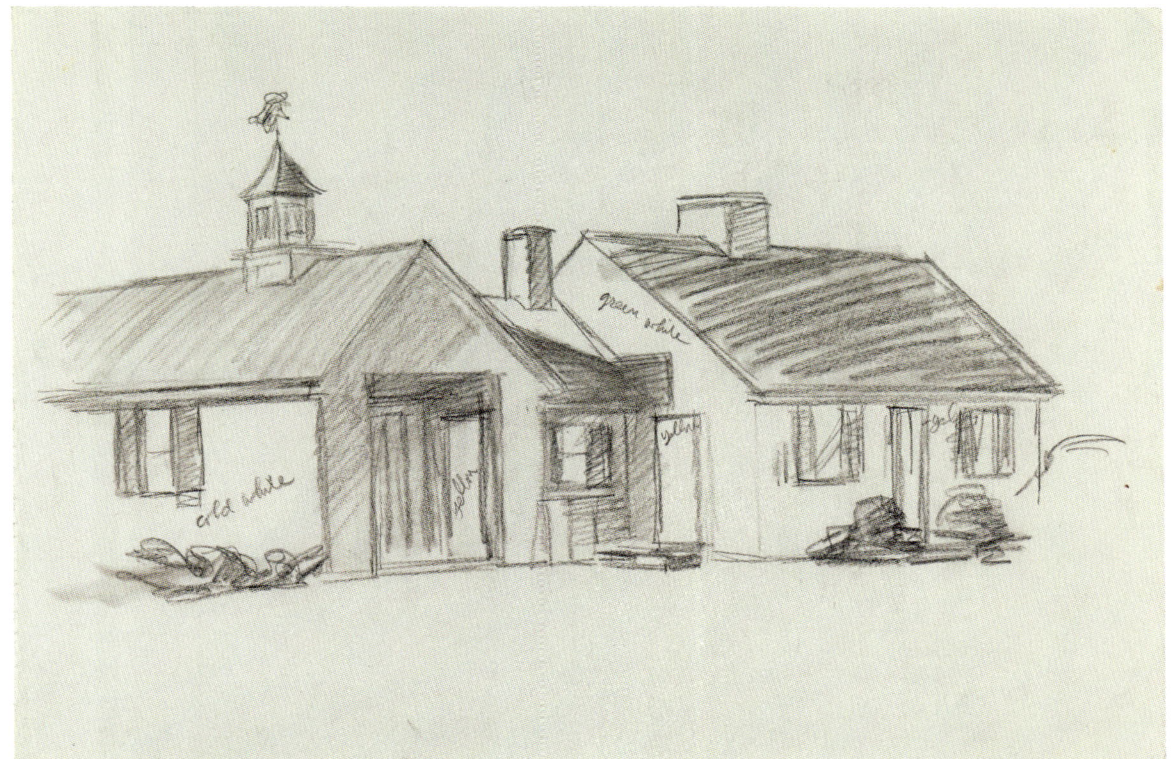

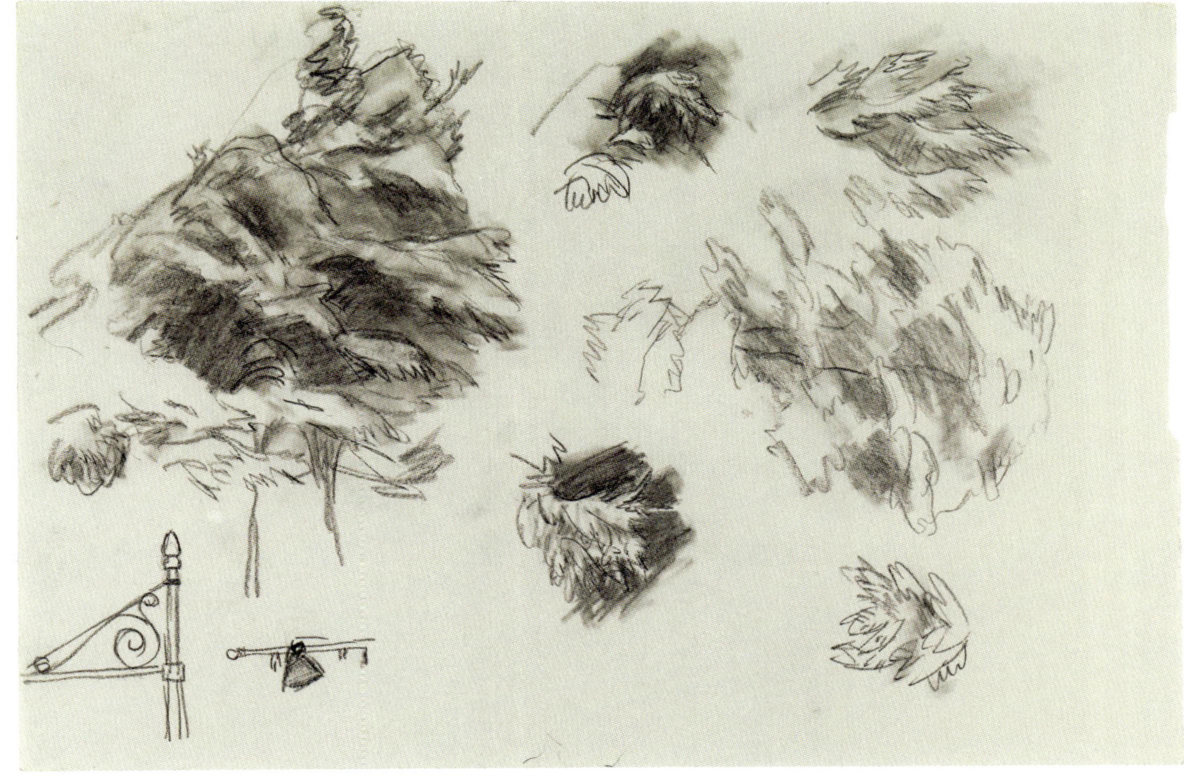

323. Study for *Gas*, 1940
Fabricated chalk on paper, 10 ½ × 16 in. (26.7 × 40.6 cm)
Josephine N. Hopper Bequest 70.226

324. Study for *Gas*, 1940
Fabricated chalk on paper, 10 ½ × 16 in. (26.7 × 40.6 cm)
Josephine N. Hopper Bequest 70.263

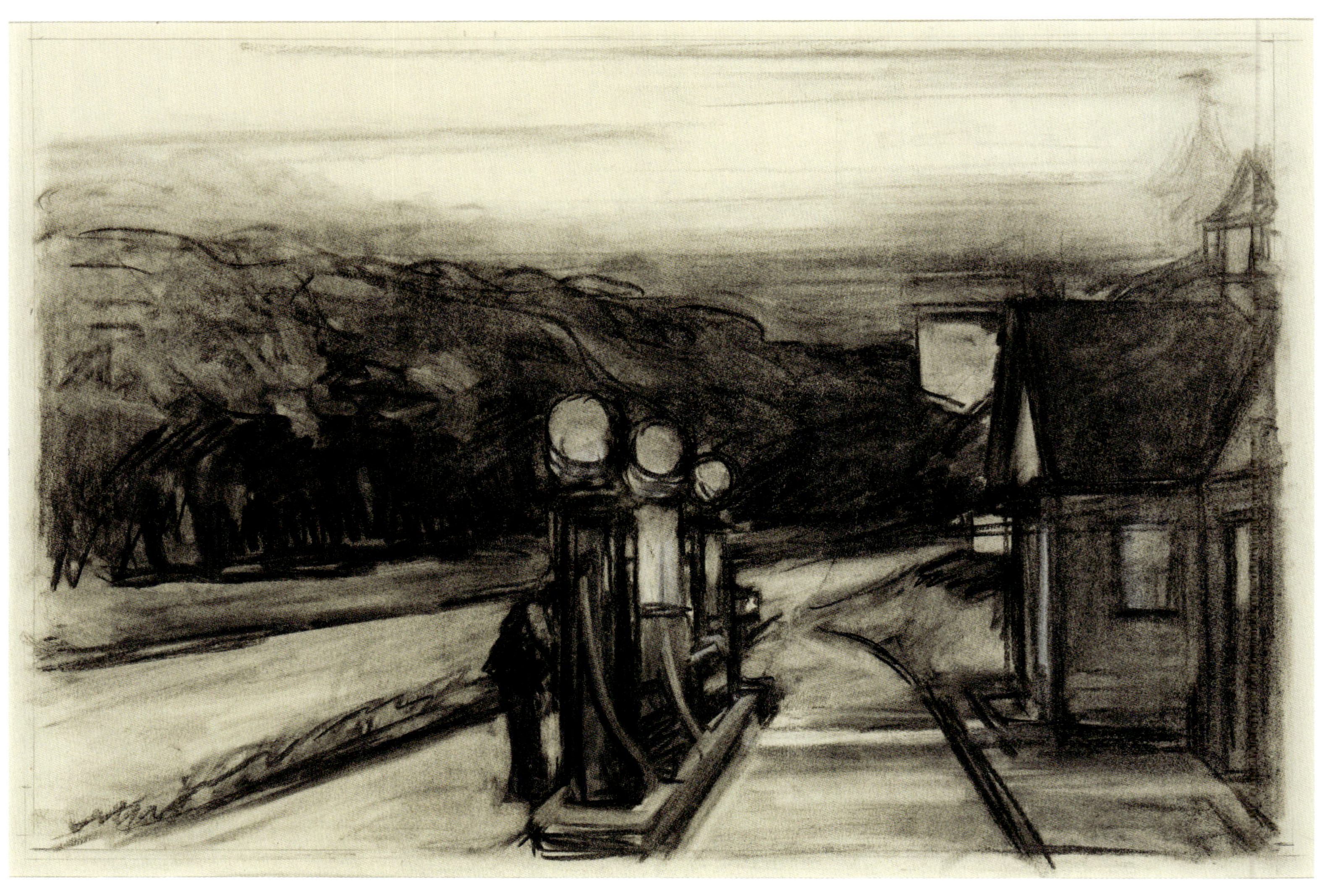

325. Study for *Gas*, 1940
Charcoal and white chalk on paper, 15 ⅛ × 22 ⅛ in.
(38.4 × 56.2 cm)
Josephine N. Hopper Bequest 70.300

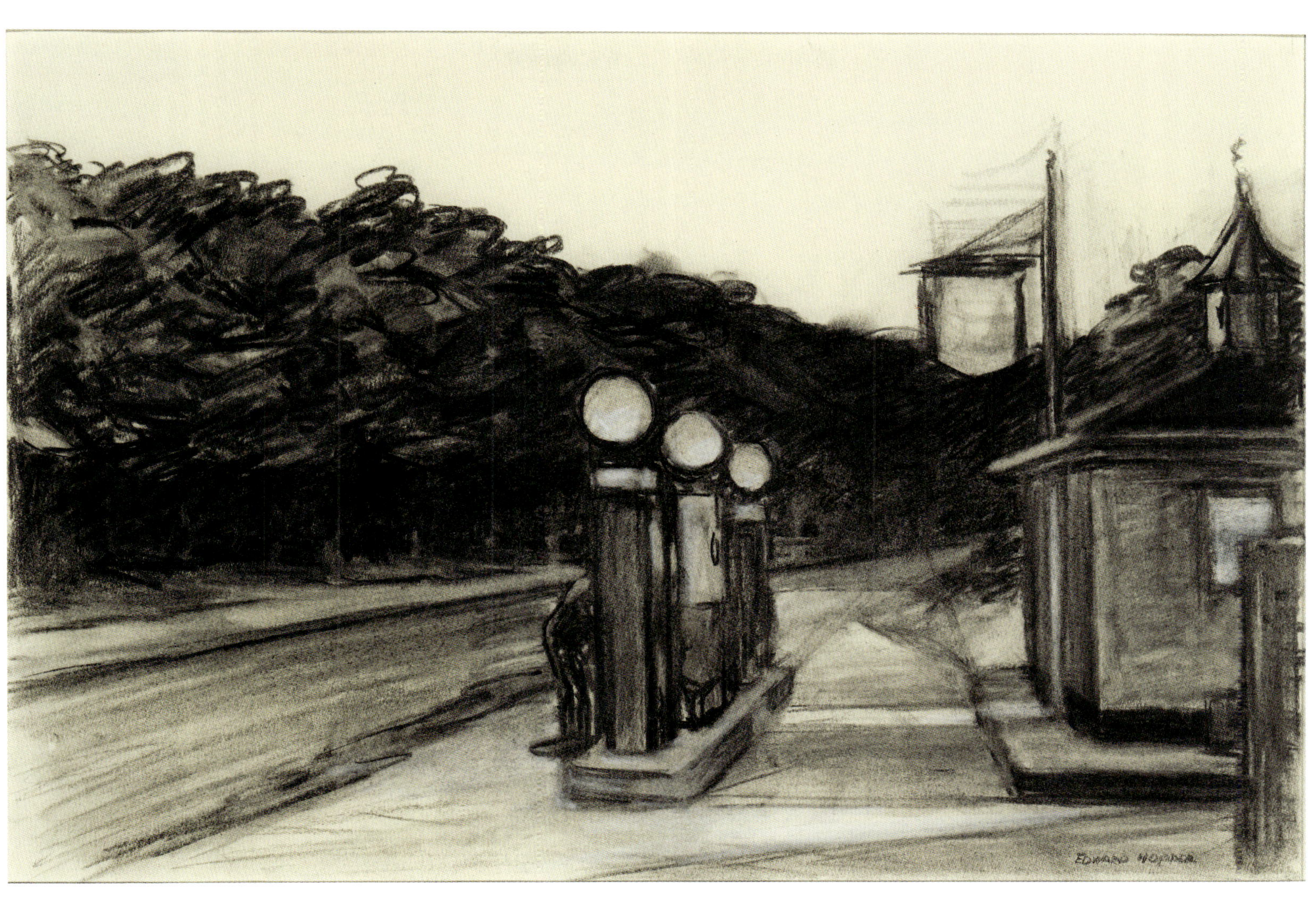

326. Study for *Gas*, 1940
Charcoal and white chalk with graphite pencil on paper, 15 1/16 × 22 1/8 in. (38.3 × 56.2 cm)
Josephine N. Hopper Bequest 70.349

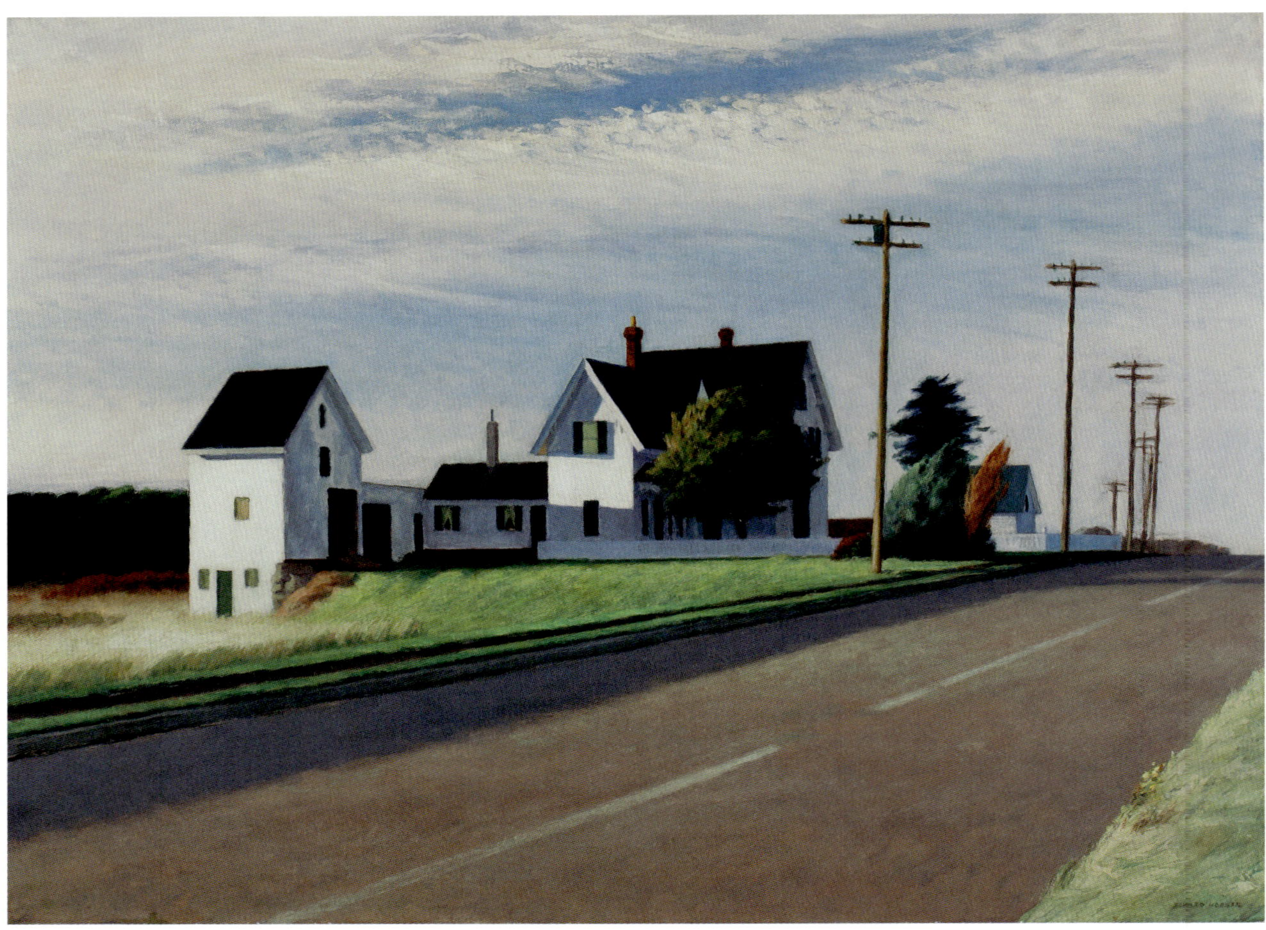

The studies track the serial movement of the ocular forms of the pumps along the road, as well as the movement of the viewer's eye through the picture. In the painting, the glow of these pumps lights and reanimates the landscape around them, as if stand-ins for the headlights of an automobile.[33] The Mobilgas sign, a suspended blankness that is even more prominent in the preparatory drawings, has been described by Alexander Nemerov as "a rare kind of concretization of [the] elusive forces" and inscrutable symbols in Hopper's work, in this case, the figure of the "fleeing" Mobilgas Pegasus set within the darkening, hushed landscape.[34] The sign, a piece of the commercial roadside landscape, is recast by its evocative, transformed surroundings into a multivalent symbol—of time's passing, of the freedom associated with the road—that elaborates our understanding of Hopper's attraction to this scene: the latent lyrical possibilities of the everyday landscape, impressed upon his memory.[35]

Painted a year after *Gas*, Hopper's *Route 6, Eastham* (fig. 327) similarly describes—and reconciles—the modern transformations of the landscape near his summer home on Cape Cod. In her diary, Jo described Eastham as "his happy hunting ground & it's the least attractive township on the Cape & could be in Westchester or N.J. almost & to think he has all these marvelous Truro hills stretched out all around us."[36] Hopper had painted those hills earlier during his time on the Cape, in works such as *Hills, South Truro* from 1930 (fig. 328), in which the rigidly linear railroad tracks, one among a set of parallel forms in an emphatically horizontal composition, announce their artificial status against the organic, undulating hills.[37] While *Hills, South Truro* addresses the beauty of the Cape Cod landscape, and the atmospheric play of color and light, that beauty is qualified, whether diminished or merely modified, by the man-made elements that Hopper accentuates. His 1931 watercolor *High Road* (fig. 329) treats the "tarred hill road," as Jo referred to it, as a kind of prospect point for the view, analogous to the rocky outcroppings in the foregrounds of Hudson River School landscapes; Hopper deploys the telephone poles ubiquitous in his work as emphatic frames for the ambiguously picturesque scene of North Truro, Massachusetts, and its surroundings beyond the crest of the road.[38]

Having begun to spend their summers in South Truro in 1930 (where they would build their house and studio in 1934), the Hoppers witnessed the beginnings of Cape Cod's shift from a semi-remote outpost to a commercial landscape that accommodated an increasing number of automobile tourists.[39] Route 6, after which the painting is titled, was paved and named in 1920; in 1938, it was widened to the four-lane highway whose lane markers are visible in one of the compositional studies for *Route 6, Eastham* (see fig. 335), although the finished painting depicts it as the two-lane road it was previously.[40] In this work, the road asserts

327. *Route 6, Eastham*, 1941
Oil on canvas, 27 ½ × 38 ¼ in. (69.9 × 97.2 cm)
Swope Art Museum, Terre Haute, Indiana 1942.01

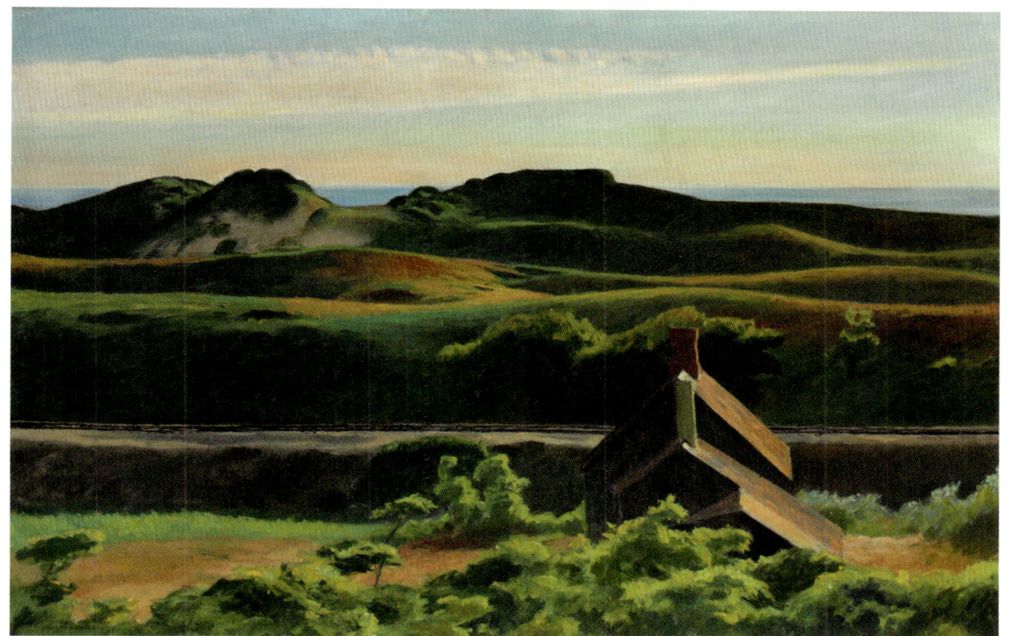

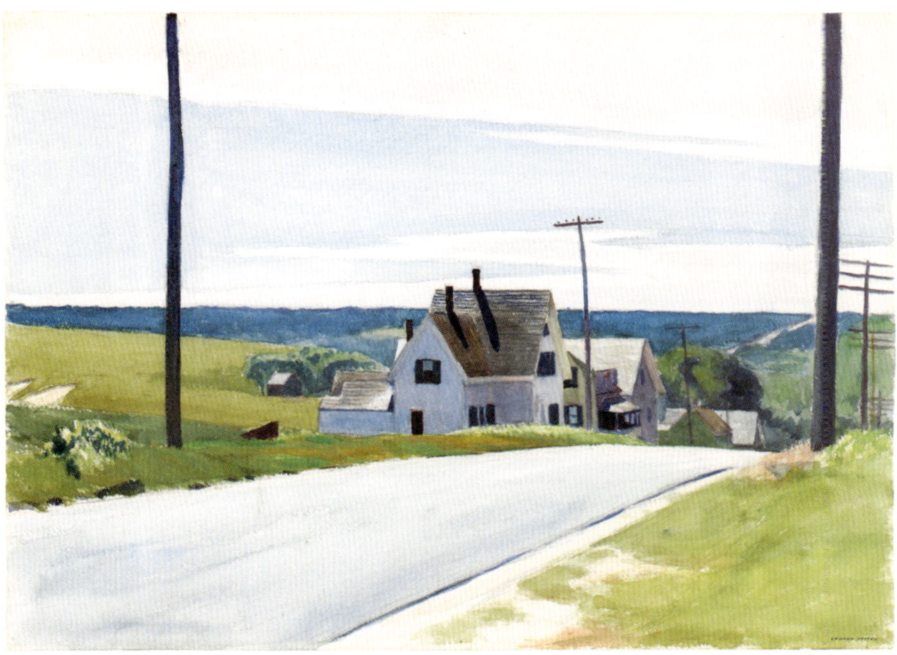

328. *Hills, South Truro*, 1930
Oil on canvas, 27 3/8 × 43 1/8 in. (69.5 × 109.5 cm)
The Cleveland Museum of Art; Hinman B. Hurlbut Collection 2647.1931

329. *High Road*, 1931
Watercolor and graphite pencil on paper, 20 × 27 15/16 in. (50.8 × 71 cm)
Josephine N. Hopper Bequest 70.1163

itself as the primary element of the work, serving as a kind of parallel landscape or space alongside its more obviously scenic surroundings.[41] As Priscilla Paton notes, while the apposition in *Route 6, Eastham* between the modernity of the asphalt road and attendant electrical poles and the vernacular Cape architecture is overt, the scene resolves: "the road and poles . . . have shifted our perspective to create a new whole."[42] That is to say, the road itself produces a new way of accessing and conceiving of the landscape, naturalizing itself even as it effects radical changes.

The dominance of the road in *Route 6, Eastham* perhaps has more to do with the artist's working method than with his intention to record changes in the built landscape. The Hoppers had just returned from their longest automobile journey to date when he began to conceive of and work on the painting, which might have embedded images of the road more firmly in his mind. Hopper painted *Route 6, Eastham* in his studio from extensive color notes and sketches, likely made from his car (figs. 330–333).[43] Jumbled over the sheet, his drawings detail significant passages: the sharp edge of the farmhouse barn against distant woods; the intricately interlocking composition of the building's gables and roofs; the double-barred top of a utility pole; the slowly curving plane of the road itself; and the small patch of tall grass that meets the road at the bottom right corner of the finished painting. These sheets provide a glimpse into Hopper's mind as he developed the picture—following his eye as it settled on particular details, which are set next to one another as fragmentary records of what he saw and which elements of the scene attracted his attention.

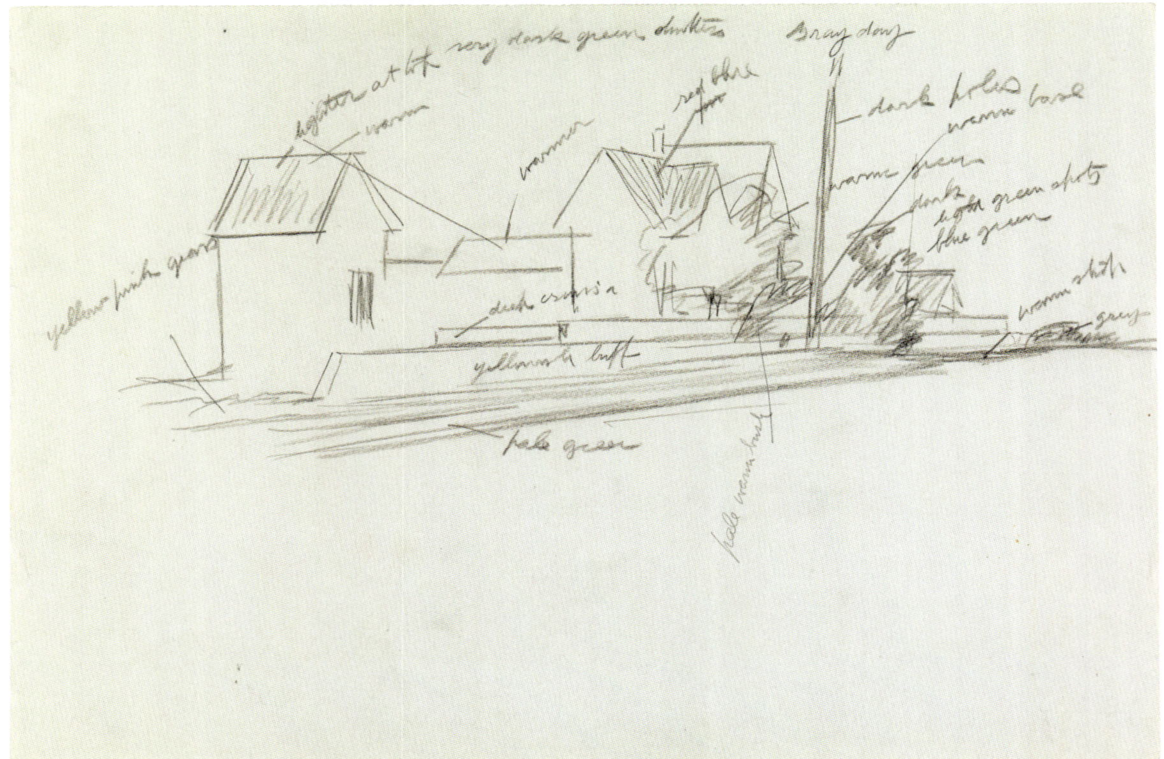

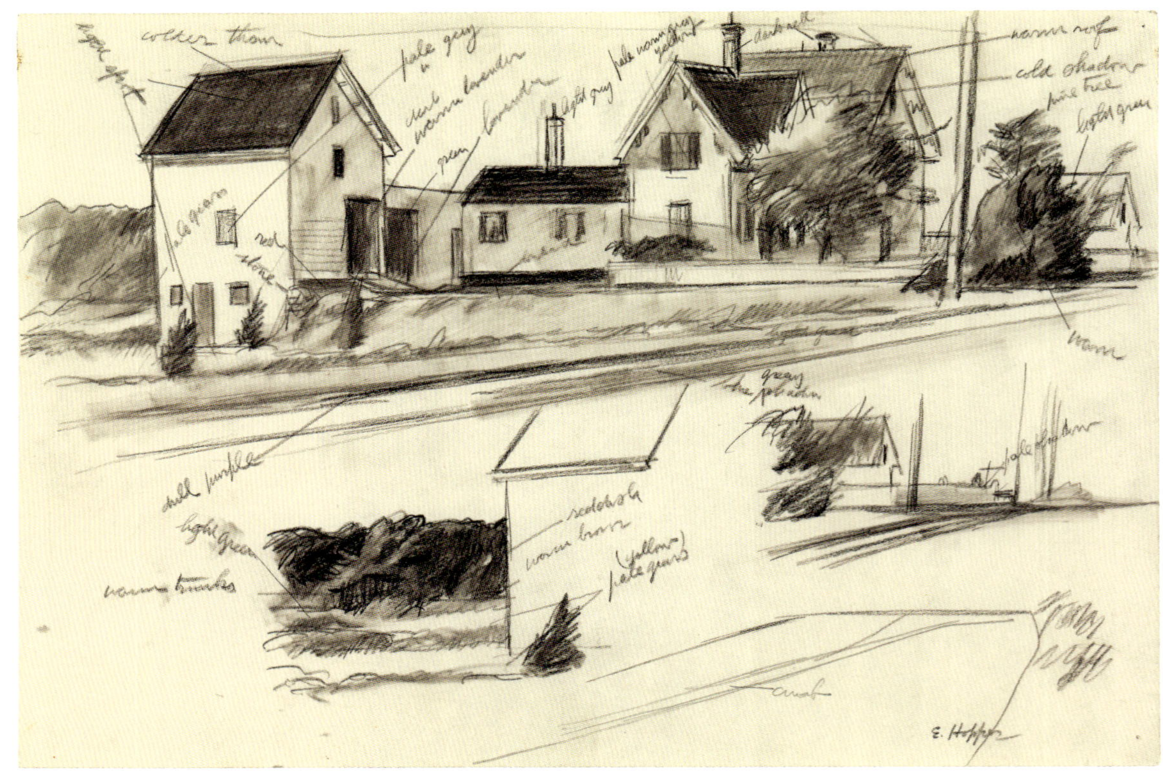

330. Study for *Route 6, Eastham*, 1941
Fabricated chalk and graphite pencil on paper,
10 ½ × 16 in. (26.7 × 40.6 cm)
Josephine N. Hopper Bequest 70.366

331. Study for *Route 6, Eastham*, 1941
Fabricated chalk, charcoal, and graphite pencil on paper,
10 ½ × 16 in. (26.7 × 40.6 cm)
Josephine N. Hopper Bequest 70.330

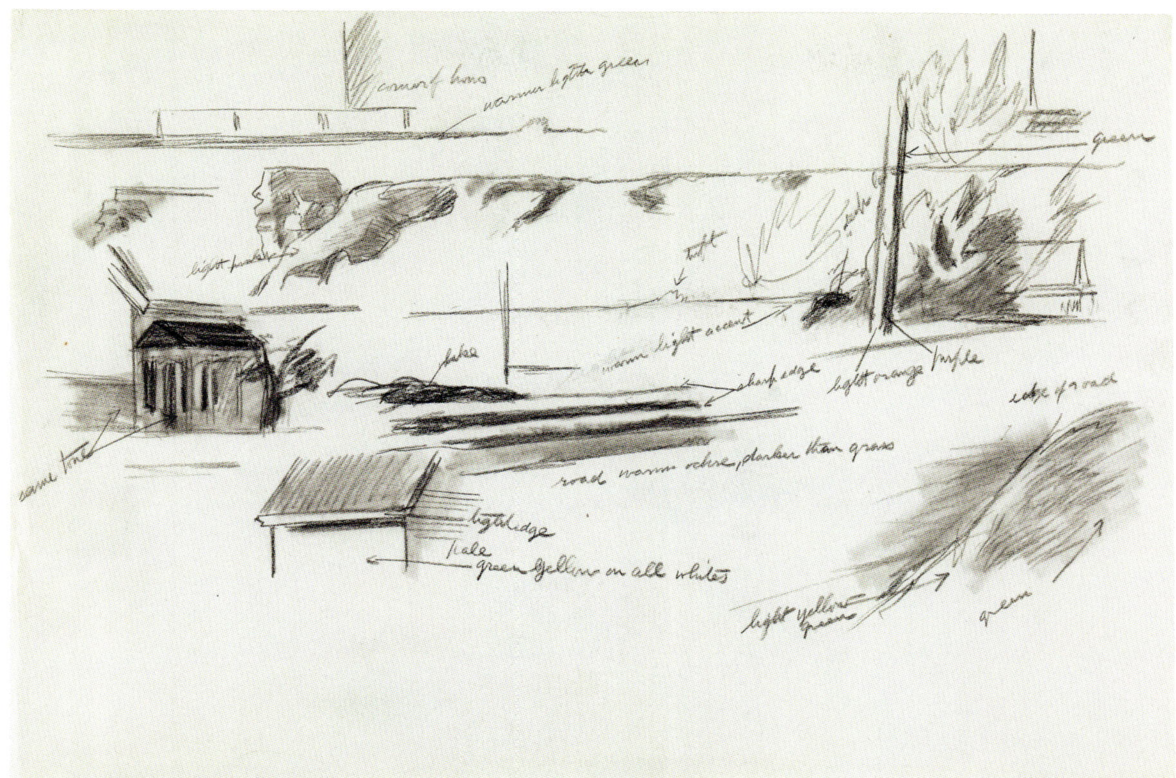

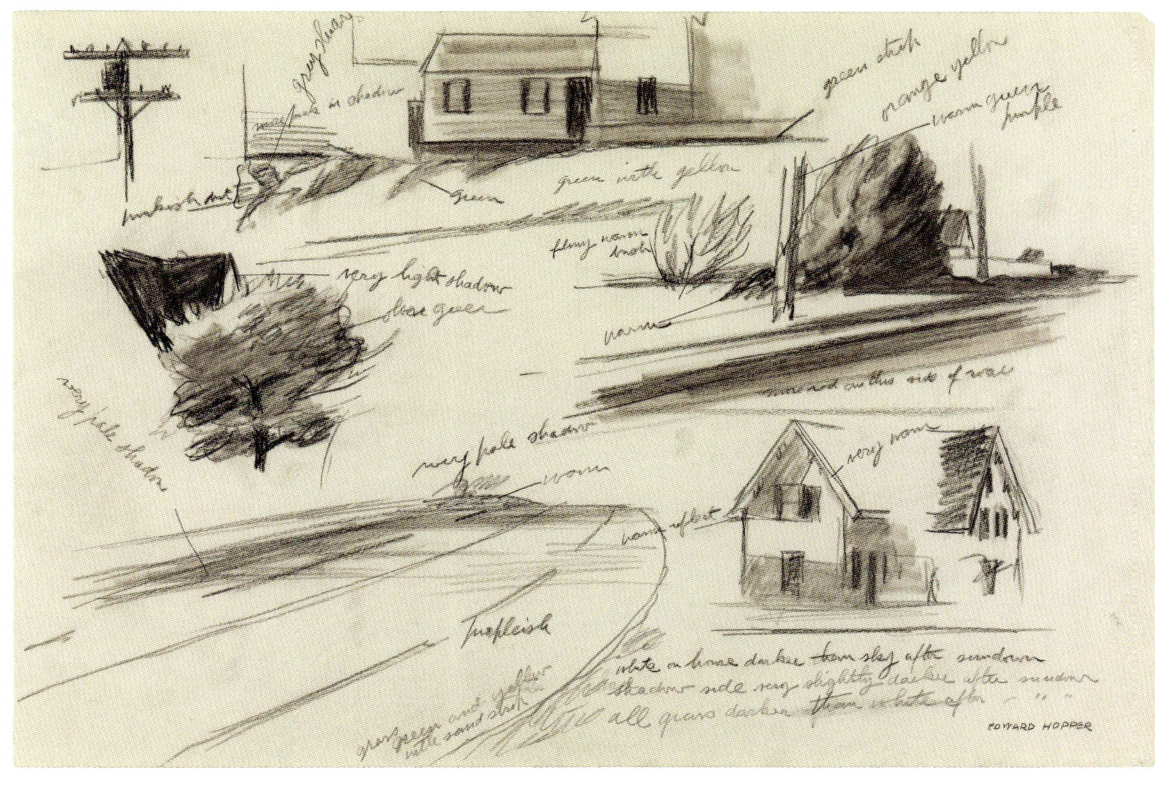

332. Study for *Route 6, Eastham*, 1941
Fabricated chalk on paper, 10 ½ × 16 in. (26.7 × 40.6 cm)
Josephine N. Hopper Bequest 70.258

333. Study for *Route 6, Eastham*, 1941
Fabricated chalk and graphite pencil on paper, 10 ½ × 16 in. (26.7 × 40.6 cm)
Josephine N. Hopper Bequest 70.369

334. Study for *Route 6, Eastham*, 1941
Fabricated chalk on paper, 10 ½ × 16 in. (26.7 × 40.6 cm)
Josephine N. Hopper Bequest 70.445

335. Study for *Route 6, Eastham*, 1941
Fabricated chalk on paper, 10 7⁄16 × 16 in. (26.5 × 40.6 cm)
Josephine N. Hopper Bequest 70.446

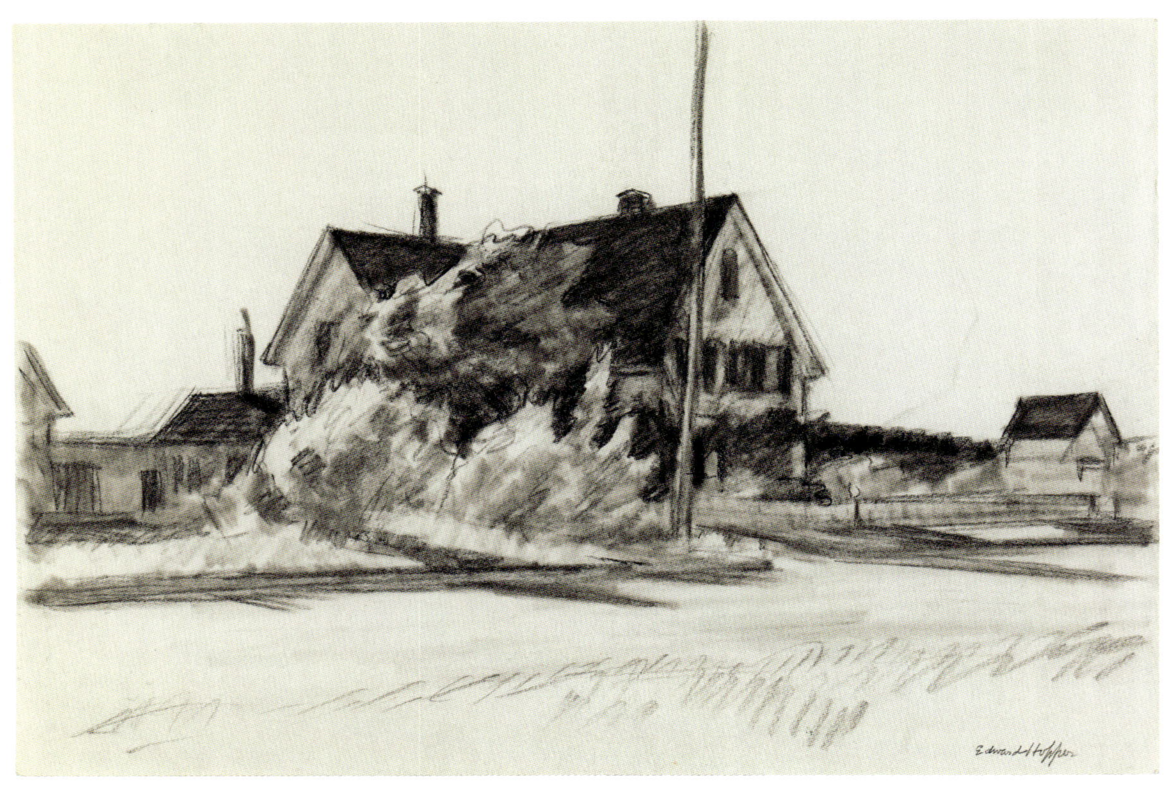

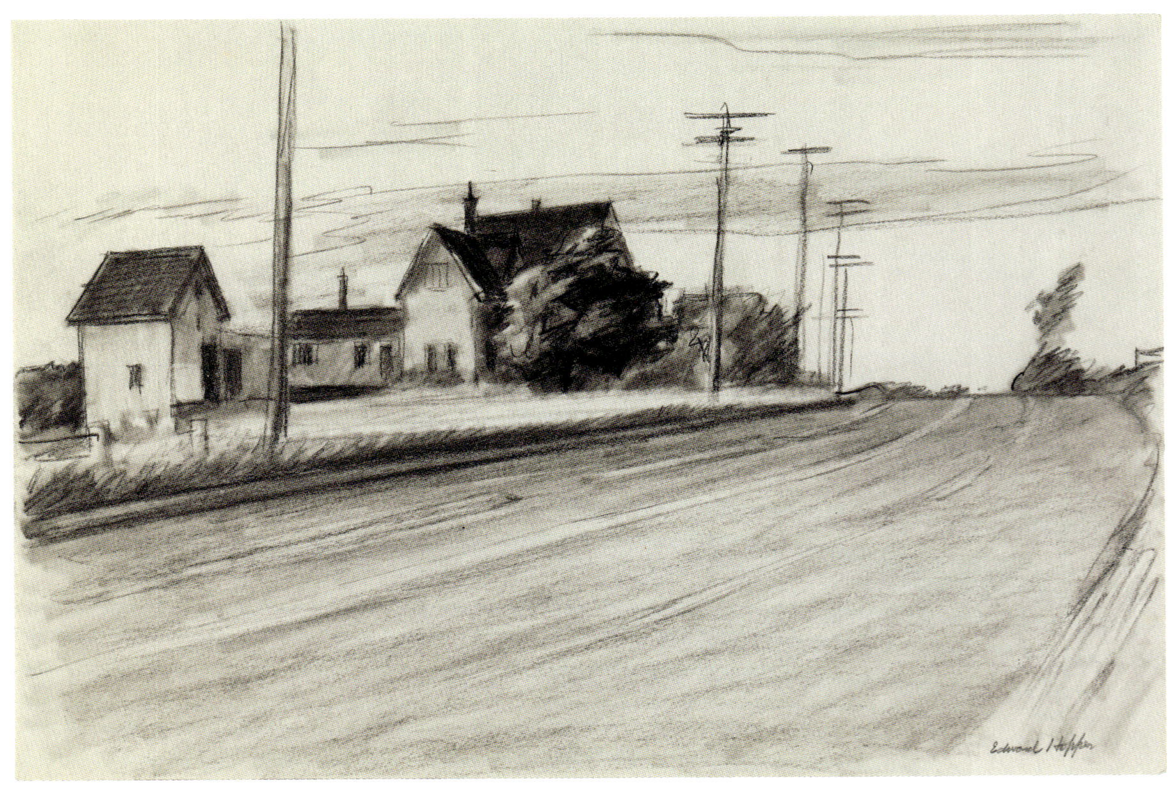

336. Study for *Route 6, Eastham*, 1941
Fabricated chalk and graphite pencil on paper,
15 1/16 × 22 3/16 in. (38.3 × 56.4 cm)
Josephine N. Hopper Bequest 70.854

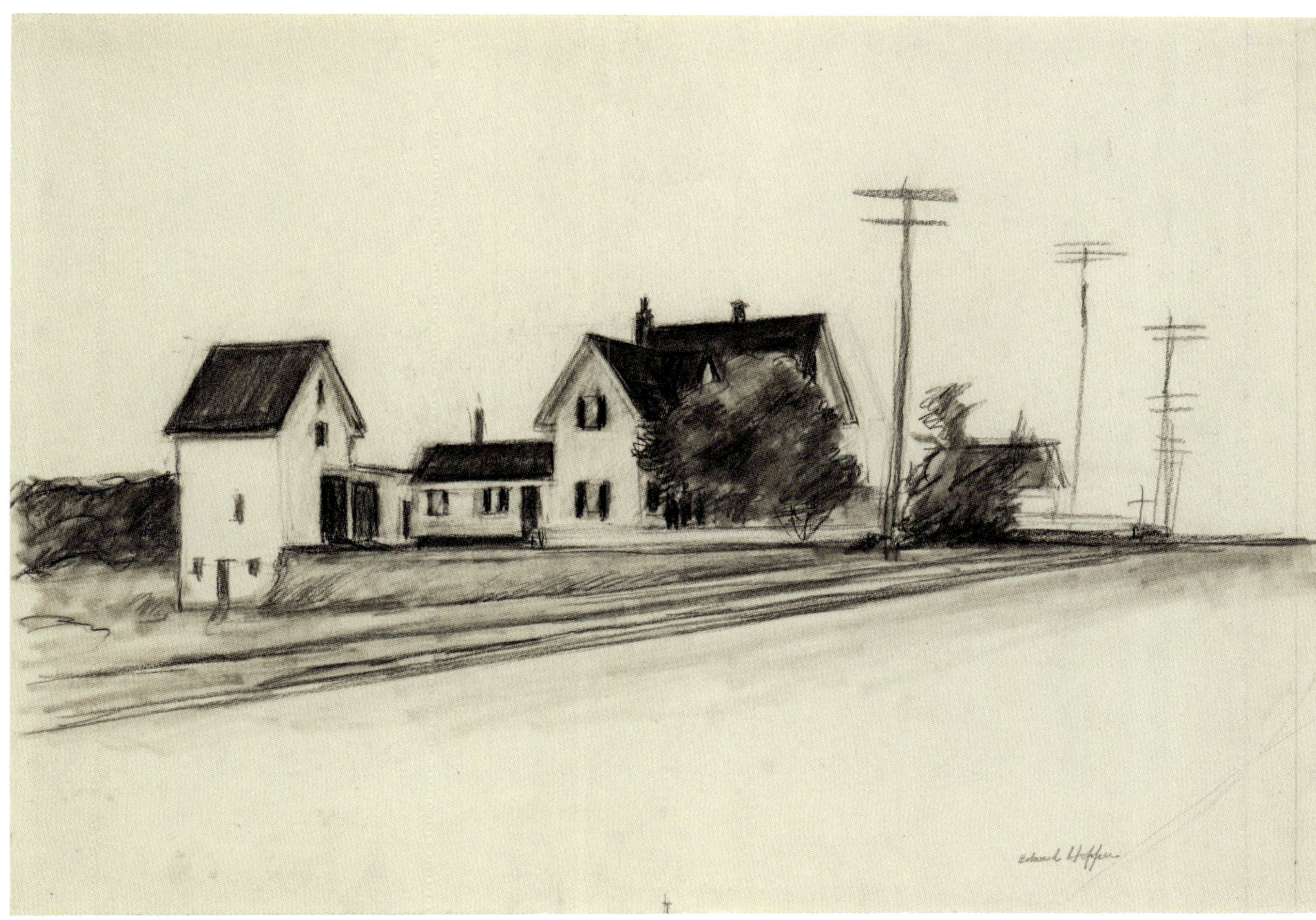

A more finished study depicts the house and barn from a slightly different viewpoint, where the road is a prominent, but not primary, element of the drawing's foreground (fig. 334). According to Jo's diary, this was this farmhouse and barn that Hopper had "had his eye on for years," and its details are the main concern of these studies.[44] In his two final drawings for the painting, however, the scene shifts and the building is set behind the bold sweep of Route 6. The building is an object—a focal point, a discrete body—in a way that the flattened road cannot be, yet Hopper also focuses attention on the easily overlooked paved surface. The low viewpoint of one study propels our gaze to the right, following the lane dividers along the shifting tonal surface of the highway (fig. 335). In another much larger and starker drawing, which might have been made in his studio, the highway is an almost-blank plane equal to the expanse of the sky (fig. 336). Although Hopper's decision to work and observe from his car along the roadside had much to do with easy access to subjects, convenience, and comfort, it also perhaps shifted the way he observed his subjects—affecting the viewpoints he chose to take, emphasizing the elements of landscape visible from the road, and therefore turning the road into a guide for his looking and for the drawings that served as his memory. In *Route 6, Eastham*, Hopper does not simply give us the viewpoint of a motorist, as he will in later works, but positions us at the highway's edge, as if just stepping out of the car to survey the house and barns. In the final painted work, the grass casts a broad shadow along the highway's left flank, imparting a strange materiality to the road's surface, extended upward by the utility poles that march along its edge.[45] The road is asserted not as an object like the house or barn, but rather as a space—an open trajectory mirrored by the blades of cirrus clouds in the sky above.

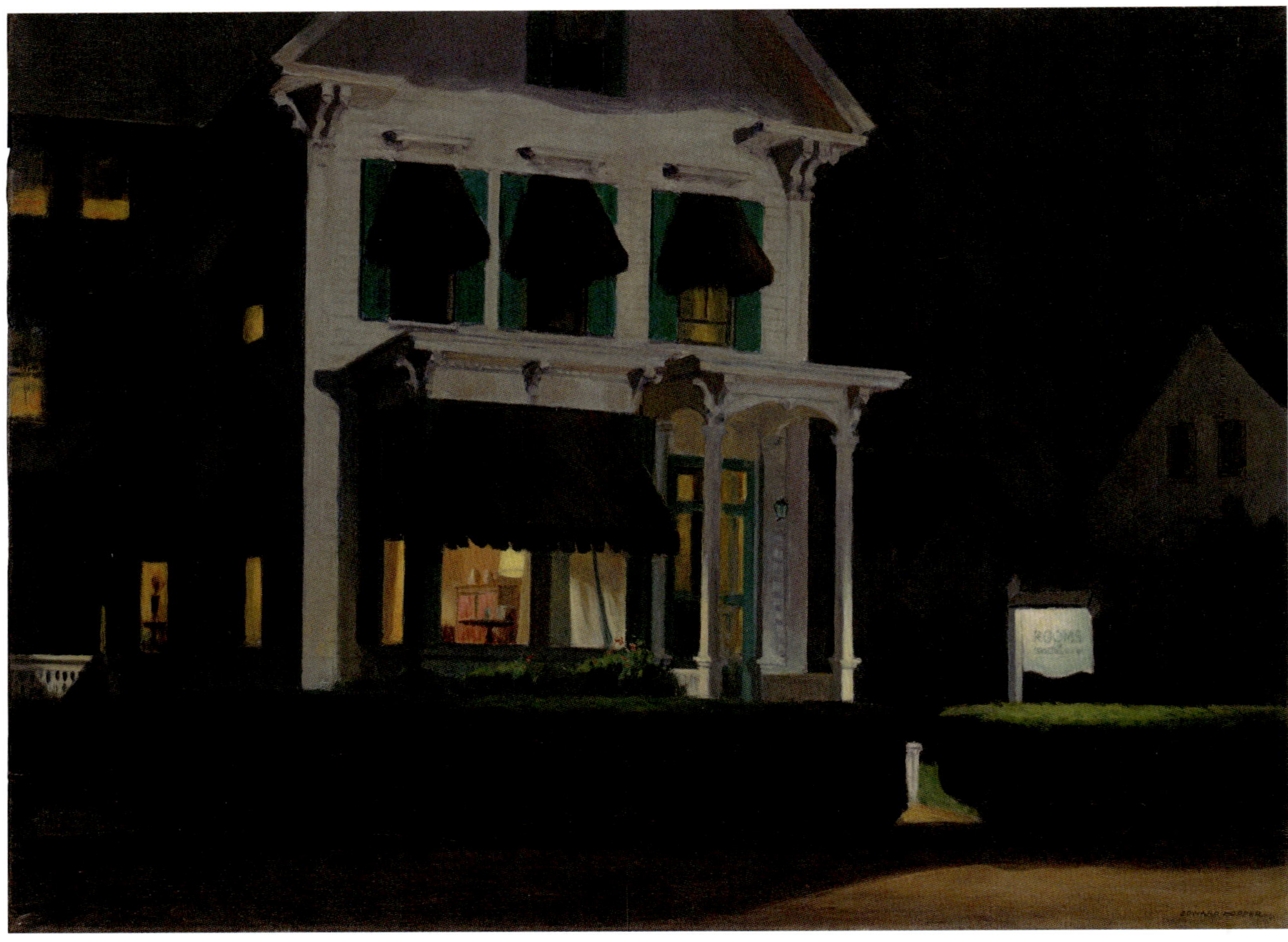

The Automobile as Frame

In 1945, Hopper painted *Rooms for Tourists* (fig. 337), a work based on a rooming house in Provincetown, Massachusetts, up the Cape from his studio in South Truro.[46] His earlier paintings of America's vernacular, "mongrel" architecture were regarded by some contemporary critics as a perverse or ironic delectation over the details of outmoded architectures.[47] Hopper's attraction to the details of ornament is very much present in this picture, and the numerous studies he made for it, many on small sketchbook paper, feature fragments of the building's structure and form, lingering on the way that a vase is framed in a bay window pane and the geometry of the building's awnings, along with precise notations of the awning fabric's hues (figs. 338–344). More compelling than these details, however, is the way the painting establishes the particular stance of the viewer—one which the writer of a 1948 review in *Time* magazine described with eloquence: "*Rooms for Tourists*, like most of Hopper's work, has the strange clarity of something seen once for an instant by a passing driver. It is a familiar vision without any of the dullness familiarity brings."[48] Though conceived to express this moment of encounter, the picture was developed over a long period of observation, as Goodrich recorded:

> [Hopper] studied the house a long time, by daylight and at night. Made sketches, some of the whole house, some of architectural details. The picture was painted in his studio, but when he was painting it he used to go almost every night in his car and park near the house and study it. (Frank Rehn told me that the people in the house wondered what it was all about.)[49]

337. *Rooms for Tourists*, 1945
Oil on canvas, 30¼ × 42⅛ in. (76.8 × 107 cm)
Yale University Art Gallery, New Haven; bequest of Stephen Carlton Clark, B.A. 1903 1961.18.30

Goodrich describes Hopper's intensive process of internalizing his visual impressions—one that sustained the artist's attenuated painting process by revivifying his subject in the exact mode of its appearance as he had encountered it on the roadside. In this instance,

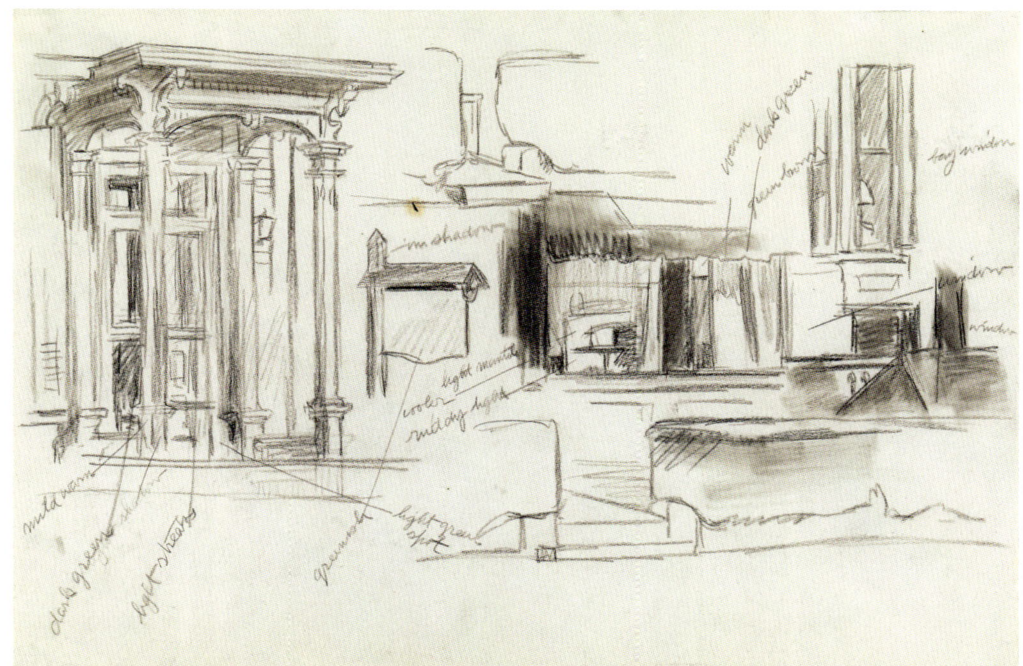

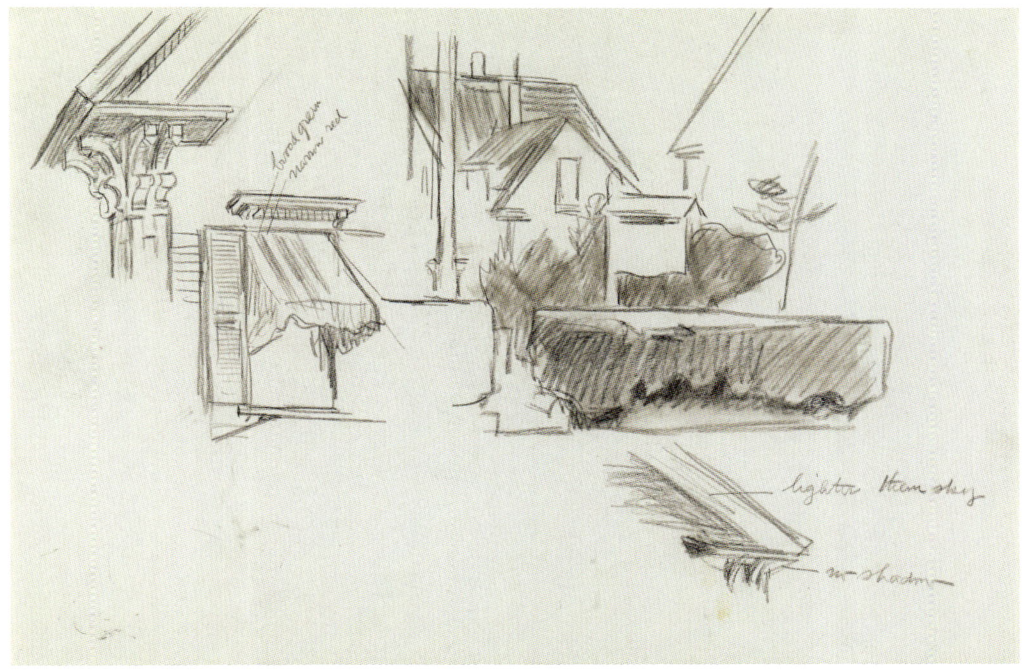

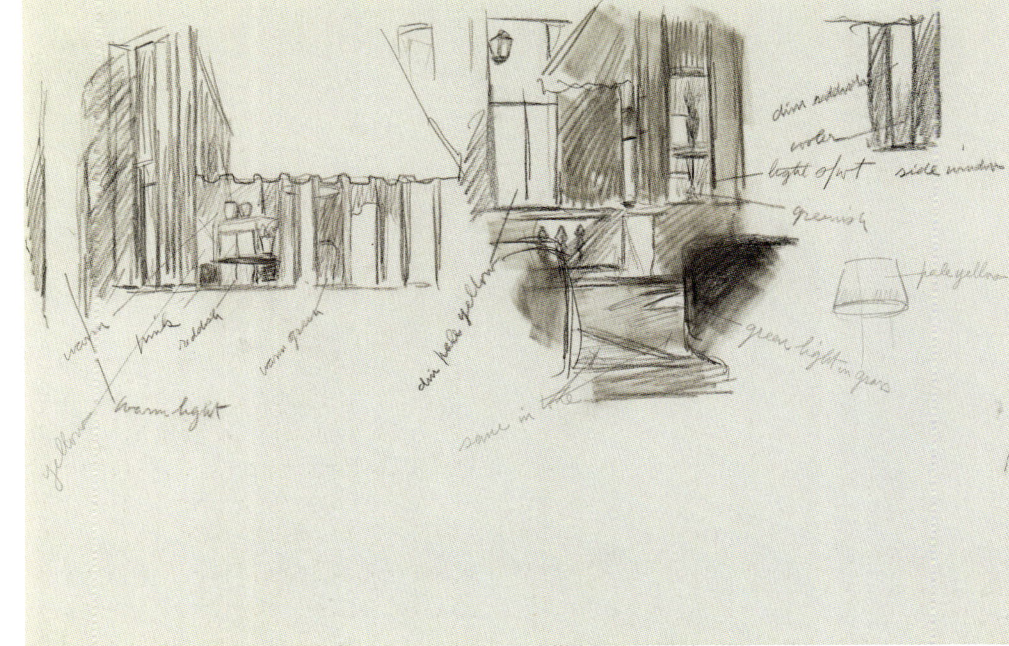

338. Study for *Rooms for Tourists*, 1945
Fabricated chalk on paper, 10 ⅜ × 15 15/16 in. (26.4 × 40.5 cm)
Josephine N. Hopper Bequest 70.221

339. Study for *Rooms for Tourists*, 1945
Fabricated chalk on paper, 10 ⅜ × 15 15/16 in. (26.4 × 40.5 cm)
Josephine N. Hopper Bequest 70.259

340. Study for *Rooms for Tourists*, 1945
Fabricated chalk and graphite pencil on paper,
10 ⅜ × 15 15/16 in. (26.4 × 40.5 cm)
Josephine N. Hopper Bequest 70.260

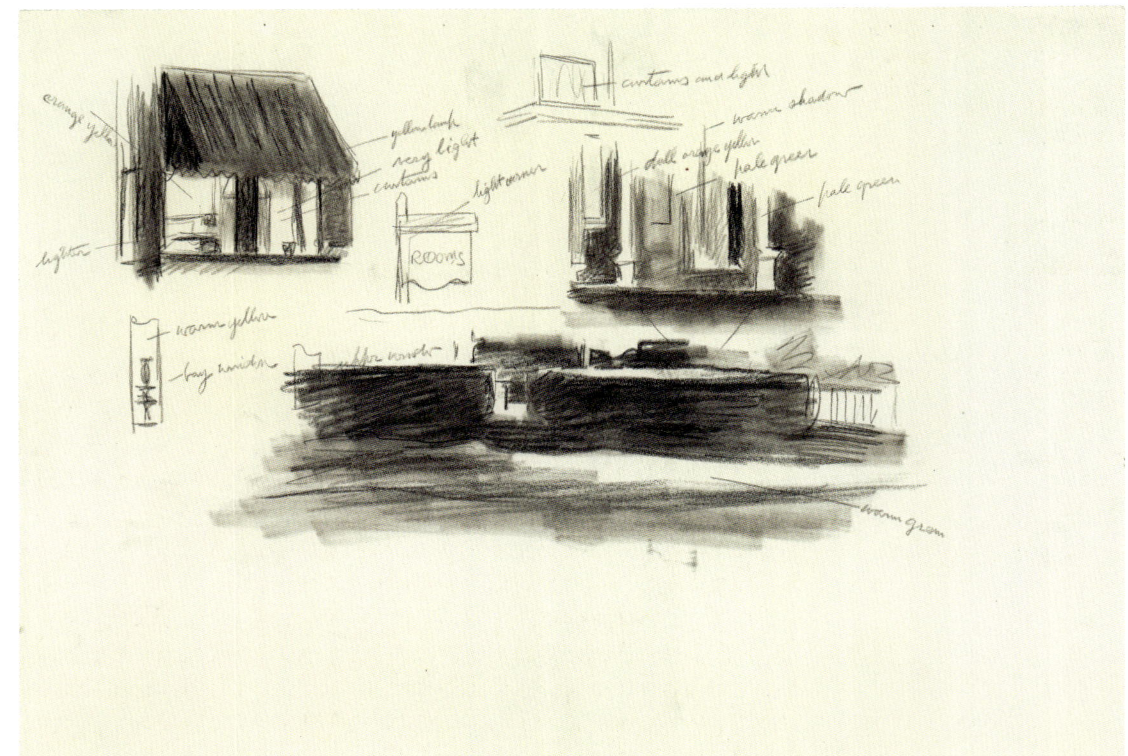
orange yellow
lighter
very light
curtains
light corner
ROOMS
curtains and light
warm shadow
dull orange yellow
pale green
pale green
warm yellow
bay window
warm green

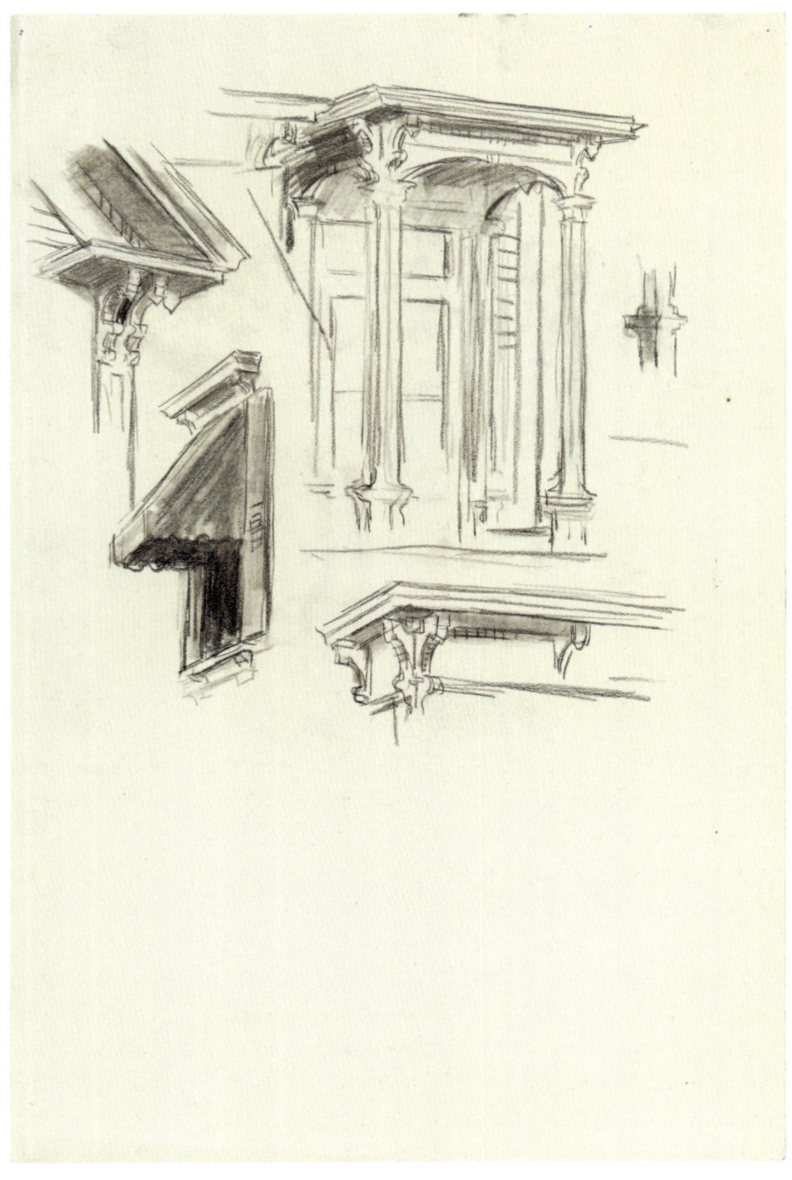

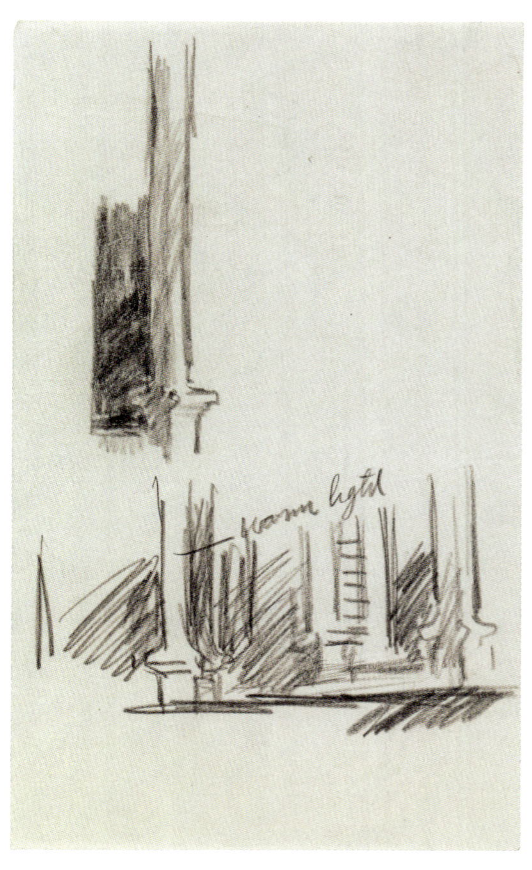
warm light

341. Study for *Rooms for Tourists*, 1945
Fabricated chalk on paper, 15 × 22 ⅛ in. (38.1 × 56.2 cm)
Josephine N. Hopper Bequest 70.1001

342. Study for *Rooms for Tourists*, 1945
Fabricated chalk on paper, 22 ⅛ × 15 1/16 in. (56.2 × 38.3 cm)
Josephine N. Hopper Bequest 70.1002

343. Study for *Rooms for Tourists*, 1945
Fabricated chalk on paper, 8 1/16 × 5 in. (20.5 × 12.7 cm)
Josephine N. Hopper Bequest 70.230

344. Study for *Rooms for Tourists*, 1945
Graphite pencil on paper, 5 × 3 in. (12.7 × 7.6 cm)
Josephine N. Hopper Bequest 70.284

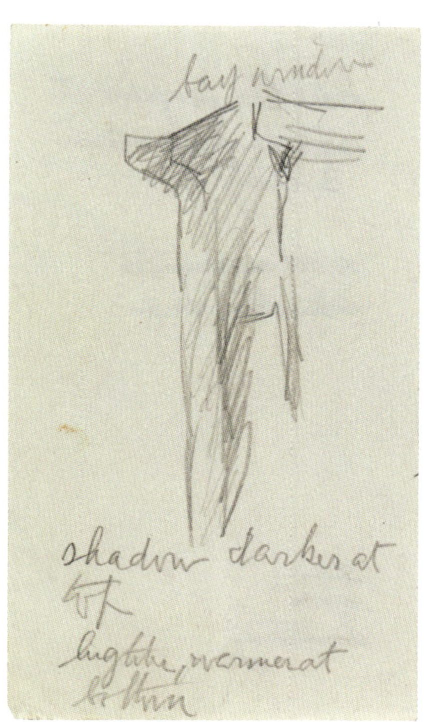

the car becomes more than a transparent tool or means of access to his subject, but rather a nonvisible frame or support for the experience Hopper attempts to enact in the painting.

Hopper's attention to the framing of his subject is evident in the two highly finished studies for *Rooms for Tourists*. In one, made in daylight, the entirety of the building's facade and receding bulk is visible (fig. 345). A formal grid, articulated by the dark blanks of the windows and the roofs of the nearby houses, structures the drawing and Hopper's conception of the spatially complex subject. On top of this drawing, Hopper laid out the faint outline of a rectangle; its upper edge intersects the gable and central window of the inn, while its right edge is established by the chimney of the adjacent building. This rectangle marks the intended framing edge of the painting and effects the dramatic shift from the placid scene of this study to the final compositional drawing. In this second sheet (fig. 346), one of Hopper's most developed and powerful preparatory works, the rooming house emerges out of thick and enveloping darkness. Rather than the formal interest expressed in the first study, the architectural form here asserts itself as a looming presence, yet we are denied a full view of the building's form. Levin and others have noted Edgar Degas's influence in Hopper's mode of composing pictures and his use of cropping, which in *Rooms for Tourists* imparts the sense of the image as a fragment in continuous, shifting, and momentary perception—the edge of embodied vision.[50] Hopper was also looking at this subject, repeatedly and over time, through a more material and obstinate frame, his car window. Certain visual and formal aspects of the picture—its unusually low perspective and lack of foreground, which contribute to the claustrophobic presence of the building—suggest that the frame of the painting and the frame of the car window are one and the same. More than that, *Rooms for Tourists* and its related drawings lead us to consider how "the frame" might be central to the visual experiences Hopper proposes in his paintings, and in particular how the automobile served an increasingly important structure for the act of seeing in Hopper's life and his work.

When asked by O'Doherty, his most insightful interlocutor, whether he thought about the frame in his paintings, Hopper replied, "The frame? I consider it forcibly."[51] As Robert Silberman argued, the frame is a central device of Hopper's pictorial language, one related to the frame of the theater and cinema, and a concern that Hopper shared with modernist conceptions of the picture plane and the status of the observer.[52] For Hopper, an articulation of the frame was not a way of calling attention to his picture's artifice, but rather a way of "forcibly" corralling diffuse experience to a distilled and particular experience of sight. In his 1939 letter to Charles Sawyer, director of the Addison Gallery of American Art, Hopper acknowledged the importance of "form, color, and design"—the structural tools of modernist painting—but emphasized that he was mainly interested in "the vast field of experience and sensation." This interest dictated his deliberations over the size and proportion of *Manhattan Bridge Loop* (1928; see fig. 153), which is "an effort to give a sensation of great lateral extent" and an attempt "to make one conscious of the spaces and elements beyond the limits of the scene itself."[53] In this way, the frame—which "belongs to the space of the observer"[54]—returns the picture to the observer as a sensation in the world.

As in many of Hopper's paintings, this sensation and this frame place the viewer of *Rooms for Tourists* in a particular position, though one suggestive of rather than insistent upon narrative—in this case, a tourist in his or her car, watching the rooming house with a measure of, perhaps, apprehension.[55] His painting *Solitude #56* (private collection) of the previous year employs the imagined frame of the windshield as a suggestion of the isolation and space for reflection afforded to the motorist-observer.[56] *Solitude #56*, which leads our eye down a paved road as it disappears at the painting's horizon, was, like *Gas*, "improvised" from his memories of similar places on Cape Cod he would have seen from his car.[57] In a diary entry of September 29, 1944, while Hopper was gestating the idea for the painting, Jo wrote that he "cares only for the common denominator in houses, roads, etc. & is not beguiled by so much individuality. He no longer cares to work out from the thing, wants only to make sketches here

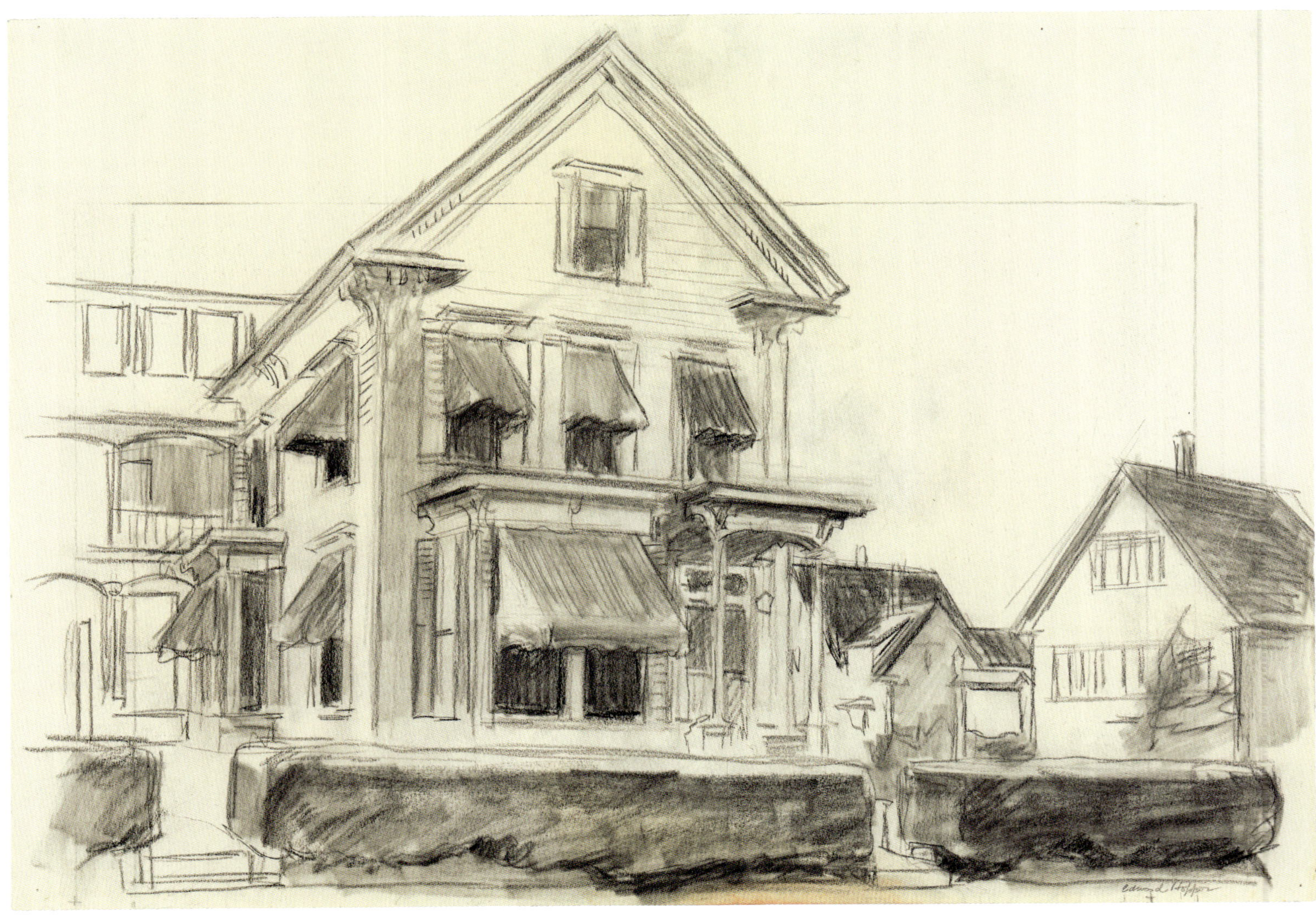

345. Study for *Rooms for Tourists*, 1945
Fabricated chalk and charcoal on paper, 15 × 22 ⅛ in.
(38.1 × 56.2 cm)
Josephine N. Hopper Bequest 70.848

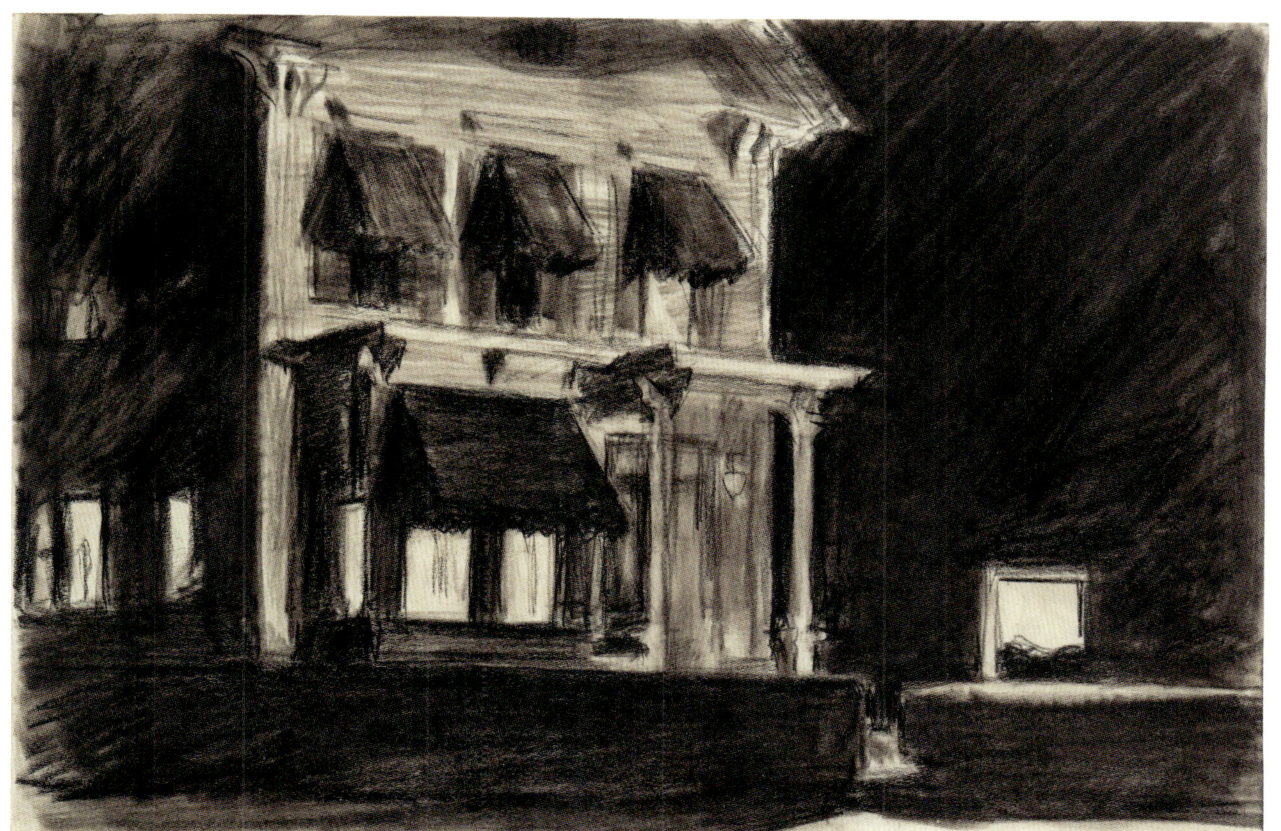

346. Study for *Rooms for Tourists*, 1945
Fabricated chalk and charcoal on paper, 10 ³⁄₈ × 16 in.
(26.4 × 40.6 cm)
Josephine N. Hopper Bequest 70.438

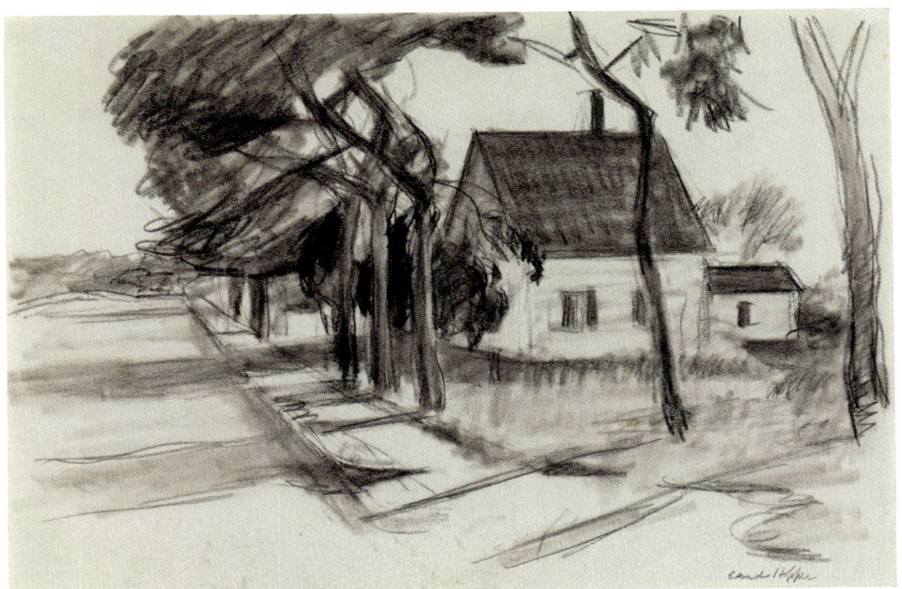

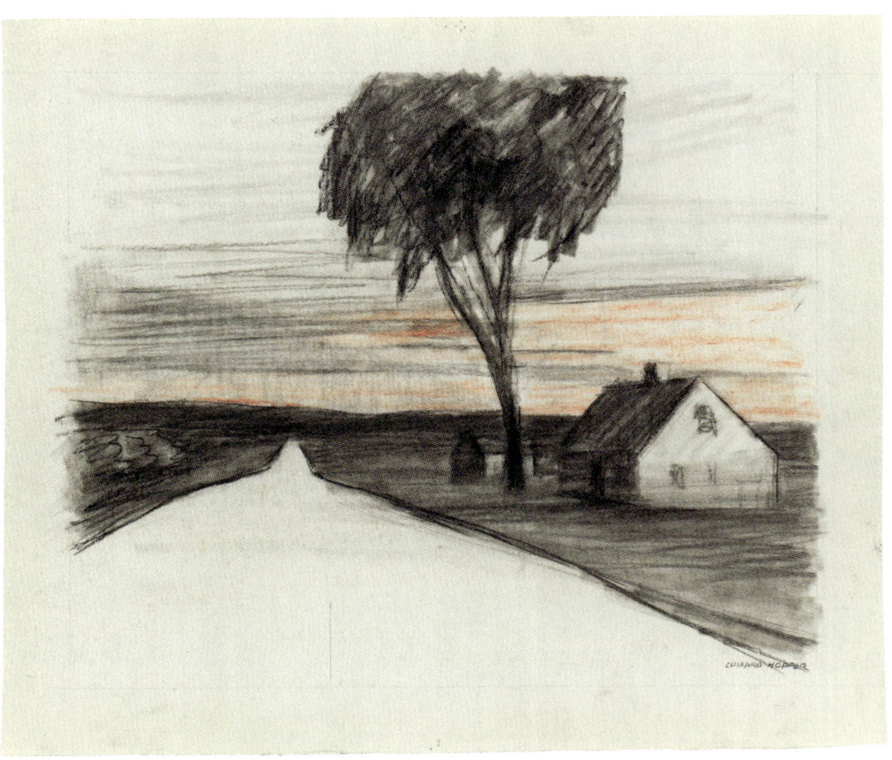

347. Study for *Solitude #56*, 1944
Fabricated chalk on paper, 10 3/8 × 16 in. (26.4 × 40.6 cm)
Josephine N. Hopper Bequest 70.443

348. Study for *Solitude #56*, 1944
Fabricated chalk, charcoal, and graphite pencil on paper, 15 × 18 1/8 in. (38.1 × 46 cm)
Josephine N. Hopper Bequest 70.685

& there & compare his own subjects in the studio which is much more comfortable, heaven knows."[58] Jo's comment on her husband's working methods at the time is perceptive of the artist's increasing shift from particularity, especially in his work on Cape Cod, to invented or "improvised" subjects that lack the markings of more precise observations. The title of the painting links it to an abstract emotional state: alone, absorptive, meditative. A suite of three related studies express, as do many of Hopper's preparatory drawings, a cinematic quality in the shifts and phenomenological adjustments that they track, as if recording the movement of the observer's head from right to left. In one sheet (fig. 347), we are led to the right toward trees that line the receding edge of the road, casting long slanted shadows. In another drawing (fig. 348), particularly bold in its reduction to essential elements, the frame is pulled back; the house stands next to an enormous tree. The road bed is left as a blank that bleeds out into the negative space surrounding the drawing, leading the viewer's eye toward a bluntly depicted sunset. The open landscape seems inflected by the wide spaces that Hopper would have seen in his first trip to the West in 1941.[59] In this drawing, the road, tree, and house are all solitary, as objects of identification for the observer. The third drawing (fig. 349), inscribed as a study for *Solitude*, falls between the other two in its orientation of the viewer's eye.

From their status as inventions distilled from observed reality, we can speculate about how the dreamlike, spare quality of these drawings reflects Hopper's incorporation and memory of his experience of driving through Cape Cod and other familiar places. For Hopper,

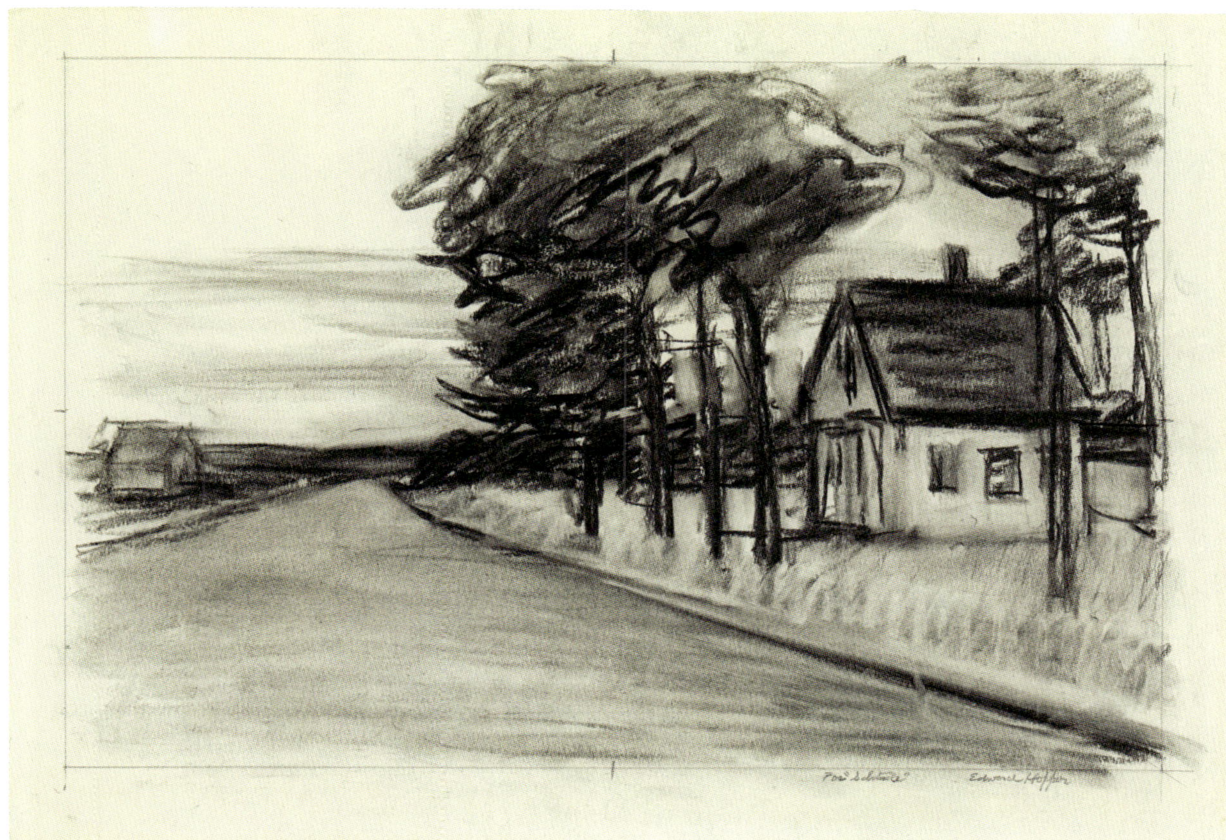

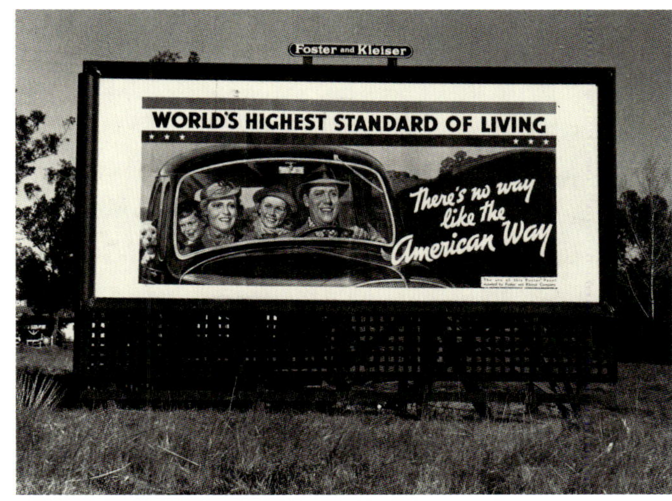

349. Study for *Solitude #56*, 1944
Fabricated chalk on paper, 15 1/16 × 22 1/8 in. (38.3 × 56.2 cm)
Josephine N. Hopper Bequest 70.855

350. Dorothea Lange (1895–1965). *Billboard on U.S. Highway 99 in California. National advertising campaign sponsored by the National Association of Manufacturers*, 1937. Black-and-white negative. Farm Security Administration – Office of War Information Photograph Collection, Library of Congress, Washington, DC

the view through the windshield of a car became a kind of structure for solitary meditation, a frame that made the familiar landscape into a responsive surface through its movement and change, offering up subjects from shifting perspectives for observation and incorporation. The particularity of the landscape is not in the sights themselves, whose banality puzzled Jo, but in the response to the moment of encounter, parsed out in these drawings through multiple viewpoints and configurations. Hopper's interest in the inward, meditative quality of driving operates at a disconnect from the way the car would be marketed and represented as an outwardly oriented technological frame.[60] For example, in the roadside billboard Dorothea Lange photographed in 1937, an archetypal American family gazes through the windshield at the prosperous national landscape, proffered (ironically, by Lange) as symbols of American identity and progress (fig. 350). In the 1956 *Time* magazine profile that cast Hopper as the "silent witness" of American life, the author recounts that the artist, upon buying a new Buick, had replaced the windshield's green glass with clear glass, claiming that Hopper "wanted to look out at an untinted America."[61] The automobile's potential as a means of accessing a national, collective identity is palpable in those terms. But the author seems to misunderstand Hopper's intention; while roads were constructed and marketed as means for Americans to discover or reconceive an expressly "modern" national landscape and their identity within it, Hopper seemed instead to increasingly internalize the view from the road as a means of exploring the self.

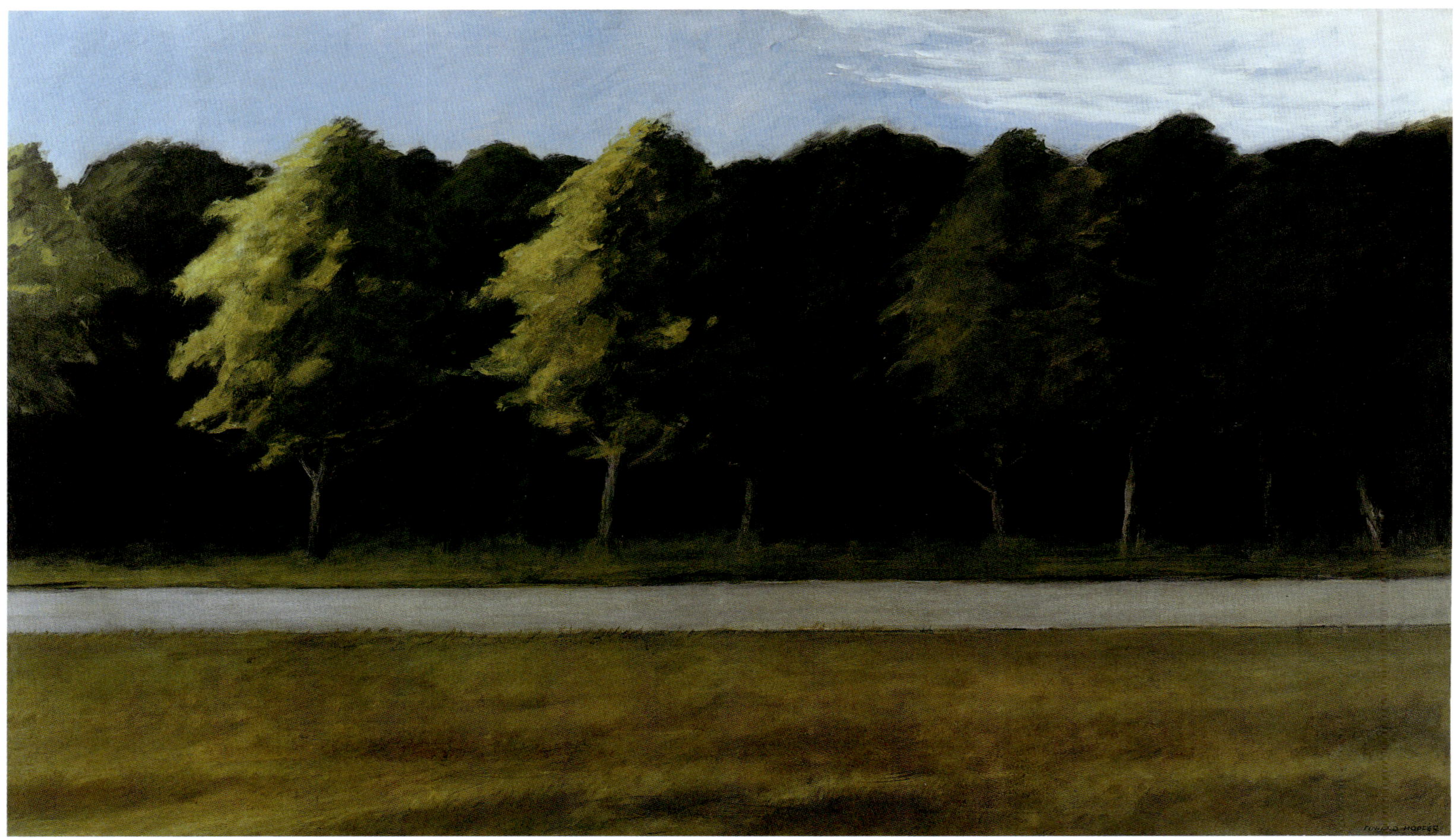

351. *Road and Trees*, 1962
Oil on canvas, 34 × 60 in. (86.4 × 152.4 cm)
Collection of Daniel W. Dietrich II

Road and Trees

There is a strange tension between motion and stillness in Hopper's final road picture, *Road and Trees* of 1962 (fig. 351); hovering between the two states, the painting appears almost to vibrate.[62] Arranged into bands, the composition has an almost semiotic simplicity: grass, road, foliage, sky. It is marked by the processes of simplification and distillation, which are also features of Hopper's other great, late work, *Sun in an Empty Room*, painted in 1963 (see fig. 385). *Road and Trees* describes the space where the road meets the natural world with an uneasy concision that suggests a missing or lacking element—yet the picture is whole and quite beautiful in its solidity, offering a toughened perceptual surface akin to the work of Gustave Courbet, an artist Hopper admired.[63] It has, as well, a curious and unexpected relationship to his *Early Sunday Morning* (see fig. 164), painted thirty-two years earlier. Nearly identical in size, the two canvases share the same absolute frontality and strangely off-kilter elements, the same foreshortened space and mass that return the gaze of its viewer back upon itself. "Look anywhere in this world," critic Parker Tyler wrote of Hopper's work in 1957, "and you meet a kind of wall, whether sky or wood, cloud, brick, or plaster."[64]

Like *Sun in an Empty Room*, *Road and Trees* represents a moment in Hopper's work in which the spaces that have functioned as stage sets or backdrops for human figures are found to be empty. The form of the landscape in this painting, a flat and extended foreground leading to a dense mass, was developed through numerous preceding works that depict the roadside. Hopper's *Four Lane Road* of 1956 (fig. 352), his most direct engagement with the postwar highway landscape, features the same gray ribbon of asphalt, beyond which lies a mutely regular mass of trees, as if one could turn one's head and observe the later painting's scene.[65] The man seated on a folding chair outside the filling station is fixed in a deep, attenuated stare, his gaze parallel to the road, his body molded allusively into the fixed position of a motorist. *Western Motel* (fig. 353), painted the next year, displays an elongated version of the same landscape, with a hill formation extruded from the California landscape beyond, visible through the expanse of the motel room's plate glass window and door.[66] *People in the Sun* of 1960 (fig. 354) multiplies and extends this vast, flat space, met here by the stares of four tourists seated on a summarily described terrace; a fifth figure is absorbed in the act of reading. Across a dun-yellow plane, aligned with the gaze of the painting's embedded viewers, is a wall-like row of mountains that, as Mark Strand noted, "seem to be looking back. Nature and civilization almost appear to be staring each other down."[67] Like *Four Lane Road*, this

352. *Four Lane Road*, 1956
Oil on canvas, 27 ½ × 41 ½ in. (69.9 × 105.4 cm)
Private collection

353. *Western Motel*, 1957
Oil on canvas, 30 ⅝ × 50 ½ in. (77.8 × 128.3 cm)
Yale University Art Gallery, New Haven; bequest of Stephen Carlton Clark, B.A. 1903 1961.18.32

354. *People in the Sun*, 1960
Oil on canvas, 40 ⅜ × 60 ⅜ in. (102.6 × 153.5 cm)
Smithsonian American Art Museum, Washington, DC; gift of S.C. Johnson & Son, Inc. 1969.47.61

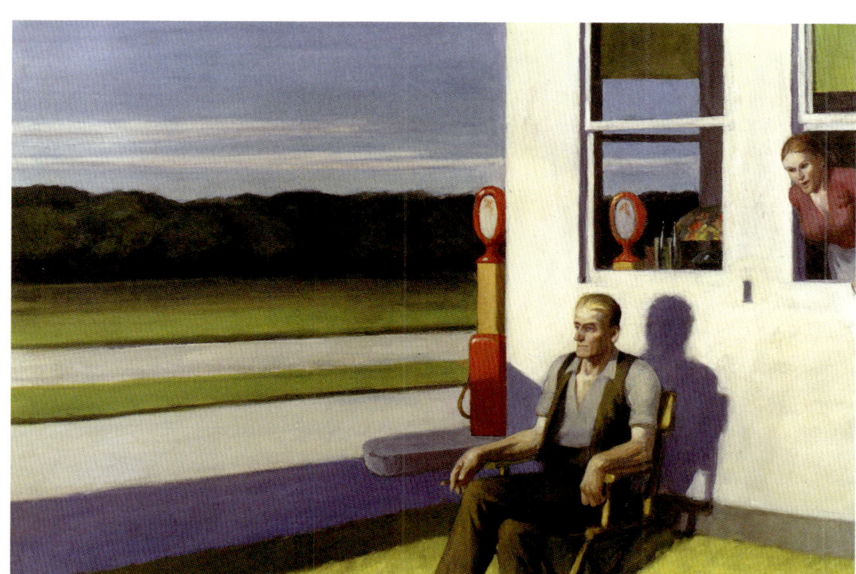

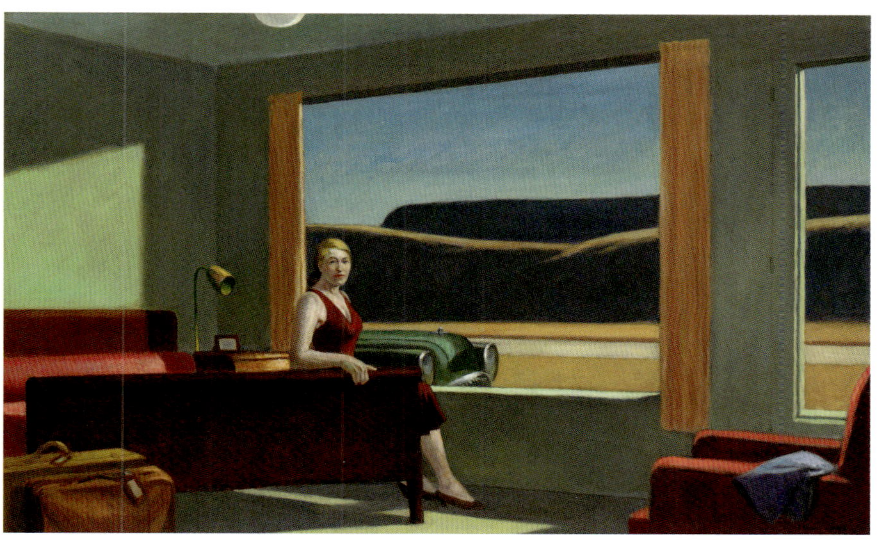

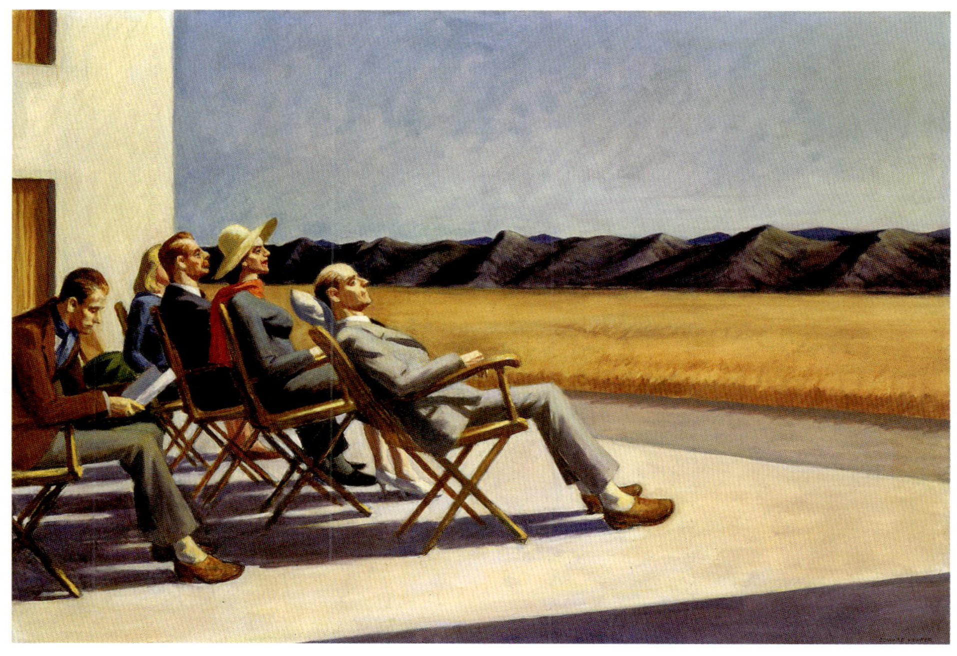

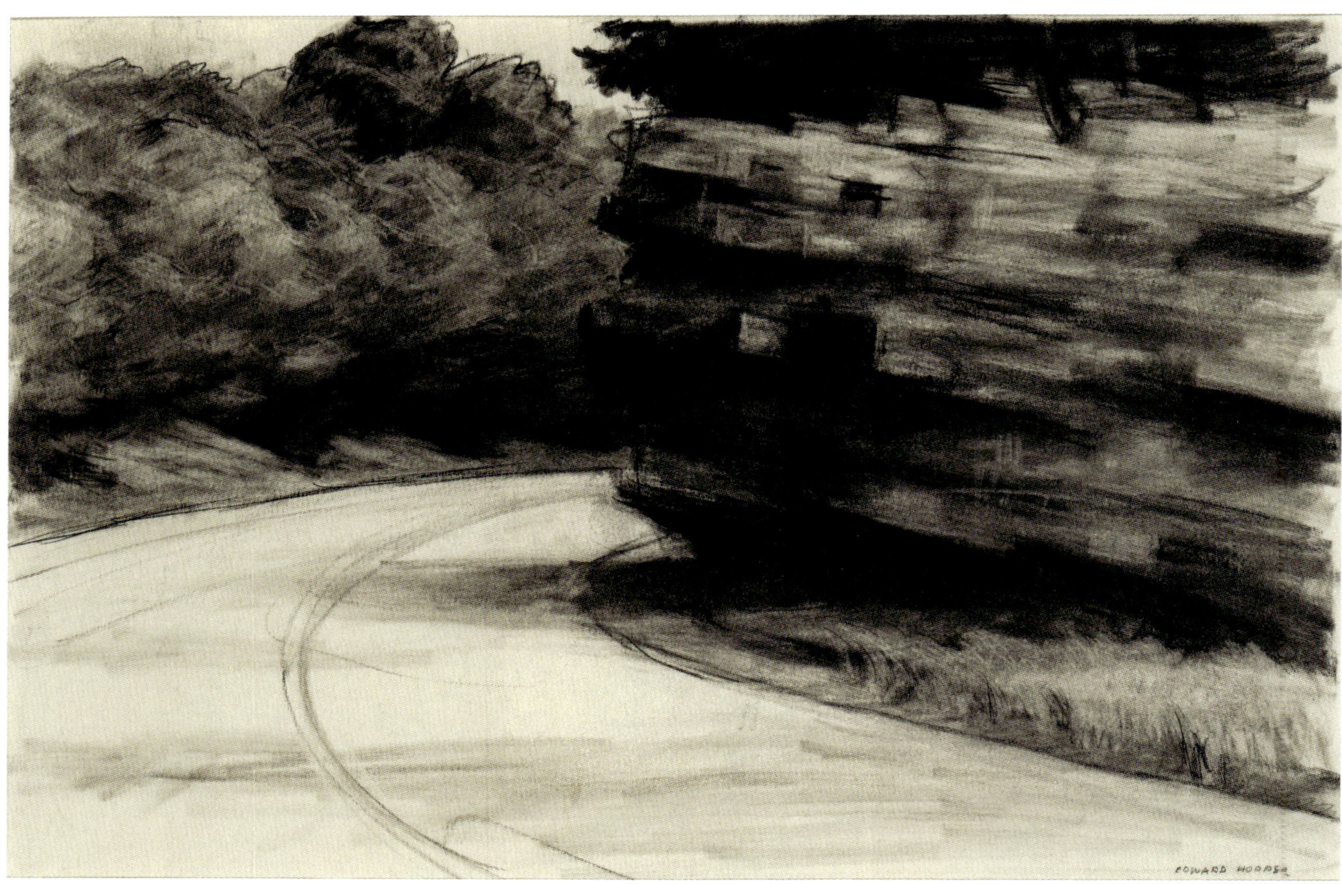

landscape was pulled from Hopper's memories of the spaces he had seen while traveling through the American West.[68] One critic wrote that Hopper's repeating motifs, whether spatial or iconographic, "tend in their references to form a closed circle—after all, they could not very well refer to anything *but* themselves," and that they were Hopper's way to "turn to form as a way out of subject, for the consummation of significance that it affords."[69] One such motif is the American roadside landscape, which Hopper absorbed and internalized during his long drives. These landscapes, seen in passing, were rearranged to form the backdrop to his series of road pictures, which culminates in the mute, yet insistent, landscape of *Road and Trees*.

What these works share as well is the prolonged, intensified, gaze of their seated surrogate observers—the man outside his gas station and his long stare; the female figure in *Western Motel*, whose eyes meet and transact with the viewer's; and the tourists in a trancelike state under the flat, strong sunlight.[70] It is this gaze, or "look," which is in question in *Road and Trees*.[71] The drawing *Road and Rocks* (fig. 355), like *Landscape with Automobile* (see fig. 317), is a drawing explicitly about the visual experience of the motorist and aids our understanding of this "look." Marked by a sense of loosening and experimentation, it is likely a late work and falls firmly in the category of Hopper's drawings that are "ideas"—works that are the artist's attempts to pull from the mind a sensate impression of the world.[72] The curve of the country road, turning out of sight, serves as the fixed point around which the roadside trees and rocky mass revolve. The artist's favored techniques of stumping and spreading his medium, as well as scraping it away to achieve lighter passages, are put to virtuosic use in this drawing. The rocks, blurred in movement, are described with long, deliberate strokes with emphatic, orthogonal outlines. The foliage and patch of grass next to the rock are defined by interlocking patterns of scraped-away chalk, representing the landscape as a texture rather than a mass.[73]

This recorded visual experience approaches a dynamism that is unusual in Hopper's work. In 1957, J. B. Jackson, author of influential investigations into the vernacular American landscape, wrote an essay questioning why the "Sunday driver" persisted in using the car for recreational purposes despite the limited contact with the natural world afforded by the country's crowded highways.[74] Investigating the thrill of speed and its effect on perception, Jackson concludes that a driver becomes "the shifting focus of a moving, abstract world.... To the perceptive individual, there can be an almost mystical quality to the experience."[75] In *Road and Rocks*, Hopper's record of the forceful transformation of the world seen by the moving eye, the material world is offered to the viewer as the memory of an impression. Anomalous as it is among Hopper's works, this drawing records the sensation of movement

355. *Road and Rocks*, c. 1962(?)
Fabricated chalk on paper, 15 × 22 ⅛ in. (38.1 × 56.2 cm)
Josephine N. Hopper Bequest 70.306

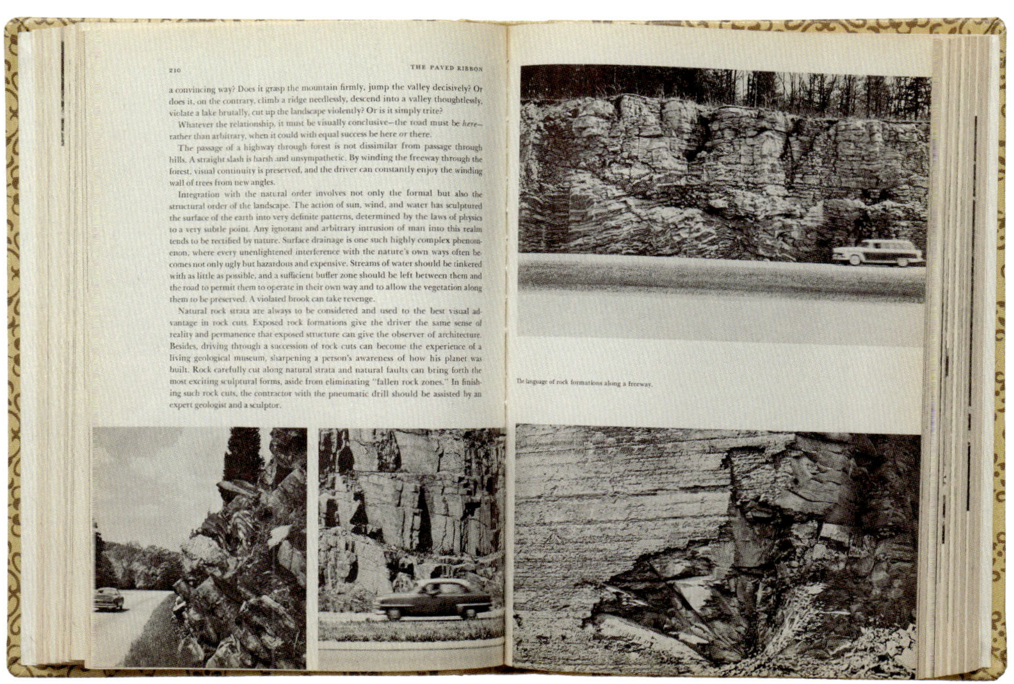

210 THE PAVED RIBBON

a convincing way? Does it grasp the mountain firmly, jump the valley decisively? Or does it, on the contrary, climb a ridge needlessly, descend into a valley thoughtlessly, violate a lake brutally, cut up the landscape violently? Or is it simply trite?

Whatever the relationship, it must be visually conclusive—the road must be *here*—rather than arbitrary, when it could with equal success be here *or* there.

The passage of a highway through forest is not dissimilar from passage through hills. A straight slash is harsh and unsympathetic. By winding the freeway through the forest, visual continuity is preserved, and the driver can constantly enjoy the winding wall of trees from new angles.

Integration with the natural order involves not only the formal but also the structural order of the landscape. The action of sun, wind, and water has sculptured the surface of the earth into very definite patterns, determined by the laws of physics to a very subtle point. Any ignorant and arbitrary intrusion of man into this realm tends to be rectified by nature. Surface drainage is one such highly complex phenomenon, where every unenlightened interference with the nature's own ways often becomes not only ugly but hazardous and expensive. Streams of water should be tinkered with as little as possible, and a sufficient buffer zone should be left between them and the road to permit them to operate in their own way and to allow the vegetation along them to be preserved. A violated brook can take revenge.

Natural rock strata are always to be considered and used to the best visual advantage in rock cuts. Exposed rock formations give the driver the same sense of reality and permanence that exposed structure can give the observer of architecture. Besides, driving through a succession of rock cuts can become the experience of a living geological museum, sharpening a person's awareness of how his planet was built. Rock carefully cut along natural strata and natural faults can bring forth the most exciting sculptural forms, aside from eliminating "fallen rock zones." In finishing such rock cuts, the contractor with the pneumatic drill should be assisted by an expert geologist and a sculptor.

The language of rock formations along a freeway.

356. Christopher Tunnard and Boris Pushkarev, *Man-Made America: Chaos or Control?* (New Haven: Yale University Press, 1963). Photographs by John Reed

with a personal intensity and interiority that recall and recalibrate Goethe's description of art-making that Hopper would refer to repeatedly: "the reproduction of the world that surrounds me by means of the world that is in me, all things being grasped, related, re-created, molded, and reconstructed in a personal form and an original manner."[76] The view from the automobile only intensified Hopper's sense that perception consisted of the interior transformation of a world seen by the engaged, ruminative eye.

Hopper's attention to the visual landscape of the highway coincided with an evolving concern about the aesthetic experience afforded by American roads, though there had been critics of roadside clutter and aesthetic disarray since the beginning of the automobile age. One of many publications addressing this question was the 1963 book *Man-Made America: Chaos or Control?* by Christopher Tunnard and Boris Pushkarev, who took up the problem of ugliness in segments of the built environment that did not typically receive aesthetic attention—the highway being a primary example.[77] In these cases, they wrote, "beauty can only emerge from a deliberate effort to express the encounter between society and environment in significant form."[78] Pushkarev, who authored the section on highway aesthetics, notes that "the moving eye perceives the form of the highway not as an engineering problem, but as an esthetic entity, a piece of sculpture or architecture, built of earth, asphalt, concrete, steel, shrubs, and trees. The highway is seen before it can be traveled upon—being seen is an integral part of its purpose."[79] The section is copiously illustrated with photographs and diagrams detailing the correct ways to "fit" the road to the landscape in order to provide a compelling visual experience within "a multidimensional work of space, time and energy."[80] On a basic level, the text reflects the ways in which the highway and heightened visuality were linked—how, as psychologist James Gibson wrote in 1950, in vehicles "visual stimulation becomes proportionally more important than bodily stimulation," and how highways dramatize and sequence vision.[81] Hopper's *Road and Rocks* and *Landscape with Automobile* also bear a curious connection to photographs by John Reed that illustrate a section of Pushkarev's text advocating for the integration of expressive, sculptural rock formations in roadway design (fig. 356).[82] Although these are images of very different kinds, Hopper's drawings and Reed's photographs address the experiences of the moving eye embedded in a world of forms animated by spatial and temporal flux as well as an evolving idea about the means of encountering and representing landscapes in the era of the automobile.

In this light, *Landscape with Automobile* and *Road and Rocks* relate to Hopper's earlier work that recovered vivid, formal beauty from urban environments and unfashionable architecture considered to be beyond aesthetic contemplation. In focusing on the intensified

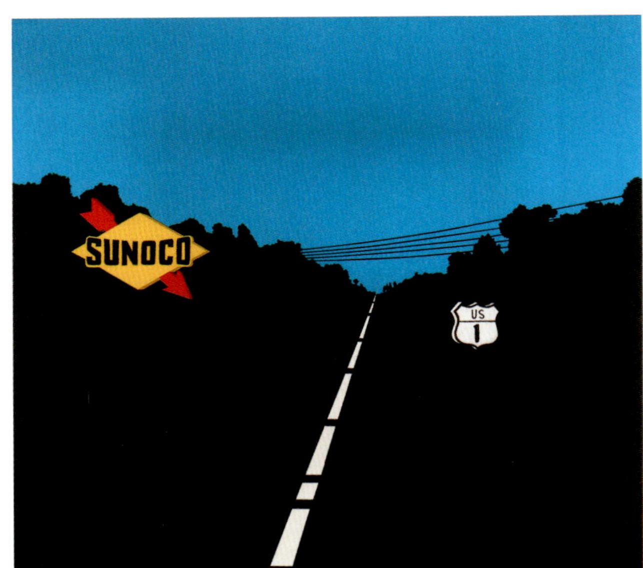

357. Allan d'Arcangelo (1930–1998)
U.S. Highway 1, 1962
Acrylic on canvas, 48 × 55 in. (121.9 × 139.7 cm)
Smithsonian American Art Museum, Washington, DC; museum purchase made possible by the American Art Forum 2011.13

relation between the motorized viewer and the moving landscape, the drawing (and the painting that followed it) responds, like Tunnard and Pushkarev, to the visually expressive possibilities of the everyday landscape. Compare Hopper's response to that of the artist Allan D'Arcangelo, who in the mid-1960s would garner critical attention for paintings that, while acknowledging the novel viewpoint of the motorist, represented the highway landscape as a configuration of flat signs and denotative planes in a reductive process very different from Hopper's (fig. 357).[83] Hopper's work was not a "cool" response to the newness of the highway's increasingly dominant presence, but rather a personal expression of the "drama of seeing" intrinsic to the highway experience—an experience that left sedimented impressions in his mind that later resurfaced in his improvised artworks.[84]

Following Hopper's death in 1967, art historians and critics would increasingly emphasize the links between his subject matter and that of Pop artists such as D'Arcangelo, Ed Ruscha, and George Segal, but Hopper's late road pictures are closer in sensibility and sensitivities to the work of a very different artist—Willem de Kooning.[85] In his paintings from the late 1950s and early 1960s, which the artist's critical champion Thomas Hess would later call "Abstract Parkway Landscapes," de Kooning attempted to contain the fluid flux of the world in canvases that featured broad, bold, enmeshed strokes of paint (fig. 358).[86] In a 1959 interview with Kenneth Snelson and Michael Sonnabend, de Kooning gave a characteristically sideways, poetic account of these works and their relation to perception, to aging, and to the expression of self:

> It seems that a lot of artists, when they get older they get simpler. . . . I'm getting more interested in my own miracle in nature . . . and I don't want to grasp the abstract, not the reason, but the experience of having moments, like I said, of being on the other side of nature. Just coming around roads, some place, and having sensation of a piece of it, a piece of nature, like a fence, something on the road. It sounds sentimental but it is such, a terrific experience, a concrete experience, where it is very clear to you.[87]

Attempting to situate himself "on the other side of nature," de Kooning connected this sensation of being in the landscape, or of having nature revealed as an event or an experience, to the experience of moving through space in a car—specifically within the parkway landscape, orchestrated and calibrated to be seen in motion.[88] Like Hopper, de Kooning

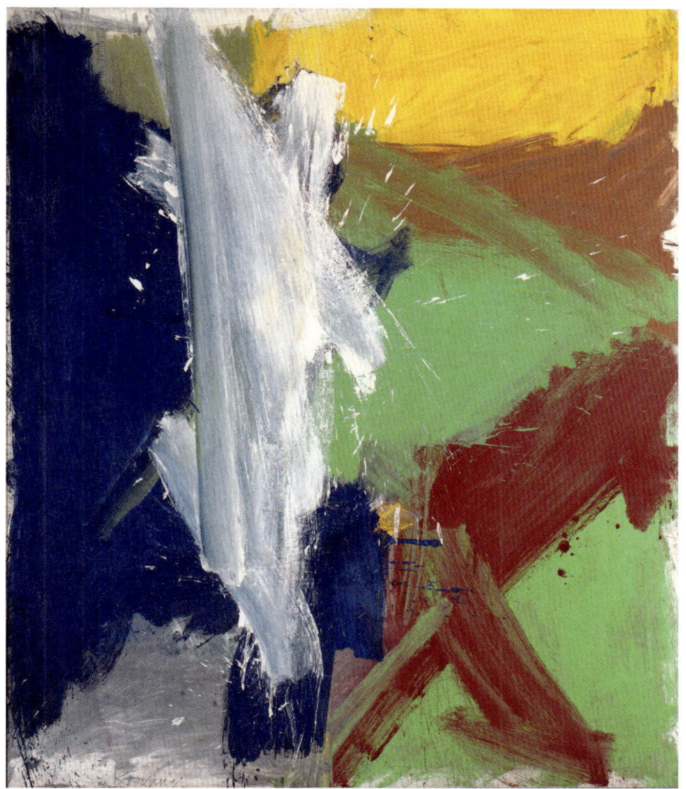

358. Willem de Kooning (1904–1997)
Merritt Parkway, 1959
Oil on canvas, 80 × 70½ in. (203.2 × 179.1 cm)
Detroit Institute of Arts; bequest of W. Hawkins Ferry
1988.177

was attracted not so much to the outward modernity or newness of the highway landscape, but rather to the vivid reality it imparted upon his perceiving eye, the idea of the world that it impressed upon him.[89] "The mystery in the world," de Kooning would tell Irving Sandler, "is to see something that is really there. I want to grab a piece of nature and make it as real as it actually is—like in my Merritt Parkway picture.... For years I had an idea of it, and then I painted it, and it is real. Hopper is the only American I know who could paint the Merritt Parkway."[90] To see the potential of Hopper's art through de Kooning's eyes is to recognize its perpetual modernity and rootedness in the artist's evolving historical moment. De Kooning and Hopper pursued different but linked versions of "the real"—of Realism—in a world that was increasingly seen, whether from the car, through the movie camera, or on the television, in fleeting and fluid encounters. "Content," as de Kooning famously said, "is a glimpse of something, an encounter... like a flash," analogous to the "fleeting" impressions that Hopper's art attempted to recover.[91] For both artists, this flux was not a process of estrangement but rather an encounter with a fresh world, newly revealed through the frame of the car, a "concrete experience" that leaves its traces on the seer.[92]

In October 1961, Jo wrote that Hopper was "casting about for a landscape"; it was not until August of the following summer that he would execute his watercolor *Mass of Trees at Eastham* (fig. 359) from the backseat of his car.[93] The stand of trees is shown at an oblique angle, curving backward along the edge of the road, with sunlight falling onto irregular sprays of foliage. It is a work that seems to lead directly to *Road and Trees* (see fig. 351), which Hopper began that October—a painting that is the summation of his lifelong exploration of the natural world framed by and encountered through the automobile. The painting returns us to de Kooning's account of his miraculous experience—what it means to be "on the other side of nature," to look out the window of an automobile for an instant and have an experience of vision that transforms both the seer and the seen. It is, of course, an encounter with the "self," a concept Hopper repeatedly insisted was at the core of his work. O'Doherty understood that Hopper pursued this self through the "preservation of the image" that is the foundation for the painting, and that his late work, *Road and Trees* included, is marked by the "intensification of the image, burning away all trivia."[94] Far from empty, the picture brims with traces of its maker and its making. Hopper told O'Doherty: "At fifty you don't think of the end much, but at eighty you think about it a lot."[95] Late in his life, it is no surprise that this question might be addressed in a work that hovers between stillness and movement, passing on while pausing to take in a sensation of the world's fullness.

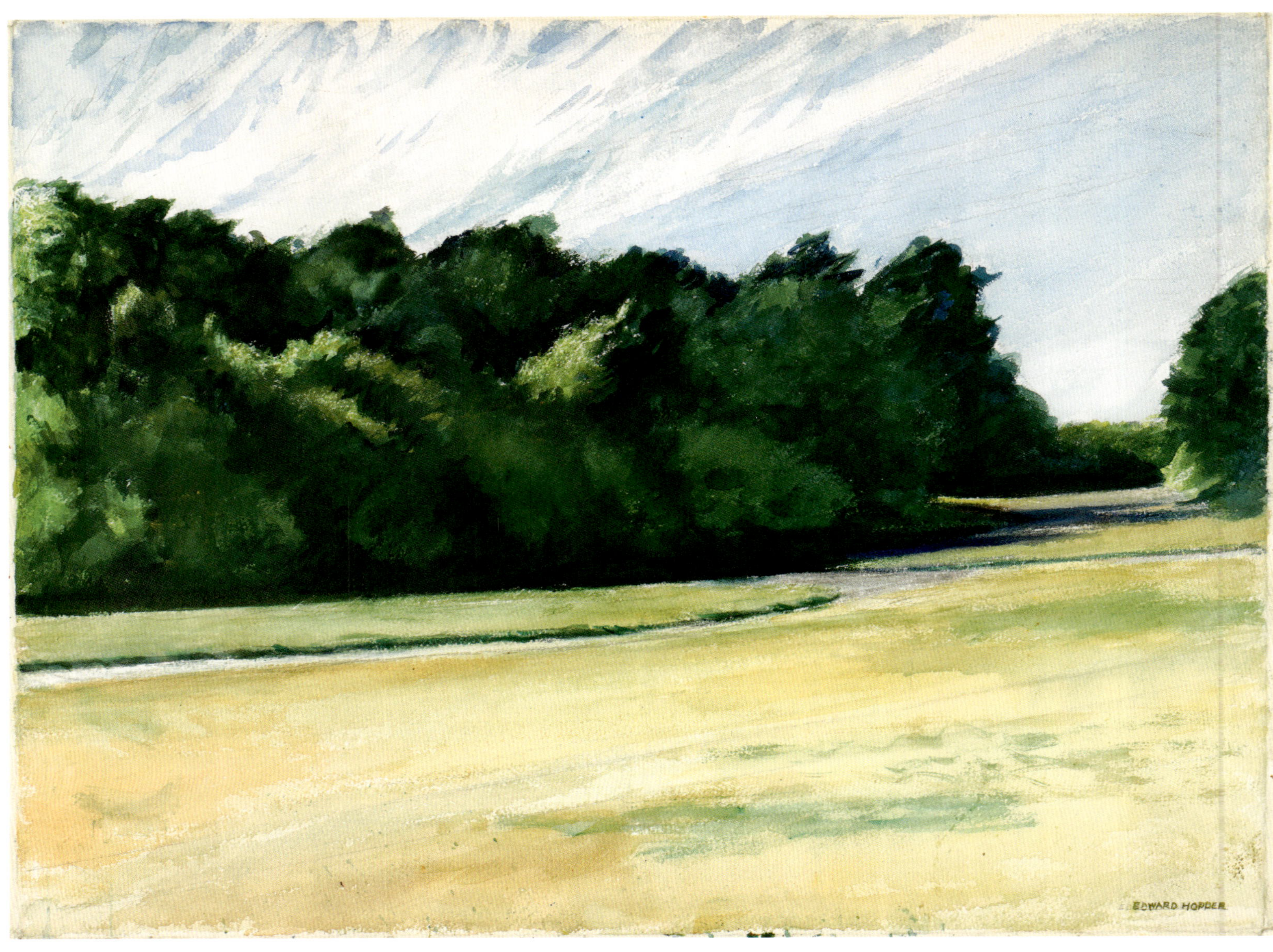

359. *Mass of Trees at Eastham*, 1962
Watercolor and graphite pencil on paper, 22 ½ × 30 ½ in.
(57.2 × 77.5 cm)
Josephine N. Hopper Bequest 70.1164

NOTES

1 Margaret Iversen provides an insightful analysis of Hopper's use of "arbitrarily cropped" pictorial elements that suggest the fleeting nature of the visions and, in suggesting the continuity of the picture with the "blind field" of the surrounding work, "[stimulate] the desire of the spectator." Iversen, "In the Blind Field: Hopper and the Uncanny," *Art History* 21, no. 3 (September 1998): 422.
2 *Edward Hopper: The Capezzera Drawings*, exh. cat. (New York: Peter Findlay Gallery, 2005), 34. On Hopper's use of paper for preparatory studies, see Carter Foster's essay in this volume (page 45).
3 Edward Hopper, letter to Norman Geske and statement about *Office at Night*, August 25, 1948, photocopy in Edward and Josephine Hopper Research Collection, 4.013, Whitney Museum of American Art Archives, New York (hereafter cited as Hopper Research Collection).
4 Robert Hobbs describes this eloquently: "Hopper transformed the sweeping glance of late nineteenth-century dandies who strolled along the recently formed grand boulevards of Paris to the strangely suspended gaze of motorists and moviegoers." Hobbs, *Edward Hopper*, exh. cat. (New York: Harry N. Abrams in association with the National Museum of American Art, 1987), 14. Others who have linked Hopper and the flâneur include Brian O'Doherty, "Hopper's Look," in Sheena Wagstaff, ed., *Edward Hopper*, exh. cat. (London: Tate Publishing, 2004), 87; Priscilla Paton, *Abandoned New England: Landscape in the Works of Homer, Frost, Hopper, Wyeth, and Bishop* (Hanover, NH: University Press of New England, 2003), 144; Lucy Fisher, "The Savage Eye: Edward Hopper and the Cinema," in *A Modern Mosaic: Art and Modernism in the United States*, ed. Townsend Ludington (Chapel Hill: University of North Carolina Press, 2000), 334–35; and Alain de Botton, *The Art of Travel* (New York: Vintage International, 2002), 27–58.
5 Hobbs, *Edward Hopper*, 14.
6 For an exploration of Hopper's road pictures and the ways in which his art addresses automobile culture, see Hobbs, *Edward Hopper*, 11–16, 91–104. Hobbs concludes that Hopper's road pictures captured the "unfeeling" and limited quality of the motorist's experience of the roadside landscape, which the artist represented as degraded in comparison with the grand vistas characteristic of nineteenth-century American landscape paintings. For a sustained and fascinating discussion of the effect of the automobile and the roadside landscape on the art of Stuart Davis and his contemporaries, including Hopper, see Carolyn Stuart, "American Autoscapes: Stuart Davis and the View from the Road, 1920–1940" (PhD diss., University of California, Los Angeles, 2010).
7 Lloyd Goodrich, "The Paintings of Edward Hopper," *The Arts* 11, no. 3 (March 1927): 137. Peter Schjeldahl describes Hopper's "profound modernity" beautifully, not as something self-consciously avant-garde but "as an objective correlative of what *lived* modern experience is like." Schjeldahl, "Hopperesque," in *Edward Hopper: Light Years*, exh. cat. (New York: Hirschl & Adler Galleries, 1988), 8.
8 Edward Hopper, quoted in "Art: A Traveling Man," *Time*, January 19, 1948, 60.
9 On Hopper's differing methods of painting in watercolor and oil, see Lloyd Goodrich, "Notes of Conversation with Hopper" (typescript, April 20, 1946), 4–5, Hopper Research Collection, 4.044.
10 On the Hoppers' purchase of their car and first use of the vehicle to paint, see Gail Levin, *Edward Hopper: An Intimate Biography* (New York: Rizzoli, 2007), 206–9.
11 See Kevin Salatino et al., *Edward Hopper's Maine*, exh. cat. (Brunswick, ME: Bowdoin College Museum of Art; Munich: Prestel, 2011).
12 Gail Levin, *Edward Hopper: A Catalogue Raisonné*, vol. 2, *Watercolors* (New York: Whitney Museum of American Art in association with W. W. Norton, 1995), 164.
13 For a useful and interesting summary of changing modes of American travel and their effect on experiences of landscapes, see David E. Nye, "Redefining the American Sublime, from Open Road to Interstate," in *Routes, Roads and Landscapes*, ed. Mari Hvattum et al. (Farnham, UK: Ashgate, 1988), 99–111. Nye writes: "Personal not corporate, never on a timetable [unlike the railroad], the automobile was understood as an escape into adventures" (103). For a more complete account, particularly of automobile travel, see John A. Jakle, *The Tourist: Travel in Twentieth-Century North America* (Lincoln: University of Nebraska Press, 1985). See also Warren Belasco, *Americans on the Road: From Autocamp to Motel, 1910–1945* (Cambridge, MA: MIT Press, 1979).
14 See Levin, *Edward Hopper: An Intimate Biography*, 206, 208, 285–86, 304–5, 372–73, 416, 429–30, 440–44, 552.
15 On the Hoppers' trip to the South, see Levin, *Edward Hopper: An Intimate Biography*, 221–23; on their 1941 travels in the West, see 337–42; on their 1956–57 stay in California, see 505–11; on their 1943 trip to Mexico, see 363–66; on their 1946 trip to Mexico, see 391–92; on their 1951 trip to Mexico, see 453–57; on their 1955 trip to Mexico, see 484–85. Their 1943 trip to Mexico was made by train due to gas rationing, which hindered Hopper's access to subjects. Writing to Frank Rehn, Hopper said of Saltillo, Mexico: "It has a nice climate and is among some interesting hills. It is pretty hard to get near then or do much of anything without a car, but I have made a few watercolors, nevertheless." Edward Hopper to Frank Rehn, August 14, 1943, Frank K. M. Rehn Galleries records, 1858–1969 (bulk 1919–68), Archives of American Art, Smithsonian Institution, box 7, reel 5857, frame 1164 (hereafter cited as Rehn Galleries records, AAA).
16 Recalling a visit from the Hoppers to Ogunquit, Maine, in 1928, Chester Chatterton, a close friend and fellow artist, described driving around with Hopper as he looked for subjects to paint: "[We] got in the car and rode around, and we came to one spot that looked like the kind of thing he would do. We stopped and looked at it... nope, didn't interest him. Wasn't quite right.... But he was that way about it." Interview with Alexander D. Ross, 1971, quoted in Levin, *Edward Hopper: An Intimate Biography*, 217.
17 Jo Hopper to Peggy Rehn, June 18–22, 1941, Rehn Galleries records, AAA, box 7, reel 5857, frames 1135–36.
18 Jo Hopper, postcard to Peggy Rehn, June 14, 1941, Rehn Galleries records, AAA, box 7, reel 5857, frame 1131. The Hoppers were following a route mapped specifically for the scenic motor tourist: the Rehn Galleries Records also include a guide to "California's Mission Trails" made for the automobile traveler, with a map of the "scenic ocean route between Los Angeles and San Francisco," which Jo likely sent to Peggy Rehn along with her enthusiastic descriptions of the sites. See "California's Mission Trails" (Los Angeles: California Mission Trails Association, Ltd.), Rehn Galleries records, AAA, box 7, reel 5857, frames 1137–40.
19 Jo Hopper to Peggy Rehn, June 18–22, 1941, Rehn Galleries records, AAA, box 7, reel 5857, frame 1134.
20 Goodrich, "Notes of Conversation with Hopper" (1946), 6.
21 See ibid., 4.
22 See Levin, *Edward Hopper: An Intimate Biography*, 392.
23 For a more extended discussion of framing and vision in *Jo in Wyoming* and Hopper's use of the automobile, see Stuart, "American Autoscapes," 25.
24 One of Hopper's more famous quotations suggests the inspiration—or relief—that cinema and its overflow of images provided for the artist: "When I don't feel in the mood for painting, I go to the movies for a week or more. I go on a regular movie binge!" Quoted in Gail Levin, *Edward Hopper: The Art and the Artist* (New York: W. W. Norton in association with the Whitney Museum of American Art, 1980), 58. Hopper was an enthusiast of *Life*; as Levin wrote, quoting from Jo Hopper's diary entry of October 20, 1941: "Once Jo found him poring over *Life* magazine and protested, why did he bother with that 'tripey' stuff. To fill his head, he said: 'it gets empty.'" Levin, *Edward Hopper: An Intimate Biography*, 345.
25 Art historian Barbara Novak, who knew Hopper, addresses the general invisibility of the automobile in American realism in her landmark text about nineteenth-century American landscape painting: "[In] art we have a fascinating history of technological inventions presenting art conventions with no option but to exclude them. The automobile in twentieth-century art provided one such example. There were few effective ways of including it within an existing realist convention until the appearance of American pop art." Novak, *Nature and Culture: American Landscape and Painting, 1825–1875* (New York: Oxford University Press, 1980), 171.
26 Goodrich, "Notes of Conversation with Hopper," 5. Gail Levin has identified one of the gas stations near Truro—owned by Jimmy De Lory, an acquaintance of the Hoppers—that the artist may have studied as he was working on *Gas*. Levin, *Edward Hopper: An Intimate Biography*, 328–29. There was another filling station in the center of Truro, owned by Ervin Tripp in the 1930s and Horace Snow in the 1940s. That station also featured the round-headed pumps and was advertised by the hanging Mobilgas Pegasus sign seen in the painting. See Susan Brennan and Diane Worthington, *Truro* (Charleston, WV: Arcadia, 2002), 46–47.
27 Brian O'Doherty, "Edward Hopper's Voice," in *American Masters: The Voice and the Myth* (New York: Random House, 1973), 24.
28 Walter Wells notes the different "resonance" that electric light would have had as "a powerful symbol of modern progress" in Hopper's time. Wells, *Silent Theater: The Art of Edward Hopper* (New York: Phaidon, 2007), 218–19. Many writers have noted the distinction between natural and artificial light in Hopper's work. In *Gas*, the apposition is between the "night-defying" light of the gasoline pumps and the soft twilight that plays over the plane of the sky. For a short history of the development of roadside America, see Karl Raitz, "American Roads, Roadside America," *Geographical Review* 88, no. 3 (July 1998): 378–85.
29 Goodrich, "Notes of Conversation with Hopper" (1946), 5.
30 See Levin, *Edward Hopper: An Intimate Biography*, 328.

31 Mark Strand notes of *Gas* that "Hopper's trees are generic. They look the way trees do when we drive by them at fifty or sixty miles an hour. Yet his woods have a peculiar and forceful identity." Strand, *Hopper* (New York: Alfred A. Knopf, 2001), 13–14.
32 Alain de Botton provides an imagined account of the motorist's encounter proposed in *Gas*, though Hopper resisted such precisely narrative readings of his work. See de Botton, *The Art of Travel*, 51–52.
33 See ibid., 52, for discussion of the interplay of artificial light in *Gas*.
34 Alexander Nemerov, "Ground Swell: Edward Hopper in 1939," *American Art* 22, no. 3 (Fall 2008): 69.
35 This lyrical dimension was evident to Museum of Modern Art curators James Thrall Soby and Dorothy C. Miller, who included *Gas* in their 1943 exhibition *Romantic Painting in America* among other works by Asher B. Durand, Albert Pinkham Ryder, and Charles Burchfield that represented, for Soby, the "triumph of Imagination over Reason." Writing about *Gas*, Soby described its "Romantic sorcery" despite the "blunt fact" of its subject matter and its overt realism—qualifying the facticity so often associated with Hopper's paintings by contemporary critics. James Thrall Soby and Dorothy C. Miller, *Romantic Painting in America*, exh. cat. (New York: Museum of Modern Art, 1943), 39.
36 Jo Hopper, diary entry of October 25, 1941, quoted in Levin, *Edward Hopper: An Intimate Biography*, 344.
37 Hobbs called this configuration, a common feature of the artist's work since etchings like *American Landscape* (1920), Hopper's "interrupted…American landscape." Hobbs, *Edward Hopper*, 53.
38 See Levin, *Edward Hopper: A Catalogue Raisonné*, 2:239. On *High Road*, see Ellen E. Roberts, "Painting the Modern Cape: Hopper in Truro," in Carol Troyen et al., *Edward Hopper*, exh. cat. (Boston: Museum of Fine Arts, 2007), 155; Virginia M. Mecklenburg, *Edward Hopper: The Watercolors*, exh. cat. (Washington, DC: National Museum of American Art, Smithsonian Institution, 1999), 108; Stuart, "American Autoscapes," 23–24.
39 "The popularization of the automobile affected the landscape of the Outer Cape more than any other social or technological trend since the days of salt works and whaling." *People and Places on the Outer Cape: A Landscape Character Study* (Amherst: University of Massachusetts, 2004), 91. See also James C. O'Connell, *Becoming Cape Cod: Creating a Seaside Resort* (Hanover, NH: University Press of New England, 2003), 47–49, 97–101.
40 Richard D. Holmes et al., *Historical Cultural Land Use Study of Lower Cape Cod* (Amherst: University of Massachusetts Archaeological Services, Environmental Institute, 1998), 37.
41 William C. Seitz wrote in 1967: "Some [of Hopper's] landscapes are dominated by the highway. Its disappearance toward the horizon is accentuated, in *Route 6, Eastham*, by a dividing strip. The presence of the road can also be suggested by a fence that one knows parallels it, or by a bridge over which the road passes. Highways and railroads have a somewhat similar meaning…. Mr. and Mrs. Hopper are both rail and automobile travelers, and have therefore observed the United States from the same moving vantage points as have millions of other tourists." Seitz, "Edward Hopper: Realist, Classicist, Existentialist," in *São Paulo 9, United States of America: Edward Hopper, Environment U.S.A., 1957–1967*, exh. cat. (Washington, DC: Smithsonian Institution Press, 1967), 22. In *Route 6, Eastham* and its metaphorical deployment of "the road," Walter Wells sees a continuation of Hopper's explorations of "mobility and rootedness." See Wells, *Silent Theater*, 180.
42 Paton, *Abandoned New England*, 154–55. See also Ellen E. Roberts, "Painting the Modern Cape: Hopper in Truro," in Troyen et al., *Edward Hopper*, 147.
43 Levin, *Edward Hopper: A Catalogue Raisonné*, 3:286.
44 Jo Hopper, diary entry of October 15, 1941, quoted in Levin, *Edward Hopper: An Intimate Biography*, 344.
45 Writing in 1955, Suzanne Burrey noted that "the more successful instances in the later phase of Hopper's art occur when he…uses space as the chief actor in the picture." Suzanne Burrey, "Edward Hopper: the Emptying Spaces," *Arts Digest* 29, no. 13 (April 1, 1955): 10.
46 Roberts notes, interestingly, that Hopper made only three works in Provincetown, which was a much livelier center for tourism and artistic production than Truro. In this sense, Hopper is here looking at a section of the Cape that has been more overtly impacted by tourism and the automobile. See Roberts, "Painting the Modern Cape," 145.
47 As Lloyd Goodrich wrote of Hopper's early "house portraits": "Never before, probably, had the American small town been subjected to such candid scrutiny. When these watercolors were first exhibited, the general reaction was that they were relentless satire. This was in large part because we were not used to seeing such commonplace and to some of us ugly material used in art. But actually, there was no overt satire; Hopper's viewpoint was objective, and on the whole affirmative." Goodrich, *Edward Hopper*, exh. cat. (New York: Whitney Museum of American Art, 1964), 19. See also Diana Tuite, "America Sits for Its Portrait: Hopper and the Critics," in Salatino et al., *Edward Hopper's Maine*, 96–97.
48 "Art: A Traveling Man," 59.
49 Goodrich, "Notes of Conversation with Hopper" (1946), 5.
50 See Gail Levin, "Edward Hopper, Francophile," *Arts Magazine* 53, no. 10 (June 1979): 119. See also Richard Kendall, "Influence in Low Places: Degas and the Ashcan Generation," in *Degas and America: The Early Collectors*, ed. Ann Dumas and David A. Brenneman, exh. cat. (Atlanta: High Museum of Art, 2000), 72–74; Sheena Wagstaff, "The Elation of Sunlight," in Wagstaff, ed., *Edward Hopper*, 18. On Hopper and the frame, see James A. Ward, *American Silences: The Realism of James Agee, Walker Evans, and Edward Hopper* (Baton Rouge: Louisiana State University Press, 1985), 176–77.
51 O'Doherty, "Hopper's Voice," 24. O'Doherty writes: "His framing…crops in ways that stimulate and frustrate attention, sometimes suggesting movement and change while fixing the subject so firmly that his best works appear like freeze-frames from a lifelong movie."
52 Robert Silberman, "Edward Hopper and the Theater of the Mind: Vision, Spectacle, and the Spectator," in *On the Edge of Your Seat: Popular Theater and Film in Early Twentieth-Century American Art*, ed. Patricia McDonnell, exh. cat. (New Haven: Yale University Press in association with Frederick R. Weisman Art Museum, University of Minnesota, 2002), 150.
53 Edward Hopper to Charles H. Sawyer, October 19, 1939, Archives of the Addison Gallery of American Art, Phillips Academy, Andover, Massachusetts.
54 Meyer Schapiro, "On Some Problems in the Semiotics of Visual Art: Field and Vehicle in Image-Signs," in *Theory and Philosophy of Art: Style, Artist, Society* (New York: George Braziller, 1994), 7.
55 As Judith Barter writes, many of Hopper's pictures from the 1940s on deal with the "apprehension that transience and impermanence produced…the implied tensions between arrival and departure, occupation and desertion." Barter, "Travels and Travails: Hopper's Late Pictures," in Troyen et al., *Edward Hopper*, 212.
56 See Levin, *Edward Hopper: A Catalogue Raisonné*, 3:304–5. See also Iversen, "In the Blind Field," 421.
57 Goodrich, "Notes of Conversation with Hopper," 5. Goodrich records: "*Solitude* [like *Gas* (1940)] was also improvised, though there were places like it on Cape Cod."
58 Quoted in Levin, *Edward Hopper: An Intimate Biography*, 371.
59 I am grateful to Carter Foster for this observation. As John Jakle writes, "Western landscapes were of a vast scale often deceptive to eastern eyes…. The mind needed to adjust when transported from region to region." Jakle, *The Tourist*, 228.
60 One of many examples of such trends would be the General Motors pavilion at the 1939 World's Fair in New York—*Futurama*, conceived by Norman Bel Geddes—which was intended to promote increased automobility and highway building as *the* central program for American modernization, which would be effected by the increased efficiency and mechanization of the automobile. See Roland Marchand, "The Designers Go to the Fair II: Norman Bel Geddes, The General Motors 'Futurama,' and the Visit to the Factory Transformed," *Design Issues* 8, no. 2 (Spring 1992): 22–40. As noted by Carter Foster in this volume, see page 119, note 33, it is possible that Hopper visited the World's Fair in 1939. On automobility and American subjectivity in the postwar period, see Cotton Seiler, *Republic of Drivers: A Cultural History of Automobility in America* (Chicago: University of Chicago Press, 2008), 69–104.
61 "Art: The Silent Witness," *Time*, December 24, 1956, 38–39.
62 See Levin, *Edward Hopper: A Catalogue Raisonné*, 3:372; Levin, *Edward Hopper: An Intimate Biography*, 552–53. O'Doherty writes of *Road and Trees* as "[engaging] problems of fixity and motion, of impact and recollection." O'Doherty, "Hopper's Voice," 25.
63 Goodrich, "Notes of Conversation with Hopper" (1946), 6. Goodrich quotes Hopper as admiring the "mechanical strength" of Courbet.
64 Parker Tyler, "Hopper/Pollock: The Loneliness of the Crowd and the Loneliness of the Universe: An Antiphonal," *ARTnews Annual* 26 (December 1957): 95.
65 Hopper spoke about making this picture to Bill Johnson, a researcher for *Time* magazine, in 1956: "I don't like it much. Of course it isn't finished yet. But you can't tell. I had this sketch…I don't remember when I made it. Last spring, I guess. It wasn't any place in particular. Just an improvisation." Quoted in Bill Johnson, "Hopper Cover Research" (unpublished typescript, October 30, 1956), 1, Hopper Research Collection, 4.043.
66 Hobbs sees a kind of degraded or quotidian aspect in the dramatic hills, noting how the picture is "a very mundane twentieth-century descendant of Alfred

Bierstadt's nineteenth-century majestic views." Hobbs, *Edward Hopper*, 98.
67 Strand, *Hopper*, 31.
68 Hopper later described the conception of this painting: "The idea was suggested by seeing people in Washington Square Park getting the sun . . . I changed the locale to a Western setting." Edward Hopper, draft of letter to Lee Nordness, July 30, 1962, quoted in Levin, *Edward Hopper: A Catalogue Raisonné*, 3:364.
69 Jerrold Lanes, "Edward Hopper: French formalist, Ash Can realist, neither, or both?" *Artforum* 7, no. 2 (October 1968): 49.
70 On Hopper's use of figures as surrogates for the artwork's viewer, see Robert Silberman, "Edward Hopper and the Implied Observer," *Art in America* 69, no. 7 (September 1981): 148–54.
71 I borrow the term "look" from O'Doherty's essay "Hopper's Look," and his eloquent discussion of the forms of looking in Hopper's pictures, which ultimately relate to Hopper's extended, reflexive and reflective look into the self. See O'Doherty, "Hopper's Look," 82–97.
72 Iversen relates Hopper's pictures that engage the subject position of the driver to the role of memory in his work and the uncanny presence of his subjects in the field of vision. She writes that *Solitude #56* (144) "represents the impression left after a quick glance at an inexplicably peculiar, isolated house. The view as if from a passing vehicle and the consequent delayed temporality of the paintings are important components of the uncanny impression made by Hopper's work in general." Iversen, "In the Blind Field," 421. Hopper's focus on situating the viewer in a particular "temporal and spatial" field beyond the edge of the picture serves, unexpectedly, "to make the scene vivid rather than, as one might expect, obscure." Ibid., 422.
73 Hopper spoke of his interest in texture to Katharine Kuh: "Trees have a different texture than houses or human flesh." Quoted in Kuh, "Edward Hopper," in *The Artist's Voice: Talks with Seventeen Artists* (New York: Harper and Row, 1962), 141.
74 J. B. Jackson, "The Abstract World of the Hot-Rodder," *Landscape in Sight: Looking at America*, ed. Helen Lefkowitz Horowitz (New Haven: Yale University Press, 1997), 199–206; originally published in *Landscape* 7, no. 2 (Winter 1957–58): 22–27.
75 Ibid., 205.
76 Hopper revealed to O'Doherty that he carried this text with him in his wallet. See O'Doherty, "Hopper's Voice," 14.
77 Christopher Tunnard and Boris Pushkarev, *Man-Made America: Chaos or Control?* (New Haven: Yale University Press, 1963). At the time, Tunnard was a professor of city planning at Yale University's School of Art and Architecture and Boris Pushkarev was a senior planner at the Regional Plan Association in New York, a nonprofit research association focused on planning and transportation in the New York metropolitan area. This volume received a fair amount of attention when it was published; it was reviewed in *Time* and the *New York Times* and received the National Book Award for Science, Philosophy and Religion in 1963.
78 Ibid., 9.
79 Ibid., 170.
80 Ibid., 171.
81 James J. Gibson, *The Perception of the Visual World* (Boston: Houghton Mifflin, 1950), 135; cited in Mitchell Schwarzer, *Zoomscape: Architecture and Media in Motion* (New York: Princeton Architectural Press, 2004), 16. See also Edward Dimendberg, "The Will to Motorization: Cinema, Highways, and Modernity," *October* 73 (Summer 1995): 90–137.
82 Tunnard and Pushkarev, *Man-Made America*, 210–11.
83 John Sandberg's 1967 article about "the traditional basis of Pop Art" links Hopper and D'Arcangelo, reproducing *Gas* (see fig. 320) and D'Arcangelo's *U.S. Highway No. 1, No. 5* (1963) next to one another, where the works' similarities in receding perspective and interest in signage are made evident. See John Sandberg, "Some Traditional Aspects of Pop Art," *Art Journal* 26, no. 3 (Spring 1967): 232. D'Arcangelo's work, along with that of Robert Indiana, George Segal, Ed Ruscha, and Tom Wesselman, featured prominently in Lawrence Alloway's 1967 article about highway culture and art, in which he writes: "The highways are, as nearly anything built for human use, new and not particularly datable. . . . They are one of the most conspicuous of the completely new environments that, every now and again, we find ourselves in." Of D'Arcangelo's landscapes, Alloway writes: "D'Arcangelo's highway paintings are always hard, new, and clean. . . . There are no foreground through background or ground plane to sky shifts and contrasts of emotional emphasis." See Lawrence Alloway, "Hi-Way Culture: Man at the Wheel," *Arts* 41, no. 4 (February 1967): 28, 32–33. See also Dan Cameron, "The Expressway Less Traveled," in *Allan D'Arcangelo: Paintings 1962–1982*, exh. cat. (New York: Mitchell-Innes and Nash, 2009), 3–5.
84 I borrow this phrase from Silberman, who writes: "Hopper's paintings are about the drama of seeing." Silberman, "Edward Hopper and the Theater of the Mind," 151.
85 Most notable is William C. Seitz, curator at the Museum of Modern Art, who organized the U.S. contribution to the 1967 São Paolo Biennial, which featured a Hopper retrospective alongside a survey of younger Pop artists. See also John Sandberg's 1967 article cited above: Sandberg, "Some Traditional Aspects of Pop Art," 228–33, 245. Hopper's pictures, and their attention to the spaces and symbols of everyday life, are often compared to those of Pop artists in more recent writing by art historians and curators. See, for example, Judith A. Barter, "Travels and Travails: Hopper's Late Pictures," 222–24; Michael Auping, "A Long Drive," in Michael Auping and Richard Prince, *Ed Ruscha: Road Tested*, exh. cat. (Fort Worth, TX: Modern Art Museum of Fort Worth in association with Hatje Cantz, 2011), 14–16; Didier Ottinger, "The Transcendental Realism of Edward Hopper," in Tomàs Llorens and Didier Ottinger, *Edward Hopper*, exh. cat. (Paris: Réunion des museés nationaux, 2012), 48–49.
86 See Thomas B. Hess, *Willem de Kooning* (New York: Museum of Modern Art, 1968), 26. On these paintings, see also Jennifer Field, "Abstract Parkway Landscapes," in *Willem de Kooning: a Retrospective*, ed. John Elderfield, exh. cat. (New York: The Museum of Modern Art, 2011), 317–22 and John J. Curley, "Running on Empty: Willem de Kooning in the Late 1950s," *Modernism/Modernity* 17, no. 1 (January 2010): 61–86.
87 Willem de Kooning, "Inner Monologue," transcript of interview with Kenneth Snelson and Michael Sonnabend, Summer 1959, 8, courtesy The Willem de Kooning Foundation, New York.
88 The Merritt Parkway, built between 1934 and 1940, was the culmination of many decades of evolving thought about highways and the kinds of aesthetic experience that they should provide—specifically, a landscape designed around a road and around the experience of the motorist. For a concise and insightful history of "the parkway idea," see Timothy Davis, "The Rise and Decline of the American Parkway," in *The World Beyond the Windshield: Roads and Landscapes in the United States and Europe*, ed. Christof Mauch and Thomas Zeller (Athens: Ohio University Press; Stuttgart: Franz Steiner Verlag, 2008), 35–58; Norman T. Newton, *Design on the Land: The Development of Landscape Architecture* (Cambridge, MA: The Belknap Press of Harvard University Press, 1971), 596–619.
89 In a conversation with David Sylvester, de Kooning said, referring the highway landscapes his paintings addressed: "This I don't particularly like, or dislike, but I wholly approve of it. . . . I'm no lover of the new; it's a personal thing." See "Willem de Kooning," in David Sylvester, *Conversations with American Artists* (New Haven: Yale University Press, 2001), 53.
90 Irving Sandler, "Conversations with de Kooning," *Art Journal* 48, no. 3 (Autumn 1989): 217.
91 Sylvester, "Willem de Kooning," 50.
92 De Kooning, "Inner Monologue," 8.
93 Jo Hopper, postcard to John Clancy, October 31, 1961, Rehn Galleries records, AAA, frame 1308. On the painting of *Mass of Trees at Eastham*, see Levin, *Edward Hopper: An Intimate Biography*, 552.
94 O'Doherty, "Hopper's Voice," 25. On Hopper and the self, O'Doherty wrote: "His art is a sort of self-reassurance. He sent out soundings whose echoes rebound from the facts, via the picture, to define and prove the existence of the self." Ibid., 14. He would later write that Hopper's oeuvre was, "if we believe his declared intention, a cumulative self-portrait." O'Doherty, "Hopper's Look," 86.
95 O'Doherty, "Hopper's Voice," 15.

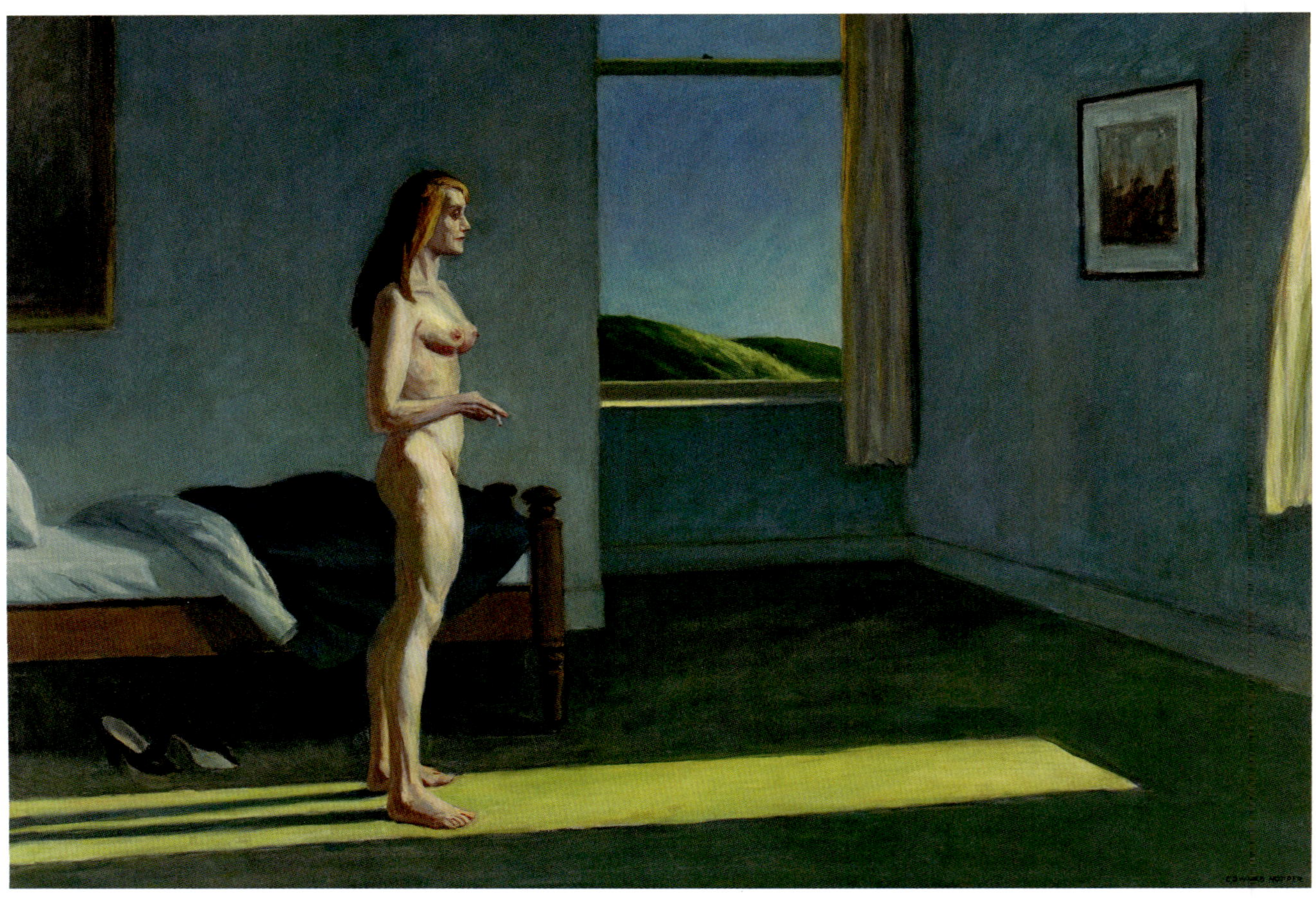

The Bedroom

CARTER E. FOSTER

"In every artist's development the germ of the later work is always found in the earlier,"[1] Edward Hopper observed in 1935, in a statement that applies well to his own output. *A Woman in the Sun* of 1961 (fig. 360) is essentially the same subject as *Summer Interior* of 1909 (see fig. 375) but a variation done more than fifty years later. In both paintings, the key elements are the same: a woman, a bed, a window, light, and the implied presence or absence of someone else. Hopper developed the bedroom into a major theme, especially in his late paintings, though he explored it throughout his career and in all mediums. His careful and close observations of reality, often made through drawing, seeded imaginative explorations, yet these were not expansive searchings of the wide world but variations on the same subjects studied again and again.

One of Hopper's main artistic pursuits was exploring a dialectic between the subjectivity of the self and the world at large—in purely formal terms, the figure's relationship to his or her surroundings. He consistently sought to make the settings his characters inhabit express something of their internal state of being. This interest is perfectly distilled in his subtly developed images of people looking out of windows, in which the metaphorical implications about the self in the world are fairly direct. More specifically, he turned the bedroom into a loaded space in which he could explore its narrative and symbolic potential with the figure in a charged, particular type of setting. It appears early in his art and remains a subject of exploration throughout his career. The bed itself, the figure's state of undress, and the relationship between interior and exterior space become the key elements for projecting mood, implying a story, and commenting on the nature of "human experience" that was the artist's stated interest.[2]

The lone figure in *A Woman in the Sun* stands with her bare, nacreous body absorbing the sunlight streaming in from an unseen window, indicated by a slightly billowing curtain.[3] The light forms a long trapezoid of harsh, acid green on the floor. Her body intersects the light, her legs casting two deep shadows. The woman's entire form is painted with a concentration of small, deliberate strokes in combinations of yellows, pinks, blues, and creamy whites and beiges. With a glistening, pearlescent beauty, these passages of paint are densely laid

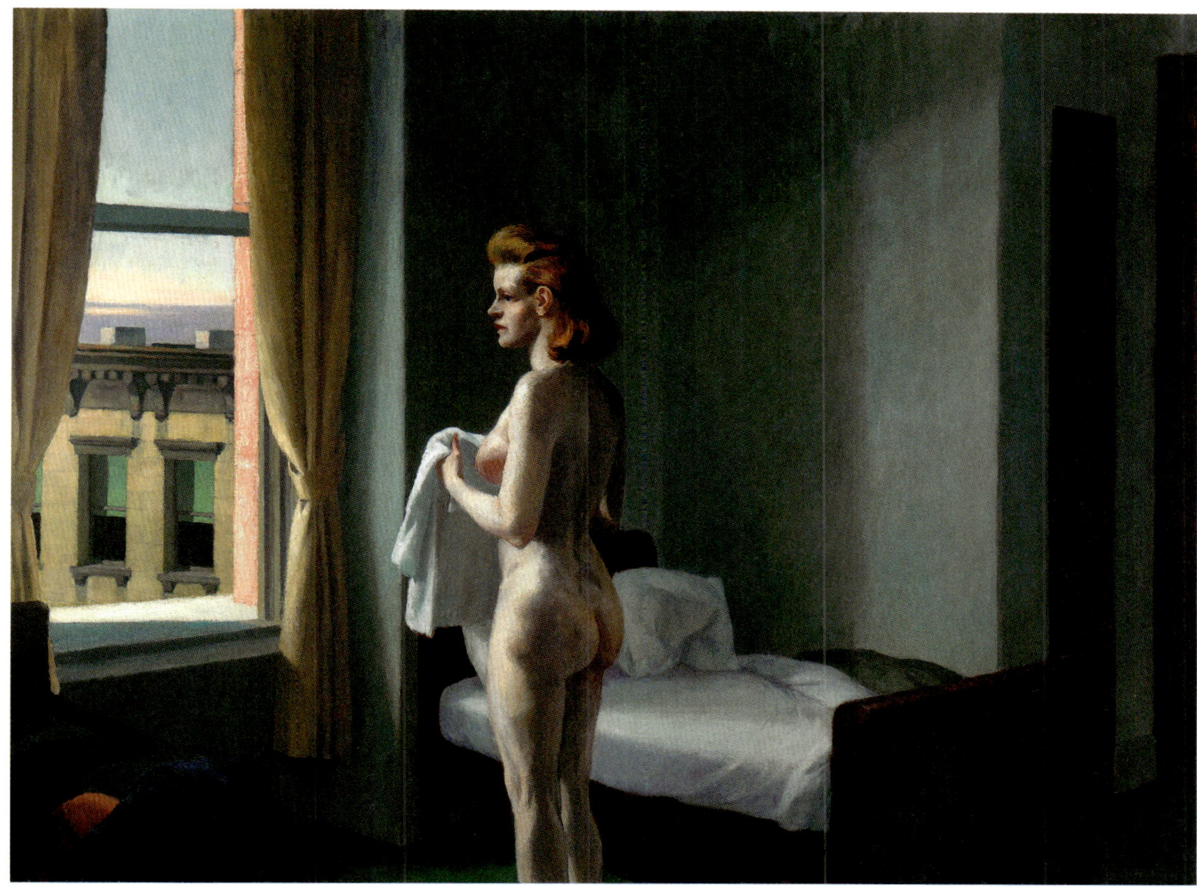

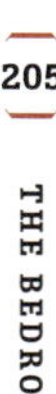

down throughout the delineations of flesh. In some places, daubs of high-keyed acrid green echo the greenish light on the floor. Hopper is sometimes described as an awkward painter (most famously by Clement Greenberg),[4] as if he somehow lacked or was not always capable of deploying his considerable technical skill. But this assumes, quite erroneously, that figures and spaces in Hopper's paintings that appear awkward were not intended by him to be such. For an artist who showed technical gifts early, excelled in art school, and painstakingly considered every stroke of paint he put to canvas,[5] it is misguided to think that irregularities of space or slightly off-looking bodies are unintentional rather than expressive. *A Woman in the Sun* is a case in point. Her strangeness is, in typical Hopper fashion, noticed secondarily but quite readily on close inspection. Although her proper left leg is shifted slightly back from the rest of her body, the upper left side of her torso is pushed forward, giving us a completely artificial view of her left breast, which extends unnaturally, cubistically, forward from her right one so that we can see both. As we know from *Office at Night* (see fig. 282), Hopper employed strange bodily torsions quite purposefully. Here, he also weirdly leaves out her left arm—we can see a hint of shoulder on that side, but once we realize we cannot find more, her strange incompleteness becomes apparent and discomfiting.[6] It is, however, perfectly consistent with the unresolved stories Hopper liked to compose. It is also not out of place in Hopper's nonlinear perspectival constructions, and in a room that, given the distant view of hills outside, seems to float or hover rather than sit firmly on the earth. Again, we notice such things secondarily, but Hopper distorted appearances to impart a disquieting atmosphere or suggest an undercurrent of uncertainty. These distortions create tensions in her body suggesting a lived life and well-inhabited flesh.

As with *Early Sunday Morning* and *Nighthawks*, Hopper seems to have made certain paintings as conceptual pendants, or at least in dialogue with others, even ones painted years apart (see figs. 164, 166). Thus *A Woman in the Sun* and 1944's *Morning in a City* (fig. 361) effectively converse, with compositions that mirror and complement their respective, similar subjects.[7] We can imagine these protagonists looking at one another across time, as if the older figure

360. *A Woman in the Sun*, 1961
Oil on canvas, 40 1/8 × 61 1/4 in. (101.9 × 155.6 cm)
50th Anniversary Gift of Mr. and Mrs. Albert Hackett in honor of Edith and Lloyd Goodrich 84.31

361. *Morning in a City*, 1944
Oil on canvas, 44 5/16 × 59 13/16 in. (112.5 × 152 cm)
Williams College Museum of Art, Williamstown, Massachusetts; bequest of Lawrence H. Bloedel, Class of 1923 77.9.7

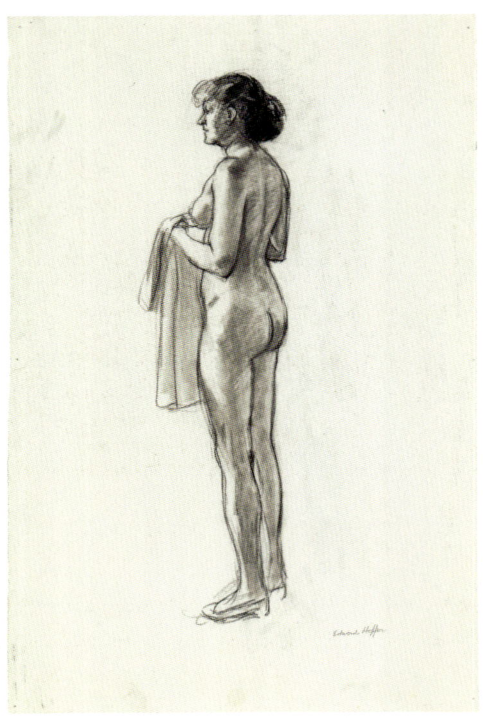

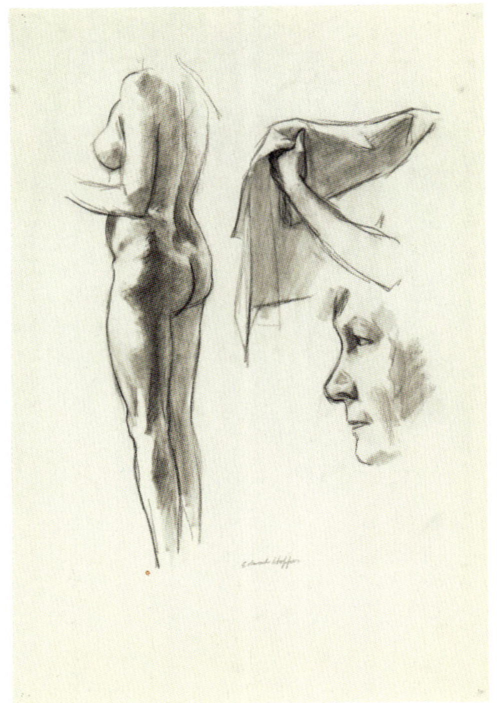

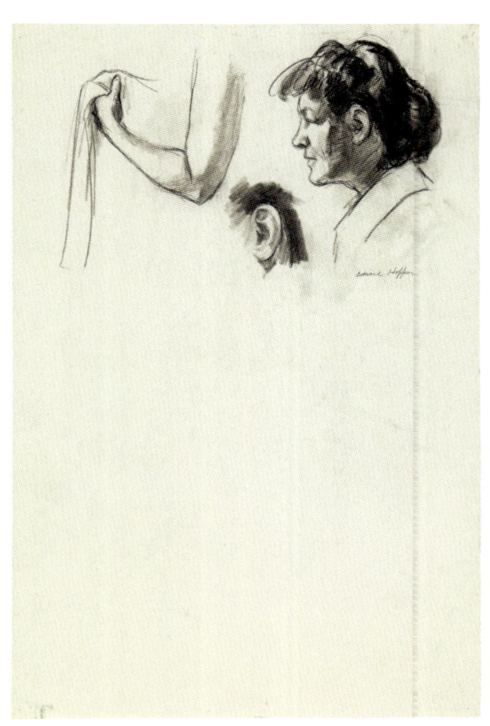

remembers her youth, or the younger one considers her place in life and her future. Both figures gaze out reflectively from an interior space, and though both look east toward the sunrise (if we believe Jo Hopper's Record Book account of *A Woman in the Sun*),[8] in the paintings themselves they look in different directions—one is tempted to say "toward" one another. Read in this way, the edge of the curtain in *A Woman in the Sun* even seems to continue the curtain cut off by the frame on the left side of *Morning in a City*. The oppositions that play out here between youth and age are also a form of continuity showing different stages in life. Though unclothed, the younger woman is turned slightly away from the viewer and projects, aided by her white towel, a purity and modesty compared to her older counterpart, whose cigarette suggests, along with her expression, that she knows quite a bit of life (figs. 362–364). (According to Jo, Hopper called her a "wise tramp," the alternate title for the work given in the Record Books.[9]) Her experienced demeanor is underscored by the suggestively, sexually configured shoes under the bed, which may comment on recent activities above, if not those from further in the past.

The bedroom is, of course, a private space, and Hopper's frequent depictions of female nudes within it usually carry an erotic charge. With empty, unmade beds, and a sense of longing suggested by contemplative window-gazing, these scenes can hint at partners potentially missing from the scene. The viewer provides the final story, but Hopper's parameters usually suggest the absence or recent presence of a lover or companion. In two paintings made a decade apart, *Summer in the City* in 1949 (fig. 365) and *Excursion into Philosophy* in 1959 (fig. 366), he explored the dynamics of couples explicitly.[10] Though different in size, they also function very well as companion pieces. The compositions mirror each other in major ways, from the light streaming in from the windows to the disposition of the adjacent beds nestled into corners. One is a city setting, one rural (as with *Morning in a City* and *A Woman in the Sun*). A man and woman inhabit a single bed in each, arrayed similarly but with reversed roles. In *Summer in the City*, the man lies face down, apparently nude, his head buried in the pillow, while his female companion sits next to him in a pink shift, looking unhappy. With *Excursion into Philosophy*'s ironic title, Hopper allowed for an injection of humor into a similar setup. Here, the woman lies on her side, her bottom half left provocatively exposed next to the book her companion has apparently put down for a moment. In both paintings, the couples are disengaged from one another despite sharing a bed. Whether the disconnection is pre- or post-coital or neither is not clear, but it becomes the dominant theme in each of these variations.

362. Study for *Morning in a City*, 1944
Fabricated chalk on paper, 22 1/8 × 15 in. (56.2 × 38.1 cm)
Josephine N. Hopper Bequest 70.294

363. Study for *Morning in a City*, 1944
Fabricated chalk on paper, 22 1/16 × 15 1/8 in. (56 × 38.4 cm)
Josephine N. Hopper Bequest 70.345

364. Study for *Morning in a City*, 1944
Fabricated chalk on paper, 22 1/16 × 15 1/16 in. (56 × 38.3 cm)
Josephine N. Hopper Bequest 70.995

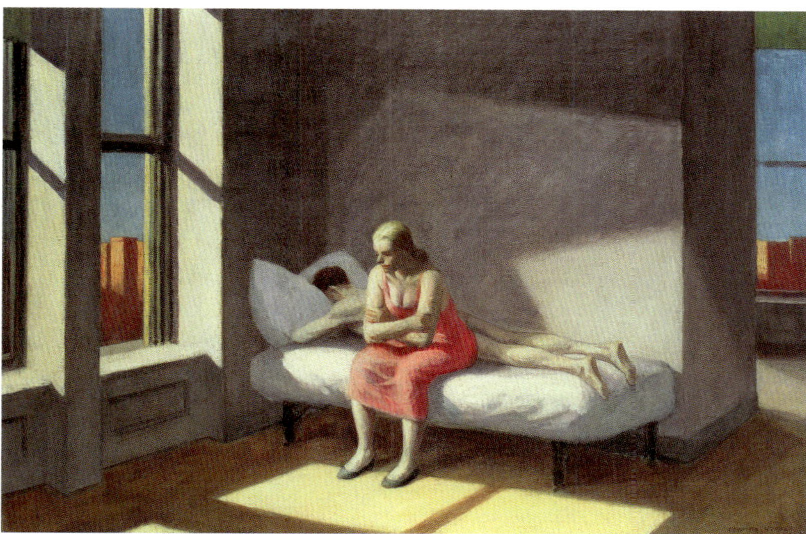

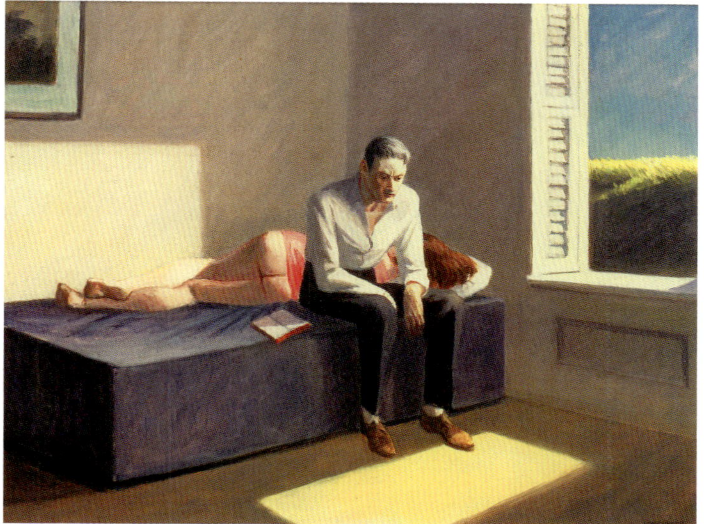

365. *Summer in the City*, 1949
Oil on canvas, 20 × 30 in. (50.8 × 76.2 cm)
Private collection

366. *Excursion into Philosophy*, 1959
Oil on canvas, 30 × 40 in. (76.2 × 101.6 cm)
Private collection

Hopper dealt explicitly with the male-female dynamic in *Summer in the City* and *Excursion into Philosophy*, but he surely thought of it in relation to other paintings as well. The fact that we can read his "bedroom" theme as a series says something important about Hopper's temperament in general. The long gestational period he needed to produce an individual painting applies as well over the course of his long career. For here is a subject on which he ruminated for decades—one could even say over the course of his entire life—ending with *A Woman in the Sun* and, finally, in 1963, *Sun in an Empty Room* (see fig. 385). When understood this way, earlier versions of the subject function like studies for later ones, whatever the medium, and drawings for one painting can even seem interchangeable with those for another. Drawings are thus a crucial form of continuity in Hopper's deep practice, a kind of binding agent that allowed him to revisit and reexamine ideas over time. He surely kept his drawings because he knew he might use them again—which he did, very specifically at times. The study of a hand holding a cigarette on one of the sheets made for *Nighthawks*'s male protagonist (see fig. 209), for example, turns up again in a very different context—the male office worker's tightly formed fingers similarly grasping a cigarette in *Office in a Small City* (see fig. 310). Hopper's lifting of this image straight from a drawing made for another painting more than a decade earlier creates a weird connection between two very different works, but one that developed naturally out of his studio use of drawings. The gorgeously tonal compositional studies for *Morning in a City* (figs. 367–369), almost painterly in their thick gestural marks, could also have served well for *Summer in the City*—and could easily have been the starting point when Hopper decided to revisit the theme. Surely the artist consulted his older studies when considering the subject afresh after years had passed. In them he had tried various positions for the woman, including one with her seated on the bed. In another, she stands but the bed contains marks that could be read as a reclining figure, implying a different variation on the couple theme. Two drawings for *Summer in the City* fit well into this group, with bedsheets and figures merging in the tangle of lines on Hopper's various beds (figs. 370, 371).

The first essay in this catalogue discusses the painting *Rooms by the Sea* as an allegory of sight and the profession of the artist. Hopper's bedrooms often have this as an undercurrent as well, and his depictions of windows and paintings hanging on walls become a crucial part of this subtext. Hopper clearly felt compelled from early on to combine his depictions of the private bedroom space with a self-conscious acknowledgment of his chosen role in the world as a painter. His first substantial bedroom scenes include two small panel paintings and a related graphite drawing done during his student years at the New York School of Art (figs. 372–374). These works deal not with erotics but with the act of looking. In the small grisaille of a half-dressed man and the related drawn study showing a male figure reading on a bed (see figs. 372, 373), he made the bedroom a place of absorptive, personal activity. In the painting of his bedroom in Nyack, New York (see fig. 374), he incorporated a portrait on the wall gazing back at us over the bed. In fact, it is one of Hopper's self-portraits (now in the Whitney's collection[11]), acknowledging us as spectator and the artist as maker of the piece: painting as a mirror of the

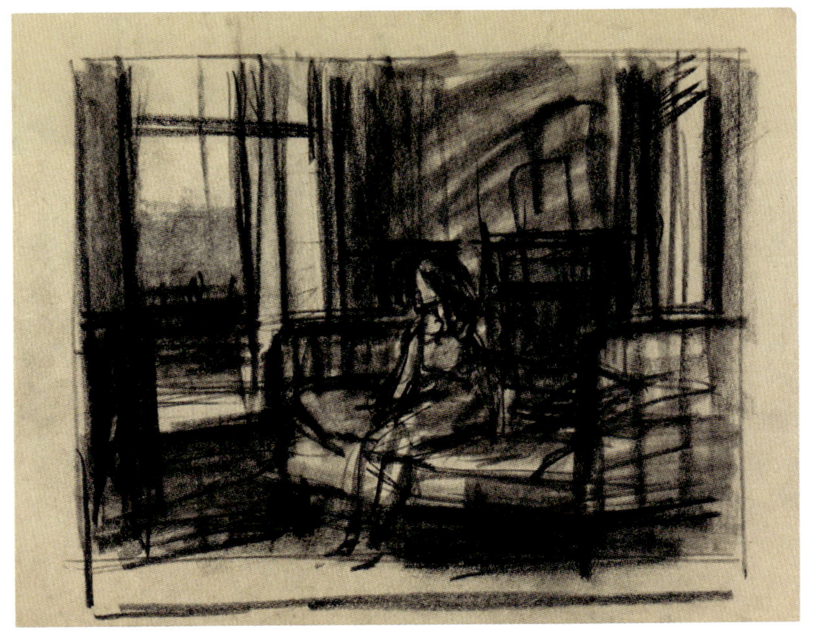

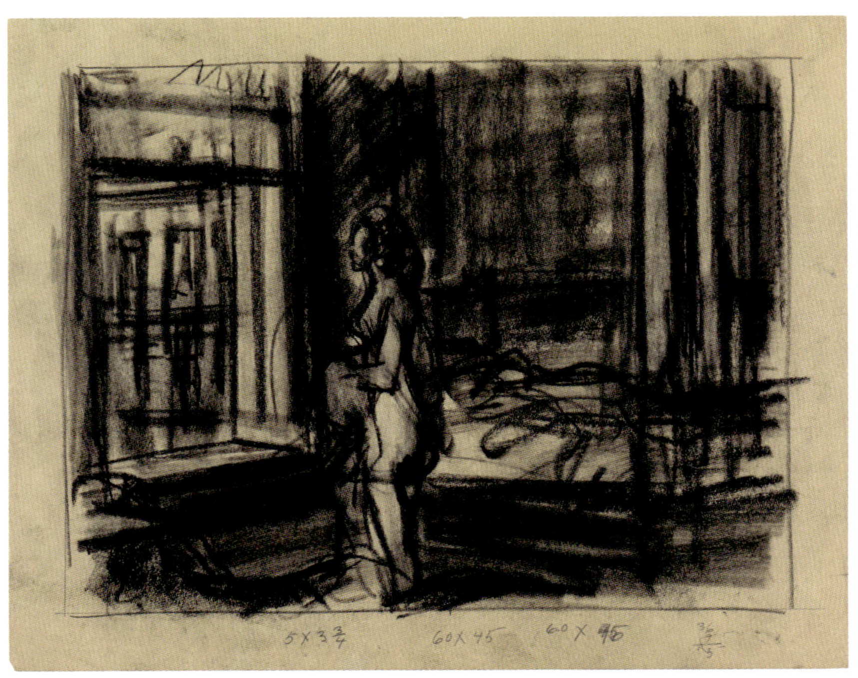
5 X 3 3/4
60 X 45
60 X 45

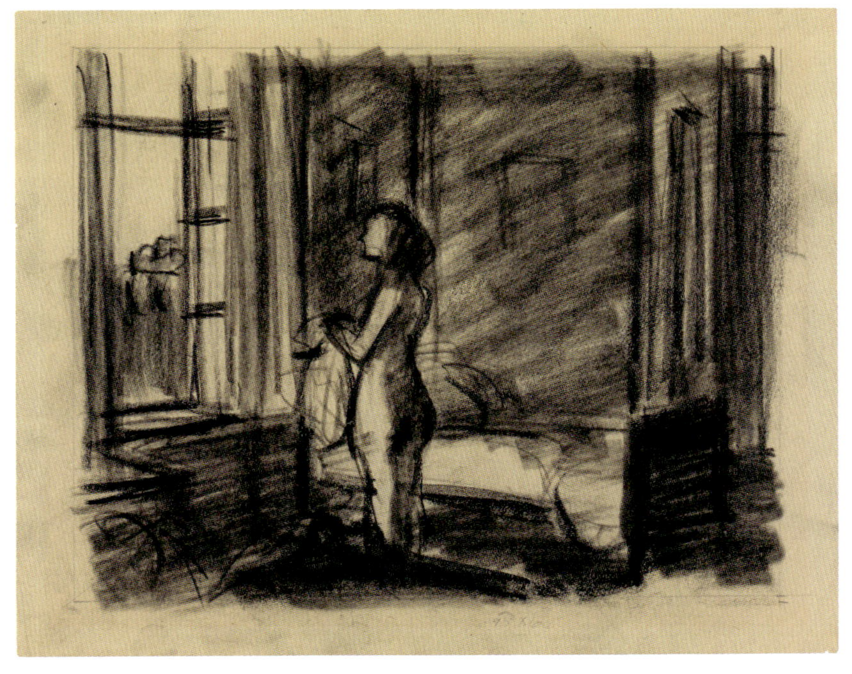

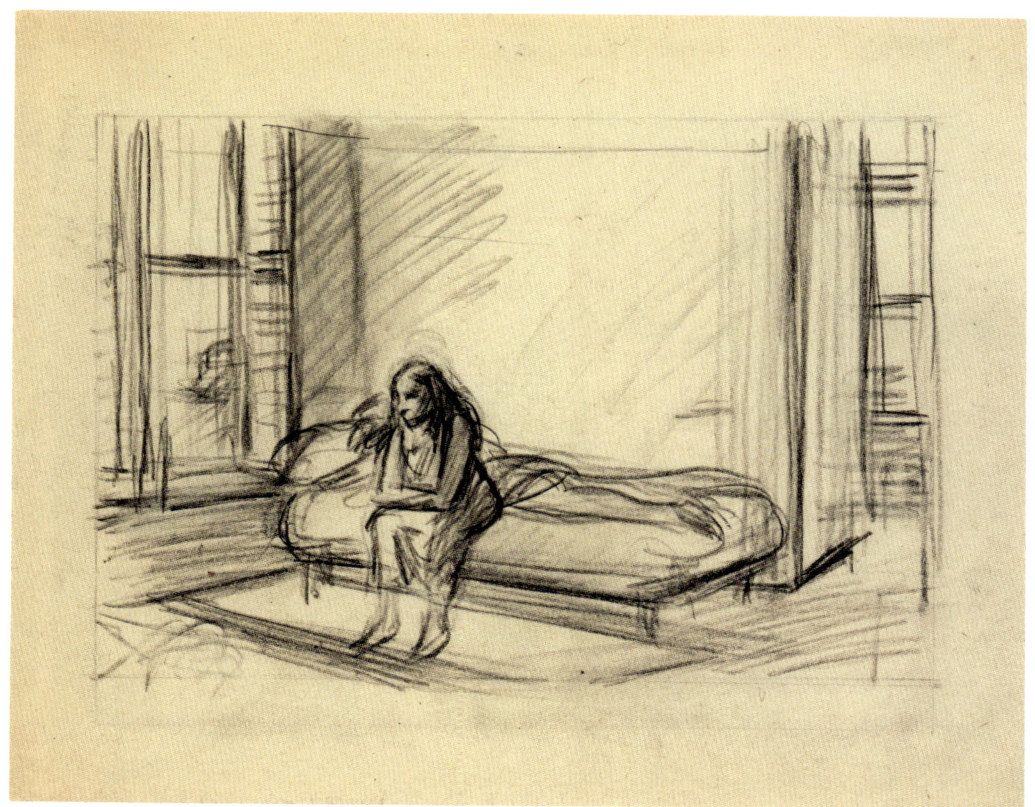

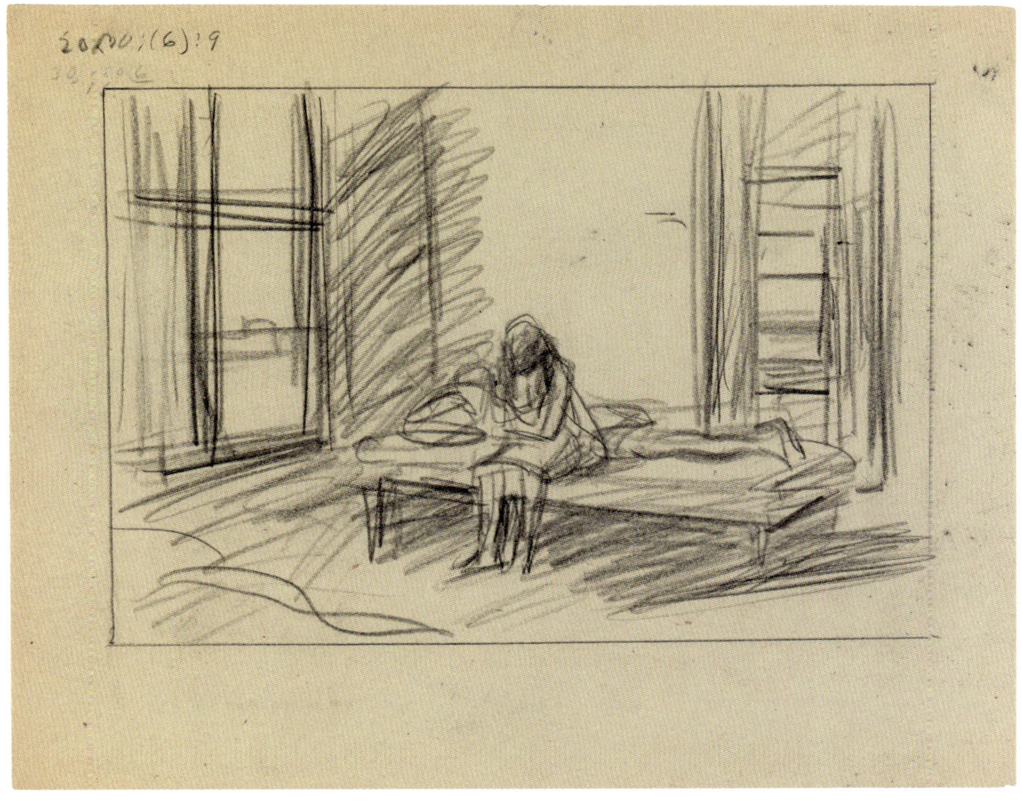

367. Study for *Morning in a City*, 1944
Fabricated chalk and graphite pencil on paper,
8½ × 11 in. (21.6 × 27.9 cm)
Josephine N. Hopper Bequest 70.205

368. Study for *Morning in a City*, 1944
Fabricated chalk and graphite pencil on paper,
8½ × 11 in. (21.6 × 27.9 cm)
Josephine N. Hopper Bequest 70.206

369. Study for *Morning in a City*, 1944
Fabricated chalk and graphite pencil on paper,
8½ × 10 15/16 in. (21.6 × 27.8 cm)
Josephine N. Hopper Bequest 70.207

370. Study for *Summer in the City*, 1949
Fabricated chalk and graphite pencil on paper,
8½ × 11 in. (21.6 × 27.9 cm)
Josephine N. Hopper Bequest 70.268

371. Study for *Summer in the City*, 1949
Fabricated chalk on paper, 8½ × 11 in. (21.6 × 27.9 cm)
Josephine N. Hopper Bequest 70.269

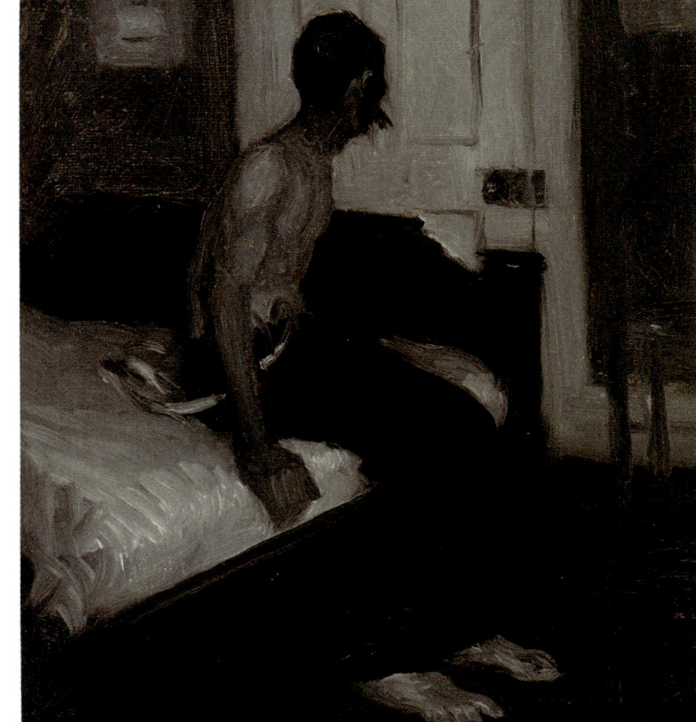

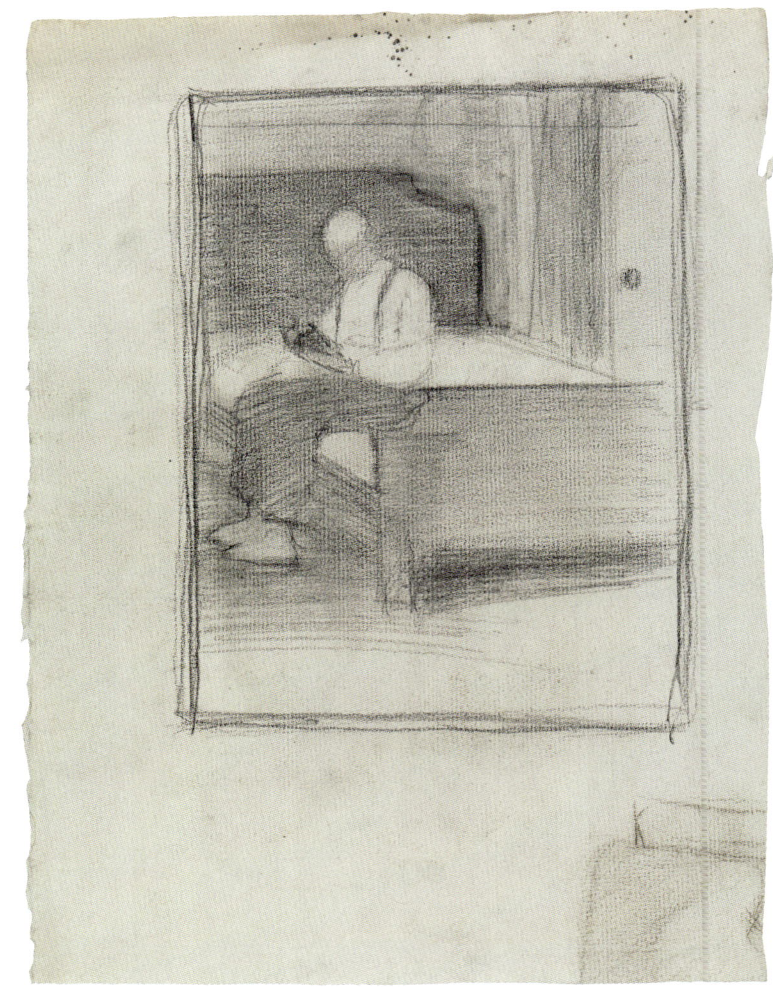

372. *Man Seated on Bed*, 1905–06
Oil on canvas mounted on board, 11 ¼ × 9 ¼ in.
(28.6 × 23.5 cm)
Josephine N. Hopper Bequest 70.1424

373. *Man Seated on Bed Reading* (recto), 1900–06
Graphite pencil on paper, 12 ¹⁄₁₆ × 9 ⅜ in. (30.6 × 23.8 cm)
Josephine N. Hopper Bequest 70.1560.44a–b

374. *The Artist's Bedroom, Nyack*, 1905–06
Oil on board, 15 ⅛ × 11 ⅛ in. (38.4 × 28.3 cm)
Josephine N. Hopper Bequest 70.1412

375. *Summer Interior*, 1909
Oil on canvas, 24 ¼ × 29 ³⁄₁₆ in. (61.6 × 74.1 cm)
Josephine N. Hopper Bequest 70.1197

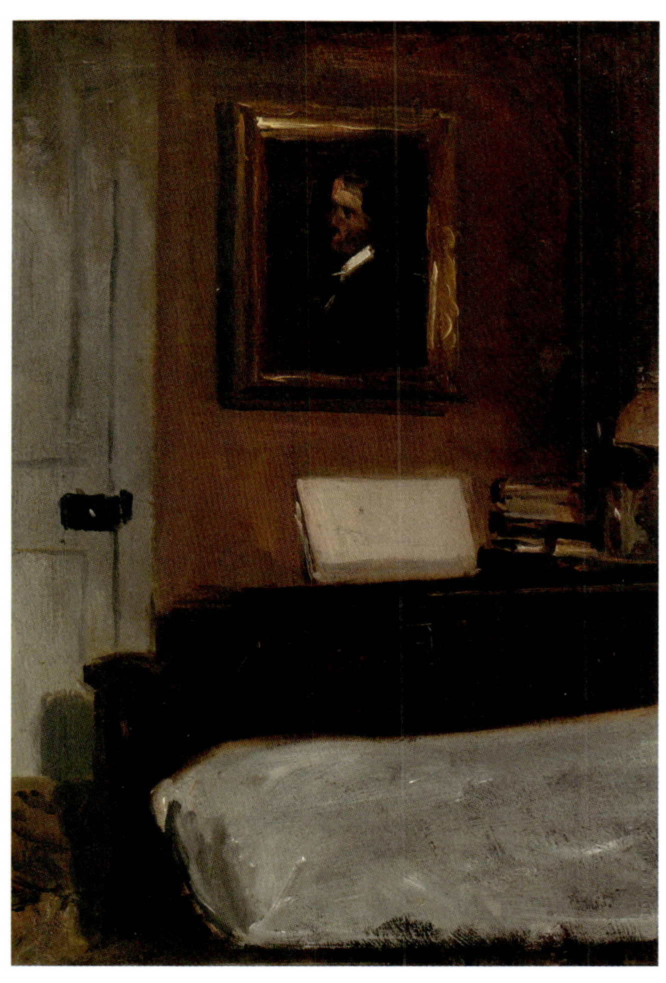

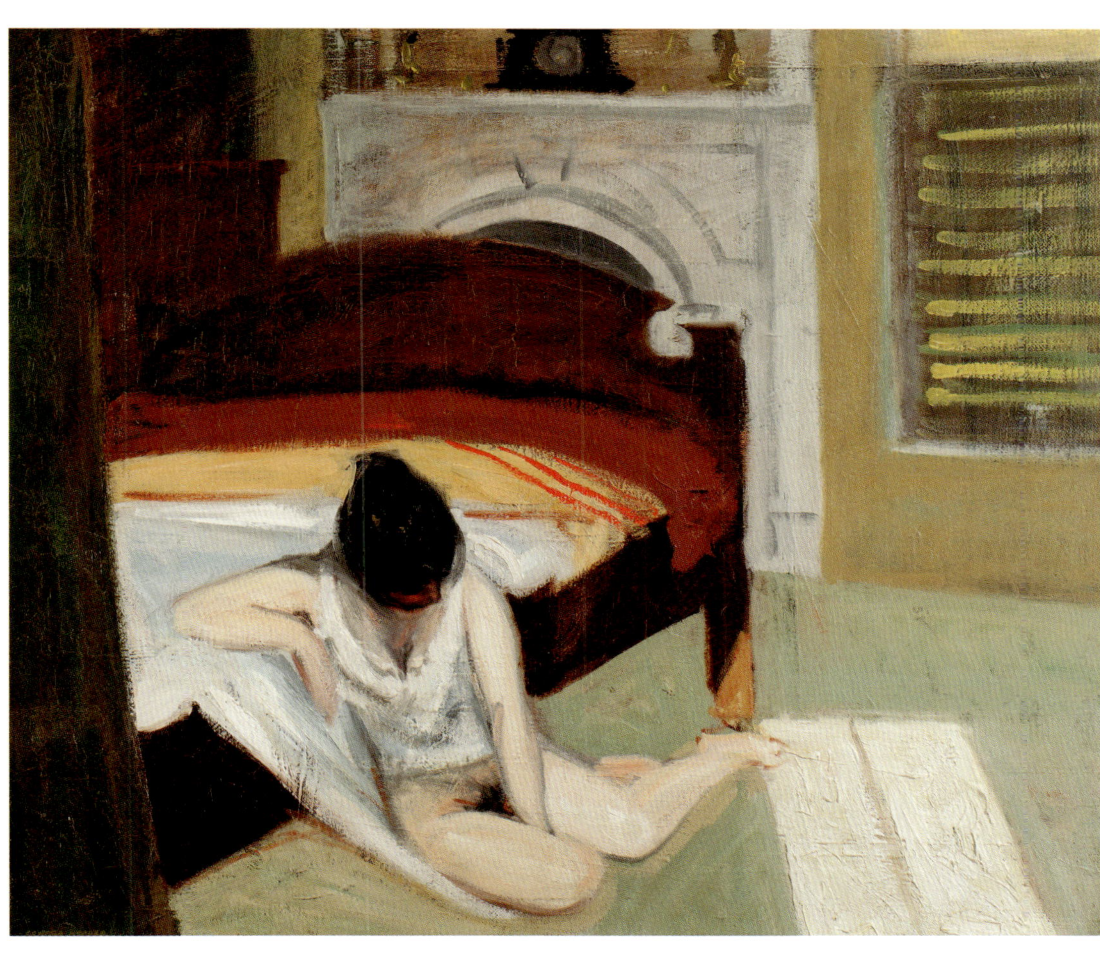

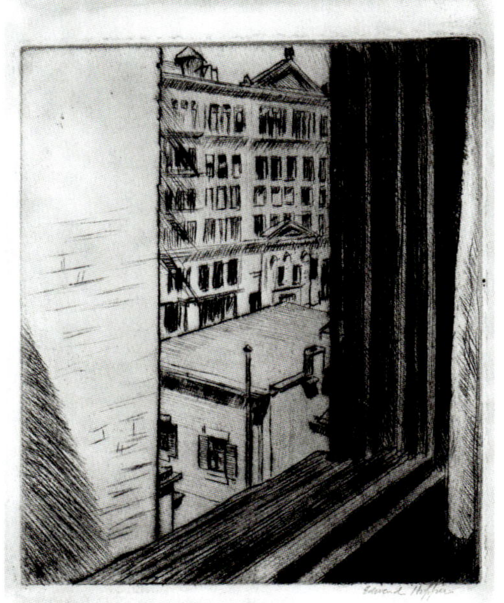

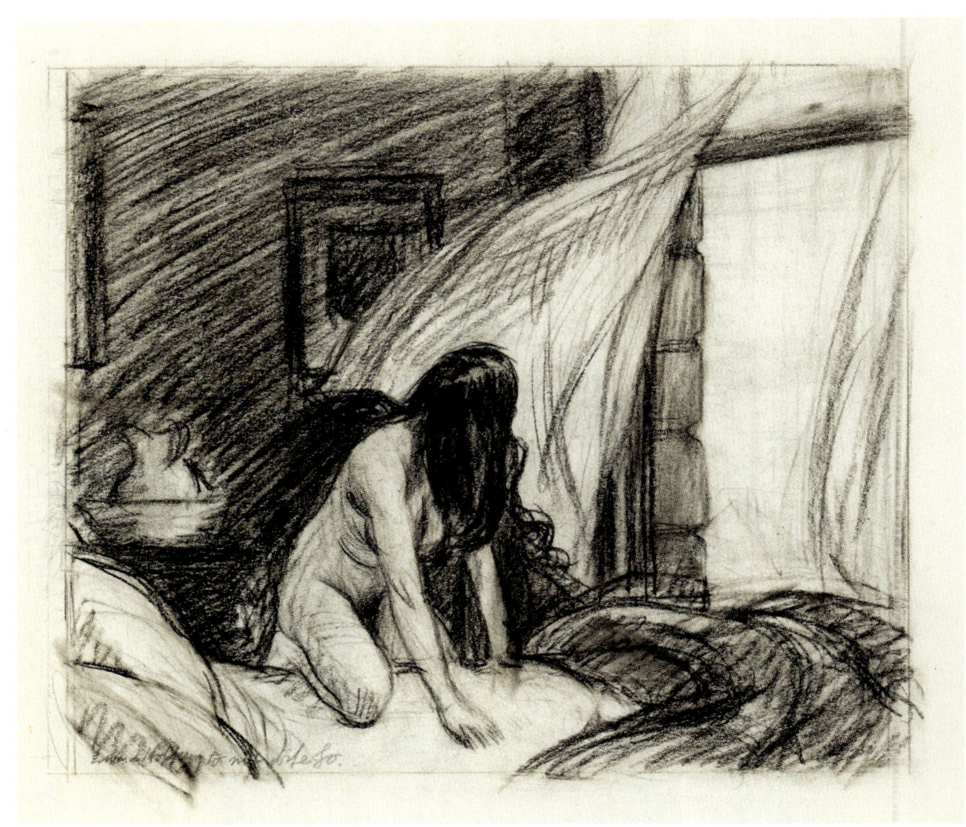

self and the world we inhabit. The spectator is implicated in a more uneasy way in one of the artist's first mature paintings, and one of the most charged and disturbing images of his career, *Summer Interior* (fig. 375).[12] Here, a green curtain creates a diagonal at left, framing the view and placing us in an uncertain status, either in or out of the room, but seemingly standing above the half-nude, strangely positioned woman on the floor. The thickly painted patch of light acknowledges an unseen window behind us, and we are thus incorporated into the space itself. The window as a boundary and threshold between outside and inside comes into play significantly here.

From My Window (fig. 376) and a group of etchings and drawings from the 1910s and early 1920s more explicitly examines the window as a boundary between private space and the world beyond. The artist's best-known rendering from this period is *Evening Wind*, an etching for which he made a complete study in black chalk (fig. 377). Two small, intimate explorations of this theme for unrealized prints give much prominence to the window itself, letting it frame the female nude, who physically inhabits its boundary between the bedroom and the city spaces beyond (figs. 378, 379). By making this boundary so prominent, the artist effectively equates interior and exterior spaces, solving a formal and conceptual problem he articulated much later as being a concern.[13] In *Evening Wind* and *The Open Window*, a small, rare etched version of a similar scene (fig. 380), he rotates the angle of the space, puts the bed prominently in the foreground, and emphasizes the interpenetration and exchange between the woman inside and the world outside through her position, her gaze, and the implied tactility of the wind blowing in from outside and caressing her nude form.

Hopper's most balanced integration of "outside and inside at the same time"[14] came much later, with his 1952 canvas *Morning Sun* (fig. 381).[15] The bedroom here becomes an echo and amplification of the woman's head, whose eyes process light in a manner physically analogous to the large window through which the sunlight streams. In three astonishing studies (figs. 382–384), we can see how Hopper developed this concept from very specific life drawings using Jo as a model, to a completely imagined composition. In the first sheet (see fig. 382), her features are recognizable and the artist has included extensive color notations that were

376. *From My Window*, 1915–18
Drypoint; sheet: 10⅜ × 8¾ in. (26.4 × 22.2 cm),
plate: 6⅞ × 5⅞ in. (17.5 × 14.9 cm)
Philadelphia Museum of Art; purchased with the Thomas Skelton Harrison Fund, 1962 1962-19-86

377. Study for *Evening Wind* (recto), 1921
Fabricated chalk on paper, 10⅛ × 13¹⁵⁄₁₆ in. (25.7 × 35.4 cm)
Josephine N. Hopper Bequest 70.343a–b

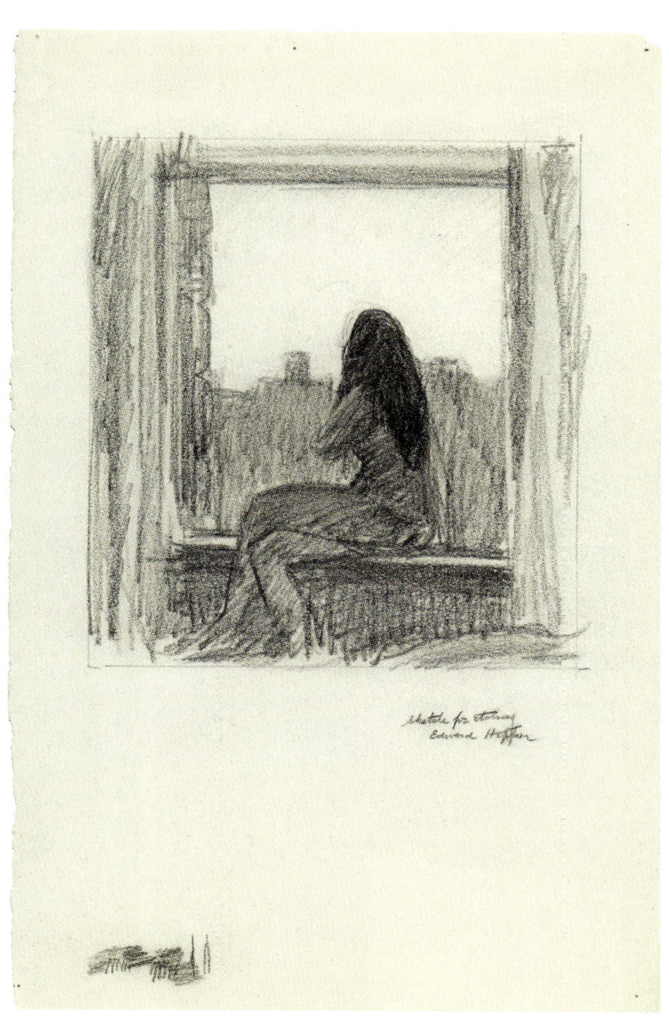

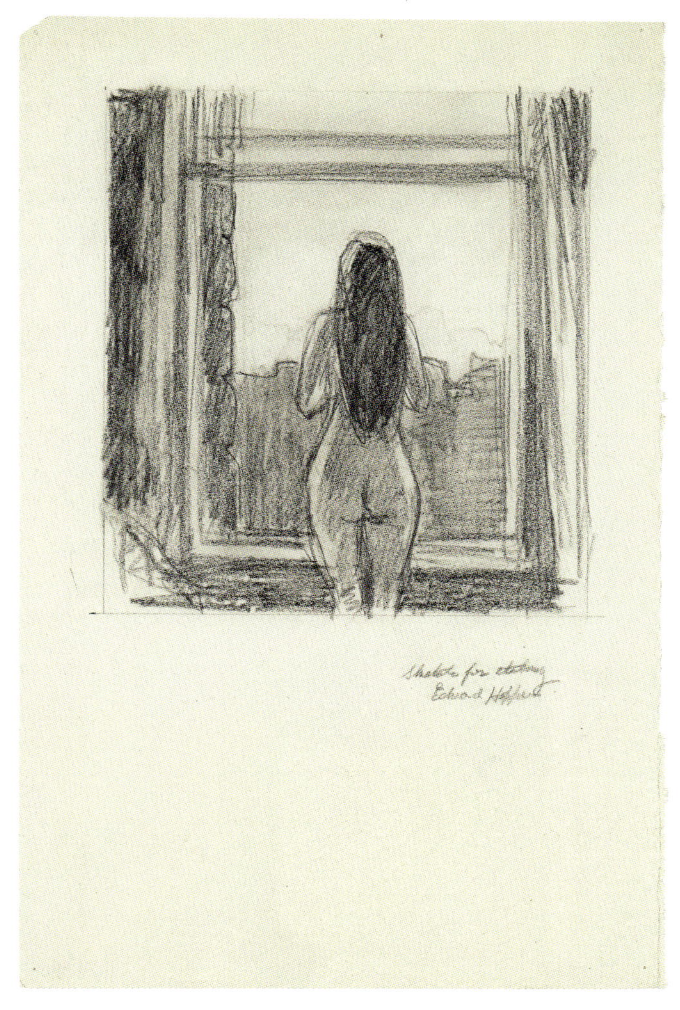

378. *Seated Female Nude by Window (Sketch for Etching)*, 1915–18
Graphite pencil on paper, 14 7/8 × 10 in. (37.8 × 25.4 cm)
Josephine N. Hopper Bequest 70.830

379. *Standing Female Nude by Window (Sketch for Etching)*, 1915–18
Graphite pencil on paper, 14 15/16 × 10 1/16 in. (37.9 × 25.6 cm)
Josephine N. Hopper Bequest 70.831

followed closely in the painting. In the second drawing (see fig. 383), her face becomes mask-like and vacant. The final compositional study (see fig. 384) blots out her features altogether as Hopper explores how to calibrate figure and setting as one. Crucially, he bisects her head with the line of reflected light on the back wall, formally linking the interiority of the mind and self with the interiority of the room and emphasizing and conflating their essential link to the outside world, through the eye/window. Hopper even changed the figure's profile from undulating curves to a plank-like straight edge, save for the nose, thereby rhyming the head's form with both the line of light and the edge of the window.

Morning Sun and *A Woman in the Sun* lead us to Hopper's last, hauntingly purged foray into this theme, *Sun in an Empty Room* (fig. 385). In suites of drawn studies for individual paintings throughout his career, Hopper typically tried multiple elements and combinations, then removed and simplified as he arrived at his final composition on the canvas.[16] This quality plays out similarly in his lifelong variations on the bedroom and in his other sustained thematic series, the "road." At the end of his long career, the artist finally felt at ease removing all but essences—for both *Sun in an Empty Room* and *Road and Trees* of the previous year (see fig. 351) provide as little as possible while remaining crucially linked to long-explored, thematically related ideas. By taking out so much, Hopper was finally able to simply "paint sunlight on the side of a house,"[17] and thereby to answer a question he'd considered decades earlier, while still a student: "When we were at school, du Bois and Rockwell Kent and others debated what a room looked like when there was nobody to see it, nobody looking in even.... I'd done so much with the figure I decided to leave the figure out."[18] The only figure remaining for *Sun in an Empty Room* is the spectator, left to consider Hopper's painting, alone in the act of looking.

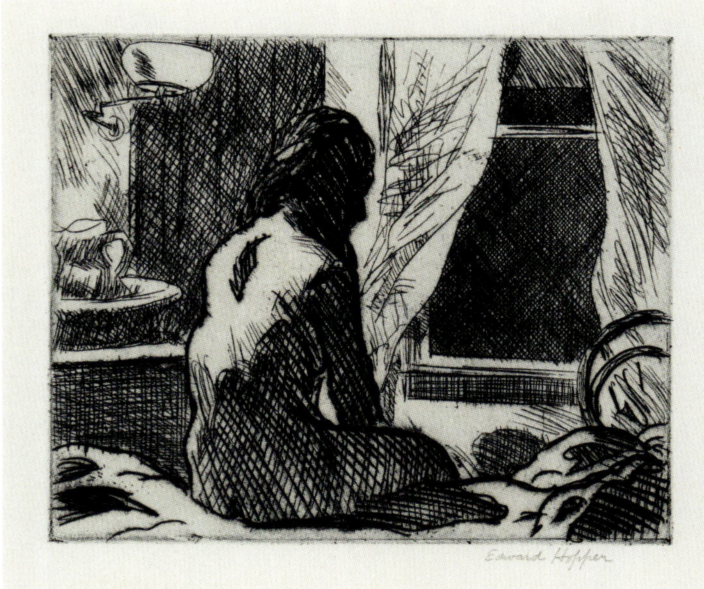

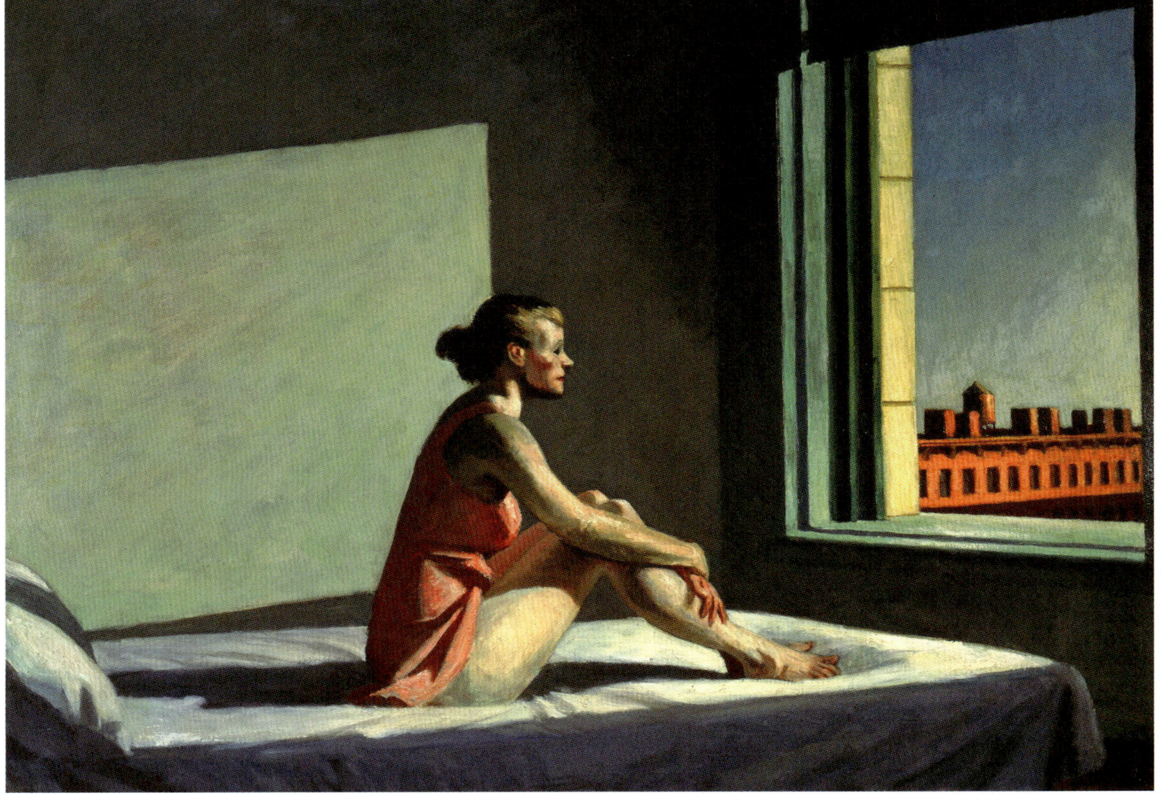

380. *The Open Window*, 1918–19
Etching; sheet: 9 1/4 × 10 1/2 in. (23.5 × 26.7 cm),
plate: 3 15/16 × 4 7/8 in. (10 × 12.4 cm)
Purchase, with funds from Brooke Garber Neidich,
Beth Rudin DeWoody, Laurie Tisch, and Joanne Leonhardt
Cassullo 2000.118

381. *Morning Sun*, 1952
Oil on canvas, 28 1/8 × 40 1/8 in. (71.4 × 101.9 cm)
Columbus Museum of Art; Howald Fund
Purchase 1954.031

382. Study for *Morning Sun*, 1952
Fabricated chalk and graphite pencil on paper,
12 1/16 × 18 15/16 in. (30.6 × 48.1 cm)
Josephine N. Hopper Bequest 70.291

383. Study for *Morning Sun*, 1952
Fabricated chalk on paper, 11 15/16 × 18 15/16 in.
(30.3 × 48.1 cm)
Josephine N. Hopper Bequest 70.290

384. Study for *Morning Sun*, 1952
Fabricated chalk on paper, 12 × 19 in. (30.5 × 48.3 cm)
Josephine N. Hopper Bequest 70.244

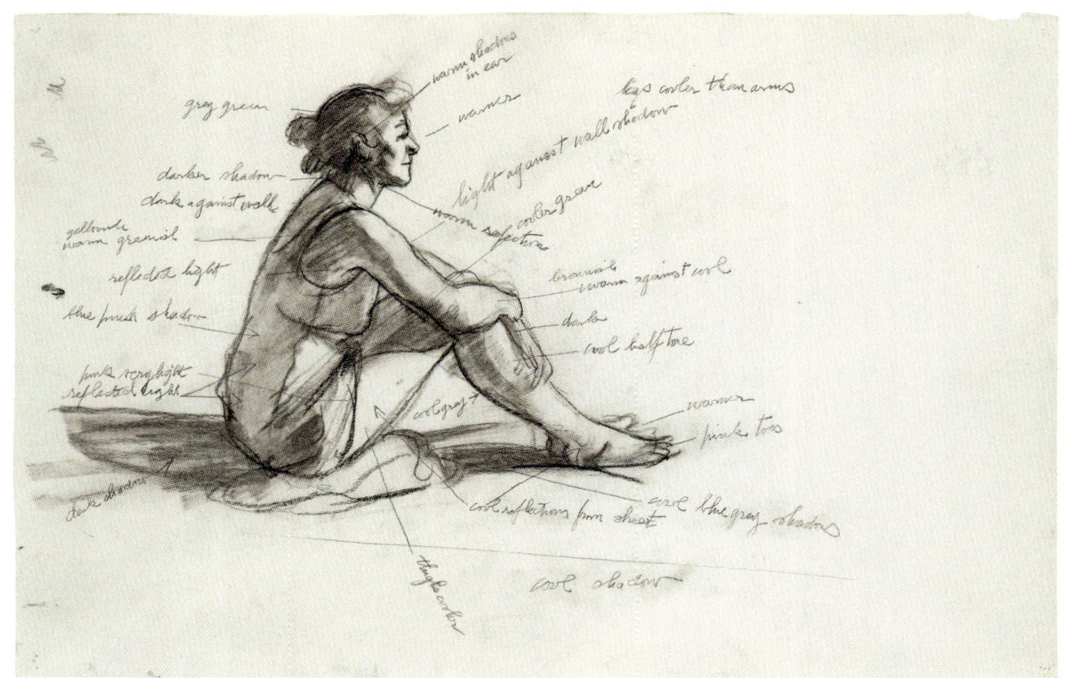
warm shadows in ear
gray green
warmer
legs cooler than arms
light against wall shadow
darker shadow
dark against wall
warm reflection
reflected light
brownish
warm against cool
dark
cool half tone
pink very light
reflected light
cool gray
warmer
pink toes
dark shadow
cool reflections from sheet
cool blue gray shadows
thigh color
cool shadow

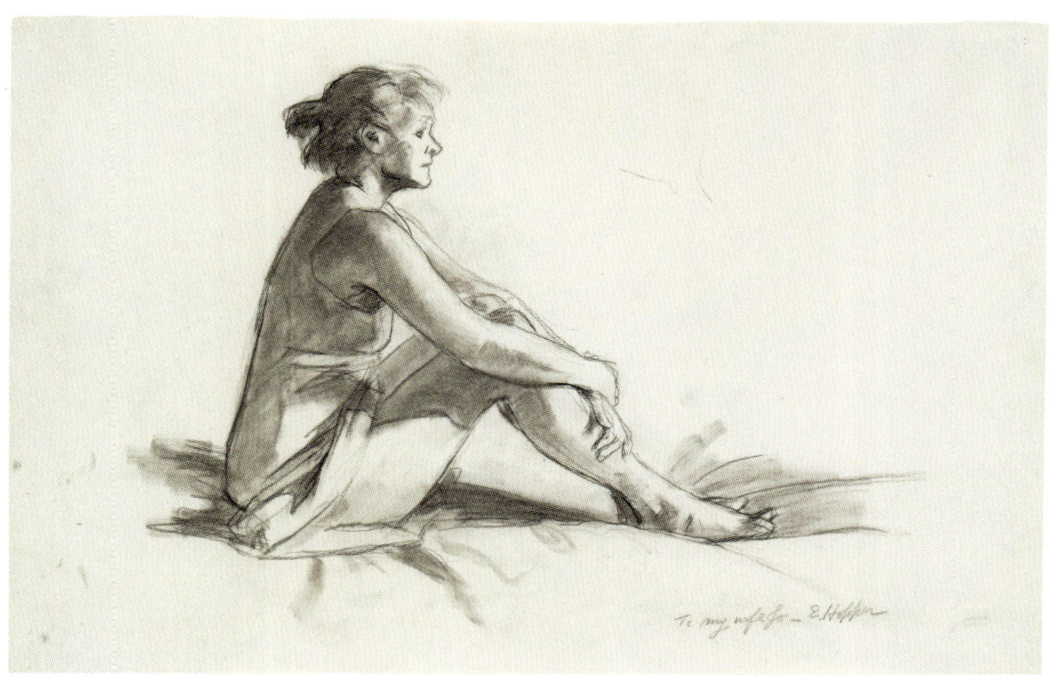
To my wife Jo — E. Hopper

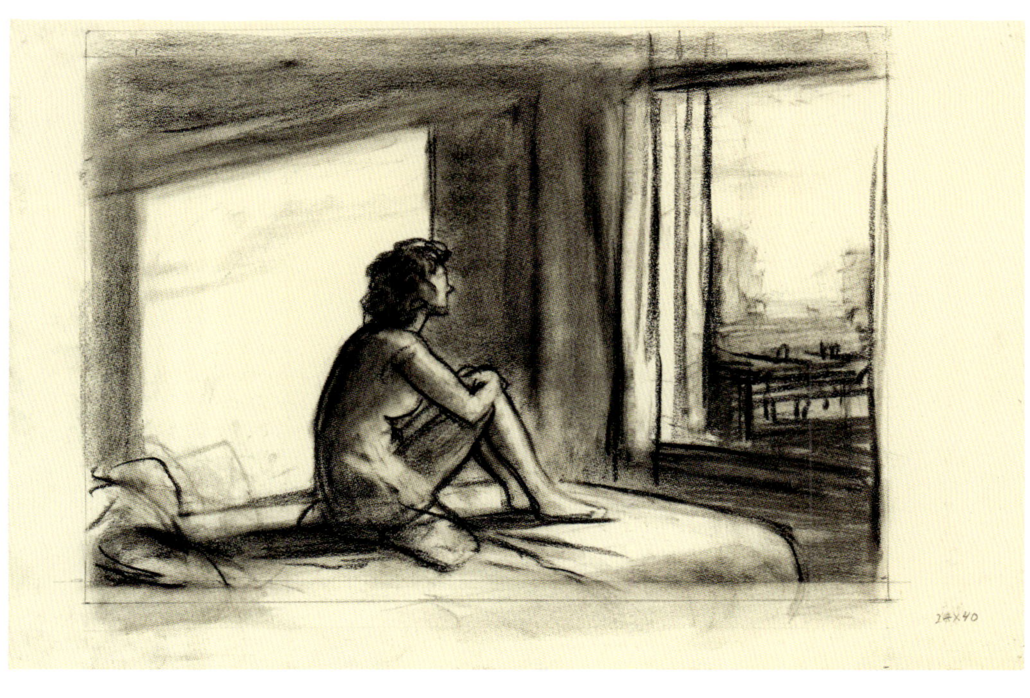

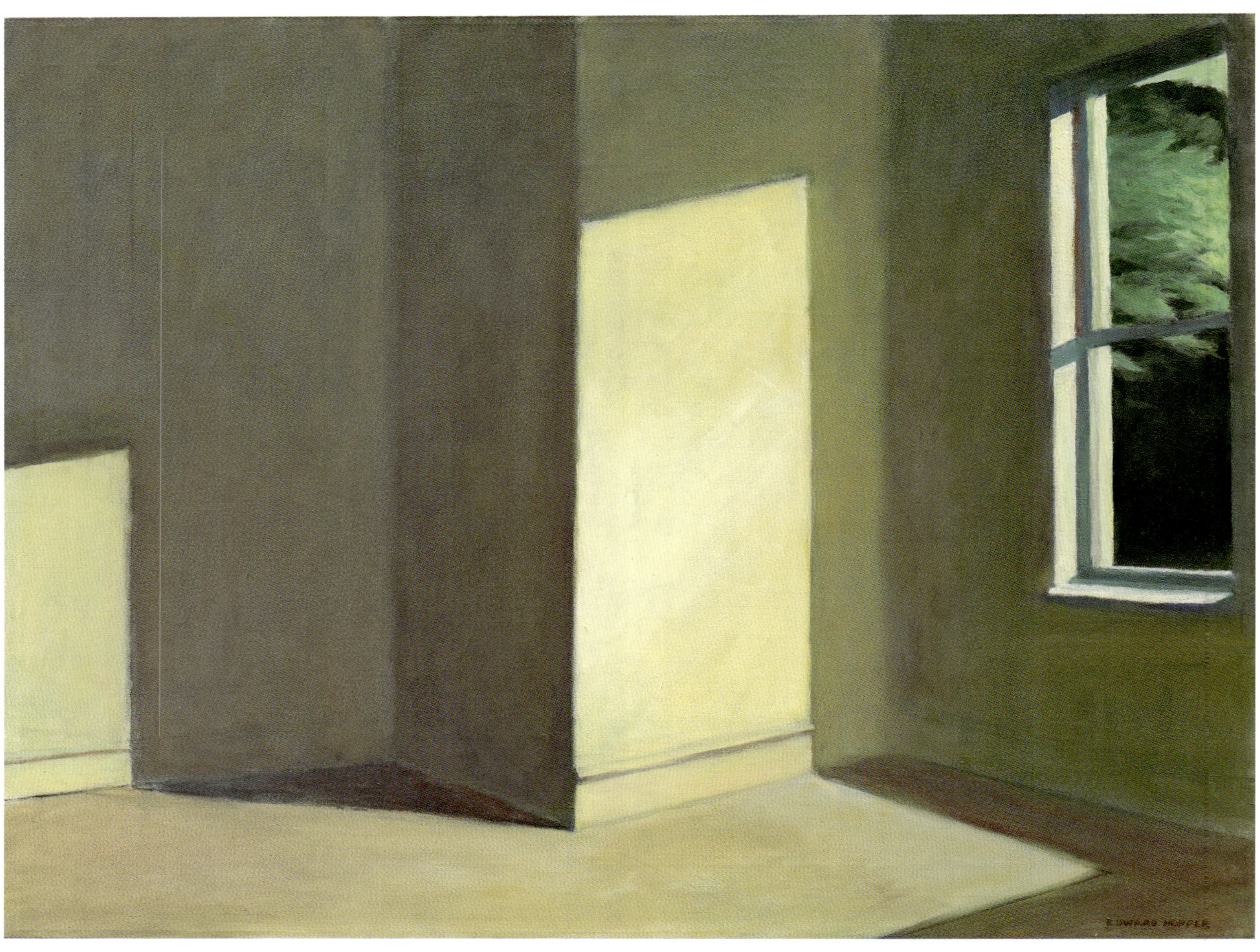

385. *Sun in an Empty Room*, 1963
Oil on canvas, 28 ¾ × 39 ½ in. (73 × 100.3 cm)
Private collection

NOTES

1 "Edward Hopper Objects," *Art of Today* 6 (February 1935): 11, cited in Gail Levin, *Edward Hopper: An Intimate Biography* (New York: Rizzoli, 2007), 266.
2 See Edward Hopper to Charles H. Sawyer, October 19, 1939, Archives of the Addison Gallery of American Art, Phillips Academy, Andover, Massachusetts.
3 On *A Woman in the Sun*, see Gail Levin, *Edward Hopper: A Catalogue Raisonné*, vol. 3, *Oils* (New York: Whitney Museum of American Art in association with W. W. Norton, 1995), 368; Levin, *Edward Hopper: An Intimate Biography*, 549–50.
4 "Hopper simply happens to be a bad painter. But if he were a better painter, he would, most likely, not be so superior an artist." Clement Greenberg, "Review of the Whitney Annual," *The Nation*, December 28, 1946, reprinted in *Clement Greenberg: The Collected Essays and Criticism*, vol. 2, *Arrogant Purpose*, ed. John O'Brian (Chicago: University of Chicago Press, 1986), 118.
5 "He said he works a long time on his oils; paints and scrapes and re-paints." Lloyd Goodrich, "Notes of Conversation with Hopper" (typescript, April 20, 1946), 4, Edward and Josephine Hopper Research Collection, 4.044, Whitney Museum of American Art Archives, New York.
6 I was alerted to this quality of the painting by the artist Richard Prince.
7 On *Morning in a City*, see Levin, *Edward Hopper: A Catalogue Raisonné*, 3:300; Levin, *Edward Hopper: An Intimate Biography*, 368; Carol Troyen, "Hopper's Women," in Troyen et al., *Edward Hopper*, exh. cat. (Boston: Museum of Fine Arts, 2007), 178–82.
8 Edward Hopper Record Book III, 75. For a facsimile of this entry, see Deborah Lyons, *Edward Hopper: A Journal of His Work* (New York: Whitney Museum of American Art in association with W. W. Norton, 1997), 89.
9 Ibid.
10 On *Summer in the City*, see Levin, *Edward Hopper: A Catalogue Raisonné*, 3:330; Levin, *Edward Hopper: An Intimate Biography*, 418–20; Walter Wells, *Silent Theater: The Art of Edward Hopper* (New York: Phaidon, 2007), 137–39. On *Excursion into Philosophy*, see Levin, *Edward Hopper: A Catalogue Raisonné*, 3:362; Levin, *Edward Hopper: An Intimate Biography*, 523–26; Wells, *Silent Theater*, 134, 136–37, 139.
11 This work, *Self-Portrait*, 1903–06, is accession number 70.1253 in the collection of the Whitney Museum of American Art, New York.
12 On *Summer Interior*, see Levin, *Edward Hopper: A Catalogue Raisonné*, 3:105; Levin, *Edward Hopper: An Intimate Biography*, 80–81; Troyen, "Hopper's Women," 177–78.
13 Brian O'Doherty, "Edward Hopper's Voice," in *American Masters: The Voice and the Myth* (New York: Random House, 1973), 26.
14 Ibid., 26.
15 On *Morning Sun*, see Levin, *Edward Hopper: A Catalogue Raisonné*, 3:340; Levin, *Edward Hopper: An Intimate Biography*, 446.
16 It is relevant to note here that Hopper's drawing for *Sun in an Empty Room*, which he discussed with O'Doherty, included a figure that the artist removed. See O'Doherty, "Hopper's Voice," 26. For the drawing, see Peter Schjeldahl, *Edward Hopper: Light Years*, exh. cat. (New York: Hirschl & Adler Galleries, 1988), 56, 58.
17 Hopper quoted in Lloyd Goodrich, *Edward Hopper: Retrospective Exhibition*, exh. cat. (New York: Whitney Museum of American Art, 1950), 6.
18 O'Doherty, "Hopper's Voice," 26.

Biographical Note

KIMIA SHAHI

Edward Hopper was born on July 22, 1882, into a middle-class family in Nyack, New York, a small town on the Hudson River just north of Manhattan. Artistically inclined from a young age, in 1899 he began to train as a commercial artist at the New York School of Illustrating. The following year, Hopper enrolled in the more prestigious New York School of Art, also known as the Chase School after its founder, the celebrated American painter William Merritt Chase. Changing his focus from illustration to painting, Hopper studied under Chase, as well as Kenneth Hayes Miller and Robert Henri, leader of the Ashcan School, a group of artists known for their realistic depictions of contemporary urban life. Working alongside classmates such as Guy Pène du Bois, Rockwell Kent, Patrick Henry Bruce, and George Bellows, Hopper excelled at life drawing; during his time as a student, he won prizes and scholarships and was given the opportunity to teach.

From 1906 to 1910, Hopper made three trips to Europe, his only travel overseas. His two extended stays in Paris—October 1906 through June 1907, and March to August of 1909—were formative for the young artist, allowing him to absorb in depth a culture that fascinated him. Hopper explored the city widely, producing paintings and drawings *en plein air* that constitute an important early body of work. Back in New York, Hopper supported himself as a freelance commercial illustrator while continuing to paint. He participated in his first exhibition in March 1908, showing with a group of Henri's former students; a few years later he sold his first painting out of the seminal 1913 Armory Show. That same year, Hopper moved to the top floor of 3 Washington Square North, which would remain his primary studio and residence for the rest of his life. By then, he had also begun to spend his summers visiting coastal towns in Maine and Massachusetts popular with other artists and making paintings and oil sketches that reflect his close observation of the natural environment.

Hopper took up etching in 1915 and earned recognition with prints that developed many of the themes and compositional strategies he would come to employ in his mature practice as a painter. He had his first one-man exhibition in 1920 at the Whitney Studio Club, but commercial success remained elusive until 1924, when dealer Frank Rehn granted Hopper his first solo gallery exhibition, from which a large group of watercolors was sold. The Rehn Gallery would represent the artist for the rest of his life. On July 9, 1924, Hopper married Josephine "Jo" Verstille Nivison, a fellow painter who had also studied at the New York School of Art. Cultured and well-read, the Hoppers lived modestly but enjoyed attending both theater and films regularly. In 1934, they finished building a house of the artist's design in South Truro, Massachusetts, on Cape Cod, which became their annual summer residence. They also traveled extensively, visiting New England and touring Mexico and the American South and West. Dividing the majority of each year between New York and the Cape, Hopper settled into the rhythm that would characterize the rest of his career. He would make watercolors and drawings "from the fact" around the Cape, during his travels across the country, and (to a lesser extent) in New York, and would work more slowly on easel paintings in oil in the studio on Washington Square and in Truro. His creative output was punctuated by periods of inactivity and long searches for subjects; in later decades Hopper averaged only about two oil paintings per year.

Though critical recognition had come slowly to his work, Hopper had begun to receive greater attention from critics, curators, and the public by the end of the 1920s. He was included in the Museum of Modern Art's second exhibition, *Nineteen Living Americans*, in 1929; the first painting to enter MoMA's permanent collection was Hopper's 1925 canvas *House by the Railroad*. When the Whitney Museum of American Art opened in 1931, Hopper's landmark painting *Early Sunday Morning* (1930) was among its important early acquisitions on display. Hopper also participated in the Whitney's first *Biennial Exhibition of Contemporary American Painting* in 1932. This rise in visibility culminated with the artist's first large-scale retrospective at MoMA, organized in 1933 by the Museum's director Alfred H. Barr, Jr. In the 1930s and 1940s, Hopper's work was increasingly defined in relation to the "American Scene," a term coined to describe

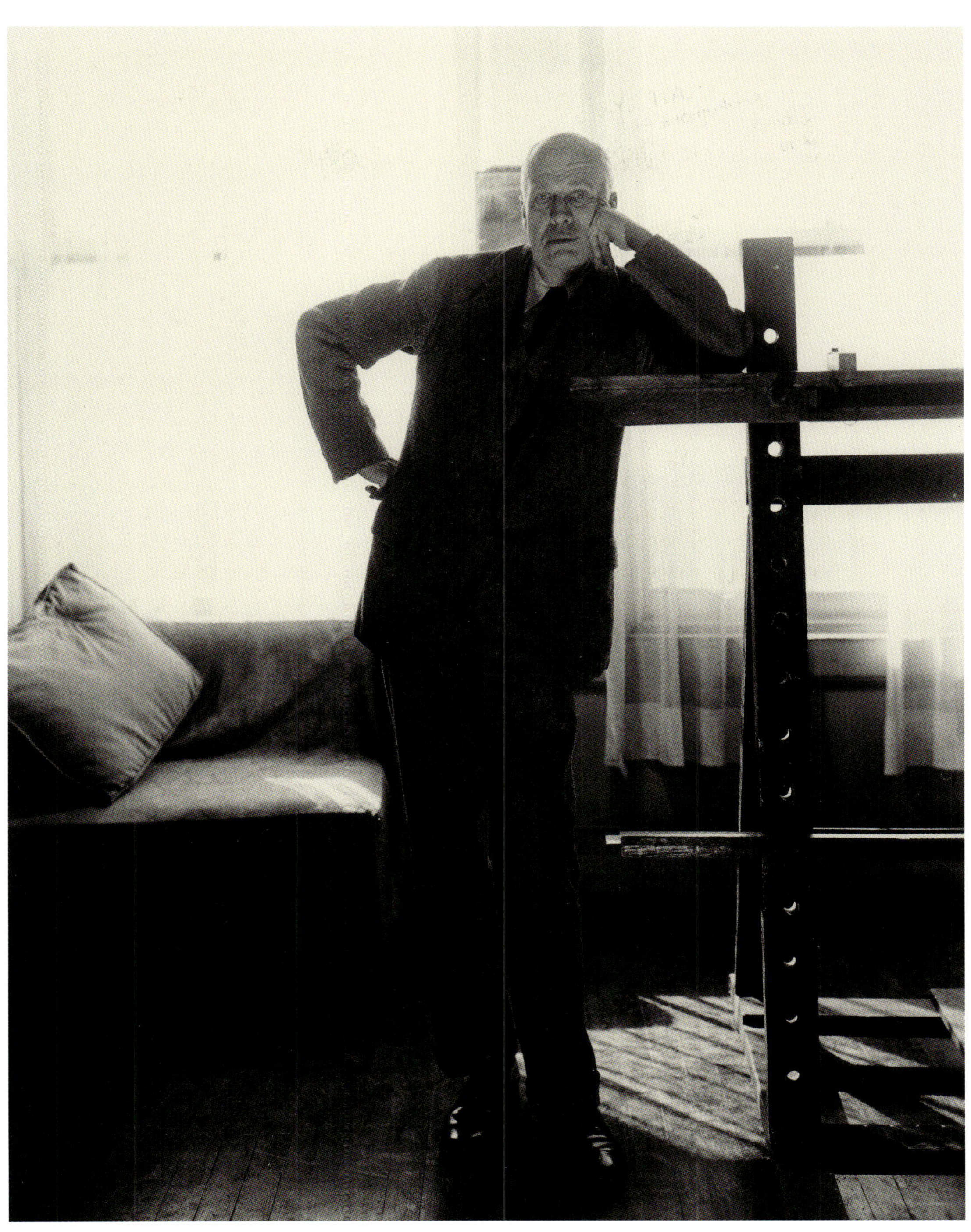

386. George Platt Lynes (1907–1955)
Portrait of Edward Hopper, February 21, 1950
Gelatin silver print, 9 13/16 × 8 1/4 in. (25 × 21 cm)
George Platt Lynes photographs, 1926–1950, Archives of American Art, Smithsonian Institution, Washington, DC; Negative #134-16

the Regionalist or Social Realist subject matter of painters such as Thomas Hart Benton, Grant Wood, and Reginald Marsh. Although Hopper chafed at this characterization, his reputation remained secure as one of the foremost representatives of modern American painting, even as representational painting's critical status declined in favor of abstract art in postwar America. One of the artist's most important advocates during his lifetime was Lloyd Goodrich, a curator at the Whitney who served as the Museum's director from 1958 to 1968. The two had a long and friendly relationship: Goodrich organized two major Hopper retrospectives at the Whitney, in 1950 and 1964, and wrote an authoritative monograph on the artist.

Hopper appeared on the cover of the December 24, 1956, issue of *Time* magazine, with a story that cast him as America's "Silent Witness." Although the artist was notoriously taciturn, he did agree to a small number of interviews, most notably those conducted in the 1960s by Brian O'Doherty, an artist, writer, and critic who befriended Edward and Jo. By the time of Hopper's death on May 15, 1967, at the age of eighty-four, his legacy was firmly cemented. That same year the exhibitions *Edward Hopper* and *Environment U.S.A., 1957–1967* were presented by the United States at the 9th São Paulo Biennial, defining Hopper as a pivotal figure in American art who bridged the divide between the early-twentieth-century realist tradition and newer approaches to representation found in Pop and conceptual art. His artworks conjure a recognizably "Hopperesque" mood and atmosphere that have had a pervasive influence on popular culture, from photography and film to advertising and design, and they endure as icons of the American visual imagination.

Lloyd Goodrich's "Notes of Conversation with Hopper, April 20, 1946"

Lloyd Goodrich (1897–1987) was one of Edward Hopper's most steadfast supporters and an incisive and thoughtful writer about his art. Goodrich began his career as a critic and art historian, and wrote an essay about Hopper early in the artist's career for the March 1927 issue of *The Arts* magazine, where Goodrich served as an editor. As associate director and later as director of the Whitney Museum of American Art, Goodrich collaborated with Hopper on two major retrospectives, in 1950 and 1964. Their long, cordial working relationship, which would extend through several decades, is evident in these notes, reproduced here for the first time, which Goodrich compiled following a series of conversations with Hopper when Goodrich was a research curator at the Museum.

Though continually guarded when speaking about his influences and, to a lesser degree, the meaning of his artworks, Hopper here gives unprecedented insight into his working methods—in particular, the relationship between his subject matter (or what he calls "the fact") and imagination or "improvisation" in his oil paintings. Also evident is the artist's marked doubt about how successfully his artworks communicate his impressions of and reactions to his subjects, a doubt that Goodrich notices and considers carefully in his notes. Many of Hopper's observations and anecdotes found here—such as his stated desire to "paint sunlight on the side of a house"—would figure in Goodrich's later foundational writing on Hopper's work, though without the intimate tone of the artist's voice.

The original typescripts are held in the Edward and Josephine Hopper Research Collection in the archives of the Whitney Museum of American Art's Frances Mulhall Achilles Library, which preserves a wide array of primary materials on Hopper's life and career and his relationship with the Whitney Museum, including an important collection of interview transcripts and statements by the artist.

Lloyd Goodrich. "Notes of Conversation with Hopper." Typescript, April 20, 1946. Series 4: Biographical and Personal Papers, 4.044: Notes: Goodrich on Hopper conversations. Edward and Josephine Hopper Research Collection, Frances Mulhall Achilles Library, Whitney Museum of American Art Archives, New York

NOTES OF CONVERSATION WITH HOPPER

APRIL 20, 1946

Mr. Hopper went over the chronology in the catalogue of the Museum of Modern Art exhibition and said that it was substantially correct. However, he said that he did not abandon oil painting between 1914 and '24. He also said that Martin Lewis was not his teacher in etching, but a friend from whom he learned a great deal about technical methods. He said that Lewis had no influence on him in such matters; that he (Hopper) had already been picturing this type of subject and he was not sure that Lewis had; he thought perhaps that he influenced Lewis.

He said that he went abroad three times. The first time he went in October 1906 and stayed through part of 1907, returning about July 1907. He was abroad about nine months. He spent most of his time in Paris but also went to England, Holland, Germany and Belgium. His second trip was in 1908 or 1909, he is not sure which. He went to France, mostly Paris, and to no other countries. He was there about six months. His third trip was in 1910, for about three or four months altogether. This time he went to France and then to Spain. He has not been abroad since 1910. He has never been to Italy.

His first trip to the west was in 1925 to New Mexico, where he spent the summer (about three or four months) in Santa Fe. He painted quite a few water colors, but no oils. He never went again to New Mexico.

His only other trip to the west was in 1941, by automobile, when he drove out to the West Coast and stayed about three months, visiting Colorado, Utah, the Yosemite, California, driving up the coast to San Francisco, then to Portland, driving back along the Columbia River through Idaho, etc., -about 10,000 miles altogether. He did not do much painting - only about four watercolors, no oils. These were his only two trips to the west. He was in Mexico in the summer of 1943, and is going back to Mexico, driving the whole way in May, 1946.

He said that he studied with Henri and Miller at the Chase school. His feeling for Henri was that he was a brilliant man and very stimulating, but I gathered that he had not learned much technically from Henri. He left the Chase school in 1907. From that time until 1925 he supported himself by commercial work and illustrating, with interruptions such as his trips abroad. In commercial work, he worked in an advertising house, but had an arrangement so that he worked three or four days a week. He said he was good at commercial work, as he could draw the figure, which most commercial artists could not. Later he took up illustration, but never liked it; he said it didn't interest him, that he didn't care about drawing people (grimacing) and posturing. "Maybe I am not very human. What I wanted to do," he said," was to paint sunlight on the side of a house," but he couldn't do that in illustration. He said that all the quality of one's work was lost in reproduction. He said that some men had a real gift for illustration and enjoyed it, but he didn't.

He said that all this time he kept on painting in his free time; he never stopped painting; as people seemed to believe. In the beginning he sent regularly to the National Academy and was rejected each time, so he finally stopped sending. He said that he couldn't get any dealer to take his work; but that he didn't try very hard. He said Rehn was the first dealer to handle him. He went to Kraushaar and Rehn, but Mr. Kraushaar was not interested.

He spoke of Nathanial Pousette-Dart's reference to his being influenced by Burchfield, and about his letter to Pousette-Dart and the latter's saying the same thing over again. He said that recently Pousette-Dart apologized to him. He said he admires Burchfield but that when he (Hopper) was paintings American subjects Burchfield was still a child.

He said that the Whitney Studio Club exhibition about 1919 was his first one-man show. He also had a show of etchings with "Pop" Hart at Sidney Phillips' Gallery shortly after the Whitney show. He also exhibited a few times at the Independents. Also at the Harmony Club on 42nd Street in 1908 - a group show of Henri students, in which he showed some Paris pictures. He said that in this show Bellows made his first reputation.

He said that the first works that he was able to get regularly into exhibitions were his etchings; that juries evidently did not mind him so much in etching as in painting.

He has been going to Truro since about 1930 in the summer.

He has never taught; feels that it takes too much out of an artist. He had one pupil once and he said it exhausted him.

He has refused to join the National Academy. Once they elected him without consulting him. A reporter from a newspaper called up in the middle of the night to give him the news. Mrs. Hopper answered the telephone and said, "You'd better not print that or he will sue you for a million dollars." He commented somewhat bitterly that the Academy rejected him when he needed it and only elected him after he was successful.

I asked him his methods of painting. He told me that practically all his watercolors were painted directly from nature (as he puts it, "from the fact."), with only one or two exceptions. He spends a long time looking for his subjects, but in his watercolors he changes the subjects very little. He seems to feel that he changes them too little, says that his watercolors are too much just portraits of places and things. As to his watercolor method, he makes a pencil drawing first, quite careful though not detailed, but takes most of it out as he paints. He said that watercolor painting was "a series of glazes." When I asked him if he ever used Chinese white, he said emphatically "Absolutely none." He scrapes with a knife to get whites where the surface has been painted. He considers his early watercolors rather thin; he works longer on his later ones. He spoke of one of the Mexican watercolors bought by a collector in Washington; it took him a month to paint it, working for a short time at a certain hour of the day, and interrupted by weather, especially showers.

He does not paint oils on his trips - only watercolors.

He said he works a long time on his oils; paints and scrapes and re-paints. The way he said it, I got the impression that oil is a difficult medium for him, that he has a hard time painting in oil (I remember that when he was painting Morning in a City he told me the great difficulties he was having with it, how he had worked and worked on it, how he felt that he was not getting what he wanted.)

As to his method of painting in oil, he says it varies. In the beginning he used to paint mostly out doors, but has not done so for a number of years. He thinks that the last oil he painted outdoors was <u>Cape Cod Afternoon</u> (1936)owned by the Carnegie Institute. <u>Freight Yard,Gloucester</u> was painted from nature. <u>Gas</u> was not painted from nature; as he puts it, it was "improvised"; there is no such place; he made it up from memories of similar places; though the gas pumps were studied from real ones. <u>Solitude</u> was also improvised, though there were places like it on Cape Cod. He spoke of his last picture, <u>Approaching a City</u>; in it he wanted to express the feeling of coming into a strange city on a train, the the sensations of interest, curiosity, fear. He said it was difficult, because of the changing, moving quality of such images and feelings, and the difficulty of expressing them in a static picture. He said he didn't think he had really succeeded.

He spoke of <u>Rooms for Tourists.</u> This is a portrait of an actual house on Cape Cod, I think at Truro. He says it is just the way the house is. He studied the house a long time, by daylight and at night. Made sketches, some of the whole house, some of architectural details. The picture was painted in his studio, but when he was painting it he used to go almost every night in his car and park near the house and study it. (Frank Rehn told me that the people in the house wondered what it was all about.)

He said he has never found the perfect method, either"from the fact" or "improvised." He said he is"torn between the two." Never satisfied. He says there is no perfect method. That the result is never quite what he wants, never quite the image he has in his mind before he starts to paint. I think his dissatisfaction is sincere and fundamental; it comes out continually in speaking of individual pictures. I got the impression of a real conflict between the inner image and outer reality. He feels that in working "from the fact" he tends to copy too much, to put in all the details, not to "synthesize" enough.

He looks a long time for his subjects - looks and looks and looks. He said this in a sort of humorous despairing way as if the finding of a subject and turning it into a picture was very hard and difficult for him.

Sometimes he makes separate drawings for his oils, but never for his watercolors. Once he used a watercolor in painting an oil, but it didn't work well. He says that in using drawings for paintings he tends too much to copy the drawing. (contrast to Homer's use of watercolors in his paintings.)

He has difficulty remembering color.

He says that abstract painting would never satisfy him; he has to create something relating closely to reality.

He admires Courbet very much; spoke of his "mechanical strength" or some such phrase, meaning the physical force and substance of his work. He seemed to feel that Courbet had this quality more than any other 19th Century painter. He contrasted it with the lack of substance in Cézanne, the papery qualtiy. He admires Homer; spoke particularly of the Winter Coast in the Philadelphia Museum. (I remember he once spoke to me of Eakins' portrait of Falconino, and how wonderful the shoes were, how much character. Also in our landscape exhibition in 1938 he admired particularly the Homer Martin Westchester Hills. He also visited our Hudson River School exhibition quite often and spoke to me particularly about Cole.)

He hates to write. He said that du Bois had asked him to write an article on American realists for the magazine that Golden is bringing out; he (Hopper) wrote one page and has never been able to get any further.

Hopper seems to me a genuinely modest man, rather insecure about his own work, not because of any sense of inferiority but because he knows that he is not realizing his conceptions to the full. This seems to bother him a good deal. Part of his extreme honesty and clear sightedness, his lack of any illusions about things. At the same time he has a considerable awareness of his own worth.

In his New York studio he has a set of carpenter's tools that are really amazing - very complete, particularly tidy and well arranged, really professional.

SELECTED BIBLIOGRAPHY

Writings, Interviews, and Archival Documents

Goodrich, Lloyd. "Notes of Conversation with Hopper." Typescript, April 20, 1946. Series 4: Biographical and Personal Papers, 4.044: Notes: Goodrich on Hopper conversations. Edward and Josephine Hopper Research Collection, Whitney Museum of American Art Archives, New York.

———. "Notes of Conversation with Hopper." Unpublished typescript, April 21, 1947. Series 4: Biographical and Personal Papers, 4.044: Notes: Goodrich on Hopper conversations. Edward and Josephine Hopper Research Collection, Whitney Museum of American Art Archives, New York.

———. "Notes on Paris oils seen at Edward Hoppers [*sic*] studio." Unpublished typescript, April 21, 1947. Series 4: Biographical and Personal Papers, 4.044: Notes: Goodrich on Hopper conversations. Edward and Josephine Hopper Research Collection, Whitney Museum of American Art Archives, New York.

Hopper, Edward. "Charles Burchfield: American." *The Arts* 14, no. 1 (July 1928): 3–12.

———. Interview by Arlene Jacobowitz. "Interview with Edward Hopper. 1966." Transcript, January 23, 1968. Series 4: Biographical and Personal Papers, 4.043: Transcripts. Edward and Josephine Hopper Research Collection, Whitney Museum of American Art Archives, New York.

———. Interview by Katharine Kuh. "Edward Hopper." In *The Artist's Voice: Talks with Seventeen Artists,* 130–42. New York: Harper and Row, 1962.

———. Interview by John Morse. "Tape Recorded Interview with Edward Hopper at the Whitney Museum, New York, New York." Unpublished transcript, June 17, 1959. Archives of American Art, Smithsonian Institution, Washington, DC.

———. Interview by Brian O'Doherty. "Brian O'Doherty Interview with Edward and Jo Hopper." Transcript, 1961. Series 4: Biographical and Personal Papers, 4.043: Transcripts. Edward and Josephine Hopper Research Collection, Whitney Museum of American Art Archives, New York.

———. Interview by Selden Rodman. "The Image of Man." In *Conversations with Artists,* 198–200. New York: Capricorn Books, 1961.

———. "John Sloan and the Philadelphians." *The Arts* 11, no. 4 (April 1927): 168–78.

———. Letter to James Biddle, January 21, 1964. Series 4: Biographical and Personal Papers, 4.018: General correspondence [1964–65]. Photocopy. Edward and Josephine Hopper Research Collection, Whitney Museum of American Art Archives, New York.

———. Letter to Norman Geske and statement about *Office at Night* (verso). August 25, 1948. Series 4: Biographical and Personal Papers, 4.013: General correspondence [1944–49]. Photocopy. Edward and Josephine Hopper Research Collection, Whitney Museum of American Art Archives, New York.

———. Letter to C. Powell Minnigerode. August 4, 1939. Series 4: Biographical and Personal Papers, 4.011: General correspondence [1937–39]. Photocopy. Edward and Josephine Hopper Research Collection, Whitney Museum of American Art Archives, New York.

———. Letter to Hermon More, January 20, 1951. Series 4: Biographical and Personal Papers, 4.014: General correspondence [1950–1954]. Photocopy. Edward and Josephine Hopper Research Collection, Whitney Museum of American Art Archives, New York.

———. "Notes on Painting." In Alfred H. Barr, Jr., et al., *Edward Hopper: Retrospective Exhibition, November 1–December 7, 1933,* 17–18. Exhibition catalogue. New York: Museum of Modern Art, 1933.

———. Review of *The Art and Craft of Drawing,* by Vernon Blake. *The Arts* 11, no. 6 (June 1927): 333–34.

Hopper, Edward, and Josephine Hopper. Interview by Joan Dye. "Luncheon Interview with Hopper and his wife Jo at Charles French Restaurant in the Village." Transcript, May 19, 1955. Series 4: Biographical and Personal Papers, 4.043: Transcripts. Edward and Josephine Hopper Research Collection, Whitney Museum of American Art Archives, New York.

Johnson, Bill. "Hopper Cover Research." Unpublished typescript, October 30, 1956. Series 4: Biographical and Personal Papers, 4.043: Transcripts. Edward and Josephine Hopper Research Collection, Whitney Museum of American Art Archives, New York.

O'Doherty, Brian. "Edward Hopper's Voice." In *American Masters: The Voice and the Myth,* 12–43. New York: Random House, 1973.

———. "Portrait: Edward Hopper." *Art in America* 52, no. 6 (December 1964): 68–88.

Periodicals

Anfam, David. "Edward Hopper—Recent Studies." *Art History* 4, no. 4 (December 1981): 457–61.

"Art: The Silent Witness." *Time*. December 24, 1956, 28–39.

Backer, Matt. "Pursuing Desire: A Lacanian Approach to the Paintings of Edward Hopper." *Oculus* 5 (2002): 54–69.

Baigell, Matthew. "The Beginnings of 'The American Wave' and the Depression." *Art Journal* 27, no. 4 (Summer 1968): 387–96, 398.

Baldinger, Wallace Spencer. "Formal Change in Recent American Painting." *The Art Bulletin* 19, no. 4 (December 1937): 580–91.

Barker, Virgil. "The Etchings of Edward Hopper." *The Arts* 5, no. 6 (June 1924): 322–27.

———. "The Search for Americanism." *The American Magazine of Art* 27, no. 2 (February 1934): 51–52.

Boyd, William. "The Best and the Worst: Notes Towards a Definition of Edward Hopper." *Modern Painters* 17 (Summer 2004): 62–65.

Brace, Ernest. "Edward Hopper." *Magazine of Art* 30, no. 5 (May 1937): 274–80.

Brown, Milton W. "The Early Realism of Hopper and Burchfield." *College Art Journal* 7, no. 1 (Autumn 1947): 3–11.

Burchfield, Charles. "Hopper: Career of Silent Poetry." *ARTnews* 49, no. 1 (March 1950): 14–17, 62–63.

Burrey, Suzanne. "Edward Hopper: the Emptying Spaces." *Arts Digest* 29, no. 13 (April 1, 1955): 8–10, 33.

Campbell, Lawrence. "Edward Hopper and the Melancholy of Robinson Crusoe." *ARTnews* 70, no. 6 (October 1971): 36–39, 78.

———. "Hopper: Painter of 'Thou Shalt Not.'" *ARTnews* 63 (October 1964): 42–45, 58.

Colleary, Elizabeth Thompson. "Josephine Nivison Hopper: Some Newly Discovered Works." *Woman's Art Journal* 25, no. 1 (Spring/Summer 2004): 3–11.

Cooledge, Dean. "Edward Hopper's Subversive Pastoralism in the Urban Landscape." *Streetnotes* 18 (Spring 2010).

Doss, Erika L. "Edward Hopper, Nighthawks, and Film Noir." *Post Script: Essays in Film and the Humanities* 2, no. 2 (Winter 1983): 14–36.

Du Bois, Guy Pène. "The American Paintings of Edward Hopper." *Creative Art* 8, no. 3 (March 1931): 187–91.

———. "Edward Hopper, Draughtsman: An Appreciation of the Work of an Etcher Who Does Not Belong to the Rank and File." *Shadowland* 7, no. 2 (October 1922): 22–23.

Fraenkel, Jeffrey, and Robert Adams. "The Difference a Painter Makes: Edward Hopper and Photography." *Aperture*, no. 195 (Summer 2009): 20–27.

Frank, Elizabeth. "Edward Hopper: Symbolist in a Hardboiled World." *ARTnews* 80, no. 2 (February 1981): 100–3.

Fryd, Vivien Green. "Edward Hopper's 'Girlie Show': Who Is the Silent Partner?" *American Art* 14, no. 2 (Summer 2000): 52–75.

———. "The Object in the Age of Theory." *American Art* 8, no. 2 (Spring 1994): 2–5.

Geldzahler, Henry. "Edward Hopper." *The Metropolitan Museum of Art Bulletin* 21, no. 3 (November 1962): 113–17.

Gillies, Jean. "The Timeless Space of Edward Hopper." *Art Journal* 31, no. 4 (Summer 1972): 404–12.

Goldberg, Itzhak. "Edward Hopper: L'Amérique en apnée." *Beaux Arts*, no. 313 (July 2010): 86–93.

Goodrich, Lloyd. "The Paintings of Edward Hopper." *The Arts* 11, no. 3 (March 1927): 134–38.

Goodrich, Lloyd, John Clancy, Helen Hayes, Raphael Soyer, Brian O'Doherty, and James Thomas Flexner. "Six Who Knew Edward Hopper." *Art Journal* 41, no. 2 (Summer 1981): 125–35.

Hankins, Evelyn C. "Edward Hopper: The Paris Years." *American Art Review* 15, no. 1 (January–February 2003): 168–73.

Hanson, Anne Coffin. "Edward Hopper, American Meaning and French Craft." *Art Journal* 41, no. 2 (Summer 1981): 142–49.

Heffner, Maura. "Edward Hopper and Urban Realism." *American Art Review* 15, no. 3 (May/June 2003): 100–5.

Hemingway, Andrew. "To 'Personalize the Rainpipe': The Critical Mythology of Edward Hopper." *Prospects* 17 (1992): 379–404.

Hollander, John. "Hopper and the Figure of Room." *Art Journal* 41, no. 2 (Summer 1981): 155–60.

Iversen, Margaret. "In the Blind Field: Hopper and the Uncanny." *Art History* 21, no. 3 (September 1998): 409–29.

Karlstrom, Paul J. "Reflections on the Automobile in American Art." *Archives of American Art Journal* 20, no. 2 (1980): 18–25.

Kazin, Alfred. "Hopper's Vision of New York." *New York Times Magazine.* September 7, 1980, 48–62.

Koob, Pamela N. "States of Being: Edward Hopper and Symbolist Aesthetics." *American Art* 18, no. 3 (Fall 2004): 52–77.

Kramer, Hilton. "Hopper: An Integrity in Realism." *New York Times.* March 19, 1971, 28.

Lanes, Jerrold. "Edward Hopper: French formalist, Ash Can realist, neither, or both?" *Artforum* 7, no. 2 (October 1968): 44–49.

Leider, Philip. "Vermeer and Hopper." *Art in America* 89, no. 3 (March 2001): 96–103.

Levin, Gail. "Edward Hopper: The Influence of Theater and Film." *Arts Magazine* 55, no. 2 (October 1980): 123–27.

———. "Edward Hopper, Francophile." *Arts Magazine* 53, no. 10 (June 1979): 114–21.

———. "Edward Hopper's 'Nighthawks.'" *Arts Magazine* 55, no. 9 (May 1981): 154–61.

———. "Edward Hopper's *Nighthawks*, Surrealism, and the War." *The Art Institute of Chicago Museum Studies* 22, no. 2 (1996): 180–95, 200.

———. "Edward Hopper's 'Office at Night.'" *Arts Magazine* 52, no. 5 (January 1978): 134–37.

———. "Edward Hopper's Process of Self-Analysis." *ARTnews* 79, no. 8 (October 1980): 144–47.

———. "Hopper's etchings: Some of the finest examples of American printmaking." *ARTnews* 78, no. 7 (September 1979): 90–93.

———. "The Office Image in the Visual Arts." *Arts Magazine* 59, no. 1 (September 1984): 98–103.

———. "Symbol and Reality in Edward Hopper's 'Room in New York.'" *Arts Magazine* 56, no. 5 (January 1982): 148–53.

Lewis, Michael J. "Homer, Hopper, and the Critics." *New Criterion* 15, no. 1 (September 1996): 74–80.

Lyons, Deborah. "By Necessity or Invention: The Record-Book Sketches of Edward Hopper." *Drawing* 18, no. 4 (Spring 1997): 101–6.

Marling, Karal Ann. "*Early Sunday Morning*." *Smithsonian Studies in American Art* 2, no. 3 (Fall 1988): 22–53.

Mecklenburg, Virginia M. "Edward Hopper: The Watercolors." *American Art Review* 12, no. 1 (January–February 2000): 128–39.

———. "Edward Hopper's Houses." *The Magazine Antiques* 156, no. 5 (November 1999): 718–25.

Mellow, James R. "The World of Edward Hopper." *New York Times Magazine*. September 5, 1971, 14–23.

Meyerowitz, Joel, George Segal, William Bailey, and Gail Levin. "Artists' Panel." *Art Journal* 41, no. 2 (Summer 1981): 150–54.

Nemerov, Alexander. "Ground Swell: Edward Hopper in 1939." *American Art* 22, no. 3 (Fall 2008): 50–71.

Nochlin, Linda. "Edward Hopper and the Imagery of Alienation." *Art Journal* 41, no. 2 (Summer 1981): 136–41.

Parks, John A. "Edward Hopper's Preliminary Drawings." *American Artist Drawing* 3, no. 8 (Winter 2006): 60–75.

Platt, Susan. "Rethinking Mr. Hopper." *The Art Book* 6, no. 1 (January 1999): 14–16.

Raynor, Vivien. "Art: Edward Hopper, Biography in Drawings." *New York Times.* March 20, 1987, C24.

Read, Helen Appleton. "Edward Hopper." *Parnassus* 5, no. 6 (November 1933): 8–10, 30.

Reece, Childe. "Edward Hopper's Etchings." *Magazine of Art* 31, no. 4 (April 1938): 226–28.

Robertson, Bryan. "Edward Hopper: Reality and Artifice." *Modern Painters* 9 (Spring 1996): 40–45.

———. "Hopper's Theater." *New York Review of Books* 17, no. 10 (December 16, 1971): 38–40.

Rothstein, Barbara. "House, Home and Hopper." *Art and Antiques* 23, no. 8 (September 2000): 102–9.

Rubin, Kate. "Edward Hopper and the American Imagination." *The Magazine Antiques* 148, no. 2 (August 1995): 166–75.

Russell, John. "The Truth in Hopper's Art." *New York Times.* May 13, 1977, C1, C22.

Sandberg, John. "Some Traditional Aspects of Pop Art." *Art Journal* 26, no. 3 (Spring 1967): 228–33, 245.

Silberman, Robert. "Edward Hopper and the Implied Observer." *Art in America* 69, no. 7 (September 1981): 148–54.

Slater, Tom. "Fear of the city 1882–1967: Edward Hopper and the discourse of anti-urbanism." *Social and Cultural Geography* 3, no. 2 (2002): 135–54.

Smith, Jacob Getlar. "Edward Hopper." *American Artist* 20, no. 1 (January 1956): 22–27.

Stein, Susan Alyson. "Edward Hopper: The Uncrossed Threshold." *Arts Magazine* 54, no. 7 (March 1980): 156–60.

Sullivan, Terry. "The Indelible Influence of Edward Hopper." *American Artist* 59 (November 1995): 60–62.

Taylor, Francis Henry. "The Romantick Revival of 1930." *Parnassus* 2, no. 6 (October 1930): 3–7.

Tillim, Sidney. "Edward Hopper and the Provincial Principle." *Arts Magazine* 39, no. 2 (November 1964): 25–31.

Troyen, Carol. "Edward Hopper and *Ryder's House*." *American Art* 20, no. 2 (Summer 2006): 4–6.

———. "Edward Hopper's Stories." *The Magazine Antiques* (April 2007): 82–91.

Tyler, Parker. "Edward Hopper: Alienation by Light." *Magazine of Art* 41, no. 8 (December 1948): 290–95.

———. "Hopper/Pollock: The Loneliness of the Crowd and the Loneliness of the Universe: An Antiphonal." *ARTnews Annual* 26 (December 1957): 86–107.

Updike, John. "Hopper's Polluted Silence." *New York Review of Books* 42, no. 13 (August 10, 1995): 19–21.

Watson, Forbes. "A Note on Edward Hopper: An Appreciation of an American Artist Whose Work Has Been Acclaimed by Critics and Public." *Vanity Fair* 31, no. 6 (February 1929): 64, 98, 107.

Zigrosser, Carl. "The Prints of Edward Hopper." *American Artist* 27, no. 9 (November 1963): 38–43, 64–65.

Zone, Ray "Emotional Triggers." *American Cinematographer* 83, no. 8 (August 2002): 32–43.

Books, Monographs, Exhibition Catalogues, and Exhibition Brochures

Achenbach Foundation for Graphic Arts. *America Observed: Etchings by Edward Hopper, Photographs by Walker Evans*. Exhibition catalogue. San Francisco: Fine Arts Museums of San Francisco, 1976.

Alacoque, Sophie. "Edward Hopper (1882–1967) et le Cinéma Américain: Rapports d'influences ou 'Fatales Coincidences.'" M.A. thesis, Université Lumière Lyon, 2001.

Badelt, Sandra. "Temporale Strukturen in den Gemälden Edward Hoppers." PhD diss., Ruhr-Universität Bochum, 2003.

Barr, Jr., Alfred H., et al. *Edward Hopper: Retrospective Exhibition, November 1–December 7, 1933*. Exhibition catalogue. New York: Museum of Modern Art, 1933.

Barter, Judith A. "Edward Hopper: *Nighthawks*." In *American Modernism at the Art Institute of Chicago: From World War I to 1955*, Judith Barter et al., 273–75. Chicago: Art Institute of Chicago; New Haven: Yale University Press, 2009.

Beck, Hubert. "Der melancholische Blick: Die Großstadt im Werk des Amerikanischen Malers Edward Hopper." PhD diss., Universität Frankfurt am Main, 1988.

———. *Edward Hopper.* Hamburg: Ellert und Richter, 1992.

Berman, Avis. *Edward Hopper: Etchings*. Exhibition catalogue. New York: Craig F. Starr Gallery, 2008.

———. *Edward Hopper: Prelude; The Nyack Years.* Exhibition catalogue. Nyack, NY: Edward Hopper Landmark Preservation Foundation, 2011.

———. *Edward Hopper's New York*. San Francisco: Pomegranate, 2005.

Brettell, Richard R. *Hopper in Paris, Collection in Context*. Exhibition brochure. New York: Whitney Museum of American Art, 1993.

Brettell, Richard R., and Éric Darragon. *Edward Hopper: Les années parisiennes 1906–1910*. Exhibition catalogue. Giverny: Musée d'Art Américain, 2004.

Bunkamura Museum of Art. *Edward Hopper.* Exhibition catalogue. Tokyo: APT International, 2000.

Cincinnati Art Museum. *An American Show*. Exhibition catalogue. Cincinnati: Cincinnati Art Museum, 1948.

Clause, Bonnie Tocher. *Edward Hopper in Vermont*. Lebanon, NH: University Press of New England, 2012.

Costantino, Maria. *Edward Hopper*. New York: Barnes and Noble Books, 1995.

Culver, Michael. "The Image of Woman in the Art of Ernest Hemingway, Edward Hopper, and Howard Hawks." PhD diss., University of Louisville, 1986.

Dreishpoon, Douglas. *Edward Hopper: Early and Late; Drawings, Watercolors, and Paintings, March 14–April 18, 1987*. Exhibition catalogue. New York: Hirschl & Adler Galleries, 1987.

Du Bois, Guy Pène. *Edward Hopper*. New York: Whitney Museum of American Art, 1931.

Fischer, Lucy. "The Savage Eye: Edward Hopper and the Cinema." In *A Modern Mosaic: Art and Modernism in the United States,* edited by Townsend Ludington, 334–56. Chapel Hill: University of North Carolina Press, 2000.

Fondation de l'Hermitage. *Edward Hopper: Exposition à la Fondation de l'Hermitage de Lausanne*. Dijon, France: Éditions Faton, 2010.

Foster, Carter E., ed. *Edward Hopper*. Exhibition catalogue. Milan: Skira, 2009.

Fraenkel Gallery. *Edward Hopper and Company.* Exhibition catalogue. San Francisco: Fraenkel Gallery, 2009.

Fryd, Vivien Green. *Art and the Crisis of Marriage: Edward Hopper and Georgia O'Keeffe*. Chicago: University of Chicago Press, 2003.

Galassi, Peter. *Walker Evans and Company*. Exhibition catalogue. New York: Museum of Modern Art, 2000.

Gibbes Museum of Art. *Edward Hopper in Charleston*. Exhibition catalogue. Charleston: Gibbes Museum of Art, 2006.

Goodrich, Lloyd. *Edward Hopper*. Exhibition catalogue. New York: Whitney Museum of American Art, 1964.

———. *Edward Hopper*. New York: Harry N. Abrams, 1971.

———. *Edward Hopper: Retrospective Exhibition*. Exhibition catalogue. New York: Whitney Museum of American Art, 1950.

———. *Edward Hopper: Selections from the Hopper Bequest to the Whitney Museum of American Art*. Exhibition catalogue. New York: Whitney Museum of American Art, 1971.

Hagerman, Gary. *Edward Hopper's Windows*. N.p.: Gary Hagerman, 2004.

Hankins, Evelyn. *Edward Hopper: The Paris Years*. Exhibition brochure. New York: Whitney Museum of American Art, 2003.

Hayward Gallery. *Edward Hopper, 1882–1967*. Exhibition catalogue. London: Arts Council of Great Britain, 1981.

Heffner, Maura. *Edward Hopper and Urban Realism*. Exhibition brochure. New York: Whitney Museum of American Art, 2002.

Hobbs, Robert. *Edward Hopper*. New York: Harry N. Abrams in association with the National Museum of American Art, Smithsonian Institution, 1987.

Junker, Patricia A. *Edward Hopper: Women*. Exhibition catalogue. Seattle: Seattle Art Museum, 2008.

Kennedy Galleries. *Edward Hopper at Kennedy Galleries*. Exhibition catalogue. New York: Kennedy Galleries, 1977.

Kiehl, David. *Edward Hopper: Printmaker*. Exhibition brochure. New York: Whitney Museum of American Art, 2000.

Költzsch, Georg-W., and Heinz Liesbrock. *Edward Hopper und die Fotografie: Die Wahrheit des Sichtbaren*. Exhibition catalogue. Essen: Museum Folkwang, 1992.

Koob, Pamela N. *Edward Hopper's "New York Movie."* Exhibition catalogue. New York: Bertha and Karl Leubsdorf Art Gallery, Hunter College, 1998.

Kranzfelder, Ivo. *Edward Hopper, 1882–1967: Vision of Reality*. Cologne: Taschen, 1995.

Levin, Gail. *The Complete Watercolors of Edward Hopper*. New York: Whitney Museum of American Art in association with W. W. Norton, 2001.

———. *The Early Drawings of Edward Hopper.* Exhibition catalogue. New York: Kennedy Galleries, 1995.

———. *Edward Hopper*. New York: Crown, 1984.

———. *Edward Hopper: A Catalogue Raisonné*. 3 vols. New York: Whitney Museum of American Art in association with W. W. Norton, 1995.

———. *Edward Hopper: An Intimate Biography*. Updated and expanded edition. New York: Rizzoli, 2007.

———. *Edward Hopper: The Art and Artist.* Exhibition catalogue. New York: W. W. Norton in association with the Whitney Museum of American Art, 1981.

———. *Edward Hopper: The Complete Prints*. Exhibition catalogue. New York: W. W. Norton in association with the Whitney Museum of American Art, 1979.

———. *Edward Hopper as Illustrator*. New York: W. W. Norton in association with the Whitney Museum of American Art, 1979.

———. *Edward Hopper, 1882–1967: Gemälde und Zeichnungen*. Exhibition catalogue. Munich: Schirmer Mosel, 1981.

———. *Hopper's Places*. New York: Alfred A. Knopf, 1989.

———. *In Black and White: Selected American Drawings and Prints—Part II; Edward Hopper: Selected Drawings.* Exhibition catalogue. Beverly Hills, CA: Louis Newman Galleries, 1989.

———. *The Poetry of Solitude: A Tribute to Edward Hopper*. New York: Universe, 1995.

Little, Carl. *Edward Hopper's New England*. San Francisco: Pomegranate, 1993.

Llorens, Tomàs, and Didier Ottinger. *Edward Hopper*. Exhibition catalogue. Paris: Réunion des musées nationaux—Grand Palais; New York: D.A.P./Distributed Art Publishers, 2012.

Lyons, Deborah. *Edward Hopper: A Journal of His Work*. New York: Whitney Museum of American Art in association with W. W. Norton, 1997.

Lyons, Deborah, and Roni Feinstein. *Edward Hopper, City, Country, Town: Selections from the Permanent Collection of the Whitney Museum of American Art*. Exhibition catalogue. New York: Whitney Museum of American Art, 1987.

Lyons, Deborah, and Susan C. Larsen. *Edward Hopper, Selections from the Permanent Collection*. Exhibition catalogue. New York: Whitney Museum of American Art, 1989.

Lyons, Deborah, and Kathleen Monaghan. *Edward Hopper and the Figure.* Exhibition catalogue. New York: Whitney Museum of American Art, 1993.

Lyons, Deborah, and Adam D. Weinberg. *Edward Hopper and the American Imagination*. Exhibition catalogue. New York: Whitney Museum of American Art in association with W. W. Norton, 1995.

Marling, Karal Ann. *Edward Hopper*. New York: Rizzoli, 1992.

Marshall Cavendish Books. *Great Artists, Their Lives and Times: Edward Hopper*. London: Marshall Cavendish, 1986.

Mecklenburg, Virginia M. *Edward Hopper: The Watercolors.* Exhibition catalogue. Washington, DC: National Museum of American Art; New York: W. W. Norton, 1999.

Modernism Gallery. *Edward Hopper/John Register: Works on Paper.* Exhibition catalogue. San Francisco: Modernism, 1996.

Mueller, Jean Gillies. "The Timeless Space of Edward Hopper." PhD diss., Northwestern University, 1971.

Musée Cantini, Marseilles. *Edward Hopper*. Exhibition catalogue. Secaucus, NJ: Wellfleet, 1989.

Musée Rath, Geneva. *Edward Hopper, 1882–1967*. Exhibition catalogue. Geneva: Musée d'art et d'histoire, 1991.

New Britain Museum of American Art. *Sound and Silence: Charles E. Burchfield, 1893–1967; Edward Hopper, 1882–1967*. Exhibition catalogue. New Britain, CT: New Britain Museum of American Art, 1973.

Palais des Beaux-Arts. *Edward Hopper, 1882–1967*. Exhibition catalogue. Brussels: Société des Expositions du Palais des Beaux-Arts, 1993.

Paton, Priscilla. "Gothic Loneliness: The Different Cases of Edward Hopper, and Andrew Wyeth." In *Abandoned New England: Landscape in the Works of Homer, Frost, Hopper, Wyeth, and Bishop*, 133–68. Hanover, NH: University Press of New England, 2003.

Peter Findlay Gallery. *Edward Hopper: The Capezzera Drawings.* Exhibition catalogue. New York: Peter Findlay Gallery, 2005.

Pontiggia, Elena. *Hopper*. Milan: Rizzoli, 2004.

Ray, Robert B. *Edward Hopper and the American Cinema*. Exhibition brochure. New York: Whitney Museum of American Art, 1995.

Read, Helen Appleton. *Robert Henri and Five of his Pupils*. Exhibition catalogue. New York: The Century Association, 1946.

Renner, Rolf Günter. *Edward Hopper, 1882–1967: Transformation of the Real*. San Diego: Thunder Bay, 1997.

Salatino, Kevin, et al. *Edward Hopper's Maine*. Exhibition catalogue. Brunswick, ME: Bowdoin College Museum of Art; Munich: Prestel, 2011.

São Paulo 9, United States of America: Edward Hopper, Environment U.S.A., 1957–1967. Exhibition catalogue. Washington, DC: Smithsonian Institution Press, 1967.

Schiffenhaus, J. Anton. *A Window into the World of Edward and Josephine Hopper*. Exhibition catalogue. Provincetown, MA: privately printed, 1996.

Schjeldahl, Peter. *Edward Hopper: Light Years.* Exhibition catalogue. New York: Hirschl & Adler Galleries, 1988.

Schmied, Wieland. *Edward Hopper: Portraits of America*. Munich: Prestel, 1995.

Silberman, Robert. "Edward Hopper and the Theater of the Mind: Vision, Spectacle, and the Spectator." In *On the Edge of Your Seat: Popular Theater and Film in Early Twentieth-Century American Art*, edited by Patricia McDonnell, 137–55. Exhibition catalogue. New Haven: Yale University Press in association with Frederick R. Weisman Art Museum, University of Minnesota, 2002.

Soby, James Thrall. "Max Weber and Edward Hopper." In *Contemporary Painters*, 28–39. New York: Museum of Modern Art, 1948.

Souter, Gerry. *Edward Hopper: Light and Dark*. New York: Parkstone Press, 2007.

Spring, Justin. *The Essential Edward Hopper*. New York: Wonderland Press, 1998.

Strand, Mark. *Hopper.* New York: Alfred A. Knopf, 2001.

Taggart, John. *Remaining in Light: Ant Meditations on a Painting by Edward Hopper*. Albany: State University of New York Press, 1993.

Theisen, Gordon. *Staying up Much Too Late: Edward Hopper's* Nighthawks *and the Dark Side of the American Psyche*. New York: Thomas Dunne Books, 2006.

Todd, Ellen Wiley. "Will (S)he Stoop to Conquer? Preliminaries toward a Reading of Edward Hopper's *Office at Night*." In *Visual Theory: Painting and Interpretation*, edited by Norman Bryson, Michael Ann Holly, and Keith Moxey, 47–53. New York: HarperCollins, 1991.

Troyen, Carol, et al. *Edward Hopper*. Exhibition catalogue. Boston: Museum of Fine Arts, 2007.

Ullmann, Antoine. *Dada Hopper*. Paris: Editions Arola, 2010.

University of Arizona, Art Gallery. *Retrospective Exhibition of Oils and Watercolors by Edward Hopper.* Exhibition catalogue. Tucson: University of Arizona, 1963.

Updike, John. "*Early Sunday Morning*." In *Still Looking: Essays on American Art,* 195–200. New York: Alfred A. Knopf, 2005.

Updike, John, Robert Adams, and Brian O'Doherty. "Edward Hopper: *Early Sunday Morning*." In *Frames of Reference: Looking at American Art, 1900–1950*, edited by Beth Venn and Adam D. Weinberg, 177–85. New York: Whitney Museum of American Art, 1999

Wagstaff, Sheena, ed. *Edward Hopper*. Exhibition catalogue. London: Tate Publishing, 2004.

Ward, Joseph Anthony. *American Silences: The Realism of James Agee, Walker Evans, and Edward Hopper.* Eaton Rouge: Louisiana State University Press, 1985.

Warkel, Harriet G. *Paper to Paint: Edward Hopper's "Hotel Lobby."* Indianapolis: Indianapolis Museum of Art, 2008.

Wells, Walter. *Silent Theater: The Art of Edward Hopper*. New York: Phaidon, 2007.

Westfälisches Landesmuseum für Kunst und Kulturgeschichte Münster. *Edward Hopper, das Frühwerk*. Exhibition catalogue. Münster: Westfälisches Landesmuseum, 1981.

Westheider, Ortrud, Barbara Haskell, et al. *Modern Life: Edward Hopper and His Time.* Exhibition catalogue. Hamburg: Bucerius Kunst Forum, 2009.

Whitney Museum of American Art. *Hopper Drawings: 44 Works from the Permanent Collection of the Whitney Museum of American Art.* Mineola, NY: Dover Publications, 1989.

William A. Farnsworth Library and Art Museum. *Edward Hopper, 1882–1967: Oils, Watercolors, Etchings*. Exhibition catalogue. Rockland, ME: William A. Farnsworth Library and Art Museum, 1971.

Wolfe, Judith. *Edward Hopper: Works on Paper; A Personal Collection*. Exhibition catalogue. East Hampton, NY: Guild Hall Museum, 1982.

Zigrosser, Carl. *The Complete Graphic Work of Edward Hopper*. N.p.: Print Council of America, 1962. Excerpted from *Prints: Thirteen Illustrated Essays on the Art of the Print*. New York: Holt, Rinehart and Winston, 1962.

CHECKLIST OF THE EXHIBITION

Artworks are listed chronologically. Groups of related works are cited in the order in which they appear in this volume; preparatory studies are similarly listed, followed by related paintings. Within groups of artworks of the same year(s), works are listed in alphabetical order if precise chronology has not been established. Titles given by the artist and descriptive titles established by the Whitney Museum are styled identically in this publication. Unless otherwise noted, all works are in the collection of the Whitney Museum of American Art.

For all dimensions, height precedes width.
Not all works traveled to all venues.

Man Leaning Against a Wall, 1899
Pen and ink and graphite pencil on board, 15 3/4 × 9 15/16 in. (40 × 25.2 cm)
Josephine N. Hopper Bequest 70.1566.49
(fig. 15)

Caricatured and Grotesque Faces, 1899–1906
Pen and ink on paper, 7 7/8 × 4 15/16 in. (20 × 12.5 cm)
Josephine N. Hopper Bequest 70.1559.26
(fig. 14)

Matchbox on Base, Bullet, and Decorative Cow (recto), 1899–1906
Fabricated chalk and charcoal on paper, 22 1/16 × 15 3/16 in. (56 × 38.6 cm)
Josephine N. Hopper Bequest 70.812a–b
(fig. 22)

Eggplant, Fruit, and Bowl (recto), 1899–1906
Fabricated chalk on paper, 22 1/16 × 15 in. (56 × 38.1 cm)
Josephine N. Hopper Bequest 70.817a–b
(fig. 23)

Figure and Character Studies by Occupation, 1899–1906
Pen and ink on paper, 8 × 5 in. (20.3 × 12.7 cm)
Josephine N. Hopper Bequest 70.1605.38
(fig. 13)

Man in Stocking-like Hat, 1899–1906
Charcoal on paper, 18 3/4 × 12 5/16 in. (47.6 × 31.3 cm)
Josephine N. Hopper Bequest 70.1507
(fig. 19)

Seated Man in Robes and Headdress (recto), 1899–1906
Fabricated chalk, colored pencil, and charcoal on paper, 12 7/8 × 9 7/8 in. (32.7 × 25.1 cm)
Josephine N. Hopper Bequest 70.1566.10a–b
(fig. 17)

Woman with Basket, Profile View, 1899–1906
Brush and ink and graphite pencil on paper, 11 15/16 × 9 in. (30.3 × 22.9 cm)
Josephine N. Hopper Bequest 70.1565.4
(fig. 16)

Woman with Gloves Viewing Painting, 1899–1906
Opaque watercolor and graphite pencil on board, 15 × 11 3/8 in. (38.1 × 28.9 cm)
Josephine N. Hopper Bequest 70.1646
(fig. 18)

Self-Portrait, 1899–1906
Charcoal on paper, 18 7/8 × 12 3/8 in. (47.9 × 31.4 cm)
Josephine N. Hopper Bequest 70.1536
(fig. 34)

Two Self-Portraits, c. 1900
Pen and ink on paper, 8 7/8 × 5 9/16 in. (22.5 × 14.1 cm)
Josephine N. Hopper Bequest 70.1561.115
(fig. 30)

Self-Portrait and Hand Studies, c. 1900
Pen and ink and graphite pencil on paper, 7 7/8 × 4 15/16 in. (20 × 12.5 cm)
Josephine N. Hopper Bequest 70.1559.28
(fig. 31)

Two Self-Portraits and Two Hand Studies, c. 1900
Pen and ink on paper, 7 7/8 × 4 15/16 in. (20 × 12.5 cm)
Josephine N. Hopper Bequest 70.1559.24
(fig. 32)

Self-Portrait and Hand Studies, c. 1900
Pen and ink on paper, 8 7/8 × 5 9/16 in. (22.5 × 14.1 cm)
Josephine N. Hopper Bequest 70.1559.21
(fig. 33)

Female Nude on Model's Platform, c. 1900–03
Charcoal on paper, 19 1/16 × 12 3/8 in. (48.4 × 31.4 cm)
Josephine N. Hopper Bequest 70.1566.118
(fig. 27)

Female Nude in Studio, Rear View, c. 1900–03
Charcoal on paper, 12 1/4 × 9 9/16 in. (31.1 × 24.3 cm)
Josephine N. Hopper Bequest 70.1560.90
(fig. 28)

Three Men at Art Exhibition, c. 1900–03
Graphite pencil on paper, 9 3/8 × 6 1/8 in. (23.8 × 15.6 cm)
Josephine N. Hopper Bequest 70.1560.51
(fig. 29)

Man Seated on Bed Reading (recto), 1900–06
Graphite pencil on paper, 12 1/16 × 9 3/8 in. (30.6 × 23.8 cm)
Josephine N. Hopper Bequest 70.1560.44a–b
(fig. 373)

Reclining Female Nude, Rear View, 1900–06
Fabricated chalk on paper, 18 3/4 × 24 7/16 in. (47.6 × 62.1 cm)
Josephine N. Hopper Bequest 70.1491
(fig. 25)

Copy after Edouard Manet's The Fifer *and Two Heads*, 1900–07
Pen and ink on paper, 10 × 7 in. (25.4 × 17.8 cm)
Josephine N. Hopper Bequest 70.1560.96
(fig. 101)

Reclining Female Nude, Rear View (recto), c. 1902–04
Fabricated chalk and graphite pencil on paper, 12 1/4 × 19 3/16 in. (31.1 × 48.7 cm)
Josephine N. Hopper Bequest 70.1534a–b
(fig. 26)

The Artist's Bedroom, Nyack, 1905–06
Oil on board, 15 1/8 × 11 1/8 in. (38.4 × 28.3 cm)
Josephine N. Hopper Bequest 70.1412
(fig. 374)

Man Seated on Bed, 1905–06
Oil on canvas mounted on board, 11 1/4 × 9 1/4 in. (28.6 × 23.5 cm)
Josephine N. Hopper Bequest 70.1424
(fig. 372)

Two Hand Studies (recto), c. 1905–06
Charcoal on paper, 18 7/8 × 12 1/16 in. (47.9 × 30.6 cm)
Josephine N. Hopper Bequest 70.1535a–b
(fig. 35)

Heads, Woman Dancing, and Man in Suit with Moustache, 1906–07
Pen and ink on paper, 8 13/16 × 5 3/4 in. (22.4 × 14.6 cm)
Josephine N. Hopper Bequest 70.1555.27
(fig. 103)

Figures in Hats, 1906–07
Pen and ink on paper, 9 7/8 × 12 7/8 in. (25.1 × 32.7 cm)
Josephine N. Hopper Bequest 70.1555.2
(fig. 116)

Four Women in Hats, 1906–07
Pen and ink on paper, 9 13/16 × 13 1/16 in. (24.9 × 33.2 cm)
Josephine N. Hopper Bequest 70.1555.7
(fig. 117)

Seated Woman, Women in Hats, Man and Woman in Conversation, and Man with Moustache, 1906–07
Pen and ink on paper, 9 13/16 × 13 1/16 in. (24.9 × 33.2 cm)
Josephine N. Hopper Bequest 70.1555.11
(fig. 118)

Two Seated Women in Profile and Women's Busts, 1906–07
Pen and ink on paper, 9 13/16 × 13 1/16 in. (24.9 × 33.2 cm)
Josephine N. Hopper Bequest 70.1555.12
(fig. 119)

Man with Moustache and Women in Dresses and Hats (recto), 1906–07
Pen and ink on paper, 9 7/8 × 12 7/8 in. (25.1 × 32.7 cm)
Josephine N. Hopper Bequest 70.1555.18a–b
(fig. 120)

Women and Man in Hats, 1906–07
Pen and ink on paper, 9 13/16 × 13 in. (24.9 × 33 cm)
Josephine N. Hopper Bequest 70.1555.13
(fig. 121)

Woman Seated at Table with Glass and Woman in Dress (recto), 1906–07
Pen and ink on paper, 8 11/16 × 6 5/8 in. (22.1 × 16.8 cm)
Josephine N. Hopper Bequest 70.1559.3a–b
(fig. 122)

Seated Woman with Opera Gloves and Two Women in Hats, 1906–07
Pen and ink on paper, 8 11/16 × 6 9/16 in. (22.1 × 16.7 cm)
Josephine N. Hopper Bequest 70.1562.4
(fig. 123)

Woman in Hat and Man's Legs, 1906–07
Pen and ink on paper, 8 11/16 × 6 7/8 in. (22.1 × 17.5 cm)
Josephine N. Hopper Bequest 70.1559.62
(fig. 124)

Four Women, 1906–07
Pen and ink on paper, 8 11/16 × 6 9/16 in. (22.1 × 16.7 cm)
Josephine N. Hopper Bequest 70.1562.7
(fig. 125)

Seated Men, Boats, Pigs, Feet, Arm, and Legs (recto), 1906–07
Pen and ink on paper, 10 1/16 × 12 3/4 in. (25.6 × 32.4 cm)
Josephine N. Hopper Bequest 70.1555.5a–b
(fig. 126)

Men in Berets, Sailors, and Man in Pointed Hat (recto), 1906–07
Pen and ink on paper, 10 1/16 × 12 3/4 in. (25.6 × 32.4 cm)
Josephine N. Hopper Bequest 70.1555.6a–b
(fig. 127)

Man in Suit, Male and Female Figures, and Men in Hats (recto), 1906–07
Pen and ink on paper, 10 1/8 × 12 7/8 in. (25.7 × 32.7 cm)
Josephine N. Hopper Bequest 70.1555.17a–b
(fig. 128)

Diver, Sailors, Male Figure, and Arm, 1906–07
Pen and ink on paper, 10 1/8 × 12 7/8 in. (25.7 × 32.7 cm)
Josephine N. Hopper Bequest 70.1555.16
(fig. 129)

Man with Moustache and Beard and Man in Hat, 1906–07
Pen and ink on paper, 8 11/16 × 6 9/16 in. (22.1 × 16.7 cm)
Josephine N. Hopper Bequest 70.1562.2
(fig. 130)

Man on Horseback, Gendarme, and Man's Head in Helmet, 1906–07
Pen and ink on paper, 8 11/16 × 6 9/16 in. (22.1 × 16.7 cm)
Josephine N. Hopper Bequest 70.1562.3
(fig. 131)

Bearded Man with Champagne Glass, Female Nude, Man in Uniform, and Man with Moustache, 1906–07
Pen and ink on paper, 8 11/16 × 6 13/16 in. (22.1 × 17.3 cm)
Josephine N. Hopper Bequest 70.1562.8
(fig. 132)

Male and Female Figures, 1906–07
Pen and ink on paper, 9 7/8 × 12 7/8 in. (25.1 × 32.7 cm)
Josephine N. Hopper Bequest 70.1555.9
(fig. 134)

Woman with Basket, Woman in Dress, and Man in Beret, 1906–07
Pen and ink on paper, 10 1/16 × 6 5/8 in. (25.6 × 16.8 cm)
Josephine N. Hopper Bequest 70.1562.11
(fig. 136)

Man in Beret and Clogs (recto), 1906–07
Pen and ink on paper, 8 11/16 × 6 3/4 in. (22.1 × 17.1 cm)
Josephine N. Hopper Bequest 70.1561.119a–b
(fig. 142)

Seated Man and Woman, Bald Men, Man with Glasses, and High Heel (recto), 1906–07
Pen and ink on paper, 8 11/16 × 6 3/4 in. (22.1 × 17.1 cm)
Josephine N. Hopper Bequest 70.1559.54a–b
(fig. 147)

Woman with Opera Glasses and Woman's Head, 1906–07
Pen and ink on paper, 4 11/16 × 6 9/16 in. (11.9 × 16.7 cm)
Josephine N. Hopper Bequest 70.1561.122
(fig. 148)

Woman with Opera Gloves, Female Figures, and Man with Beard, 1906–07
Pen and ink on paper, 8 11/16 × 6 9/16 in. (22.1 × 16.7 cm)
Josephine N. Hopper Bequest 70.1562.5
(fig. 149)

Le Militaire, 1906–07
Watercolor on paper, 11 3/4 × 9 1/4 in. (30 × 23.5 cm)
The Dayton Art Institute, Ohio; bequest of Virginia Rike Haswell, 1977.51
(fig. 106)

At the Café, 1906–07
Watercolor and graphite pencil on paper, 11 7/8 × 9 1/2 in. (30.2 × 24.1 cm)
Josephine N. Hopper Bequest 70.1321
(fig. 108)

Parisian Woman Walking, 1906–07
Watercolor and graphite pencil on board, 11 7/8 × 9 3/8 in. (30.2 × 23.8 cm)
Josephine N. Hopper Bequest 70.1322
(fig. 109)

Fille de Joie, 1906–07
Transparent and opaque watercolor and graphite pencil on paper, 11 13/16 × 8 7/16 in. (30 × 24 cm)
Josephine N. Hopper Bequest 70.1324
(fig. 110)

Woman, 1906–07
Watercolor and graphite pencil on paper, 11 7/8 × 9 5/16 in. (30.2 × 23.7 cm)
Josephine N. Hopper Bequest 70.1325
(fig. 111)

Parisian with Wine Bottle and Loaf of Bread, 1906–07
Watercolor and graphite pencil on paper, 26 1/8 × 10 1/2 in. (66.4 × 26.7 cm)
Josephine N. Hopper Bequest 70.1329
(fig. 113)

Woman at Café Table, 1906–07
Watercolor and graphite pencil on board, 19 15/16 × 14 7/8 in. (50.6 × 37.8 cm)
Josephine N. Hopper Bequest 70.1372
(fig. 115)

French Woman with Basket, 1906–07
Watercolor and graphite pencil on paper, 14 13/16 × 10 7/16 in. (37.6 × 26.5 cm)
Josephine N. Hopper Bequest 70.1331
(fig. 137)

Parisian Workman, 1906–07
Watercolor and graphite pencil on paper, 15 1/16 × 10 5/8 in. (38.3 × 27 cm)
Josephine N. Hopper Bequest 70.1333
(fig. 143)

Couple Drinking, 1906–07
Transparent and opaque watercolor, graphite pencil, and fabricated chalk on paper, 13 1/2 × 19 7/8 in. (34.3 × 50.5 cm)
Josephine N. Hopper Bequest 70.1340
(fig. 145)

Waiter and Diners, 1906–07
Brush and ink, watercolor, and fabricated chalk on paper, 14 15/16 × 22 1/16 in. (37.9 × 56 cm)
Josephine N. Hopper Bequest 70.1443
(fig. 150)

Boy and Moon, c. 1906–10
Pen, brush and ink, and transparent and opaque watercolor on paper, 21 13/16 × 14 13/16 in. (55.4 × 37.6 cm)
Josephine N. Hopper Bequest 70.1349
(fig. 141)

New York and Its Houses, c. 1906–10
Brush and ink, transparent and opaque watercolor, and graphite pencil on paper, 21 13/16 × 14 13/16 in. (55.4 × 37.6 cm)
Josephine N. Hopper Bequest 70.1347
(fig. 38)

Dome, c. 1907
Fabricated chalk and wash on paper, 21 3/8 × 19 15/16 in. (54.3 × 50.6 cm)
Josephine N. Hopper Bequest 70.1434
(fig. 37)

Le Quai des Grands Augustins, 1909
Oil on canvas, 23 11/16 × 28 3/4 in. (60.2 × 73 cm)
Josephine N. Hopper Bequest 70.1173
(fig. 97)

Le Pont Royal, 1909
Oil on canvas, 24 × 29 1/16 in. (61 × 73.8 cm)
Josephine N. Hopper Bequest 70.1175
(fig. 98)

Le Bistro or *The Wine Shop*, 1909
Oil on canvas, 24 × 28 7/8 in. (61 × 73.3 cm)
Josephine N. Hopper Bequest 70.1187
(fig. 102)

Summer Interior, 1909
Oil on canvas, 24 1/4 × 29 3/16 in. (61.6 × 74.1 cm)
Josephine N. Hopper Bequest 70.1197
(fig. 375)

Un Maquereau, 1914
Fabricated chalk and charcoal on paper, 10 9/16 × 8 3/8 in. (26.8 × 21.3 cm)
Josephine N. Hopper Bequest 70.318
(fig. 138)

Soir Bleu, 1914
Oil on canvas, 36 × 72 in. (91.4 × 182.9 cm)
Josephine N. Hopper Bequest 70.1208
(fig. 95)

Seated Female Nude by Window (Sketch for Etching), 1915–18
Graphite pencil on paper, 14 7/8 × 10 in. (37.8 × 25.4 cm)
Josephine N. Hopper Bequest 70.830
(fig. 378)

Standing Female Nude by Window (Sketch for Etching), 1915–18
Graphite pencil on paper, 14 15/16 × 10 1/16 in. (37.9 × 25.6 cm)
Josephine N. Hopper Bequest 70.831
(fig. 379)

Monhegan, 1916–19
Fabricated chalk on paper, 10 1/2 × 16 in. (26.7 × 40.6 cm)
Josephine N. Hopper Bequest 70.679
(fig. 42)

Monhegan Island, 1916–19
Fabricated chalk on paper, 12 9/16 × 16 1/8 in. (31.9 × 41 cm)
Josephine N. Hopper Bequest 70.363
(fig. 43)

The Open Window, 1918–19
Etching; sheet: 9 1/4 × 10 1/2 in. (23.5 × 26.7 cm), plate: 3 15/16 × 4 7/8 in. (10 × 12.4 cm)
Purchase, with funds from Brooke Garber Neidich, Beth Rudin DeWoody, Laurie Tisch, and Joanne Leonhardt Cassullo 2000.118
(fig. 380)

Guy du Bois, 1919
Fabricated chalk on paper, 21 × 16 in. (53.3 × 40.6 cm)
Josephine N. Hopper Bequest 70.907
(fig. 63)

My Mother, c. 1920
Fabricated chalk on paper, 20 15/16 × 15 15/16 in. (53.2 × 40.5 cm)
Josephine N. Hopper Bequest 70.298
(fig. 62)

Tree Trunk, c. 1920
Fabricated chalk on paper, 14 × 10 in. (35.6 × 25.4 cm)
Josephine N. Hopper Bequest 70.730
(fig. 51)

Two Hand Studies, c. 1920
Fabricated chalk on paper, 10 5/8 × 8 in. (27 × 20.3 cm)
Josephine N. Hopper Bequest 70.631
(fig. 93)

Standing Female Nude with Arm Behind Back, Rear View, 1920–25
Fabricated chalk on paper, 22 × 15 in. (55.9 × 38.1 cm)
Josephine N. Hopper Bequest 70.315
(fig. 54)

Standing Female Nude, 1920–25
Fabricated chalk on paper, 17 15/16 × 11 1/2 in. (45.6 × 29.2 cm)
Josephine N. Hopper Bequest 70.320
(fig. 55)

Study for *Evening Wind* (recto), 1921
Fabricated chalk on paper, 10 1/8 × 13 15/16 in. (25.7 × 35.4 cm)
Josephine N. Hopper Bequest 70.343a–b
(fig. 377)

Study for *East Side Interior* (recto), 1922
Fabricated chalk and charcoal on paper, 9 × 11 1/2 in. (22.9 × 29.2 cm)
Josephine N. Hopper Bequest 70.342a–b
(fig. 41)

Drawing for The Maine Coast, 1923
Charcoal on paper, 10 3/4 × 12 1/2 in. (27.3 × 31.8 cm)
Collection of Aaron I. Fleischman
(fig. 52)

The Henry Ford on the Ways, Gloucester, 1923
Charcoal on paper, 12 × 17 15/16 in. (30.5 × 45.6 cm)
Josephine N. Hopper Bequest 70.837
(fig. 46)

Study for *The Henry Ford*, 1923
Fabricated chalk and charcoal on paper, 15 1/16 × 18 3/16 in. (38.3 × 46.2 cm)
Josephine N. Hopper Bequest 70.680
(fig. 53)

Victorian House on a Wooded Street, c. 1923–25
Fabricated chalk on paper, 16 × 17 1/2 in. (40.6 × 44.5 cm)
Josephine N. Hopper Bequest 70.901
(fig. 61)

Hopper's Hat on His Etching Press, after 1924
Fabricated chalk on paper, 11 1/16 × 15 1/8 in. (28.1 × 38.4 cm)
Josephine N. Hopper Bequest 70.344
(fig. 94)

"*What's this?... Don't, don't—Hannah!*" 1925
Illustration for Emerson Low, "The Man Who Had Been Away," *Scribner's Magazine* 77 (May 1925)
Fabricated chalk and charcoal on paper, 19 7/8 × 29 13/16 in. (50.5 × 75.7 cm)
Josephine N. Hopper Bequest 70.1450
(fig. 40)

Three Men in an Interior Space, c. 1925(?)
Fabricated chalk on paper, 11 1/8 × 15 1/8 in. (28.3 × 38.4 cm)
Josephine N. Hopper Bequest 70.836
(fig. 47)

Jo Hopper Reclining on a Couch, 1925–30
Fabricated chalk on paper, 15 9/16 × 18 in. (39.5 × 45.7 cm)
Josephine N. Hopper Bequest 70.296
(fig. 89)

Harbor Landscape with Docks, Boats, and Buildings, c. 1926
Fabricated chalk on paper, 11 13/16 × 18 1/16 in. (30 × 45.9 cm)
Josephine N. Hopper Bequest 70.304
(fig. 44)

The Lily Apartments, 1926
Watercolor on paper, 14 × 20 in. (35.6 × 50.8 cm)
Private collection
(fig. 159)

Study for *From Williamsburg Bridge*, 1928
Fabricated chalk on paper, 8 9/16 × 11 1/16 in. (21.7 × 28.1 cm)
Josephine N. Hopper Bequest 70.457
(fig. 162)

From Williamsburg Bridge, 1928
Oil on canvas, 29 × 43 in. (73.7 × 109.2 cm)
The Metropolitan Museum of Art, New York; George A. Hearn Fund, 1937 37.44
(fig. 161)

Study for *Manhattan Bridge Loop*, 1928
Crayon on paper, 8 1/2 × 11 1/16 in. (21.6 × 28.1 cm)
Addison Gallery of American Art, Phillips Academy, Andover, Massachusetts; gift of the artist 1940.71
(fig. 156)

Study for *Manhattan Bridge Loop*, 1928
Fabricated chalk on paper, 6 3/8 × 11 1/4 in. (16.2 × 28.6 cm)
Addison Gallery of American Art, Phillips Academy, Andover, Massachusetts; gift of the artist 1940.72
(fig. 157)

Street Lamp (Study for *Manhattan Bridge Loop*), 1928
Fabricated chalk on paper, 8 7/8 × 9 7/16 in. (22.5 × 24 cm)
Josephine N. Hopper Bequest 70.235
(fig. 158)

Manhattan Bridge Loop, 1928
Oil on canvas, 35 × 60 in. (88.9 × 152.4 cm)
Addison Gallery of American Art, Phillips Academy, Andover, Massachusetts; gift of Stephen C. Clark, Esq. 1932.17
(fig. 153)

Study of the Upper Stories of 82 Washington Square East, c. 1928
Fabricated chalk on paper, 8 7/8 × 11 7/8 in. (22.5 × 30.2 cm)
Josephine N. Hopper Bequest 70.234
(fig. 163)

Salem, 1929
Fabricated chalk on paper, 15 × 22 1/16 in. (38.1 × 56 cm)
Josephine N. Hopper Bequest 70.307
(fig. 45)

Topsfield, 1929
Fabricated chalk on paper, 15 × 22 1/16 in. (38.1 × 56 cm)
Josephine N. Hopper Bequest 70.682
(fig. 48)

Study for *Early Sunday Morning*, 1930
Fabricated chalk on paper, 6 × 4 in. (15.2 × 10.2 cm)
Josephine N. Hopper Bequest 70.823
(fig. 175)

Early Sunday Morning, 1930
Oil on canvas, 35 3/16 × 60 in. (89.4 × 152.4 cm)
Purchase, with funds from Gertrude Vanderbilt Whitney 31.426
(fig. 164)

Cobb's Barns, South Truro, 1930–33
Fabricated chalk and wax crayon on paper, 15 1/16 × 22 1/8 in. (38.3 × 56.2 cm)
Josephine N. Hopper Bequest 70.684
(fig. 49)

The Camel's Hump, 1931
Fabricated chalk on paper, 11 7/8 × 17 15/16 in. (30.2 × 45.6 cm)
Josephine N. Hopper Bequest 70.858
(fig. 59)

High Road, 1931
Watercolor and graphite pencil on paper, 20 × 27 15/16 in. (50.8 × 71 cm)
Josephine N. Hopper Bequest 70.1163
(fig. 329)

Study for *Barber Shop*, 1931
Fabricated chalk and charcoal on paper, 12 1/2 × 17 5/8 in. (31.8 × 44.8 cm)
Josephine N. Hopper Bequest 70.853
(fig. 58)

Hillside Landscape with Trees, c. 1936–38
Fabricated chalk on paper, 15 × 22 1/8 in. (38.1 × 56.2 cm)
Josephine N. Hopper Bequest 70.305
(fig. 50)

Study for *Compartment C, Car 293* (recto), 1938
Fabricated chalk and charcoal on paper, 8 1/16 × 10 1/2 in. (20.5 × 26.7 cm)
Josephine N. Hopper Bequest 70.431a–b
(fig. 68)

Study for *New York Movie* (Globe Theatre), 1938
Fabricated chalk on paper, 7 1/4 × 4 7/16 in. (18.4 × 11.3 cm)
Josephine N. Hopper Bequest 70.77
(fig. 221)

Study for *New York Movie* (Globe Theatre), 1938
Fabricated chalk on paper, 7 1/4 × 4 7/16 in. (18.4 × 11.3 cm)
Josephine N. Hopper Bequest 70.79
(fig. 222)

Study for *New York Movie* (Globe Theatre), 1938
Fabricated chalk on paper, 7 9/16 × 4 7/16 in. (19.2 × 11.3 cm)
Josephine N. Hopper Bequest 70.86
(fig. 223)

Study for *New York Movie* (Republic Theatre), 1938
Fabricated chalk and graphite pencil on paper, 7 1/4 × 4 7/16 in. (18.4 × 11.3 cm)
Josephine N. Hopper Bequest 70.92
(fig. 224)

Study for *New York Movie* (Republic Theatre), 1938
Fabricated chalk on paper, 4 7/16 × 7 1/4 in. (11.3 × 18.4 cm)
Josephine N. Hopper Bequest 70.91
(fig. 225)

Study for *New York Movie* (Republic Theatre), 1938
Fabricated chalk on paper, 7 1/4 × 4 7/16 in. (18.4 × 11.3 cm)
Josephine N. Hopper Bequest 70.147
(fig. 226)

Study for *New York Movie* (Republic Theatre), 1938
Fabricated chalk on paper, 7 1/4 × 4 7/16 in. (18.4 × 11.3 cm)
Josephine N. Hopper Bequest 70.150
(fig. 227)

Study for *New York Movie* (Strand Theatre), 1938
Fabricated chalk on paper, 4 1/2 × 7 1/8 in. (11.4 × 18.1 cm)
Josephine N. Hopper Bequest 70.81
(fig. 228)

Study for *New York Movie* (Strand Theatre), 1938
Fabricated chalk on paper, 4 1/2 × 7 1/8 in. (11.4 × 18.1 cm)
Josephine N. Hopper Bequest 70.82
(fig. 229)

Study for *New York Movie* (Strand Theatre), 1938
Fabricated chalk on paper, $7\frac{1}{4} \times 4\frac{1}{2}$ in. (18.4 × 11.4 cm)
Josephine N. Hopper Bequest 70.83
(fig. 230)

Study for *New York Movie* (Strand Theatre), 1938
Fabricated chalk on paper, $4\frac{1}{2} \times 7\frac{3}{16}$ in. (11.4 × 18.3 cm)
Josephine N. Hopper Bequest 70.87
(fig. 231)

Study for *New York Movie*, 1938
Graphite pencil on paper, $7\frac{1}{4} \times 4\frac{7}{16}$ in. (18.4 × 11.3 cm)
Josephine N. Hopper Bequest 70.84
(fig. 233)

Study for *New York Movie*, 1938
Graphite pencil on paper, $7\frac{1}{4} \times 4\frac{7}{16}$ in. (18.4 × 11.3 cm)
Josephine N. Hopper Bequest 70.85
(fig. 234)

Study for *New York Movie*, 1938
Fabricated chalk on paper, $7\frac{1}{8} \times 4\frac{1}{2}$ in. (18.1 × 11.4 cm)
Josephine N. Hopper Bequest 70.80
(fig. 235)

Study for *New York Movie*, 1938
Fabricated chalk on paper, $7\frac{1}{4} \times 4\frac{7}{16}$ in. (18.4 × 11.3 cm)
Josephine N. Hopper Bequest 70.88
(fig. 236)

Study for *New York Movie* (Palace Theatre), 1938
Fabricated chalk on paper, $7\frac{1}{8} \times 4\frac{7}{16}$ in. (18.1 × 11.3 cm)
Josephine N. Hopper Bequest 70.152
(fig. 237)

Study for *New York Movie* (Palace Theatre), 1938
Charcoal on paper, $4\frac{7}{16} \times 7\frac{1}{8}$ in. (11.3 × 18.1 cm)
Josephine N. Hopper Bequest 70.78
(fig. 238)

Study for *New York Movie* (Palace Theatre), 1938
Fabricated chalk on paper, $4\frac{7}{16} \times 7\frac{1}{8}$ in. (11.3 × 18.1 cm)
Josephine N. Hopper Bequest 70.148
(fig. 239)

Study for *New York Movie* (Palace Theatre), 1938
Fabricated chalk on paper, $7\frac{1}{8} \times 4\frac{1}{2}$ in. (18.1 × 11.4 cm)
Josephine N. Hopper Bequest 70.90
(fig. 240)

Study for *New York Movie* (Palace Theatre), 1938
Fabricated chalk on paper, $7\frac{1}{8} \times 4\frac{7}{16}$ in. (18.1 × 11.3 cm)
Josephine N. Hopper Bequest 70.149
(fig. 241)

Study for *New York Movie* (Palace Theatre), 1938
Fabricated chalk on paper, $7\frac{1}{8} \times 4\frac{7}{16}$ in. (18.1 × 11.3 cm)
Josephine N. Hopper Bequest 70.151
(fig. 242)

Study for *New York Movie* (Palace Theatre), 1938
Fabricated chalk on paper, $7\frac{1}{8} \times 4\frac{1}{2}$ in. (18.1 × 11.4 cm)
Josephine N. Hopper Bequest 70.76
(fig. 243)

Study for *New York Movie* (Palace Theatre), 1938
Fabricated chalk on paper, $4\frac{1}{2} \times 7\frac{1}{4}$ in. (11.4 × 18.4 cm)
Josephine N. Hopper Bequest 70.89
(fig. 244)

Study for *New York Movie* (Palace Theatre), 1938
Fabricated chalk on paper, $8\frac{13}{16} \times 11\frac{13}{16}$ in.
(22.4 × 30 cm)
Josephine N. Hopper Bequest 70.110
(fig. 245)

Study for *New York Movie* (Palace Theatre), 1938
Fabricated chalk on paper, $8\frac{7}{8} \times 11\frac{13}{16}$ in.
(22.5 × 30 cm)
Josephine N. Hopper Bequest 70.106
(fig. 250)

Study for *New York Movie* (Palace Theatre), 1938
Fabricated chalk and graphite pencil on paper,
$11\frac{7}{8} \times 8\frac{7}{8}$ in. (30.2 × 22.5 cm)
Josephine N. Hopper Bequest 70.105
(fig. 251)

Study for *New York Movie* (Palace Theatre), 1938
Fabricated chalk on paper, $11\frac{13}{16} \times 8\frac{13}{16}$ in.
(30 × 22.4 cm)
Josephine N. Hopper Bequest 70.103
(fig. 252)

Study for *New York Movie* (Palace Theatre), 1938
Fabricated chalk on paper, $8\frac{13}{16} \times 11\frac{7}{8}$ in.
(22.4 × 30.2 cm)
Josephine N. Hopper Bequest 70.108
(fig. 253)

Study for *New York Movie* (Palace Theatre), 1938
Fabricated chalk on paper, $11\frac{13}{16} \times 8\frac{13}{16}$ in.
(30 × 22.4 cm)
Josephine N. Hopper Bequest 70.102
(fig. 254)

Study for *New York Movie* (Palace Theatre), 1938
Fabricated chalk on paper, $8\frac{7}{8} \times 11\frac{7}{8}$ in. (22.5 × 30.2 cm)
Josephine N. Hopper Bequest 70.107
(fig. 255)

Study for *New York Movie* (Palace Theatre), 1938
Fabricated chalk on paper, $11\frac{7}{8} \times 8\frac{13}{16}$ in.
(30.2 × 22.4 cm)
Josephine N. Hopper Bequest 70.104
(fig. 256)

Study for *New York Movie* (Palace Theatre), 1938
Fabricated chalk on paper, $8\frac{7}{8} \times 11\frac{7}{8}$ in. (22.5 × 30.2 cm)
Josephine N. Hopper Bequest 70.111
(fig. 257)

Study for *New York Movie* (Palace Theatre), 1938
Fabricated chalk on paper, $8\frac{13}{16} \times 11\frac{13}{16}$ in.
(22.4 × 30 cm)
Josephine N. Hopper Bequest 70.109
(fig. 258)

Study for *New York Movie*, 1938 or 1939
Fabricated chalk on paper, $8\frac{3}{4} \times 10\frac{7}{8}$ in. (22.2 × 27.6 cm)
Josephine N. Hopper Bequest 70.93
(fig. 259)

Study for *New York Movie*, 1938 or 1939
Fabricated chalk and graphite pencil on paper,
$10\frac{7}{8} \times 8\frac{3}{8}$ in. (27.6 × 21.3 cm)
Josephine N. Hopper Bequest 70.98
(fig. 262)

Study for *New York Movie*, 1938 or 1939
Fabricated chalk on paper, $10\frac{7}{8} \times 8\frac{3}{8}$ in. (27.6 × 21.3 cm)
Josephine N. Hopper Bequest 70.99
(fig. 263)

Study for *New York Movie*, 1938 or 1939
Fabricated chalk on paper, $10\frac{3}{16} \times 8\frac{7}{16}$ in.
(25.9 × 21.4 cm)
Josephine N. Hopper Bequest 70.96
(fig. 264)

Study for *New York Movie*, 1938 or 1939
Fabricated chalk on paper, $11\frac{1}{8} \times 15$ in. (28.3 × 38.1 cm)
Josephine N. Hopper Bequest 70.276
(fig. 265)

Study for *New York Movie* (recto and verso),
1938 or 1939
Fabricated chalk and charcoal on paper,
$11\frac{1}{8} \times 15\frac{1}{16}$ in. (28.3 × 38.3 cm)
Josephine N. Hopper Bequest 70.274a–b
(recto: fig. 266; verso: fig. 260)

Study for *New York Movie*, 1938 or 1939
Charcoal on paper, $11\frac{1}{16} \times 15$ in. (28.1 × 38.1 cm)
Josephine N. Hopper Bequest 70.275
(fig. 267)

Study for *New York Movie*, 1938 or 1939
Fabricated chalk on paper, $10\frac{7}{8} \times 8\frac{3}{8}$ in. (27.6 × 21.3 cm)
Josephine N. Hopper Bequest 70.95
(fig. 268)

Study for *New York Movie* (recto and verso),
1938 or 1939
Fabricated chalk on paper, $8\frac{3}{8} \times 10\frac{7}{8}$ in. (21.3 × 27.6 cm)
Josephine N. Hopper Bequest 70.94a–b
(recto: fig. 269; verso: fig. 261)

Study for *New York Movie*, 1938 or 1939
Fabricated chalk on paper, $10\frac{5}{16} \times 8\frac{3}{8}$ in.
(26.2 × 21.3 cm)
Josephine N. Hopper Bequest 70.97
(fig. 270)

Study for *New York Movie*, 1938 or 1939
Fabricated chalk on paper, $11\frac{1}{8} \times 15$ in. (28.3 × 38.1 cm)
Josephine N. Hopper Bequest 70.277
(fig. 271)

Study for *New York Movie*, 1938 or 1939
Fabricated chalk on paper, $8\frac{3}{8} \times 10\frac{15}{16}$ in.
(21.3 × 27.8 cm)
Josephine N. Hopper Bequest 70.100
(fig. 272)

Study for *New York Movie*, 1938 or 1939
Fabricated chalk on paper, $10\frac{7}{8} \times 8\frac{3}{8}$ in. (27.6 × 21.3 cm)
Josephine N. Hopper Bequest 70.101
(fig. 273)

Study for *New York Movie*, 1939
Fabricated chalk on paper, $15\frac{1}{2} \times 7\frac{3}{4}$ in. (39.4 × 19.7 cm)
Josephine N. Hopper Bequest 70.447
(fig. 275)

Study for *New York Movie*, 1939
Fabricated chalk on paper, $15 \times 11\frac{1}{8}$ in. (38.1 × 28.3 cm)
Josephine N. Hopper Bequest 70.278
(fig. 276)

Study for *New York Movie*, 1939
Fabricated chalk on paper, $15 \times 11\frac{3}{16}$ in. (38.1 × 28.4 cm)
Josephine N. Hopper Bequest 70.273
(fig. 277)

Study for *New York Movie*, 1939
Fabricated chalk and charcoal on paper, $15 \times 11\frac{1}{16}$ in.
(38.1 × 28.1 cm)
Josephine N. Hopper Bequest 70.272
(fig. 278)

Study for *New York Movie*, 1939
Fabricated chalk and charcoal on paper,
$14\frac{15}{16} \times 11\frac{1}{8}$ in. (37.9 × 28.3 cm)
Josephine N. Hopper Bequest 70.452
(fig. 279)

Study for *New York Movie*, 1939
Fabricated chalk and charcoal on paper, 15 × 11 1/8 in. (38.1 × 28.3 cm)
Josephine N. Hopper Bequest 70.455
(fig. 280)

New York Movie, 1939
Oil on canvas, 32 1/4 × 40 1/8 in. (81.9 × 101.9 cm)
The Museum of Modern Art, New York; given anonymously 396.1941
(fig. 214)

Study for *Bridle Path*, 1939
Fabricated chalk on paper, 8 13/16 × 11 13/16 in. (22.4 × 30 cm)
Josephine N. Hopper Bequest 70.463
(fig. 70)

Study for *Bridle Path* (recto), 1939
Fabricated chalk and charcoal on paper, 22 1/16 × 15 in. (56 × 38.1 cm)
Josephine N. Hopper Bequest 70.857a–b
(fig. 71)

Study for *Ground Swell*, 1939
Fabricated chalk, charcoal, and graphite pencil on paper, 15 × 22 1/8 in. (38.1 × 56.2 cm)
Josephine N. Hopper Bequest 70.339
(fig. 84)

Study for *Pretty Penny*, 1939
Fabricated chalk on paper, 15 1/16 × 25 3/16 in. (38.3 × 64 cm)
Josephine N. Hopper Bequest 70.658
(fig. 69)

Study for *Office at Night*, 1940
Fabricated chalk on paper, 8 1/2 × 11 in. (21.6 × 27.9 cm)
Josephine N. Hopper Bequest 70.169
(fig. 302)

Study for *Office at Night* (recto), 1940
Fabricated chalk on paper, 8 1/2 × 11 in. (21.6 × 27.9 cm)
Josephine N. Hopper Bequest 70.167a–b
(fig. 304)

Study for *Office at Night*, 1940
Fabricated chalk on paper, 8 7/16 × 10 15/16 in. (21.4 × 27.8 cm)
Josephine N. Hopper Bequest 70.168
(fig. 305)

Study for *Office at Night*, 1940
Fabricated chalk and charcoal on paper, 15 1/16 × 19 5/8 in. (38.3 × 49.8 cm)
Josephine N. Hopper Bequest 70.340
(fig. 306)

Study for *Office at Night*, 1940
Fabricated chalk and graphite pencil on paper, 15 1/16 × 18 3/8 in. (38.3 × 46.7 cm)
Josephine N. Hopper Bequest 70.341
(fig. 307)

Study for *Office at Night* (recto), 1940
Fabricated chalk on paper, 22 × 15 1/16 in. (55.9 × 38.3 cm)
Josephine N. Hopper Bequest 70.815a–b
(fig. 308)

Office at Night, 1940
Oil on canvas, 22 3/16 × 25 1/8 in. (56.4 × 63.8 cm)
Walker Art Center, Minneapolis; gift of the T. B. Walker Foundation, Gilbert M. Walker Fund, 1948 1948.21
(fig. 282)

Study for *Gas*, 1940
Fabricated chalk on paper, 8 7/8 × 11 13/16 in. (22.5 × 30 cm)
Josephine N. Hopper Bequest 70.224
(fig. 321)

Study for *Gas*, 1940
Fabricated chalk on paper, 8 7/8 × 11 7/8 in. (22.5 × 30.2 cm)
Josephine N. Hopper Bequest 70.225
(fig. 322)

Study for *Gas*, 1940
Fabricated chalk on paper, 10 1/2 × 16 in. (26.7 × 40.6 cm)
Josephine N. Hopper Bequest 70.226
(fig. 323)

Study for *Gas*, 1940
Fabricated chalk on paper, 10 1/2 × 16 in. (26.7 × 40.6 cm)
Josephine N. Hopper Bequest 70.263
(fig. 324)

Study for *Gas*, 1940
Charcoal and white chalk on paper, 15 1/8 × 22 1/8 in. (38.4 × 56.2 cm)
Josephine N. Hopper Bequest 70.300
(fig. 325)

Study for *Gas*, 1940
Charcoal and white chalk with graphite pencil on paper, 15 1/16 × 22 1/8 in. (38.3 × 56.2 cm)
Josephine N. Hopper Bequest 70.349
(fig. 326)

Gas, 1940
Oil on canvas, 26 1/4 × 40 1/4 in. (66.7 × 102.2 cm)
The Museum of Modern Art, New York; Mrs. Simon Guggenheim Fund 577.1943
(fig. 320)

Perkins Youngboy Dos Passos, 1941
Fabricated chalk on paper, 15 × 22 in. (38.1 × 55.9 cm)
Josephine N. Hopper Bequest 70.659
(fig. 87)

Study for *Girlie Show*, 1941
Fabricated chalk and charcoal on paper, 22 1/8 × 15 3/16 in. (56.2 × 38.6 cm)
Josephine N. Hopper Bequest 70.997
(fig. 85)

Study for *Route 6, Eastham*, 1941
Fabricated chalk and graphite pencil on paper, 10 1/2 × 16 in. (26.7 × 40.6 cm)
Josephine N. Hopper Bequest 70.366
(fig. 330)

Study for *Route 6, Eastham*, 1941
Fabricated chalk, charcoal, and graphite pencil on paper, 10 1/2 × 16 in. (26.7 × 40.6 cm)
Josephine N. Hopper Bequest 70.330
(fig. 331)

Study for *Route 6, Eastham*, 1941
Fabricated chalk on paper, 10 1/2 × 16 in. (26.7 × 40.6 cm)
Josephine N. Hopper Bequest 70.258
(fig. 332)

Study for *Route 6, Eastham*, 1941
Fabricated chalk and graphite pencil on paper, 10 1/2 × 16 in. (26.7 × 40.6 cm)
Josephine N. Hopper Bequest 70.369
(fig. 333)

Study for *Route 6, Eastham*, 1941
Fabricated chalk on paper, 10 1/2 × 16 in. (26.7 × 40.6 cm)
Josephine N. Hopper Bequest 70.445
(fig. 334)

Study for *Route 6, Eastham*, 1941
Fabricated chalk on paper, 10 7/16 × 16 in. (26.5 × 40.6 cm)
Josephine N. Hopper Bequest 70.446
(fig. 335)

Study for *Route 6, Eastham*, 1941
Fabricated chalk and graphite pencil on paper, 15 1/16 × 22 3/16 in. (38.3 × 56.4 cm)
Josephine N. Hopper Bequest 70.854
(fig. 336)

Route 6, Eastham, 1941
Oil on canvas, 27 1/2 × 38 1/4 in. (69.9 × 97.2 cm)
Swope Art Museum, Terre Haute, Indiana 1942.01
(fig. 327)

Study for *Nighthawks*, 1941 or 1942
Fabricated chalk on paper, 4 7/16 × 7 3/16 in. (11.3 × 18.3 cm)
Josephine N. Hopper Bequest 70.192
(fig. 190)

Study for *Nighthawks*, 1941 or 1942
Fabricated chalk on paper, 7 3/16 × 4 7/16 in. (18.3 × 11.3 cm)
Josephine N. Hopper Bequest 70.188
(fig. 191)

Study for *Nighthawks*, 1941 or 1942
Fabricated chalk on paper, 7 1/4 × 4 7/16 in. (18.4 × 11.3 cm)
Josephine N. Hopper Bequest 70.189
(fig. 192)

Study for *Nighthawks*, 1941 or 1942
Fabricated chalk on paper, 7 1/4 × 4 7/16 in. (18.4 × 11.3 cm)
Josephine N. Hopper Bequest 70.186
(fig. 193)

Study for *Nighthawks*, 1941 or 1942
Fabricated chalk on paper, 7 1/4 × 4 7/16 in. (18.4 × 11.3 cm)
Josephine N. Hopper Bequest 70.187
(fig. 194)

Study for *Nighthawks*, 1941 or 1942
Fabricated chalk on paper, 7 3/16 × 4 7/16 in. (18.3 × 11.3 cm)
Josephine N. Hopper Bequest 70.190
(fig. 195)

Study for *Nighthawks*, 1941 or 1942
Fabricated chalk on paper, 7 3/16 × 4 7/16 in. (18.3 × 11.3 cm)
Josephine N. Hopper Bequest 70.191
(fig. 196)

Study for *Nighthawks* (verso), 1941 or 1942
Fabricated chalk on paper, 8 7/16 × 11 in. (21.4 × 27.9 cm)
Josephine N. Hopper Bequest 70.200a–b
(fig. 197)

Study for *Nighthawks* (verso), 1941 or 1942
Study for *Office at Night* (recto), 1940
Fabricated chalk on paper, 8 1/2 × 10 15/16 in. (21.6 × 27.8 cm)
Josephine N. Hopper Bequest 70.166a–b
(verso: fig. 198; recto: fig. 303)

Study for *Nighthawks*, 1941 or 1942
Fabricated chalk on paper, 8 7/16 × 10 15/16 in. (21.4 × 27.8 cm)
Josephine N. Hopper Bequest 70.193
(fig. 199)

Study for *Nighthawks* (recto), 1941 or 1942
Fabricated chalk on paper, 8 1/2 × 11 in. (21.6 × 27.9 cm)
Josephine N. Hopper Bequest 70.194a–b
(fig. 200)

Study for *Nighthawks*, 1941 or 1942
Fabricated chalk on paper, 8 1/2 × 11 1/16 in. (21.6 × 28.1 cm)
Josephine N. Hopper Bequest 70.195
(fig. 201)

Study for *Nighthawks*, 1941 or 1942
Charcoal and white chalk on paper, 5 × 8 1/2 in. (12.7 × 21.6 cm)
Collection of Mr. and Mrs. Larry Magid
(fig. 203)

Study for *Nighthawks*, 1941 or 1942
Charcoal on paper, 4 1/2 × 8 1/2 in. (11.4 × 21.6 cm)
Collection of Mr. and Mrs. Larry Magid
(fig. 204)

Study for *Nighthawks*, 1941 or 1942
Fabricated chalk on paper, 10 7/16 × 8 in. (26.5 × 20.3 cm)
Josephine N. Hopper Bequest 70.255
(fig. 205)

Study for *Nighthawks*, 1941 or 1942
Fabricated chalk and charcoal on paper, 8 1/8 × 8 in. (20.6 × 20.3 cm)
Josephine N. Hopper Bequest 70.253
(fig. 206)

Study for *Nighthawks*, 1941 or 1942
Fabricated chalk and charcoal on paper, 11 13/16 × 8 7/8 in. (30 × 22.5 cm)
Josephine N. Hopper Bequest 70.254
(fig. 207)

Study for *Nighthawks*, 1941 or 1942
Fabricated chalk and charcoal on paper, 15 1/16 × 11 1/16 in. (38.3 × 28.1 cm)
Josephine N. Hopper Bequest 70.256
(fig. 209)

Study for *Nighthawks*, 1941 or 1942
Fabricated chalk and charcoal on paper, 11 1/8 × 15 in. (28.3 × 38.1 cm)
Purchase and gift of Josephine N. Hopper by exchange 2011.65
(fig. 211)

Nighthawks, 1942
Oil on canvas, 33 1/8 × 60 in. (84.1 × 152.4 cm)
The Art Institute of Chicago; Friends of American Art Collection 1942.51
(fig. 166)

Study for *Dawn in Pennsylvania*, 1942
Charcoal, fabricated chalk, and graphite pencil on paper, 15 × 22 1/8 in. (38.1 × 56.2 cm)
Josephine N. Hopper Bequest 70.850
(fig. 78)

Study for *Dawn in Pennsylvania*, 1942
Charcoal on paper, 11 × 15 in. (27.9 × 38.1 cm)
Josephine N. Hopper Bequest 70.851
(fig. 79)

Study for *Dawn in Pennsylvania*, 1942
Charcoal on paper, 11 1/16 × 15 1/16 in. (28.1 × 38.3 cm)
Josephine N. Hopper Bequest 70.852
(fig. 80)

Dawn in Pennsylvania, 1942
Oil on canvas, 24 3/8 × 44 1/4 in. (61.9 × 112.4 cm)
Terra Foundation for American Art; Daniel J. Terra Collection 1999.77

Study for *Hotel Lobby*, 1942
Fabricated chalk on paper, 10 13/16 × 8 7/16 in. (27.5 × 21.4 cm)
Josephine N. Hopper Bequest 70.112
(fig. 75)

Study for *Hotel Lobby* (recto), 1942
Fabricated chalk on paper, 8 1/2 × 11 in. (21.6 × 27.9 cm)
Josephine N. Hopper Bequest 70.114a–b
(fig. 76)

Study for *Hotel Lobby*, 1942
Fabricated chalk and graphite pencil on paper, 8 7/16 × 10 15/16 in. (21.4 × 27.8 cm)
Josephine N. Hopper Bequest 70.117
(fig. 77)

Study for *Hotel Lobby*, 1942
Fabricated chalk and charcoal on paper, 15 × 22 3/16 in. (38.1 × 56.4 cm)
Josephine N. Hopper Bequest 70.996
(fig. 86)

Hotel Lobby, 1943
Oil on canvas, 32 1/2 × 40 3/4 in. (82.6 × 103.5 cm)
Indianapolis Museum of Art; William Ray Adams Memorial Collection 47.4

Study for *Summertime*, 1943
Fabricated chalk and graphite pencil on paper, 8 3/8 × 10 15/16 in. (21.3 × 27.8 cm)
Josephine N. Hopper Bequest 70.458
(fig. 81)

Study for *Summertime*, 1943
Fabricated chalk on paper, 8 3/8 × 11 in. (21.3 × 27.9 cm)
Josephine N. Hopper Bequest 70.459
(fig. 82)

Study for *Summertime*, 1943
Fabricated chalk on paper, 8 13/16 × 11 13/16 in. (22.4 × 30 cm)
Josephine N. Hopper Bequest 70.460
(fig. 83)

Three Hand Studies (*Hands* or *The Artist's Hands, Three Views*), 1943
Fabricated chalk, charcoal, and graphite pencil on paper, 22 1/8 × 15 in. (56.2 × 38.1 cm)
Josephine N. Hopper Bequest 70.337
(fig. 92)

Study for *Morning in a City*, 1944
Fabricated chalk and graphite pencil on paper, 8 1/2 × 11 in. (21.6 × 27.9 cm)
Josephine N. Hopper Bequest 70.205
(fig. 367)

Study for *Morning in a City*, 1944
Fabricated chalk and graphite pencil on paper, 8 1/2 × 11 in. (21.6 × 27.9 cm)
Josephine N. Hopper Bequest 70.206
(fig. 368)

Study for *Morning in a City*, 1944
Fabricated chalk and graphite pencil on paper, 8 1/2 × 10 15/16 in. (21.6 × 27.8 cm)
Josephine N. Hopper Bequest 70.207
(fig. 369)

Study for *Morning in a City*, 1944
Fabricated chalk on paper, 22 1/8 × 15 in. (56.2 × 38.1 cm)
Josephine N. Hopper Bequest 70.294
(fig. 362)

Study for *Morning in a City*, 1944
Fabricated chalk on paper, 22 1/16 × 15 1/8 in. (56 × 38.4 cm)
Josephine N. Hopper Bequest 70.345
(fig. 363)

Study for *Morning in a City*, 1944
Fabricated chalk on paper, 22 1/16 × 15 1/16 in. (56 × 38.3 cm)
Josephine N. Hopper Bequest 70.995
(fig. 364)

Morning in a City, 1944
Oil on canvas, 44 5/16 × 59 13/16 in. (112.5 × 152 cm)
Williams College Museum of Art, Williamstown, Massachusetts; bequest of Lawrence H. Bloedel, Class of 1923 77.9.7
(fig. 361)

Study for *Solitude #56*, 1944
Fabricated chalk on paper, 10 3/8 × 16 in. (26.4 × 40.6 cm)
Josephine N. Hopper Bequest 70.443
(fig. 347)

Study for *Solitude #56*, 1944
Fabricated chalk, charcoal, and graphite pencil on paper, 15 × 18 1/8 in. (38.1 × 46 cm)
Josephine N. Hopper Bequest 70.685
(fig. 348)

Study for *Solitude #56*, 1944
Fabricated chalk on paper, 15 1/16 × 22 1/8 in. (38.3 × 56.2 cm)
Josephine N. Hopper Bequest 70.855
(fig. 349)

Self-Portrait, 1945
Fabricated chalk and charcoal on paper, 22 × 14 15/16 in. (55.9 × 37.9 cm)
Josephine N. Hopper Bequest 70.287
(fig. 90)

Self-Portrait, 1945
Fabricated chalk and charcoal on paper, 22 1/8 × 15 in. (56.2 × 38.1 cm)
Josephine N. Hopper Bequest 70.336
(fig. 91)

Study for *Rooms for Tourists*, 1945
Fabricated chalk on paper, 10 3/8 × 15 15/16 in. (26.4 × 40.5 cm)
Josephine N. Hopper Bequest 70.221
(fig. 338)

Study for *Rooms for Tourists*, 1945
Fabricated chalk on paper, 10 3/8 × 15 15/16 in. (26.4 × 40.5 cm)
Josephine N. Hopper Bequest 70.259
(fig. 339)

Study for *Rooms for Tourists*, 1945
Fabricated chalk and graphite pencil on paper, 10 3/8 × 15 15/16 in. (26.4 × 40.5 cm)
Josephine N. Hopper Bequest 70.260
(fig. 340)

Study for *Rooms for Tourists*, 1945
Fabricated chalk on paper, 15 × 22 1/8 in. (38.1 × 56.2 cm)
Josephine N. Hopper Bequest 70.1001
(fig. 341)

Study for *Rooms for Tourists*, 1945
Fabricated chalk on paper, 22 1/8 × 15 1/16 in. (56.2 × 38.3 cm)
Josephine N. Hopper Bequest 70.1002
(fig. 342)

Study for *Rooms for Tourists*, 1945
Fabricated chalk on paper, 8 1/16 × 5 in. (20.5 × 12.7 cm)
Josephine N. Hopper Bequest 70.230
(fig. 343)

Study for *Rooms for Tourists*, 1945
Graphite pencil on paper, 5 × 3 in. (12.7 × 7.6 cm)
Josephine N. Hopper Bequest 70.284
(fig. 344)

Study for *Rooms for Tourists*, 1945
Fabricated chalk and charcoal on paper,
15 × 22 1/8 in. (38.1 × 56.2 cm)
Josephine N. Hopper Bequest 70.848
(fig. 345)

Study for *Rooms for Tourists*, 1945
Fabricated chalk and charcoal on paper,
10 3/8 × 16 in. (26.4 × 40.6 cm)
Josephine N. Hopper Bequest 70.438
(fig. 346)

Rooms for Tourists, 1945
Oil on canvas, 30 1/4 × 42 1/8 in. (76.8 × 107 cm)
Yale University Art Gallery, New Haven; bequest
of Stephen Carlton Clark, B.A. 1903 1961.18.30
(fig. 337)

Jo Hopper, 1945–50
Charcoal on paper, 18 × 15 7/16 in. (45.7 × 39.2 cm)
Josephine N. Hopper Bequest 70.288
(fig. 88)

Study for *Approaching a City*, 1946
Fabricated chalk and charcoal on paper,
15 3/16 × 22 3/16 in. (38.6 × 56.4 cm)
Josephine N. Hopper Bequest 70.869
(fig. 72)

Study for *Corn Belt City*, 1946 or 1947
Charcoal on paper, 14 15/16 × 22 1/8 in. (37.9 × 56.2 cm)
Josephine N. Hopper Bequest 70.840
(fig. 67)

Study for *Conference at Night*, 1948 or 1949
Fabricated chalk on paper, 8 1/2 × 11 in. (21.6 × 27.9 cm)
Josephine N. Hopper Bequest 70.172
(fig. 292)

Study for *Conference at Night*, 1948 or 1949
Fabricated chalk on paper, 8 1/2 × 10 15/16 in. (21.6 × 27.8 cm)
Josephine N. Hopper Bequest 70.173
(fig. 293)

Study for *Conference at Night*, 1948 or 1949
Fabricated chalk on paper, 8 1/2 × 10 15/16 in. (21.6 × 27.8 cm)
Josephine N. Hopper Bequest 70.174
(fig. 294)

Study for *Conference at Night*, 1948 or 1949
Fabricated chalk on paper, 8 1/2 × 10 15/16 in. (21.6 × 27.8 cm)
Josephine N. Hopper Bequest 70.170
(fig. 295)

Study for *Conference at Night*, 1948 or 1949
Fabricated chalk on paper, 8 1/2 × 10 15/16 in. (21.6 × 27.8 cm)
Josephine N. Hopper Bequest 70.171
(fig. 296)

Study for *Conference at Night* (recto), 1949
Fabricated chalk and charcoal on paper,
15 1/16 × 22 1/16 in. (38.3 × 56 cm)
Josephine N. Hopper Bequest 70.842a–b
(fig. 297)

Study for *Conference at Night*, 1948 or 1949
Fabricated chalk on paper, 8 5/8 × 11 5/8 in. (21.9 × 29.5 cm)
Josephine N. Hopper Bequest 70.844
(fig. 298)

Study for *Conference at Night*, 1948 or 1949
Fabricated chalk on paper, 11 5/8 × 8 5/8 in. (29.5 × 21.9 cm)
Josephine N. Hopper Bequest 70.843
(fig. 299)

Study for *Conference at Night*, 1948 or 1949
Fabricated chalk and charcoal on paper, 8 1/8 × 5 in.
(20.6 × 12.7 cm)
Josephine N. Hopper Bequest 70.845
(fig. 300)

Study for *Conference at Night*, 1948 or 1949
Fabricated chalk and charcoal on paper, 8 1/8 × 5 in.
(20.6 × 12.7 cm)
Josephine N. Hopper Bequest 70.846
(fig. 301)

Conference at Night, 1949
Oil on canvas, 28 1/4 × 40 5/16 in. (72.8 × 102.4 cm)
Wichita Art Museum; Roland P. Murdock
Collection M100.52
(fig. 291)

Study for *Stairway*, 1949
Fabricated chalk and graphite pencil on paper,
19 1/4 × 12 3/16 in. (48.9 × 31 cm)
Josephine N. Hopper Bequest 70.849
(fig. 73)

Stairway, 1949
Oil on wood, 16 × 11 7/8 in. (40.6 × 30.2 cm)
Josephine N. Hopper Bequest 70.1265
(fig. 74)

Study for *Summer in the City*, 1949
Fabricated chalk and graphite pencil on paper,
8 1/2 × 11 in. (21.6 × 27.9 cm)
Josephine N. Hopper Bequest 70.268
(fig. 370)

Study for *Summer in the City*, 1949
Fabricated chalk on paper, 8 1/2 × 11 in. (21.6 × 27.9 cm)
Josephine N. Hopper Bequest 70.269
(fig. 371)

Study for *Morning Sun*, 1952
Fabricated chalk and graphite pencil on paper,
12 1/16 × 18 15/16 in. (30.6 × 48.1 cm)
Josephine N. Hopper Bequest 70.291
(fig. 382)

Study for *Morning Sun*, 1952
Fabricated chalk on paper, 11 15/16 × 18 15/16 in.
(30.3 × 48.1 cm)
Josephine N. Hopper Bequest 70.290
(fig. 383)

Study for *Morning Sun*, 1952
Fabricated chalk on paper, 12 × 19 in. (30.5 × 48.3 cm)
Josephine N. Hopper Bequest 70.244
(fig. 384)

Morning Sun, 1952
Oil on canvas, 28 1/8 × 40 1/8 in. (71.4 × 101.9 cm)
Columbus Museum of Art; Howald Fund
Purchase 1954.031
(fig. 381)

Study for *Hotel by a Railroad*, 1952
Fabricated chalk on paper, 12 × 19 in. (30.5 × 48.3 cm)
Josephine N. Hopper Bequest 70.427
(fig. 64)

Study for *Hotel by a Railroad*, 1952
Fabricated chalk on paper, 7 9/16 × 5 in. (19.2 × 12.7 cm)
Josephine N. Hopper Bequest 70.428
(fig. 65)

Study for *Hotel by a Railroad*, 1952
Fabricated chalk on paper, 19 × 12 in. (48.3 × 30.5 cm)
Josephine N. Hopper Bequest 70.874
(fig. 66)

A Woman in the Sun, 1961
Oil on canvas, 40 1/8 × 61 1/4 in. (101.9 × 155.6 cm)
50th Anniversary Gift of Mr. and Mrs. Albert Hackett
in honor of Edith and Lloyd Goodrich 84.31
(fig. 360)

Landscape with Automobile (Study for *Road and Trees*),
c. 1962
Charcoal on paper, 8 15/16 × 11 in. (22.7 × 27.9 cm)
Peter Findlay Gallery, New York
(fig. 317)

Road and Rocks, c. 1962(?)
Fabricated chalk on paper, 15 × 22 1/8 in. (38.1 × 56.2 cm)
Josephine N. Hopper Bequest 70.306
(fig. 355)

Mass of Trees at Eastham, 1962
Watercolor and graphite pencil on paper,
22 1/2 × 30 1/2 in. (57.2 × 77.5 cm)
Josephine N. Hopper Bequest 70.1164
(fig. 359)

Road and Trees, 1962
Oil on canvas, 34 × 60 in. (86.4 × 152.4 cm)
Collection of Daniel W. Dietrich II
(fig. 351)

Artist's Ledger—Book II, 1907–62
Pen and ink and graphite pencil on paper,
11 13/16 × 7 1/2 in. (30 × 19.1 cm)
Drawings by Edward Hopper. Text and inscriptions
by Edward Hopper and Josephine Nivison Hopper
(1883–1968)
Gift of Lloyd Goodrich 96.209
(fig. 217)

Sun in an Empty Room, 1963
Oil on canvas, 28 3/4 × 39 1/2 in. (73 × 100.3 cm)
Private collection
(fig. 385)

As of February 19, 2013

INDEX

Page numbers in italics refer to illustrations.

All works are by Edward Hopper unless otherwise indicated.

PHOTOGRAPHIC CREDITS

The copyright holders, photographers, and sources of visual material other than those indicated in the captions are as follows. Every effort has been made to credit the copyright holders, photographers, and sources; if there are errors or omissions, please contact the Whitney Museum of American Art so that corrections can be made in any subsequent edition.

Unless otherwise indicated below, all artworks by Edward Hopper in the collection of the Whitney Museum of American Art are © Heirs of Josephine N. Hopper, licensed by the Whitney Museum of American Art, New York; digital images © Whitney Museum of American Art, New York.

Art © Arnold Newman Collection / Getty Images (fig. 178)
Photographs © The Art Institute of Chicago (figs. 105, 107, 166)
Art © Artists Rights Society (ARS), New York / ADAGP, Paris; digital image © The Museum of Modern Art/ Licensed by SCALA / Art Resource, NY (fig. 135)
Photograph © The Cleveland Museum of Art (fig. 328)
Art © Estate of Allan D'Arcangelo/Licensed by VAGA, New York, NY; image credit: Smithsonian American Art Museum, Washington, DC / Art Resource, NY (fig. 357)
Text © 2012 Lisa de Kooning (quotes by Willem de Kooning, pp. 198–99, 203n89)
Art © 2012 The Willem de Kooning Foundation / Artists Rights Society (ARS), New York; image source: Bridgeman Art Library (fig. 358)
Design © Editions Flammarion, Paris, 1989; image of artwork © The Metropolitan Museum of Art, New York (fig. 316)
Digital image © Private collection, courtesy Fraenkel Gallery, San Francisco, and Pace Gallery, New York (fig. 96)
Art © Estate of George Platt Lynes; image source: Archives of American Art, Smithsonian Institution, Washington, DC (fig. 386)
Art © 2012 Estate of Reginald Marsh / Art Student's League, New York / Artists Rights Society (ARS), New York. Photograph by Geoffrey Clements (fig. 216)
Digital image © The Metropolitan Museum of Art, New York; image source: Art Resource, NY (figs. 140, 161, 310)
Art © Milstein Division of United States History, Local History and Genealogy, The New York Public Library, Astor, Lenox and Tilden Foundations (figs. 160, 169, 202)
Digital image © The Museum of Modern Art/ Licensed by SCALA / Art Resource, NY (figs. 133, 214, 320)
Map © The Sanborn Library LLC; image source: The New York Public Library, Astor, Lenox and Tilden Foundations; used with permission of The Sanborn Library (figs. 165, 168)
Design © Time-Life Inc. Photographs by Sheldan C. Collins (figs. 210, 315)
Digital images © Whitney Museum of American Art, New York (figs. 56, 215)
Art © Whitney Museum of American Art, New York. Photographs by Sheldan C. Collins (figs. 164, 360)
Art © Whitney Museum of American Art, New York; digital image © Whitney Museum of American Art, New York (figs. 211, 284, 380)
Design © Yale University Press, New Haven and London; photograph by Sheldan C. Collins (fig. 356)

Image sources:
Academic Film Archive of North America and Carson Davidson (figs. 286–289)
Addison Gallery of American Art, Phillips Academy, Andover, Massachusetts (figs. 153–157)
Bridgeman Art Library (fig. 365)
The Dayton Art Institute, Ohio (fig. 106)
Hirshhorn Museum and Sculpture Garden, Smithsonian Institution, Washington, DC; photograph by Lee Stalsworth (fig. 311)
Erich Lessing / Art Resource, NY (figs. 139, 152)
The Library of Congress, Washington, DC (fig. 350)
The Museum of the City of New York / Art Resource, NY (fig. 232)
New-York Historical Society (figs. 167, 170–174, 181–189); reprinted with permission from the *New York Post*, NYP Holdings; image source The New York Public Library, Astor, Lenox and Tilden Foundations (fig. 281)
The New York Public Library, Astor, Lenox and Tilden Foundations (figs. 176, 177, 179, 180, 285)
Newark Museum / Art Resource, NY (fig. 213)
Philadelphia Museum of Art / Art Resource, NY (figs. 151, 274, 376)
The Phillips Collection, Washington, DC (fig. 309)
Smithsonian American Art Museum, Washington, DC / Art Resource, NY (fig. 354)
Swope Art Museum, Terre Haute, Indiana (fig. 327)
Theatre Historical Society of America, Elmhurst, Illinois (figs. 246–249)
Walker Art Center, Minneapolis (figs. 282, 314)
Wichita Art Museum (fig. 291)
Williams College Museum of Art, Williamstown, MA (fig. 361)
Yale University Art Gallery, New Haven (figs. 1, 99, 337, 353)

Photograph by Ron Amstutz (fig. 317)
Photographs by Sheldan C. Collins (figs. 95, 102, 212, 283, 290, 375, pp. 217–25)
Photograph by Lee R. Ewing (fig. 52)
Photograph by Alex Jamison (fig. 385)
Photograph by Eric Pollitzer (fig. 352)
Photographs by Jason Wierzbicki (figs. 203, 204)

LENDERS TO THE EXHIBITION

Addison Gallery of American Art, Phillips Academy, Andover, Massachusetts
The Art Institute of Chicago
Columbus Museum of Art, Ohio
The Dayton Art Institute, Ohio
Daniel W. Dietrich II
Aaron I. Fleischman
Indianapolis Museum of Art
Mr. and Mrs. Larry Magid
The Metropolitan Museum of Art, New York
The Museum of Modern Art, New York
Peter Findlay Gallery, New York
Swope Art Museum, Terre Haute, Indiana
Terra Foundation for American Art, Chicago
Walker Art Center, Minneapolis
Whitney Museum of American Art, New York
Wichita Art Museum
Williams College Museum of Art, Williamstown, Massachusetts
Yale University Art Gallery, New Haven

Private collections

Alison Abreu-Garcia
Jay Abu-Hamda
Stephanie Adams
Adrienne Alston
Martha Alvarez-LaRose
Amanda Angel
Marilou Aquino
Emily Arensman
Morgan Arenson
I. D. Aruede
Bernadette Baker
John Balestrieri
Michael Baptist
Wendy Barbee-Lowell
Courtney Bassett
Ingrid Baumanis
Caroline Beasley
Justine Benith
Harry Benjamin
Jeffrey Bergstrom
Megan Berkey
Caitlin Bermingham
Alberto Betancourt
Stephanie Birmingham
Ivy Blackman
Hillary Blass
Richard Bloes
Andrea Bonin
Leigh Brawer
Jeffrey Britton
Keri Bronk
Carda Burke
Douglas Burnham
Patrick Burns
Ron Burrell
Christopher Burton
Garfield Burton
Jocelyn Cabral
Pablo Caines
Margaret Cannie
Amanda Carrasco
Inde Cheong
Ramon Cintron
Randy Clark
Ron Clark
Correna Cohen
Melissa Cohen
John Collins
Arthur Conway
Heather Cox
Kenneth Cronan
Mia Curran
Donna De Salvo
Margo Delidow
Anthony DeMercurio
Kristen Denner
Eduardo Diaz
Kate Dietrick
Lauren DiLoreto
Lisa Dowd
Delano Dunn
Anita Duquette
Raquel Echanique
Alvin Eubanks
Eileen Farrell
Richard Fett
Rich Flood
Seth Fogelman
Meghan Forsyth
Carter E. Foster
Samuel Franks
Murlin Frederick
Annie French
Donald Garlington
John Gatti
Larissa Gentile
Claire Gerhard
Robert Gerhardt
Liz Gillroy
Hilary Greenbaum
Peter Guss
Kate Hahm
Kiowa Hammons
Greta Hartenstein
Barbara Haskell
Maura Heffner
Dina Helal
Peter Henderson
Claire Henry
Jennifer Heslin
Ann Holcomb
Nicholas S. Holmes
Abigail Hoover
Sarah Hromack
Karen Huang
Wycliffe Husbands
Beth Huseman
Chrissie Iles
Jennifer Isaac
Carlos Jacobo
Julia Johnson
Dolores Joseph
Chris Ketchie
David Kiehl
Melissa Kim
Kathleen Koehler
Irene Koo
Tom Kraft
Larissa Kunynskuj
Amber LaCasse
Eunice Lee
Sang Soo Lee
Kristen Leipert
Monica Leon
Jen Leventhal
Jeffrey Levine
Danielle Linzer
Kelley Loftus
Robert Lomblad
Sarah Lookofsky
Brianna O'Brien Lowndes
Kevin Lu
Doug Madill
Trista Mallory
Elyse Mallouk
Carol Mancusi-Ungaro
Louis Manners
Joseph Mannino
Anna Martin
Heather Maxson
Madeline McGrath
Gene McHugh
Michael McQuilkin
Kate McWatters
Sandra Meadows
Sarah Meller
Bridget Mendoza
Graham Miles
Dana Miller
David Miller
Christa Molinaro
Becca Morgan
Victor Moscoso
Eleonora Nagy
Sakina Namazi
Pablo Narvaez
Ruben Negron
Graham Newhall
Carlos Noboa
Thomas Nunes
Suzanna Okie
Rose O'Neill-Suspitsyna
Nelson Ortiz
Barbara Padolsky
Jane Panetta
Christiane Paul
Ailen Pedraza
Jessica Pepe
Laura Phipps
Angelo Pikoulas
Mary Potter
Kathryn Potts
Linda Priest
Frank Procaccini
Vincent Punch
Christy Putnam
Jessica Ragusa
Julie Rega
Natalee Reid
Gregory Reynolds
Emanuel Riley
Ariel Rivera
Felix Rivera
Nicholas Robbins
Jeffrey Robinson
Georgianna Rodriguez
Gina Rogak
Justin Romeo
Adrienne Rooney
Joshua Rosenblatt
Jamie Rosenfeld
Amy Roth
Scott Rothkopf
Carol Rusk
Angelina Salerno
Leo Sanchez
Jay Sanders
Galina Sapozhnikova
Lynn Schatz
Arielle Schraeter
Peter Scott
Michelle Sealey
David Selimoski
Jason Senquiz
Ai Wee Seow
Amy Sharp
Elisabeth Sherman
Kasey Sherrick
Sasha Silcox
Matt Skopek
Joel Snyder
Michele Snyder
Stephen Soba
Veronica Speck
Barbi Spieler
Carrie Springer
John Stanley
Mark Steigelman
Berry Stein
Minerva Stella
Betty Stolpen
Hillary Strong
Jillian Suarez
Emilie Sullivan
Denis Suspitsyn
Elisabeth Sussman
Catherine Taft
Christine Taguines
Kean Tan
Ellen Tepfer
Latasha Thomas
Phyllis Thorpe
Ana Torres
Beth Turk
Lauren Turner
Ray Vega
Snigdha Verma
Eric Vermilion
Billie Rae Vinson
Farris Wahbeh
Cecil Weekes
Adam D. Weinberg
Margie Weinstein
Alexandra Wheeler
Michelle Wilder
John Williams
Katie Wright
Liza Zapol
Sefkia Zekiroski
Kayla Zemsky

As of January 2, 2013

This catalogue was published on the occasion of the exhibition *Hopper Drawing*, curated by Carter E. Foster, Steven and Ann Ames Curator of Drawing, with the assistance of Nicholas Robbins, curatorial assistant, Whitney Museum of American Art, New York.

Whitney Museum of American Art, New York
May 23–October 6, 2013

Dallas Museum of Art
November 17, 2013–February 16, 2014

Walker Art Center, Minneapolis
March 15–June 22, 2014

Significant support for this exhibition is provided by the National Endowment for the Arts, The Dietrich Foundation, The Selz Foundation, Barney A. Ebsworth, Steve Martin and Anne Stringfield, The Robert Lehman Foundation, Jane Carroll, The Aaron I. Fleischman Foundation, Arlene and Robert Kogod, Sarah and Seth Glickenhaus, and an anonymous donor.

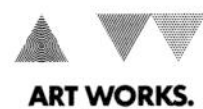

Support for the catalogue is provided by the Wyeth Foundation for American Art and Furthermore: a program of the J. M. Kaplan Fund.

All works are in the collection of the Whitney Museum of American Art, New York, unless otherwise noted.

Whitney Museum of American Art
945 Madison Avenue
New York, NY 10021
whitney.org

Distributed by
Yale University Press
302 Temple Street
P.O. Box 209040
New Haven, CT 06520-9040
yalebooks.com/art

This publication was produced by the publications department at the Whitney Museum of American Art, New York: Beth A. Huseman, director of publications; Beth Turk, associate editor; Anita Duquette, manager, rights and reproductions; Kiowa Hammons, rights and reproductions assistant.

Project manager: Beth A. Huseman
Editor: David Updike
Designer: McCall Associates, New York
Production: The Production Department
Proofreader: Susan Richmond
Indexer: Susan G. Burke

Printing and binding: Trifolio SRL, Verona
Typeset in Hoefler Text; Enclave by Terminal Design, Linotype Didot
Printed on 150gsm Sappi Galerie Art Volume

Library of Congress Cataloging-in-Publication Data
Foster, Carter E.
Hopper drawing / Carter E. Foster ; with contributions by Daniel S. Palmer ... [et al.].
p. cm.
Catalog of an exhibition held at the Whitney Museum of American Art, New York, May 23–Oct. 6, 2013; Dallas Museum of Art, Nov. 17, 2013–Feb. 16, 2014; Walker Art Center, Minneapolis, Mar. 15–June 22, 2014.
Includes bibliographical references and index.
ISBN 978-0-300-18149-4
1. Hopper, Edward, 1882–1967—Exhibitions. 2. Whitney Museum of American Art—Exhibitions. 3. Drawing—New York (State)—New York—Exhibitions. I. Palmer, Daniel S. II. Whitney Museum of American Art. III. Dallas Museum of Art. IV. Walker Art Center. V. Title.
NC139.H65A4 2013
741.973—dc23
2012047722

Printed and bound in Italy
10 9 8 7 6 5 4 3 2 1

Jacket illustration: Study for *Nighthawks*, 1941 or 1942 (detail) (fig. 211)

Front endpapers: Study for *Route 6, Eastham*, 1941 (detail) (fig. 331); Study for *New York Movie*, 1939 (detail) (fig. 280)

Illustration, page 4: *Three Men at Art Exhibition*, c. 1900–03 (fig. 29)

Illustration, page 6: Study for *Summertime*, 1943 (detail) (fig. 83)

Illustration, page 10: *Victorian House on a Wooded Street*, c. 1923–25 (detail) (fig. 61)

Illustration, pages 14 and 15: *Road and Rocks*, c. 1962(?) (detail) (fig. 355)

Back endpapers: *Self-Portrait*, 1945 (detail) (fig. 91); *Hopper's Hat on His Etching Press*, after 1924 (detail) (fig. 94)

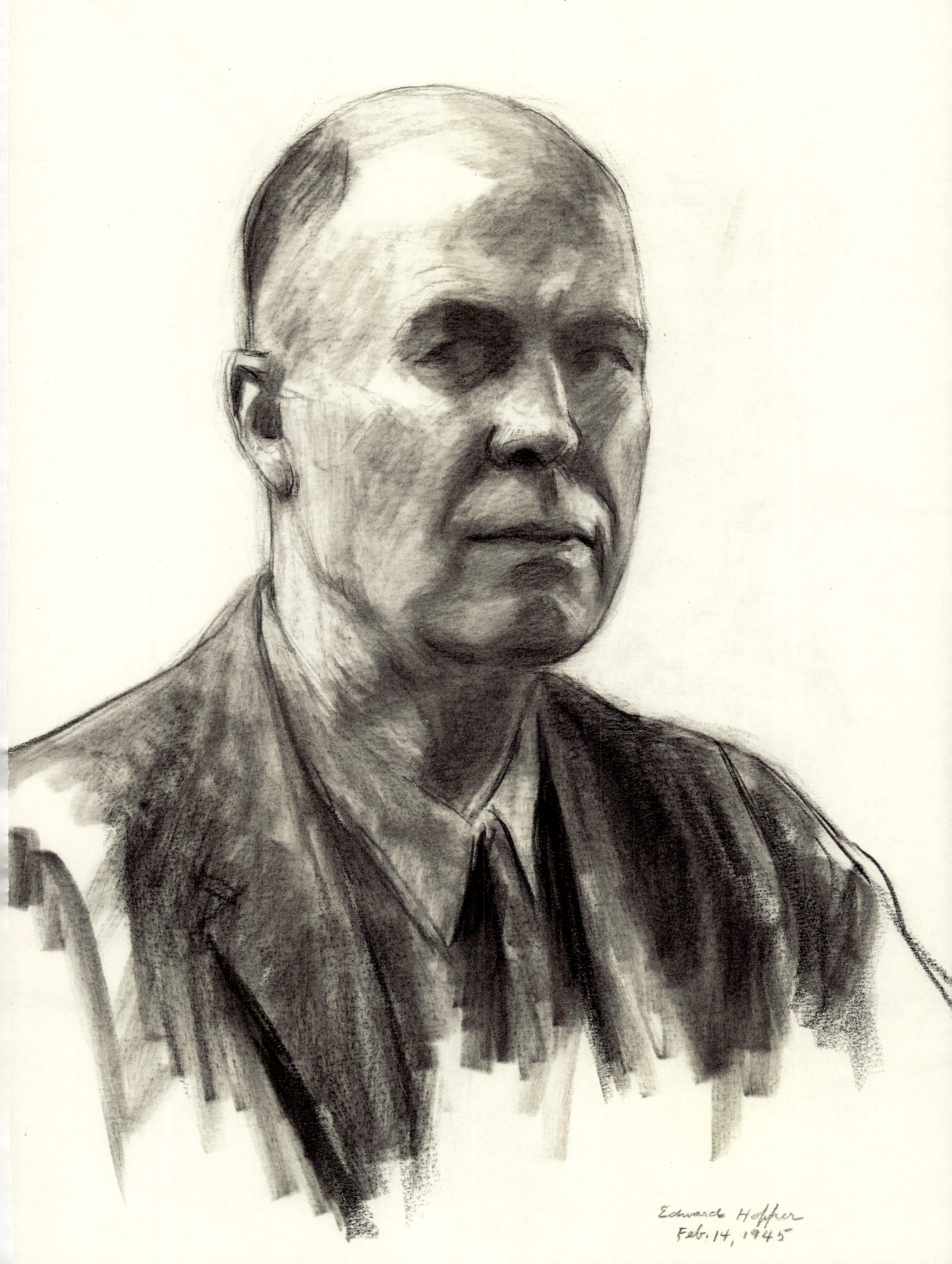
Edward Hopper
Feb. 14, 1945

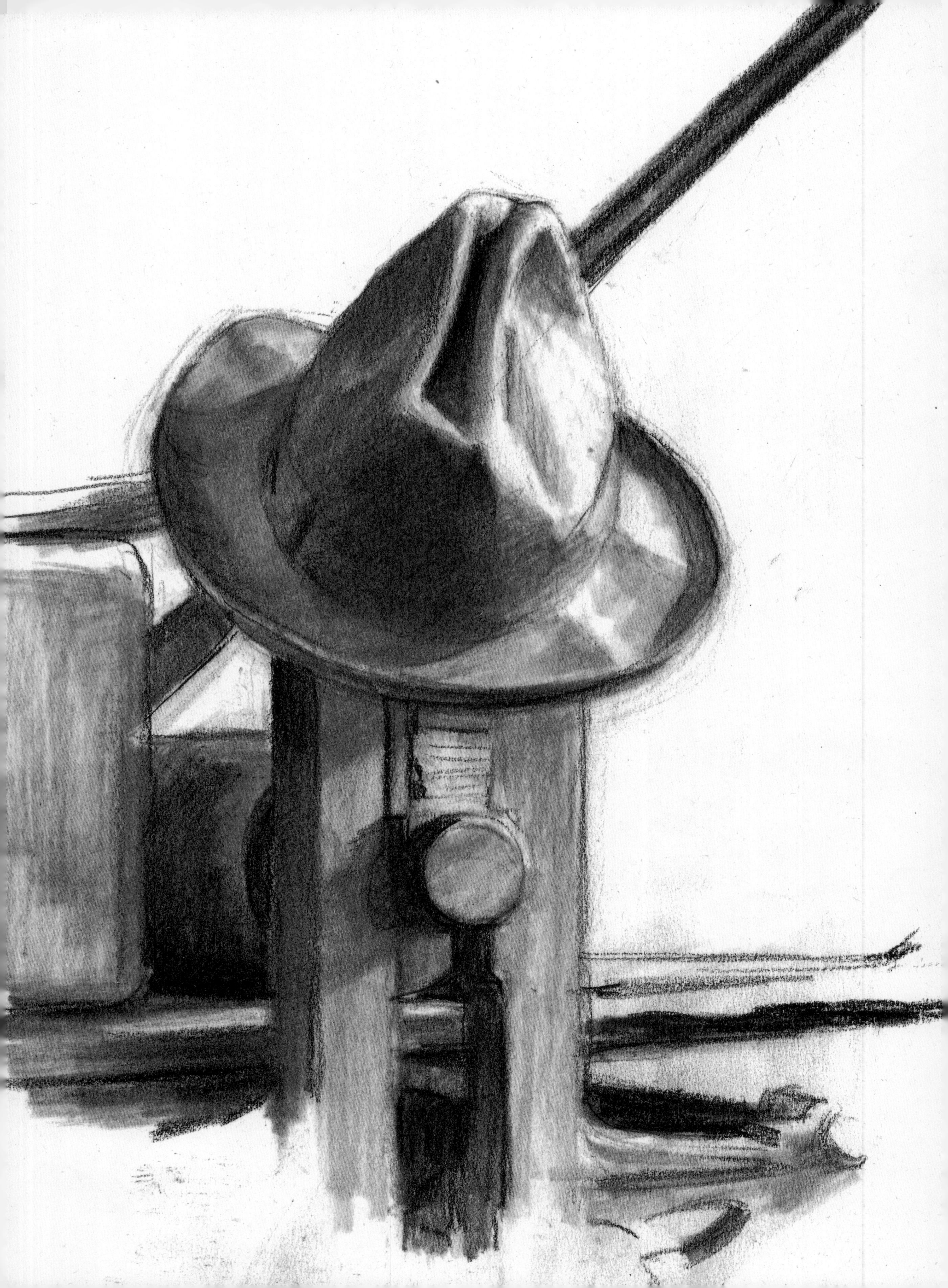